This book is due for return on or before the last date shown below.

Hand/ On DarkBASIC Pro
Volume 1

A Self-Study Guide to Games Programming

Alistair Stewart

DIGITAL SKILLS
Milton
Barr
Girvan
Ayrshire
KA26 9TY

www.digital-skills.co.uk

Cover Design by Neil King 2007

Printed September 2005
2nd Printing November 2005
3rd Printing January 2006
4th Printing November 2006
5th Printing February 2007
6th Printing September 2007
7th Printing February 2008

Title   : Hands On DarkBASIC Pro Volume 1

ISBN   : 1-874107-08-4
ISBN-13 978-1-874107-08-8

Other Titles Available:

Hands On DarkBASIC Pro Volume 2
Hands On Pascal
Hands On C++
Hands On Java
Hands On XHTML

Table Of Contents

Chapter 3   Data

Chapter 4   Selection

Chapter 5   Iteration

Chapter 6   Drawing Statements

Chapter 7   Modular Programming

Chapter 8   String Functions

Chapter 9   Hangman

Chapter 10   Arrays

Chapter 11   Bull and Touch

Chapter 12   Advanced Data Types and Operators

Chapter 13   Bitmaps

Chapter 14   Video Cards and the Screen

Chapter 15   File Handling

Chapter 16   Handling Music Files

Chapter 17   Displaying Video Files

Chapter 18   Accessing the Keyboard

Chapter 19   Mathematical Functions

Chapter 20   Images

Chapter 21   Sprites1

Chapter 22	Sprites 2

Chapter 23   Animated Sprites

Chapter 24   Sound

Chapter 25   2D Vectors

Chapter 26   Space Duel

Chapter 27   Using the Mouse

Chapter 28   Pelmanism

Chapter 29   Using a Joystick

Acknowledgements

I would like to thank all those who helped me prepare the final draft of this book.

In particular, Virginia Marshall who proof-read the original script and Michael Kerr who did an excellent job of checking the technical contents.

Any errors that remain are probably due to the extra few paragraphs I added after all the proof-reading was complete!

Thanks also to The Game Creators Ltd for producing an excellent piece of software - DarkBASIC Professional - known as DarkBASIC Pro to its friends.

Finally, thank you to every one of you who has bought this book. Any constructive comments would be most welcome.

Email me at *alistair@digital-skills.co.uk.*

Introduction

Welcome to a book that I hope is a little different from any other you've come across. Instead of just telling you about software design and programming, it makes you get involved. There's plenty of work for you to do since the book is full of exercises - most of them programming exercises - but you also get a full set of solutions, just in case you get stuck!

Learn by Doing

The only way to become a programming expert is to practice. No one ever learned any skill by just reading about it! Hence, this is not a text book where you can just sit back in a passive way and read from cover to cover whilst sitting in your favourite chair. Rather it is designed as a teaching package in which you will do most of the work.

The tasks embedded in the text are included to test your understanding of what has gone before and as a method of helping you retain the knowledge you have gained. It is therefore important that you tackle each task as you come to it. Also, many of the programming exercises are referred to, or expanded, in later pages so it is important that you are familar with the code concerned.

What You Need

You'll obviously need a PC and a copy of DarkBASIC Pro.

You don't need any experience of programming, but knowing your bits from your bytes and understanding binary and hexadecimal number systems would be useful.

How to Get the Most out of this Text

Experience has shown that readers derive most benefit from this material by approaching its study in an organised way. The following strategy for study is highly recommended:

1. Read a chapter or section through without taking notes or worrying too much about topics that are not immediately clear to you. This will give you an overview of the contents of that chapter/section.

2. Re-read the chapter. This time take things slowly; make notes and summaries of the material you are reading (even if you understand the material, making notes helps to retain the facts in your long-term memory); re-read any parts you are unclear about.

3. Embedded in the material are a series of activities. Do each task as you reach it (on the second reading). These activities are designed to test your knowledge and understanding of what has gone before. Do not be tempted to skip over them, promise to come back to them later, or to make only a half-hearted attempt at tackling them before looking up the answer (there are solutions at the end of each chapter). Once you have attempted a task, look at the solution given. Often there will be important points emphasised in the solution which will aid higher understanding.

4. As you progress through the book, go back and re-read earlier chapters, since you will often get something new from them as your knowledge increases.

Language Syntax Diagrams

The text contains many syntax diagrams which give a visual representation of the format of various statements allowed in DarkBASIC Professional. These diagrams make no attempt to be complete, but merely act as a guide to the format most likely to be used. The accompanying text and example should highlight the more complex options available. Below is a typical diagram:

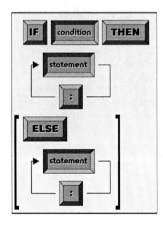

Each tile in the diagram holds a **token** of the statement. Raised tiles represent fixed terms in the statement, which must be entered exactly as shown. Sunken tiles represent tokens whose exact value is decided by you, the programmer, but again these values must conform to some stated rule.

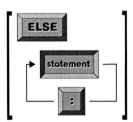

Items enclosed in brackets may be omitted if not required. In this example we can see that ELSE and all the terms that follow may be omitted.

Where one or more tokens in a diagram may be repeated indefinitely, this is shown using the arrowed line. This example shows that any number of statements can be used so long as a colon appears between each statement.

Occasionally, a single line of code will have to be printed over two or more lines because of paper width restrictions; these lines are signified by a ↳ symbol. Enter these lines without a break when testing any of the programs in which they are used. For example, the code

```
SPRITE crosshairs,(JOYSTICK X()+1000)*xpixels#,
↳(JOYSTICK Y()+1000)*ypixels#,1
```

should be entered as a single line.

1

Designing Algorithms

Boolean expressions

Data Variables

Designing Algorithms

Desk Checking

IF Control Structure

FOR Control Structure

REPEAT Control Structure

Stepwise Refinement

Testing

WHILE Control Structure

Designing Algorithms

Following Instructions

Activity 1.1

Carry out the following set of instructions in your head.

Think of a number between 1 and 10
Multiply that number by 9
Add up the individual digits of this new number
Subtract 5 from this total
Think of the letter at that position in the alphabet
Think of a country in Europe that starts with that letter
Think of a mammal that starts with the second letter of the country's name
Think of the colour of that mammal

Congratulations! You've just become a human computer. You were given a set of instructions which you have carried out (by the way, did you think of the colour grey?).

That's exactly what a computer does. You give it a set of instructions, the machine carries out those instructions, and that is ALL a computer does. If some computers seem to be able to do amazing things, that is only because someone has written an amazingly clever set of instructions. A set of instructions designed to perform some specific task is known as an **algorithm**.

There are a few points to note from the algorithm given above:

➢ There is one instruction per line

➢ Each instruction is unambiguous

➢ Each instruction is as short as possible

Activity 1.2

This time let's see if you can devise your own algorithm.

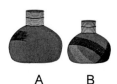

A   B

The task you need to solve is to measure out exactly 4 litres of water. You have two containers. Container A, if filled, will hold exactly 5 litres of water, while container B will hold 3 litres of water. You have an unlimited supply of water and a drain to get rid of any water you no longer need. It is not possible to know how much water is in a container if you only partly fill it from the supply.

If you managed to come up with a solution, see if you can find a second way of measuring out the 4 litres.

As you can see, there are at least two ways to solve the problem given in Activity 1.2. Is one better than the other? Well, if we start by filling container A, the solution needs less instructions, so that might be a good guideline at this point when choosing which algorithm is best.

However, the algorithms that a computer carries out are not written in English like the instructions shown above, but in a more stylised form using a **computer programming language**. DarkBASIC Pro is one such language. The set of program language instructions which make up each algorithm is then known as a **computer program** or **software**.

Just as we may perform a great diversity of tasks by following different sets of instructions, so the computer can be made to carry out any task for which a program exists.

Computer programs are normally copied (or **loaded**) from a magnetic disk into the computer's memory and then executed (or **run**). Execution of a program involves the computer performing each instruction in the program one after the other. This it does at impressively high rates, possibly exceeding 2,000 million (or 2 billion) instructions per second (2,000 mips).

Depending on the program being run, the computer may act as a word processor, a database, a spreadsheet, a game, a musical instrument or one of many other possibilities. Of course, as a programmer, you are required to design and write computer programs rather than use them. And, more specifically, our programs in this text will be mainly games-related; an area of programming for which DarkBASIC Pro has been specifically designed.

Activity 1.3

1. A set of instructions that performs a specific task is known as what?

2. What term is used to describe a set of instructions used by a computer?

3. The speed of a computer is measured in what units?

Control Structures

Although writing algorithms and programming computers are certainly complicated tasks, there are only a few basic concepts and statements which you need to master before you are ready to start producing software. Luckily, the concepts are already familiar to you in everyday situations. If you examine any algorithm, no matter how complex, you will find it consists of three basic structures:

> **Sequence**   where one statement follows on from another.

> **Selection**   where a choice is made between two or more alternative actions.

> **Iteration**   where one or more instructions are carried out over and over again.

These are explained in detail over the next few pages. All that is needed is to formalise the use of these structures within an algorithm. This formalisation better matches the structure of a computer program.

Sequence

A set of instructions designed to be carried out one after another, beginning at the first and continuing, without omitting any, until the final instruction is completed, is known as a **sequence**. For example, instructions on how to play Monopoly might begin with the sequence:

Choose your playing piece
Place your piece on the GO square
Get £1,500 from the bank

The set of instructions given earlier in Activity 1.1 is also an example of a sequence.

Activity 1.4

Re-arrange the following instructions to describe how to play a single shot during a golf game:

Swing club forwards, attempting to hit ball
Take up correct stance beside ball
Grip club correctly
Swing club backwards
Choose club

Selection

Binary Selection

Often a group of instructions in an algorithm should only be carried out when certain circumstances arise. For example, if we were playing a simple game with a young child in which we hide a sweet in one hand and allow the child to have the sweet if she can guess which hand the sweet is in, then we might explain the core idea with an instruction such as

Give the sweet to the child if the child guesses which hand the sweet is in

Notice that when we write a sentence containing the word IF, it consists of two main components:

a condition   :   *the child guesses which hand the sweet is in*
and
a command   :   *give the sweet to the child*

A **condition** (also known as a **Boolean expression**) is a statement that is either true or false. The command given in the statement is only carried out if the condition is true and hence this type of instruction is known as an **IF** statement and the command as a **conditional instruction**. Although we could rewrite the above instruction in many different ways, when we produce a set of instructions in a formal manner, as we are required to do when writing algorithms, then we use a specific layout as shown in FIG-1.1 always beginning with the word IF.

FIG-1.1

The IF Statement

Notice that the layout of this instruction makes use of three terms that are always included. These are the words IF, which marks the beginning of the instruction; THEN, which separates the condition from the command; and finally, ENDIF which marks the end of the instruction.

The indentation of the command is important since it helps our eye grasp the structure of our instructions. Appropriate indentation is particularly valuable in aiding readability once an algorithm becomes long and complex. Using this layout, the instruction for our game with the child would be written as:

```
IF the child guesses which hand the sweet is in THEN
        Give the sweet to the child
ENDIF
```

Sometimes, there will be several commands to be carried out when the condition specified is met. For example, in the game of Scrabble we might describe a turn as:

```
IF you can make a word THEN
        Add the word to the board
        Work out the points gained
        Add the points to your total
        Select more letter tiles
ENDIF
```

Of course, the conditional statement will almost certainly appear in a longer sequence of instructions. For example, the instructions for playing our guessing game with the young child may be given as:

```
Hide a sweet in one hand
Ask the child to guess which hand contains the sweet
IF the child guesses which hand the sweet is in THEN
        Give the sweet to the child
ENDIF
Ask the child if they would like to play again
```

This longer sequence of instructions highlights the usefulness of the term ENDIF in separating the conditional command, Give the sweet to the child, from subsequent unconditional instructions, in this case, Ask the child if they would like to play again.

Activity 1.5

A simple game involves two players. Player 1 thinks of a number between 1 and 100, then Player 2 makes a single attempt at guessing the number. Player 1 responds to a correct guess by saying *Correct*. The game is then complete and Player 1 states the value of the number.

Write the set of instructions necessary to play the game.

In your solution, include the statements:

```
Player 1 says "Correct"
Player 1 thinks of a number
IF guess matches number THEN
```

The IF structure is also used in an extended form to offer a choice between two alternative actions. This expanded form of the IF statement includes another formal term, ELSE, and a second command. If the condition specified in the IF statement is true, then the command following the term THEN is executed, otherwise that following ELSE is carried out.

For instance, in our earlier example of playing a guessing game with a child, nothing happened if the child guessed wrongly. If the person holding the sweet were to eat it when the child's guess was incorrect, we could describe this setup with the following statement:

```
IF the child guesses which hand the sweet is in THEN
    Give the sweet to the child
ELSE
    Eat sweet yourself
ENDIF
```

The general form of this extended IF statement is shown in FIG-1.2.

FIG-1.2

The IF ... ELSE Statement

Activity 1.6

Write an IF statement containing an ELSE section which describes the alternative actions to be taken when playing Hangman and the player trying to guess the word suggests a letter.

In the solution include the statements:
    Add letter at appropriate position(s)
    Add part to hanged man

Choosing between two alternative actions is called **binary selection**.

When we have several independent selections to make, then we may use several IF statements. For example, when playing Monopoly, we may buy any unpurchased property we land on. In addition, we get another turn if we throw a double. This part of the game might be described using the following statements:

```
Throw the dice
Move your piece forward by the number indicated
IF you land on an unpurchased property THEN
    Buy the property
ENDIF
IF you threw doubles THEN
    Throw the dice again
ELSE
    Hand the dice to the next player
ENDIF
```

This set of instructions is not complete and is shown here only to illustrate the use of multiple IF statements in an algorithm.

Multi-way Selection

Although a single IF statement can be used to select one of two alternative actions, sometimes we need to choose between more than two alternatives (known as **multi-way selection**). For example, imagine that the rules of the simple guessing game mentioned in Activity 1.5 are changed so that there are three possible responses to Player 2's guess; these being:

➤ Correct

➤ Too low

➤ Too high

One way to create an algorithm that describes this situation is just to employ three separate IF statements:

```
IF the guess is equal to the number you thought of THEN
        Say "Correct"
ENDIF
IF the guess is lower than the number you thought of THEN
        Say "Too low"
ENDIF
IF the guess is higher than the number you thought of THEN
        Say "Too high"
ENDIF
```

This will work, but would not be considered a good design for an algorithm since, when the first IF statement is true, we still go on and check if the conditions in the second and third IF statements are true. After all, only one of the three conditions can be true at any one time.

Where only one of the conditions being considered can be true at a given moment in time, these conditions are known as **mutually exclusive** conditions.

The most effective way to deal with mutually exclusive conditions is to check for one condition, and only if this is not true, are the other conditions tested. So, for example, in our algorithm for guessing the number, we might begin by writing:

```
IF guess matches number THEN
        Say "Correct"
ELSE
        ***Check the other conditions***
ENDIF
```

Of course a statement like ***Check the other conditions*** is too vague to be much use in an algorithm (hence the asterisks). But what are these other conditions? They are *the guess is lower than the number you thought of* and *the guess is higher than the number you thought of*.

We already know how to handle a situation where there are only two alternatives: use an IF statement. So we can chose between *Too low* and *Too high* with the statement

```
IF guess is less than number THEN
        Say "Too low"
ELSE
        Say "Too high"
ENDIF
```

Now, by replacing the phrase ***Check the other conditions*** in our original algorithm with our new IF statement we get:

```
IF guess matches number THEN
        Say "Correct
ELSE
        IF guess is less than number THEN
            Say "Too low"
        ELSE
            Say "Too high"
        ENDIF
ENDIF
```

Notice that the second IF statement is now totally contained within the ELSE section of the first IF statement. This situation is known as **nested** IF statements. Where there are even more mutually exclusive alternatives, several IF statements may be nested in this way. However, in most cases, we're not likely to need more than two nested IF statements.

As you can see from the solution to Activity 1.7, although nested IF statements get the job done, the general structure can be rather difficult to follow. A better method would be to change the format of the IF statement so that several, mutually exclusive, conditions can be declared in a single IF statement along with the action required for each of these conditions. This would allow us to rewrite the solution to Activity 1.7 as:

```
IF
    crossbow is too high:
        Say "Down a bit"
    crossbow is too low:
        Say "Up a bit"
    crossbow is too far right:
        Say "Left a bit"
    crossbow is too far left:
        Say " Right a bit"
    crossbow is on target:
        Say "Fire"
ENDIF
```

Each option is explicitly named (ending with a colon) and only the one which is true will be carried out, the others will be ignored.

Of course, we are not limited to merely five options; there can be as many as the situation requires.

When producing a program for a computer, all possibilities have to be taken into account. Early adventure games, which were text based, allowed the player to type a command such as *Go East*, *Go West*, *Go North*, *Go South* and this moved the player's character to new positions in the imaginary world of the computer program. If the player typed in an unrecognised command such as *Go North-East* or *Move faster*, then the game would issue an error message. This setup can be described by adding an ELSE section to the structure as shown below:

```
IF
    command is Go East:
        Move player's character eastward
    command is Go West:
        Move player's character westward
    command is Go North:
        Move player's character northward
    command is Go South:
        Move player's character southward
    ELSE
        Display an error message
ENDIF
```

The additional ELSE option will be chosen only if none of the other options are applicable. In other words, it acts like a catch-all, handling all the possibilities not explicitly mentioned in the earlier conditions.

This gives us the final form of this style of the IF statement as shown in FIG-1.3:

FIG-1.3

The Third Version of the IF Statement

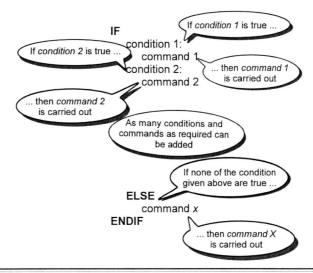

Complex Conditions

Often the condition given in an IF statement may be a complex one. For example, in the TV game Family Fortunes, you only win the star prize if you get 200 points and guess the most popular answers to a series of questions. This can be described in our more formal style as:

```
IF at least 200 points gained AND all most popular answers have been guessed THEN
    winning team get the star prize
ENDIF
```

The AND Operator

Note the use of the word AND in the above example. AND (called a **Boolean operator**) is one of the terms used to link simple conditions in order to produce a more complex one (known as a **complex condition**). The conditions on either side of the AND are called the operands. Both operands must be true for the overall result to be true. We can generalise this to describe the AND operator as being used in the form:

```
condition 1   AND   condition 2
```

The result of the AND operator is determined using the following rules:

1. Determine the truth of condition 1
2. Determine the truth of condition 2
3. IF both conditions are true THEN
        the overall result is true
   ELSE
        the overall result is false
   ENDIF

For example, if we assume the group reaching the final of the game show Family Fortunes has amassed 230 points but have not guessed all of the most popular answers, then a computer would determine the overall result of the IF statement given earlier as shown in FIG-1.4.

FIG-1.4

Calculating the Result of an AND Operation

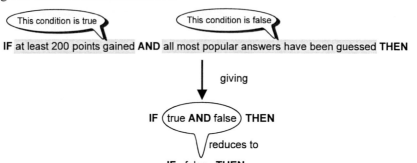

With two conditions there are four possible combinations. The first possibility is that both conditions are false; another possibility is that *condition 1* is false but *condition 2* is true.

Activity 1.9

What are the other two possible combinations of true and false?

The results of the AND operator are summarised in TABLE-1.1.

TABLE-1.1

The AND Operator

condition 1	condition 2	condition 1 AND condition 2
false	false	false
false	true	false
true	false	false
true	true	true

Activity 1.10

In the card game Snap, you win the cards on the table if you are first to place your hand over those cards, and the last two cards laid down are of the same value.

Write an IF statement, which includes the term AND, summarising this situation.

The OR Operator

Simple conditions may also be linked by the Boolean OR operator. Using OR, only one of the conditions needs to be true in order to carry out the action that follows. For example, in the game of Monopoly you go to jail if you land on the *GoTo Jail* square or if you throw three doubles in a row. This can be written as:

```
IF player lands on Go To Jail OR player has thrown 3 pairs in a row THEN
    Player goes to jail
ENDIF
```

Like AND, the OR operator works on two operands:

```
condition 1   OR   condition 2
```

When OR is used, only one of the conditions involved needs to be true for the overall result to be true. Hence the results are determined by the following rules:

```
1.    Determine the truth of condition 1
2.    Determine the truth of condition 2
3.    IF any of the conditions are true THEN
          the overall result is true
      ELSE
          the overall result is false
      ENDIF
```

For example, if a player in the game of Monopoly has not landed on the *Go To Jail* square, but has thrown three consecutive pairs, then the result of the IF statement given above would be determined as shown in FIG-1.5.

FIG-1.5

Calculating the Result of an OR Operation

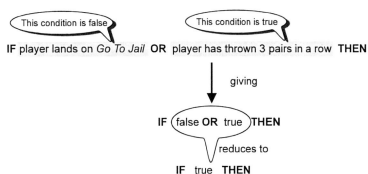

The results of the OR operator are summarised in TABLE-1.2.

TABLE-1.2

The OR Operator

condition 1	condition 2	condition 1 OR condition 2
false	false	false
false	true	true
true	false	true
true	true	true

Activity 1.11

In Monopoly, a player can get out of jail if he throws a double or pays a £50 fine.

Express this information in an IF statement which makes use of the OR operator.

The NOT Operator

The final Boolean operator which can be used as part of a condition is NOT. This operator is used to reverse the meaning of a condition. Hence, if *property mortgaged* is true, then *NOT property mortgaged* is false.

Notice that the word NOT is always placed at the start of the condition and not where it would appear in everyday English (*property NOT mortgaged*).

In Monopoly a player can charge rent on a property as long as that property is not mortgaged. This situation can be described with the statement:

```
IF NOT property mortgaged THEN
     Rent can be charged
ENDIF
```

The NOT operator works on a single operand:

```
NOT condition
```

When NOT is used, the result given by the original condition is reversed. Hence the results are determined by the following rules:

1. Determine the truth of the condition
2. Complement the result obtained in step 1

For example, if a player lands on a property that is not mortgaged, then the result of the IF statement given above would be determined as shown in FIG-1.6.

FIG-1.6

Calculating the Result of
a NOT Operation

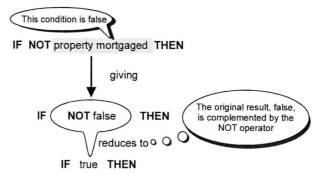

The results of the NOT operator are summarised in TABLE-1.3.

TABLE-1.3

The NOT Operator

condition	NOT condition
false	true
true	false

Complex conditions are not limited to a single occurrence of a Boolean operator, hence it is valid to have statements such as:

```
IF player lands on Go To Jail OR player has thrown 3 pairs in a row OR
   player lifts a Go To Jail card
THEN
     Player goes to jail
ENDIF
```

Although us humans might be able to work all of this out in our heads without even a conscious thought, computers deal with such complex conditions in a slow, but methodical way.

To calculate the final result of the condition given above, the computer requires several operations to be performed. These are performed in two stages:

1. Determine the truth of each condition
2. Determine the result of each OR operation, starting with the left-most OR

FIG-1.7

Using More than One
OR Operator

For example, if a player lifts a *Go To Jail* card from the *Chance* pack, then the result of the IF statement given above would be determined as shown in FIG-1.7.

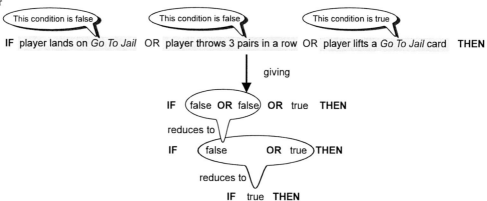

That might seem a rather complicated way of achieving what was probably an obvious result, but when the conditions become even more complex, this methodical approach is necessary.

Notice that when a complex condition contains only a single Boolean operator type (OR in the example above), that the expression is worked out from left to right. However, should the condition contain a mixture of OR, AND and NOT operators, NOT operations are performed first, ANDs second, and ORs last.

For example, if a game has the following rule

```
IF player has a magic sword AND player has magic armour OR
player has taken invisibility potion AND player possesses sleep spell
THEN
      Player can kill dragon
ENDIF
```

and a player has magic armour and has drunk the invisibility potion, then to determine if the player can kill the dragon, the process shown in FIG-1.8 is followed.

FIG-1.8

AND Operators have
Priority

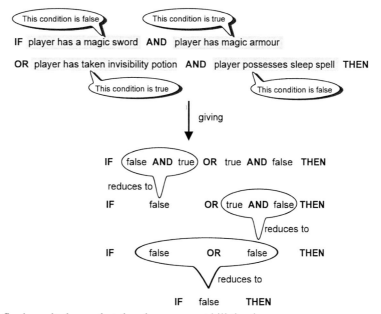

The final result shows that the player cannot kill the dragon.

Sometimes the priority of operators works against what we are trying to express. For example, if a player receives a bonus if he lands on a red, green or blue square after throwing 7 on a pair of dice, then we might be tempted to write:

```
IF landed on red OR landed on green OR landed on blue AND thrown 7 THEN
    Add bonus to player's score
ENDIF
```

We would not expect a player landing on a red square after throwing 9 to receive the bonus. But, if we look at the calculation for such a situation, we get the result shown in FIG-1.9 which means that the bonus is incorrectly added to the player's score.

FIG-1.9

How the Final Result is
Calculated

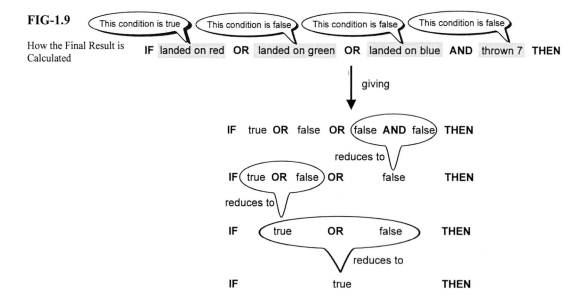

To achieve the correct results, we need the OR operations to be performed first and this can be done by giving the OR operators a higher priority than the AND. Luckily, operator priority can be modified by using parentheses. Operations in parentheses are always performed first. So, by rewriting our instruction as

```
IF (landed on red OR landed on green OR landed on blue) AND thrown 7 THEN
    Add bonus to player's score
ENDIF
```

the condition is calculated as shown in FIG-1.10.

FIG-1.10

Using Parentheses to Modify Operator Priority

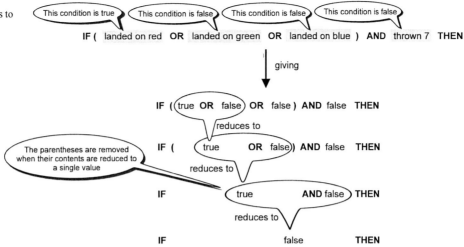

Boolean operator priority is summarised in TABLE-1.4.

TABLE-1.4

Operator Priority

Priority	Operator
1	( )
2	NOT
3	AND
4	OR

Activity 1.13

The rules for winning a card game are that your hand of 5 cards must add up to exactly 43 (faces =10, Ace = 11) or you must have four cards of the same value. In addition, a player cannot win unless he has a Queen in his hand.

Express these winning conditions as an IF statement.

Activity 1.14

1. Name the three types of control structures.

2. Another term for condition is what?

3. Name the two types of selection.

4. What does the term *mutually exclusive conditions* mean?

5. Give an example of a Boolean operator.

6. If the terms AND and OR are included in a single complex condition, which of these operators will be performed first?

7. How can the order in which operations in a complex condition be changed?

Iteration

There are certain circumstances in which it is necessary to perform the same sequence of instructions several times. For example, let's assume that a game involves throwing a dice three times and adding up the total of the values thrown. We could write instructions for such a game as follows:

```
Set the total to zero
Throw dice
Add dice value to total
Throw dice
Add dice value to total
Throw dice
Add dice value to total
Call out the value of total
```

You can see from the above that two instructions,

```
Throw dice
Add dice value to total
```

are carried out three times, once for each turn taken by the player. Not only does it seem rather time-consuming to have to write the same pair of instructions three times, but it would be even worse if the player had to throw the dice 10 times!

What is required is a way of showing that a section of the instructions is to be repeated a fixed number of times. Carrying out one or more statements over and over again is known as **looping** or **iteration**. The statement or statements that we want to perform over and over again are known as the **loop body**.

Activity 1.15

What statements make up the loop body in our dice problem given above?

FOR..ENDFOR

When writing a formal algorithm in which we wish to repeat a set of statements a specific number of times, we use a **FOR..ENDFOR** structure.

There are two parts to this statement. The first of these is placed just before the loop body and in it we state how often we want the statements in the loop body to be carried out. For the dice problem our statement would be:

```
FOR 3 times DO
```

Generalising, we can say this statement takes the form

```
FOR value times DO
```

where *value* would be some positive number.

Next come the statements that make up the loop body. These are indented:

```
FOR 3 times DO
    Throw dice
    Add dice value to total
```

Finally, to mark the fact that we have reached the end of the loop body statements we add the word ENDFOR:

Note that ENDFOR is left-aligned with the opening FOR statement.

```
FOR 3 times DO
    Throw dice
    Add dice value to total
ENDFOR
```

Now we can rewrite our original algorithm as:

```
Set the total to zero
FOR 3 times DO
    Throw dice
    Add dice value to total
ENDFOR
Call out the value of total
```

The instructions between the terms FOR and ENDFOR are now carried out three times.

Activity 1.16

You can find the average of the 10 numbers by dividing the final total by 10.

If the player was required to throw the dice 10 times rather than 3, what changes would we need to make to the algorithm?
If the player was required to call out the average of these 10 numbers, rather than the total, show what other changes are required to the set of instructions.

We are free to place any statements we wish within the loop body. For example, the last version of our number guessing game produced the following algorithm

```
Player 1 thinks of a number between 1 and 100
Player 2 makes an attempt at guessing the number
IF guess matches number THEN
    Player 1 says "Correct
ELSE
    IF guess is less than number THEN
        Player 1 says "Too low"
    ELSE
        Player 1 says "Too high"
    ENDIF
ENDIF
```

player 2 would have more chance of winning if he were allowed several chances at guessing player 1's number. To allow several attempts at guessing the number, some of the statements given above would have to be repeated.

Activity 1.17

What statements in the algorithm above need to be repeated?

To allow for 7 attempts our new algorithm becomes:

```
Player 1 thinks of a number between 1 and 100
FOR 7 times DO
    Player 2 makes an attempt at guessing the number
    IF guess matches number THEN
        Player 1 says "Correct
    ELSE
        IF guess is less than number THEN
            Player 1 says "Too low"
        ELSE
            Player 1 says "Too high"
        ENDIF
    ENDIF
ENDFOR
```

Occasionally, we may have to use a slightly different version of the FOR loop.
Imagine we are trying to write an algorithm explaining how to decide who goes first
in a game. In this game every player throws a dice and the player who throws the
highest value goes first. To describe this activity we know that each player does the
following task:

    Player throws dice

But since we can't know in advance how many players there will be, we write the
algorithm using the statement

    FOR every player DO

to give the following algorithm

    FOR every player DO
        Throw dice
    ENDFOR
    Player with highest throw goes first

If we had to save the details of a game of chess with the intention of going back to
the game later, we might write:

```
FOR each piece on the board DO
    Write down the name and position of the piece
ENDFOR
```

The general form of the FOR statement is shown in FIG-1.11.

FIG-1.11

The FOR Loop

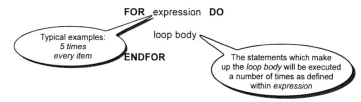

Although the FOR loop allows us to perform a set of statements a specific number of times, this statement is not always suitable for the problem we are trying to solve. For example, in the guessing game we stated that the loop body was to be performed 7 times, but what if player 2 guesses the number after only three attempts? If we were to follow the algorithm exactly (as a computer would), then we must make four more guesses at the number even after we know the correct answer!

To solve this problem, we need another way of expressing looping which does not commit us to a specific number of iterations.

REPEAT.. UNTIL

The REPEAT .. UNTIL statement allows us to specify that a set of statements should be repeated until some condition becomes true, at which point iteration should cease. The word REPEAT is placed at the start of the loop body and, at its end, we add the UNTIL statement. The UNTIL statement also contains a condition, which, when true, causes iteration to stop. This is known as the **terminating** (or **exit**) **condition**. For example, we could use the REPEAT.. UNTIL structure rather than the FOR loop in our guessing game algorithm. The new version would then be:

```
Player 1 thinks of a number between 1 and 100
REPEAT
      Player 2 makes an attempt at guessing the number
      IF guess matches number THEN
            Player 1 says "Correct
      ELSE
            IF guess is less than number THEN
                  Player 1 says "Too low"
            ELSE
                  Player 1 says "Too high"
            ENDIF
      ENDIF
UNTIL player 2 guesses correctly
```

We could also use the REPEAT..UNTIL loop to describe how a slot machine (one-armed bandit) is played:

```
REPEAT
      Put coin in machine
      Pull handle
      IF you win THEN
            Collect winnings
      ENDIF
UNTIL you want to stop
```

The general form of this structure is shown in FIG-1.12.

FIG-1.12

The REPEAT Loop

REPEAT

loop body

UNTIL condition

> The *loop body* statements will be executed continuously until *condition* is true

The terminating condition may use the Boolean operators AND, OR and NOT as well as parentheses, where necessary.

Activity 1.21

A one-armed bandit costs 50p per play. A player has several 50p pieces and is determined to play until his coins are gone or until he wins at least £10.00. Write an algorithm describing the steps in this game. The algorithm should make use of the following statements:

Collect winnings
Place coin in machine
Pull arm
UNTIL all coins are gone OR winnings are at least £10.00

There is still a problem with our number-guessing game. By using a REPEAT .. UNTIL loop we are allowing player 2 to have as many guesses as needed to determine the correct number. That doesn't lead to a very interesting game. Later we'll discover how we might solve this problem.

WHILE.. ENDWHILE

A final method of iteration, differing only subtly from the REPEAT.. UNTIL loop, is the WHILE .. ENDWHILE structure which has an **entry condition** at the start of the loop.

The aim of the card game of Pontoon is to attempt to make the value of your cards add up to 21 without going over that value. Each player is dealt two cards initially but can repeatedly ask for more cards by saying "twist". One player is designated the dealer. The dealer must twist while his cards have a total value of less than 16. So we might write the rules for the dealer as:

```
Calculate the sum of the initial two cards
REPEAT
    Take another card
    Add new card's value to sum
UNTIL sum is greater than or equal to 16
```

But this solution implies that the dealer must take at least one card before deciding to stop. Using the WHILE..ENDWHILE structure we could describe the logic as

```
Calculate sum of the initial two cards
WHILE sum is less than 16 DO
    Take another card
    Add new card's value to sum
ENDWHILE
```

Now determining if the sum is less than 16 is performed before *Take another card* instruction. If the dealer's two cards already add up to 16 or more, then the *Take another card* instruction will be ignored.

The general form of the WHILE.. ENDWHILE statement is shown in FIG-1.13.

FIG-1.13

The WHILE Loop

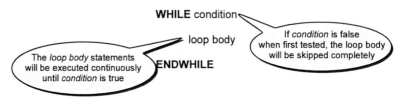

WHILE condition

loop body

ENDWHILE

The *loop body* statements will be executed continuously until *condition* is true

If *condition* is false when first tested, the loop body will be skipped completely

In what way does this differ from the REPEAT statement? There are two differences:

> The condition is given at the beginning of the loop.

> Looping stops when the condition is false.

The main consequence of this is that it is possible to bypass the loop body of a WHILE structure entirely without ever carrying out any of the instructions it contains, whereas the loop body of a REPEAT structure will always be executed at least once.

Activity 1.22

A game involves throwing two dice. If the two values thrown are not the same, then the dice showing the lower value must be rolled again. This process is continued until both dice show the same value.

Write a set of instructions to perform this game.

Your solution should contain the statements

      Roll both dice

and

      Choose dice with lower value

Activity 1.23

1. What is the meaning of the term iteration?

2. Name the three types of looping structures.

3. What type of loop structure should be used when looping needs to occur an exact number of times?

4. What type of loop structure can bypass its loop body without ever executing it?

5. What type of loop contains an exit condition?

Data

Almost every game requires the players to remember or record some facts and figures. In our number guessing game described earlier, the players needed to remember the original number and the guesses made; in Hangman the word being guessed and the letters guessed so far must be remembered.

These examples introduce the need to process facts and figures (known as **data**). Every computer game has to process data. This data may be the name of a character, the speed of a missile, the strength of a blow, or some other factor.

Every item of data has two basic characteristics :

      a name

and   a value

The name of a data item is a description of the type of information it represents. Hence character's *title*, *strength* and *charisma* are names of data items; *"Fred the Invincible"*, *3*, and *9* are examples of the actual values which might be given to these data items.

In programming, a data item is often referred to as a **variable**. This term arises from the fact that, although the name assigned to a data item cannot change, its value may vary. For example, the value assigned to a variable called *lives remaining*, will be reduced if the player's character is killed.

Activity 1.24

List the names of four data items that might be held about a player in a game of Monopoly.

Operations on Data

There are four basic operations that a computer can do with data. These are:

Input

This involves being given a value for a data item. For example, in our number-guessing game, the player who has thought of the original number is given the value of the guess from the second player. When playing Noughts and Crosses adding an X (or O) changes the set up on the board. When using a computer, any value entered at the keyboard, or any movement or action dictated by a mouse or joystick would be considered as data entry. This type of action is known as an **input operation**.

Calculation

Most games involve some basic arithmetic. In Monopoly, the banker has to work out how much change to give a player buying a property. If a character in an adventure game is hit, points must be deducted from his strength value. This type of instruction is referred to as a **calculation operation**.

Comparison

Often values have to be compared. For example, we need to compare the two numbers in our guessing game to find out if they are the same. This is known as a **comparison operation**.

Output

The final requirement is to communicate with others to give the result of some calculation or comparison. For example, in the guessing game player 1 communicates with player 2 by saying either that the guess is *Correct*, *Too high* or *Too low*.

In a computer environment, the equivalent operation would normally involve displaying information on a screen or printing it on paper. For instance, in a racing game your speed and time will be displayed on the screen. This is called an **output operation**.

When describing a calculation, it is common to use arithmetic operator symbols rather than English. Hence, instead of writing the word *subtract* we use the minus sign (-). A summary of the operators available are given in TABLE-1.5.

TABLE-1.5

Mathematical Operators

English	Symbol
Multiply	*
Divide	/
Add	+
Subtract	-

Similarly, when we need to compare values, rather than use terms such as is less than, we use the less than symbol (<). A summary of these relational operators is given in TABLE-1.6.

TABLE-1.6

Relational Operators

English	Symbol
is less than	<
is less than or equal to	<=
is greater than	>
is greater than or equal to	>=
is equal to	=
is not equal to	<>

As well as replacing the words used for arithmetic calculations and comparisons with symbols, the term *calculate* or *set* is often replaced by the shorter but more cryptic symbol := between the variable being assigned a value and the value itself. Using this abbreviated form, the instruction:

Calculate time to complete course as distance divided by speed

becomes

time := distance / speed

Although the long-winded English form is more readable, this more cryptic style is briefer and is much closer to the code used when programming a computer.

Below we compare the two methods of describing our guessing game; first in English:

```
Player 1 thinks of a number between 1 and 100
REPEAT
    Player 2 makes an attempt at guessing the number
    IF guess matches number THEN
        Player 1 says "Correct
    ELSE
        IF guess is less than number THEN
            Player 1 says "Too low"
        ELSE
            Player 1 says "Too high"
        ENDIF
    ENDIF
UNTIL player 2 guesses correctly
```

Using some of the symbols described earlier, we can rewrite this as:

```
Player 1 thinks of a number between 1 and 100
REPEAT
    Player 2 makes an attempt at guessing the number
    IF guess = number THEN
        Player 1 says "Correct
    ELSE
        IF guess < number THEN
            Player 1 says "Too low"
        ELSE
            Player 1 says "Too high"
        ENDIF
    ENDIF
UNTIL guess = number
```

Activity 1.26

1. What are the two main characteristics of any data item?

2. When data is input, from where is its value obtained?

3. Give an example of a relational operator.

Levels of Detail

When we start to write an algorithm in English, one of the things we need to consider is exactly how much detail should be included. For example, we might describe how to record a programme on a video recorder as:

```
Put new tape in video
Set timer details
```

However, this lacks enough detail for anyone unfamiliar with the operation of the machine. We could replace the first statement with:

```
Press the eject button
IF there is a tape in the machine THEN
    Remove it
ENDIF
Place the new tape in the machine
```

and the second statement could be substituted by:

```
Switch to timer mode
Enter start time
Enter finish time
Select channel
```

This approach of starting with a less detailed sequence of instructions and then, where necessary, replacing each of these with more detailed instructions can be used to good effect when tackling long and complex problems.

By using this technique, we are defining the original problem as an equivalent sequence of simpler tasks before going on to create a set of instructions to handle each of these simpler problems. This divide-and-conquer strategy is known as **stepwise refinement**. The following is a fully worked example of this technique:

Problem:
Describe how to make a cup of tea.

Outline Solution:

1. Fill kettle
2. Boil water
3. Put tea bag in teapot
4. Add boiling water to teapot
5. Wait 1 minute
6. Pour tea into cup
7. Add milk and sugar to taste

This is termed a **LEVEL 1 solution**.

As a guideline we should aim for a LEVEL 1 solution with between 5 and 12 instructions. Notice that each instruction has been numbered. This is merely to help with identification during the stepwise refinement process.

Before going any further, we must assure ourselves that this is a correct and full (though not detailed) description of all the steps required to tackle the original problem. If we are not happy with the solution, then changes must be made before going any further.

Next, we examine each statement in turn and determine if it should be described in more detail. Where this is necessary, rewrite the statement to be dealt with, and below it, give the more detailed version. For example. *Fill kettle* would be expanded thus:

1. Fill kettle
   1.1 Remove kettle lid
   1.2 Put kettle under tap
   1.3 Turn on tap
   1.4 When kettle is full, turn off tap
   1.5 Place lid back on kettle

The numbering of the new statement reflects that they are the detailed instructions pertaining to statement 1. Also note that the number system is not a decimal fraction so if there were to be many more statements they would be numbered 1.6, 1.7, 1.8, 1.9, 1.10, 1.11, etc.

It is important that these sets of more detailed instructions describe how to perform only the original task being examined - they must achieve no more and no less. Sometimes the detailed instructions will contain control structures such as IFs, WHILEs or FORs. Where this is the case, the whole structure must be included in the detailed instructions for that task.

Having satisfied ourselves that the breakdown is correct, we proceed to the next statement from the original solution.

2. Boil water
   2.1 Plug in kettle
   2.2 Switch on power at socket
   2.3 Switch on power at kettle
   2.4 When water boils switch off kettle

The next two statements expand as follows:

3. Put tea bag in teapot
   3.1 Remove lid from teapot
   3.2 Add tea bag to teapot

4. Add boiling water to teapot
   4.1 Take kettle over to teapot
   4.2 Add required quantity of water from kettle to teapot

But not every statement from a level 1 solution needs to be expanded. In our case there is no more detail to add to the statement

     5. Wait 1 minute

and therefore, we leave it unchanged.

The last two statements expand as follows:

     6. Pour tea into cup
         6.1 Take teapot over to cup
         6.2 Pour required quantity of tea from teapot into cup

     7. Add milk and sugar as required
         7.1 IF milk is required THEN
         7.2   Add milk
         7.3 ENDIF
         7.4 IF sugar is required THEN
         7.5   Add sugar
         7.6   Stir tea
         7.7 ENDIF

Notice that this last expansion (step 7) has introduced IF statements. Control structures (i.e. IF, WHILE, FOR, etc.) can be introduced at any point in an algorithm.

Finally, we can describe the solution to the original problem in more detail by substituting the statements in our LEVEL 1 solution by their more detailed equivalent:

     1.1 Remove kettle lid
     1.2 Put kettle under tap
     1.3 Turn on tap
     1.4 When kettle is full, turn off tap
     1.5 Place lid back on kettle
     2.1 Plug in kettle
     2.2 Switch on power at socket
     2.3 Switch on power at kettle
     2.4 When water boils switch off kettle
     3.1 Remove lid from teapot
     3.2 Add tea bag to teapot
     4.1 Take kettle over to teapot
     4.2 Add required quantity of water from kettle to teapot
     5.   Wait 1 minute
     6.1 Take teapot over to cup
     6.2 Pour required quantity of tea from teapot into cup
     7.1 IF milk is required THEN
     7.2   Add milk
     7.3 ENDIF
     7.4 IF sugar is required THEN
     7.5   Add sugar
     7.6   Stir tea
     7.7 ENDIF

This is a LEVEL 2 solution. Note that a level 2 solution includes any LEVEL 1 statements which were not given more detail (in this case, the statement Wait 1 minute).

For some more complex problems it may be necessary to repeat this process to more levels before sufficient detail is achieved. That is, statements in LEVEL 2 may need to be given more detail in a LEVEL 3 breakdown.

Activity 1.27

The game of battleships involves two players. Each player draws two 10 by 10 grids. Each of these have columns lettered A to J and rows numbered 1 to 10. In the first grid each player marks squares in the first grid to mark the position of warships. Ships are added as follows

    1 aircraft carrier 4 squares
    2 destroyers   3 squares each
    3 cruisers   2 squares each
    4 submarines   1 square each

The squares of each ship must be adjacent and must be vertical or horizontal.

The first player now calls out a grid reference. The second player responds to the call by saying HIT or MISS. HIT is called if the grid reference corresponds to a position of a ship. The first player then marks this result on his second grid using an o to signify a miss and x for a hit (see diagram below).

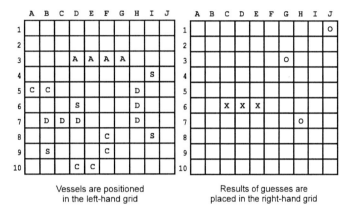

Vessels are positioned   Results of guesses are
in the left-hand grid   placed in the right-hand grid

If the first player achieves a HIT then he continues to call grid references until MISS is called. In response to a HIT or MISS call the first player marks the second grid at the reference called: 0 for a MISS, X for a HIT.

When the second player responds with MISS the first player's turn is over, and the second player has his turn.

The first player to eliminate all segments of the opponent's ships is the winner. However, each player must have an equal number of turns, and if both sets of ships are eliminated in the same round the game is a draw.

The algorithm describing the task of one player is given in the instructions below. Create a LEVEL 1 algorithm by assembling the lines in the correct order, adding line numbers to the finished description.

    Add ships to left grid
    Call grid position(s)
    REPEAT
    Respond to other player's call(s)
    Draw grids
    UNTIL there is a winner

continued on next page

Activity 1.27 (continued)

To create a LEVEL 2 algorithm, some of the above lines will have to be expanded to give more detail. More detailed instructions are given below for the statements *Call grid position(s)* and *Respond to other player's call(s)*. By reordering and numbering the lines below create LEVEL 2 details for these two statements

```
UNTIL other player misses
Mark position in second grid with X
Get other player's call
Get reply
Get reply
ENDIF
Call HIT
Call MISS
Mark position in second grid with 0
WHILE reply is HIT DO
Call grid reference
Call grid reference
IF other player's call matches position of ship THEN
ENDWHILE
REPEAT
ELSE
```

Checking for Errors

Once we've created our algorithm we would like to make sure it is correct. Unfortunately, there is no foolproof way to do this! But we can at least try to find any errors or omissions in the set of instructions we have created.

We do this by going back to the original description of the task our algorithm is attempting to solve. For example, let's assume we want to check our number guessing game algorithm. In the last version of the game we allowed the second player to make as many guesses as required until he came up with the correct answer. The first player responded to each guess by saying either "too low", "too high" or "correct".

To check our algorithm for errors we must come up with typical values that might be used when carrying out the set of instructions and those values should be chosen so that each possible result is achieved at least once.

So, as well as making up values, we need to predict what response our algorithm should give to each value used. Hence, if the first player thinks of the value 42 and the second player guesses 75, then the first player will respond to the guess by saying "Too high".

Our set of test values must evoke each of the possible results from our algorithm. One possible set of values and the responses are shown in TABLE-1.7.

TABLE-1.7

Test Data for the Number
Guessing Game Algorithm

Test Data	Expected Results
number = 42	
guess = 75	Says "Too high"
guess = 15	Says "Too low"
guess = 42	Says "Correct"

Once we've created test data, we need to work our way through the algorithm using that test data and checking that we get the expected results. The algorithm for the number game is shown below, this time with instruction numbers added.

```
1. Player 1 thinks of a number between 1 and 100
2. REPEAT
3.    Player 2 makes an attempt at guessing the number
4.    IF guess = number THEN
5.       Player 1 says "Correct"
6.    ELSE
7.       IF guess < number THEN
8.          Player 1 says "Too low"
9.       ELSE
10.         Player 1 says "Too high"
11.      ENDIF
12.   ENDIF
13. UNTIL guess = number
```

Next we create a new table (called a **trace table**) with the headings as shown in FIG-1.14.

FIG-1.14

The Components of a Trace Table

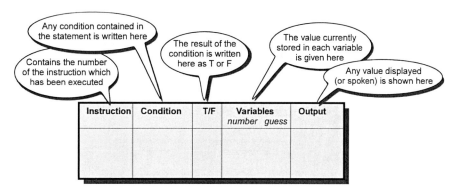

Now we work our way through the statements in the algorithm filling in a line of the trace table for each instruction.

Instruction 1 is for player 1 to think of a number. Using our test data, that number will be 42, so our trace table starts with the line shown in FIG-1.15.

FIG-1.15

Tracing the First Statement

Instruction	Condition	T/F	Variables number guess	Output
1			42	

The REPEAT word comes next. Although this does not cause any changes, nevertheless a 2 should be entered in the next line of our trace table. Instruction 3 involves player 2 making a guess at the number (this guess will be 75 according to our test data). After 3 instructions our trace table is as shown in FIG-1.16.

FIG-1.16

Moving through the Trace

Instruction	Condition	T/F	Variables number guess	Output
1			42	
2				
3			75	

Instruction 4 is an IF statement containing a condition. This condition and its result are written into columns 2 and 3 as shown in FIG-1.17.

FIG-1.17

Tracing a Condition

Instruction	Condition	T/F	Variables number guess	Output
1			42	
2				
3			75	
4	guess = number	F		

Because the condition is false, we now jump to instruction 6 (the ELSE line) and on to 7. This is another IF statement and our table now becomes that shown in FIG-1.18.

FIG-1.18

Tracing a Second Condition

Instruction	Condition	T/F	Variables number guess	Output
1			42	
2				
3			75	
4	guess = number	F		
6				
7	guess < number	F		

Since this second IF statement is also false, we move on to statements 9 and 10. Instruction 10 causes output (speech) and hence we enter this in the final column as shown in FIG-1.19.

FIG-1.19

Recording Output

Instruction	Condition	T/F	Variables number guess	Output
1			42	
2				
3			75	
4	guess = number	F		
6				
7	guess < number	F		
9				
10				Too high

Now we move on to statements 11,12 and 13 as shown in FIG-1.20.

FIG-1.20

Reaching the end of the REPEAT .. UNTIL Structure

Instruction	Condition	T/F	Variables number guess	Output
1			42	
2				
3			75	
4	guess = number	F		
6				
7	guess < number	F		
9				
10				Too high
11				
12				
13	guess = number	F		

Since statement 13 contains a condition which is false, we return to statement 2 and then onto 3 where we enter 15 as our second guess (see FIG-1.21).

FIG-1.21

Showing Iteration

Instruction	Condition	T/F	Variables number	guess	Output
1			42		
2					
3				75	
4	guess = number	F			
6					
7	guess < number	F			
9					
10					Too high
11					
12					
13	guess = number	F			
2					
3				15	

This method of checking is known as **desk checking** or **dry running**.

Activity 1.28

Create your own trace table for the number-guessing game and, using the same test data as given in TABLE-1.7 complete the testing of the algorithm.

Were the expected results obtained?

Summary

- Computers can perform many tasks by executing different programs.

- An algorithm is a sequence of instructions which solves a specific problem.

- A program is a sequence of computer instructions which usually manipulates data and produces results.

- Three control structures are used in programs :

    ➢ Sequence

    ➢ Selection

    ➢ Iteration

- A sequence is a list of instructions which are performed one after the other.

- Selection involves choosing between two or more alternative actions.

- Selection is performed using the IF statement.

- There are three forms of IF statement:

```
IF condition THEN
    instructions
ENDIF

IF condition THEN
    instructions
ELSE
    instructions
ENDIF
```

```
IF
    condition 1:
        instructions
    condition 2:
        instructions
    condition x :
        instructions
    ELSE
        instructions
ENDIF
```

● Iteration is the repeated execution of one or more statements.

● Iteration is performed using one of three instructions:

```
FOR number of iterations required DO
    instructions
ENDFOR

REPEAT
    instructions
UNTIL condition

WHILE condition DO
    instructions
ENDWHILE
```

● A condition is an expression which is either true or false.

● Simple conditions can be linked using AND or OR to produce a complex condition.

● The meaning of a condition can be reversed by adding the word NOT.

● Data items (or variables) hold the information used by the algorithm.

● Data item values may be:

> Input
> Calculated
> Compared
> or Output

● Calculations can be performed using the following arithmetic operators:

Multiplication	*	Addition	+
Division	/	Subtraction	-

● The order of priority of an operator may be overridden using parentheses.

● Comparisons can be performed using the relational operators:

Less than	$<$
Less than or equal to	$<=$
Greater than	$>$
Greater than or equal to	$>=$
Equal to	$=$
Not equal to	$<>$

- The symbol := is used to assign a value to a data item. Read this symbol as *is assigned the value*.

- In programming, a data item is referred to as a variable.

- The divide-and-conquer strategy of stepwise refinement can be used when creating an algorithm.

- LEVEL 1 solution gives an overview of the sub-tasks involved in carrying out the required operation.

- LEVEL 2 gives a more detailed solution by taking each sub-task from LEVEL 1 and, where necessary, giving a more detailed list of instructions required to perform that sub-task.

- Not every statement needs to be broken down into more detail.

- Further levels of detail may be necessary when using stepwise refinement for complex problems.

- Further refinement may not be required for every statement.

- An algorithm can be checked for errors or omissions using a trace table.

Solutions

Activity 1.1

No solution required.

Activity 1.2

One possible solution is:

```
Fill A
Fill B from A
Empty B
Empty A into B
Fill A
Fill B from A
```

Activity 1.3

1. An algorithm
2. A Computer program
3. mips (millions of instructions per second)

Activity 1.4

```
Choose club
Take up correct stance beside ball
Grip club correctly
Swing club backwards
Swing club forwards, attempting to hit ball
```

The second and third statements could be interchanged.

Activity 1.5

```
Player 1 thinks of a number
Player 2 makes a guess at the number
IF guess matches number THEN
  Player 1 says "Correct"
ENDIF
Player 1 states the value of the number
```

Activity 1.6

```
IF letter appears in word THEN
  Add letter at appropriate position(s)
ELSE
  Add part to hanged man
ENDIF
```

Activity 1.7

```
IF the crossbow is on target THEN
  Say "Fire"
ELSE
  IF the crossbow is pointing too high THEN
     Say "Down a bit"
  ELSE
     IF the crossbow is pointing too low THEN
        Say "Up a bit"
     ELSE
        IF crossbow is too far left THEN
           Say "Right a bit"
        ELSE
           Say "Left a bit"
        ENDIF
     ENDIF
  ENDIF
ENDIF
```

Activity 1.8

```
IF
  you know the phrase:
     Make guess at phrase
  there are many unseen letters:
     Guess a consonant
  ELSE
     Buy a vowel
ENDIF
```

Activity 1.9

Other possibilities are:

Both conditions are true
condition 1 is true and condition 2 is false

Activity 1.10

```
IF you are first to place your hand over
those cards AND the last two cards laid
down are of the same value
THEN
  You win the cards already played
ENDIF
```

Activity 1.11

```
IF  double thrown OR fine paid THEN
  Player gets out of jail
ENDIF
```

Activity 1.12

Assuming the player has one Ace and one Knave the statement

```
IF a player has an Ace AND player has
King OR player has two Knaves
THEN
```

would reduce to

```
IF true AND false OR false THEN
```

The AND operation is then performed giving:

```
IF  false OR false THEN
```

Next, the OR operation is completed giving a final value of

```
IF false THEN
```

and, therefore the player does not pick up an extra card.

Activity 1.13

```
IF (total of cards held is 43 OR hand has
4 cards of the same value ) AND hand
contains a Queen THEN
```

Activity 1.14

1. Sequence
   Selection
   Iteration

2. Boolean expression

3. Binary selection
   Multi-way selection

4. No more than one of the conditions can be true at any given time.

5. Boolean operators are: AND, OR, and NOT.

6. AND is performed before OR .

7. The order in which operations in a complex condition are calculated can changed by using parentheses.

Activity 1.15

```
Throw dice
Add dice value to total
```

Activity 1.16

Only one line, the FOR statement, would need to be changed, the new version being:

```
FOR 10 times DO
```

To call out the average, the algorithm would change to

```
Set the total to zero
FOR 10 times DO
  Throw dice
  Add dice value to total
ENDFOR
Calculate average as total divided by 10
Call out the value of average
```

Activity 1.17

In fact, only the first line of our algorithm is not repeated, so the lines that need to be repeated are:

```
Player 2 makes an attempt at guessing the
number
IF guess matches number THEN
  Player 1 says "Correct "
ELSE
  IF guess is less than number THEN
     Player 1 says "Too low"
  ELSE
     Player 1 says "Too high"
  ENDIF
ENDIF
```

Activity 1.18

The FOR loop forces the loop body to be executed exactly 7 times. If the player guesses the number in less attempts, the algorithm will nevertheless continue to ask for the remainder of the 7 guesses.

Later, we'll see how to solve this problem.

Activity 1.19

```
FOR 6 times DO
  Pick out ball
  Call out number on the ball
ENDFOR
```

Activity 1.20

```
FOR every card in player's hand DO
  IF card is a knight THEN
     Remove card from hand
  ENDIF
ENDFOR
```

Activity 1.21

```
REPEAT
  Place coin in machine
  Pull arm
  IF a win THEN
     Collect winnings
  ENDIF
UNTIL all coins are gone OR winnings are
at least £10.00
```

Activity 1.22

```
Roll both dice
WHILE both dice do not match in value DO
  Choose dice with lower value
  Roll the chosen dice
ENDWHILE
```

Activity 1.23

1. Iteration means executing a set of instructions over and over again.
2. The three looping structures are:

```
FOR .. ENDFOR
REPEAT .. UNTIL
WHILE .. ENDWHILE
```

3. The FOR .. ENDFOR structure.
4. The WHILE .. ENDWHILE structure.
5. The REPEAT .. UNTIL structure.

Activity 1.24

Number of properties held
Amount of money held
The playing token being used
The position on the board

Activity 1.25

Input:
  Letter guessed
  Word guessed
Calculations:
  Where to place a correctly guessed letter
  The number of wrong guesses made
Comparisons:
  The letter guessed with the letters in the word
  The word guessed with the word to be guessed
  The number of wrong guesses with the value 6
  (6 wrong guesses completes the drawing of the hanged man)
Output:
  Hyphens indicating each letter in the word
  Gallows
  Body parts of the hanged man
  Correctly guessed letters

Activity 1.26

1. Name and value
2. From outside the system. In a computerised system this is often via a keyboard.
3. The relational operators are:
   $<$, $<=$, $>$, $>=$, $=$, and $<>$

Activity 1.27

The LEVEL 1 is coded as:

```
1. Draw grids
2. Add ships to left grid
3. REPEAT
4.      Call grid position(s)
5.      Respond to other player's call(s)
6. UNTIL there is a winner
```

The expansion of statement 4 would become:

```
4.1 Call grid reference
4.2 Get reply
4.3 WHILE reply is HIT DO
4.4      Mark position in second grid with X
4.5      Call grid reference
4.6      Get reply
4.7 ENDWHILE
4.8 Mark position in second grid with O
```

The expansion of statement 5 would become:

```
5.1.REPEAT
5.2      Get other player's call
5.3      IF other player's call matches position of ship THEN
5.4          Call HIT
5.5      ELSE
5.6          Call MISS
5.7      ENDIF
5.8 UNTIL other player misses
```

Activity 1.28

Instruction	Condition	T/F	Variables number guess	Output
1			42	
2				
3			75	
4	guess = number	F		
6				
7	guess < number	F		
9				
10				Too high
11				
12				
13	guess = number	F		
2				
3			15	
4	guess = number	F		
6				
7	guess < number	T		
8				Too low
11				
12				
13	guess = number	F		
2				
3			42	
4	guess = number	T		
5				Correct
11				
12				
13	guess = number	T		

The expected results were obtained.

2

Starting DarkBASIC Pro

Correcting Errors

Creating a Project in DarkBASIC Pro

Executing a Program

Screen Output

Text Colour, Size, Font, and Style

The Compilation Process

Transparent and Opaque Text

Using the DarkBASIC Pro Editor

Programming a Computer

Introduction

In the last chapter we created algorithms written in a style of English known as structured English. But if we want to create an algorithm that can be followed by a computer, then we need to convert our structured English instructions into a programming language.

There are many programming languages; C++, Java, C#, and Visual Basic being amongst the most widely used. So how do we choose which programming language to use? Probably the most important consideration is the area of programming that is best suited to a given language. For example, Java is designed to create programs that can be executed on a variety of different computers, while C++ was designed for fast execution times.

We are going to use a language known as DarkBASIC Professional or just DarkBASIC Pro, which was designed specifically for writing computer games. Because of this, it has many unique commands for displaying graphics, controlling joysticks, and creating three dimensional images.

The Compilation Process

As we will soon see, DarkBASIC Pro uses statements that retain some English terms and phrases, so we can look at the set of instructions and make some sense of what is happening after only a relatively small amount of training.

Binary is a method of representing numbers using only the digits 0 and 1.

Unfortunately, the computer itself only understands instructions given in a **binary code** known as **machine code** and has no capability of directly following a set of instructions written in DarkBASIC Pro. But this need not be a problem. If we were given a set of instructions written in Russian we could easily have them translated into English and then carry out the translated commands.

This is exactly the approach the computer uses. We begin the process of creating a new piece of software by mentally converting our structured English into DarkBASIC Pro commands. These commands are entered using a **text editor** which is nothing more than a simple word-processor-like program allowing such basic operations as inserting and deleting text. Once the complete program has been entered, we get the machine itself to translate those instructions into machine code. The original code is known as the **source code**; the machine code equivalent is known as the **object code**.

The translator (known as a **compiler**) is simply another program installed in the computer. After typing in our program instructions, we feed these to the compiler which produces the equivalent instructions in machine code. These instructions are then executed by the computer and we should see the results of our calculations appear on the screen (assuming there are output statements in the program).

The compiler is a very exacting task master. The structure, or **syntax**, of every statement must be exactly right. If you make the slightest mistake, even something as simple as missing out a comma or misspelling a word, the translation process will fail. When this happens in DarkBASIC Pro the incorrect command is highlighted in red.

A failure of this type is known as a **syntax error** - a mistake in the grammar of your commands. Any syntax errors have to be corrected before you can try compiling the program again.

As we work on the computer entering a DarkBASIC Pro program, we need to save this source code to a file. This ensures that we have a copy of our work should there be a power cut or we accidentally delete the program from the computer's memory. DarkBASIC Pro refers to this as the **source file**.

But a second file, known as the **project file** is also produced. This second file is created automatically by DarkBASIC Pro and contains details of any images, sounds or other resources that might be used by your program.

When we compile our program (translating it from source code to object code), yet another file is produced. This third file, the **executable file**, contains the object code and is, again, created automatically.

To run our program, the source code in the executable file is loaded into the computer's memory (RAM) and the instructions it contains are carried out.

The whole process is summarised in FIG-2.1.

FIG-2.1

Creating Software

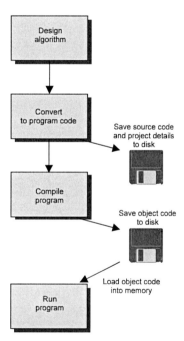

If we want to make changes to the program, we load the source code into the editor, make the necessary changes, then save and recompile our program, thereby replacing the old version of all three files.

Activity 2.1

1. What type of instructions are understood by a computer?

2. What piece of software is used to translate a program from source code to object code?

3. Misspelling a word in your program is an example of what type of error?

Starting DarkBASIC Pro

Introduction

DarkBASIC Pro is based on one of the earliest computer languages, BASIC, but has been enhanced specifically to aid the creation of games programs.

The language was invented by Lee Bamber who formed a company to sell DarkBASIC Pro. Over the last few years the company has grown in size and expanded to sell other DarkBASIC related products, such as DarkMatter, which contains many 3D objects that can be used in DarkBASIC programs.

In fact, there are two versions of the language: DarkBASIC and DarkBASIC Professional. It's this second, enhanced version of the language we will be using here.

DarkBASIC Pro Files

Because a typical program written in DarkBASIC Pro is likely to contain images, sounds and even video, the DarkBASIC Pro package has to save much more than the set of instructions that make up your program; it also needs to store details of these images, sounds, etc.

To do this DarkBASIC Pro creates two files every time you produce a new program (see FIG-2.2).

The first of these files, known as the **project file**, contains details of the images and sounds used by your program, as well as other information such as the screen resolution and number of colours used. This file has a *.dbpro* extension.

The second file, known as the **source file**, contains only the program's code written in the DarkBASIC Pro language. This file has a *.dba* extension.

FIG-2.2

The Two Files Created by a
DarkBASIC Pro Program

Getting Started with DarkBASIC Pro

When you first start up DarkBASIC Pro you should see one of the screens shown in FIG-2.3. Exactly which one you see depends on how often DarkBASIC Pro has been run on your computer. The first time the program is run, the display will match that shown on the left of FIG-2.3; every other time your screen will match that shown on the right.

FIG-2.3

The Start-Up Screen in DarkBASIC Pro

DarkBASIC Pro Start-Up Screen (First Start-Up Only)   DarkBASIC Pro Start-Up Screen (Subsequent Start-Ups)

First Start-Up

If this is the first time DarkBASIC Pro has been run on your machine, as well as the main window, the **Assistant Window** also shows on the right-hand side.

If you close down the Assistant Window the display changes to match that shown in FIG-2.4, showing the Project Dialog box.

FIG-2.4

The Project Dialog Box

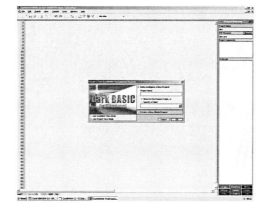

Subsequent Start-Ups

Click on this icon to show the *New Project* dialog

When DarkBASIC Pro is started up for the second (or subsequent) time, use the **FILE | NEW PROJECT** option from the main menu, or click on the *New Project* icon near the top left corner, to display the *Project Dialog* box.

Specifying a Project

The next stage is to create a project file by filling in the details required by the Project Dialog box.

First the name to be given to the project is entered. This should be something meaningful like *Hangman* or *SpaceMonsters*.

Next the *Specify a Folder* radio button is selected and the folder in which the DarkBASIC Pro projects are to be saved is entered. The folder specified must already exist. See FIG-2.5 for a summary of these steps.

FIG-2.5

Filling in the *New Project* Dialog Box

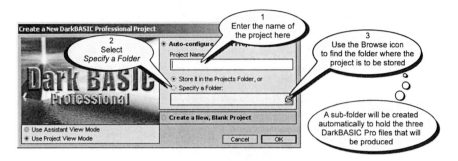

Once the OK button in the Project Dialog box is clicked, the dialog box disappears and you are left with the main edit area where the program code is entered. Line numbers appear to the left of this area.

A First Program

Before we begin looking in detail at the commands available in DarkBASIC Pro, we'll have a quick look at a simple program and show you how to type it in, run it and save the code.

The program in LISTING-2.1 gets you to enter your name at the keyboard and then displays a greeting on the screen.

LISTING-2.1

A First Program

```
Rem Project: First
Rem Created: 02/10/2004 07:35:27
Rem ***** Main Source File *****

REM *** A program to read and display your name ***
INPUT "Enter your name : ",name$
PRINT "Hello " ,name$, " welcome to DarkBASIC Pro."
WAIT KEY
END
```

An Explanation of the Code

DarkBASIC Pro allows words to be given in either upper or lower case.

REM

This is short for REMARK and is used to indicate a comment within the program. Comments are totally ignored when the source code is translated into object code and are only included for the benefit of anybody examining the program code, giving an explanation of what the program does.

When you type in a program, you'll see that the instructions are colour-coded with keywords appearing in blue.

INPUT

This is a keyword in DarkBASIC Pro. Keywords are words recognised by the programming language as having a specific meaning.

All keywords are shown throughout this text in uppercase, but lowercase characters are also acceptable.

The INPUT keyword tells the computer to allow the user to enter a value from the keyboard.

The need for a space after the colon will become clear when you run this program.

`"Enter your name:"`   This message is displayed on the screen as a prompt, telling the user what information is to be entered.

Messages are always enclosed in double quotes (" ") and are more generally known as **strings**.

`name$`   This is the variable in which the value entered by the user will be stored.

`PRINT`   This command is used to tell the computer to display information on the screen.

`"Hello "`   This is the first piece of information to be displayed

`,`   Items of data are separated from each other by commas.

`name$`   The value held in the variable *name$* is to be displayed. This will be whatever value the user typed in when the earlier INPUT statement was executed.

`" welcome to DarkBASIC Pro."`
Another data item to be displayed.

`WAIT KEY`   This command contains two key words which tell the computer to wait for a key to be pressed before continuing to the next instruction.

`END`   Marks the end of the program.

Activity 2.2

In this Activity you are going to type in and run the program given in LISTING-2.1.

Create a folder in the C: drive (or elsewhere) named *DarkBasicProjects*

Start up DarkBASIC Pro.

Bring up the Project Dialog box shown in FIG-2.4.

Name the project *first.dbpro*, select *Specify a Folder*; browse to your *DarkBASICProjects* folder and click OK.

The first three lines of the program will appear automatically (only the date and time will differ from that in LISTING-2.1).

Type in the remainder of the program as shown in LISTING-2.1.

Execute the program by pressing the F5 key or clicking on the Run icon.

When requested, type in your name. You should then see a message including your name displayed on the screen.

Finally, press any key to finish the program and return to the editor.

Click on this icon to execute your program

If we use Windows Explorer to examine our *DarkBasicProjects* folder we'll see that a new sub-folder called *first* has been created.

Inside that new folder are three files (see FIG-2.6).

FIG-2.6

Files Created by
DarkBASIC Pro

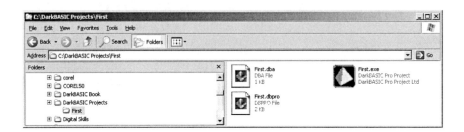

first.dbpro	This is the project file.
first.dba	This is the file containing the source code.
first.exe	This is the machine code version of your program. It's the code in this file that is actually executed when you run your program.

If you ever want to give away your completed programs to other people, you only need to give them a copy of the .exe file. This contains everything they need to run your program without allowing them to see your original DarkBASIC Pro code.

When opening the file in Notepad, change the *File of Type* entry to *All Files*.

Saving Your Project

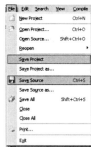

When you've typed in your program you need to save both the project and the source files. To do this, select **FILE|SAVE PROJECT** and then **FILE|SAVE SOURCE**.

First Statements in DarkBASIC Pro

Introduction

Learning to program in DarkBASIC Pro is very simple compared to other languages such as C++ or Java. Unlike most other programming languages, it has no rigid structure that must be adhered to. In fact, there are only two statements that you should include at this stage. These are given below.

Ending a Program

The END Statement

The first statement we examine is the one that should come at the end of any program you write. It consists of the single keyword END and, as you might have guessed, marks the end of your program.

We have already seen this statement in LISTING-2.1.

Some of the statements available in DarkBASIC Pro have quite a complex syntax so, to help show exactly what options are available when using a statement, we'll use informal syntax diagrams. FIG-2.7 shows a syntax diagram for the END statement.

FIG-2.7

The END Statement

These diagrams contain one or more tiles. A raised tile (like the one above) signifies a DarkBASIC Pro keyword. The order of the tiles signifies the order in which the keywords must be placed when using this statement in your program.

So the diagram above tells us that the END statement contains only the single word END.

The WAIT KEY Statement

We can make a program pause until a key is pressed using the WAIT KEY statement. The program will only continue after a key has been pressed. Any key on the keyboard will do.

For example, in the program given in LISTING-2.1, the computer will pause after the PRINT statement is executed.

For most simple programs, you need to include a WAIT KEY statement immediately before the END statement, otherwise your program will finish and close down before you get a chance to view what is being displayed on the screen.

The syntax for this statement is shown in FIG-2.8.

FIG-2.8

The WAIT KEY Statement

Adding Comments

It is important that you add comments to any programs you write. These comments should explain what each section of code is doing. It's also good practice, when writing longer programs, to add comments giving details such as your name, date, programming language being used, hardware requirements of the program, and version number.

Comments are totally ignored by the translation process as it turns DarkBASIC Pro statements into machine code. The purpose of comments is to make a program more readable to other people who may have to modify a program after you've moved on to other things.

In DarkBASIC Pro there are three ways to add comments:

> ➤ Add the keyword REM. The remainder of the line becomes a comment (see FIG-2.9).

FIG-2.9

The REM Comment

Notice that this syntax diagram introduces the sunken tile. Sunken tiles signify details that are determined by the programmer. Hence, the programmer gets to choose exactly what comment should be added after the keyword REM. For example:

Adding asterisks to a comment helps it to stand out.

```
REM *** Program to display numbers ***
```

> ➤ Add an opening quote character (you'll find this on the top left key, just next to the 1). Again the remainder of the line is treated as a comment (see FIG-2.10).

FIG-2.10

The ' Comment

For example:

```
' Get details from keyboard
```

> ➤ Add several lines of comments by starting with the term REMSTART and ending with REMEND. Everything between these two words is treated as a comment (see FIG-2.11).

FIG-2.11

The REMSTART ..
REMEND Comment

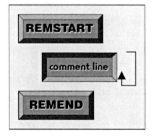

This diagram introduces another symbol - a looping arrowed line. This is used to indicate a section of the structure that may be repeated if required. In the diagram above it is used to signify that any number of comment lines can be placed between the REMSTART and REMEND keywords.

For example, we can use this statement to create the following comment which contains three comment lines:

```
REMSTART
    This program is designed to play the game of
    battleships. Two peer-to-peer computers are
    required.
REMEND
```

Activity 2.6

1. How are keywords shown in a syntax diagram?

2. What does a sunken tile in a syntax diagram represent?

3. How is a repeatable element in a statement represented in a syntax diagram?

Outputting to the Screen

Introduction

Even the simplest program will require information to be displayed on the screen.

In DarkBASIC Pro the simplest way to display information on the screen is to use the PRINT statement. Other statements exist which allow changes to the colour, font and style of displayed characters to be specified.

A description of most of these statements are given over the next few pages

The PRINT Statement

As we saw in LISTING-2.1, information can be displayed using the PRINT statement.

To use it, we start with the keyword PRINT, followed by whatever information we want to display. For example, the statement

```
PRINT "Hello"
```

displays the word *Hello* on the screen. The quotes themselves are not displayed. Absolutely any set of characters can appear between the quotes, including spaces.

Although a set of characters, or strings, must be enclosed in double quotes, if you want to display a number, quotes are not required. For example, the following are valid statements:

```
PRINT 12
PRINT 3.1416
PRINT -7.0
```

It is possible to display several pieces of information using a single PRINT statement by separating each value to be displayed by a comma:

```
PRINT 12,7,1.2
```

Unfortunately, all the values in this statement will be displayed without any spaces between them giving the impression of one large number (1271.2) rather than three separate values.

To solve this problem we need to display some spaces between the numbers:

```
PRINT 12,"   ",7,"   ",1.2
```

Spaces are just strings - like any other sequence of characters - and must be enclosed in double quotes.

When several values are displayed by a single PRINT statement they appear on a single line of the screen, but by using several PRINT statements we can make the data appear over several lines:

```
PRINT 12
PRINT 1
PRINT 1.2
```

To turn this into a complete program we just need to add the WAIT KEY and END statements as shown in LISTING-2.2.

LISTING-2.2

Displaying Numbers

REM statements generated when you start a new project have been omitted from the listing.

```
REM *** Print some numbers ***
PRINT 12
PRINT 7
PRINT 1.2

REM *** End program ***
WAIT KEY
END
```

Activity 2.7

Start up a new DarkBASIC Pro project.

To do this select File | **New Project**.

In the *Project* dialog box that appears, call the project *printing.dbpro*; select *Specify a Folder*; browse to your *DarkBASICProjects* folder and click OK.

Type in and test the program given in LISTING-2.2.

Remember to save the Source and Project files when you have finished.

Creating Blank Lines

The PRINT statement can even be used without any data values being given, as in the line

```
PRINT
```

This has the effect of creating a blank line on the screen. Hence, the lines

```
PRINT 1
PRINT
PRINT 2
```

would display the values 1 and 2 with a blank line between them.

Activity 2.8

Modify your last program so that a blank line appears between each number displayed.

Ending the PRINT Statement with a Semicolon

If you end a PRINT statement with a string and a semicolon, the output produced by the next PRINT statement will be displayed on the same line. For example, the lines:

```
PRINT 12,"";
PRINT 7
PRINT 1.2
```

would produce the output

```
127
1.2
```

As you will see later, this apparently useless option can be used to great effect.

DarkBASIC Pro: Starting DarkBASIC Pro 49

The format of the PRINT statement is shown in FIG-2.12.

FIG-2.12

The PRINT Statement

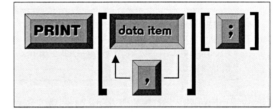

This diagram introduces two new concepts. Items within the brackets are optional
and may be omitted. Any number of data items can be displayed, but each must be
separated from the next by a comma.

Positioning Text on the Screen

In DarkBASIC Pro the screen is treated like a piece of paper divided into thousands of small squares, as shown in FIG-2.13. These small invisible squares are known as **pixels** (derived from the phrase **picture elements**). An individual pixel is identified by giving its position on the screen.

A pixel's position is given by the column number (also known as the position on the x-axis) followed by the row number (the position on the y-axis) separated by a comma.

The top left pixel is at position (0,0). This point is known as the **origin**.

FIG-2.13

The Screen is Made Up of Pixels

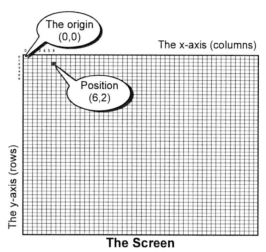

Exactly how many pixels are on the screen depends on the screen resolution (which we will examine later) but there will be at least 640 columns by 480 rows.

The SET CURSOR Statement

Normally, the first text that we output to the screen will start at the origin, but we can change this by using the SET CURSOR statement which allows us to specify where on the screen the next PRINT statement will begin its output. For example, the statements

```
SET CURSOR 350, 100
PRINT "HELLO"
```

displays the word HELLO, with the top-left corner of the H starting at position (350,100) (i.e. at column 350, row 100) as shown in FIG-2.14.

FIG-2.14

Positioning Text Using the SET CURSOR Statement

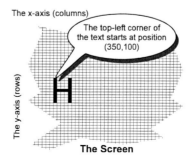

The format for the SET CURSOR statement is shown in FIG-2.15.

FIG-2.15

The SET CURSOR
Statement

In the diagram above:

x,y   is a pair of integer values specifying the
                                     position to which the cursor is to be moved.

Activity 2.12

Create a new project (*corners.dbpro*) that displays the letters A, B, C and D so
that one letter appears at each corner of the screen.

(You'll have to use trial and error to find the correct positions)

Activity 2.13

Since we can output at any position on the screen, this allows us to display
different values at the same position on the screen.

Create a new project (*overwrite.dbpro*) containing the following code:

```
REM *** Output two strings at the same location ***
SET CURSOR 100,100
PRINT "Hello"
WAIT KEY
SET CURSOR 100,100
PRINT "Goodbye"
REM *** End program ***
WAIT KEY
END
```

Check the output produced by running this program.

The TEXT Statement

The effects of the SET CURSOR and PRINT statements are combined in the TEXT
command which takes both the value to be displayed and the position at which the
data is to be displayed. For example, the statement

```
TEXT 350, 100, "HELLO"
```

has the same effect as the SET CURSOR example given earlier, although you may
find that the program uses a different screen resolution when the output is displayed.

Your screen will almost
certainly use a different
resolution when using the
TEXT statement than it
did in previous programs.
This means that in this
Activity you'll have to
change the coordinates
from those used in the
previous example.

Activity 2.14

Change your *corners.dbpro* project so that it uses the TEXT command to
position the letters in the corners of the screen.

There are a few differences between the PRINT and TEXT commands.

Firstly, TEXT makes use of a graphics display mode to create output, PRINT does not. Because of this, the screen resolution in Activity 2.14 may differ from that used by the PRINT statement and how output is handled will change.

Activity 2.15

Change your *overwrite.dbpro* project replacing the SET CURSOR and PRINT commands with equivalent TEXT statements.

How does the result differ from before?

The second difference is that the TEXT command will only display strings, so a line such as

```
TEXT 100, 100, 12
```

where the statement attempts to display the value 12 is not acceptable and will cause an error message to appear when you attempt to run the program. Of course, by enclosing the 12 in quotes you turn it from a number into a string and this would be accepted:

```
TEXT 100, 100, "12"
```

A final difference is that the TEXT command can only be used to display a single value at a time. Hence, a statement such as

```
TEXT 100, 100, "Hello", "again"
```

would fail since there are two strings in the command. Again, this could be corrected, this time by joining the two strings:

```
TEXT 100, 100, "Hello again"
```

The syntax for the TEXT statement is given in FIG-2.16.

FIG-2.16

The TEXT Statement

In the diagram above:

x,y	is a pair of integer values specifying the position to which the cursor is to be moved.
string	is the string value to be displayed on the screen. All strings should be enclosed in double quotes.

The CENTER TEXT Command

Like most programming languages, DarkBASIC Pro keywords use American spelling. Hence, CENTER and not CENTRE.

Whereas the TEXT command starts output at the specified position, CENTER TEXT, which uses the same format as TEXT, centres the output horizontally round the value given for the x-axis. Hence, the statement

```
CENTER TEXT 350, 150, "Hello"
```

will display the word *Hello* as shown in FIG-2.17.

FIG-2.17

Positioning Text Using
CENTER TEXT

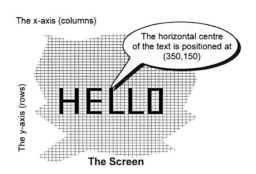

Activity 2.16

Write a program (project *centre.dbpro*) to place the word *MIDDLE* at the centre of the screen.

The format of the CENTER TEXT statement is given in FIG-2.18.

FIG-2.18

The CENTER TEXT
Statement

In the diagram above:

    x,y   is a pair of integer values specifying the position where the horizontal centre of the string is to be output.

    string   is the string value to be displayed on the screen.

Changing the Output Font

When you display text on your computer, you can choose the size, style, and font of that text.

We can change the font style and size used when outputting text by using the SET TEXT FONT and SET TEXT SIZE commands. Once a new font and size has been set, any subsequent output statements will be done in this style.

The SET TEXT FONT Statement

You have to add a font name in quotes to the end of this statement. Any values output after this will be shown in that font. For example,

```
SET TEXT FONT "Courier New"
```

will result in the Courier New font being used by any subsequent output.

The format for this instruction is given in FIG-2.19.

FIG-2.19

The SET TEXT FONT
Statement

In the diagram above:

font name   is a string (enclosed in quotes) giving the name of the font to be used for subsequent output.

The SET TEXT SIZE Statement

The text size is given in **points** (a point being 1/72 of an inch). For example,

```
SET TEXT SIZE 20
```

will result in subsequent output using characters that are 20/72 of an inch tall.

The format of this statement is given in FIG-2.20.

FIG-2.20

The SET TEXT SIZE
Statement

In the diagram above:

point size   is an integer value specifying the size of font (in points) to be used for subsequent output.

The SET TEXT TO Statement

You can also set the text style to produce italics, bold, or bold italics output as well as the normal default style. This is achieved using the SET TEXT TO commands. There are four options:

```
SET TEXT TO BOLD
SET TEXT TO ITALIC
SET TEXT TO BOLDITALIC
SET TEXT TO NORMAL
```

The following program (LISTING-2.3) outputs the word *HELLO* in large, bold, Courier New font:

LISTING-2.3

Setting Text Size, Font
and Style

```
REM *** Use Courier New size 20 bold ***
SET TEXT FONT "Courier New"
SET TEXT SIZE 20
SET TEXT TO BOLD
PRINT "HELLO"
WAIT KEY

REM *** Change to italics ***
SET TEXT TO ITALIC
PRINT "HELLO"
WAIT KEY

REM *** Change to bold italics ***
SET TEXT TO BOLDITALIC
PRINT "HELLO"
WAIT KEY

REM *** Change to normal ***
SET TEXT TO NORMAL
PRINT "HELLO"
REM *** End the program ***
WAIT KEY
END
```

The format for this statement is shown in FIG-2.21.

FIG-2.21

The SET TEXT TO Statement

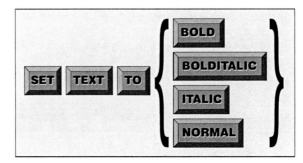

This diagram introduces another new feature. The braces are used to enclose items which are mutually exclusive alternatives. In other words, the statement is completed by choosing one of the options given in the braces.

Changing Colours

So far we've had white text on a black background, but you're free to choose any colours you want for both the text and the background. Before we see how to do that in DarkBASIC Pro, let's start with some basic facts about colour.

How Colours are Displayed

Have a close look at your computer monitor. It's in full colour, showing almost every colour and shade your eye is capable of seeing. And yet your screen can generate only three basic colours: red, green and blue.

Every other colour that you see on the screen is made up from those three colours. For example, to show the colour yellow, the screen combines the colours red and green; red, green and blue together produce white; when all three basic colours are switched off, we have black.

This is known as the **additive colour process** and the colours red, green and blue are known as the **primary colours**. The basic colours that can be constructed from these three primary colours are shown in FIG-2.22.

FIG-2.22

The Additive Colour Process

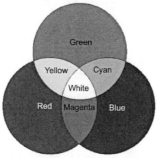

As you can see from the figure above, green and blue combine to give a colour called cyan, while red and blue give magenta.

To create other colours and shades we need only to vary the brightness of the primary colours. Hence, to create orange we use an intense red, a less intense green, and no blue.

In computer systems the colour of any spot on the screen is recorded as a series of three numbers. These numbers represent the intensities of the red, green and blue (RGB) components (in that order) that make up the colour of the spot. Each number can range between 0 and 255; 0 means that the colour is not used, while 255 means that the colour is at full brightness. Hence, a bright yellow spot on the screen will be recorded as 255, 255, 0, meaning that the red and green are at full intensity, and the blue is switched off.

The RGB Statement

In DarkBASIC Pro we can define any colour using the RGB statement. This statement takes three values, enclosed in parentheses. These values define the intensities of the red, green and blue components that make up the required colour. The RGB statement combines these three components into a single integer value which it returns as a result of calling this statement. For example, the statement

```
PRINT RGB(255,255,0)
```

will display the integer value representing the colour yellow.

Activity 2.18

Create a new project (*colours.dbpro*) containing the following code:

```
PRINT RGB (255,255,0)
WAIT KEY
END
```

What value is displayed?

Change the values in the RGB command to 255,0,255. What value is displayed this time?

The syntax for the RGB statement is shown in FIG-2.23.

FIG-2.23

The RGB Statement

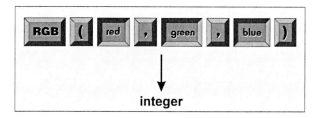

In the diagram:

red	is an integer value between 0 and 255
green	is an integer value between 0 and 255
blue	is an integer value between 0 and 255.

The arrowed line and the term *integer* signify that this statement returns an integer value.

How do you find out the red, green and blue values of some particularly nice shade of orange? Luckily, the DarkBASIC Pro editor can help. If you are busy typing in a program and suddenly need to supply the three values required by an RGB statement, you can simply right-click in the edit window. The resulting pop-up menu (see FIG-2.24) has an RGB Color Picker option which, when selected, displays a colour palette (see FIG-2.25).

FIG-2.24

The DarkBASIC Pro
Editor's Pop-Up Menu

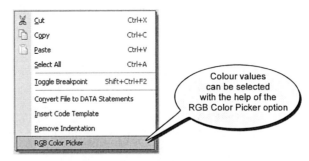

FIG-2.25

The Colour Palette Box

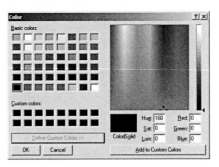

Selecting a colour from this palette and clicking OK automatically produces an RGB statement in your program code with the appropriate values to match the colour selected. We'll use this in the next Activity.

The INK Statement

In DarkBASIC Pro we can change both the colour used when writing text onto the screen (known as the foreground colour) and the colour behind that text (known as the background colour) using the INK. command. This command takes the general form shown in FIG-2.26.

FIG-2.26

The INK Statement

In the diagram:

    foreground   is an integer value representing the colour to be used for the foreground.

    background   is an integer value representing the colour to be used for the background.

The colour values themselves are created using the RGB command. So to have our text output in yellow on a red background we would use the command:

```
                        INK RGB(255,255,0), RGB(255,0,0)
```

Where you want to use black, rather than use RGB (0, 0, 0) you may simply enter
the value zero. For example, to change the foreground to blue and the background
to black, we would use the statement

```
            INK RGB(0,0,255) ,0
```

Once you have set the ink colour, any output you do to the screen will be in that
colour. For example, we would expect the program in LISTING-2.4 to display the
word *HELLO* in yellow on a red background.

LISTING-2.4

Setting Foreground and
Background Colours

```
REM *** Set yellow foreground and red background ***
INK RGB(255,255,0) , RGB(255,0,0)
PRINT "HELLO"

REM *** End program ***
WAIT KEY
END
```

Activity 2.19

Type in and execute the program in LISTING-2.4 (project *colours2.dbpro*).

What colour is the background on the screen?

Delete the first RGB command within the INK statement and use the *RGB
Color Picker* option to replace it with a colour of your choice.

Notice that the background colour in the INK command was set to red and yet the
colour behind the letters is still black. If you want to know why, read on!

There are two main areas to any text that appears on the computer screen: the text
and the text background (see FIG-2.27).

FIG-2.27

Text Areas

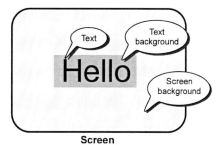

Screen

The foreground colour setting determines the colour of the text itself while the
background colour sets the colour used in the text background. However, normally
the text background is transparent so setting the background colour appears to have
no effect. Usually, a transparent background will be exactly what we want, since it
allows us to do things such as place text on top of an image, and have the image
still show through the text (see FIG-2.28) but, as we'll see in a moment, we can
change this transparent background setting.

Activity 2.20

Modify your previous program so that the word *GOODBYE* is displayed in
green after the existing word *HELLO*.

FIG-2.28

Text with a Transparent
Background

The Scottish Highlands

We'll see how to place
images on the screen later.

The SET TEXT OPAQUE Statement

We can create a block of colour around any text we display by using the SET TEXT
OPAQUE command. The colour used in the text background will be that defined
as the background colour in your INK command. This statement has the format
shown in FIG-2.29.

FIG-2.29

The SET TEXT
OPAQUE Statement

For example, if a program contains the statements

```
SET TEXT OPAQUE
INK RGB(0,0,255), RGB(255,255,0)
PRINT "Hello"
```

the word *Hello* should appear in blue with a yellow background around the text.

Activity 2.21

Add the line SET TEXT OPAQUE to start of your previous program.

Change the program so that the word *GOODBYE* shows in cyan with a
magenta background.

The SET TEXT TRANSPARENT Statement

Although text normally has a transparent background, if you use the SET TEXT
OPAQUE command, every output statement executed later will have a coloured
background. To return to a transparent background you need to use the statement
SET TEXT TRANSPARENT which has the format shown in FIG-2.30.

FIG-2.30

The SET TEXT
TRANSPARENT
Statement

For example, if a program contains the statements

```
SET TEXT OPAQUE
INK RGB(0,0,255), RGB(255,255,0)
PRINT "Hello"
SET TEXT TRANSPARENT
PRINT "Goodbye"
```

Hello will have a yellow background while the word *Goodbye* would be surrounded by the black background of the screen.

The CLS Statement

Although when you first run your program it will start with a blank screen, you can clear everything from the screen at any point in your program by using the CLS statement (derived from **CL**ear **S**creen). To use the command, just write the term:

```
CLS
```

This gives a empty black screen. However, if you don't want the screen to be black, you can clear the screen to another colour by specifying a colour setting in conjunction with the CLS statement. For example, to create a green screen, use the line:

```
CLS RGB(0,255,0)
```

The format for this statement is shown in FIG-2.31.

FIG-2.31

The CLS Statement

In the diagram:

> *colour*   is an integer value representing a colour. The screen will be filled with this colour after the CLS statement has been executed.

The program in LISTING-2.5 displays the word HELLO several times using both opaque and transparent modes. The screen colour is set to red.

LISTING-2.5

Using Transparent and Opaque Text

```
REM *** clear screen to red ***
CLS RGB(255,0,0)
REM *** Change text to yellow and the background to green ***
INK RGB(255,255,0), RGB(0,255,0)

REM *** Output the word HELLO with a transparent background ***
PRINT "HELLO"

REM *** Output the word HELLO twice with opaque background ***
SET TEXT OPAQUE
PRINT "HELLO"
PRINT "HELLO"

REM *** Return to transparent output ***
SET TEXT TRANSPARENT
PRINT "HELLO"

REM *** End the program ***
WAIT KEY
END
```

The output from this program is shown in FIG-2.32.

FIG-2.32

Changing Background Transparency

Summary

- The CLS statement clears the screen using a given colour.

- The PRINT statement can be used to print any type of value.

- A single PRINT statement can display many values.

- The PRINT statement moves the cursor to a new line unless it finishes with a semicolon.

- The SET CURSOR statement moves the cursor to any position on the screen.

- The TEXT statement will output a single string at any position on the screen.

- The CENTER TEXT statement will output a string centred round a specified position.

- The INK statement sets the foreground and background colours used.

- The SET TEXT FONT statement sets the font to be used when displaying information.

- The SET TEXT SIZE statement sets the size to be used in text output.

- The text size is given in points (1/72 of an inch).

- The SET TEXT BOLD statement sets the text style to be used for output to bold.

- The SET TEXT BOLDITALIC statement sets the text style to be used for output to bold italics.

- The SET TEXT ITALIC statement sets the style to be used for output to italics.

- The SET TEXT NORMAL statement sets the style to be used for output to normal.

- The SET TEXT OPAQUE statement creates a background colour round any text that is output.

- The SET TEXT TRANSPARENT statement makes text background transparent.

- The WAIT KEY statement causes the program to halt until any key is pressed.

- The END statement marks the end of the program.

Some Display Techniques

Screen Resolution

Earlier in this chapter you saw how the screen resolution changed when we started using the TEXT command in place of PRINT and SET CURSOR.

Luckily, we can choose which resolution we want the program's output to use by clicking on the brown *Settings* button at the bottom right of screen. In the resulting *Configure EXE Settings* window we can choose the resolution we want to use (see FIG-2.33).

FIG-2.33

Setting the Screen Resolution

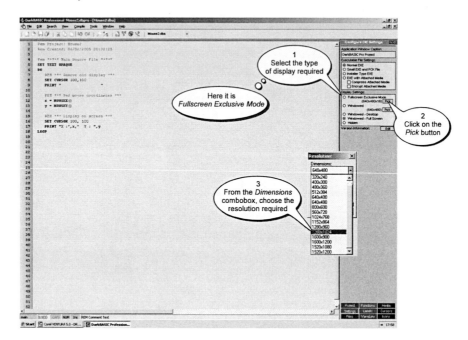

You should consider the following when choosing a resolution.

> ➢ Output looks better in higher screen resolutions.

> ➢ Everything looks smaller in higher resolutions.

> ➢ The memory on your video card may limit what resolutions can be used.

> ➢ High resolutions take longer to update, so a visually complex game may seem slower in higher resolutions.

The SET DISPLAY MODE Statement

It is also possible to set the screen resolution and colour depth from within your program using the SET DISPLAY MODE statement which has the format shown in FIG-2.34.

FIG-2.34

The SET DISPLAY MODE Statement

In the diagram:

width	is an integer value representing the width of the display mode required given in pixels.
height	is an integer value representing the height of the display mode required given in pixels.
depth	is an integer value representing the number of bits used to represent a single pixel on the screen. Typical values are 16, 24 or 32.

To set the screen to a resolution of 1280 by 1024 using 32 bit pixels we would use the line

```
SET DISPLAY MODE 1280,1024,32
```

It is only valid to chose a resolution which can be achieved by your video card and screen. Attempt to set an invalid resolution will produce an error message.

Choosing a Text Font

The SET TEXT FONT statement allows us to choose a font for any text that we intend to output. However, that choice depends on what fonts are available on your computer. You need to also consider what fonts are available on any other computers that your final software is to be run on. If your game makes use of a font such as *Kidnap* and that font is not available to someone who has bought your program, then the *Kidnap* font will be missing when your game runs on the buyer's machine.

Most fonts are **proportional fonts**. That is, the horizontal width of a character depends on what that character is. Hence, w's take up more width than i's. You can see this in the two lines below:

wwwwww
iiiiii

But some fonts are **mono-spaced**. In this style every character takes up the same width, as you can see below:

```
wwwwww
iiiiii
```

When you're working in the DarkBASIC Pro editor entering the lines of your program, the text is displayed in a mono-spaced font, but the default font used by your program when outputting to the screen is a proportional font.

Erasing Text

Back in Activity 2.15, we saw that when the TEXT command is used to output more than one item to the same area of the screen it created an unreadable blob. We need some way of getting rid of the old text before outputting new text at the same position.

There are two ways to erase text from the screen.

The first of these is to overwrite the text with spaces with the text background set to opaque. This is demonstrated in LISTING-2.6.

LISTING-2.6

Erasing Text Using Opaque Spaces

```
REM *** Set background colour ***
CLS RGB (126,126,126)

REM *** Set text font, size, and background colour ***
SET TEXT FONT "Arial"
SET TEXT SIZE 36
INK RGB(255,0,0),RGB(126,126,126)

REM *** Output Text ***
TEXT 100,100,"Hello"
WAIT KEY

REM *** Remove text by writing opaque spaces ***
REM *** at the same position as the original text ***
SET TEXT OPAQUE
TEXT 100,100,"     "

REM *** End program ***
WAIT KEY
END
```

Activity 2.24

Type in and test the program given above (*TextGone*).

There should be 5 spaces between the quotes in the second TEXT statement.

What problem arises? Try to cure the problem.

A second method of erasing text is to overwrite with exactly the same text, but this time in the background colour. The logic of our strategy is:

    Clear screen in required background colour
    Set text font, size and colour
    Output text
    Set foreground colour to match background colour
    Output text at same position as before

This logic is implemented in LISTING-2.7.

LISTING-2.7

Erasing Text Using The Same Text in the Background Colour

```
REM *** Set background colour ***
CLS RGB (126,126,126)

REM *** Set text font, size, and background colour ***
SET TEXT FONT "Arial"
SET TEXT SIZE 36
INK RGB(255,0,0),0

REM *** Output Text ***
TEXT 100,100,"Hello"
WAIT KEY

REM ** Remove text by writing it again in background colour ***
INK RGB(126,126,126),0
TEXT 100,100,"Hello"

REM *** End program ***
WAIT KEY
END
```

Shadow Text

We can create shadowed text by writing the same text in different colours at slightly offset positions. This needs the following logic:

```
Set foreground colour to black
Output text
Set foreground colour to red (or some other colour)
Output text at a slightly different position from before
```

which is coded as:

```
REM *** Shadow Text ***
INK RGB(0,0,0),0
TEXT 102, 102, "Hello"
INK RGB(255,0,0) ,0
TEXT 100, 100, "Hello"
```

Embossed Text

By creating two versions of a text, we achieved shadowed text; by creating three copies, we can produce an embossed effect.

To do this we need the following logic:

```
Clear the screen to grey (or some other colour)
Set foreground to black
Output required text
Set foreground to white
Output required text at an offset position
Set foreground to match background
Output required text at a position between the black and white output.
```

The code for this is:

```
CLS RGB(126,126,126)
REM *** Embossed Text ***
INK RGB(0,0,0),0
TEXT 201,201,"Goodbye"
INK RGB(255,255,255),0
TEXT 199,199,"Goodbye"
INK RGB(126,126,126),0
TEXT 200,200,"Goodbye"
```

Activity 2.27

Add the code above to your existing program.

Try modifying the font, size and colours used as well as the offset values to create the best effect.

Summary

- The screen resolution used by your program can be set manually using the Settings button.

- The screen resolution can be set from within your program using the SET DISPLAY MODE statement.

- In proportional fonts the width of a character depends on the shape of the character.

- In mono-spaced fonts all characters have the same width.

- Text can be erased from the screen by overwriting it with opaque spaces.

- Text can be removed from the screen by overwriting it with the same text in the background colour.

- Shadow text can be created by outputting a darker version of the text and then overwriting it with the same text slightly offset from the original and in a different colour.

- Embossed text can be created by outputting dark, light, and background coloured versions of the text. The dark version is written first, then the offset light text and finally the background coloured text at a mid point between the dark and light text.

Solutions

Activity 2.1

    1. Machine code (or object code) instructions
    2. Compiler
    3. A syntax error

Activity 2.2

No solution required.

Activity 2.3

    1. A keyword
    2. Strings
    3. Causes the program to pause until a key is pressed.

Activity 2.4

No solution required.

Activity 2.5

No solution required.

Activity 2.6

    1. Keywords are shown in raised tiles

    2. A sunken tile represent information whose exact value is determined by the programmer.

    3. Repeatable elements are shown using a looping arrowed line.

Activity 2.7

No solution required.

Activity 2.8

The program code is:

```
REM *** Print some numbers ***
PRINT 12
PRINT
PRINT 7
PRINT
PRINT 1.2
REM *** End program ***
WAIT KEY
END
```

Activity 2.9

Version 1:

```
REM *** Display numbers on the same line ***
PRINT 1, " ", 2, " ", 3
REM *** End program ***
WAIT KEY
END
```

Version 2:

```
REM *** Display numbers on the separate
lines
PRINT 1
PRINT 2
PRINT 3
REM *** End program ***
WAIT KEY
END
```

Version 3:

```
REM *** Display numbers on the separate
lines ***
PRINT 1
WAIT KEY
PRINT 2
WAIT KEY
PRINT 3
REM *** End program ***
WAIT KEY
END
```

Activity 2.10

Program code:

```
REM *** Shape 1 ***
PRINT "**********"
PRINT "**********"
PRINT "**********"
PRINT "**********"
WAIT KEY
REM *** Shape 2 ***
PRINT "*"
PRINT "**"
PRINT "***"
PRINT "****"
PRINT "*****"
WAIT KEY
REM *** Shape 3 ***
PRINT "    *"
PRINT "   **"
PRINT "  ***"
PRINT " ****"
PRINT "*****"
REM *** End program ***
WAIT KEY
END
```

The last shape may not be exact. See Choosing a Text Font later in this chapter.

Activity 2.11

None of the PRINT statements are invalid

Activity 2.12

The exact values will vary according to your screen resolution.

The following code will fit a 1280 by 1024 screen

```
REM *** A top left ***
PRINT "A"
REM *** B top right ***
SET CURSOR 1260,0
PRINT "B"
```

```
REM *** C bottom left ***
SET CURSOR 0,990
PRINT "C"
REM *** D bottom right ***
SET CURSOR 1260,990
PRINT "D"
REM *** End program ***
WAIT KEY
END
```

Activity 2.13

The word *Goodbye* overwrites and removes the word *Hello* from the screen.

Activity 2.14

The code for a resolution of 1280 by 1024 is:

```
REM *** A top left ***
TEXT 0,0,"A"
REM *** B top right ***
TEXT 1260,0,"B"
REM *** C bottom left ***
TEXT 0,990,"C"
REM *** D bottom right ***
TEXT 1260,990,"D"
REM *** End program ***
WAIT KEY
END
```

You may find that this program uses a different resolution than the earlier version did.

Activity 2.15

The program code is:

```
REM *** Output two strings at same
location ***
TEXT 100, 100, "Hello"
WAIT KEY
TEXT 100, 100, "Goodbye"
REM *** End program ***
WAIT KEY
END
```

The second string writes on top of the first without removing it. We'll see a cure for this later in the chapter.

Activity 2.16

For 1248 by 1024, the program code is:

```
CENTER TEXT 623,500, "MIDDLE"
REM *** End program ***
WAIT KEY
END
```

Activity 2.17

The second line of the LISTING-2.3 should be changed to

```
SET TEXT FONT "Times New Roman"
```

Activity 2.18

```
PRINT RGB(255,255,0)
```

displays the value 4294967040

```
PRINT RGB(255,0,255)
```

displays 4294902015

Activity 2.19

The background remains black.

Activity 2.20

The program code is:

```
INK RGB(255,255,0), RGB(255,0,0)
PRINT "Hello"
REM *** Set green foreground ***
INK RGB(0,255,0),0
PRINT "Goodbye"
REM *** End program ***
WAIT KEY
END
```

Activity 2.21

```
REM *** Yellow foreground and red background
***
SET TEXT OPAQUE
INK RGB(255,255,0), RGB(255,0,0)
PRINT "Hello"
REM *** Cyan foreg'nd & magenta backg'nd ***
INK RGB(0,255,255),RGB(255,0,255)
PRINT "Goodbye"
REM *** End program ***
WAIT KEY
END
```

Activity 2.22

No solution required

Activity 2.23

The program code is:

```
REM *** Clear screen to red ***
CLS RGB(255,0,0)
REM *** Set text characteristics ***
SET TEXT FONT "Courier New"
SET TEXT TO BOLD
SET TEXT SIZE 20
REM *** Set colours (yellow and red) ***
INK RGB(255,255,0),RGB(255,0,0)
REM *** Output box ***
TEXT 0, 0, "**********"
TEXT 0,20, "*        *"
TEXT 0,40, "**********"
REM *** Set opaque text ***
SET TEXT OPAQUE
REM *** Set colours (blue and black) ***
INK RGB(0,0,255),RGB(0,0,0)
REM *** Output text ***
TEXT 34,18,"BOX"
REM *** End program
WAIT KEY
END
```

Activity 2.24

The problem can be cured by adding more spaces to the second TEXT statement.

Activity 2.25

```
REM *** Set background colour ***
CLS RGB(126,126,126)
REM *** Set text font and size ***
SET TEXT FONT "Arial"
SET TEXT SIZE 36
INK RGB (255, 0,0) ,0
REM *** Output Text ***
TEXT 100,80, "Goodbye"
WAIT KEY
REM ** Remove text by writing it again in
background colour ***
INK RGB(126,126,126),0
TEXT 100,80, "Goodbye"
REM *** End program ***
WAIT KEY
END
```

```
REM *** Embossed Text ***
INK RGB(0,0,0),0
TEXT 201, 201, "Goodbye"
INK RGB(255,255,255),0
TEXT 199, 199, "Goodbye"
INK RGB(126,126,126),0
TEXT 200, 200, "Goodbye"
REM *** End program ***
WAIT KEY
END
```

Activity 2.26

Existing code is in grey:

```
REM *** Set background colour ***
CLS RGB (126,126,126)
SET TEXT SIZE 36
REM *** Set text font and size ***
SET TEXT FONT "Arial"
SET TEXT SIZE 36
INK RGB (255, 0,0) ,0
REM *** Output Text ***
TEXT 100,80, "Goodbye"
WAIT KEY
REM ** Remove text by writing it again in
background colour ***
INK RGB(126,126,126),0
TEXT 100,80, "Goodbye"
WAIT KEY
REM *** Shadow text ***
INK RGB (0,0,0) ,0
TEXT 102,102, "Hello"
INK RGB (255, 0,0) ,0
TEXT 100, 100, "Hello"
REM *** End program ***
WAIT KEY
END
```

Activity 2.27

Existing code is in grey:

```
REM *** Set background colour ***
CLS RGB (126,126,126)
SET TEXT SIZE 36
REM *** Set text font and size ***
SET TEXT FONT "Arial"
SET TEXT SIZE 36
INK RGB (255, 0,0) ,0
REM *** Output Text ***
TEXT 100,80, "Goodbye"
WAIT KEY
REM ** Remove text by writing it again in
background colour ***
INK RGB(126,126,126),0
TEXT 100,80, "Goodbye"
WAIT KEY
REM *** Shadow text ***
INK RGB (0,0,0) ,0
TEXT 102,102, "Hello"
INK RGB (255, 0,0) ,0
TEXT 100, 100, "Hello"
```

8

Data

Arithmetic Operators

Assignment Statement

Constants

Creating Random Numbers

Input Statement

RANDOMIZE and RND Statements

READ, DATA and RESTORE Statements

String Operations

Testing Sequential Structures

Variables

Variable Names

Program Data

Introduction

Every computer game has to store and manipulate facts and figures (more commonly known as **data**). For example, a program may store the name of a player, the number of lives remaining or the time the player has remaining in which to complete a task.

We group information like this into three basic types:

> **integer** - any whole number, positive, negative or zero
> **real** - any number containing a decimal point
> **strings** - any collection of characters (may include numeric characters)

For example, if player *Daniel McLaren* had *3* lives and *10.6* minutes to complete a game, then:

> *3*   is an example of an integer value,
> *10.6*   is a real value,
> and   *Daniel McLaren* is an example of a string.

Activity 3.1

Identify which type of value each of the following is:

a) -9	f) 0
b) abc	g) -3.0
c) 18	h) Mary had a little lamb
d) 12.8	i) 4 minutes
e) ?	j) 0.023

Constants

When a specific value appears in a computer program's code it is usually referred to as a **constant**. Hence, in the statement

```
PRINT 7
```

the value 7 is a constant. More specifically, we may refer to constant's type. In the line

```
PRINT "Charlotte", 15, 42.7
```

Charlotte is a **string constant**, *15*, an **integer constant**, and *42.7*, a **real constant**. Note that in DarkBASIC Pro, string constants always appear within double quotes.

Activity 3.2

Identify the constant types in the following line of code:

```
PRINT "Mary is ", 12, " years old"
```

Variables

Most programs not only need to display data, but also need to store data and calculate results. To do this in DarkBASIC Pro we need to use a **variable**. A variable is simply somewhere to store a value. Every variable in a program is assigned a unique name and can store a single value. That value might be an integer, a real or a string but each variable is designed to store only one type of value. Hence, a variable designed to store an integer value cannot store a string.

Integer Variables

In DarkBASIC Pro variables are created automatically as soon as we mention them in our code. For example, let's assume we want to store the number of lives allocated to a game player in a variable called *lives*. To do this in DarkBASIC Pro we simply write the line:

```
lives = 3
```

This sets up a variable called *lives* and stores the value 3 in that variable (see FIG-3.1)

FIG-3.1

Storing Data in a Variable

This is known as an **assignment statement** since we are assigning a value (3) to a variable (*lives*).

You are free to change the contents of a variable at any time by just assigning it a different value. For example, we can change the contents of *lives* with a line such as:

```
lives = 2
```

When we do this any previous value will be removed and the new value stored in its place (see FIG-3.2).

FIG-3.2

Changing the Value in a Variable

The variable *lives* is designed to store an integer value. In the lines below, a, b, c, d, and e are also integer variables. So the following assignments are correct

```
a = 200
b = 0
c = -8
```

but the lines below are wrong

```
d = 3.14
e = -1.9
```

since they attempt to store real constants in variables designed to hold an integers. DarkBASIC Pro won't actually report an error if you try out these last two examples, it simply ignores the fractional part of the numbers and ends up storing 3 in *d* and 1 in *e* (see FIG-3.3).

FIG-3.3

Trying to Copy a Real
Value to an Integer
Variable

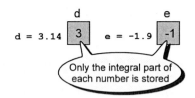

Real Variables

If you want to create a variable capable of storing a real number, then we must end the variable name with the hash (#) symbol. For example, if we write

```
d# = 3.14
e# = -1.9
```

we have created variables named d# and e#, both capable of storing real values(see FIG-3.4).

FIG-3.4

Creating Real Variables

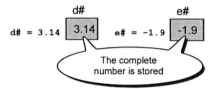

Any number can be stored in a real variable, so we could also write a statement such as:

```
d# = 12
```

and this will be stored as 12.0.

If any value can be stored in a real variable, why bother with integer variables? Actually, you should always use integer values wherever possible because the computer is much faster at handling integer values than reals which require much more processing whenever you want to do any calculations. Also, real numbers can be slightly inaccurate because of rounding errors within the machine. For example, the value 2.3 might be stored as 2.2999987.

String Variables

Finally, if you want to store a string value, you need to use a string variable. String variable names must end with a dollar ($) sign. The value to be stored must be enclosed in double quotes. We could create a string variable named *player$* and store the name *Liz Heron* in it using the statement:

```
player$ = "Liz Heron"
```

The double quotes are not stored in the variable (see FIG-3.5).

FIG-3.5

Creating String
Variables

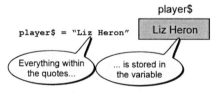

Absolutely any value can be stored in a string variable as long as that value is enclosed in double quotes. Below are a few examples:

```
a$ = "?>%"
b$ = "Your spaceship has been destroyed"
c$ = "That costs $12.50"
```

Activity 3.3

Which of the following are valid DarkBASIC Pro statements that will store
the specified value in the named variable?

```
a) a = 6              d) d# = 5
b) b = 12.89          e) e$ = 'Goodbye'
c) c$ = Hello         f) f# = -12.5
```

Using Meaningful Names

It is important that you use meaningful names for your variables when you write a
program. This helps you remember what a variable is being used for when you go
back and look at your program a month or two after you wrote it.

So, rather than write statements such as

```
a = 3
b = 120
c = 2000
```

a better set of statements would be

```
lives = 3
points = 120
timeremaining = 2000
```

which give a much clearer indication of what the variables are being used for.

Naming Rules

DarkBASIC Pro, like all other programming languages, demands that you follow
a few rules when you make up a variable name. These rules are:

> ➤ The name should start with a letter.

> ➤ Subsequent characters in the name can be a letter, number, or underscore

> ➤ The final character can be a # (when creating real variables) or $ (when
> creating string variables).

> ➤ Upper or lower case letters can be used, but such differences are ignored.
> Hence, the terms *total* and *TOTAL* refer to the same variable.

> ➤ The name cannot be a DarkBASIC Pro keyword.

This means that variable names such as

```
a
bc
de_2
fgh$
iJKlmnp#
```

are valid, while names such as

are invalid.

The most common mistake people make is to have a space in their variable names (e.g. *fuel level*). This is not allowed. As a valid alternative, you can replace the space with an underscore (*fuel_level*) or join the words together (*fuellevel*). Using capital letters for the joined words is also popular (*FuelLevel*).

Note that the names *no*, *no#* and *no$* represent three different variables; one designed to hold an integer value (*no*), one a real value (*no#*) and the last a string (*no$*).

Activity 3.4

Which of the following are invalid variable names:

a) `x`   e) `total score`
b) `5`   f) `ts#o`
c) `"total"`   g) `end`
d) `a12$`   h) `G2_F3`

Summary

- Fixed values are known as constants.
- There are three types of constants: integer, real and string.
- String constants are always enclosed in double quotes.
- The double quotes are not part of the string constant.
- A variable is a space within the computer's memory where a value can be stored.
- Every variable must have a name.
- A variable's name determines which type of value it may hold.
- Variables that end with the # symbol can hold real values.
- Variables that end with the $ symbol can hold string values.
- Other variables hold integer values.
- The name given to a variable should reflect the value held in that variable.
- When naming a variable the following rules apply:

  The name must start with a letter
  Subsequent characters in the name can be numeric, alphabetic or the underscore character.
  The name may end with a # or $ symbol.
  The name must not be a DarkBASIC Pro keyword.

Allocating Values to Variables

Introduction

There are several ways to place a value in a variable. The DarkBASIC Pro statements available to achieve this are described below.

The Assignment Statement

In the last few pages we've used DarkBASIC Pro's assignment statement to store a value in a variable. This statement allows the programmer to place a specific value in a variable, or to store the result of some calculation.

In its simplest form the assignment statement has the form shown in FIG-3.6.

FIG-3.6

The Assignment Statement

The value copied into the variable may be one of the following types:

> ➢ a constant
>
> ➢ another variable
>
> ➢ an arithmetic expression

Examples of each are shown below.

Assigning a Constant

This is the type of assignment we've seen earlier, with examples such as

```
name$ = "Liz Heron"
```

where a fixed value (a constant) is copied into the variable. Make sure that the constant is the same type as the variable. For instance, the statement

```
desc = "tall"
```

is invalid since it attempts to copy a string constant ("tall") into an integer variable (*desc*). Not every mistake will be signalled by the compiler. For example, if we try to assign a real constant to an integer variable as in the statement

```
result = 12.79
```

the integer variable result stores only the integral part of the constant (i.e. 12), the fractional part being lost.

However, an integer value may be copied into a real variable, as in the line:

```
result# = 33
```

The program deals with this by storing the value assigned to *result#* as 33.0.

Copying a Variable's Value

Once we've assigned a value to a variable in a statement such as

```
no1 = 12
```

we can copy the contents of that variable into another variable with a command such as:

```
no2 = no1
```

The effect of these two statements is shown in FIG-3.7.

FIG-3.7

Copying One Variable's
Value to Another
Variable

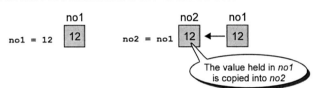

The value held in *no1*
is copied into *no2*

As before, you must make sure the two variables are of the same type, although the contents of an integer variable may be copied to a real variable as in the lines:

```
ans# = no1
```

Although not invalid, trying this the other way round (real copied to integer) as in

```
ans# = 12.94
no1 = ans#
```

will cause *no1* to store only the integral part of *ans#* contents (i.e. 12).

Copying the Result of an Arithmetic Expression

Another variation for the assignment statement is to perform a calculation and store the result of that calculation. Hence we might write

```
no1 = 7 + 3
```

which would store the value 10 in the variable *no1*.

The example shows the use of the addition operator, but there are 5 possible operators that may be used when performing a calculation. These are shown in TABLE-3.1.

Operator	Function	Example
+	Addition	no1 = no2 + 5
-	Subtraction	no1 = no2 - 9
*	Multiplication	ans = no1 * no2
/	Division	r1# = no1 / 2
mod	Remainder	ans = no2 mod 3
^	Power	ans = 2 ^ 24

The result of most statements should be obvious. For example, if a program begins with the statements

```
no1 = 12
no2 = 3
```

and then contains the line

```
total = no1 - no2
```

then the variable *total* will contain the value 9, while the line

```
product = no1 * no2
```

stores the value 36 in the variable *product*.

The remainder operator (mod) is used to find the integer remainder after dividing one integer into another. For example,

```
ans = 9 mod 5
```

assigns the value 4 to the variable *ans* since 5 divides into 9 once with a remainder of 4. Other examples are given below:

```
6 mod 3        gives 0
7 mod 9        gives 7
123 mod 10     gives 3
```

If the first value is negative, then any remainder is also negative:

```
-11 mod 3      gives -2
```

Activity 3.7

What is the result of the following calculations:

a) `12 mod 5`   c) `5 mod 11`
b) `-7 mod 2`   d) `-12 mod -8`

The power operator (^) allows us to perform a calculation of the form x^y. For example, a 24-bit address bus on the microprocessor of your computer allows 2^{24}

memory addresses. We could calculate this number with the statement:

```
addresses = 2^24
```

However, the results of some statements are not quite so obvious. The line

```
ans# = 19/4
```

will result in the value 4.0 being stored in *ans#* since the division operator always returns an integer result if the two values involved are both integer. On the other hand, if we write

```
ans# = 19/4.0
```

and thereby use a real value, then the result stored in *ans#* will be 4.75.

When a real value is copied into an integer variable, the fractional part of the value being copied is lost. For example, the variable *result* would contain the value 4 after executing the line

```
result = 19/4.0
```

When using the division operator, a second situation that you must guard against is division by zero. In mathematics, dividing any number by zero gives an undefined result, so computers get quite upset if you try to get them to perform such a calculation. Hence, the line

```
ans = 10/0
```

would cause a program to crash when it attempted to perform that line in the program. You might be tempted to think that you would never write such a statement, but a more likely scenario is that your program contains a line such as

```
ans = no1 / no2
```

and if *no2* contains the value zero attempting to execute the line will still cause the program to terminate.

Some statements may not appear to make sense if you are used to traditional algebra. For example, what is the meaning of a line such as:

```
no1 = no1 + 3
```

In fact, it means *add 3 to no1*. See FIG-3.8 for a full explanation.

FIG-3.8

Adding to a Variable's Contents

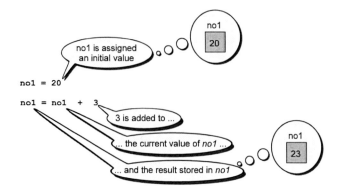

Another unusual assignment statement is:

```
no1 = -no1
```

The effect of this statement is to change the sign of the value held in *no1*. For example, if *no1* contained the value 12, the above statement would change that value to -12. Alternatively, if *no1* started off containing the value -12, the above statement would change *no1*'s contents to 12.

Activity 3.8

Assuming a program starts with the lines:

```
no1 = 2
v# = 41.09
```

what will be the result of the following instructions?

a) `no2 = no1^4`   d) `no4 = no1 + 7`
b) `x# = v#*2`   e) `m# = no1/5`
c) `no3 = no1/5`   f) `v2# = v# - 0.1`

Of course, an arithmetic expression may have several parts to it as in the line

```
answer = no1 - 3 / v# * 2
```

and, how the final result of such lines is calculated is determined by **operator precedence**.

Operator Precedence

If we have a complex arithmetic expression such as

```
answer# = 12 + 18 / 3^2 - 6
```

then there's a potential problem about what should be done first. Will we start by adding 12 and 18 or subtracting 6 from 2, raising 3 to the power 2, or even dividing 18 by 3. In fact, calculations are done in a very specific order according to a fixed set of rules. The rules are that the power operation ($\wedge$) is always done first. After that comes multiplication and division with addition and subtraction done last. The power operator ($\wedge$) is said to have a higher priority than multiplication and division; they in turn having a higher priority than addition and subtraction.

So, to calculate the result of the statement above the computer begins by performing the calculation `3^2` which leaves us with:

```
answer = 12 + 18 / 9 - 6
```

Next the division operation is performed (18/9) giving

```
answer = 12 + 2 - 6
```

The remaining operators, + and -, have the same priority, so the operations are performed on a left-to-right basis meaning that we next calculate 12+2 giving

```
answer = 14 - 6
```

Finally, the last calculation (14 -6) is performed leaving

```
answer = 8
```

and the value 8 stored in the variable *answer*.

Activity 3.9

What is the result of the calculation   `12 - 5 * 12 / 10 - 5`

Using Parentheses

If we need to change the order in which calculations within an expression are performed, we can use parentheses. Expressions in parentheses are always done first. Therefore, if we write

```
answer = (12 + 18) / 9 - 6
```

then 12+18 will be calculated first, leaving:

```
answer = 30 / 9 - 6
```

This will continue as follows:

```
answer = 3.3333 - 6
answer = -2.6667
```

An arithmetic expression can contain many sets of parentheses. Normally, the computer calculates the value in the parentheses by starting with the left-most set.

Activity 3.10

Show the steps involved in calculating the result of the expression
`8 * (6-2) / (3-1)`

If sets of parentheses are placed inside one another (this is known as **nested parentheses**) , then the contents of the inner-most set is calculated first. Hence, in the expression

```
12 / (3 * (10 - 6) + 4)
```

the calculation is performed as follows:

```
(10 - 6)    giving 12 / (3*4+4)
3 * 4       giving 12 / (12 + 4)
12 + 4      giving 12 / 16
12 / 16     giving 0.75
```

Activity 3.11

Assuming a program begins with the lines
```
no1 = 12
no2 = 3
no3 = 5
```
what would be the value stored in *answer* as a result of the line
```
answer = no1/(4 + no2 - 1)*5 - no3^2 ?
```

Variable Range

When first learning to program, a favourite pastime is to see how large a number the computer can handle, so people write lines such as:

```
no1 = 1234567890
```

They are often disappointed when the program crashes at this point.

There is a limit to the value that can be stored in a variable. That limit is determined by how much memory is allocated to a variable, and that differs from language to language. The range of values that can be stored in DarkBASIC Pro variables is shown in TABLE-3.2.

TABLE-3.2

Variable Range

Variable Type	Range of Values
integer	-2,147,483,648 to + 2,147,483,647
real	±3.4 E ± 38

String Operations

The + operator can also be used on string values to join them together. For example, if we write

```
a$ = "to" + "get"
```

then the value *toget* is stored in variable *a$*. If we then continue with the line

```
b$ = a$ + "her"
```

b$ will contain the value *together*, a result obtained by joining the contents of a$ to the string constant "her".

Activity 3.12

What value will be stored as a result of the statement
```
term$ = "abc"+"123"+"xyz"
```

The PRINT Statement Again

We've already seen that the PRINT command can be used to display values on the screen using lines such as:

```
PRINT 12
PRINT "Hello"
```

We can also get the PRINT statement to display the answer to a calculation. Hence,

```
PRINT 7+3
```

will display the value 10 on the screen, while the statement

```
PRINT "Hello " + "again"
```

displays *Hello again*.

The PRINT statement can also be used to display the value held within a variable. This means that if we follow the statement

```
number = 23
```

by the line

```
PRINT number
```

our program will display the value 23 on the screen, this being the value held in *number*. Real and string variables can be displayed in the same way. Hence the lines

```
name$ = "Charlotte"
weight# = 95.3
PRINT name$
PRINT weight#
```

will produce the output

```
Charlotte
95.3
```

Activity 3.13

A program contains the following lines of code:
```
number = 23
PRINT "number"
PRINT number
```
What output will be produced by the two PRINT statements?

Activity 3.14

Type in and test the following program (don't bother to save the program):

```
number = 23
PRINT number
WAIT KEY
END
```

Change the program by removing the first two lines and replacing this with two statements which will assign the value *Jessica McLaren* to a variable called *name$* and then display the contents of *name$* on the screen.

The PRINT statement can display more than one value at a time. For example, we can get it to display the number *12* and the word *Hello* at the same time by writing

```
PRINT 12,"Hello"
```

Each value we want displayed must be separated from the next by a comma. We can use this to display a message alongside the contents of a variable. For example, the lines

```
capital$ = "Washington"
PRINT "The capital of the USA is ", capital$
```

produce the following output on the screen:

```
The capital of the USA is Washington
```

Other Ways to Store a Value in a Variable

The INPUT Statement

There will be many values which we cannot know when we are writing the program. For example, we can't know the name of the player until someone sits down at the computer and begins to play our game. The only way we can get access to that sort of information is to ask the player to type in the information the program requires. This is done with the INPUT statement. In its simplest form the INPUT keyword is followed by the name of the variable where we'd like to store the information the player types in. For example, we might write

```
INPUT name$
```

expecting the person at the keyboard to type in their name and then storing what they type in the variable *name$*. Of course, the player has to be told what sort of information they are expected to enter, so we could precede the INPUT statement with a message telling them what to type in :

```
PRINT "Please enter your name "
INPUT name$
```

DarkBASIC Pro makes things simpler than this by allowing us to include the message we want displayed as part of the INPUT statement. Hence, we can achieve the same effect as the two statements above using the line:

```
INPUT "Please enter your name ", name$
```

This gives us the final format for the INPUT statement as shown in FIG-3.9.

FIG-3.9

The INPUT Statement

In the diagram:

message	is a string (enclosed in double quotes) which is displayed before any data from the keyboard is accepted.
variable	is a variable name. The value entered by the user at the keyboard will be assigned to this variable. It is the user's responsibility to enter a value of the correct type.

We can use the INPUT statement anywhere in our program and as often as necessary.

The READ and DATA Statements

There are times when we want to assign a value to a variable, but we don't want to have to enter that value from the keyboard. For example, let's say a variable, *daysinmonth*, is used to store how many days are in January. The contents of *daysinmonth* is then to be displayed. After this the program stores within *daysinmonth* the number of days in a normal February. Again, the contents of *daysinmonth* is displayed. This continues until every month of the year has been dealt with.

We could start the coding for this as:

```
daysinmonth = 31
PRINT daysinmonth
daysinmonth = 28
PRINT daysinmonth
daysinmonth = 31
PRINT daysinmonth
```

Alternatively, we can set up the values we intend to assign to *daysinmonth* in a DATA statement:

```
DATA 31,28,31,30,31,30,31,31,30,31,30,31
```

and then use a READ statement every time we want to assign a value to *daysinmonth*.

```
READ daysinmonth
```

The value given to *daysinmonth* by the READ statement will be the first value listed in the DATA statement. When another READ statement is executed, the second value from the DATA statement will be used. We can therefore rewrite the statements given earlier as:

```
DATA 31,28,31,30,31,30,31,31,30,31,30,31
READ daysinmonth
PRINT daysinmonth
READ daysinmonth
PRINT daysinmonth
READ daysinmonth
PRINT daysinmonth
```

The operation of these statements is shown in FIG-3.10.

FIG-3.10

Using DATA and READ

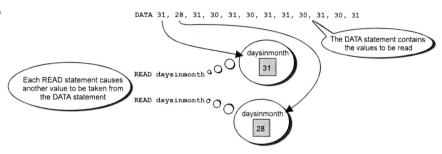

Is this second approach any better than the first? You should have noticed that by using the DATA/READ approach we repeat exactly the same statements over and over again. In a later chapter we will see that this code can be shortened by using a loop statement which would not be possible with the first approach.

Several DATA statements may be used by a program, so we might write:

```
DATA 31, 28
DATA 31, 30
```

The computer simply groups the values given in the DATA statements into a single list, so the two DATA statements above have exactly the same effect as:

```
DATA 31,28,31,30
```

The DATA statement can contain values of any type. The next example stores the names of the first three days of the week:

```
DATA "Sunday", "Monday","Tuesday"
```

Of course, when you read from this DATA statement, the variable being assigned the value must be a string:

```
READ day$
```

The type of values in a DATA statement can even be mixed, containing integer, real or string constants in any order. It is only important that READ statements use the type of variable appropriate to the next value coming from the DATA statement.

We might write

```
DATA 12, 2.7, "Hello"
```

followed by

```
READ no1
READ x#
READ word$
```

and this would be acceptable because variables and values being read are of matching types. That is, the first READ statement would assign the integer value 12 to the integer variable *no1*; the second READ would assign the real value 2.7 to the real variable *x#* and the third READ would assign the string "Hello" to the string variable *word$*. It's also possible to read the value of more than one variable in a single READ statement. Hence, we could reduce the three statements above to the single line:

```
READ no1, x#, word$
```

A DATA statement can be placed anywhere in your program. Often it is placed at the start or end of a program where it can easily be found should the values it holds need to be examined or changed.

The format for the DATA statement is shown in FIG-3.11 and the format of the READ statement is shown in FIG-3.12.

FIG-3.11

The DATA Statement

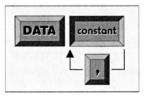

In the diagram:

    constant   represents any fixed value. This value can be an integer, real, or string.

FIG-3.12

The READ Statement

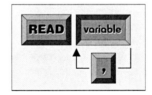

In the diagram:

    variable   is any variable name. The variable named will be assigned the next available value from the DATA statement.

An error will be reported if your program contains a READ statement but no DATA statement. An error will also occur if a READ statement is executed after all the values in the DATA statement have been used.

Activity 3.19

Write a short program (*days01.dbpro*) which displays the names of the days of the week. Start with Sunday.

The names should be set up in a DATA statement, then accessed using a series of READ statements.

The RESTORE Statement

DarkBASIC Pro knows which value is to be used next from a DATA statement by keeping a marker which indicates which value in the statement is to be used when the next READ statement is executed.

Initially this marker points to the first value in the first DATA statement. After each READ the marker moves on one position. However, it is possible to return the marker to the start of the DATA list by executing the RESTORE statement.

For example, in the code

```
DATA 3,6,9,12
READ no1
READ no2
RESTORE
READ no3
```

the variable *no3* will be assigned the value *3* because the RESTORE statement will have moved the DATA marker back to the first value in the list.

The RESTORE statement has the format shown in FIG-3.13.

FIG-3.13

The RESTORE Statement

Activity 3.20

Modify your last program so that after all the days of the week have been displayed the word *Sunday* is displayed for a second time.

You can achieve this result by adding a RESTORE statement, another READ statement and a PRINT statement to your program.

The Time and Date

The TIMER Statement

DarkBASIC Pro contains a command that lets you find out how long your computer has been switched on. This is the TIMER statement which returns an integer specifying the number of milliseconds that have passed since your machine was last powered up. This information is actually maintained by the operating system and the DarkBASIC Pro statement interrogates the area of computer memory where this data is held.

The TIMER statement has the format given in FIG-3.14.

FIG-3.14

The TIMER Statement

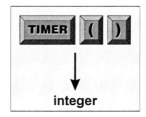

Notice that the parentheses must be included in the statement even though no information is placed within them. DarkBASIC Pro's general syntax demands that any statement that returns a value must always have parentheses.

So the TIMER statement could be used to display how long your machine has been on with the single line

```
PRINT TIMER ()
```

but this would be in milliseconds. Perhaps a better option would be to save the value returned by TIMER and convert that value to seconds, as in the lines:

```
millisecondsPassed = TIMER()
seconds = millisecondsPassed / 1000
PRINT "Your computer has been on for ", seconds, " seconds"
```

> **Activity 3.21**
>
> Create a project (*minutes.dbpro*) which displays how many minutes have passed since your computer was last switched on.

By using TIMER before and after some event we can measure how long that event lasts. For example, we could create a simple reaction time game by seeing how quickly the user can press a key after being told to do so. Such a program requires the following logic:

```
Display "Press any key"
Record the start time
Wait for a key press
Record the finish time
Calculate the duration as finish time minus the start time
Display the duration
```

> **Activity 3.22**
>
> Create a project (*reaction.dbpro*) that implements the logic given above.

The GET TIME$ Statement

If we need to get the actual time of day then we can use the TIME$ statement which returns a string giving the current time (as obtained from the system clock) in the form HH:MM:SS, where HH is the hour (0 to 23), MM is the minutes, and SS the seconds.

The format for this statement is given in FIG-3.15.

FIG-3.15

The GET TIME$ Statement

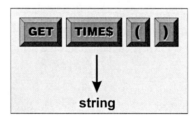

For example, we could display the current time using the line:

```
PRINT GET TIME$()
```

The GET DATE$ Statement

The current date can be returned as a string using the GET DATE$ statement which has the format shown in FIG-3.16.

FIG-3.16

The GET DATE$
Statement

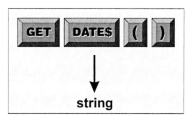

string

The string returned is in the American form MM/DD/YY. For example, when run at the time of writing, the statement

```
PRINT GET DATE$()
```

displayed the output 07/16/05.

Generating Random Numbers

Often in a game we need to throw a dice, choose a card or think of a number. All of these are random events. That is to say, we cannot predict what value will be thrown on the dice, what card will be chosen, or what number some other person will think of.

The RND Statement

There is a need to get computer programs to emulate this randomness and this is done using the RND statement. In fact, like RGB, RND is a function. It will generate an integer value within a specified range and return that generated value. For example, if we wanted to display a random number between 0 and 10, we could write

```
PRINT RND(10)
```

RND has to be supplied with a value enclosed in parentheses. This value lets the command know what range of possible values may be generated. Notice that the lowest value that can be generated is always zero, while the largest value is equal to the number given in the brackets.

Activity 3.23

What expression would we use if we wanted to create a random number in the range 0 to 48?

The format for the RND statement is given m FIG-3.17.

FIG-3.17

The RND Statement

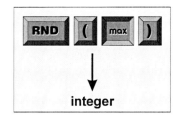

integer

In the diagram:

max is any positive integer value. The command will return an integer in the range 0 to *max*.

The value given within the parentheses can also be a variable or arithmetic expression, as in the lines:

```
num = 25
PRINT RND (num)        '0 to 25
PRINT RND (num*2-3)    '0 to 47
```

The value returned by RND could be stored in a variable using a statement such as:

```
number = RND(10)
```

If RND(5) generates a number between 0 and 5, how are we going to emulate a dice throw which gives values 1 to 6? Often people suggest writing RND(6), but this gives values in the range 0 to 6, not 1 to 6.

Instead we have to generate a value between 0 and 5 and then add 1 to that number.

We could do this with the line

```
diceThrow = RND(5)+1
```

and follow this with a PRINT statement displaying the contents of *diceThrow*:

```
PRINT "You threw a ",diceThrow
```

The RANDOMIZE Statement

Computers can't really think of a random number all by themselves. Actually, they cheat and use a mathematical formula to calculate an apparently random number. As long as you don't know that formula, you won't be able to predict what number the computer is going to come up with.

But to get the mathematics started correctly, we need to supply it with a start up value or **seed value**. Effectively this seed value determines what numbers the computer is going to generate when RND is used.

The seed value is set up using the RANDOMIZE statement which has the format shown in FIG-3.18.

FIG-3.18

The RANDOMIZE Statement

In the diagram:

seed is an integer value which is used as a start-up value for the random number generator.

Exactly what seed value you use doesn't really matter, but if you start with the same seed value every time, you'll always get the same set of values from RND. For example, if a program contained the lines

```
RANDOMIZE 12345
PRINT RND(50)
PRINT RND(12)
```

every time that program is executed, the same numbers would be displayed.

To stop this happening we need to make sure that the seed value is different every time we run a program. We can achieve this using the TIMER statement. So if we write

```
number = TIMER()
RANDOMIZE number
```

then, since TIMER will return a different value every time it's carried out (remember the time in your computer is being updated 1000 times per second), the seed value for RANDOMIZE will always be different. Actually, we can combine the two statements above into one:

```
RANDOMIZE TIMER()
```

Now we are ready to write a program using random numbers. The program in LISTING-3.1 simulates a dice throw and displays the number generated.

LISTING-3.1

Displaying a Random Number

```
REM *** Generate random number ***
RANDOMIZE TIMER()
number = RND(5)+1

REM *** Display number ***
PRINT number

REM *** End program ***
WAIT KEY
END
```

Activity 3.24

Type in and run the program given above (*random.dbpro*).
Modify the program so that it generates a number between 1 and 49.

Activity 3.25

Write a program (*guess01.dbpro*) that performs the following logic:

Computer thinks of a number between 1 and 100
User (you) enters their guess at what the number is
The computer displays both the guess and the original number

Structured English and Programs

When we write a structured English algorithm with the intention of turning that algorithm into a computer program, we always write the algorithm as if we are telling the computer what it has to do. Therefore, the rather long winded algorithm in the Activity above would be better written as:

Generate a random integer between 1 and 100
Get user's guess
Display number and guess

Using Variables to Store Colour Values

We've seen how the value generated by the RND statement can be stored in a variable with a statement such as:

```
number = RND(5)+1
```

Since the RGB statement also returns a value, we can use that same approach there. So rather than write

```
INK RGB(255,0,0),RGB(0,255,0)
```

we could write

```
colour1 = RGB(255,0,0)
colour2 = RGB(0,255,0)
INK colour1, colour2
```

Activity 3.26

Write a program (*colours03.dbpro*) that performs the following operations

Assigns the colour red to a variable called *scarlet*;
Assigns the colour blue to a variable called *sky*;
Clears the screen to create red blank screen (use *scarlet*);
Writes the word *Ocean* in blue on the screen (use *sky*)

Named Constants

When a program uses a fixed value which has an important role (for example, perhaps the value 1000 is the score a player must achieve to win a game), then we have the option of assigning a name to that value using the #CONSTANT statement.

The format of this statement is shown in FIG-3.19.

FIG-3.19

The #CONSTANT statement

In the diagram:

name   is the name to be assigned to the constant value.

value   is the constant value being named.

For example, we can name the value 1000 *WinningScore* using the line:

```
#CONSTANT WinningScore = 1000
```

Since the equal sign (=) is optional, it is also valid to write:

```
#CONSTANT WinningScore 1000
```

Real and string constants can also be named, but the names assigned must NOT end with # or $ symbols. Therefore the following lines are valid

```
#CONSTANT Pi = 3.14159265
#CONSTANT Vowels = "aeiou"
```

The value assigned to a name cannot be changed, so having written

```
#CONSTANT WinningScore = 1000
```

it is not valid to try to assign a new value with a line such as:

```
WinningScore = 1900
```

The two main reasons for using named constants in a program are:

1) Aiding the readability of the program. For example, it is easier to understand the meaning of the line

    ```
    IF playerscore >= WinningScore
    ```

    than

    ```
    IF playerscore >= 1000
    ```

2) If the same constant value is used in several places throughout a program, it is easier to change its value if it is defined as a named constant. For example, if, when writing a second version of a game we decide that the winning score has to be changed from 1000 to 2000, then we need only change the line

    ```
    #CONSTANT WinningScore = 1000
    ```

    to

    ```
    #CONSTANT WinningScore = 2000
    ```

    On the other hand, if we've used lines such as

    ```
    IF playerscore >= 1000
    ```

    throughout our program, every one of those lines will have to be changed so that the value within them is changed from 1000 to 2000.

Testing Sequential Code

The programs in this chapter are very simple ones, with the statements being executed one after the other, starting with the first and ending with the last. In other words, the programs are **sequential** in structure.

Every program we write needs to be tested. For a simple sequential program that involves input, the minimum testing involves thinking of a value to be entered, predicting what result this value should produce, and then running the program to check that we do indeed obtain the expected result.

The program below (see LISTING-3.2) reads in a value from the keyboard and displays the square root of that number.

LISTING-3.2

Calculating the Square
Root of a Value

```
INPUT "Please enter your number : ", number#
squareroot# = number#^0.5
PRINT "The square root of ", number#, " is ",squareroot#
WAIT KEY
END
```

To test this program we might decide to enter the value 16 with the expectation of the result being 4.

Activity 3.27

Type in the program given above (*root.dbpro*) and test it by inputting the value 16.

Perhaps that would seem sufficient to say that the program is functioning correctly. However, a more cautious person might try a few more values just to make sure. But what values should be chosen? Should we try 25 or 9, 3 or 7?

As a general rule it is best to think carefully about what values you choose as test data. A few carefully chosen values may show up problems when many more randomly chosen values show nothing.

When the test data is numeric, the most obvious choices are to use a typical value (in the case of the above program, 16 falls into this category), a very large value, a negative value and zero. But in each case it is important that you work out the expected result before entering your test data into the program - otherwise you have no way of knowing if the results you are seeing on the screen are correct.

Activity 3.28

What results would you expect from *root.dbpro* if your test data was

  401286
    0
    -9

Run the program with these test values and check that the expected results are produced.

When entering string test values, an empty string (just press Enter when asked to enter the data), a single character string, and a multicharacter string should do.

These suggestions for creating test data may need to be modified depending on the nature of the program you are testing.

Summary

- The assignment statement takes the form

    `variable = value`

- *value* can be a constant, other variable, or an expression.

- The value assigned should be of the same type as the receiving variable.

- Arithmetic expressions can use the following operators:

  ```
  ^ * / + - mod
  ```

- Calculations are performed on the basis of highest priority operator first and a left-to-right basis.

- The power operator has the highest priority; multiplication and division and the mod operator the next highest, followed by addition and subtraction.

- Terms enclosed in parentheses are always performed first.

- The + operator can be used to join strings.

- The INPUT statement reads a value from the keyboard and places that value in a named variable.

- The INPUT statement can display a message designed to inform the user what has to be entered.

- The DATA and READ statements can be used to assign a listed value to a variable.

- The RESTORE statement forces a return to the start of the first DATA statement.

- The TIMER statement returns the time in milliseconds from switch on.

- The GET TIME$ statement returns the current time as a string.

- The GET DATE$ statement returns the current date as a string.

- The RND statement generates a random integer number in the range 0 to a specified maximum.

- The RANDOMIZE statement ensures that the numbers created by the RND are truly random.

- The value returned by statements such as RND and RGB can be assigned to a variable.

- A named constant can be created using the #CONSTANT statement.

- The name assigned to a constant must not end with a # or $ symbol.

Determining Current Settings

Introduction

Let's say we want to place the title of our new game in the centre of the screen. We know that we can place text at any position using TEXT or CENTER TEXT, but how are we to discover where the centre of the screen is? If we're working in an 800 by 600 display mode, then the centre is at 400,300 - but how can we be sure what display mode is being used? Luckily, DarkBASIC Pro has many statements that allow us to find out this, and other, information. Some of these are given below, others we'll discuss in later chapters.

Screen Settings

The SCREEN HEIGHT Statement

The SCREEN HEIGHT statement returns the height of the output screen in pixels and has the format shown in FIG-3.20.

FIG-3.20

The SCREEN HEIGHT
Statement

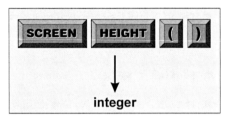

For example, the statement

```
PRINT SCREEN HEIGHT()
```

would display the value 600, assuming the screen resolution was set to 800 by 600.

The SCREEN WIDTH Statement

This statement returns the width of the output screen in pixels. The statement has the format shown in FIG-3.21.

FIG-3.21

The SCREEN WIDTH
Statement

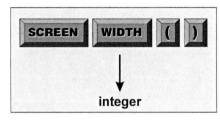

For example, the statement

```
screenwidth = SCREEN WIDTH()
```

would assign the value 800 to the variable *screenwidth*, assuming the screen resolution was set to 800 by 600.

The program in LISTING-3.3 displays the word WELCOME at the centre of the screen.

LISTING-3.3

Centring Text

```
REM *** Find centre of screen ***
centrex = SCREEN WIDTH()/2
centrey = SCREEN HEIGHT()/2

REM *** Display text at centre ***
CENTER TEXT centrex, centrey, "WELCOME"

REM *** End program ***
WAIT KEY
END
```

Activity 3.29

Type in and test the program above (*centred*.dbpro).

Is the text correctly centred both vertically and horizontally?

The SCREEN DEPTH Statement

The number of bits used to represent a single pixel on the screen determines the maximum number of colours that can be shown on the screen. For example, if a single bit was used to represent a pixel, that bit could have the value 0 or 1, hence only two colours can be shown. With two bits per pixel, four colours are possible, represented by the bit patterns 00, 01, 10, and 11.

The SCREEN DEPTH statement returns the number of bits used per pixel and has the format shown in FIG-3.22.

FIG-3.22

The SCREEN DEPTH Statement

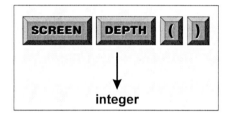

If a call to this statement returns the value 16, then the number of colours that can be shown is calculated as 2^{16}. The code required to perform this calculation is:

```
noofcolours = 2^SCREEN DEPTH()
```

Colour Components

If we were to generate a random colour with the lines

```
RANDOMIZE TIMER()
colour = RGB(RND(255),RND(255),RND(255))
```

we could find out the settings of the red, green and blue components of that colour using the following statements.

The RGBR Statement

The RGBR statement returns an integer specifying the red component of a specified colour. The statement has the format shown in FIG-3.23.

FIG-3.23

The RGBR Statement

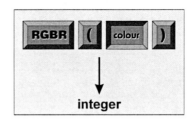

In the diagram:

> *colour*   is an integer value representing a colour. This value will probably have been generated using the RGB statement.

Hence, assuming the variable colour had been set using the line given earlier, we could extract the red component of that colour with the line

```
redvalue = RGBR(colour)
```

The RGBG Statement

The RGBG statement returns an integer specifying the green component of a specified colour. The statement has the format shown in FIG-3.24.

FIG-3.24

The RGBG Statement

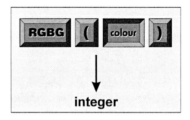

In the diagram:

> *colour*   is an integer value representing a colour. This value will probably have been generated using the RGB statement.

The RGBB Statement

The RGBB statement returns an integer specifying the blue component of a specified colour. The statement has the format shown in FIG-3.25.

FIG-3.25

The RGBB Statement

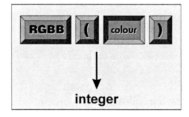

In the diagram:

> *colour*   is an integer value representing a colour. This value will probably have been generated using the RGB statement.

The three statements are used in LISTING-3.4 to display the component values of a randomly generated colour.

LISTING-3.4

Colour Component Values

```
REM *** Create random colour ***
RANDOMIZE TIMER()
colour = RGB(RND(255),RND(255),RND(255))

REM *** Extract components of this colour ***
red = RGBR(colour)
green = RGBG(colour)
blue = RGBB(colour)

REM *** Use the new colour ***
INK colour,0

REM *** Display the colour details ***
PRINT "The generated colour has the following settings"
PRINT "Red component : ",red
PRINT "Green component : ",green
PRINT "Blue component : ",blue

REM *** End program ***
WAIT KEY
END
```

Activity 3.30

Type in and test the program (*colours03.dbpro*) in LISTING-3.4.

Text Settings

Details of the text font, size and style currently being used by a program can be retrieved using the following statements.

The TEXT BACKGROUND TYPE Statement

We can discover the current text background mode (opaque or transparent) using the TEXT BACKGROUND TYPE statement which has the format shown in FIG-3.26.

FIG-3.26

The TEXT
BACKGROUND
Statement

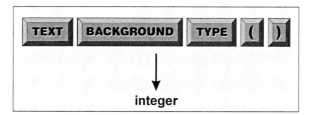

The statement returns the value zero if a transparent background is being used; 1 is returned when the background setting is opaque.

The TEXT STYLE Statement

The style of font, (bold, italic, etc.) can be determined using the TEXT STYLE statement which has the format shown in FIG-3.27.

The integer value returned lies between 0 and 3 (0 - normal; 1 - italic; 2 - bold; 3 - bold italic).

FIG-3.27

The TEXT STYLE
Statement

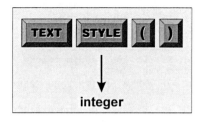

integer

The TEXT SIZE Statement

The TEXT STYLE statement returns the current text size setting in points. This statement has the format shown in FIG-3.28.

FIG-3.28

The TEXT SIZE
Statement

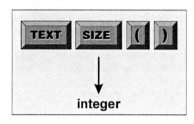

integer

The TEXT FONT$ Statement

The TEXT FONT$ statement returns a string giving the name of the font currently being used. For example, it would return the string "Arial", assuming this font had been selected earlier, using the SET TEXT FONT statement. The TEXT FONT$ statement has the format shown in FIG-3.29.

FIG-3.29

The TEXT FONT$
Statement

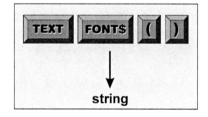

string

The TEXT WIDTH Statement

When placing text on the screen it can be very useful to know in advance just how many pixels wide that piece of text is going to be. The exact width of the text will obviously depend on the text itself, *goodbye* being wider than *hello*, but text font, style and size settings are also going to effect the width of the text. We can find out the exact width of any text to be displayed using the TEXT WIDTH statement. This has the format shown in FIG-3.30.

FIG-3.30

The TEXT WIDTH
Statement

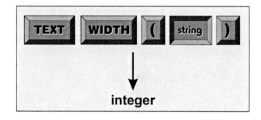

integer

In the diagram:

string   is the string whose width is to be determined.

The TEXT HEIGHT Statement

The number of pixels from the lowest point on a piece of text (typically at the bottom of letters such as *g* and *y*) to the highest point (on letters such as *t* and *l*) can be found using the TEXT HEIGHT statement, which has the format shown in FIG-3.31.

FIG-3.31

The TEXT HEIGHT
Statement

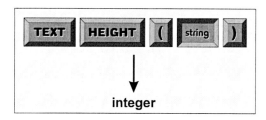

In the diagram:

> *string*   is the string whose height is to be determined.

The program in LISTING-3.5 demonstrates the use of the statements in this section.

LISTING 3.5

Display Text
Characteristics

```
REM *** Set text characteristics ***
SET TEXT FONT "Arial"
SET TEXT TO BOLD
SET TEXT SIZE 20
SET TEXT OPAQUE

REM *** Read in text ***
INPUT "Enter text : ", text$

REM *** Display details ***
PRINT "Font used is ",TEXT FONT$()
PRINT "Font style is ",TEXT STYLE()," 0 - normal, 1 - italic, 2
- bold, 3 - bold italic"
PRINT "Font size is ", TEXT SIZE()," points"
PRINT "Text background ",TEXT BACKGROUND TYPE()," 0 - transparent
1 - opaque"
PRINT text$," is ",TEXT WIDTH(text$)," pixels wide"
PRINT text$," is ",TEXT HEIGHT(text$)," pixels high"

REM *** End program ***
WAIT KEY
END
```

Activity 3.31

Type in and test the program in LISTING-3.5 (*textdetails.dbpro*).

Summary

- Use SCREEN WIDTH to find the current screen width setting.

- Use SCREEN HEIGHT to find the current screen height setting.

- Use SCREEN DEPTH to find how many bits are used to represent one screen pixel.

- Use RGBR to find the value of the red component in a specified colour.

- Use RGBG to find the value of the green component in a specified colour.

- Use RGBB to find the value of the blue component in a specified colour.

- Use TEXT BACKGROUND TYPE to determine if transparent or opaque backgrounds are being used with text output.

- Use TEXT STYLE to determine the current text style setting.

- Use TEXT SIZE to determine the current text size setting.

- Use TEXT FONT$ to determine the current text font name.

- Use TEXT WIDTH to determine the width of a specified piece of text.

- Use TEXT HEIGHT to determine the height of a specified piece of text.

Solutions

Activity 3.1

a) Integer
b) String
c) Integer
d) Real
e) String
f) Integer
g) Real
h) String
i) String
j) Real

Activity 3.2

"Mary is"	-	string
12	-	integer
" years old"	-	string

Activity 3.3

a) Valid
b) Invalid. Integer variable will store 12
c) Invalid. Hello should be enclosed in double quotes("Hello")
d) Valid
e) Invalid. Must be double quotes, not single quotes
f) Valid

Activity 3.4

a) Valid
b) Invalid. Must start with a letter
c) Invalid. Names cannot be within quotes.
d) Valid
e) Invalid. Spaces are not allowed in a name
f) Valid
g) Invalid, **end** is a DarkBASIC Pro keyword
h) Valid

Activity 3.5

```
1.    desc$="tall"
2.    result#= 12.34
```

Activity 3.6

a) Valid
b) Invalid. Fraction part lost
c) Invalid. A string cannot be copied to an integer variable
d) Valid
e) Invalid. A real cannot be copied to a string variable
f) Invalid. A string cannot be copied to a real variable

Activity 3.7

a) 2
b) -1
c) 5
d) -4

Activity 3.8

a) no2 is 16
b) x# is 82.18
c) no3 is zero
d) no4 is 9
e) m# is 0.4
f) v2# is 40.99

Activity 3.9

The result is 1

The expression is calculated as follows:

```
12-5* 12/10-5
12-60/10-5
12-6-5
6-5
```

Activity 3.10

Steps

```
8*(6-2)/(3-1)
8*4/(3-1)
8*4/2
32/2
16
```

Activity 3.11

```
answer = no1 / (4 + no2 - 1) * 5 - no3 ^ 2
answer = 12  / (4 + 3   - 1) * 5 - 5   ^ 2
answer = 12  / (7        - 1) * 5 - 5   ^ 2
answer = 12  / 6             * 5 - 5   ^ 2
answer = 12  / 6             * 5 - 25
answer = 2                   * 5 - 25
answer = 10                      - 25
answer = -15
```

Activity 3.12

term$ will hold the string *abc123xyz*

Activity 3.13

Output:

```
number
23
```

Activity 3.14

The final version of the program should read:

```
name$ = "Jessica McLaren"
PRINT name$
WAIT KEY
END
```

Activity 3.15

```
REM *** Assign name to variable & display
it ***
name$ = "Jessica McLaren"
PRINT "Hello, ",name$,", how are you today?"
REM *** End program ***
WAIT KEY
END
```

Activity 3.16

a) Valid
b) Valid
c) Invalid. The comma is missing after the message.

Activity 3.17

No solution required.

Activity 3.18

```
REM *** Get name ***
INPUT "Player 1, enter your name ", name$
INPUT "Enter your age ", age
PRINT "Hello, ", name$, ", I see you are
",age," years old"
REM *** End program ***
WAIT KEY
END
```

Activity 3.19

```
REM *** Set up names of days of the week ***
DATA
"Sunday","Monday","Tuesday","Wednesday",
"Thursday","Friday","Saturday"
REM *** Read and display each day ***
READ day$
PRINT day$
READ day$
PRINT day$
READ day$
PRINT day$
READ day$
PRINT day$
READ day$
PRINT day$
READ day$
PRINT day$
READ day$
PRINT day$
REM *** End program ***
WAIT KEY
END
```

Activity 3.20

Existing lines are in grey.

```
REM *** Set up names of days of the week ***
DATA
"Sunday","Monday","Tuesday","Wednesday",
"Thursday","Friday","Saturday"
REM *** Read and display each day ***
READ day$
PRINT day$
READ day$
PRINT day$
READ day$
PRINT day$
READ day$
```

```
PRINT day$
READ day$
PRINT day$
READ day$
PRINT day$
READ day$
PRINT day$
REM *** Go back to the start of the data ***
RESTORE
REM *** Read and display the first day ***
READ day$
PRINT day$
REM *** End program ***
WAIT KEY
END
```

Activity 3.21

```
millisecondsPassed = TIMER()
seconds = millisecondsPassed / 1000
minutes = seconds / 60
PRINT "Your computer has been on for "
,minutes, " minutes"
WAIT KEY
END
```

This could be reduced to just

```
minutes = TIMER()/60000
PRINT "Your computer has been on for "
,minutes, " minutes"
WAIT KEY
END
```

Activity 3.22

```
REM *** Display message ***
PRINT "Press any key"
REM *** Record start time ***
start = TIMER()
REM *** Wait for key press ***
WAIT KEY
REM *** Record finish time ***
finish = TIMER()
REM *** Calculate and display duration ***
duration = finish - start
PRINT "You took ", duration, " milliseconds"
REM *** End program ***
WAIT KEY
END
```

Activity 3.23

```
RND(48)
```

Activity 3.24

The RND line needs to be changed to read:

```
RND(48) + 1
```

Activity 3.25

```
REM *** Generate random value ***
RANDOMIZE TIMER()
number = RND(99)+1
REM *** Guess the number ***
INPUT "Enter your guess (1 to 100) : "
,guess
REM *** Display both values
PRINT "Number was ", number," Guess was "
,guess
```

```
REM *** End program ***
WAIT KEY
END
```

Activity 3.26

```
REM *** Assign colours ***
scarlet = RGB(255,0,0)
sky = RGB(0,0,255)
CLS scarlet
INK sky, scarlet
PRINT "Ocean"
REM *** End program ***
WAIT KEY
END
```

Activity 3.27

No solution required.

Activity 3.28

Test Value	Expected Result
401286	633.471
0	0
-9	Undefined

Activity 3.29

The text is not centred vertically since the CENTER TEXT statement positions the top of the text at the y-ordinate specified. To be correctly centred, the middle of the text would have to positioned at this y-ordinate.

Activity 3.30

No solution required

Activity 3.31

No solution required.

4

Selection

AND, OR and NOT Operators

Boolean Conditions

IF..ENDIF Statement

IF..THEN Statement

Nested IF Statements

Relational Operators

SELECT Statement

Testing Selective Structures

Binary Selection

Introduction

As we saw in structured English, many algorithms need to perform an action only when a specified condition is met. The general form for this statement was:

```
IF condition THEN
    action
ENDIF
```

Hence, in our guessing game we described the response to a correct guess as:

```
IF guess = number THEN
    Say "Correct"
ENDIF
```

As we'll see, DarkBASIC Pro also makes use of an IF statement to handle such situations.

The IF Statement

In its simplest form the IF statement in DarkBASIC Pro takes the format shown in FIG-4.1.

FIG-4.1

The Simple IF Statement

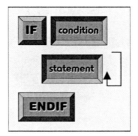

Notice that DarkBASIC Pro's IF statement does not contain the word THEN

In the diagram:

condition	is any term which can be reduced to a true or false value.
statement	is any executable DarkBASIC Pro statement.

If condition evaluates to true, then the set of statements between the IF and ENDIF terms are executed; if condition evaluates to false, then the set of statements are ignored and execution moves on to the statements following the ENDIF term.

An unlimited number of statements may be placed between the IF and ENDIF terms.

Condition

Generally, the condition will be an expression in which the relationship between two quantities is compared. For example, the condition

```
no < 0
```

will be true if the content of the variable *no* is less than zero (i.e. negative).

A condition is sometimes referred to as a **Boolean expression** and has the general format given in FIG-4.2.

FIG-4.2

A Boolean Expression

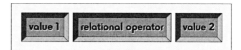

In the diagram:

value1 and *value2*   may be constants, variables, or expressions

relational operator   is one of the symbols given in TABLE-4.1.

TABLE-4.1

Relational Operators

English	Symbol
is less than	<
is less than or equal to	<=
is greater than	>
is greater than or equal to	>=
is equal to	=
is not equal to	<>

The values being compared should be of the same type, but it is acceptable to mix integer and real numeric values as in the conditions:

```
v > x#
t# < 12
```

However, numeric and string values cannot be compared. Therefore, conditions such as

```
name$ = 34
no1 <> "16"
```

are invalid.

Activity 4.1

Which of the following are not valid Boolean expressions?

```
a) no1 < 0            d) v# => 12.0
b) name$ = "Fred"     e) total <> "0"
c) no1 * 3 >= no2 - 6 f) address$ = 14 High Street
```

When two strings are checked for equality as in the condition

```
IF name$ = "Fred"
```

the condition will only be considered true if the match is an exact one (see FIG-4.3), even the slightest difference between the two strings will return a false result.

FIG-4.3

Comparing Strings

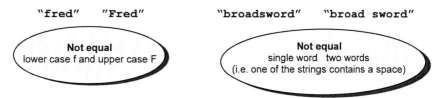

Not only is it valid to test if two string values are equal, or not, as in the conditions

```
IF name$ = "Fred"
IF village$ <> "Turok"
```

it is also valid to test if one string value is greater or less than another. For example, it is true that

```
"B" > "A"
```

Such a condition is considered true not because B comes after A in the alphabet, but because the coding used within the computer to store a "B" has a greater numeric value than the code used to store "A".

The method of coding characters is known as **ASCII** (American Standard Code for Information Interchange). This coding system is given in Appendix A at the back of the book.

If you are comparing strings which only contain letters, then one string is less than another if that first string would appear first in an alphabetically ordered list. Hence,

```
"Aardvark"   is less than   "Abolish"
```

But watch out for upper and lower case letters. All upper case letters are less than all lower case letters. Hence, the condition

```
"A" < "a"
```

is true.

If two strings differ in length, with the shorter matching the first part of the longer as

```
"abc" < "abcd"
```

then the shorter string is considered to be less than the longer string. Also, because the computer compares strings using their internal codes, it can make sense of a condition such as

```
"$" < "?"
```

which is also considered true since the $ sign has a smaller value than the ? character in the ASCII coding system.

Activity 4.2

Determine the result of each of the following conditions (true or false). You may have to examine the ASCII coding at the end of the book for part f).

a) `"wxy" = "w xy"`   d) `"cat" = "cat."`
b) `"def" < "defg"`   e) `"dog" = "Dog"`
c) `"AB" < "BA"`   f) `"*" > "&"`

TABLE-4.2 shows some Structured English IF statements and the DarkBASIC Pro equivalents.

TABLE-4.2

Examples of Simple IF
Statements

Structured English	DarkBASIC Pro Code

IF *no* is negative THEN
   make *no* positive
ENDIF
	IF no < 0
	   no = -no
	ENDIF

IF *day* is zero THEN
   Display "Sunday"
ENDIF
	IF day = 0
	   PRINT "Sunday"
	ENDIF

IF *value* is even THEN
   Subtract 1 from *value*
ENDIF
	IF value mod 2 = 0
	   value = value - 1
	ENDIF

The program in LISTING-4.1 reads in two numbers and displays a message if the numbers are equal. The program employs the following logic:

```
Get values for no1 and no2
IF no1 = no2 THEN
      Display "Numbers are equal"
ENDIF
```

LISTING-4.1

Using a Simple IF
Statement

```
REM *** Read in two numbers ***
INPUT "Enter first value : ",no1
INPUT "Enter second value ",no2

REM *** IF both numbers are the same THEN Display message ***
IF no1 = no2
    PRINT "Numbers are equal"
ENDIF

REM *** End program ***
WAIT KEY
END
```

Notice the use of indentation in the program listings. DarkBASIC Pro does not demand that this be done, but indentation makes a program easier to read - this is particularly true when more complex programs are written.

Activity 4.3

Type in and test the program in LISTING-4.1 (Call the project *same.dbpro*)

Modify the program you created for project *guess.dbpro*, so that, after the player has typed in his guess, the program displays the word *Correct* if the guess and number are equal.

In the next program (see LISTING-4.2) a real value representing the radius of a circle is read from the keyboard. As long as a valid value has been entered (i.e. a value greater than zero) then the area of the circle is calculated and displayed.

Notice that this time we have more than one statement within the IF structure.

LISTING-4.2

Placing Several
Statements within the
IF..ENDIF Structure

```
REM *** Read radius of circle ***
INPUT "Enter radius : ", radius#

REM *** IF valid radius THEN ***
IF radius# > 0
    REM *** Calculate and display area ***
    area# = 3.14159 * radius# * radius#
    PRINT "Area of circle is ",area#
ENDIF
```
continued on next page

LISTING-4.2
(continued)

Placing Several
Statements within the
IF..ENDIF Structure

```
REM *** End program ***
WAIT KEY
END
```

Activity 4.5

Write separate DarkBASIC Pro programs for each of the following tasks:
(Name the projects *act4_5_1.dbpro*, *act4_5_2.dbpro*, etc.)

1. Read in an integer number (*no1*) and display the message "Negative value" if the number is less than zero.

2. Read in a real number representing the width and height of a square. If the number is greater than zero, calculate and display the area of the square.

3. Read in a word. If the word is "yes", display the message "Access granted".

4. Read in an integer value and display the word "Even" if it is an even number (HINT: an even number gives no remainder when divided by 2).

Compound Conditions - the AND and OR Operators

Two or more simple conditions (like those given earlier) can be combined using either the term AND or the term OR (just as we did in structured English in Chapter 1).

The term AND should be used when we need two conditions to be true before an action should be carried out. For example, if a game requires you to throw two sixes to win, this could be written as:

```
RANDOMIZE TIMER ()
dice1 = RND(5) + 1
dice2 = RND(5) + 1
IF dice1 = 6 AND dice2 = 6
    PRINT "You win!"
ENDIF
```

The statement PRINT "You win!" will only be executed if both conditions, *dice1* = 6 and *dice2* = 6, are true.

Activity 4.6

Using the code given above, if *dice1* = 6 and *dice2* = 5, will the statement PRINT "You win!" be carried out?

You may recall from Chapter 1 that there are four possible combinations for an IF statement containing two simple expressions. Because these two conditions are linked by the AND operator, the overall result will only be true when both conditions are true. These combinations are shown in TABLE-4.3.

TABLE-4.3

The AND Operator

condition 1	condition 2	condition 1 AND condition 2
false	false	false
false	true	false
true	false	false
true	true	true

We link conditions using the OR operator when we require only one of the conditions given to be true. For example, if a dice game produces a win when the total of two dice is either 7 or 11, we could write the code for this as:

```
RANDOMIZE TIMER ()
dice1 = RND(5) + 1
dice2 = RND(5) + 1
total = dice1 + dice2
IF total = 7 OR total = 11
    PRINT "You win!"
ENDIF
```

Again, the computer reduces the individual Boolean expressions to either true or false. If at least one of the individual conditions is true, then the overall result is also true. This time the four possible combinations give the results shown in TABLE-4.4

TABLE-4.4

The OR Operator

condition 1	condition 2	condition 1 OR condition 2
false	false	false
false	true	true
true	false	true
true	true	true

Activity 4.7

If *no1* =10 and *no2* = 7, which of the following IF statements will evaluate to true?

```
a)  IF no1 < no2 OR no2 = 8
b)  IF no1 + no2 > 15 OR no1 < 9
c)  IF no2 - no1 > 0 OR no1 / no2 > 1
d)  IF no1 >= 10 OR no2 <= 10
```

There is no limit to the number of conditions that can be linked using AND and OR. For example, a statement of the form

```
IF condition1 AND condition2 AND condition3
```

means that all three conditions must be true, while the statement

```
IF condition1 OR condition2 OR condition3
```

means that at least one of the conditions must be true.

Activity 4.8

A game requires 3 dice to be thrown. If at least two dice show the same value, the player has won.

Write a program (*dice.dbpro*) which contains the following logic:

```
Throw all three dice
IF any two dice match THEN
    Display "You win!"
ENDIF
Display the value of each dice
```

Once we start to create conditions containing both AND and OR operators, we must remember that the AND operator takes precedence over the OR operator. Therefore, the statement

```
IF dice = 5 OR dice = 2 AND card$ = "Ace"
```

means that throwing a dice value of 5 is sufficient to give us an overall result of true and it does not matter what value *card$* is. However, it we don't throw a 5, then we must throw a 2 and *card$* must be equal to "Ace" to achieve an overall true result.

The normal rule of performing the AND operation before OR can be modified by the use of parentheses. Expressions within parentheses are always evaluated first. Hence, if we write

```
IF (dice = 5 OR dice = 2) AND card$ = "Ace"
```

the expression will be calculated as follows:

```
      (true OR false)     AND     false
  =        true           AND     false
  =   false
```

The NOT Operator

DarkBASIC Pro's NOT operator works in exactly the same way as that described in Chapter 1. It is used to negate the final result of a Boolean expression.

If we assume *dice* = 4, then the line

```
IF NOT (dice = 5 OR dice = 2)
```

will evaluate as

```
      NOT (false OR false)
  =   NOT        false
  =   true
```

ELSE - Creating Two Alternative Actions

In its present form the IF statement allows us to perform an action when a given condition is met. But sometimes we need to perform an action only when the condition is not met. For example, when the user has to guess the number generated by the computer, we use an IF statement to display the word "Correct" when the user guesses the number correctly:

```
IF guess = number
    PRINT "Correct"
ENDIF
```

However, shouldn't we display an alternative message when the player is wrong?

One way to do this is to follow the first IF statement with another testing the opposite condition:

```
IF guess = number
    PRINT "Correct"
ENDIF
IF NOT guess = number
    PRINT "Wrong"
ENDIF
```

Although this will work, it's not very efficient since we always have to test both conditions - and the second condition can't be true if the first one is!

As an alternative, we can add the word ELSE to our IF statement and follow this by the action we wish to have carried out when the stated condition is false:

```
IF guess = number
    PRINT "Correct"
ELSE
    PRINT "Wrong"
ENDIF
```

Activity 4.12

Modify *act4_5_1.dbpro* to display the phrase "Positive number" if the variable *no1* is greater than or equal to zero and displays the phrase "Negative number" if *no1* contains a value less than zero.

This gives us the longer version of the IF statement format as shown in FIG-4.4.

FIG-4.4

The IF..ELSE Statement

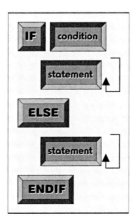

The Other IF Statement

DarkBASIC Pro actually offers a second version of the IF statement which has the format shown in FIG-4.5.

FIG-4.5

The Alternative IF
Statement

Although the syntax diagram shows the IF statement spread over several lines, this statement must be entered as a single line in your program.

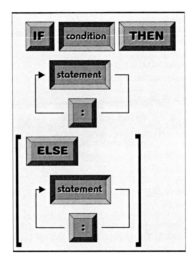

As you can see from the diagram, this version uses the word THEN but omits the ENDIF term. You can have as many statements as you need in each section (after THEN and ELSE) but these must be separated by colons.

A major restriction when using this version of the IF statement is that the keyword ELSE, if used, must appear on the same line as the term IF. Hence, it is invalid to write:

```
IF no1 < 0 THEN
    PRINT "Negative"
ELSE
    PRINT "Positive"
```

Instead you must write

```
IF no1 < 0 THEN PRINT "Negative" ELSE PRINT "Positive"
```

Activity 4.16

Rewrite the IF statement you created in Activity 4.12 to use this alternative version of the IF statement.

It is probably best to avoid this version of the IF statement, since the requirement to place the IF and ELSE terms on the same line does not allow a good layout for the program code.

Activity 4.17

1. What is a Boolean expression?

2. How many relation operators are there?

3. If a condition contains both AND and OR operators, which will be performed first?

Summary

- Conditional statements are created using the IF statement.

- A Boolean expression is one which gives a result of either true or false.

- Conditions linked by the AND operator must all be true for the overall result to be true.

- Only one of the conditions linked by the OR operator needs to be true for the overall result to be true.

- When the NOT operation is applied to a condition, it reverses the overall result.

- The statements following a condition are only executed if that condition is true.

- Statements following the term ELSE are only executed if the condition is false.

- A second version of the IF statement is available in DarkBASIC Pro in which IF and ELSE must appear on the same line.

Multi-Way Selection

Introduction

A single IF statement is fine if all we want to do is perform one of two alternative actions, but what if we need to perform one action from many possible actions? For example, what if we need to select from three or more alternative actions? How can we create code to deal with such a situation? In structured English we use a modified IF statement of the form:

```
IF
        condition 1:
                action1
        condition 2:
                action 2
        ELSE
                action 3
ENDIF
```

However, this structure is not available in DarkBASIC Pro and hence we must find some other way to implement multi-way selection.

Nested IF Statements

One method is to use nested IF statements - where one IF statement is placed within another. For example, let's assume in our number guessing game that we want to display one of three messages: *Correct, Your guess is too high*, or *Your guess is too low*. Our previous solution allowed for two alternative messages: *Correct* or *Wrong* and was coded as:

```
IF guess = number
    PRINT "Correct"
ELSE
    PRINT "Wrong"
ENDIF
```

In this new problem the `PRINT "Wrong"` statement needs to be replaced by the two alternatives: *Your guess is too high*, or *Your guess is too low*. But we already know how to deal with two alternatives - use an IF statement. In this case, our IF statement

```
IF guess > number
    PRINT "Your guess is too high"
ELSE
    PRINT "Your guess is too low"
ENDIF
```

If we now remove the `PRINT "Wrong"` statement from our earlier code and substitute the four lines given above, we get:

```
IF guess = number
    PRINT "Correct"
ELSE
    IF guess > number
        PRINT "Your guess is too high"
    ELSE
        PRINT "Your guess is too low"
    ENDIF
ENDIF
```

There is no limit to the number of IF statements that can be nested. Hence, if we required four alternative actions, we might use three nested IF statements, while four nested IF statements could handle five alternative actions. To demonstrate this we'll take our number guessing game a stage further and display the message *Your guess is slightly too high* if the guess is no more than 5 above the original number; the message *Your guess is slightly too low* will be displayed if the guess is no more than 5 below the original number.

We'll start by working out the difference between our guess and the computer's number using the line

```
difference = guess - number
```

Now, if we've guessed the number correctly, then *difference* will be zero. However, if we've gone too high, then *difference* will be a positive number. On the other hand, a low guess will result in difference being negative. When difference is a small value (either positive or negative) then guess must be close to number. The complete program is given in LISTING-4.3.

LISTING-4.3

The Number Guessing Game Again

```
REM *** Generate number ***
RANDOMIZE TIMER()
number = RND(99)+1
REM *** Get guess ***
INPUT "Enter your guess (1 - 100) ", guess
REM *** Calculate difference between the two values ***
difference = guess - number
REM *** Display appropriate message ***
IF difference = 0
        PRINT "Correct"
ELSE
   IF difference > 0
       IF difference <= 5
           PRINT "Your guess is slightly too high"
       ELSE
           PRINT "Your guess is too high"
       ENDIF
   ELSE
       IF difference >= -5
           PRINT "Your guess is slightly too low"
       ELSE
           PRINT "Your guess is too low"
       ENDIF
   ENDIF
ENDIF
```

The SELECT Statement

An alternative, and often clearer, way to deal with choosing one action from many is to employ the SELECT statement. The simplest way to explain the operation of the SELECT statement is simply to give you an example. In the code snippet given below we display the name of the day of week corresponding to the number entered. For example, entering 1 results in the word *Sunday* being displayed.

```
INPUT "Enter a number between 1 and 7 ", day
SELECT day
    CASE 1
        PRINT "Sunday"
    ENDCASE
    CASE 2
        PRINT "Monday"
    ENDCASE
    CASE 3
        PRINT "Tuesday"
    ENDCASE
    CASE 4
        PRINT "Wednesday"
    ENDCASE
    CASE 5
        PRINT "Thursday"
    ENDCASE
    CASE 6
        PRINT "Friday"
    ENDCASE
    CASE 7
        PRINT "Saturday"
    ENDCASE
ENDSELECT
```

Once a value for *day* has been entered, the SELECT statement chooses the CASE statement that matches that value and executes the code given within that section. All other CASE statements are ignored and the instruction following the END SELECT statement (not shown above) is the next to be executed. For example, if *day* = 3, then the statement given beside CASE 3 will be executed (i.e. PRINT "Tuesday"). If *day* were to be assigned a value not given in any of the CASE statements (i.e. a value outside the range 1 to 7), the whole SELECT statement would be ignored and no part of it executed.

Optionally, a special CASE statement can be added at the end of the SELECT statement. This is the CASE DEFAULT option which is used to catch all other values which have not been mentioned in previous CASE statements. For example, if we modified our SELECT statement above to end with the code

```
        CASE 7
            PRINT "Saturday"
        ENDCASE
        CASE DEFAULT
            PRINT "Invalid day"
        ENDCASE
    ENDSELECT
```

then, if a value outside the range 1 to 7 is entered, this last CASE statement will be executed. FIG-4.6 shows how the SELECT statement is executed.

FIG-4.6

How the SELECT
statement operates

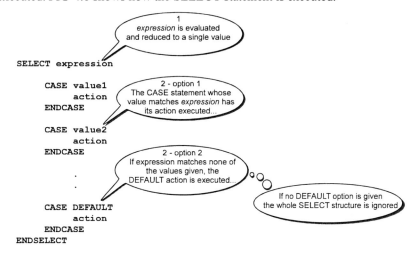

Several values can be specified for each CASE option. If the SELECT value matches any of the values listed, then that CASE option will be executed. For example, using the lines

```
    INPUT "Enter a number " , num
    SELECT num
        CASE 1, 3, 5, 7, 9
            PRINT "Odd"
        ENDCASE
        CASE 2,4,6,8,10
            PRINT "Even"
        ENDCASE
    ENDSELECT
```

the word *Odd* would be displayed if any odd number between 1 and 9 was entered.

The values given beside the CASE keyword may also be a string as in the example below:

```
    INPUT "Enter your name ", name$ `
    SELECT name$
        CASE "Liz","John"
            PRINT "Hello friend"
        ENDCASE
        CASE DEFAULT
            PRINT "I do not know your name"
        ENDCASE
    ENDSELECT
```

Although the value may also be a real value as in the line

it is a bad idea to use these since the machine cannot store real values accurately. If a real variable contained the value 1.52000001 it would not match with the CASE value given above.

The general format of the SELECT statement is given in FIG-4.7.

FIG-4.7

The SELECT Statement

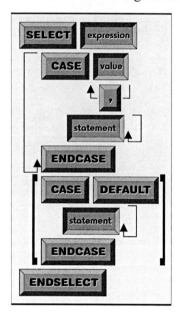

In the diagram:

expression	is a variable or expression which reduces to a single integer, real or string value.
value	is a constant of any type (integer, real or string).
statement	is any valid DarkBASIC Pro statement (even another SELECT statement!).

Activity 4.22

Rewrite the *Items* program so that it uses a SELECT structure when determining which message is to be displayed.

Activity 4.23

Write a project (*Grading*) which accepts a score from the keyboard and displays the grade assigned according to the following rules:

Score 0-99	grade: Pathetic
Score 100-199	grade: Beginner
Score 200 - 299	grade: Apprentice
Score 300-399	grade: Competent
Score 400-499	grade: Master
Score 500-599	grade: Grand Master
Other values	Invalid score

Testing Selective Code

When a program contains IF or SELECT structures, our test strategy has to change to cope with these structures. In the case of an IF statement, we must create two test values: one which results in the IF statement being true, the other in the IF statement being false. For example, if a program contained the lines

```
INPUT no
IF no <= 0
    PRINT "This is a negative number"
ENDIF
```

then we need to have a test value for *no* which is less than zero and another which is not less than zero. Perhaps the values -8 and 3.

Another important test is to find out what happens when the variable's value is exactly equal to the value against which it is being tested. In the above case that would mean testing the code with *no* set to 0. Very often this is the only value which will highlight a problem in the code.

Activity 4.24

If *no* is zero, will the message *"This is a negative number"* be displayed by the code given above?

Since zero is not a negative number we have discovered an error in our code. The line

```
IF no <= 0
```

should actually read

```
IF no < 0
```

We would not have detected this error if we hadn't used zero as our test value.

When an IF statement contains more than one condition linked with AND or OR operators, testing needs to check each possible combinations of true and false settings. For example, if a program contained the line

```
IF dice1 = 6 AND dice2 = 6
```

then our tests should include all possible combinations for the two conditions as shown in TABLE-4.5.

TABLE-4.5

Testing Complex
Conditions

dice1 = 6	dice2 = 6	dice1 = 6 AND dice2 = 6
false	false	false
false	true	false
true	false	false
true	true	true

So our test values, chosen to meet these combinations, might be

dice1 = 3	dice2 = 5
dice1 = 4	dice2 = 6
dice1 = 6	dice2 = 1
dice1 = 6	dice2 = 6

If the dice values are randomly generated in the program we would have to change lines such as

```
dice1 = RND(5) +1
```

to

```
INPUT "Enter value for dice 1 :  ",dice1
```

to allow the test to take place. Once the tests have been completed, the INPUT lines would be replaced by the original code.

In a complex condition it is sometimes not possible to create every theoretical combination of true and false combinations. For example, if a program contains the line

```
IF dice = 5 OR dice = 2 AND card$ = "Ace"
```

then the combinations of true and false are shown in TABLE-4.6.

TABLE-4.6

Dealing with Impossible Combinations

dice = 5	dice = 2	card$="Ace"		dice = 5 OR dice = 2 AND card$="Ace"
false	false	false		false
false	false	true		false
false	true	false		false
false	true	true		true
true	false	false		true
true	false	true		true
true	true	false	*	true
true	true	true	*	true

But the last two combinations in the table are impossible to achieve since the variable *dice* cannot contain the values 5 and 2 at the same time. So our test data will have test values which create only the remaining 6 combinations.

When testing nested IF statements, as in the lines

```
IF guess = number
    PRINT "Correct"
ELSE
    IF guess > number
        PRINT "Your guess is too high"
    ELSE
        PRINT "Your guess is too low"
    ENDIF
ENDIF
```

then each path through the structure must be tested. For the above code this means that we must test for the following conditions being true:

guess = number
guess > number
guess < number

To test a SELECT structure, then every value mentioned in every CASE option must be tested. Hence, the lines

```
INPUT "Enter a number "  , num
SELECT num
    CASE 1, 3, 5, 7, 9
        PRINT "Odd"
    ENDCASE
    CASE 2,4,6,8,10
```

```
                    PRINT "Even"
            ENDCASE
        ENDSELECT
```

need to be tested using the values 1, 2, 3, 4, 5, 6, 7, 8, and 9. In addition, at least one test should specify a value not given in any of the CASE statements. This will check that the DEFAULT option is executed as expected (assuming there is a DEFAULT option), or that the whole SELECT structure is bypassed as expected.

Summary

- The term nested IF statements refers to the construct where one IF statement is placed within the structure of another IF statement.

- Multi-way selection can be achieved using either nested IF statements or the SELECT statement.

- The SELECT statement can be based on integer, real or string values.

- The CASE line can have any number of values, each separated by a comma.

- The CASE DEFAULT option is executed when the value being searched for matches none of those given in the CASE statements.

- Testing a simple IF statement should ensure that both true and false results are tested.

- Where a specific value is mentioned in a condition (as in no < 0) , that value should be part of the test data.

- When a condition contains AND or OR operators, every possible combination of results should be tested.

- Nested IF statements should be tested by ensuring that every possible path through the structure is executed by the combination of test data.

- SELECT structures should be tested by using every value specified in the CASE statements.

- SELECT should also be tested using a value that does not appear in any of the CASE statements.

Solutions

Activity 4.1

a) Valid
b) Valid
c) Valid
d) Invalid. => is not a relational operator (should be >=)
e) Invalid. Integer variable compared with string.
f) Invalid. 14 High Street should be in double quotes.

Activity 4.2

a) False. Only the second string contains a space.
b) True. "def is shorter and matches the first three characters of "defg".
c) True A comes before B.
d) False Only the second string contains a full stop.
e) False Only the second string contains a capital D.
f) True. * has a greater ASCII coding than &

Activity 4.3

No solution required.

Activity 4.4

```
REM *** Generate random value ***
RANDOMIZE TIMER ()
number = RND (99)+1
REM *** Guess the number ***
INPUT "Enter your guess (1 to 100) : "
,guess
REM *** IF the guess is correct THEN ***
REM *** Display "Correct" ***
IF guess = number
  PRINT "Correct"
ENDIF
REM *** Display both values ***
PRINT "Number was ", number," Guess was "
,guess
REM *** End program ***
WAIT KEY
END
```

Activity 4.5

1.

```
REM *** Read in integer ***
INPUT "Enter a number : ", no1
REM *** IF neg THEN Display message ***
IF no1 < 0
  PRINT "Negative value"
ENDIF
REM *** End program ***
WAIT KEY
END
```

2.

```
REM *** Read in real ***
INPUT "Enter length of side : ", side#
REM *** IF greater than zero THEN ***
IF side# > 0
  REM *** Calculate and display area ***
  area# = side# * side#
  PRINT "Area of square is ",area#
ENDIF
```

```
REM *** End program ***
WAIT KEY
END
```

3.

```
REM *** Read in word ***
INPUT "Enter a word : ",word$
IF word$ = "yes"
  PRINT "Access allowed"
ENDIF
REM *** End program ***
WAIT KEY
END
```

4.

```
REM *** Read in an integer ***
INPUT "Enter a number : ",no1
REM *** IF an even number THEN Display
"Even" ***
IF no1 mod 2=0
  PRINT "Even"
ENDIF
REM *** End program ***
WAIT KEY
END
```

Activity 4.6

No, the PRINT statement is not executed.
The condition
    dice1 = 6 AND dice2 = 6
reduces to
    true AND false
which further reduces to
    false

Activity 4.7

a) false OR false = false
b) true OR false = true
c) false OR true = true
d) true OR true = true

Activity 4.8

```
REM *** Throw dice ***
RANDOMIZE TIMER ()
dice1 = RND(5)+1
dice2 = RND(5)+1
dice3 = RND(5)+1
REM *** IF at least two dice match THEN
display message ***
IF dice1 = dice2 OR dice1 = dice3 OR dice2
= dice3
  PRINT "You win"
ENDIF
REM *** Display dice values ***
PRINT "Dice 1 was ", dice1
PRINT "Dice 2 was ", dice2
PRINT "Dice 3 was ", dice3
REM *** End program ***
WAIT KEY
END
```

Activity 4.9

```
REM *** Read in word ***
INPUT "Enter a word : ",word$
IF word$ = "yes" OR word$ = "YES"
  PRINT "Access granted"
ENDIF
REM *** End program ***
WAIT KEY
END
```

Activity 4.10

Substituting true and false we get:

```
(false OR true) AND (false OR true)
= true AND true
        =true
```

Activity 4.11

Substituting true and false we get:

```
  NOT (true AND true)
= NOT true
= false
```

Activity 4.12

```
IF no1 >= 0
  PRINT* "Positive number"
ELSE
  PRINT "Negative number"
ENDIF
```

Activity 4.13

```
REM *** Generate random value ***
RANDOMIZE TIMER ()
number = RND(99)+1
REM *** Guess the number ***
INPUT "Enter your guess (1 to 100) :
",guess
REM *** IF the guess is correct THEN
Display

"Correct" ***
IF guess = number
  PRINT "Correct"
ELSE
  PRINT "Wrong"
ENDIF
REM *** Display both values ***
PRINT "Number was ", number," Guess was
",guess
REM *** End program ***
WAIT KEY
END
```

Activity 4.14

```
REM *** Read in two numbers ***
INPUT "Enter first number : ", no1
INPUT "Enter second number : ", no2
IF no1 < no2
  PRINT "Smallest number is ", no1
ELSE
  PRINT "Smallest number is ",no2
ENDIF
REM *** End program ***
WAIT KEY
END
```

Activity 4.15

```
REM *** Read in an integer ***
INPUT "Enter a number : ",no1
REM *** IF even THEN Display "Even" ***
IF no1 mod 2 = 0
  PRINT "Even"
ELSE
  PRINT "Odd"
ENDIF
REM *** End program ***
WAIT KEY
END
```

Activity 4.16

```
IF no1 >= 0 THEN PRINT "Positive number"
ELSE PRINT "Negative number"
```

(this is entered in a single line)

Activity 4.17

1. A Boolean expression is an expression which reduces to either true or false.

2. Six ($<, <=, >, >=, =, <>$)

3. AND is always performed first unless the OR is enclosed in parentheses.

Activity 4.18

```
REM *** Generate random value ***
RANDOMIZE TIMER()
number = RND(99)+1
REM *** Guess the number ***
INPUT "Enter your guess (1 to 100) : ",guess
REM *** Respond to guess ***
IF guess = number
  PRINT "Correct"
ELSE
  IF guess > number
      PRINT "Your guess is too high"
  ELSE
      PRINT "Your guess is too low"
  ENDIF
ENDIF
REM *** Display both values ***
PRINT "Number was ", number," Guess was
",guess
REM *** End program ***
WAIT KEY
END
```

Activity 4.19

```
REM *** Read in a number ***
INPUT "Enter number ", no1
REM *** Display appropriate message ***
IF no1 > 0
  PRINT "Positive number"
ELSE
  IF no1 = 0
      PRINT "Zero"
  ELSE
      PRINT "Negative number"
  ENDIF
ENDIF
REM *** End program ***
WAIT KEY
END
```

Activity 4.20

No solution required.

Activity 4.21

```
REM *** Get number ***
INPUT "Enter item number (1 - 4) : ", no
IF no = 1
  PRINT "A sword"
ELSE
  IF no = 2
      PRINT "A wand"
  ELSE
      IF no = 3
          PRINT "A bag of dragon's teeth"
      ELSE
          IF no = 4
              PRINT "A water skin"
          ELSE
              PRINT "Unknown item"
          ENDIF
      ENDIF
  ENDIF
ENDIF
```

Activity 4.22

```
REM *** Get number ***
INPUT "Enter item number (1 - 4) : ", no
REM *** Display appropriate message ***
SELECT no
  CASE 1
      PRINT "A sword"
  ENDCASE
  CASE 2
      PRINT "A wand"
  ENDCASE
  CASE 3
      PRINT "A bag of dragon's teeth"
  ENDCASE
  CASE 4
      PRINT "A water skin"
  ENDCASE
  CASE DEFAULT
      PRINT "Unknown item"
  ENDCASE
ENDSELECT
REM *** End program ***
WAIT KEY
END
```

Activity 4.23

```
REM *** Get numberRead score
INPUT "Enter your score : ", score
REM *** Display appropriate message ***
SELECT score / 100
  CASE 0
      PRINT "Pathetic"
  ENDCASE
  CASE 1
      PRINT "Beginner"
  ENDCASE
  CASE 2
      PRINT "Apprentice"
  ENDCASE
  CASE 3
      PRINT "Competent
  ENDCASE
  CASE 4
      PRINT "Master"
  ENDCASE
  CASE 5
      PRINT "Grand master"
```

```
  ENDCASE
  CASE DEFAULT
      PRINT "Invalid score"
  ENDCASE
ENDSELECT
REM *** End program ***
WAIT KEY
END
```

Activity 4.24

Yes. The condition no <= 0 is true and hence the PRINT statement is executed.

5

Iteration

DO .. LOOP Construct

EXIT Statement

FOR .. NEXT Construct

REPEAT .. UNTIL Construct

SLEEP Statement

Testing Iterative Structures

Using DATA and READ in a FOR .. NEXT Construct

WAIT Statement

WHILE .. ENDWHILE Construct

Iteration

Introduction

Iteration is the term used when one or more statements are carried out repeatedly. As we saw in Chapter 1, structured English has three distinct iterative structures: FOR .. ENDFOR, REPEAT .. UNTIL and WHILE .. ENDWHILE.

DarkBASIC Pro, on the other hand, has four iterative structures. Most of these take the same form as their structured English equivalent, but others differ slightly and therefore care should be taken when translating structured English statements to DarkBASIC Pro.

The WHILE .. ENDWHILE Construct

The WHILE statement is probably the easiest of DarkBASIC Pro's loop structures to understand, since it is identical in operation and syntax to the WHILE loop in structured English. For example, if a wizard uses 25 units of power every time he casts a spell to shrink an enemy's height by 10%, a burst of spell casting could be described using the logic:

```
WHILE energy available >= 25 DO
      Reduce enemy's height by 10%
      Reduce energy available by 25
ENDWHILE
```

which can be coded in DarkBASIC Pro as:

```
WHILE energyavailable >= 25
    enemyheight = enemyheight * 0.9
    energyavailable = energyavailable - 25
ENDWHILE
```

The syntax of the WHILE .. ENDWHILE construct is shown in FIG-5.1.

FIG-5.1

The WHILE ..
ENDWHILE Construct

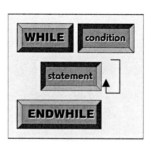

In the diagram:

condition	is a Boolean expression and may include AND, OR, NOT and parentheses as required.
statement	is any valid DarkBASIC Pro statement.

A visual representation of how this loop operates is shown in FIG-5.2. Note that the loop body may never be executed if *condition* is false when first tested.

FIG-5.2

Executing a WHILE ..
ENDWHILE Construct

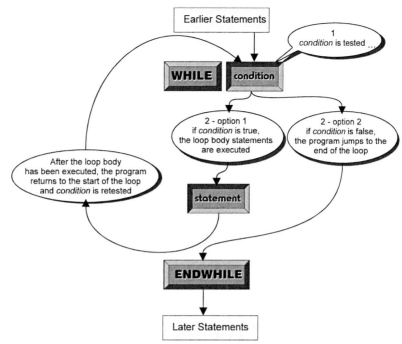

A common use for this loop statement is validation of input. So, for example, in our number guessing game, we might ensure that the user types in a value between 1 and 100 when entering their guess by using the logic

```
Get guess
WHILE guess outside the range 1 to 100 DO
      Display error message
      Get guess
ENDWHILE
```

which can be coded in DarkBASIC Pro as:

```
INPUT "Enter your guess (1 - 100) : ",guess
WHILE guess < 1 OR guess > 100
    PRINT "Your guess must be between 1 and 100"
    INPUT "Enter your guess again (1 - 100) : ",guess
ENDWHILE
```

Activity 5.1

Modify your *guess01.dbpro* project to incorporate the code given above.

Check that the program works correctly by attempting to make guesses which are outside the range 1 to 100.

Activity 5.2

Using a WHILE statement similar to that given above, modify project *items.dbpro* (which you created in the last chapter) so that the value entered from the keyboard is checked to be in the range 1 to 4.

An invalid value should result in the message "Invalid selection. Please re-enter" being displayed and require the user to re-enter the value.

Check that the program correctly deals with invalid entries.

TABLE-5.1 gives examples of structured English WHILE statements and the equivalent DarkBASIC Pro code.

TABLE-5.1

WHILE Examples

Structured English	DarkBASIC Pro Code

Get month
WHILE month outside the range 1 to 12 DO
   Display "Invalid month"
   Get month
ENDWHILE
	INPUT "Enter month ",month
	WHILE month < 1 OR month > 12
	   PRINT "Invalid month"
	   INPUT "Enter month ",month
	ENDWHILE

Get value
WHILE value not zero DO
   Add value to total
   Get value
ENDWHILE
	INPUT "Enter value ",value
	WHILE value <> 0 DO
	   total = total + value
	   INPUT "Enter value ",value
	ENDWHILE

Activity 5.3

Write the DarkBASIC Pro equivalent of the following structured English:

```
Get no1
Get no2
WHILE no1 <> no2 DO
    Set no1 equal to no2
    Get no2
ENDWHILE
```

Under what conditions will the WHILE loop terminate?

Activity 5.4

A simple dice game involves counting how many times in a row a pair of dice can be thrown to produce a value of 8 or less. The game stops as soon as a value greater than 8 is thrown.

Write a DarkBASIC Pro project (*dice01.dbpro*) to perform this task. (You will need RANDOMIZE and RND to simulate dice throws.)

The REPEAT .. UNTIL Construct

Like structured English, DarkBASIC Pro has a REPEAT..UNTIL statement. The two structures are identical. Hence, if in structured English we write

```
Set total to zero
REPEAT
    Get a number
    Add number to total
UNTIL number is zero
```

then the same logic would be coded in DarkBASIC Pro as

```
total = 0
REPEAT
    INPUT "Enter a number : ", number
    total = total + number
UNTIL number = 0
```

The REPEAT..UNTIL statement is an **exit-controlled** loop structure. That is, the action within the loop is executed and then an exit condition is tested. If that condition is found to be true, then looping stops, otherwise the action specified within the loop is executed again. Iteration continues until the exit condition is true.

The syntax of the REPEAT statement is shown in FIG-5.3.

FIG-5.3

The REPEAT .. UNTIL Construct

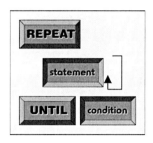

In the diagram:

condition	is a Boolean expression and may include AND, OR, NOT and parentheses as required.
statement	is any valid DarkBASIC Pro statement.

The operation of the REPEAT .. UNTIL construct is shown graphically in FIG-5.4.

FIG-5.4

Executing the REPEAT .. UNTIL Construct

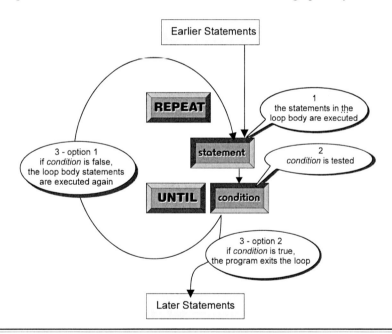

Activity 5.5

Create a project (*total.dbpro*) to read in a series of integer values, stopping only when a zero is entered. The values entered should be totalled and that total displayed at the end of the program.

Activity 5.6

Modify project *guess01.dbpro* to allow the player to keep guessing until the correct number is arrived at.

TABLE-5.2 gives some examples of structured English REPEAT..UNTIL loops and the DarkBASIC Pro equivalents.

TABLE-5.2

REPEAT .. UNTIL
Examples

Structured English	DarkBASIC Pro Code

Set target to 401
REPEAT
   Get Score
   Subtract score from target
UNTIL target zero or less
	target = 401
	REPEAT
	   INPUT "Enter score: ",score
	   target = target - score
	UNTIL target <= 0

Set total to zero
Set count to zero
REPEAT
   Get number
   Add 1 to count
UNTIL count is 10 or number is zero
	total = 0
	count = 0
	REPEAT
	   INPUT "Enter number:", number
	   count = count +1
	UNTIL count = 10 OR number = 0

The FOR..NEXT Construct

In structured English, the FOR loop is used to perform an action a specific number of times. For example, we might describe dealing seven cards to a player using the logic:

```
FOR 7 times DO
    Deal card
ENDFOR
```

Sometimes the number of times the action is to be carried out is less explicit. For example, if each player in a game is to pay a £10 fine we could write:

```
FOR each player DO
    Pay £10 fine
ENDFOR
```

However, in both examples, the action specified between the FOR and ENDFOR terms will be executed a known number of times.

In DarkBASIC Pro the FOR construct makes use of a variable to keep a count of how often the loop is executed and takes the form:

```
FOR variable = start_value TO finish_value
```

Hence, if we want a FOR loop to iterate 7 times we would write

```
FOR c = 1 TO 7
```

In this case c would be assigned the value 1 when the FOR loop is about to start. Each time the action within the loop is performed, c will be incremented, and eventually, once the action is performed with c equal to 7, iteration stops.

The variable used in a FOR loop is known as the **loop counter**.

Activity 5.7

Write the first line of a FOR loop that is to be executed 10 times, using a variable j which is to start with a value of 1.

While structured English marks the end of a FOR loop using the term ENDFOR, in DarkBASIC Pro the end of the loop is indicated by the term NEXT followed by the name of the loop counter variable used in the FOR statement.

The action to be performed within the loop (known as the **loop body**) can consist of any number of statements. For example, the code

```
FOR k = 1 TO 10
    PRINT "*"
NEXT k
```

contains a single statement within the loop body and will display a column of 10 asterisks.

Activity 5.8

What would be displayed by the code

```
FOR p = 1 TO 10
    PRINT p
NEXT p
```

The loop counter in a FOR loop can be made to start and finish at any value, so it is quite valid to start a loop with the line

```
FOR m = 3 TO 12
```

When executed, the loop counter *m* will contain the value 3 when the loop is first executed and finish with the value 12. The loop will be executed exactly 10 times.

If the start and finish values are identical as in the line

```
FOR r = 10 TO 10
```

then the loop is executed once only.

Where the start value is greater than the finish value, the loop will not be executed at all as in the line

```
FOR k = 10 TO 9
```

Normally, one is added to the loop counter each time the loop body is performed. However, we can change this by adding a STEP value to the FOR loop as shown below:

```
FOR c = 2 TO 10 STEP 2
```

In this last example the loop counter, *c*, will start at 2 and then increment to 4 on the next iteration. The program in LISTING-5.1 uses the STEP option to display the 7 times table from 1 x 7 to 12 x 7.

LISTING-5.1

Using the FOR .. NEXT Structure

```
REM *** Display 7 times table ***
FOR c = 7 TO 84 STEP 7
    PRINT c
NEXT c
REM *** End program ***
WAIT KEY
END
```

By using the STEP keyword with a negative value, it is even possible to create a FOR loop that reduces the loop counter on each iteration as in the line:

```
FOR d = 10 TO 0 STEP -1
```

This last example causes the loop counter to start at 10 and finish at 0.

It is possible that the step value given may cause the loop counter never to match the finish value. For example, in the line

```
FOR c = 1 TO 12 STEP 5
```

the variable *c* will take on the values 1, 6, and 11. The loop will always stop before the variable passes the finishing value.

The start, finish and even step values of a FOR loop can be defined using a variable or arithmetic expression as well as a constant. For example, in LISTING-5.2 below the user is allowed to enter the upper limit of the FOR loop.

LISTING-5.2

FOR Loops Using a
Variable Limit

```
REM *** Get a number ***
PRINT "I will display all of the values between 1 and any number
you give me"
INPUT "Please enter your number : ",num

REM *** Display values ***
FOR c = 1 TO num
    PRINT c
NEXT c

REM *** End program ***
WAIT KEY
END
```

The program will display every integer value between 1 and the number entered by the user.

The FOR loop counter can also be specified as a real value with a STEP value of less than 1 as in the lines:

```
FOR ch# = 1.0 TO 2.0 STEP 0.1
    PRINT ch#
NEXT ch#
```

Activity 5.12

Create a project (*forloops02.dbpro*) containing the code given above and check out the result.

Notice that most of the values displayed by the last Activity are slightly out. For example, instead of the second value displayed being 1.1, it displays as 1.10000002384. This difference is caused by rounding errors when converting from the decimal values that we use to the binary values favoured by the computer.

Although we might have expected the FOR loop to perform 11 times (1.0,1.1,1.2, etc. to 2.0), in fact, it only performs 10 times up to 1.90000021458. Again, this discrepancy is caused by the rounding error problem.

Activity 5.13

Modify *forloop02.dbpro* so that the upper limit of the loop is 2.01.

How many times is the iteration performed now?

The format of the FOR..NEXT construct is shown in FIG-5.5.

FIG-5.5

The FOR .. NEXT
Structure

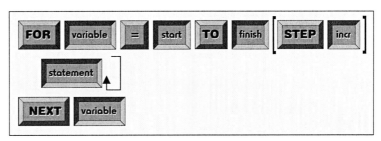

In the diagram:

variable	is either an integer or real variable. Both variable tiles refer to the same variable. Hence the name used after the keywords FOR and NEXT should be the same. This variable is known as the loop counter.
start	is the initial value of the loop counter. The loop counter will contain this value the first time the statements within the loop are executed.
finish	is the final value of the loop variable. The loop variable will usually contain this value the last time the loop body is executed.
incr	is the value to be added to the loop counter after each iteration. If this value is omitted then a value

of 1 is added to the loop counter on each iteration.

statement   is any valid DarkBASIC Pro statement.

The operation of the FOR statement is shown graphically in FIG-5.6.

FIG-5.6

Executing a FOR
.. NEXT Construct

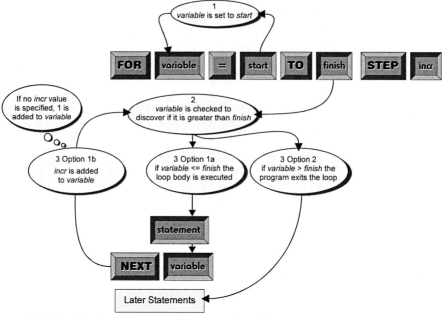

TABLE-5.3 gives examples of structured English FOR loops and their DarkBASIC Pro equivalents.

TABLE-5.3

FOR .. NEXT Examples

Structured English	DarkBASIC Pro Code

Set total to zero
FOR each value between 1 and 10 DO
   Add that value to total
ENDFOR
Display total
	total = 0
	FOR c = 1 TO 10
	   total = total + c
	NEXT c
	PRINT total

Set total to zero
Get number of players
FOR each player DO
   Get player's score
   Add score to total
ENDFOR
Calculate average as total / players
Display average
	total = 0
	INPUT "Enter number of players:", players
	FOR c = 1 TO players
	   INPUT "Enter score:", score
	   total = total + score
	NEXT c
	average = total / players
	PRINT average

Activity 5.14

Create a new project (*total.dbpro*) which reads in and displays the total of 12 numbers.

Finding the Smallest Value in a List of Values

There are several tasks you will find yourself (and your programs) having to do over and over again. One of these is finding the smallest number in a list of numbers. If someone writes down a list of values on a piece of paper and asks you which value is the smallest, you shouldn't have any problem giving them the correct answer. But if they ask how you managed to come up with the correct answer, you might have more of a problem trying to describe in precise terms how you did it.

When the list contains only a few, small numbers, then our brain seems to be able to take them all in at one go and instantly come up with an answer. On the other hand if the numbers were large (several digits long) and you were only shown one number every day over a period of several months, you'd have to think of a more organised strategy to ensure you came up with the correct answer.

The best approach would be to write down the first number you see on a piece of paper and, every day when you are shown a new number, compare this new value with what is written on the paper. If you are shown a smaller number than before, erase the old number from your paper and write in the new one. Do this every day and, by the end, the piece of paper will have a copy of the smallest number you saw throughout the period.

This is exactly how we tackle the problem in a computer program. We set up one variable to hold the smallest value we've come across and if a later value is smaller, it is copied into this variable. The algorithm used is given below and assumes 10 numbers will be entered in total:

```
Get first number
Set smallest to first number
FOR 9 times DO
    Get next number
    IF number < smallest THEN
        Set smallest to number
    ENDIF
ENDFOR
Display smallest
```

Activity 5.15

Create a new project called *smallest.dbpro*. In this program implement the logic shown above to display the smallest of 10 integer values entered at the keyboard.

Modify the program to find the largest, rather than the smallest, of the numbers entered.

Activity 5.16

In ice skating, a number of judges (N) award marks. The highest and lowest of these are ignored and the others averaged to give a result. Write a program *(skating.dbpro)* to input N (the number of judges), followed by N marks (the mark given by each judge), and display the average score ignoring the highest and lowest mark. (Scores range from 0.0 to 6.0 in increments of 0.1.)
The logic required by the program is:

```
Get value for N
Get value for score
Set highestscore to score
Set lowestscore to score
Set total to score
FOR N-1 times DO
    Get value for score
    Add score to total
    IF score > highestscore THEN
        Set highestscore to score
```

continued on next page

Using FOR with READ and DATA

The FOR statement can be useful when reading values from a DATA list. For example, back in Chapter 3 we set up a DATA statement containing the names of the days of the week and then displayed these using the code:

```
DATA "Sunday", "Monday", "Tuesday", "Wednesday",
DATA "Thursday", "Friday", "Saturday"
READ day$
PRINT day$
READ day$
PRINT day$
    etc.
```

But we can simplify this whole process by rewriting the code as

```
DATA "Sunday", "Monday", "Tuesday", "Wednesday",
DATA "Thursday","Friday", "Saturday"
FOR c = 1 TO 7
    READ day$
    PRINT day$
NEXT c
```

Each time the FOR loop body is executed, the next value in the DATA statement is retrieved by the READ statement, and so all 7 day names are displayed.

Once you've played the latest version of the guessing game a few times, you will have encountered a problem. If you guess the number in less than seven attempts, you still need to keep going until all seven attempts have been completed. Obviously, it makes more sense to stop as soon as the number has been guessed. The next statement gives us a way of doing just that.

The EXIT Statement

The EXIT statement is used to exit from a loop structure, making the next statement to be executed the one immediately after the end of the loop. Normally, the EXIT statement will appear within an IF statement. The EXIT statement takes the form shown in FIG-5.7.

FIG-5.7

The EXIT Statement

The EXIT statement can be used in any loop structure, not just FOR loops.

For example, in a dice game we are allowed to throw a pair of dice 5 times and our score is the total of the five throws. However, if during our throws we throw a 1, then our turn ends and our final score becomes the total achieved up to that point (excluding the throw containing a 1). We could code this game as shown in LISTING-5.3.

LISTING-5.3

Using the EXIT Statement

```
REM ** Seed random number generator ***
RANDOMIZE TIMER ()

REM *** Set total to zero ***
total = 0

REM *** FOR 5 times DO ***
FOR c = 1 TO 5
    PRINT "Hit any key to roll the dice"
    WAIT KEY
    REM *** Throw both dice ***
    dice1 = RND(5)+1
    dice2 = RND(5)+1
    REM *** Display throw number and dice values ***
    PRINT "Throw : ",c," Dice 1 : ",dice1," Dice 2 : ",dice2
    REM *** IF either dice is a 1 THEN quit loop ***
    IF dice1 = 1 OR dice2 = 1
        EXIT
    ENDIF
    REM *** Add dice throws to total ***
    total = total + dice1 + dice2
NEXT c

REM *** Display final score ***
PRINT "Your final score was : ", total

REM *** End program ***
WAIT KEY
END
```

Activity 5.19

Create a new project (*dicetotal01.dbpro*) containing the code given above.

Run the program and check that the loop exits if a 1 is thrown.

Modify the program to exit only if both dice are 1's during a throw.

The DO .. LOOP Construct

The DO..LOOP construct is a rather strange loop structure, since, while other loops are designed to terminate eventually, the DO .. LOOP structure will continue to repeat its loop body indefinitely.

It has a very simple structure. In the example below, the code causes the word *Hello* to be displayed over and over again:

```
DO
    PRINT "Hello"
LOOP
```

The nearest equivalent to this in Structured English would be to write

Since *false* is never true, the REPEAT..UNTIL loop will execute forever.

```
REPEAT
    Display "Hello"
UNTIL false
```

Although there seems little likelihood that such a loop would be useful, it is, in fact, often used to implement the main part of a game program with logic often following the pattern:

```
DO
    Get player's command
    Update player's situation in the game
    Update video display
LOOP
```

The DO .. LOOP Statement takes the format shown in FIG-5.8.

FIG-5.8

The DO .. LOOP
Construct

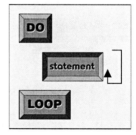

DarkBASIC Pro will allow the user to escape from a DO .. LOOP structure by pressing the Escape key.

Alternatively, an EXIT statement can be included within the loop to allow the loop to be exited when a given condition occurs.

Activity 5.20

Create a new project (*randomstops.dbpro*) which positions full stops of a random colour at random positions on the screen. The program requires the following logic:

```
Seed the random number generator
DO
    Set the cursor to a random position
    Set the foreground to a random colour
    Display a full stop
LOOP
```
continued on next page

The WAIT *milliseconds* Statement

The loop in your last program may have iterated quickly with dots appearing very rapidly (how quickly, depends on the hardware you're using). However, there's a way to slow the machine down. We've already encountered the WAIT KEY statement where the computer stops and waits for a key to be pressed, but there is a second version of the WAIT statement that waits a specific number of milliseconds (thousandth of a second) before continuing. This statement takes the form shown in FIG-5.9.

FIG-5.9

The WAIT *milliseconds* Statement

In the diagram:

time   is an integer value representing the number of milliseconds the program is to wait at this statement before continuing.

A typical example of the statement in use would be

```
WAIT 1000
```

which would cause the computer to pause for 1 second.

The SLEEP Statement

The SLEEP statement has exactly the same effect as the WAIT statement described above, pausing a program for a specified amount of time. This statement takes the format shown in FIG-5.10.

FIG-5.10

The SLEEP Statement

Nested Loops

A common requirement is to produce nested loops, that is situations where one loop control structure appears within another. For example, to read in six game scores (each between 0 and 100) and then calculate their average, the logic required is:

```
1.   Set total to zero
2.   FOR 6 times DO
3.       Get valid score
4.       Add score to total
5.   ENDFOR
6.   Calculate average as total / 6
7.   Display average
```

This appears to have only a single loop structure beginning at statement 2 and ending at statement 5. However, if we add detail to statement 3, this gives us

```
3. Get valid score
   3.1   Read score
   3.2   WHILE score is invalid DO
   3.3       Display "Score must be between 0 to 100"
   3.4       Read score
   3.5   ENDWHILE
```

which, if placed in the original solution, results in a nested loop structure, where a WHILE loop appears inside a FOR loop.

```
1.    Set total to zero
2.    FOR 6 times DO
3.1       Read score
3.2       WHILE score is invalid DO
3.3           Display "Score must be between 0 to 100"
3.4           Read score
3.5       ENDWHILE
4.        Add score to total
5.    ENDFOR
6.    Calculate average as total / 6
7.    Display average
```

Nested FOR Loops

Perhaps the most troublesome situation is where FOR loops are nested. The following example demonstrates the characteristics of such a structure. Consider the first two digits of a car's odometer. Initially, they are set to 00. As the car moves, the least-significant digit (*units*) increments while the most significant digit (*tens*) remains unchanged. But when the *units* value reaches 9, the *tens* value increments and the *units* value is reset to zero (see FIG-5.11).

FIG-5.11

Incrementing the *Units*
Loop Counter

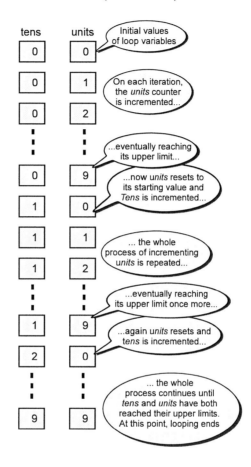

This situation is matched exactly by the following code:

```
FOR tens = 0 TO 9
    FOR units = 0 TO 9
        PRINT tens,units
    NEXT units
NEXT tens
```

The *tens* loop is known as the **outer loop,** while the *units* loop is known as the **inner loop.** A few points to note about nested FOR loops:

➤ The inner loop increments fastest.

➤ Only when the inner loop is complete does the outer loop variable increment.

➤ The inner loop counter is reset to its starting value each time the outer loop counter is incremented.

Testing Iterative Code

We need a test strategy when looking for errors in iterative code. Where possible, it is best to create at least three sets of test data:

> ➢ test data that causes the loop to execute zero times.

> ➢ test data that causes the loop to execute once.

> ➢ test data that causes the loop to execute multiple times.

For example, in project *guess01.dbpro* we checked that the player was entering a number between 1 and 100 using the code:

```
INPUT "Enter your guess (1 - 100) : ",guess
WHILE guess < 1 OR guess > 100
    PRINT "Your guess must be between 1 and 100"
    INPUT "Enter your guess again (1 - 100) : ",guess
ENDWHILE
```

To test the WHILE loop in this section of code we could use the test data shown in TABLE-5.4.

TABLE-5.4

Test Data for a WHILE Loop

Test Run	Test Data	Iterations
1	guess = 77	0
2	guess = 0 guess = 98	1
3	guess = 101 guess = -9 guess = 50	2

The WHILE loop is only executed if *guess* is outside the range 1 to 100, so Test 1, which uses a value in that range, will skip the WHILE loop - giving zero iterations.

Test 2 uses an invalid value for *guess*, causing the WHILE loop body to be executed, and then uses a valid value. This loop is therefore exited after only one iteration.

Test 3 uses two invalid values, causing the WHILE loop to execute twice.

Activity 5.26

The following code is meant to calculate the average of a sequence of numbers. The sequence ends when the value zero is entered. This terminating zero is not considered to be one of the numbers in the sequence.

```
total = 0
count = 0
INPUT "Enter number (end with 0) : ", num
WHILE num <> 0
    total = total + num
    count = count + 1
    INPUT "Enter number (end with 0): ", num
ENDWHILE
average = total / count
PRINT average
WAIT KEY
END
```

Make up a set of test values (similar in construct to TABLE-5.4) for the WHILE loop in the code.

Create a new project (*average.dbpro*) containing the code given above and use the test data to find out if the code functions correctly.

All three tests are not always possible. For example, a REPEAT loop cannot execute zero times and, in this case, we have to satisfy ourselves with single and multiple iteration tests.

A FOR loop, when written for a fixed number of iterations can only be tested for that number of iterations. So a loop beginning with the line

```
FOR c = 1 TO 10
```

can only be tested for multiple iterations (10 iterations in this case). The exception being if the loop body contains an EXIT statement, in which case zero and one iteration tests may also be possible.

However, a FOR loop which is coded with a variable upper limit as in

```
FOR c = 1 TO max
```

may be fully tested by making sure *max* has the values 0, 1, and more than 1 during testing.

A DO loop can only be tested for zero and one iterations if it contains an EXIT statement.

Summary

- DarkBASIC Pro contains four iteration constructs:

```
WHILE . . ENDWHILE
REPEAT . . UNTIL
```

- The WHILE..ENDWHILE construct executes a minimum of zero times and exits when the specified condition is false.

- The REPEAT..UNTIL construct executes at least once and exits when the specified condition is true.

- The FOR..NEXT construct is used when iteration has to be done a specific number of times.

- A STEP size may be included in the FOR statement. The value specified by the STEP term is added to the loop counter on each iteration.

- If no STEP size is given in the FOR statement, a value of 1 is used.

- FOR loops counters can be integer or real.

- The start, finish and STEP values in a FOR loop can be defined using variables or arithmetic expressions.

- If the start value is equal to the finish value, a FOR loop will execute only once.

- If the start value is greater than the finish value and the STEP size is a positive value, a FOR loop will execute zero times.

- Using the DO..LOOP structure creates an infinite loop.

- The EXIT statement can be used to exit from any loop.

- One loop structure can be placed within another loop structure. Such a structure is known as a nested loop.

- Loops should be tested by creating test data for zero, one and multiple iterations during execution whenever possible.

Solutions

Activity 5.1

```
RANDOMIZE TIMER()
number = RND(99)+1
REM *** Guess the number ***
INPUT "Enter your guess (1 to 100) : "
,guess
WHILE guess < 1 OR guess > 100
  PRINT "Your guess must be between 1 and
  100"
  INPUT "Enter your guess again (1-100) : "
  , guess
ENDWHILE
REM *** Respond to guess **"
IF guess = number
  PRINT "Correct"
ELSE
  IF guess > number
    PRINT "Your guess is too high"
  ELSE
    PRINT "Your guess is too low"
  ENDIF
ENDIF
REM *** Display both values ***
PRINT "Number was ", number," Guess was "
,guess
REM *** End program ***
WAIT KEY
END
```

Activity 5.2

```
REM *** Get number ***
INPUT "Enter item selected : ",no
WHILE no < 1 OR no > 4
  PRINT "Invalid selection. Please
  re-enter."
  INPUT "Enter item number (1-4) : ", no
ENDWHILE
REM *** Display name of item ***
SELECT no
  CASE 1
    PRINT "A sword"
  ENDCASE
  CASE 2
    PRINT "A wand"
  ENDCASE
  CASE 3
    PRINT "A bag of dragon's teeth"
  ENDCASE
  CASE 4
    PRINT "A water skin"
  ENDCASE
  CASE DEFAULT
    PRINT "Unknown item"
  ENDCASE
ENDSELECT
REM *** End program ***
WAIT KEY
END
```

Activity 5.3

```
INPUT "Enter a number : ",no1
INPUT "Enter a number : ",no2
WHILE no1 <> no2
  no1 = no2
  INPUT "Enter a number : ",no2
ENDWHILE
```

The loop will terminate when *no1* and *no2* both contain the same value.

Activity 5.4

```
REM *** Seed random number generator ***
RANDOMIZE TIMER ()
REM *** Set number of throws to zero ***
throws = 0
REM *** Throw both dice ***
dice1 = RND(5)+1
dice2 = RND(5)+1
REM *** WHILE 8 or less DO  ***
WHILE dice1 + dice2 <= 8
  REM *** Add 1 to throws achieved ***
  throws = throws + 1
  REM *** Throw dice again ***
  dice1 = RND(5)+1
  dice2 = RND(5)+1
ENDWHILE
REM *** Display the number of throws
achieved ***
PRINT "You managed ",throws," throws"
REM *** End program ***
WAIT KEY
END
```

Activity 5.5

```
REM *** Set total to zero ***
total = 0
REPEAT
  REM *** Read a number ***
  INPUT "Enter a value (0 to stop ) : ", no
  REM *** Add number to total ***
  total = total + no
UNTIL no = 0
REM *** Display total ***
PRINT "Total of values entered is ", total
REM *** End program ***
WAIT KEY
END
```

Activity 5.6

```
REM *** Generate random value ***
RANDOMIZE TIMER()
number  = RND(99)+1
REPEAT
  REM *** Guess the number ***
  INPUT "Enter your guess (1 to 100) : ",guess
  WHILE guess < 1 OR guess > 100
    PRINT "Your guess must be between 1 and
    100"
    INPUT "Enter your guess again (1-100): ",
    guess
  ENDWHILE
  REM *** Respond to guess ***
  IF guess = number
    PRINT "Correct"
  ELSE
    IF guess > number
      PRINT "Your guess is too high"
    ELSE
      PRINT "Your guess is too low"
    ENDIF
  ENDIF
UNTIL guess = number
REM  *** Display both values ***
PRINT "Number was ", number," Guess was "
,guess
REM *** End program ***
WAIT KEY
END
```

Activity 5.7

```
FOR j = 1 TO 10
```

Activity 5.8

This code would display the values 1 to 10

Activity 5.9

```
REM *** Display 12 times table ***
FOR c = 12 TO 144 STEP 12
  PRINT c
NEXT c
REM *** End program ***
WAIT KEY
END
```

Activity 5.10

```
REM *** 12 times table backwards! ***
FOR c = 144 TO 12 STEP -12
  PRINT c
NEXT c
REM *** End program ***
WAIT KEY
END
```

Activity 5.11

The second version of the program should be:

```
REM *** Get limit of FOR loop ***
PRINT "I will display all of the values
between any two numbers you give me"
INPUT "Enter start value : ",start
INPUT "Enter finish value : ", num
FOR c = start TO num
  PRINT c
NEXT c
REM *** End program ***
WAIT KEY
END
```

The final version is:

```
PRINT "I will display the appropriate
values between any two numbers you give me"
INPUT "Enter start value : ",start
INPUT "Enter finish value : ", num
INPUT "Enter the step size : ", size
FOR c = start TO num STEP size
  PRINT c
NEXT c
REM *** End program ***
WAIT KEY
END
```

Activity 5.12

The values displayed are:

```
1
1.10000002384
1.20000004768
1.30000007153
1.40000009537
1.50000011921
1.60000014305
1.70000016689
1.80000019073
1.90000021458
```

The discrepancy is caused by rounding errors when converting decimal to binary. (Binary is the number system used by the computer.)

Activity 5.13

The iteration now performs the expected 11 times, the last value displayed being 2.00000023842

Activity 5.14

```
REM *** Set total to zero ***
total = 0
REM *** FOR 12 times DO ***
FOR c = 1 TO 12
  REM *** Get a number ***
  INPUT "Enter a number : ",num
  REM *** Add number to total ***
  total = total + num
NEXT c
PRINT "The total of the 12 numbers is "
,total
REM *** End program ***
WAIT KEY
END
```

Activity 5.15

Smallest:

```
REM *** Get first number ***
INPUT "Enter number : ", num
REM *** Set smallest to first number ***
smallest = num
REM *** FOR 9 times DO ***
FOR c = 2 TO 10
  REM *** Get next number ***
  INPUT "Enter a number : ", num
  REM *** IF smaller, store in smallest ***
  IF num < smallest
      smallest = num
  ENDIF
NEXT c
REM *** Display smallest ***
PRINT "The smallest number entered was ",
smallest
REM *** End program ***
WAIT KEY
END
```

Largest:

```
REM *** Get first number ***
INPUT "Enter number : ", num
REM *** Set largest to first number ***
largest = num
REM *** FOR 9 times DO ***
FOR c = 2 TO 10
  REM *** Get next number ***
  INPUT "Enter a number : ", num
  REM *** IF larger, store in largest ***
  IF num > largest
      largest = num
  ENDIF
NEXT c
REM *** Display largest ***
PRINT "The largest number entered was ",
largest
REM *** End program ***
WAIT KEY
END
```

Activity 5.16

```
REM *** Get the number of judges ***
INPUT "Enter the number of judges : ", n
REM *** Get first score ***
INPUT "Enter score of first judge : ",
score#
REM *** Set highest, lowest, total to score
***
highestScore# = score#
lowestScore# = score#
total# = score#
REM *** FOR N-1 times DO ***
FOR c = 1 TO N-1
  REM *** Get next score ***
  INPUT "Enter next judge's score : ",score#
  REM *** Add score to total ***
  total# = total# + score#
  REM *** Check highest and lowest ***
  IF score# > highestScore#
      highestScore# = score#
  ELSE
      IF score# < lowestScore#
          lowestScore# = score#
      ENDIF
  ENDIF
NEXT c
REM *** Subtract highest & lowest from
total ***
total# = total# - (highestScore# +
lowestScore#)
REM *** Calculate and display average ***
average# = total# / (N-2)
PRINT "The average score was : ", average#
REM *** End program ***
WAIT KEY
END
```

No attempt at validation has been made. You could have added WHILE loops to make sure the number of judges and the scores were within acceptable limits.

Activity 5.17

```
REM *** Set up day names ***
DATA "Sunday", "Monday", "Tuesday",
"Wednesday", "Thursday", "Friday","Saturday"
REM *** Read and display each day ***
FOR c = 1 TO 7
  READ day$
  PRINT day$
NEXT c
REM *** End program ***
WAIT KEY
END
```

Activity 5.18

```
REM *** Generate random value ***
RANDOMIZE TIMER()
number = RND(99)+1
FOR c = 1 TO 7
  REM *** Guess the number ***
  INPUT "Enter your guess (1 to 100) : ",
  guess
  WHILE guess < 1 OR guess > 100
      PRINT "Your guess must be between 1
      and 100"
      INPUT "Enter your guess again (1-100):",
      guess
  ENDWHILE
  REM *** Respond to guess ***
  IF guess = number
      PRINT "Correct"
  ELSE
```

```
      IF guess > number
          PRINT "Your guess is too high"
      ELSE
          PRINT "Your guess is too low"
      ENDIF
  ENDIF
NEXT c
REM *** Display both values ***
PRINT "Number was ", number," Guess was "
,guess
REM *** End program ***
WAIT KEY
END
```

Activity 5.19

```
REM *** Seed random number generator ***
RANDOMIZE TIMER()
REM *** Set total to zero ***
total= 0
REM *** FOR 5 times DO ***
FOR c = 1 TO 5
  PRINT "Hit any key to roll the dice"
  WAIT KEY
  REM *** Throw both dice ***
  dice1 = RND(5) +1
  dice2 = RND(5) +1
  REM *** Display throw & dice values ***
  PRINT "Throw : ",c,"    Dice 1 : ",dice1,
  "   Dice 2 : ",dice2
  REM *** IF both dice are 1 THEN exit ***
  IF dice1 = 1 AND dice2 = 1
      EXIT
  ENDIF
  REM *** Add dice throws to total ***
  total = total + dice1 + dice2
NEXT c
REM *** Display final score ***
PRINT "Your final score was : ", total
REM *** End program ***
WAIT KEY
END
```

Activity 5.20

First version:

```
REM *** Seed random number generator ***
RANDOMIZE TIMER()
DO
  REM *** Generate random position ***
  x = RND(799)
  y = RND(599)
  REM *** Move cursor to position ***
  SET CURSOR x,y
  REM *** Create random foreground colour ***
  INK RGB(RND(255) ,RND(255) ,RND(255) ) ,0
  REM *** Display full stop ***
  PRINT "."
LOOP
REM *** End program ***
WAIT KEY
END
```

Second version:

```
REM *** Seed random number generator ***
RANDOMIZE TIMER()
DO
  REM *** Generate random position ***
  x = RND(799)
  y = RND(599)
  REM *** IF (100,100) THEN Exit loop ***
  IF x = 100 AND y = 100
      EXIT
```

```
        ENDIF
        REM *** Move cursor to position ***
        SET CURSOR x,y
        REM *** Create random foreground colour ***
        INK RGB(RND(255),RND(255),RND(255) ) ,0
        REM *** Display full stop ***
        PRINT "."
    LOOP
    REM *** End program ***
    WAIT KEY
    END
```

Activity 5.21

```
    REM *** Seed random number generator ***
    RANDOMIZE TIMER()
    DO
        x = RND(799)
        y = RND(599)
        IF x = 100 AND y = 100
            EXIT
        ENDIF
        SET CURSOR x,y
        INK RGB (RND (255) ,RND (255) ,RND (255)) ,0
        PRINT "."
        WAIT 500
    LOOP
    REM *** End program ***
    WAIT KEY
    END
```

Activity 5.22

A one second delay:

```
    REM *** Wait 1 second ***
    SLEEP 1000
    REM *** Display message ***
    PRINT "Press any key"
    REM *** Record start time ***
    start = TIMER()
    REM *** Wait for key press ***
    WAIT KEY
    REM *** Record finish time *"*
    finish = TIMER()
    REM *** Calculate and display duration ***
    duration = finish - start
    PRINT "You took ", duration, " milliseconds"
    REM *** End program ***
    WAIT KEY
    END
```

A variable delay:

```
    REM *** Seed random number generator ***
    RANDOMIZE TIMER ()
    REM *** Wait 1 second ***
    SLEEP 1000 + RND(2000)
    REM *** Display message ***
    PRINT "Press any key"
    REM *** Record start time ***
    start = TIMER()
    REM *** Wait for key press ***
    WAIT KEY
    REM "** Record finish time ***
    finish = TIMER()
    REM "** Calculate and display duration ***
    duration = finish - start
    PRINT "You took ", duration, " milliseconds"
    REM *** End program ***
    WAIT KEY
    END
```

Activity 5.23

```
    REM *** Set total to zero ***
    total = 0
    REM *** FOR 6 times DO ***
    FOR c = 1 TO 6
        REM ***, Get valid score ***
        INPUT "Enter score : ",score
        WHILE score < 0 OR score > 100
            PRINT "Score must be between 0 and 100"
            INPUT "Re-enter score : ", score
        ENDWHILE
        REM *** Add score to total ***
        total = total + score
    NEXT c
    REM *** Calculate and display average ***
    average = total / 6
    PRINT "Average score is ", average
    REM *** End program ***
    WAIT KEY
    END
```

Activity 5.24

Output would be:

```
    -20
    -21
    -22
    -23
    -10
    -11
    -12
    -13
    00
    01
    02
    03
    10
    11
    12
    13
```

Activity 5.25

```
    REM *** FOR each player DO ***
    FOR player = 1 TO 4
        PRINT "Enter scores for player ", player
        REM *** Set total to zero ***
        total = 0
        REM *** FOR 6 times DO ***
        FOR game = 1 TO 6
            REM *** Get valid score ***
            INPUT "Enter score : ",score
            WHILE score < 0 OR score > 100
                PRINT "Score must be between 0 and
                100"
                INPUT "Re-enter score : ", score
            ENDWHILE
            REM *** Add score to total ***
            total = total + score
        NEXT game
        REM *** Calculate and display average ***
        average = total / 6
        PRINT "Average score is ", average
    NEXT player
    REM *** End program ***
    WAIT KEY
    END
```

Notice that the line

```
    PRINT "Enter scores for player ", player
```

displays the player's number. This helps the user keep
tabs on whose set of game scores is being entered.

Activity 5.26

Possible test data is shown below:

Test Run	Test Data	Iterations
1	num = 0	0
2	num = 50 num = 0	1
3	num = 12 num = 8 num = 0	2

The first test run should highlight a problem with the code. The line

```
average = total / count
```

will be calculated as

```
average = 0 / 0
```

and division by zero is an invalid operation which causes the program to terminate.

Drawing Statements

A First Look at Animation Techniques

Drawing Basic Shapes on the Screen

Erasing Shapes

Drawing On The Screen

Introduction

As well as outputting text to the screen, DarkBASIC Pro contains various commands which allow us to draw basic shapes such as lines circles, and boxes on the screen. Like output text, we can select the colour of these shapes.

Basic Drawing Commands

The DOT Statement

This command draws a single pixel at a specified point. The pixel will be drawn in the current foreground colour (as set using the INK command). The statement takes the format shown in FIG-6.1.

FIG-6.1

The DOT Statement

In the diagram:

x,y
are integer values specifying the coordinates of the pixel to be drawn. These values should specify a position within the bounds of the current screen resolution. For example, if the screen is set to 800 by 600, then the coordinates of the pixel can range from (0,0) to (799,599).

To draw a yellow pixel at position (100,80) on the screen we would use the following statements:

```
REM *** Change foreground colour to yellow ***
INK RGB(255,255,0),0
REM *** Draw the pixel ***
DOT 100,80
```

The program in LISTING-6.1 places 1000 randomly coloured dots at random positions on the screen using the following logic:

```
Clear the screen
FOR 1000 times DO
    Change to a randomly chosen foreground colour
    Choose a random position on the screen
    Place pixel at that position
ENDFOR
```

LISTING-6.1

Random Dots

```
REM *** Seed random number generator ***
RANDOMIZE TIMER()
REM *** Clear the screen ***
CLS
FOR c = 1 TO 1000
   REM *** Choose a colour at random ***
   colour = RGB(RND(255),RND(255),RND(255))
```

continued on next page

LISTING-6.1
(continued)

Random Dots

```
        INK colour,0
        REM *** Choose random position on screen ***
        x = RND(800)
        y = RND(600)
        REM *** Draw pixel on screen ***
        DOT x,y
NEXT c
REM *** End program ***
WAIT KEY
END
```

Activity 6.1

Type in and test the program in LISTING-6.1 (*dots01.dbpro*).

Modify the program so that 10,000 dots are drawn.

Activity 6.2

dots01.dbpro assumes a screen resolution of 800 by 600. If you are using a different resolution the pixels will not be spread correctly over the whole screen.

Modify *dots01.dbpro* to make sure the random dots occupy the whole screen no matter what resolution is being used.

(HINT: You'll need to use SCREEN WIDTH and SCREEN HEIGHT)

The POINT Statement

We can discover the colour of any pixel on the screen using the POINT command. This statement returns the colour of specified pixel on the screen and has the format shown in FIG-6.2.

FIG-6.2

The POINT Statement

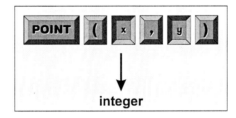

In the diagram:

x,y   is a pair of integer values giving the position of the screen pixel whose colour is to be returned.

Colours are represented by large integer values (as we saw when using the RGB statement back in Chapter 2). Therefore, to check if a pixel is a specific colour, say, red, then we need to use a statement such as:

```
IF POINT(100,100) = RGB(255,0,0)
    PRINT "The pixel is red"
```

Alternatively, we might use the colour returned by the POINT statement to set the foreground (or background) colour with a statement such as:

```
INK POINT(200,5),0
```

The LINE Statement

The LINE statement draws a line between two points. The line is drawn using the foreground colour. The statement takes the format shown in FIG-6.3.

FIG-6.3

The LINE Statement

In the diagram:

x1, y1	are the coordinates of the starting point of the line.
x2, y2	are the coordinates of the end point of the line.

For example, the statements

The background colour is not used when drawing shapes.

```
CLS RGB(0,0,255)
INK RGB(255,255,0),0
LINE 80,50,300,90
```

would produce a yellow line on a blue background as shown in FIG-6.4.

FIG-6.4

Drawing a Line on the Screen

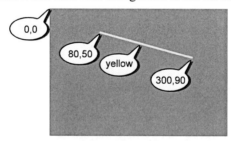

The program in LISTING-6.2 demonstrates the use of the LINE command by drawing an arrow constructed from three lines.

LISTING-6.2

Using the LINE Statement

```
REM *** Clear the screen ***
CLS
REM *** Set foreground colour to red ***
INK RGB(255,0,0),0

REM *** Draw lines ***
LINE 50,50,250,50
LINE 250,50,200,25
LINE 250,50,200,75

REM *** End program ***
WAIT KEY
END
```

Activity 6.4

Type in and test LISTING-6.2 (*arrow01.dbpro*).

Activity 6.5

Write a program (*gallows01.dbpro*) to draw the following shape:

You may find it useful to draw the gallows on some squared paper before starting to code.

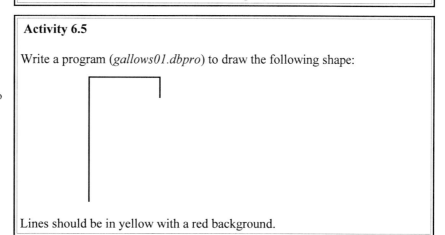

Lines should be in yellow with a red background.

The BOX Statement

The BOX statement is used to draw a filled-in rectangle. There are two versions of this statement. Using the simplest form, the coordinates of the top-left corner and bottom-right corner of the required box must be supplied. For example, we could create a box shown in FIG-6.5 using the statement:

```
BOX 100,120,400,180
```

FIG-6.5

Using the BOX Statement

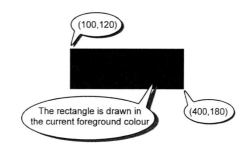

Activity 6.6

Modify *gallows01.dbpro* so that the output produced now looks as follows:

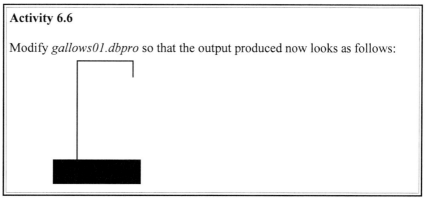

The second, longer version of the BOX statement can create a much more colourful rectangle. This statement takes four additional colour parameters which are used to fill in the four corners of the rectangle. Away from the corners the colours merge into each other. The effect is rather psychedelic!

An example of the fill effect is shown in the following code

```
c1 = RGB(255,0,0)
c2 = RGB(0,255,0)
c3 = RGB(0,0,255)
c4 = RGB(255,255,0)
BOX 10,10,100,100,c1,c2,c3,c4
```

Activity 6.7

Modify your *gallows01.dbpro* project so that the box is filled with various colours.
Feel free to experiment with the colours you use.

FIG-6.6

The BOX Statement

The format for the BOX statement is shown in FIG-6.6.

In the diagram:

x1,y1	represent the coordinates of the top-left corner of the box.
x2,y2	represent the coordinates of the bottom-right corner of the box.
c1,c2,c3,c4	represent the fill colours used in the four corners of the box.

Activity 6.8

By creating a short program, identify which corner is assigned to each of the colour parameters in the BOX statement.

The CIRCLE Statement

You can draw a circle using the CIRCLE statement. Unlike the rectangle created by the BOX command, CIRCLE creates an outline only; the inside of the circle is not filled. The centre of the circle and its radius must be specified. For example,

```
CIRCLE 100,120,50
```

creates the circle shown in FIG-6.7.

FIG-6.7

Using the CIRCLE Statement

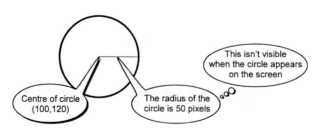

The statement has the format shown in FIG-6.8.

FIG-6.8

The CIRCLE Statement

In the diagram:

x,y   are the coordinates of the centre of the circle.

radius   is an integer value giving the radius of the circle (in pixels).

Activity 6.9

Modify your *gallows01.dbpro* program so that your display now displays the figure shown below.

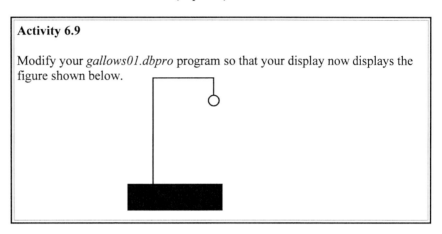

The ELLIPSE Statement

You can draw an ellipse using the ELLIPSE statement. Like the CIRCLE command, ELLIPSE creates an outline only. The ELLIPSE command takes four parameters detailing the centre of the ellipse, the horizontal radius and the vertical radius. For example, the line

```
ELLIPSE 300,200,120,80
```

will create output similar to that in FIG-6.9.

FIG-6.9

Using the ELLIPSE Statement

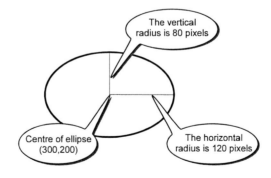

The format of the ELLIPSE statement is shown in FIG-6.10.

FIG-6.10

The ELLIPSE Statement

In the diagram:

x,y	are the coordinates of the centre of the ellipse.
hradius	is an integer value giving the horizontal radius of the ellipse (in pixels).
vradius	is an integer value giving the vertical radius of the ellipse (in pixels).

Activity 6.10

Using an ellipse and four more lines, complete the "hangman" symbol as shown below.

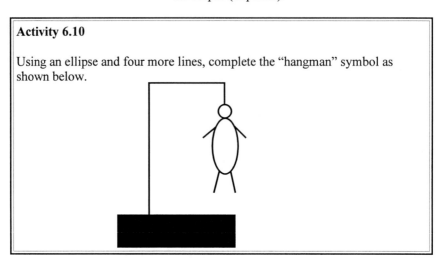

Summary

- The DOT x,y statement places a single pixel on the screen at position (x,y) using the current foreground colour.

- The POINT (x,y) statement returns the colour currently showing at position (x,y) on the screen.

- Use LINE x1,y1,x2,y2 to draw a line between $(x1,y1)$, $(x2,y2)$.

- Use BOX x1,y1,x2,y2 to draw a filled rectangle with top-left corner at the point $(x1,y1)$ and bottom-right corner at $(x2,y2)$.

- Use BOX x1,y1, x2, y2,c1,c2,c3,c4 to draw a filled box using colours *c1, c2, c3* and *c4* which radiate from the four corners of the rectangle.

- Use CIRCLE x,y,r to draw the outline of a circle with centre (x,y) radius *r*.

- Use ELLIPSE x,y,hr,vr to draw the outline of an ellipse with centre (x,y), horizontal radius *hr* and vertical radius *vr*.

Demonstrating Basic Shapes

Introduction

This section contains the longest program we've created so far. It allows the user to select any basic graphics shape (from those described on the previous pages); choose a colour for the shape, and then draw the requested object on the screen.

The program uses the following logic:

```
Display a menu of possible shapes
Get the user's choice of shape
Display a menu of possible colours
Get the user's choice of colour
Set foreground colour to the one selected
Display the requested object
```

The implementation of the program is given in LISTING-6.3.

LISTING-6.3

Displaying Basic
Graphics Shapes

```
REM *** Display menu of possible shapes ***
PRINT "Choose from the following shapes"
PRINT "1 - Pixel "
PRINT "2 - Line"
PRINT "3 - Box"
PRINT "4 - Circle"
PRINT "5 - Ellipse"

REM *** Get user's choice ***
INPUT "Enter option : ", choiceshape
WHILE choiceshape < 1 OR choiceshape > 5
    PRINT "That was an invalid choice. 1 to 5 only"
    INPUT "Enter option : ",choiceshape
ENDWHILE

REM *** Display possible colours ***
PRINT "Choose from the following colours"
PRINT "1 - Red"
PRINT "2 - Green"
PRINT "3 - Blue"
PRINT "4 - Yellow"
PRINT "5 - Cyan"
PRINT "6 - Magenta"

REM *** Get user's choice ***
INPUT "Enter option : ", choicecolour
WHILE choicecolour < 1 OR choicecolour > 6
    PRINT "That was an invalid choice. 1 to 6 only"
    INPUT "Enter option : ",choicecolour
ENDWHILE

REM *** Change to selected colour ***
SELECT choicecolour
    CASE 1
        foreground = RGB(255,0,0)
    ENDCASE
    CASE 2
        foreground = RGB(0,255,0)
    ENDCASE
    CASE 3
        foreground = RGB(0,0,255)
    ENDCASE
```

continued on next page

LISTING-6.3
(continued)

Displaying Basic
Graphics Shapes

```
      CASE 4
         foreground = RGB(255,255,0)
      ENDCASE
      CASE 5
         foreground = RGB(0,255,255)
      ENDCASE
      CASE 6
         foreground = RGB(255, 0,255)
      ENDCASE
ENDSELECT

REM *** Set foreground colour, clear screen and draw shape ***
INK foreground,0
CLS
SELECT choiceshape
      CASE 1 '*** Pixel ***
         DOT 300,250
      ENDCASE
      CASE 2 '*** Line ***
         LINE 20,50,300,120
      ENDCASE
      CASE 3 '*** Rectangle ***
         BOX 20,50,300,150
      ENDCASE
      CASE 4 '*** Circle ***
         CIRCLE 300,250,50
      ENDCASE
      CASE 5 '*** Ellipse ***
         ELLIPSE 300,250,50,15
      ENDCASE
ENDSELECT

REM *** End program ***
WAIT KEY
END
```

Activity 6.11

Type in and test the program in LISTING-6.3 (*shapes01.dbpro*).

Modify the program so that, once a shape has been displayed, the user can
select other shapes and colours. To do this add a loop structure to the code and
insert a QUIT option to the shapes menu. The program should terminate when
this quit option is chosen.

A First Look at Animation

Basic Concepts

To animate a simple object on the screen we need to draw the image on the screen, wait for a fraction of a second (so that your brain gets time to register that something has appeared on the screen) and then make the object disappear. These three steps are repeated, drawing the object in a slightly different position on each occasion.

How to Remove an Object from the Screen

Back in Chapter 2 we saw how to remove text from the screen by overwriting the text with an exact duplicate of itself using the background colour. This same technique can also be used to remove drawings from the screen.

If we draw a yellow circle on a black background, we can make that circle disappear by drawing a black circle in exactly the same place. This technique is demonstrated in LISTING-6.4 which employs the following logic:

```
Set the foreground colour to yellow
Draw a circle
Wait for a key press
Set the foreground colour to black
Draw a circle
```

LISTING-6.4

Removing an Object from the Screen

```
REM *** Set foreground to yellow ***
foreground = RGB (255,255,0)
INK foreground, 0

REM *** Draw the circle ***
x = 300
y = 250
CIRCLE x, y, 5

REM *** Wait for a key press ***
WAIT KEY

REM *** Change foreground colour to black ***
foreground = RGB (0,0,0)

REM *** Draw the circle in black ***
INK foreground, 0
CIRCLE x, y, 5

REM *** End program ***
WAIT KEY
END
```

Activity 6.12

Type in and test the program in LISTING-6.4 (*disappear.dbpro*)

Modify the program to use a box rather than a circle.

Notice that the circle in project *disappear.dbpro* is not removed until a key is pressed. However, an alternative approach is to remove the circle automatically after a given amount of time has passed. We have two statements that can make the machine halt for a given time - SLEEP and WAIT (as described in the last chapter).

> **Activity 6.13**
>
> Modify your last program by removing the WAIT KEY statement between displaying and hiding the yellow circle and replacing it with a SLEEP statement that waits 1 second before making the circle disappear.

How to Move an Object

The next stage in the animation process is to redraw our object at a different position. If we write a program which uses the following logic

```
y = 250
FOR x = 1 TO 600 DO
      Show circle at position (x,y)
      Wait 20 milliseconds
      Hide circle at position (x,y)
ENDFOR
```

then we should see the circle travel across the middle of the screen. This logic is coded in LISTING-6.5.

LISTING-6.5

Animating an Object

```
REM *** Set y-ordinate of object ***
y = 250

REM *** FOR x-ordinate varies from 1 TO 600 DO
FOR x = 1 TO 600
   REM *** Set foreground to yellow ***
   foreground = RGB(255,255,0)
   INK foreground,0
   REM *** Draw the circle ***
   CIRCLE x,y,5
   REM *** Wait for 20 milliseconds ***
   WAIT 20
   REM *** Change foreground colour to black ***
   foreground = RGB(0,0,0)
   REM *** Draw the circle ***
   INK foreground,0
   CIRCLE x,y,5
NEXT x

REM *** End program ***
WAIT KEY
END
```

> **Activity 6.14**
>
> Type in and test the program in LISTING-6.5 (*moving.dbpro*).
>
> Modify the program so that the circle moves faster.
>
> Modify the program so that the circle moves vertically rather than horizontally.

This gives you some idea of how we can give the impression of movement on the screen. However, we don't want too spend too much time using this approach to animation since DarkBASIC Pro has a much better way of doing this type of operation using sprites which we'll find out about in a later chapter.

Solutions

Activity 6.1

The modified version of the program is:

```
REM *** Seed random number generator ***
RANDOMIZE TIMER()
CLS
FOR c = 1 TO 10000
  REM *** Choose a colour at random ***
  colour = RGB(RND(255),RND(255),RND(255))
  INK colour,0
  REM *** Choose random position ***
  x = RND(800)
  y = RND(600)
  DOT x, y
NEXT c
REM *** End program ***
WAIT KEY
END
```

Activity 6.2

The code for this new version of *Dots* is:

```
REM *** Seed random number generator ***
RANDOMIZE TIMER()
REM *** Get the screen dimensions ***
width = SCREEN WIDTH()
height = SCREEN HEIGHT()
REM *** Clear the screen ***
CLS
FOR c = 1 TO 10000
  colour = RGB(RND(255),RND(255),RND(255))
  INK colour,0
  x = RND(width)
  y = RND(height)
  REM *** Draw a pixel on screen ***
  DOT x,y
NEXT c
REM *** End program ***
WAIT KEY
END
```

Activity 6.3

```
REM *** Seed random number generator ***
RANDOMIZE TIMER ()
REM *** Get the screen dimensions ***
width = SCREEN WIDTH ()
height = SCREEN HEIGHT()
REM *** Clear the screen ***
CLS
FOR c = 1 TO 10000
  REM *** Choose a colour at random ***
  colour = RGB(RND(255),RND(255),RND(255))
  INK colour,0
  REM *** Choose random position ***
  x = RND(width)
  Y = RND(height)
  REM *** Draw a pixel on screen ***
  DOT x, y
NEXT c
REM *** Check colour of random pixel ***
x = RND(width)
y = RND(height)
IF POINT(x,y) = RGB(0,0,0)
  PRINT "The pixel at position (",x,",",y,
  ")is black"
ELSE
  PRINT "The pixel at position (",x,",",y,
  ")is not black"
ENDIF
```

```
REM *** End program ***
WAIT KEY
END
```

Activity 6.4

No solution required.

Activity 6.5

The code for *gallows01.dbpro* is :

```
REM *** Set colours ***
paint = RGB(255,255,0)
paper = RGB(255,0,0)
REM *** Create a red screen ***
CLS paper
REM *** Set drawing colour
INK paint,paper
REM *** Draw long vertical ***
LINE 50,100,50,200
REM *** Draw horizontal ***
LINE 50,100,100,100
REM *** Draw short vertical ***
LINE 100,100,100,120
REM *** End program ***
WAIT KEY
END
```

Obviously, you will have used different coordinates from the ones given in this solution.

Activity 6.6

```
REM *** Set colours ***
paint = RGB(255,255,0)
paper = RGB(255,0,0)
REM *** Create a red screen ***
CLS paper
REM *** Set drawing colour
INK paint,paper
REM *** Draw long vertical ***
LINE 50,100,50,200
REM *** Draw horizontal ***
LINE 50,100,100,100
REM *** Draw short vertical ***
LINE 100,100,100,120
REM *** Draw platform ***
BOX 10,200,100,230

REM *** End program ***
WAIT KEY
END
```

Activity 6.7

```
An example of the new BOX line would be:

BOX(10,200,100,230,RGB(0,255,255),
RGB(0,255,0),RGB(0,0,255),RGB(255,0,255)
```

Activity 6.8

The colours are used in the following order:

```
c1 = bottom left
c2 = top left
c3 = bottom right
c4 = top right
```

Activity 6.9

From the coordinates used in the Gallows project so far, drawing the head requires the lines:

```
REM *** Draw head ***
CIRCLE 100,125,5
```

Activity 6.10

```
REM *** Set colours ***
paint = RGB(255,255,0)
paper = RGB(255,0,0)
REM *** Create a red screen ***
CLS paper
REM *** Set drawing colour
INK paint,paper
REM *** Draw long vertical ***
LINE 50,100,50,200
REM *** Draw horizontal ***
LINE 50,100,100,100
REM *** Draw short vertical ***
LINE 100,100,100,120
REM *** Draw head ***
CIRCLE 100,125,5

REM *** Draw body ***
ELLIPSE 100,145,7,15
REM *** Left leg ***
LINE 97,156,90,176
REM *** Right leg ***
LINE 103,156,110,176
REM *** Left arm ***
LINE 97,132,85,150
REM *** Right arm ***
LINE 103,132,115,150

REM *** End program ***
WAIT KEY
END
```

Activity 6.11

The program needs a few small additions to add the required feature. These additions are highlighted.

```
REPEAT
  REM *** Display menu of possible shapes ***
  PRINT "Choose from the following shapes"
  PRINT "1 - Pixel "
  PRINT "2 - Line"
  PRINT "3 - Box"
  PRINT "4 - Circle"
  PRINT "5 - Ellipse"
  PRINT "6 - QUIT"

  REM *** Get user's choice ***
  INPUT "Enter option : ", choiceshape
  WHILE choiceshape < 1 OR choiceshape > 6
      PRINT "That was an invalid choice.
      1 to 6 only"
      INPUT "Enter option : ",choiceshape
  ENDWHILE

  REM *** Display possible colours ***
  PRINT "Choose from the following colours"
  PRINT "1 - Red"
  PRINT "2 - Green"
  PRINT "3 - Blue"
  PRINT "4 - Yellow"
  PRINT "5 - Cyan"
  PRINT "6 - Magenta"

  REM *** Get user's choice ***
  INPUT "Enter option : ", choicecolour
```

```
  WHILE choicecolour < 1 OR choicecolour > 6
      PRINT "That was an invalid choice.
      1 to 6    only"
      INPUT "Enter option : ",choicecolour
  ENDWHILE

  REM *** Change to selected colour ***
  SELECT choicecolour
      CASE 1
          foreground = RGB (255,0,0)
      ENDCASE
      CASE 2
          foreground = RGB (0,255,0)
      ENDCASE
      CASE 3
          foreground = RGB (0,0,255)
      ENDCASE
      CASE 4
          foreground = RGB (255,255,0)
      ENDCASE
      CASE 5
          foreground = RGB (0,255,255)
      ENDCASE
      CASE 6
          foreground = RGB (255, 0,255)
      ENDCASE
  ENDSELECT

  REM *** Set foreground colour, ***
  REM *** clear screen and draw shape ***
  INK foreground, 0
  CLS
  SELECT choiceshape
      CASE 1 '*** Pixel ***
          DOT 300,250
      ENDCASE
      CASE 2 '*** Line ***
          LINE 20,50,300,120
      ENDCASE
      CASE 3 '*** Rectangle ***
          BOX 20,50,300,150
      ENDCASE
      CASE 4 '*** Circle ***
          CIRCLE 300,250,50
      ENDCASE
      CASE 5 '*** Ellipse ***
          ELLIPSE 300,250,50,15
      ENDCASE
  ENDSELECT
  PRINT "Press any key to continue"
  WAIT KEY
UNTIL choiceshape = 6

REM *** End program ***
WAIT KEY
END
```

Activity 6.12

```
REM *** Set foreground to yellow ***
foreground = RGB(255,255,0)
INK foreground,0

REM *** Draw the box ***
x1 = 300
y1 = 250
x2 = 400
y2 = 280
BOX x1,y1,x2,y2

REM *** Wait for key press ***
WAIT KEY

REM *** Set foreground colour to black ***
foreground = RGB(0,0,0)

REM *** Draw the box in black ***
```

```
INK foreground, 0
BOX x1,y1,x2,y2

REM *** End program ***
WAIT KEY
END
```

Activity 6.13

```
REM *** Set foreground to yellow ***
foreground = RGB(255,255,0)
INK foreground,0

REM *** Draw the box ***
x1 = 300
y1 = 250
x2 = 400
y2 = 280
BOX x1,y1,x2,y2

REM *** Wait for 1 second ***
SLEEP 1000

REM *** Set foreground colour to black ***
foreground = RGB(0,0,0)

REM *** Draw the box in black ***
INK foreground, 0
BOX x1,y1,x2,y2

REM *** End program ***
WAIT KEY
END
```

Activity 6.14

To increase the speed, the delay should be reduced:

```
REM *** Set y-ordinate of object ***
y = 250

REM *** FOR x-ordinate varies from 1 TO
600 DO
FOR x = 1 TO 600 DO
  REM *** Set foreground to yellow ***
  foreground = RGB (255,255,0)
  INK foreground,0
  REM *** Draw the circle ***
  CIRCLE x, y, 5
  REM *** Wait for 5 milliseconds ***
  WAIT 5
  REM *** Change foreground to black ***
  foreground = RGB (0,0,0)
  REM *** Draw the circle ***
  INK foreground, 0
  CIRCLE x, y, 5
NEXT x

REM *** End program ***
WAIT KEY
END
```

To make the circle move vertically, the x-ordinate must remain fixed while the y-ordinate value changes:

```
REM *** Set x-ordinate of object ***
x = 250

REM *** FOR y-ordinate varies from 1 TO
600 DO
FOR y = 1 TO 600 DO
  REM *** Set foreground to yellow ***
  foreground = RGB (255,255,0)
  INK foreground,0
  REM *** Draw the circle ***
```

```
  CIRCLE x, y, 5
  REM *** Wait for 5 milliseconds ***
  WAIT 5
  REM *** Change foreground to black ***
  foreground = RGB (0,0,0)
  REM *** Draw the circle ***
  INK foreground, 0
  CIRCLE x, y, 5
NEXT y

REM *** End program ***
WAIT KEY
END
```

7

Modular Programming

Creating Functions

Global Variables

GOSUB Statement

Local Variables

Mini-Specs

Modular Programming

Parameter Passing

Pre-Conditions

Post-Conditions

Return Values

Functions

Introduction

Look at the computer in front of you. Notice how it is made up of several separate components: keyboard, screen, mouse, and inside the main casing are other discreet pieces such as the hard disk and CDROM.

Why are computers made this way, as a collection of separate pieces rather than have everything encased in a single frame?

Well, there are several reasons. Firstly, by using separate components each can be designed to perform just one specific task such as: get information from the user (keyboard); display information (the screen); store information (the disk) etc. This allows all of these items to be made and tested separately.

Also, if a component breaks down or needs to be replaced, you simply have to unplug that component and replace it with a new one.

Why is all of this relevant to creating games programs? Years of experience have shown that the advantages of this modular approach to construction doesn't just apply to physical items such as computers, it also applies to software.

Rather than create programs as one continuous set of instructions, we can split the program into several **routines** (also known as **modules** or **subroutines**), each routine being designed to perform just one specific function. This is particularly important in long programs and when several programmers are involved in creating the software.

In fact, routines in DarkBASIC Pro are often referred to as functions, and that's the term we'll use from here on in.

We'll demonstrate this technique by rewriting the Basic Shapes program (LISTING-6.3) that we created in the last chapter in a modular fashion.

Functions

Designing a Function

The first stage in creating a function is to decide on what task the function has to perform. For example, we might want a function to display a set of menu options (look back at LISTING-6.3 and you'll see examples of several simple menus).

When a team of people is involved in creating the software, it is important that the exact purpose of each routine is written out in detail so there can be no misconceptions between the people designing the routine and those programming it.

Functions must also be given a name. This name should reflect the purpose of the function and usually starts with a verb, since functions perform tasks.

Coding a Function

So, let's start by creating a function called *ShowShapeMenu* which displays the various shapes that can be drawn on the screen. The code for this function is shown below:

```
FUNCTION ShowShapeMenu()
    PRINT "Choose from the following options"
    PRINT "1 - Pixel"
    PRINT "2 - Line"
    PRINT "3 - Box"
    PRINT "4 - Circle"
    PRINT "5 - Ellipse"
ENDFUNCTION
```

Notice that the module begins with the keyword FUNCTION and ends with the keyword ENDFUNCTION.

The first line also contains the name of the function, *ShowShapesMenu*, and an empty set of parentheses.

Between the first and last lines go the set of instructions that perform the task the function has been designed to do.

Calling a Function

When you type in a program's code, place any functions you have at the end of that code (see LISTING-7.1).

LISTING-7.1

Adding a Function

```
REM *** Display a message ***
PRINT "Shape drawing program"

REM *** End program ***
WAIT KEY
END

REM *** Display shape options ***
FUNCTION ShowShapeMenu()
    PRINT "Choose from the following options"
    PRINT "1 - Pixel"
    PRINT "2 - Line"
    PRINT "3 - Box"
    PRINT "4 - Circle"
    PRINT "5 - Ellipse"
ENDFUNCTION
```

Activity 7.1

Type in and run the program given in LISTING-7.1 (*functions01.dbpro*).

NOTE: The menu will not appear when you run the program.

As you've just had demonstrated, functions are totally ignored when you run your program. You might as well have saved yourself some typing for all the good it did! It's only the code before the function, known as the **main** section, that is executed.

The code within a function is only executed if you **make a call** to that function.

Calling a function is taken as a request to execute the code within a function, and you make that call by simply giving the function name (including the parentheses) at the point in the main program where you'd like the function's lines to be executed. So, to execute the code within the *ShowShapeMenu* function we use the line:

```
ShowShapeMenu()
```

An updated version of the program is shown in LISTING-7.2.

LISTING-7.2

Calling a Function

```
REM *** Display a message ***
PRINT "Shape drawing program"

REM *** Call function ***
ShowShapeMenu()

REM *** End program ***
WAIT KEY
END

REM *** Display shape options ***
FUNCTION ShowShapeMenu ()
    PRINT "Choose from the following options"
    PRINT "1 - Pixel"
    PRINT "2 - Line"
    PRINT "3 - Box"
    PRINT "4 - Circle"
    PRINT "5 - Ellipse"
ENDFUNCTION
```

Activity 7.2

Modify your project to match LISTING-7.2 and check that the menu is displayed.

Notice that when you ran the program the message *Shape drawing program* appeared before the menu options. This is because the PRINT statement appears before the line

```
ShowShapeMenu()
```

which executes the function.

FIG-7.1

How a Function is Executed

FIG-7.1 shows what's happening when a function is executed.

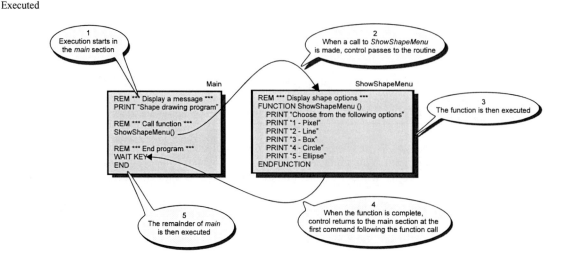

DarkBASIC Pro: Modular Programming

Another Example

We'll leave the shape program for the moment and have a look at another example. The function in LISTING-7.3 (*DrawTextLine()*) draws a line of asterisks on the screen.

LISTING-7.3

Calling the
DrawTextLine() Function

```
REM *** Draw a line of asterisks ***
DrawTextLine ()
REM *** Display a message ***
PRINT " Hello"
REM *** End program ***
WAIT KEY
END

REM *** Draw a line of asterisks ***
FUNCTION DrawTextLine ()
    PRINT "*******************"
ENDFUNCTION
```

You can call a function as often as you want from the main program. All you have to do is repeat the calling line. Hence, if we change the main program in project *testline.dbpro* to

```
DrawTextLine()
PRINT "   Hello"
DrawTextLine()
```

the *DrawTextLine()* function will be called twice and we will see a row of asterisks both above and below the word *Hello*.

Parameters

Sometimes we need to supply information to a function. For example, the DarkBASIC Pro statement DOT is actually a function and, when it is called, we need to supply it with details of where we want the pixel to be displayed. Each piece of information that we give to a function is known as a **parameter** to that function.

We'll see how parameters work by rewriting the *DrawTextLine()* so that the number of asterisks that are to appear in the line can be specified.

When a function needs to be supplied with information, we give that piece of information a name and place it in the parentheses following the function name. In *DrawTextLine()* we want to specify the size of the line to be drawn, so we'll supply it with a parameter called *size*. That makes the first line of our function now read:

```
FUNCTION DrawTextLine(size)
```

To make use of this information we'll have to rewrite the code for our function so that a single asterisk is output *size* times. Our new version of the routine is coded as:

```
FUNCTION DrawTextLine(size)
    FOR c = 1 TO size
        PRINT "*";
    NEXT c
    PRINT
ENDFUNCTION
```

Now, if we're going to call the function, we need to supply a value for *size*. Hence,

```
DrawTextLine (25)
```

FIG-7.2

Passing a Parameter to a Function

causes the *DrawTextLine()* function to be executed and sets the value of *size* to 25 (thereby drawing a line of 25 asterisks). The mechanism involved is shown visually in FIG-7.2.

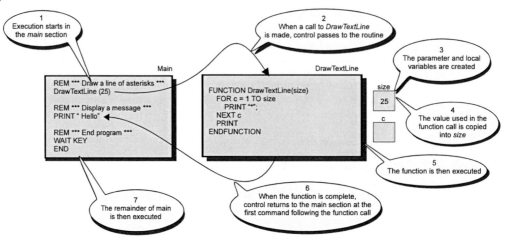

A function can have as many parameters as you require and these parameters can be of any type: integer, real or string. To demonstrate this we'll write yet another version of the *DrawTextLine()* function in which the character used to construct the line is also passed as a parameter.

```
FUNCTION DrawTextLine (size, char$)
    REM *** Display size characters ***
    FOR c = 1 TO size
        PRINT char$;
    NEXT c
    REM *** Move cursor to next line ***
    PRINT
ENDFUNCTION
```

Notice that parameters are separated from each other by commas. We can tell that the second parameter is a string by the fact that its name ends with the dollar ($).

We have to supply two values when we call the function; one to be given to *size*, the other to *char$*. A typical call would be

```
DrawTextLine (20, "=")
```

which would assign the value 20 to *size* and the string "=" to *char$* and thereby produce a line on the screen created from twenty = symbols.

It's important that you put the values in the correct order when you call up the function. For example, the line

```
DrawTextLine ("=" ,20)
```

would be invalid since the function expects the first value given in the parentheses is the integer to be assigned to the *size* parameter.

Pre-conditions

When a function uses parameters, we will often need to restrict the range of values which may sensibly be assigned to the parameter. For example, when we specify what length of line we want *DrawTextLine()* to produce, it doesn't make sense to specify negative value for the parameter *size*. Equally, it makes little sense to request a line hundreds of characters long since there is a limit to how many characters can fit on a single line of the screen. We might therefore expect the value specified for *size* to be in a range such as 0 to 80.

When we place limitations on the conditions under which a function can operate successfully, these limitations are known as the **pre-conditions** of the function. We can therefore state that the pre-condition for *DrawTextLine()* is that *size* lies between 0 and 80.

Now we need some way of enforcing this limit. We do this by adding an IF statement at the beginning of the *DrawTextLine()* function which causes that function to be aborted if the value of size is outside the acceptable range.

The EXITFUNCTION Statement

The EXITFUNCTION statement is designed to be placed within a function. When executed, this statement causes the remaining statements in the function to be ignored, ending execution of the routine and returning to the code which called the function in the first place.

We can make use of this statement to terminate execution of a function when its parameter(s) fall outside an acceptable range. In the case of *DrawTextLine()*, we would add the following statement to check the value of *size:*

```
REM *** IF size outside range 0 to 80, terminate function ***
IF size < 0 OR size > 80
    EXITFUNCTION
ENDIF
```

The complete routine is now coded as

```
FUNCTION DrawTextLine(size, char$)
    REM *** IF size invalid, terminate function ***
    IF size < 0 OR size >80
        EXITFUNCTION
    ENDIF
    REM *** Display size characters ***
    FOR c = 1 TO size
        PRINT char$;
    NEXT c
    REM *** Move cursor to next line ***
    PRINT
ENDFUNCTION
```

Now, if we were to make a call to this function with a line such as

```
DrawTextLine (95, "-")
```

the function will abort since the value assigned to *size* will be outside the range 0 to 80, and no line will be drawn on the screen.

Return Types

Not only can we supply values to a function (in the form of parameters), but some functions also return results. For example, in the *SumIntegers()* function that we designed earlier, we actually limit the usefulness of the routine by displaying the result rather than returning it. After all, the main program may have wanted to use the answer in some calculation rather than have it displayed on the screen.

To return a value from a DarkBASIC Pro function we add the value to be returned immediately after the term ENDFUNCTION. A new version of *SumIntegers()* is shown below:

```
FUNCTION SumIntegers(number)
    total = 0
    FOR c = 1 TO number
        total = total + c
    NEXT c
ENDFUNCTION total
```

Notice that the pre-condition check has been removed from the function - more about that later.

When a function is designed to return a value, then the main program which calls that function will want to do something with the value that is returned. For example, we could still display the result of summing the numbers 1 to 10 by using the line:

```
PRINT SumIntegers(10)
```

This line causes the *SumIntegers()* function to be executed and then displays the value returned by the function.

We could store the value returned in a variable with a line such as:

```
ans = SumIntegers(10)
```

If required, we could use the returned value in a calculation:

```
result = SumIntegers (10) / 2
```

or in an IF statement:

```
IF SumIntegers(12) > 1000
```

Activity 7.13

Create a project called *testfact.dbpro* and in it write a function called *Factorial()* which takes a single integer parameter, *v*, and returns the values produced by multiplying every number between 1 and *v*. For example, if *v* had the value 5 then the value returned would be the result of the calculation 1x2x3x4x5.

Test the function to make sure it operates correctly.

If a function returns a string value, then the name of the function must end with a dollar sign. For example, the function *FilledString$(ch$, num)* returns a string containing *num* copies of *ch$*:

A function that returns a string is often referred to as a **string function**.

```
FUNCTION FilledString$ (ch$, num)
    result$ = ""
    FOR c = 1 TO num
        result$ = result$ + ch$
    NEXT c
ENDFUNCTION result$
```

Why was the pre-condition check for *SumIntegers()* removed? Well, by creating a return value, we introduced a problem. It is no longer sufficient to write

```
IF number < 1 OR number > 50
    EXITFUNCTION
```

because *SumIntegers()* is now designed to return a value, and it is no longer legal to exit that function without returning that value. This means that the EXITFUNCTION statement as shown above is no longer valid since it attempts to exit the return without returning a value. Luckily, the statement format allows for a value to be specified after the keyword EXITFUNCTION. But that just leaves us with another problem - what value should we return when the routine does not meet its pre-conditions?

We can return any value we like, but usually this is handled by returning some special value which cannot occur when the function's pre-conditions are met. For example, here we could return the value -1, since it is an impossible result to achieve when *number* does lie between 1 and 50. We would do this with the line:

```
EXITFUNCTION -1
```

This allows us to add back the pre-condition to our routine, the final version of the code being:

```
FUNCTION SumIntegers(number)
    IF number < 1 OR number > 50
        EXITFUNCTION -1
    total = 0
    FOR c = 1 TO number
        total = total + c
    NEXT c
ENDFUNCTION total
```

Activity 7.14

Modify your *Factorial()* function from the last Activity so that it implements the pre-condition that *v* must lie between 1 and 25.

When a function such as *SumIntegers()* (which returns a dummy result if its pre-condition has not been met) is called, you must check that it has performed correctly. This is done with code such as:

```
INPUT "Enter your number ", number
result = SumIntegers(number)
IF result = -1
    PRINT "The program could not calculate the sum 1 to ",number
ELSE
    PRINT "1 to ",number,"= ", result
ENDIF
```

Better still, the program should make sure the value passed is acceptable before making a call to *SumIntegers ()*. We could do this with the code:

```
INPUT "Enter your number ", number
WHILE number < 1 OR number > 50
    PRINT "Invalid number, must be between 1 and 50"
    INPUT "Re-enter number : ", number
ENDWHILE
result = SumIntegers(number)
```

We've introduced three new function-related statements in this section; the format of these are given in FIG-7.3, FIG-7.4 and FIG-7.5.

FIG-7.3

The FUNCTION
Statement

In the diagram:

function name	is the name of the function. The name chosen must conform to the rules of identifier name creation. If a string value is returned by the function, the name should end with a dollar symbol.

parameter		is the name of any value passed to the function. Names should be appropriate for the type of value being passed.

FIG-7.4

The ENDFUNCTION Statement

In the diagram:

return value		is the value returned by the function. This can be specified using a variable, constant or expression.

FIG-7.5

The EXITFUNCTION Statement

In the diagram:

return value		is the value returned by the function. This can be specified using a variable, constant or expression.

Local Variables

When you make use of a variable inside a function (other than a parameter), that variable exists only within that function. If you look at the code for *SumIntegers()* you'll see two variables which are used within the function: *c* and *total*. This type of variable is known as a **local variable**: it exists only while the function is being executed. Once the function has been executed, these local variables cease to exist. We can prove this with a little experiment shown in the code below:

```
REM *** The main program ***
num = 10
Test()
PRINT num
WAIT KEY
END

FUNCTION Test()
    num = 15
ENDFUNCTION
```

Function *Test()* assigns the value 15 to a variable called *num*. The main program assigns the value 10 to *num*, executes *Test()* and then displays the value in *num*. What value do you think appears on the screen?

Activity 7.15

Type in the code given above (*local.dbpro*) and check out what value is displayed on the screen.

There are in fact two variables called *num*. One of these exists only within *Test()* and, although it is assigned the value 15, that variable ceases to exist when *Test()* has been completed. When execution returns from the function back to the main program, we have come back to the part of the program where the other variable called *num* exists - and that variable still contains the value 10 as assigned to it.

The program doesn't have a problem with there being two variables of the same name: it's like having two students called John - as long as they are in different classes then there's no problem if the tutor calls on John he is obviously referring to the one in the class he is currently teaching.

There is no way to access the main program's variable called *num* from within *Test()* and there is no way to access *Test()*'s *num* from within the main program (although you could access it's value by returning *num* at the end of the function).

FIG-7.6 gives a visual representation of this situation.

FIG-7.6

Local Variables

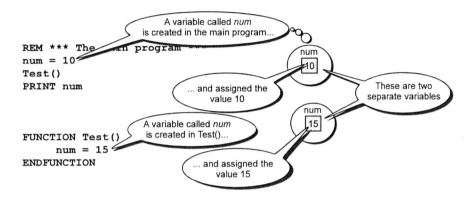

Global Variables

It is possible to make a variable available anywhere in a program by using the term GLOBAL when the variable is created. So, if we change the previous example to now read

```
REM *** The main program ***
GLOBAL num = 10
Test()
PRINT num
WAIT KEY
END

FUNCTION Test()
    num = 15
ENDFUNCTION
```

by declaring *num* as GLOBAL, it is no longer possible to create a local variable named *num*, and therefore the program lines

```
GLOBAL num = 10
num = 15
PRINT num
```

now all refer to the same variable.

Activity 7.16

Add the word GLOBAL to the appropriate line in your *local.dbpro* program and find out what difference this makes to the value displayed.

Designing Routines

In the real world we have to design routines before we can think of turning them into code. So far, we've been quite informal in how we've described a routine before going on to write it. However, any company involved in creating software will have a precise standard for designing routines. One possible design is given below using the *SumIntegers()* function as an example.

```
NAME              :    SumIntegers
PARAMETERS
   IN             :    num : integer
   OUT            :    result : integer
PRE-CONDITION     :    1 <= num <= 50
DESCRIPTION       :    The routine sets result to the sum of all integer values
                       between 1 and num.
OUTLINE LOGIC     :    Set result to zero
                       FOR c = 1 TO num DO
                           Add c to result
                       ENDFOR
```

This specification of a routine is often known as a **mini-spec**. Most of its contents should be self-explanatory. We start with the routine's name, followed by the parameters. Notice that the value returned by the routine is given as an OUT parameter.

The pre-condition specifies any limits imposed on an IN parameter. Here, for example, it states that *num* must lie between 1 and 50. If a routine is passed a value which does not meet the stated pre-condition, then the routine will fail to perform the task for which it is designed.

The Description explains in English *what* the routine should do, while the Outline Logic describes in structured English *how* the task should be done.

Specifying a Post-Condition

Some mini-specs make use of a **post-condition** statement which specifies what should be true when the routine has been successfully executed. For example, the pre-condition for *SumIntegers* would be:

POST-CONDITION : *result* = sum of the integer values between 1 and *num*.

Often a post-condition will be very similar to the description. When used, the post-condition statement follows immediately after the pre-condition statement.

The *DrawTextLine* Mini-Spec

Overleaf are the mini-specs for the first and last versions of *DrawTextLine()*.

```
NAME              :    DrawTextLine
PARAMETERS
   IN             :    None
   OUT            :    None
```

PRE-CONDITION	:	None
DESCRIPTION	:	The routine draws a horizontal line of 20 asterisks.
OUTLINE LOGIC	:	Display "********************"

NAME	:	DrawTextLine
PARAMETERS		
IN	:	*size* : integer
		ch : character
OUT	:	None
PRE-CONDITION	:	0<=*size*<=80
DESCRIPTION	:	The routine draws a horizontal line constructed from *size* occurrences of *ch*.
OUTLINE LOGIC	:	FOR *c* = 1 TO *size* DO
		Display *ch* (keep cursor on same line)
		ENDFOR
		Move cursor to start of next line

In the last example, notice that the second parameter does not contain a dollar sign as part of its name and that its type is declared as character, not string. This is because a design should be independent of the programming language that you finally use to implement that design. DarkBASIC Pro-specific requirements, such as ending string variable names with a dollar symbol, or reals with the hash character, having string functions end their name with a dollar sign, or using only integer, real and string types, should be avoided in your designs.

So, just what are you allowed to use in a design? Names (functions and variables) should conform to the following rules:

➢ Must begin with a letter

➢ Can continue with letter or numeric characters

Variable types can be any of the following:

➢ integer

➢ real

➢ string

➢ character   (a single character)

➢ Boolean   (a variable that is set to *true* or *false*)

Even the main section of the program should be designed in the form of a mini-spec. For example, in order to test the *DrawTextLine()* function, we could create a main program which implements the following specification:

NAME	:	Main
PARAMETERS		
IN	:	None
OUT	:	None
PRE-CONDITION	:	None
DESCRIPTION	:	The routine is designed to test *DrawTextLine()*. It allows the length and character making up the line

> to be entered from the keyboard and passes these as parameters when the *DrawTextLine()* is called. The program terminates when -99 is entered.

OUTLINE LOGIC :
```
REPEAT
    Get size
    Get character
    Call DrawTextLine(size, character)
UNTIL size = -99
```

The implementation of both the *DrawTextLine* and *Main* mini-specs is shown in LISTING-7.4.

LISTING-7.4

Displaying the Menu

```
REPEAT
    INPUT "Enter size of line (-99 to end) : ", size
    INPUT "Enter character used in line creation : ", ch$
    DrawTextLine(size,ch$)
UNTIL size = -99
END

REM *** Draw a line of characters ***
FUNCTION DrawTextLine(size, ch$)
    REM *** IF pre-condition not met THEN exit routine ***
    IF size < 0 OR size > 80
        EXITFUNCTION
    ENDIF
    REM *** Draw line ***
    FOR c = 1 TO size
        PRINT ch$;
    NEXT c
    REM *** Move cursor to start of next line ***
    PRINT
ENDFUNCTION
```

Activity 7.17

Write a DarkBASIC Pro function (in a project called *testsmallest.dbpro*) which implements the following design:

```
NAME            :   Smallest
PARAMETERS
    IN          :   no1 : integer
                    no2 : integer
                    no3 : integer
    OUT         :   result : integer
PRE-CONDITION :   None
DESCRIPTION   :   The routine sets result equal to the the smallest
                    of the values no1, no2, and no3.
                    IF all three values are the same, that value
                    should be returned in result.
OUTLINE LOGIC :   IF no1 < no2 AND no1 < no3 THEN
                        result := no1
                    ELSE
                        IF no2 < no1 AND no2 < no3 THEN
                            result := no2
                        ELSE
                            result := no3
                        ENDIF
                    ENDIF
```

Activity 7.18

Create a design for a main section to test function *Smallest()*.
Implement your design and use it to check that *Smallest()* functions correctly.

Creating Modular Software

Now that we know the basic techniques required to design and implement functions in DarkBASIC Pro, we're ready to rewrite the *shapes.dbpro* project that we produced in the last program. The original program is listed again below (see LISTING-7.5).

LISTING-7.5

The Original
shapes.dbpro Program

```
REM *** Display menu of possible shapes ***^
PRINT "Choose from the following shapes"
PRINT "1 - Pixel "
PRINT "2 - Line"
PRINT "3 - Box"
PRINT "4 - Circle"
PRINT "5 - Ellipse"

REM *** Get user's choice ***
INPUT "Enter option : ", choiceshape
WHILE choiceshape < 1 OR choiceshape > 5
    PRINT "That was an invalid choice. 1 to 5 only"
    INPUT "Enter option : ",choiceshape
ENDWHILE

REM *** Display possible colours ***
PRINT "Choose from the following colours"
PRINT "1 - Red"
PRINT "2 - Green"
PRINT "3 - Blue"
PRINT "4 - Yellow"
PRINT "5 - Cyan"
PRINT "6 - Magenta"

REM *** Get user's choice ***
INPUT "Enter option : ", choicecolour
WHILE choicecolour < 1 OR choicecolour > 6
    PRINT "That was an invalid choice. 1 to 6 only"
    INPUT "Enter option : ",choicecolour
ENDWHILE

REM *** Save foreground colour ***
SELECT choicecolour
    CASE 1
        foreground = RGB (255,0,0)
    ENDCASE
    CASE 2
        foreground = RGB (0,255,0)
    ENDCASE
    CASE 3
        foreground = RGB (0,0,255)
    ENDCASE
    CASE 4
        foreground = RGB (255,255,0)
    ENDCASE
    CASE 5
        foreground = RGB (0,255,255)
    ENDCASE
    CASE 6
        foreground = RGB (255, 0,255)
    ENDCASE
```

continued on next page

LISTING-7.5
(continued)

The Original
shapes.dbpro Program

```
ENDSELECT
REM *** Set foreground colour, clear screen and draw shape ***
INK foreground, 0
CLS
SELECT choiceshape
    CASE 1 '*** Pixel ***
        DOT 300,250
    ENDCASE
    CASE 2 '*** Line ***
        LINE 20,50, 300, 120
    ENDCASE
    CASE 3 '*** Rectangle ***
        BOX 20,50,300,150
    ENDCASE
    CASE 4 '*** Circle ***
        CIRCLE 300,250,50
    ENDCASE
    CASE 5 '*** Ellipse ***
        ELLIPSE 300,250,50,15
    ENDCASE
ENDSELECT
REM *** End program ***
WAIT KEY
END
```

Since the code is already divided into obvious sections, each doing a specific job, it's quite easy to see what functions are required. The mini-spec for each identified routine is shown below.

NAME	:	Main
PARAMETERS		
IN	:	None
OUT	:	None
PRE-CONDITION	:	None
DESCRIPTION	:	The program displays a selected shape in a specified colour. The user selects which shape is required. (pixel, line, rectangle, circle or ellipse) and the colour to be used (red, green, blue, yellow, cyan or magenta).
OUTLINE LOGIC	:	Display shapes menu
		Get user's choice
		Display colour menu
		Get user's choice
		Draw chosen shape

NAME	:	ShowShapeMenu
PARAMETERS		
IN	:	None
OUT	:	None
PRE-CONDITION	:	None
DESCRIPTION	:	The routine displays the option available to the user when choosing a shape to be displayed. The display should show the following options: 1 - Pixel; 2 - Line; 3 - Box; 4 - Circle; 5 - Ellipse
OUTLINE LOGIC	:	Display "1 - Pixel"
		Display "2 - Line"
		Display "3 - Box"
		Display "4 - Circle"
		Display "5 - Ellipse"

```
┌─────────────────────────────────────────────────────────────────────┐
│ NAME             :   GetUserChoice                                    │
│ PARAMETERS                                                            │
│     IN           :   max : integer                                    │
│     OUT          :   choice : integer                                 │
│ PRE-CONDITION    :   0<=max<=72                                       │
│ DESCRIPTION      :   The routine gets an integer value from the keyboard │
│                      which is returned in choice.                     │
│                      The value entered must lie between 1 and max     │
│                      otherwise an error message is displayed and the user │
│                      must re-enter the value.                         │
│ OUTLINE LOGIC    :   Display "Enter choice 1 - ",max                  │
│                      Get choice                                       │
│                      WHILE choice < 1 OR choice > max DO              │
│                          Display "That is an invalid choice. 1 to ",max," only" │
│                          Get choice                                   │
│                      ENDWHILE                                         │
└─────────────────────────────────────────────────────────────────────┘
```

Notice that the above specification is flexible enough to be used to get the user's choice of both shape and colour.

```
┌─────────────────────────────────────────────────────────────────────┐
│ NAME             :   ShowColourMenu                                   │
│ PARAMETERS                                                            │
│     IN           :   None                                             │
│     OUT          :   None                                             │
│ PRE-CONDITION    :   None                                             │
│ DESCRIPTION      :   The routine displays the option available to the user │
│                      when choosing the colour of the shape.           │
│                      The display should show the following options:   │
│                      1 - Red; 2 - Green; 3 - Blue; 4 - Yellow; 5 - Cyan; │
│                      6 - Magenta.                                     │
│ OUTLINE LOGIC    :   Display "1 - Red"                                │
│                      Display "2 - Green"                              │
│                      Display "3 - Blue"                               │
│                      Display "4 - Yellow"                             │
│                      Display "5 - Cyan"                               │
│                      Display "6 - Magenta""                           │
└─────────────────────────────────────────────────────────────────────┘
```

This specification for *ShowColourMenu* is similar to the one for *ShowShapeMenu*, but since the actual options offered differ between the two routines, we are forced to write separate mini-specs for each.

```
┌─────────────────────────────────────────────────────────────────────┐
│ NAME             :   SetInkColour                                     │
│ PARAMETERS                                                            │
│     IN           :   choice : integer                                 │
│     OUT          :   result : integer (colour value)                  │
│ PRE-CONDITION    :   1 <= choice <= 6                                 │
│ DESCRIPTION      :   The routine sets result to a colour value based on │
│                      choice. Settings are as follows:                 │
│                              choice      colour                       │
│                                1           red                        │
│                                2           green                      │
│                                3           blue                       │
└─────────────────────────────────────────────────────────────────────┘
```

		4	yellow
		5	cyan
		6	magenta
OUTLINE LOGIC	:	IF	
		choice = 1:	result := red
		choice = 2:	result := green
		choice = 3:	result := blue
		choice = 4:	result := yellow
		choice = 5:	result := cyan
		choice = 6:	result := magenta
		ENDIF	

NAME	:	DisplayChosenShape
PARAMETERS		
IN	:	choice : integer
		colour : integer
OUT	:	None
PRE-CONDITION	:	1 <= choice <= 5
DESCRIPTION	:	The routine displays the shape chosen by the user. The screen is cleared and the foreground colour set to *colour*.
		If *choice* is 1, a pixel is drawn at (300,250)
		If *choice* is 2, a line is drawn from (20,50) to (300,120)
		If *choice* is 3, a rectangle is drawn with top-left at (20,50) and bottom-right at (300,150)
		If *choice* is 4, a circle is drawn with its centre at (300,250). Its radius is 50.
		If *choice* is 5, an ellipse is drawn. Its centre is at (300,250). The horizontal radius is 50; the vertical radius, 15.
OUTLINE LOGIC	:	Set foreground colour to *colour*
		Clear the screen
		IF
		choice = 1: Draw pixel at (300,250)
		choice = 2: Draw line between points (20,50) and (300,120)
		choice = 3: Draw a rectangle between points (20,50) and (300,150)
		choice = 4: Draw a circle of radius 50 and centred at (300,250)
		choice = 5: Draw an ellipse with centre at (300,250). The horizontal radius is 50 and the vertical radius 15.
		ENDIF

Now we're ready to start turning our design into a program.

There are various ways to tackle this. If we had several people working on the program, we could give each a separate routine to work on at the same time. It would then just be a matter of bringing together the separate routines to give us the final program.

On the other hand, if only one person is working on the coding, the routines are coded one after another, usually starting with *Main*.

Top-Down Programming

When we code our routines one at a time, starting with *Main*, this is known as **top-down programming**. The name is used because we start with the main part of the program (the top) and then work our way through the routines called by that main part. We'll see how it's done below.

Step 1

We start by turning the outline logic given in the mini-spec for *Main* into DarkBASIC Pro program code. An important point to note is that the program code must match that logic in the mini-spec exactly. If we find we have to deviate from this logic then we must go back and modify the details given in that mini-spec. Actually, the code for *Main* becomes little more than a set of calls to the other routines:

```
Rem ***** Main Section *****
ShowShapeMenu()
shapeoption = GetUserOption(5)
ShowColourMenu()
colouroption = GetUserOption(6)
DisplayChosenShape(shapeoption,colouroption)

REM *** End program ***
WAIT KEY
END
```

Notice that *Main* really doesn't do any of the detailed work, it leaves that to the routines. *Main* only has to call up each of the routines in the correct order and save any values returned by one function to pass it on to another function. For example, it saves the user's choice of shape (in *shapeoption*) from *GetUserOption()* and then passes that value on to *DisplayChosenShape()*.

In order to write *Main* you need to know the names and purposes of the other routines as well as what parameters are passed and what values are returned from those routines. We should test our program, even at this early stage in its development, to ensure that the routines are executed in the correct order and that the proper parameters are passed between the routines. But there's a problem. The program can't run without the routines that *Main* is attempting to call. The compiler will simply complain about calls to non-existent routines.

Activity 7.19

Create a new project called *shapes2.dbpro*.

Type in *Main* as given above and attempt to compile it.

Step 2

To get *Main* to run we must write code for the routines that are called. And yet, if we do that, it would appear that the whole program will need to be completed before the program can be executed for the first time.

The way round this problem is to write empty routines with the required names, parameters and return values as shown below.

```
FUNCTION ShowShapeMenu()
    PRINT "DisplayShapesMenu"
ENDFUNCTION
FUNCTION GetUserOption(max)
    PRINT "GetUserOption"
ENDFUNCTION 1
FUNCTION ShowColourMenu()
    PRINT "DisplayColourMenu"
ENDFUNCTION
FUNCTION SetInkColour(choice)
    PRINT "SetInkColour"
    result = RGB(255,0,0)
ENDFUNCTION result
FUNCTION DisplayChosenShape(choice,colour)
    PRINT "DisplayChosenShape"
ENDFUNCTION
```

DarkBASIC Pro will not accept the line

`ENDFUNCTION RGB(255,0,0)`

and hence, the test stub for *SetInkColour()* has had an extra line added to set up a viable return value.

Take a moment to look at this code. Each function displays its own name, takes parameters, and returns a value where necessary. Again, we need to make sure that the names, parameter names and return types match with those given in the mini-specs. These empty routines are known as **test stubs**, and are written so that we can test *Main* without having the final code for any of the routines which *Main* has to call.

Activity 7.20

Add the stubs given above to your *shapes2.dbpro* project.

Attempt to run the program again.

Does it execute this time?

Step 3

Now we can begin to remove the stubs in our project and replace them with the final version of each routine, always testing as each new routine is added to make sure the new routine, and the program as a whole, are working correctly.

Activity 7.21

We have already written the *ShowShapeMenu()* function.

Replace the stub for this routine with its full code.

Run the program again and check that the appropriate menu is displayed on the screen.

The code for *GetUserOption()* is:

```
FUNCTION GetUserOption (max)
    INPUT "Enter option : ",choice
    WHILE choice < 1 OR choice > max
        PRINT "That was an invalid choice. 1 to ",max," only"
        INPUT "Enter option : ",choice
    ENDWHILE
ENDFUNCTION choice
```

Bottom-Up Programming

If you're working as part of a team of programmers, then you're likely to get landed with having to code a specific routine which, when completed, will be handed over to the team leader. He will then add your routine to the main program.

So let's assume we've just been landed with the job of writing the *GetUserOption()* function. How do we go about doing this job? Well, it's just a matter of getting hold of the mini-spec for the routine and turning it into a coded function. In the case of *GetUserOption()* we should end up with the following code:

```
FUNCTION GetUserOption(max)
    INPUT "Enter option : ", choice
    WHILE choice < 1 OR choice > max
        PRINT "That was an invalid choice. 1 to ",max," only."
        INPUT "Enter option : ", choice
    ENDWHILE
ENDFUNCTION choice
```

Although we might be tempted to think our job is done at this point, we really need to check that our routine is operating correctly. It won't do your reputation as a programmer any good if you hand over code which contains obvious faults.

To test a routine, we start by making sure that what we've written conforms to the requirements of the mini-spec. Once we're happy with that, then the code itself must be tested. Since a function only executes when called by another piece of code, we need to write a main program which will call up the function we want to test. This main program, known as a **test driver**, needs to perform four main tasks:

➢ Supply a value for any parameters required by the function

➢ Execute the function

➢ Display the value of any parameters passed to the function

➢ Display any value returned by the function

So, our test driver for *GetUserOption()* could be coded as follows:

```
DO
    REM *** Get a value for parameter ***
    INPUT "Enter a value for max : ",max
    REM *** IF -1 entered, exit loop ***
    IF max = -1
        EXIT
    ENDIF
    REM *** Call function being tested ***
    returnedvalue = GetUserOption(max)
    REM *** Display function parameters ***
    PRINT "max = ",max
```

```
                    REM *** Display value returned ***
                    PRINT "Value returned by GetUserOption() = ",returnedvalue
              LOOP
              REM *** End program ***
              WAIT KEY
              END
```

Notice that the main code is in a loop so that several tests can be carried out in a single run.

Activity 7.24

Create a new project (*bottomup.dbpro*) and type in the code for *GetUserOption()* and its test driver as given above.

Run the program and check that *GetUserOption()* is returning the expected results.

Structure Diagrams

As we begin to develop more complex programs containing several routines, it can be useful to retain an overview of the program's structure, showing which routine is called by which, and the values that pass between them. This is done with a **structure diagram**.

FIG-7.7

A Graphical Representation of the Routines in the System

A structure diagram contains one rectangle for each routine in a program, including a rectangle representing Main. These rectangles contain the name of the routine they represent. The collection of rectangles for the *shapes2.dbpro* project is shown in FIG-7.7.

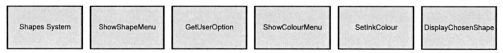

Only *Main* has been renamed, with a new title to reflect the overall purpose of the system.

The rectangles are now set in a series of levels, with *Shapes System* (the renamed *Main*) at the top. On the second level are routines called by *Shapes System*. On the third level are any routines called by second level routines. In addition, lines are drawn between the rectangles to reflect which routine calls which (see FIG-7.8).

FIG-7.8

The Calling Hierarchy of the Routines

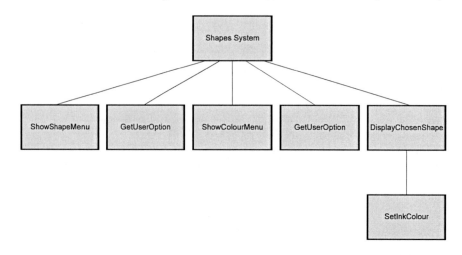

For example, from the diagram we can see that *DisplayChosenShape* calls the routine *SetInkColour*.

Another point to note is that *GetUserOption* has been included twice. This is because that routine is used to get two different items of data: on its first call it returns the choice of shape, on the second call, the choice of colour.

Finally, we add any parameters passed between the routines (see FIG-7.9).

FIG-7.9

The Complete
Structure Diagram
Showing Parameters

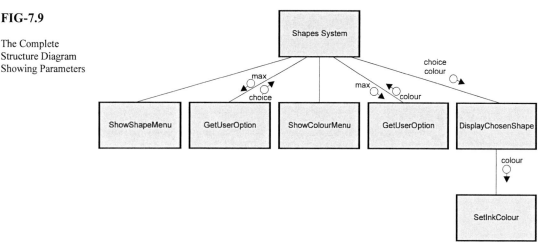

The circle with arrowed line symbol in the diagram is used to show the direction in which data is passed, with IN values pointing towards a routine and OUT parameters pointing away from the routine.

Summary

- Good programming technique requires program code to be partitioned into routines.

- Each routine should perform a single task.

- A routine's name should reflect the purpose of that routine.

- Mini-specs should be produced when designing a routine.

- A mini-spec should include the name of the routine, its parameters, restrictions of the range of values a parameter may take, a detailed description of the routine's purpose, and an outline logic specifying how the routine is to operate.

- A mini-spec may contain a post-condition which states what should be true once the routine has been successfully executed.

- Where possible, a routine should be made as flexible as possible so that it can be used in situations which differ slightly from the original requirement.

- DarkBASIC Pro allows us to write routines using the FUNCTION keyword.

- A function is executed by specifying the function name followed by parentheses.

- Values may be passed to a function as parameters.

- Where the value of a parameter must fall within a limited range, this restriction should be tested for at the start of the function.

- Variables used within a function are normally local to that function.

- The term GLOBAL can be used to create a variable which can be accessed anywhere within a program.

- Top-down programming begins by coding the main routine.

- Top-down programming using stubs in place of completed routines.

- Bottom-up programming starts by coding individual routines.

- Bottom-up programming uses test drivers to check that completed routines are operating correctly.

- A structure diagram shows every routine in a program, how they are called, and the values that pass between them.

Subroutines

Introduction

Using functions is probably the best way to create modular software in DarkBASIC Pro, but the language does offer another way to achieve a similar effect, and that is to use subroutines. Although we've used the term subroutine earlier to mean any modular section of code, in DarkBASIC Pro the word has a more specific meaning as we'll see below.

Creating a Subroutine

The fact that we are going to use DarkBASIC Pro subroutines rather than functions makes no difference to the design stage of a project - we still need to create mini-specs identical to those shown earlier. But when we come to implement these designs in DarkBASIC Pro, we will use subroutines instead of functions.

The start of a subroutine is marked with a label giving the name of the subroutine. This will be the name given in the mini-spec.

A label is just a valid name followed by a colon, for example:

```
ShowShapeMenu:
```

Next comes the code of the routine:

```
ShowShapeMenu:
    PRINT "Choose from the following shapes"^
    PRINT "1 - Pixel "
    PRINT "2 - Line"
    PRINT "3 - Box"
    PRINT "4 - Circle"
    PRINT "5 - Ellipse"
```

Finally, we end with the keyword RETURN:

```
ShowShapeMenu:
    PRINT "Choose from the following shapes"^
    PRINT "1 - Pixel "
    PRINT "2 - Line"
    PRINT "3 - Box"
    PRINT "4 - Circle"
    PRINT "5 - Ellipse"
RETURN
```

The overall structure is shown in FIG-7.10.

FIG-7.10

The Subroutine Construct

Calling a Subroutine

The GOSUB Statement

To execute a subroutine we use the GOSUB statement (the term being a shortening of *GO to SUBroutine*). This statement has the format shown in FIG-7.11.

FIG-7.11

The GOSUB Statement

In the diagram:

> *label*   is the label name previously assigned to the subroutine which is to be executed.

For example, the statement

```
GOSUB ShowShapesMenu
```

would cause the subroutine labelled *ShowShapesMenu* to be executed.

When the execution reaches the RETURN statement, the program jumps back from the subroutine and continues by executing the line following the call to the subroutine.

Activity 7.25

Create a project called *subroutines.dbpro* containing the *ShowShapesMenu* subroutine as given earlier.

At the start of the program add the following lines:

```
REM *** Call subroutine ***
GOSUB ShowShapesMenu
REM *** End program ***
WAIT KEY
END
```

Run the program and check that the subroutine is correctly executed.

Subroutines are quite restricting since they cannot accept parameters nor return a value.

This means that a routine such as *GetUserChoice* which has both an IN parameter and a return value (OUT parameter) cannot be coded efficiently using a subroutine.

Variables in a Subroutine

Also, it is not possible to create local variables within a subroutine. When variables of the same name are used in both the main program and a subroutine, these are assumed be one and the same variable.

Activity 7.26

Create a new project (*subvariables.dbpro*) and enter the following code:

```
REM *** The main program ***
num = 10
GOSUB Test
PRINT num
WAIT KEY
END


REM *** Subroutine ***
Test:
    num = 15
RETURN
```

Execute the program and check out what value is displayed on the screen.

As a general rule, it is best to avoid the use of DarkBASIC Pro's subroutines and stick with functions since they offer a much greater flexibility.

Summary

- Subroutines are a group of instructions which begin with a label and end with the term RETURN.

- A subroutine is called using the term GOSUB.

- A subroutine cannot accept parameters.

- A subroutine cannot return a value.

- A subroutine cannot contain local variables.

Solutions

Activity 7.1

No solution required.

Activity 7.2

No solution required.

Activity 7.3

This time the message appears after the function has been executed.

Activity 7.4

No solution required.

Activity 7.5

```
REM *** Call function ***
DrawTextBox()
REM *** End program ***
WAIT KEY
END
REM *** Draw box of asterisks ***
FUNCTION DrawTextBox()
    PRINT "*****"
    PRINT "*****"
    PRINT "*****"
    PRINT "*****"
    PRINT "*****"
ENDFUNCTION
```

Activity 7.6

Line above and below text:

```
REM *** Execute function ***
DrawTextLine()
REM *** Display a message ***
PRINT "    Hello"
REM *** Execute function again ***
DrawTextLine()
REM *** End program ***
WAIT KEY
END

REM *** Draw a line of asterisks ***
FUNCTION DrawTextLine()
    PRINT "************************"
ENDFUNCTION
```

Line above and two lines below text:

```
REM *** Execute function ***
DrawTextLine()
REM *** Display a message ***
PRINT "    Hello"
REM *** Execute function again ***
DrawTextLine()
DrawTextLine()
REM *** End program ***
WAIT KEY
END

REM *** Draw a line of asterisks ***
FUNCTION DrawTextLine()
    PRINT "************************"
ENDFUNCTION
```

Activity 7.7

```
REM *** Execute function ***
DrawTextLine(5)
REM *** Display a message ***
PRINT "    Hello"
REM *** Execute function again ***
DrawTextLine(15)
DrawTextLine(15)
REM *** End program ***
WAIT KEY
END

REM *** Draw a line of asterisks ***
FUNCTION DrawTextLine(size)
    FOR c = 1 TO size
        PRINT "*";
    NEXT c
    PRINT
ENDFUNCTION
```

Activity 7.8

```
REM *** Get value from user ***
INPUT "Enter number : ", num
REM *** Call function using value input ***
DrawTextBox(num)
REM *** End program ***
WAIT KEY
END

REM *** Draw box of asterisks ***
FUNCTION DrawTextBox(height)
    FOR c = 1 TO height
        PRINT "*****"
    NEXT c
ENDFUNCTION
```

Activity 7.9

```
REM *** Get values from user ***
INPUT "Enter number : ", num
INPUT "Enter character : ", c$
REM *** Call function; use values input ***
DrawTextBox(num,c$)
REM *** End program ***
WAIT KEY
END
REM *** Draw box of characters ***
FUNCTION DrawTextBox(height,ch$)
    FOR c = 1 TO height
        FOR k = 1 TO 5
            PRINT ch$;
        NEXT k
        PRINT
    NEXT c
ENDFUNCTION
```

Activity 7.10

```
Rem ***** Main Source File *****
INPUT "Enter size : ", sz
REM *** Execute function ***
DrawTextLine(sz)
REM *** Display a message ***
PRINT "    Hello"
REM *** Execute function again ***
DrawTextLine(sz)
DrawTextLine(sz)
REM *** End program ***
WAIT KEY
END
```

```
REM *** Draw a line of asterisks ***
FUNCTION DrawTextLine(size)
   IF size < 0 OR size > 80
      EXITFUNCTION
   ENDIF
   FOR c = 1 TO size
      PRINT "*";
   NEXT c
   PRINT
ENDFUNCTION
```

Activity 7.11

```
REM *** Get values from user ***
INPUT "Enter number : ", num
INPUT "Enter character : ", c$
REM *** Call function using values input ***
DrawTextBox(num,c$)
REM *** End program ***
WAIT KEY
END

REM *** Draw box of characters ***
FUNCTION DrawTextBox(height,ch$)
   IF height < 0 OR height > 24
      EXITFUNCTION
   ENDIF
   FOR c = 1 TO height
      FOR k = 1 TO 5
         PRINT ch$;
      NEXT k
      PRINT
   NEXT c
ENDFUNCTION
```

Activity 7.12

```
REM *** Read in a number ***
INPUT "Enter a value : ", value
REM *** Continue while number not zero ***
WHILE value <> 0
   REM *** Execute function ***
   SumIntegers(value)
   REM *** Get another number ***
   INPUT "Enter a value : ", value
ENDWHILE
REM *** End program ***
WAIT KEY
END

REM *** Sum values between 1 and number ***
FUNCTION SumIntegers(number)
   REM *** IF pre-cond not met, exit ***
   IF number < 1 OR number > 50
      EXITFUNCTION
   ENDIF
   REM *** Start sum at zero ***
   total = 0
   REM *** FOR all values 1 to number DO ***
   FOR c = 1 TO number
      REM *** Add that number to sum ***
      total = total + c
   NEXT c
   REM *** Display sum ***
   PRINT total
ENDFUNCTION
```

Activity 7.13

```
REM *** Get a value ***
INPUT "Enter a value : ", num
REM *** Call function and display result ***
PRINT "The product of the numbers 1 to ",
num," is ",Factorial(num)
REM *** End program ***
```

```
WAIT KEY
END

REM *** Calculate product of 1 to v ***
FUNCTION Factorial(v)
   REM *** Start product at 1 ***
   product = 1
   REM *** FOR all values  1 to v DO ***
   FOR c = 1 TO v
      REM *** Multiply product by value ***
      product = product * c
   NEXT c
ENDFUNCTION product
```

Activity 7.14

```
INPUT "Enter a value : ", num
REM *** Call function and display result ***
PRINT "The product of the numbers 1 to ",
num," is ",Factorial(num)
REM *** End program ***
WAIT KEY
END

REM *** Calculate product of 1 to v ***
FUNCTION Factorial(v)
   IF v < 1 OR v > 25
      EXITFUNCTION -1
   ENDIF
   REM *** Start product at 1 ***
   product = 1
   REM *** FOR all values 1 to v DO ***
   FOR c = 1 TO v
      REM *** Multiple product by that
value ***
      product = product * c
   NEXT c
ENDFUNCTION product
```

Activity 7.15

The value 10 is displayed.

Activity 7.16

The value displayed is 15.

The function is now accessing the same variable (*num*) as the main program.

Activity 7.17

```
REM *** Find smallest of three values ***
FUNCTION Smallest(no1,no2,no3)
   IF no1 < no2 AND no1 < no3
      result = no1
   ELSE
      IF no2 < no1 AND no2 < no3
         result = no2
      ELSE
         result = no3
      ENDIF
   ENDIF
ENDFUNCTION result
```

Activity 7.18

The main section uses a WHILE loop to allow as many tests of the function as required. The program stops if -99 is entered as the first of the three values.

```
REM *** Get three numbers ***
INPUT "Enter first number : ", n1
WHILE n1 <> -99
  INPUT "Enter second number : ", n2
  INPUT "Enter third number : ", n3
  REM *** Call function & display result ***
  PRINT "The smallest value is "
  ,Smallest(n1,n2,n3)
  REM *** Read first number again ***
  INPUT "Enter first number : ",n1
ENDWHILE
REM *** End program ***
WAIT KEY
END

REM *** Find smallest of three values ***
FUNCTION Smallest(no1,no2,no3)
  IF no1 < no2 AND no1 < no3
    result = no1
  ELSE
    IF no2 < no1 AND no2 < no3
        result = no2
    ELSE
        result = no3
    ENDIF
  ENDIF
ENDFUNCTION result
```

Activity 7.19

The program will not run since the functions it calls have not yet been written.

Activity 7.20

The program will now execute.

The PRINT statement in every function causes the name of each routine called to be displayed on the screen.

Activity 7.21

The *ShowShapeMenu()* function now displays the list of user options on the screen.

Activity 7.22

No solution required.

Activity 7.23

The complete solution is given below:

```
REM *** Main program ***
ShowShapeMenu()
shapeoption = GetUserOption(5)
ShowColourMenu()
colouroption = GetUserOption(6)
DisplayChosenShape(shapeoption,colouroption)
REM *** End program ***
WAIT KEY
END

REM *** Display menu of possible shapes ***
FUNCTION ShowShapeMenu()
  PRINT "Choose from the following shapes"
  PRINT "1 - Pixel "
  PRINT "2 - Line"
  PRINT "3 - Box"
  PRINT "4 - Circle"
  PRINT "5 - Ellipse"
ENDFUNCTION
```

```
REM *** Get user's choice ***
FUNCTION GetUserOption(max)
  INPUT "Enter option : ", choice
  WHILE choice < 1 OR choice > max
    PRINT "That was an invalid choice.
    1 to ",max," only"
    INPUT "Enter option : ",choice
  ENDWHILE
ENDFUNCTION choice

REM *** Display possible colours ***
FUNCTION ShowColourMenu()
  PRINT "Choose from the following
    colours"
  PRINT "1 - Red"
  PRINT "2 - Green"
  PRINT "3 - Blue"
  PRINT "4 - Yellow"
  PRINT "5 - Cyan"
  PRINT "6 - Magenta"
ENDFUNCTION

REM *** Draw shape in selected colour***
FUNCTION DisplayChosenShape(choice, colour)
  INK SetInkColour(colour),0
  CLS
  SELECT choice
    CASE 1 '*** Pixel ***
      DOT 300,250
    ENDCASE
    CASE 2 '*** Line ***
      LINE 20,50,300,120
    ENDCASE
    CASE 3 '*** Rectangle ***
      BOX 20,50,300,150
    ENDCASE
    CASE 4 '*** Circle ***
      CIRCLE 300,250,50
    ENDCASE
    CASE 5 '*** Ellipse ***
      ELLIPSE 300,250,50,15
    ENDCASE
  ENDSELECT
ENDFUNCTION

REM *** Change to selected colour ***
FUNCTION SetInkColour(choice)
  SELECT choice
    CASE 1
      result = RGB (255,0,0)
    ENDCASE
    CASE 2
      result = RGB (0,255,0)
    ENDCASE
    CASE 3
      result = RGB (0,0,255)
    ENDCASE
    CASE 4
      result = RGB (255,255,0)
    ENDCASE
    CASE 5
      result = RGB (0,255,255)
    ENDCASE
    CASE 6
      result = RGB (255, 0,255)
    ENDCASE
  ENDSELECT
ENDFUNCTION result
```

Activity 7.24

```
REM *** Test driver ***
DO
  REM *** Get a value for parameter ***
  INPUT "Enter a value for max : ",max
  IF max = -1
```

```
        EXIT
      ENDIF
      REM *** Call function being tested ***
      returnedvalue = GetUserOption(max)
      REM *** Display function parameters ***
      PRINT "max = ",max
      REM *** Display value returned ***
      PRINT "Value returned by GetUserOption() = ",
      returnedvalue
   LOOP
   REM *** End program ***
   WAIT KEY
   END

   FUNCTION GetUserOption(max)
      INPUT "Enter option : " ,choice
      WHILE choice < 1 OR choice > max
         PRINT "That was an invalid choice. 1 to ",
         max," only"
         INPUT "Enter option : ",choice
      ENDWHILE
   ENDFUNCTION choice
```

Activity 7.25

No solution required.

Activity 7.26

The value 15 is displayed. This is because the *num* referred to in the
main program and *num* in the subroutine are the same variable.

String Functions

Creating a Library of Functions

Including Existing Code in a New Project

String Handling Functions Native to DarkBASIC Pro

User-Defined String-Handling Functions

Standard String Functions

Introduction

Unlike numeric variables which hold only a single value, strings can hold a whole collection of characters, perhaps several words or even sentences. For example, it's quite valid to write:

```
poem$ = "Mary had a little lamb"
```

Because a string can contain so many characters, there are several operations that programmers find themselves needing to do with strings. For example, we might want to find out how many characters are in the string, convert a string to uppercase, or extract part of a string.

DarkBASIC Pro contains many statements to help us perform some of these tasks, as we shall see in the following pages.

String Operations

The LEN Statement

The LEN statement is a function which returns the number of characters in a string. The string to be examined is given in parentheses. For example, the expression

```
LEN("Hello")
```

would return the value 5 since there are 5 characters in the word *Hello*.

The LEN statement has the format shown in FIG-8.1.

FIG-8.1

The LEN Statement

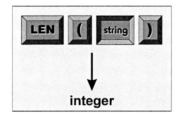

In the diagram:

string   is a string constant, string variable, or string expression.

As with any function that returns a value, this value can be displayed, assigned to a variable, or used in an expression. Hence each of the following lines are valid:

```
PRINT LEN("Hello")         'displays 5
result = LEN("Hello")      'sets result equal to 5
ans = LEN("Hello") *3      'sets ans to 15 (5 x 3)
IF LEN("Hello") > 3        'condition is true since 5 > 3
```

Of course, it's much more likely that you'll use a string variable as an argument rather than a string constant. For example, the code

```
INPUT "Enter your name : ",name$
PRINT "There are ",LEN(name$), " characters in your name."
```

uses the variable *name$* as the argument to LEN().

Activity 8.1

Create a project (*stringlength.dbpro*) containing the two lines given above and
test out the program.

Activity 8.2

Write a project (*comparelengths.dbpro*) which reads in two strings and
displays the shorter of the two.

The UPPER$ Statement

The UPPER$ statement takes a string argument and returns the uppercase version
of that string. Notice that the statement name ends with a dollar sign ($). This is an
indication that the statement returns a string and not the more usual integer.

```
PRINT UPPER$ ("Hello")
```

would display the word *HELLO*.

Any characters in the string that are not letters are returned unchanged by this
statement. Hence,

```
PRINT UPPER$("abc123")
```

would display *ABC123*.

As in all of these statements in this section, the argument can be a string constant,
variable or expression. The value returned by the function can be stored in a string
variable.

Activity 8.3

What value would be stored in *b$* after the following statements are executed?

```
a$ = "1-by-1"
b$ = UPPER$(a$)
```

The UPPER$ statement has the format shown in FIG-8.2.

FIG-8.2

The UPPER$ Statement

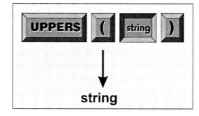

In the diagram:

    string   is any string value.

The LOWER$ Statement

The LOWER$ statement takes a string argument and returns the lowercase version of that string. Any non-alphabetic characters in the string are returned unchanged.

```
PRINT LOWER$(" Hello")
```

would display the word *hello*.

This statement has the format shown in FIG-8.3.

FIG-8.3

The LOWER$ Statement

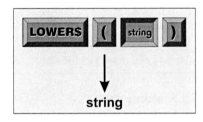

string

In the diagram:

    string   is any string value.

The LEFT$ Statement

It's possible to extract the left section of a string using the LEFT$ statement. This time you need to include two parameters: the first is the string itself, and the second is the number of characters you want to extract. For example,

```
PRINT LEFT$ ("abcdef" , 2)
```

would display *ab* on the screen, LEFT$ having returned the left two characters from the string *abcdef*.

If the number given is larger than the number of characters in the string as in

```
ans$ = LEFT$("abcdef",10)
```

then the complete string is returned (i.e. *abcdef*)

Should a zero, or negative value be given as in

```
result$ = LEFT$("abcdef",0)
```

then the returned string contains no characters. That is, *result$* will hold an empty string.

The LEFT$ statement has the format shown in FIG-8.4.

FIG-8.4

The LEFT$ Statement

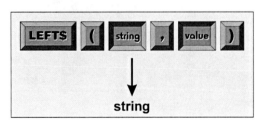

string

In the diagram:

string   is any string value.

value   is a positive integer value in the range 1 to the
                            number of characters in *string*.

The RIGHT$ Statement

If we want to extract the right-hand part of a string we can use the RIGHT$
statement. For example, the statement

```
PRINT RIGHT$("abcdef",2)
```

would display *ef* on the screen.

The statement has the format shown in FIG-8.5.

FIG-8.5

The RIGHT$ Statement

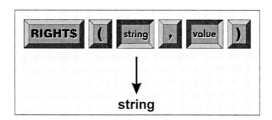

In the diagram:

string   is any string value.

value   is a positive integer value in the range 1 to the
                            number of characters in *string*.

The MID$ Statement

This statement extracts only one character from the specified string. The position
of the character to be extracted is given as the second argument to the function. For
example, the statement

```
letter$ = MID$("abcdef",4)
```

would place the value *d* in *letter$*.

We can use this statement to access each character in a string. For example, the code
snippet

```
INPUT "Enter a word : ",word$
FOR c = 1 TO LEN(word$)
    PRINT MID$ (word$,c)
NEXT c
```

will display each character of the string stored in *word$* on a separate line.

The format for this statement is given in FIG-8.6.

FIG-8.6

The MID$ Statement

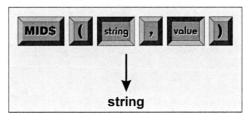

In the diagram:

string	is any string value.
value	is a positive integer value in the range 1 to the number of characters in *string*.

The ASC Statement

This statement returns an integer value representing the ASCII value of the first character in the string supplied. A typical statement such as

```
PRINT ASC("ABC")
```

would display the value 65 since this is the ASCII code for a capital A. Using this function on an empty string as in the line

```
result = ASC("")
```

returns the value zero.

The format for this statement is given in FIG-8.7.

FIG-8.7

The ASC Statement

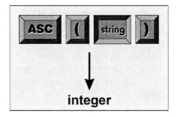

In the diagram:

string	is any string value, but only the first character is used by the function.

The CHR$ Statement

The CHR$ statement complements the ASC function by returning the character whose ASCII code matches the specified value. For example, the line

```
PRINT CHR$(65)
```

would display the capital letter A since the ASCII code for a capital A is 65.

The value given should lie between 0 and 127. However, only characters with an ASCII code of 32 to 126 are displayable; other values are used for various control purposes and attempting to display such values has no visible effect in DarkBASIC Pro.

We could display all the letters of the alphabet using the lines

Alternatively.

```
FOR c = 65 TO 90
   PRINT CHR$(c)
NEXT c
```

```
FOR c = 1 TO 26
   PRINT CHR$(64+c)
NEXT c
```

The format for this statement is given in FIG-8.8.

FIG-8.8

The CHR$ Statement

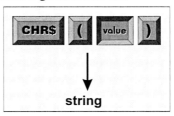

string

In the diagram:

> *value* is an integer value. This value must be between 0 and 255, but is more likely to be between 32 and 126, these being the ASCII range of values for all displayable characters.

Activity 8.5

Create a project (*ASCIITable*) which displays the numbers 32 to 126 beside the corresponding ASCII character.

The STR$ Statement

The STR$ statement takes an integer argument and returns a string containing the same digits as the integer argument. For example, the line

```
result$ = STR$(123)
```

will store the string *123* in the variable *result$*. This statement has the format shown in FIG-8.9.

FIG-8.9

The STR$ Statement

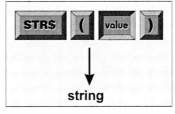

string

In the diagram:

value   is any integer value.

Activity 8.6

Write a project (*countdigits.dbpro*) which reads in a number and displays how
many zeros are in the number.

(HINT: Change the number into a string and examine each character to check
if it's a zero.)

In fact, the STR$ does accept real values, but because of rounding errors, the string
returned will be inaccurate.

The VAL Statement

This statement takes a string argument and returns the integer equivalent. The string
must contain only numeric characters. For example,

```
result = VAL("123")
```

Strings containing real values can also be converted, but again you'll have problems
with rounding errors. So the line

```
ans = VAL("123.45")
```

gives *ans* a value of 123.449996948 when displayed.

The VAL statement has the format shown in FIG-8.10.

FIG-8.10

The VAL Statement

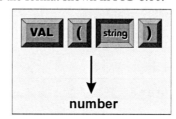

In the diagram:

string   is a string containing only numeric characters, a
                             decimal point, or a sign (+ or -).

The value returned depends on the nature of the string: if no decimal point is
included an integer value is returned, otherwise a real value is returned.

If the string contains a mixture of numeric and non-numeric characters, the value
returned is constructed from all numeric characters preceding the first non-numeric
character. For example,

```
VAL("12ABC3")
```

returns the value 12.

If the string starts with a non-numeric character (other than a sign or decimal point)
then the function returns zero.

The SPACE$ Statement

Although it is easy enough to create a string full of spaces with a line such as

```
text$ = "                              "
```

if you want an exact number of spaces in your string, then it's easier to use the SPACE$ function which returns a string containing a specified number of spaces.

```
text$ = SPACE$(23)
```

assigns a string containing 23 spaces to the variable *text$*. The format for this statement is shown in FIG-8.11.

FIG-8.11

The SPACE$ Statement

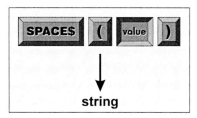

In the diagram:

value   is a positive integer which specifies the number of spaces in the string returned by the function.

The BIN$ Statement

As you know, the computer uses the binary number system when storing programs and data. If you'd like to see what a specific integer value looks like in binary, this function will do the job for you. It returns a 32 character string showing the binary representation of a specified integer value. For example, the instruction

```
binary$ = BIN$(65)
```

would assign the string *%00000000000000000000000001000001* (the binary equivalent of 65 stored over 32 bits) to the variable *binary$*. The percent sign at the start of the string is how DarkBASIC Pro signifies a binary number.

2's complement is the term used to describe how the computer stores negative numbers.

If a negative value is used, the string returned is in **2's complement** form. This means that the instruction

```
PRINT BIN$(-15)
```

would display the string *%11111111111111111111111111110001*. The format for this function is shown in FIG-8.12.

FIG-8.12

The BIN$ Statement

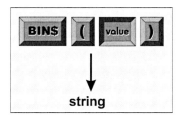

In the diagram:

value   is an integer value.

The HEX$ Statement

Another widely used number system is hexadecimal which uses the letters A to F to represent values 10 to 15. The HEX$ function returns an 8 character string containing the hexadecimal equivalent of a specified integer value. For example,

```
hexadecimal$ = HEX$(65)
```

assigns the string *41* to the variable *hexadecimal$*.

For negative values, the hexadecimal string returned is the equivalent of the 2's complement form. Therefore,

```
PRINT HEX$(-15)
```

displays the string *FFFFFFF1*.

The format of this function is shown in FIG-8.13.

FIG-8.13

The HEX$ Statement

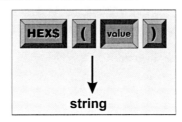

In the diagram:

value   is an integer value.

Activity 8.7

Write a program (*Conversions*) which reads in an integer value and displays its equivalent binary and hexadecimal value.

Summary

- The LEN() function returns the number of characters in a specified string.

- The UPPER$() function returns the uppercase equivalent of a specified string.

- The LOWER$() function returns the lowercase equivalent of a specified string.

- The LEFT$() function returns a left-hand sub-string from a specified string.

- The RIGHT$() function returns a right-hand sub-string from a specified string.

- The MID$() function returns a single character from a given position in a specified string.

- The ASC() function returns the ASCII code of a specified character.

- The CHR$() function returns the character whose ASCII code matches a specified value.

- The STR$() function returns the string equivalent of a specified number.

- The VAL() function returns the numeric equivalent of a specified string.

- The SPACE$() function returns a string containing a specified number of spaces.

- The BIN$() function returns a string representing the binary equivalent of a specified integer.

- The HEX$() function returns a string representing the hexadecimal equivalent of a specified integer.

User-Defined String Functions

Introduction

There are several more operations which would be useful to have when manipulating strings, and, although DarkBASIC Pro does not contain commands to perform these operations, we can easily write them ourselves. Some of these are described below.

Creating New String Functions

The Pos() Function

The *Pos()* function returns the position of a specified character in a specified string.

```
place = Pos("abcd","c")
```

would assign the value 3 to *place*, since *c* occurs at position 3 in the string *abcd*.

If the character being searched for occurs more than once in the string, then it is the position of the first occurrence that is returned. Hence,

```
Pos("abcdc","c")
```

would return the value 3.

If the character being searched for does not occur within the string, then a value of -1 is returned.

The code for this function is shown in LISTING-8.1.

LISTING-8.1

Using the *Pos()* Function

```
FUNCTION Pos(s$, c$)
   REM *** result stays at -1 if no match found ***
   result = -1
   REM *** Make sure we're looking for a single character ***
   first$ = MID$(c$,1)

   REM *** FOR each character in s$ DO ***
   FOR c = 1 TO LEN(s$)
      REM *** IF that character matches what we're after THEN ***
      IF MID$(s$,c) = first$
         REM *** set result to this position and exit loop ***
         result = c
         EXIT
      ENDIF
   NEXT c
ENDFUNCTION result
```

Because DarkBASIC Pro only allows string variables, we cannot be sure that when the function *Pos()* is called, the second argument contains only a single character. For example, the line

```
result$ = Pos("abcdef","ei")
```

would be valid, even though there is more than one character in the second parameter. But by including the line

```
                    first$ = MID$(c$,1)
```

in *Pos()*, we extract the first character from *c$*. It is this first character that we then search for in *s$*.

The Occurs() Function

The *Occurs()* function returns how often a specified character appears within a specified string. Hence, the expression

```
Occurs("abcdc","c")
```

would return 2 since *c* occurs twice within *abcdc*.

The code for this function is shown in LISTING-8.2.

LISTING-8.2

The *Occurs()* Function

```
FUNCTION Occurs(s$,c$)
   REM *** None found so far ***
   result = 0

   REM *** Make sure only one character ***
   first$ = MID$(c$,1)

   REM *** FOR each character in s$ DO ***
   FOR c = 1 TO LEN(s$)
       REM *** IF it matches req'd character, add 1 to result ***
       IF MID$(s$,c) = first$
           result = result + 1
       ENDIF
   NEXT c
ENDFUNCTION result
```

The Insert$() Function

The *Insert$()* function returns a string created by inserting one string into another, starting at a specified position. For example, the line

```
PRINT Insert$("abcdef ","xy", 4)
```

would display the string *abcxydef* having inserted the string *xy* into string *abcdef* starting at position 4.

If an attempt is made to insert the second string at an invalid position, then the returned string is an exact match of the first string.

The code for this routine is given in LISTING-8.3.

LISTING-8.3

The *Insert$()* Function

```
FUNCTION Insert$ (s1$,s2$,post)
   REM *** IF invalid position, result is original string ***
   IF post < 1 OR post> LEN(S1$)+1
       result$ = s1$
   ELSE
       REM *** Split s1$ into two parts & insert s2$ in between ***
       result$ = LEFT$(s1$,post-1)
       result$ = result$ + s2$
       result$ = result$+ RIGHT$(s1$,LEN(s1$)-(post-1))
   ENDIF
ENDFUNCTION result$
```

Notice that the main logic in the function involves splitting the first string into two parts and inserting the second string in between these parts.

The Delete$() Function

The *Delete$()* function returns a string created by deleting a specified section of an original string. For example, the line

```
temp$ = Delete$("abcdefghi",2,4)
```

would set *temp$* to *afghi*. this being created by removing 4 characters, starting at position 2, from the original string *abcdefghi*.

If the start position is invalid, a copy of the original string is returned. If the number of characters to be deleted is too large, then as many characters as possible are removed.

The code for this routine is given in LISTING-8.4.

LISTING-8.4

The *Delete$()* Function

```
FUNCTION Delete$(s$, start, num)
   REM *** IF invalid position, result is original string ***
   IF start < 1 OR start > LEN(s$)
      result$ = s$
   ELSE
      REM *** Construct result from left of deleted section ***
      REM *** and right of deleted section ***
      result$ = LEFT$(s$, start-1)
      result$ = result$+RIGHT$(s$,LEN(s$)-(start+num-1))
   ENDIF
ENDFUNCTION result$
```

The Replace$() Function

The *Replace$()* function is designed to return a string constructed by replacing a single character at a specified position in an original string. Therefore the line

```
ans$ = Replace$("abcdef","x",4)
```

sets *ans$* equal to *abcxef* having replaced the fourth character in *abcdef* with an *x*.

If an invalid position is specified, then the original string is returned.

The code for this function is shown in LISTING-8.5.

LISTING-8.5

The *Replace$()* Function

```
FUNCTION Replace$(s$, c$, post)
   REM *** IF invalid position, result is original string ***
   IF post < 1 OR post > LEN(s$)
      result$ = s$
   ELSE
      REM *** Make sure only one character is being replaced ***
      first$ = MID$(c$,1)
      REM *** Result is original string with new character at ***
      REM *** specified position ***
      result$ = LEFT$(s$,post-1)+first$+RIGHT$(s$,LEN(s$)-post)
   ENDIF
ENDFUNCTION result$
```

The Copy$() Function

The *Copy$()* function is designed to return a copy of part of a specified string. For example, the statement

```
result$ = Copy$("abcdefghi",3,5)
```

would copy a part of the string *abcdefghi* starting at the 3rd character. A total of 5 characters would be copied, so *result$* would end up containing the value *cdefg*.

The mini-spec for this operation is given below.

NAME	:	Copy
PARAMETERS		
IN	:	s : string
		start : integer
		number : integer
OUT	:	result : string
PRE-CONDITION	:	None
DESCRIPTION	:	The routine sets *result* to a sub-string copied from *s*. The sub-string contains characters from positions *start* to (*start*+*number* - 1) in *s*. If *start* is less than 1 or greater than the number of characters in *s*, an empty string is assigned to *result*. If (start+number-1) is greater than the length of s, then *result* contains the characters from *start* to LEN(*s*).
OUTLINE LOGIC	:	IF start < 1 OR start > LEN(s) THEN

```
                    result := ""
                ELSE
                    IF start + number - 1 > LEN(s) THEN
                        lastposition := LEN(s)
                    ELSE
                        lastposition := start+number-1
                    ENDIF
                        FOR c := start TO lastposition  DO
                            result := result + s[c]
                        ENDFOR
                ENDIF
```

Activity 8.8

Create a new project called *TestCopy* and write a program containing a *Copy$()* function which implements the logic given in the mini-spec above.

Write a test driver to make sure the function operates correctly.

Using Your Routines in Other Programs

The #INCLUDE Statement

The functions created here (such as *Copy$()*, *Insert$()*, etc.) are so useful that you're likely to employ them in many other programs. Although we can do this by simply copying and pasting the code for these routines into any new project that needs them, a better approach is to use DarkBASIC Pro's #INCLUDE statement.

#INCLUDE allows us to automatically include a set of routines within a new project without the need to use copy and paste.

We now have our collection of string functions in a single source file, *StringLibrary.dba.*

The program doesn't execute because the code for our function *Pos()* is not present and therefore attempting to execute the function causes an error.

There are two ways to make the code of *Pos()* available to the program without resorting to a copy and paste job.

The first method involves copying the *StringLibrary.dba* file into your current directory and then add the line

```
#INCLUDE "StringLibrary.dba"
```

at the start of your program. When you compile the program, the code in the named file will automatically be included in your project.

The second method, which uses the editor to load the *StringLibrary* file into your project, is shown in FIG-8.14.

Once the three steps have been performed, your project will contain the source files *TestLibrary.dba* and *StringLibrary.dba* with the source of *StringLibrary.dba* now showing in the edit window.

The source code displayed in the editor can be changed by clicking on the required filename (see FIG-8.15).

FIG-8.14

Loading the *StringLibrary* Source into your Project.

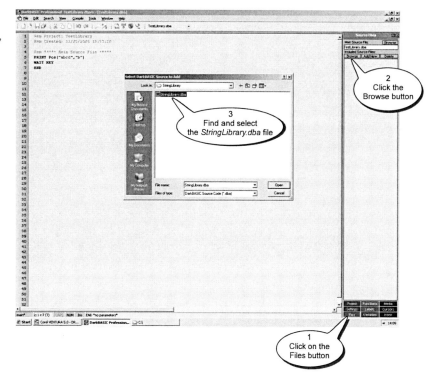

FIG-8.15

Changing the Source File Displayed in the Edit Window

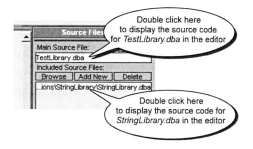

Activity 8.12

Remove the #INCLUDE line from your *TestLibrary* program.

Remove the *StringLibrary.dba* file from the *TestLibrary* folder.

Include the *StringLibrary.dba* file in your project using the method described above.

Try to execute the main program again.

Summary

- A set of functions which has been designed to be used in a range of programs can be saved as a separate file.

- A saved set of functions can be included in another project by copying its source file (*.dba*) into the current folder and using the #INCLUDE statement at the start of your program.

- Alternatively, the source code file can be included in the current project by using the Files|Browse option

Solutions

Activity 8.1

No solution required.

Activity 8.2

```
REM *** Read in two strings **
INPUT "Enter some text : ", s1$
INPUT "Enter more text : ", s2$
REM *** Display shorter string ***
IF LEN(s1$) < LEN(s2$)
    PRINT "Shorter text is ",s1$
ELSE
    PRINT "Shorter text is ", s2$
ENDIF
REM *** End program ***
WAIT KEY
END
```

Activity 8.3

b$ will contain the string *1-BY-1*

Activity 8.4

To display characters in reverse order:

```
REM *** Get string ***
INPUT "Enter a word : ",word$
REM *** Display chars in reverse order ***
FOR c = LEN(word$) TO 1 STEP -1
    PRINT MID$(word$,c)
NEXT c
REM *** End program ***
WAIT KEY
END
```

To count number of lowercase e's

```
REM *** Get string ***
INPUT "Enter a word : ",word$
REM *** Set count to zero ***
count = 0
REM *** FOR each character in word ***
FOR c = 1 TO LEN(word$)
    REM *** IF it's e, add 1 to count ***
    IF MID$(word$,c) = "e"
        count = count + 1
    ENDIF
NEXT c
REM *** Display count ***
PRINT "There are ",count," e's in ",word$
REM *** End program ***
WAIT KEY
END
```

To count upper and lowercase e's:

```
REM *** Get string ***
INPUT "Enter a word : ",word$
REM *** Set count to zero ***
count = 0
REM *** FOR each character in word ***
FOR c = 1 TO LEN(word$)
    REM *** IF it's E, add 1 to count ***
    IF UPPER$(MID$(word$,c)) = "E"
        count = count + 1
    ENDIF
NEXT c
REM *** Display count ***
PRINT "There are ",count," e's in ",word$
```

```
REM *** End program ***
WAIT KEY
END
```

Activity 8.5

```
REM *** FOR each code ***
FOR c = 32 TO 126
    REM *** Convert to a character ***
    ch$ = CHR$(c)
    REM *** and display ***
    PRINT c," ",ch$
NEXT c
REM *** End program ***
WAIT KEY
END
```

The following version pauses after every 24 characters:

```
REM *** FOR each code ***
FOR c = 1 TO 95
    REM *** Convert to a character ***
    ch$ = CHR$(c+31)
    REM *** and display ***
    PRINT c+31," ",ch$
    REM *** Pause every 24 characters ***
    IF c mod 24 = 0
        WAIT KEY
    ENDIF
NEXT c
REM *** End program ***
WAIT KEY
END
```

Activity 8.6

```
REM *** Get number ***
INPUT "Enter a number : ", num
REM *** Covert number to string ***
num$ = STR$(num)
REM *** Start count at zero ***
count = 0
REM *** FOR each character in string ***
FOR c = 1 TO LEN(num$)
    REM *** IF it's zero, add 1 to count ***
    IF MID$(num$,c) = "0"
        count = count + 1
    ENDIF
NEXT c
REM *** Display results ***
PRINT "The number ", num, " contains "
,count," zeros"
REM *** End program ***
WAIT KEY
END
```

Activity 8.7

```
REM *** Get value **
INPUT "Enter a number : ",num
REM *** Display in binary and hex ***
PRINT num," in binary is ",BIN$(num)
PRINT num," in hexadecimal is ",HEX$(num)
REM *** End program ***
WAIT KEY
END
```

Activity 8.8

```
REM *** Get a string ***
INPUT "Enter text : ", words$
REM *** Get start of copy position ***
INPUT "Input start position : ", st
REM *** get number of chars to copy ***
INPUT "Number of chars to copy : ", num
substring$ = Copy$(words$,st,num)
PRINT "substring returned was ",substring$
REM *** End program ***
WAIT KEY
END

REM *** Copy section of string ***
FUNCTION Copy$(s$, start, number)
   REM *** IF start invalid, return ***
   REM *** empty string ***
   IF start < 1 OR start > LEN(s$)
      result$ =""
   ELSE
      REM *** IF number copied too big, ***
      REM *** copy up to end of string ***
      IF start+number -1 > LEN(s$)
         lastposition = LEN(s$)
      ELSE
         REM *** Calc position of last  ***
         REM *** char to copy ***
         lastposition = start+number-1
      ENDIF
      REM *** Copy selected chars to ***
      REM *** result ***
      FOR c = start TO lastposition
         result$ = result$ + MID$(s$,c)
      NEXT c
   ENDIF
ENDFUNCTION result$
```

Activity 8.9

No solution required.

Activity 8.10

No solution required.

Activity 8.11

No solution required.

Activity 8.12

No solution required.

Hangman

Adding Global Variables to a Design

Black Box Testing

Designing a Complete Game

Equivalence Classes

Named Constants

Programming a Complete Game

White Box Testing

Creating a First Game

Introduction

By this stage we've covered quite a bit about programming. Most of it has been fairly conventional - no sprites, sound or 3D graphics - yet! However, it is time we had a go at producing a complete game.

If we are creating a new game, then, of course, we need to write a description of the game; how it is won and the rules. But, for our first attempt, we'll stick with an existing game which already has a set of rules - Hangman.

The Rules of the Game

Just in case there are any of you out there who don't know the rules of Hangman, here's a quick summary.

In Hangman one player thinks of a word or phrase and writes down a line of dashes; one dash for each letter in the word (or phrase). The same player also draws a set of gallows.

Player two then attempts to guess a letter that appears in the word. If he guesses correctly, player one overwrites the dashes with the letter at the appropriate place(s) in the word; if the letter does not appear, then part of the hanged man is drawn in.

Any non-alphabetic characters in a phrase, such as apostrophes, should be shown from the start.

Player two can attempt to guess the whole word at any time. If he gets it wrong another part is added to the hanged man; if he gets it right, he has won the game.

Player one wins the game if the hanged man is completed before the word is guessed.

There are six parts to the hanged man: head, torso, left arm, right arm, left leg, and right leg.

What Part the Computer Plays in the Game

In some games the computer will become one of the players. For example, if you buy a computer chess game, the computer itself becomes your opponent, taking control of one set of pieces.

In other games such as Solitaire, the computer displays the cards and makes sure you keep to the rules, but it doesn't become one of the players in the game.

You must decide at the start of your project exactly what part the computer is going to play.

For the Hangman game the computer will always be the player that chooses the word, responds to your guesses and draws the gallows and the hanged figure.

Designing the Screen Layout

How the game appears on the screen makes an important contribution to a player's enjoyment of a game.

We have to begin by deciding what information we want to see on the screen. If you've had experience of this game, the obvious answer to this task is that we need to see the hyphens, gallows and, as the game is played, the parts of the hanged man and those letters that have been guessed correctly.

But remember, we are doing this on a computer. This allows us to add more information, such as the number of guesses made so far, which letters have already been guessed and how long the game has been running. So we need to think carefully before we come up with a final design.

Of course, your programming ability might restrict what design options are available, but as a general rule you should create the best design possible without considering what programming problems will arise. If obstacles come up that cannot be solved, then you may have to modify your design later.

For this first attempt at a game, we'll keep the design simple (see FIG-9.1).

FIG-9.1

The Game's Screen Layout

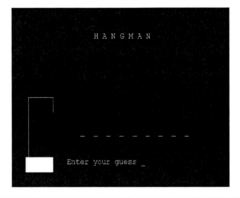

Game Data

We will need to decide what information we are going to store in the program. Some of this should be obvious. For example, the word to be guessed and the guessed letter.

Unlike us, the computer can't "see" that the hanged man is complete or that all the letters in the word have been filled in, so we need some method of knowing when these events have occurred.

We could do this by keeping a count of how many letters in the word are showing on the screen (when that count is equal to the number of characters in the word, the word will have been guessed) and, by recording how many wrong guesses have been made, we'll know when the hanged man is complete (it takes 6 wrong guesses to complete the drawing). These new data items should be added to our list of game data and the game logic should be modified to mention them.

We will also discover the need to define a few fixed values which will be used at various points throughout the program. For example, the name, size and colour of the font being used in the program and the screen resolution to be used. These values, which will not be changed within the program, are known as **named constants**.

However, minor variables such as a loop counter variable need not be considered at this stage. This type of variable will be local to the relevant routine and can be considered when that routine is being coded.

A list of the main variables and constants for our Hangman game are shown in TABLE-9.1.

TABLE-9.1

The Main Data Items and Constants Needed in the Game

Name	Type/Value	Description
Variables		
word	string	word to be guessed
guess	character	player's guess
wrongguesses	integer	number of wrong guesses made
correctletters	integer	number of letters in *word* that have been guessed
Constants		
screenwidth	800	screen width in pixels
screenheight	600	screen height in pixels
fontname	"Courier New"	name of font used
fontsize	30	font height in points
fontcolour	white	colour of font

It's a bit unrealistic to expect to come up with all the main data items and constants on the first attempt. This is a table we'll change as the project progresses and we become aware of our values that need to be added to the table.

Game Logic

We need to use structured English to create a brief description of how the game is played. A first attempt at explaining Hangman might be as follows:

```
Think of a word
Draw a hyphen for each letter
Draw the gallows
REPEAT
    Get guess letter
    Check for letter in word
    IF letter is in word THEN
        Add letter at appropriate position(s) above hyphens
    ELSE
        Add section to hanged man
    ENDIF
UNTIL word guessed OR hanged man complete
```

However, for a computer version of the game, we need a slightly different description which will take into account the need to set up details such as the screen resolution, the text font, size and colour. Also, drawing the gallows and the hyphens is just part of drawing the initial screen display. At the end of most games, a final screen appears. This might display a message of congratulations or commiseration. So a second attempt at the algorithm might be:

```
Initialise game
Think of a word
Draw initial screen
REPEAT
    Get guess letter
    Check for letter in word
    IF letter is in word THEN
        Add letter at appropriate position(s) above hyphens
    ELSE
        Add section to hanged man
    ENDIF
UNTIL word guessed OR hanged man complete
Display Game Over screen
```

Whereas in Chapter 1 we added more detail to our algorithm by using stepwise refinement, a better method when dealing with larger projects, such as this, is to identify which steps in the algorithm might be complex enough to be turned into separate functions and hence should be described using a mini-spec.

For our game, the following steps could be coded as functions:

```
Initialise game
Think of a word
Draw initial screen
Get guess letter
Check for letter in word
Add letter at appropriate position(s) above hyphens
Add section to hanged man
Word guessed
Hanged man complete
```

An initial set of mini-specs for each of these routines is given in the next section.

Game Documentation

NAME	:	Main
PARAMETERS		
IN	:	None
OUT	:	None
PRE-CONDITION	:	None
DESCRIPTION	:	Plays the game of Hangman. The program thinks of a word and displays a set of hyphens representing the letters in the word. Gallows are drawn. The player guesses a letter in the word.
		If the letter appears in the word, it is added above each appropriate hyphen. If not, then a section is added to the hanged man.
		The game finishes when all parts of the hanged man have been drawn or when the word has been guessed. There are six parts to the hanged man: head, torso, legs and arms.
OUTLINE LOGIC	:	Initialise game

```
                        Initialise game
                        Think of  a word
                        Draw  initial screen
                        REPEAT
                            Get guess letter
                            Check for letter in word
                            IF letter is in word THEN
                                Add letter at appropriate position(s) above
                                hyphens
                            ELSE
                                Add section to hanged man
                            ENDIF
                        UNTIL word guessed OR hanged man complete
                        Display Game Over screen
```

When a program makes use of global variables, a routine accessing any of these variables should specify this in its mini-spec.

```
NAME              :   InitaliseGame
PARAMETERS
   IN             :   None
   OUT            :   None
GLOBALS
   READ           :   screenwidth
                      screenheight
                      fontname
                      fontsize
                      fontcolour
   WRITTEN        :   wrongguesses
                      correctletters
PRE-CONDITION     :   None
DESCRIPTION       :   This routine sets the screen resolution to screenwidth
                      by screenheight. The font details are set to fontname
                      and fontsize. The foreground colour is set to
                      fontcolour. The global variables wrongguesses and
                      correctletters are set to zero. The random number
                      generator is seeded.
OUTLINE LOGIC     :   Set display mode to screenwidth x screenheight
                      Set text font to fontname
                      Set text size to fontsize
                      Set foreground colour to fontcolour
                      Set wrongguesses to 0
                      Set correctletters to 0
                      Seed random number generator
```

Notice that the global values accessed are listed under GLOBALS in the mini-spec
above. Any global whose value is unchanged by the routine is listed under READ,
while those whose values are modified in any way are listed under WRITTEN.

As you can see, the *InitialiseGame* routine is used to perform all the things that need
be done only once at the start of the game. Generally, these fall into two categories:
initialising data items and getting the visual items, such as display mode, colours
and fonts, into the correct mode.

```
NAME              :   ThinkOfWord
PARAMETERS
   IN             :   None
   OUT            :   None
GLOBALS
   READ           :   None
   WRITTEN        :   word
PRE-CONDITION     :   None
DESCRIPTION       :   The routine sets word to a word chosen at random
                      from a list of words.
OUTLINE LOGIC     :   Set up list of 20 lowercase words
                      Choose a position at random (between 1 and 20)
                      Set word equal to the word in the list at position chosen
```

NAME	:	DrawInitialScreen
PARAMETERS		
IN	:	None
OUT	:	None
GLOBALS		
READ	:	None
WRITTEN	:	None
PRE-CONDITION	:	None
DESCRIPTION	:	This routine creates the screen layout as shown in the screen design.
OUTLINE LOGIC	:	Display "H A N G M A N"
		Draw a hyphen for each letter in the word
		Draw the gallows

NAME	:	GuessLetter
PARAMETERS		
IN	:	None
OUT	:	None
GLOBALS		
READ	:	None
WRITTEN	:	guess
PRE-CONDITION	:	None
DESCRIPTION	:	*guess* is set to the lowercase version of any letter entered at the keyboard.
		If a non-alphabetic character is entered, or more than one letter is entered, then an error message should be displayed and the player made to re-enter their guess.
OUTLINE LOGIC	:	Display "Please enter your guess :"
		Get *guess*
		WHILE *guess* not a single letter DO
		Display "Single letters only"
		Get *guess*
		ENDWHILE
		Convert *guess* to lowercase

NAME	:	CheckForLetter
PARAMETERS		
IN	:	None
OUT	:	letterfound : integer
GLOBALS		
READ	:	word
		guess
WRITTEN	:	None
PRE-CONDITION	:	None
DESCRIPTION	:	*letterfound* is set to 1 if *guess* appears in *word*; otherwise *letterfound* is set to 0.
OUTLINE LOGIC	:	Set letterfound to zero
		FOR each character in word DO
		IF character = guess THEN
		Set letterfound to 1
		ENDIF
		ENDFOR

NAME	:	DrawLetter
PARAMETERS		
IN	:	None
OUT	:	None
GLOBALS		
READ	:	word
		guess
WRITTEN	:	correctletters
PRE-CONDITION	:	None
DESCRIPTION	:	This routine displays a letter above each hyphen where *guess* appears in *word*. *correctletters* is incremented by the number of times *guess* occurs in *word*.
OUTLINE LOGIC	:	Move cursor above first hyphen

```
FOR each character in word DO
    IF character = guess THEN
        Display letter
        Add 1 to correctletters
    ENDIF
    Move cursor over next hyphen
ENDFOR
```

NAME	:	AddToHangedMan
PARAMETERS		
IN	:	None
OUT	:	None
GLOBALS		
READ	:	wrongguesses
WRITTEN	:	None
PRE-CONDITION	:	None
DESCRIPTION	:	This routine adds another part to the hanged man. Which part is added is dependent on the value of *wrongguesses*.
OUTLINE LOGIC	:	IF

```
    wrongguesses = 1:
        Draw head
    wrongguesses = 2:
        Draw torso
    wrongguesses = 3:
        Draw left leg
    wrongguesses = 4:
        Draw right leg
    wrongguesses = 5:
        Draw left arm
    wrongguesses = 6:
        Draw right arm
ENDIF
```

NAME	:	WordGuessed
PARAMETERS		
IN	:	None
OUT	:	result : integer

continued on next page

```
GLOBALS
    READ           :   correctletters
                       word
    WRITTEN        :   None
PRE-CONDITION      :   None
DESCRIPTION        :   This routine sets result to 1 if correctletters =
                       number of characters in word; otherwise result
                       is set to zero.
OUTLINE LOGIC      :   IF correctletters = LEN(word) THEN
                            Set result to 1
                       ELSE
                            Set result to 0
                       ENDIF
```

```
NAME               :   HangedManComplete
PARAMETERS
    IN             :   None
    OUT            :   result
GLOBALS
    READ           :   wrongguesses
    WRITTEN        :   None
PRE-CONDITION      :   None
DESCRIPTION        :   This routine sets result to 1 if wrongguesses = 6;
                       otherwise result is set to zero.
OUTLINE LOGIC      :   IF wrongguesses = 6 THEN
                            Set result to 1
                       ELSE
                            Set result to 0
                       ENDIF
```

Implementing the Design

Since this is going to be a long program (by the standards of what we've done so far) we'll add a full set of comments at the start of the program giving details such as the date, version number, author and hardware requirements. Next, we'll start the actual program code by declaring the data items (named constants and global variables) along with the main section (see LISTING-9.1).

LISTING-9.1

Defining the Data and
Main Logic for Hangman

```
REM **************************************
REM *** Program    : Hangman           ***
REM *** Version    : 0.1               ***
REM *** Date       : 15/3/2005         ***
REM *** Author     : A. Stewart        ***
REM *** Language   : DarkBASIC Pro     ***
REM *** Hardware   : PC at least 800 by ***
REM ***              600 display       ***
REM *** Purpose    : Plays the game of ***
REM ***              Hangman.          ***
REM**************************************
REM *** Global Constants ***
#CONSTANT screenwidth = 800
#CONSTANT screenheight = 600
#CONSTANT fontname = "Courier New"
#CONSTANT fontsize = 30
#CONSTANT fontcolour = RGB(255,255,255)
```

continued on next page

LISTING-9.1
(continued)

Defining the Data and
Main Logic for Hangman

```
REM *** Global variables ***
GLOBAL word$                       'word to be guessed
GLOBAL guess$                      'player's guess
GLOBAL wrongguesses                'number of wrong guesses made
GLOBAL correctletters              'number of letters in word$ that have
                                   'been guessed


REM *** Main program ***
InitialiseGame()                   'Set display and globals
ThinkOfWord()                      'Think of word
DrawInitialScreen()                'Draw start-up screen
REPEAT
   GetGuess()                      'Get player's guess
   letterfound = CheckForLetter()  'Check if letter in word
   IF letterfound = 1
      DrawLetter()                 'Add letter at each point
   ELSE
      AddToHangedMan()             'Add section to hanged man
   ENDIF
UNTIL WordGuessed() OR HangedManComplete()
GameOver()                         'Game Over message
WAIT KEY
END
```

Activity 9.1

Create a new project called *hangman.dbpro* and enter the program given
above.

Add stubs for each of the missing routines.

Each stub should display its own name.

Since *CheckForLetter()*, *WordGuessed()* and *HangedManComplete()* all
return a value, their stubs will also have to return a value. Set this returned
value to 1 in each case.

Adding *InitialiseGame()*

With the program running correctly, we can now begin to replace the stubs with the
actual code for each routine. The code for *InitialiseGame()*, derived from that
routine's mini-spec, is shown below:

```
FUNCTION InitialiseGame
   SET DISPLAY MODE screenwidth,screenheight,16
   SET TEXT FONT fontname
   SET TEXT SIZE fontsize
   INK fontcolour,0
   wrongguesses = 0
   correctletters = 0
   RANDOMIZE TIMER()
ENDFUNCTION
```

Activity 9.2

Add the code for *InitialiseGame()* to your project and recompile the program
to check that there are no errors in the code.

Adding *ThinkOfWord()*

We've just added *InitialiseGame()* to our program, but how can we be sure that it performs as expected without testing it? Answer - we can't. We'll just have to wait until we run the completed program and hope for the best.

Obviously, we need to make sure a routine is working properly before we go any further. Exactly how we do that will vary from routine to routine. Let's add the next routine and think about how it can be tested.

The code for *ThinkOfWord()* is

```
FUNCTION ThinkOfWord()
   REM *** Words to choose from ***
   DATA "london", "glasgow", "blackpool", "edinburgh",
   DATA "boston", "berlin", "moscow", "sydney"
   DATA "wellington", "washington", "rome", "amsterdam"
   DATA "stockholm", "oslo", "lisbon", "madrid"
   DATA "prague", "bonn", "budapest", "vienna"

   REM *** Choose word from list ***
   num = RND(19) + 1
   FOR c = 1 TO num
      READ word$
   NEXT c
ENDFUNCTION
```

The letters in the names are all in lowercase to help with comparisons later.

If we add the code for this routine directly into our program, we'll have no way of knowing if it functions correctly until several more routines have been added, so a better approach would be to create a new project just to test *ThinkOfWord()* before it is inserted into the main section.

The complete code for the test program is given in LISTING-9.2.

LISTING-9.2

Testing ThinkOfWord()

```
GLOBAL word$        'Global variable referenced in ThinkOfWord

REM *** Test Driver for ThinkOfWord ***
REM *** Seed random number generator ***
RANDOMIZE TIMER()
REM *** Call function being tested ***
ThinkOfWord()

REM *** Display word generated ***
PRINT word$

REM *** End program ***
WAIT KEY
END

REM *** Think of a word ***
FUNCTION ThinkOfWord()
   REM *** Words to choose from ***
   DATA "london", "glasgow", "blackpool", "edinburgh"
   DATA "boston", "berlin", "moscow", "sydney"
   DATA "wellington", "washington", "rome", "amsterdam"
   DATA "stockholm", "oslo", "lisbon", "madrid"
   DATA "prague", "bonn", "budapest", "vienna"

   REM *** Choose word from list ***
   num = RND(19)+1
   FOR c = 1 TO num
      READ word$
   NEXT c
ENDFUNCTION
```

The test driver actually calls the function and displays the word chosen.

Activity 9.3

Create a new project called *testthinkofword.dbpro* and enter the code given above.

The trouble with the test driver is that *ThinkOfWord()* is called only once, so only one word is shown. Perhaps there is a fault and the routine chooses the same word every time! To check for this we'll need to run our test program again. Even now, how can we be sure that every word in the list is equally likely to be chosen? Well, we could run the test program many times and make sure every word gets chosen eventually.

But an easier approach would be to get the test driver itself to execute the function several times, displaying which word is chosen on each occasion. Perhaps we could change the test driver code to:

```
REM *** Test Driver for ThinkOfWord ***
RANDOMIZE TIMER()
REM *** FOR 10 times DO ***
FOR c = 1 TO 10
    REM *** Call function being tested ***
    ThinkOfWord()
    REM *** Display word generated ***
    PRINT word$
NEXT c
REM *** End program ***
WAIT KEY
END
```

Activity 9.4

Change your test driver to match the code given above and run the program. Do you see 10 words listed?

Only one or two words appear when you run the program. Why is this? The words are read from the DATA statement(s), and, when the function has been executed once or twice, all the values in the DATA statements will have been used up. When no more data is available for the READ statement, *word$* is set to an empty string. Luckily, we can solve this problem quite easily by restoring the data before each call to *ThinkOfWord()*. This requires the code shown below:

```
REM *** Test Driver for ThinkOfWord ***
RANDOMIZE TIMER()
REM *** FOR 10 times DO ***
FOR c = 1 TO 10
    RESTORE
    REM *** Call function being tested ***
    ThinkOfWord()
    REM *** Display word generated ***
    PRINT word$
NEXT c
REM *** End program **
WAIT KEY
END*
```

Notice, we've settled for 20 city names. Since the mini-spec didn't say which words were to be used, the program has the freedom to choose any set of words.

Now that we feel happy with the *ThinkOfWord()* routine, it can be added to the original program.

Adding *DrawInitialScreen()*

If we look at the mini-spec for *DrawInitialScreen*, we can see that there are three main parts to this routine:

```
Draw the title
Draw the gallows
Draw the hyphens
```

We saw in Chapter 6 that it takes several lines of code to draw the gallows. It will also takes several lines of code to produce the hyphens. So rather, than do all this in a single routine, we'll create two new routines: one to draw the gallows and one to draw the hyphens. *DrawInitialScreen* can then be coded to draw the title and then call the other routines to perform the more complicated tasks. What we're really doing here is the same stepwise refinement process that identified the routines we needed for the game as a whole.

Now that we've recognised the need for new routines we'll start by creating mini-specs for them.

NAME	:	DrawHyphens
PARAMETERS		
IN	:	None
OUT	:	None
GLOBALS		
READ	:	word
WRITTEN	:	None
PRE-CONDITION	:	None
DESCRIPTION	:	Draws a hyphen on the screen for each character in word.

OUTLINE LOGIC	:	Move cursor to appropriate position on screen
		FOR each letter in word DO
		    Display a hyphen on screen
		ENDFOR

NAME	:	DrawGallows
PARAMETERS		
IN	:	None
OUT	:	None

continued on next page

```
GLOBALS
    READ         :   None
    WRITTEN      :   None
PRE-CONDITION    :   None
DESCRIPTION      :   This routine draws the gallows on the screen.
OUTLINE LOGIC    :   Draw gallows at appropriate position
```

Now we can code *DrawInitialScreen()* and create stubs for *DrawGallows()* and *DrawHyphens()*:

```
FUNCTION DrawInitialScreen()
    SET CURSOR 300,80
    PRINT "H A N G M A N"
    DrawGallows()                    'Draw gallows
    DrawHyphens()                    'Draw hyphens
ENDFUNCTION

FUNCTION DrawGallows()
    PRINT "DrawGallows"
ENDFUNCTION

FUNCTION DrawHyphens()
    PRINT "DrawHyphens"
ENDFUNCTION
```

Since the *DrawInitialScreen()* creates output, this time we can test our new code by just adding it to the main project and running it.

Activity 9.7

Add the above code to your program and execute it.

Activity 9.8

Replace the stub for *DrawGallows()* with actual code for the routine. Use the coordinates given in the diagram below.

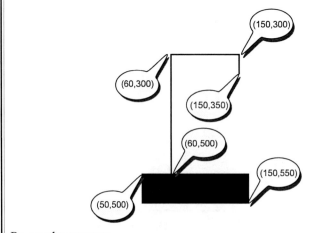

Re-run the program.

Are the gallows displayed on the screen?

The code for *DrawHyphens()* is as follows:

```
FUNCTION DrawHyphens()
    REM *** Position cursor ***
    SET CURSOR 250,400
    REM *** Draw hyphens ***
    FOR C = 1 TO LEN(word$)
        PRINT "_   ";
    NEXT c
ENDFUNCTION
```

Activity 9.9

As usual, replace the stub for the appropriate routine with the code given above.

Run the program.

Do the hyphens display correctly?

Although you may see the hyphens appearing on the screen, we can't really be sure that *DrawHyphens()* is operating correctly unless we know what word has been chosen; then we can check that we have the correct number of hyphens.

We can do this by adding the line

```
PRINT word$
```

as the last statement inside the *DrawInitialScreen()* function.

Activity 9.10

Add the line suggested above at the required position.

Run the program again and check that the number of hyphens displayed matches the number of characters in the word.

Run the program a few times just to check that the results are always correct.

Once you are satisfied that the *DrawHyphens()* routine is operating correctly, remove the `PRINT word$` line from *DrawInitialScreen()*.

As we can see, it is sometimes necessary to add statements to the program simply to help with program testing. Some languages allow these statements to be marked in a special way so that the final compilation ignores these **debug statements**. Since DarkBASIC Pro doesn't have that feature, we should remove these debug statements as soon as we have finished with them. That way there's little chance of them accidentally being left in the final version of the program.

Adding *GetGuess()*

Working our way through the main program, the next routine we come to is *GetGuess()*. This is the first routine that we can actually think about creating test data for since it accepts input from the keyboard.

We should think about testing at two main stages. The first of these is during development after the mini-spec has been created. At this time we have a description of what task a routine should perform. From that description we should be able to think of a set of test values.

To help us do this, we start by examining what different response we can elicit from the routine. There are two:

> Input accepted

> Input rejected

Accepted input falls into two sub-categories:

> Uppercase letter

> Lowercase letter

with uppercase letters being converted to lowercase.

Rejected input can also be broken into two sub-categories:

> Single, non-alphabetic characters

> Multiple characters

Now that we've identified the possible response of the routine, we need to choose test values from each category and sub-category. But how many values should we choose from each section? To test *Input accepted - uppercase letters* should we try every single letter, A to Z, just one letter, or a few letters?

All the values which give the same response from a routine are collectively known as an **equivalence class**.

Therefore, all the capital letters , A to Z, make up the equivalence class for the *Input accepted - uppercase letter* category. To test that this response is functioning correctly, we need choose just a few values from the equivalence class. If all of these values give the response we expect, then it is likely (but not guaranteed) that all the other values in that equivalence class will respond in the expected way also.

When the members of an equivalence class have an order (A is the first member ; Z the last) it is usual to use these first and last values within the class as well as some other random value from the group as test data. In addition, another value from near the middle of the class is also selected.

So, to test the *Input accepted -uppercase letter* response we could choose the test values A, Z, and P.

Similarly, for the response *Input accepted - lowercase letter*, we could use the values a, z, and k.

As well as testing that valid input is handled correctly, it is necessary to make sure that invalid input is also handled as expected. To test the *Input rejected - single non-alphabetic* character we have to select values from the equivalence class values that fall into this category. A sample of invalid single characters is 2 , ?, ^, +.

Unlike the *Input accepted* equivalence classes, this time there is no obvious order to the characters that make up this class. For example, we cannot say that the character ! is the first member of the class and ? the last. So we have no guide as to which test values should be chosen. Without this guideline we need to pick three values representative of the group. Perhaps 3, $ and a space.

The last grouping: *Input reject - multiple characters* again has no obvious order for the infinite number of values that fall into this category, but we could try a two character string with letters "AB", a two character string without letters "2@" and a five characters string "a1234".

Choosing test values based on the description of the routine given in the mini-spec is known as **black box testing**. This term being used since, at this stage we have no idea how the internals of the box (i.e. the routine that is to be created) operates - it's a black box.

The test data is presented in tabular form, giving the reason why each test value was chosen and the way in which the routine is expected to react to each of these test values (see TABLE-9.2).

TABLE-9.2

Black Box Test Data for *GetGuess()*

Test Number	Test Data	Reason for Test	Expected Result	Actual Result
1	guess = "A"	To check that valid capital letters are accepted and converted to lowercase	guess = "a"	
2	guess = "Z"	To check that valid capital letters are accepted and converted to lowercase	guess = "z"	
3	guess = "P"	To check that valid capital letters are accepted and converted to lowercase	guess = "p"	
4	guess = "a"	To check that valid lowercase letters are accepted	guess="a"	
5	guess = "z"	To check that valid lowercase letters are accepted	guess="z"	
6	guess = "k"	To check that valid lowercase letters are accepted	guess="k"	
7	guess = "3"	To check that non-alphabetic characters are rejected	Error message displayed User required to re-enter	
8	guess = "$"	To check that non-alphabetic characters are rejected	Error message displayed User required to re-enter	
9	guess = " "	To check that non-alphabetic characters are rejected	Error message displayed User required to re-enter	
10	guess = "AB"	To check that strings of more than one character are rejected	Error message displayed User required to re-enter	
11	guess = "2@"	To check that strings of more than one character are rejected	Error message displayed User required to re-enter	
12	guess = "a1234"	To check that strings of more than one character are rejected	Error message displayed User required to re-enter	

Notice that the final column, *Actual Result*, is left blank. This column will finally be filled in when the function is coded and run using the test data values supplied. When the result matches the expectation, then the last column contains the phrase "as expected". If we don't get the expected results, and it's the program that's at fault a message such as "see entry 12 in test log" should be added to the *Actual result* column. We'll talk about **test logs** later in this chapter.

With the black box test data ready, it's time to code up this routine from the mini-spec's outline logic. The necessary code is given below:

```
FUNCTION GetGuess()
    REM *** Use opaque text mode ***
    SET TEXT OPAQUE
    REM *** Remove any text already at this position ***
    SET CURSOR 200,500
    PRINT "                              ";
    REM *** Get guess ***
    SET CURSOR 200,500
    INPUT "Enter your guess ",guess$
    REM *** Change guess to lowercase ***
    guess$ = LOWER$(guess$)
    REM *** WHILE guess invalid DO ***
    WHILE LEN(guess$)<>1 OR guess$<"a" OR guess$ > "z"
        REM *** Display error message ***
        SET CURSOR 200,500
```

```
            PRINT "                         "
            SET CURSOR 200,500
            PRINT "single letters only"
            REM *** Wait one second ***
            WAIT 1000
            REM *** Remove error message ***
            SET CURSOR 200,500
            PRINT "                         ";
            REM *** Get guess ***
            SET CURSOR 200,500
            INPUT "Enter your guess ",guess$
            guess$ = LOWER$(guess$)
        ENDWHILE
        REM *** Return to transparent text mode ***
        SET TEXT TRANSPARENT
    ENDFUNCTION
```

This seems to be quite a long routine, and, if we check the routine's outline logic

```
Display "Please enter your guess :"
Get guess
WHILE guess not a single letter DO
        Display "Single letters only"
        Get guess
ENDWHILE
Convert guess to lowercase
```

we can see that there's more to the code than might be assumed from the outline logic. Also, the conversion to lowercase is done at a different place in the code than it is in the mini-spec.

What are the differences? Well, some of the extra statements have come about because we need to place the display at a certain position on the screen and hence the need for SET CURSOR statements. In addition, it is necessary to remove any old message before attempting to write a new one, otherwise it is possible that not all of the old text will be removed from the screen. These details might reasonably be omitted from the outline logic, but other differences are more fundamental. The conversion to lowercase has been moved in order to make it easier to check if the input is a letter.

Because the actual code is so different from the outline logic, that outline logic needs to be modified so that it agrees with the final code that is to be used in the program. Hence, we may rewrite the mini-spec's outline logic as:

```
Change to opaque text mode
Remove any text already at this position
Display "Please enter guess"
Get guess
Change guess to lowercase
 WHILE guess invalid DO
        Display "Single letters only" for one second
        Display "Please enter guess"
        Get guess
        Change guess to lowercase
ENDWHILE
Return to transparent text mode
```

Now that the function has been coded, we can create more test data based solely on that code. You should recall from previous previous chapters that we have specific ways of testing selection and iteration structures. This routine contains one structure; a WHILE loop, which should be tested in such a way that zero, one and multiple iterations are performed during these tests. Possible test data for the *GetGuess()* routine is given in TABLE 9.3.

TABLE-9.3

White Box Test Data for
GetGuess()

Test Number	Test Data	Reason for Test	Expected Result	Actual Result
1	guess = "A"	Zero iterations of WHILE loop	guess = "a"	
2	guess = "3" guess = "Z"	One iteration of WHILE loop	First value rejected Re-entered value accepted guess = "z"	
3	guess = "$" guess = " " guess = "P"	Multiple iterations of WHILE	First two values rejected Third value accepted guess = "p"	

Notice that the values used here match some of those from the black box test data. This is deliberate. If we can make the same data value test two or more situations, then we have reduced the number of test runs we're going to have to perform.

Finally, we can combine the black box and white box test data to give a list of the actual test runs that will be performed on the routine (see TABLE-9.4).

TABLE-9.4

The Final Test Data for
GetGuess()

Test Run	Test Data	Reason for Test	Expected Result	Actual Result
1	guess = "A"	Zero iterations of WHILE loop	guess = "a"	
2	guess = "3" guess = "Z"	One iteration of WHILE loop	First value rejected Re-entered value accepted guess = "z"	
3	guess = "$" guess = " " guess = "AB" guess = "2@" guess = "al234" guess = "P"	Multiple iterations of WHILE	First 5 values rejected Sixth value accepted guess = "p"	
4	guess = "a"	To check that valid lowercase letters are accepted	guess="a"	
5	guess = "z"	To check that valid lowercase letters are accepted	guess="z"	
6	guess = "k"	To check that valid lowercase letters are accepted	guess="k"	

We've managed to keep the number of separate test run to six by increasing the number of iterations in the last test of the WHILE loop, thereby using up all the invalid tests we wanted to carry out in the black box testing.

To check that the routine is assigning the correct value to the program's *guess$* we could add the statement PRINT guess$ at the end of the routine.

Activity 9.11

Add the *GetGuess()* routine to your project.

Add a PRINT guess$ statement to the end of the routine.

Test your program using the values given in TABLE-9.4.

Are all the results as expected?

Remove the PRINT guess$ statement from the program.

Adding *CheckForLetter()*

The code for *CheckForLetter()* is

```
FUNCTION CheckForLetter()
    letterfound = 0
    FOR c = 1 TO LEN(word$)
```

```
        IF guess$ = MID$(word$,c)
            letterfound = 1
            correctletters = correctletters + 1
        ENDIF
    NEXT c
    IF letterfound = 0
        wrongguesses = wrongguesses + 1
    ENDIF
ENDFUNCTION letterfound
```

Although there is no direct input to this routine, nevertheless it can be tested.

The routine can react to the value of *guess$* in two ways. The first of these is to set *letterfound* to true and increment *correctletters*; the second to set *letterfound* to false and increment *wrongguesses*. This means we need one test where *guess$* is in *word$* and a second test where *guess$* is not in *word$*.

The code contains three control structures: a FOR and two IF's.

Although the number of iterations the FOR loop will execute depends on the length of *word$* it is still impractical to test for zero and one iteration of the loop since no word chosen will create these conditions.

The IF statements need to be tested for both true and false conditions, but these requirements are already handled by the black box test data given earlier.

Activity 9.12

Create a test driver for *CheckForLetter()*.

The driver should allow the value for *word$* and *guess$* to be entered from the keyboard making it easy to ensure that the test conditions are met.

Using both black box and white box techniques, construct a set of test data for this routine.

Once testing is complete, add the routine to your main program.

Adding *DrawLetter()*

The code for *DrawLetter()* is:

```
FUNCTION DrawLetter()
    SET CURSOR 250, 400
    FOR c = 1 TO LEN(word$)
        IF guess$ = MID$(word$,c)
            PRINT guess$,"   ";
        ELSE
            PRINT "    ";
        ENDIF
    NEXT c
ENDFUNCTION
```

Activity 9.13

Add this routine to your project and check that it is operating correctly.

Adding *AddToHangedMan()*

> **Activity 9.14**
>
> A diagram of the hanged man is shown below.
>
> NOTE: The diagram is not to scale.
>
>
> Using the outline logic given in the mini-spec and the coordinates given above, write the code for *AddToHangedMan()* and add the routine to your project.
>
> Check that it is operating correctly with a body part being added each time a wrong letter is guessed.

Adding *WordGuessed()*

The word has been guessed if the variable *correctletters* has a value equal to the number of letters in *word$*, so the code for this routine is:

```
FUNCTION WordGuessed()
    IF correctletters = LEN(word$)
        EXITFUNCTION 1
    ENDIF
ENDFUNCTION 0
```

Adding *HangedManComplete()*

The game is over if the figure of the hanged man has been completed. We can detect this state by checking if the value of *wrongguesses* is 6, that is, the number of parts in the hanged figure. This is coded as:

```
FUNCTION HangedManComplete()
    IF wrongguesses = 6
        EXITFUNCTION 1
    ENDIF
ENDFUNCTION 0
```

Adding *GameOver()*

The *GameOver* routine displays a "GAME OVER" message and is coded as:

```
FUNCTION GameOver()
    SET CURSOR 330,200
    PRINT "GAME OVER"
ENDFUNCTION
```

Keeping a Test Log

A test log is little more than a formalised diary specifying which routines are being tested and what test data is being used. When an unexpected result is obtained during a test run, the test log should describe what result actually appeared and what was expected. In addition, the changes made to the code must be documented. An extract from a test log is shown in TABLE-9.5. Test run numbers are obtained from the values used in the test data tables.

TABLE-9.5

An Extract from a Test Log

Test Log for Hangman Program

Date	Unit Tested	Test Run	Comments
1/7/2005	GetGuess	1	OK
		2	OK
		3	OK
		4	"a" rejected as valid
			Added line
			guess$ = LOWER$(guess$)

Flaws in the Game

Omissions from the Code

Some errors can be very difficult to find and can easily slip through the testing process unnoticed.

The problem here is that, if you enter the same letter, it will continue to add to *correctletters*, which will eventually have a value equal to the number of letters in *word$* and the *WordGuessed()* routine will take this to mean that you have won and that the game is over.

To cure this problem, we need to make sure the player is not allowed to enter the same letter twice.

One way of achieving this is to remember every letter that has been guessed and reject any attempt at repeating a previous letter. We can store every letter entered in a string, adding one more letter every time a valid guess is entered. And we can check for a repeated letter by searching this string to determine if the guessed letter already appears there. The logic we need is

```
Set lettersguessed to an empty string
Get guess
Check for guess in lettersguessed
```

```
        WHILE letter is in lettersguessed DO
            Display "You've already used that letter"
            Get guess
        ENDWHILE
        Add guess to lettersguessed
```

To implement this we'll need to set up another global variable, *lettersguessed$*, and set it to an empty string in *InitialiseGame()*. The remainder of the logic will be incorporated into *GetGuess()* which will now be coded as

```
FUNCTION GetGuess()
    SET CURSOR 200,500
    SET TEXT OPAQUE
    PRINT "                                    ";
    SET CURSOR 200,500
    INPUT "Enter your guess ",guess$
    guess$ = LOWER$(guess$)
    alreadyused = Pos(lettersguessed$,guess$)
    WHILE LEN(guess$)<>1 OR guess$<"a" OR guess$ > "z"
    OR alreadyused <> -1
        SET CURSOR 200,500
        IF LEN(guess$)<>1 OR guess$<"a" OR guess$ > "z"
            PRINT "single letters only"
        ELSE
            PRINT "You've already entered that letter"
        ENDIF
        WAIT 2000
        SET CURSOR 200,500
        PRINT "                                    ";
        SET CURSOR 200,500
        INPUT "Enter your guess ",guess$
        guess$ = LOWER$(guess$)
        alreadyused = Pos(lettersguessed$,guess$)
    ENDWHILE
    lettersguessed$ = lettersguessed$ + guess$
    SET TEXT TRANSPARENT
ENDFUNCTION
```

Notice that the routine makes use of the *Pos()* function we created in the previous chapter to search for *guess$* in *lettersguessed$*. For this to work we'll need to copy the *StringLibrary.dba* file into the current folder and use the #INCLUDE "stringlibrary.dba" statement at the start of our program.

Activity 9.17

Make the necessary changes to your program as described above and check that the program correctly rejects repeated letters.

Although we won't show it here, the min-spec for the *GetGuess* routine will need to be updated to reflect the new logic.

Deviating from the Original Specifications

If we look back at the original remit for the game we've been developing, it stated that the program should allow the player to play the game of Hangman. In that game's rules, the player who is attempting to guess the word may enter a single letter or attempt to guess the complete word. Our program does not allow the player to guess at the complete word and therefore deviates from the original specifications.

Correcting this fault will not be a trivial matter. In fact, we may need to rethink the whole logic of the game. So be very careful when implementing software that you have stuck to the original statement of requirements. Realising you've made this type of mistake when you've almost finished a project can result in a significant amount of reworking. In a commercial situation this will cost time and money.

Final Testing

Once all the specified testing is complete, the program needs to be handed over to other testers. They may simply play the game several hundreds of times without having any specific test situations in mind.

Any errors or problems (game running too slowly, sound not synchronised to actions, etc.) that may crop up will be reported and the appropriate changes made to the software.

Summary

- When creating a game, begin by setting out the rules of the game.

- Decide what part the computer is going to play in the game.

- Design the various screen layouts that may appear as part of the game.

- Identify the main data that is used in the game.

- Describe the overall logic of the game.

- Make sure this logic meets the complete requirements of the game.

- Identify which parts of the logic can be written as routines.

- Create mini-specs for each routine.

- Create black box test data for each routine.

- If required, create some lower level routines which are to be called by the main routines.

- Code the routines using top-down, bottom-up, or a mixture of both techniques.

- Create white box test data for each routine.

- Combine black and white box test data to create the actual tests that will be carried out on each routine.

- Keep adding routines to the program until the final product has been produced.

- Hand over the completed program to tester who can perform non-specific tests on the game, looking for any problems that have not previously been detected.

Solutions

Activity 9.1

```
REM **************************************
REM *** Program   : Hangman          ***
REM *** Version   : 0.1              ***
REM *** Date      : 15/3/2005        ***
REM *** Author    : A. Stewart       ***
REM *** Language  : DarkBASIC Pro    ***
REM *** Hardware  : PC at least 800 by ***
REM ***              600 display      ***
REM *** Purpose   : Plays the game of  ***
REM ***              Hangman.         ***
REM **************************************

REM *** Global Constants ***
#CONSTANT screenwidth = 800
#CONSTANT screenheight = 600
#CONSTANT fontname = "Courier New"
#CONSTANT fontsize = 30
#CONSTANT fontcolour = RGB(255,255,255)

REM *** Global variables ***
GLOBAL word$
GLOBAL guess$
GLOBAL wrongguesses
GLOBAL correctletters
GLOBAL lettersguessed$

REM *** Main program ***
InitialiseGame()
ThinkOfWord()
DrawInitialScreen()
REPEAT
  GetGuess()
  letterfound = CheckForLetter()
  IF letterfound = 1
     DrawLetter()
  ELSE
     AddToHangedMan()
  ENDIF
UNTIL WordGuessed() OR HangedManComplete()
GameOver()
WAIT KEY
END
```

```
REM *** Initialises game ***
FUNCTION InitialiseGame()
   PRINT "InitialiseGame"
ENDFUNCTION

REM *** Think of word ***
FUNCTION ThinkOfWord()
   PRINT "ThinkOfWord"
ENDFUNCTION

REM *** Set up the screen ***
FUNCTION DrawInitialScreen()
   PRINT "DrawInitialScreen"
ENDFUNCTION

REM *** Get player's guess ***
FUNCTION GetGuess()
PRINT "GetGuess"
ENDFUNCTION

REM *** Returns 1 if letter is in word ***
FUNCTION CheckForLetter()
   PRINT "CheckForLetter"
ENDFUNCTION 1
```

```
REM *** Add letter above hyphens***
FUNCTION DrawLetter()
   PRINT "DrawLetter"
ENDFUNCTION

REM *** Add section to hanged man ***
FUNCTION AddToHangedMan()
   PRINT "AddToHangedMan"
ENDFUNCTION

REM *** Returns 1 if player has won ***
FUNCTION WordGuessed()
   PRINT "WordGuessed"
ENDFUNCTION 1

REM *** Returns 1 if player has lost ***
FUNCTION HangedManComplete()
   PRINT "HangedManComplete"
ENDFUNCTION 1

REM *** Display the game over message ***
FUNCTION GameOver()
   PRINT "GameOver"
ENDFUNCTION
```

Activity 9.2

No solution required.

Activity 9.3

No solution required.

Activity 9.4

Only one or two words appear - you may get three or four but certainly not 10.

Activity 9.5

10 words are displayed. However, there may be some duplicated words.

Activity 9.6

No solution required.

Activity 9.7

No solution required.

Activity 9.8

The complete code for *DrawGallows()* is:

```
FUNCTION DrawGallows()
   BOX 50,500,150,550
   LINE 60,500,60,300
   LINE 60,300,150,300
   LINE 150,300,150,350
ENDFUNCTION
```

The gallows should be displayed correctly.

Activity 9.9

The hyphens should be displayed as expected.

Activity 9.10

No solution required.

Activity 9.11

Results should be as expected.

Activity 9.12

The code for the routine and test driver is:

```
REM *** Driver for CheckForLetter() ***
REM *** Globals accessed ***
GLOBAL word$
GLOBAL guess$
REM *** Run test until end entered ***
REPEAT
    INPUT "Enter word : ", word$
    INPUT "Enter guess : ", guess$
    result = CheckForLetter()
    PRINT "Value returned by
    CheckForLetter() = ",result
UNTIL LOWER$(word$) = "end"
REM *** End program ***
WAIT KEY
END

FUNCTION CheckForLetter()
    letterfound = 0
    FOR c = 1 TO LEN(word$)
        IF guess$ = MID$(word$,c)
            letterfound = 1
            correctletters = correctletters +1
        ENDIF
    NEXT c
    IF letterfound = 0
        wrongguesses = wrongguesses +1
    ENDIF
ENDFUNCTION letterfound
```

Black Box Test Data

Possible response from routine:

letterfound = 1	-	found
letterfound = 0	-	not found

Test for found:
    word$ = london
    guess$ = l
Test for not found
    word$ = london
    guess$ = x

White Box Test Data

Constructs to be tested:

    FOR
    IF guess$
    IF letterfound

Test FOR:

Zero iterations	word$=""
1 iteration	word$ = "a"
1+ iterations	word$ = "london"

Test IF guess$ = MID$(word$,c):
    true
        word$ = "london", c = 1, MID$(word$,c) = "l",
        guess$ = "l"
    false
        word$ = "london", c = 2, MID$(word$,c) = "o",
        guess$ ="l"

Test IF letterfound = 0:

true	word$ = "a", guess$ = "a"
false	word$ = "london",guess$="x"

Tests can be combined (and in some cases the test values changed) to give us a final set of test data which covers all the tests required:

Test Run	Test Data	Reason for Test	Expected Result	Actual Result
1	word = "" guess="x"	Zero iterations of FOR IF letterfound = 1 (False)	letterfound = 0 wrongguesses incr'd	
2	word ="a" guess="a"	One iteration of FOR IF letterfound = 1 (True) IF guess=MID$(word,c) (true)	letterfound = 1 correctletters incr'd	
3	word="london" guess="l"	Multi-iteration of FOR IF guess=MID$(word,c)(false)	letterfound = 1 correctletters incr'd	

Activity 9.13

No solution required.

Activity 9.14

```
FUNCTION AddToHangedMan()
    SELECT wrongguesses
        CASE 1
                    CIRCLE 150,360,10
        ENDCASE
        CASE 2
                    ELLIPSE 150,400,10,30
        ENDCASE
        CASE 3
            LINE 145,428,135,460
        ENDCASE
        CASE 4
            LINE 155,428,165,460
        ENDCASE
        CASE 5
            LINE 143,380,133,410
        ENDCASE
        CASE 6
            LINE 157,380,167,410
        ENDCASE
    ENDSELECT
ENDFUNCTION
```

Testing can be carried out by adding the routine to the main project.

Activity 9.15

No solution required.

Activity 9.16

By entering the same letter over and over again, the program can be fooled into thinking that the player has won the game.

Activity 9.17

The completed program is shown below:

```
#INCLUDE "StringLibrary.dba"

REM *** Global Constants ***
#CONSTANT screenwidth = 800
#CONSTANT screenheight = 600
#CONSTANT fontname = "Courier New"
#CONSTANT fontsize = 30
#CONSTANT fontcolour = RGB(255,255,255)

REM *** Global variables ***
GLOBAL word$
GLOBAL guess$
GLOBAL wrongguesses
GLOBAL correctletters
GLOBAL lettersguessed$

REM *** Main program ***
InitialiseGame()
ThinkOfWord()
DrawInitialScreen()
REPEAT
    GetGuess()
    letterfound = CheckForLetter()
    IF letterfound = 1
        DrawLetter()
    ELSE
        AddToHangedMan()
    ENDIF
UNTIL WordGuessed() OR
↳HangedManComplete()
GameOver()
WAIT KEY
END


REM *** Initialises game ***
FUNCTION InitialiseGame
    SET DISPLAY MODE
        screenwidth,screenheight,16
    SET TEXT FONT fontname
    SET TEXT SIZE fontsize
    INK fontcolour,0
    wrongguesses = 0
    correctletters = 0
    lettersguessed$=""
    RANDOMIZE TIMER()
ENDFUNCTION

REM *** Think of word ***
FUNCTION ThinkOfWord()
    REM *** Words to choose from **
    DATA "london", "glasgow", "blackpool"
    DATA "edinburgh", "boston", "berlin"
    DATA "moscow", "sydney", "wellington"
    DATA "washington", "rome","amsterdam"
    DATA "stockholm", "oslo", "lisbon"
    DATA "madrid", "prague", "bonn"
    DATA "budapest", "vienna"
    REM *** Choose word from list ***
    num = RND(19)+1
    FOR c = 1 TO num
        READ word$
    NEXT c
ENDFUNCTION

REM *** Set up the screen ***
FUNCTION DrawInitialScreen()
    SET CURSOR 300,80
    PRINT "H A N G M A N"
    DrawGallows()
    DrawHyphens()
ENDFUNCTION
```

```
REM *** Returns 1 if player has won ***
FUNCTION WordGuessed()
    IF correctletters = LEN(word$)
        EXITFUNCTION 1
    ENDIF
ENDFUNCTION 0

REM *** Returns 1 if player has lost ***
FUNCTION HangedManComplete()
    IF wrongguesses = 6
        EXITFUNCTION 1
    ENDIF
ENDFUNCTION 0

REM *** Display game over message ***
FUNCTION GameOver()
    SET CURSOR 330,200
    PRINT "GAME OVER"
ENDFUNCTION

REM *** Draw the gallows ***
FUNCTION DrawGallows()
    BOX 50,500,150,550
    LINE 60,500,60,300
    LINE 60,300,150,300
    LINE 150,300,150,350
ENDFUNCTION

REM *** Draw hyphen for each letter ***
FUNCTION DrawHyphens()
    REM *** Position cursor ***
    SET CURSOR 250,400
    REM *** Draw hyphens ***
    FOR C = 1 TO LEN(word$)
        PRINT "_  ";
    NEXT c
ENDFUNCTION

REM *** Get player's guess ***
FUNCTION GetGuess()
    SET CURSOR 200,500
    SET TEXT OPAQUE
    PRINT"                        ";
    SET CURSOR 200,500
    INPUT "Enter your guess ",guess$
    guess$ = LOWER$(guess$)
    alreadyused = Pos(lettersguessed$,
                    guess$)
    WHILE LEN(guess$)<>1 OR guess$<"a"
    ↳OR guess$ > "z" OR alreadyused <> -1
        SET CURSOR 200,500
        IF LEN(guess$)<>1 OR guess$<"a" OR
        guess$ > "z"
            PRINT "single letters only"
        ELSE
            PRINT "You've already entered
                    that letter"
        ENDIF
        WAIT 2000
        SET CURSOR 200,500
        PRINT "                        ";
        SET CURSOR 200,500
        INPUT "Enter your guess ",guess$
        guess$ = LOWER$(guess$)
        alreadyused = Pos(lettersguessed$,
                        guess$)
    ENDWHILE
    lettersguessed$ = lettersguessed$+guess$
    SET TEXT TRANSPARENT
ENDFUNCTION

REM *** Returns 1 if letter is in word ***
FUNCTION CheckForLetter()
    letterfound = 0
    FOR c = 1 TO LEN(word$)
        IF guess$ = MID$(word$,c)
            letterfound = 1
        ENDIF
```

```
        NEXT c
        IF letterfound=0
            wrongguesses = wrongguesses + 1
        ENDIF
ENDFUNCTION letterfound

REM *** Add letter where it occurs in word
***
FUNCTION DrawLetter()
    SET CURSOR 250, 400
    FOR c = 1 TO LEN(word$)
        IF guess$ = MID$(word$,c)
            PRINT guess$," ";
            correctletters = correctletters+1
        ELSE
            PRINT "   ";
        ENDIF
    NEXT c
ENDFUNCTION

REM *** Add section to hanged man ***
FUNCTION AddToHangedMan()
    SELECT wrongguesses
        CASE 1:
                CIRCLE 150,360,10
        ENDCASE
        CASE 2
                ELLIPSE 150,400,10,30
        ENDCASE
        CASE 3
                LINE 145,428,135,460
        ENDCASE
        CASE 4
                LINE 155,428,165,460
        ENDCASE
        CASE 5
                LINE 143,380,133,410
        ENDCASE
        CASE 6
                LINE 157,380,167,410
        ENDCASE
    ENDSELECT
ENDFUNCTION
```

10

Arrays

Accessing Array Elements

Adding Values to an Array

Declaring Arrays

Deleting Arrays

Deleting Values from an Array

Dynamically Sized Arrays

Generating a Set of Unique Values

Multi-Dimensional Arrays

Searching an Array

Sorting an Array

Shuffling a Pack of Cards

Using Arrays for Counting

Arrays

Introduction

There are certain tasks which are very difficult or long-winded when we try to do them using the normal variables we've been dealing with up to now.

For example, it's common for a game to retain the top scores but, from what we know at the moment, we'd have to set up one variable for each score to be saved (see FIG-10.1).

FIG-10.1

Saving the Top Ten Scores

The top five scores held in 5 separate variables

When a player finishes a game, the program has to decide if the player's score should be recorded in the top five and, if so, at what position.

If the new score is held in a variable called *newscore* and has a value of 2100, then, since this is a high score, the end result should be that the top five scores are now recorded as shown in FIG-10.2.

FIG-10.2

The Top Five Scores

Notice that what had been the second, third and fourth highest scores have now moved down one position and that the score of 1220 has been lost from the top five.

We need to develop an algorithm which can perform the above task for all possible values. It could start with the lines:

```
IF
    newscore > score1:
        score5 := score4
        score4 := score3
        score3 := score2
        score2 := score1
        score1 := newscore
    newscore > score2:
        score5 := score4
        score4 := score3
        score3 := score2
        score2 := newscore
    newscore > score3:
        score5 := score4
        score4 := score3
        score3 := newscore
    newscore > score4:
        score5 := score4
        score4 := newscore
    newscore > score5:
        score5 = newscore
ENDIF
```

The algorithm is a bit long-winded, but just about acceptable. Now imagine that we had the top ten scores to retain. What would the algorithm look like then? It's going to be long - very long. Luckily, there is a better way to achieve what we're after - arrays.

Creating Arrays

The DIM Statement

If we need to store a list of values, such as the top ten scores or a set of words, then often the best way to do this will be to set up an **array**. An array is a named data variable capable of storing several values at the same time. We can compare an array to the pigeon holes that we might find at the reception area in a hotel. The storage areas in an array are known as **cells** or **elements**. Each cell is capable of storing a single value. Like the pigeon holes in the hotel, array cells are numbered. The first cell is numbered cell zero, the next cell 1, etc. Exactly how many cells an array contains is determined when it is first set up. If we need an array called *topscores* which needs to store 11 integer values, then we would use the line:

```
DIM topscores(10)
```

In this line DIM is short for dimension (i.e. the size), *topscores* is the name of the variable, and 10 is the number assigned to the last cell in the array. FIG-10.3 shows a visual impression of the variable created by the instruction.

FIG-10.3

Creating an Array

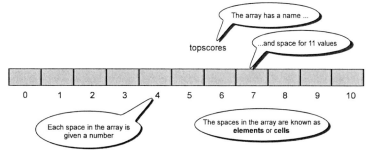

So, unlike normal variables, an array must be set up (or declared) before it can be used. This allows the program to determine how much space must be set up to hold the values placed in the array.

The format of the DIM statement is shown in FIG-10.4.

FIG-10.4

The DIM Statement

In the diagram:

name is the name assigned to the array. Array names conform to that of normal variables. End the array name with a # sign if the array is to hold real numbers and with a $ symbol if strings are to be stored.

size is a positive integer value specifying the number to be assigned to the last element in the array. Since cell numbers start at zero, the array will contain *size* + 1 cells.

Every value held in an array must be of the same type; we cannot have the first element hold an integer value while the second holds a string.

Activity 10.2

Write a line of code to define an array for each of the following:

a) An array called *list* which stores up to 20 integer values
b) An array called *names$* which stores up to 5 strings.
c) An array called *weights#* which stores up to 100 real values.

Having an element zero in an array can often lead to some confusion. After all, the natural inclination is to place the first value in cell 1 and the second in cell 2, etc. Because of this it is quite common to ignore the existence of cell zero when writing a program. For the most part, that is the approach used in the programs given here.

Of course, if we're going to ignore cell zero, we'll need to make the array one element bigger. So to store 10 numbers, we need an 11 element array.

When a numeric array is created, every element is automatically set to zero; the elements of a string array contain empty (zero character) strings.

Accessing Array Elements

Each cell or element in the array is capable of holding a value. To get a value into a cell we need to specify the variable's name and, in parentheses, the number of the cell we wish to access. Hence the lines

```
DIM numbers(10)
numbers(1) = 250
```

sets up an array called *numbers* containing 11 elements and then stores the value 250 in cell 1 of that array (see FIG-10.5).

FIG-10.5

Storing a Value in an Array Element

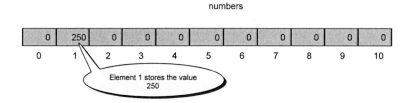

The value in the parentheses is known as the **array subscript**, and specifies which element of the array is to be accessed.

Activity 10.3

What line would be used to store the value 1500 in cell 3 of an array called *numbers*?

In fact, as long as you give the array name and the element number, you can do anything with a single array element that you can with a normal variable. For example, each of the following examples are all valid:

These lines assume that the array *numbers* has been previously declared using a DIM statement.

```
1.  numbers(9) = numbers(1) + numbers(3)

2.  PRINT numbers(1)

3.  IF value > numbers(1) THEN
        PRINT value , " is larger than ", numbers(1)
    ENDIF

4.  numbers(2) = value
```

Activity 10.4

Assuming a twenty-element array (0 to 19) called *list* has been created, write DarkBASIC Pro statements to perform each of the following:

a) Store the value 12 in element 15
b) Store the value -7 in element 3
c) Add the contents of elements 15 and 3, storing the result in element 1
d) Display the contents of element 1 on the screen.
e) Double any value held in element 15.

Variable Subscripts

If what we've seen so far was the limit of an array's abilities, their usefulness would be limited since using them wouldn't reduce the complexity of any code that we had to write. However, the real power of an array lies in the fact that the subscript may be specified using an integer variable. For example, in the lines

```
p = 5
numbers(p) = 23
```

the value 23 is stored in element 5 of the *numbers* array.

The program looks at the array subscript to determine which element of the array is to be accessed, But since the subscript is given as a variable (p), the program must first discover the value of that variable (5) and then use that value as the element to be accessed. So in the lines

```
k = 10
numbers(k) = -12
```

the value -12 is stored in element 10 of the *numbers* array.

In that last Activity we saw how the subscript variable could be incremented to reference the next element of an array hence

```
p = 15
list(p) =   99
```

accessed element 15 of the array, but by incrementing p

```
p = p + 1
```

we then accessed element 16 with the statement:

```
list(p) = 5
```

We can take this idea one stage further and use a FOR loop counter to access every element of an array in turn. Hence, the lines

This time we're making use of element zero in the array.

```
DIM list(20)
FOR p = 0 TO 20
    list(p) = 12
NEXT p
```

will store the value 12 in every element of the array *list*, since as *p* changes on each iteration of the FOR loop, a different element of the array is accessed each time.

A FOR loop is often used to read a value into every element of an array, the code for this being

```
FOR p = 0 TO 20
    INPUT" Enter a number ",list(p)
NEXT p
```

or for displaying the complete contents of an array:

```
FOR p = 0 TO 20
    PRINT list(p)
NEXT p
```

The program in LISTING-10.1 makes use of these techniques to read in 6 city names and then displays the values entered.

LISTING-10.1

Reading into an Array
and Displaying Its
Contents

```
REM *** Set up a seven element string array ***
DIM cities$(6)

REM *** Read a value into each element ***
FOR c = 1 TO 6
   INPUT "Enter city name : ",cities$(c)
NEXT c

REM *** Display the values entered ***
FOR c = 1 TO 6
   PRINT cities$(c)
NEXT c

REM *** End program ***
WAIT KEY
END
```

Activity 10.6

Type in and test the program (*arrays01.dba*) given in LISTING-10.1.

Modify the program so that 8 names are read and displayed.

Did you notice that, when typing in several values, you become unsure as to just how many values you've entered? It would be more helpful if the program stated which name was required - first, second, third, etc. We can do this by making a slight modification to the program as shown in LISTING-10.2.

LISTING-10.2

Displaying the Element
Number

```
REM *** Set up a seven element string array ***
DIM cities$(6)

REM *** Read a value into each element ***
FOR c = 1 TO 6
   PRINT "Enter city name ",c," : ";
   INPUT cities$(c)
NEXT c

REM *** Display the values entered ***
FOR c = 1 TO 6
   PRINT cities$(c)
NEXT c

REM *** End program ***
WAIT KEY
END
```

Activity 10.7

Modify your own program to match that given above (but still with 8 elements rather than 6) and check that it operates correctly.

Make a second change to your program so that the array element number is displayed beside each city name.

If we know in advance what values we want to place in an array, for example, the words used in our Hangman game, we can use DATA and READ statements to set up those values.

Once the DATA statement has been set up, this needs little more than to replace the INPUT statement with a READ statement as shown in LISTING-10.3.

LISTING-10.3

Using DATA and READ
with an Array

```
REM Set up array to hold 20 words ***
DIM words$(20)

REM *** Words to be placed in array **
DATA "london", "glasgow", "blackpool", "edinburgh", "boston"
DATA "berlin", "moscow", "sydney", "wellington", "washington"
DATA "rome", "amsterdam", "stockholm", "oslo", "lisbon"
DATA "madrid", "prague", "bonn","budapest","vienna"

REM *** Place words in array***
FOR c = 1 TO 20
   READ words$(c)
NEXT c

REM *** Display the contents of the array ***
FOR c = 1 TO 20
   PRINT words$(c)
NEXT c

REM *** End program ***
WAIT KEY
END
```

Activity 10.8

Type in and test the program given in LISTING-10.3 (*arrays02.dba*).

Activity 10.9

Create a new program (*arrays03.dba*) containing two arrays: *monthnames$*
(a 13 element string array) and *daysinmonth* (a 13 element integer array).
In *monthnames$* place, in order, the names of each month of the year. In
daysinmonth store, in order, the number of days in each month (set month 2 to
28).
The program should end by displaying 12 lines. Each of these lines should
contain a month of the year and the number of days in that month as shown
below:

> January 31
> February 28
> etc.

Basic Algorithms that Use Arrays

There are several operations involving arrays that crop up over and over again in
many programming situations, some of these are described below.

Calculating the Sum of the Values in an Array

To calculate the sum of all the values held in a numeric array, we start by setting a
variable, *sum*, to zero and then adding the value held in each element of the array
to this variable. The logic required is

```
Set sum to zero
FOR each element in the array DO
    Add its value to sum
ENDFOR
```

The coding, which includes the reading in of the array's values, is given in
LISTING-10.4.

LISTING-10.4

Summing the Values in
an Array

```
REM *** Set up a 10 element array ***
DIM numbers(10)

REM *** Read a value into each element ***
FOR c = 1 TO 10
    PRINT "Enter number ", c," : ";
    INPUT numbers(c)
NEXT c

REM *** set sum to zero ***
sum = 0

REM *** FOR each element in the array DO ***
FOR p = 1 TO 10
    REM *** Add that element's value to sum ***
    sum = sum + numbers(p)
NEXT p

REM *** Display the result ***
PRINT "The sum of the numbers is ", sum

REM *** End program ***
WAIT KEY
END
```

Activity 10.10

Type in and test the program given above (*arrays04.dba*).

Modify the program so that the array contains 8 values rather than 10.

Modify the program so that the average, rather than the sum, of the numbers is displayed. Make the average a real value.

Finding the Smallest Value in an Array

Another common requirement is finding the smallest value in an array. The logic for this algorithm is:

```
Set smallest equal to the value held in element one of the array
FOR every other element in the array DO
        IF its value is less than smallest THEN
                Set smallest equal to that value
        ENDIF
ENDFOR
Display the value in smallest
```

The DarkBASIC Pro code is given in LISTING-10.5.

LISTING-10.5

Finding the Smallest
Value in an Array

```
REM *** Set up a 10 element array ***
DIM numbers(10)
REM *** Read a value into each element ***
FOR c = 1 TO 10
    PRINT " Enter number ", c," : ";
    INPUT numbers(c)
NEXT c

REM *** set smallest to numbers(1) ***
smallest = numbers(1)

REM *** FOR each element in the array DO ***
FOR p = 2 TO 10
```
continued on next page

LISTING-10.5
(continued)

Finding the Smallest
Value in an Array

```
   REM *** IF value is smaller, change contents of smallest ***
   IF numbers(p) < smallest
      smallest = numbers(p)
   ENDIF
NEXT p

REM *** Display the result ***
PRINT "The smallest value is ", smallest

REM *** End program ***
WAIT KEY
END
```

Activity 10.11

Type in and test the program given in LISTING-10.5 (*arrays05.dba*).

Modify the program so that it displays the largest value in the array.

Searching For a Value in an Array

Searching an array to find out if it contains a specific value is another common requirement. For example, if we want to search *cities$*, an array containing a set of city names, for the word *london*, then the program would use the following logic:

```
Set up the array to contain the city names
Get the name of the city to be searched for
Starting at position 1 in the array
WHILE the value at the current position in the array does not match the required name
DO
     Move to the next position in the array
ENDWHILE
```

A visual representation of a typical search is shown in FIG-10.6.

FIG-10.6

Searching an Array

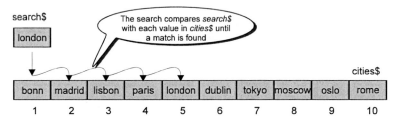

Actually, the algorithm assumes that a match will eventually be found, but, of course, this may not be the case. If we searched the same array for the word *berlin*, no match would be found. The fact that no match is to be found only becomes obvious when we have compared the required value (*berlin*) with every entry in the array. Because there is a possibility that the searched for item may not be found, the WHILE loop in our algorithm needs a second terminating condition: reaching the end of the array. So the algorithm changes to:

```
Set up the array to contain the city names
Get the name of the city to be searched for
Starting at position 1 in the array
WHILE the value at the current position in the array does not match the required name
AND not yet reached the end of the array
DO
     Move to the next position in the array
ENDWHILE
```

Since there are two possible outcomes: *match found* and *no match found* we have to decide on which of these possibilities is actually the case. This is achieved by ending the algorithm with an IF statement:

```
IF value at current position matches name being searched for THEN
        Display "Match found"
ELSE
        Display "No match found"
ENDIF
```

The implementation of the algorithm is shown in LISTING-10.6.

LISTING-10.6

Searching an Array

```
REM ***Set up array ***
DIM cities$(20)

REM *** Words to be placed in array ***
DATA "london", "glasgow", "blackpool", "edinburgh", "boston"
DATA "berlin", "moscow", "sydney", "wellington", "washington"
DATA "rome", "amsterdam", "stockholm", "oslo", "lisbon"
DATA "madrid", "prague", "bonn", "budapest", "vienna"

REM *** Place words in array***
FOR c = 1 TO 20
    READ cities$(c)
NEXT c

REM *** Get name to be searched for ***
INPUT "Enter the city to be searched for ",search$
search$ = LOWER$(search$)

REM *** Search for match ***
p = 1
WHILE cities$(p) <> search$ AND p < 20
    p = p + 1
ENDWHILE

REM *** Display result ***
IF cities$(p) = search$
    PRINT "Match found"
ELSE
    PRINT "No match found"
ENDIF

REM *** End program ***
WAIT KEY
END
```

Activity 10.12

Type in and test the program in LISTING-10.6. (*arrays06.dba*).

Keeping an Array's Values in Order

We started this chapter by looking at how we could store the top scores achieved in a game. Perhaps you've guessed by now that an array would be a useful structure to use in coming up with a short algorithm for this problem. FIG-10.7 shows the stages involved in adding a new value to an array containing the high scores. All of this can be described in the following algorithm:

```
Get newscore
Find insert position
Move lower values along one place
Insert new score
```

FIG-10.7

Maintaining Order
Within an Array

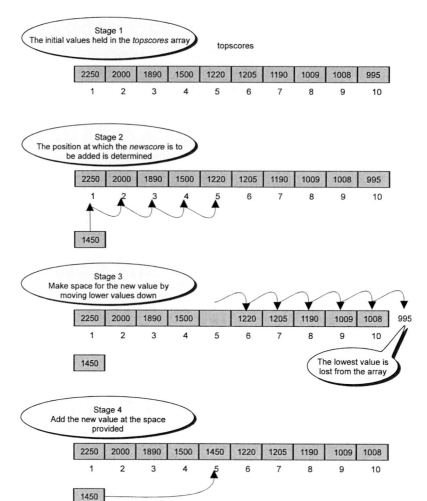

This is an example of a
list in **descending** order
(highest value first).

Values can also be held
in **ascending** order with
the lowest value first.

LISTING-10.7 gives the DarkBASIC Pro code for this algorithm.

LISTING-10.7

Maintaining an Array in
Descending Order

```
REM ***Set up topscores array ***
DIM topscores(10)
REM *** Current top score values to be placed in array ***
DATA 2250,2000,1890,1500,1220,1205,1190,1009,1008,995

REM *** Place top scores in array***
FOR c = 1 TO 10
   READ topscores(c)
NEXT c

REM *** Get new score ***
INPUT "Enter new score ",newscore

REM *** Display the current top scores ***
FOR c = 1 TO 10
   PRINT topscores(c), " ";
NEXT c
PRINT

REM *** Search for value less than new score ***
p = 1
WHILE topscores(p) >= newscore
   p = p + 1
ENDWHILE
```
continued on next page

DarkBASIC Pro: Arrays

LISTING-10.7
(continued)

Maintaining an Array in
Descending Order

```
insertposition = p
REM *** Move values between insertposition and end down ***
FOR c = 9 TO insertposition STEP - 1
   topscores(c+1) = topscores(c)
NEXT c

REM *** Insert new score at the position created ***
topscores(insertposition) = newscore

REM *** Display the new top scores order ***
FOR c = 1 TO 10
   PRINT topscores(c), " ";
NEXT c

REM *** End program ***
WAIT KEY
END
```

The program begins by setting up values in the *topscores* array. In a real game the *topscores* array would initially be filled with zeros (or scores achieved by fictional players). These would then be displaced by the scores achieved by the first ten games played.

Activity 10.13

Type in and test the program in Activity 10.11 (*arrays07.dbpro*).

Modify the program so that the top scores are in ascending order.

Using an Array for Counting

In the Hangman game the computer generated a random number between 1 and 20 when choosing the word to be used in the game. For the game to work correctly, each number (and hence each word) should have an equal chance of being chosen. So, if we get the computer to choose a word one thousand times, each word should be chosen around fifty times. Of course, this can't be exact, but if several words were to be chosen 10 times or less, then we might worry that the words were not being chosen on a truly random basis.

We can find out which words are being chosen by recording how often each number between 1 and 20 is generated. To do this we need to set up 20 different counts. One to count how often a 1 is generated, another to count how often 2 is generated, etc.

The simplest way to do this is by using a 20 element array with each element being used as a separate count. Element 1 would record how often a 1 is generated; element 2 how often a 2 was generated, etc. The algorithm we need then becomes:

The algorithm specifies setting all elements of counts to zero even though this is done automatically in DarkBASIC Pro. However, not all languages set array elements to zero without explicit instructions to do so.

```
Seed random number generator
Set up the counts array
Set all elements of counts to zero
FOR 1000 times DO
     Generate the random number used for choosing word
     Add1 to the count corresponding to the number generated
ENDFOR
Display all the counts
```

The code for the program is given in LISTING-10.8.

LISTING-10.8

Using Array Elements as
Counters

```
REM *** Set up globals ***
GLOBAL word$
GLOBAL DIM counts(20)

REM *** Seed number generator ***
RANDOMIZE TIMER()

REM *** Set all counts to zero ***
FOR p = 1 TO 20
   counts(p) = 0
NEXT p

REM *** FOR 1000 times DO ***
FOR c = 1 TO 1000
   REM *** Generate the number ***
   num = RND(19)+1
   REM *** Add 1 to the corresponding count ***
   counts(num) = counts(num) + 1
NEXT c

REM *** Display counts ***
FOR p = 1 TO 20
   PRINT counts(p)
NEXT p

REM *** End program ***
WAIT KEY
END
```

***

Activity 10.14

Type in and test the program in LISTING-10.12 (*arrays08.dbpro*).

***

Associating Numbers with Strings

In Chapter 4 we introduced the SELECT statement by demonstrating how a number
representing the day of the week (1 for Sunday; 7 for Saturday) could be used to
determine what word should be displayed on the screen. The code began with the
lines:

```
INPUT "Enter a number between 1 and 7 : ", day
SELECT day
    CASE 1
        PRINT "Sunday"
    ENDCASE
```

We can achieve the same sort of result using an array of strings. First we set up the
words in the array:

```
DIM daysofweek$(7)
DATA "Sunday","Monday","Tuesday","Wednesday"
DATA "Thursday", "Friday", "Saturday"
FOR p = 1 TO 7
    READ daysofweek$(p)
NEXT p
```

That's the hard work done. Now all we need to do is read in the day as a number
and display the corresponding element in the array. That is, if the user enters a 5 we
display the contents of element 5 in the array. Entering 2 will display element 2,
etc. The code is:

```
INPUT "Enter a number between 1 and 7 : ", day
```

```
PRINT daysofweek$(day)
```

Activity 10.15

Write a program (*arrays09.dbpro*) which will accept a value between 1 and 12 and display the corresponding month of the year by name.

Card Shuffling

An obvious use for an array in a game is to hold a deck of playing cards.

We have to start by thinking of a way to represent the individual card values and suit. Since there are 13 cards in a suit we could use the numbers 1 to 13 to represent these cards with 1 being the representation of an Ace and 13 the code for a King. We could then represent the suits by adding 100, 200, 300, or 400 to a card's basic value to represent Spades, Hearts, Diamonds, Clubs respectively. Using this system the Queen of Spades would be represented by the number 112 while the Queen of Clubs would be 412.

Activity 10.16

What values would be used to represent the following cards?

a) 8 of Diamonds
b) 2 of Hearts
c) The King of Spades

If a variable is assigned a value with the line

```
card = 311
```

we can tell from the 300 part that it's a Diamond and from the 11 that it's a Knave (Jack). In the program these two pieces of information can be extracted using the lines:

```
suit = card / 100
value = card mod 100
```

With a little bit of effort we can display a cards value in words. This time we need to set up two arrays: one containing the suit names and the other the card names:

```
REM *** Create arrays ***
DIM suits$(4)
DIM cardnames$(13)
REM *** Values for each array ***
DATA "Spades", "Hearts", "Diamonds", "Clubs"
DATA "Ace","Deuce","Three","Four","Five","Six","Seven"
DATA "Eight","Nine","Ten","Knave","Queen","King"
REM *** Read in suits ***
FOR p = 1 TO 4
    READ suits$(p)
NEXT p
REM *** Read card names ***
FOR p = 1 TO 13
    READ cardnames$(p)
NEXT p
```

Just to prove the code works, we could generate a number and display the card it represents using the lines:

```
REM *** Pick a card at random ***
RANDOMIZE TIMER()
card = (RND(3)+1)*100 + RND(12)+1

REM *** Display the card's value ***
suit = card / 100
value = card mod 100
PRINT "Card is ", card ," which is the ",cardnames$(value),
" of ",suits$(suit)
```

Activity 10.17

Using the appropriate lines from above, create a program (*arrays10.dbpro*) which generates a playing card at random and displays its name and suit.

The whole pack can be held in a 52 element array which can be set up with the following code:

```
DIM pack(52)
p = 0
FOR suit = 100 TO 400 STEP 100
    FOR card = 1 TO 13
        p = p + 1
        pack(p) = suit + card
    NEXT card
NEXT suit
```

and displayed using the lines

```
FOR p = 1 TO 52
    suit = pack(p) / 100
    value = pack(p) mod 100
    PRINT "Card is ", pack(p) ," which is the ",
    cardnames$(value)," of ",suits$(suit)
NEXT p
```

Activity 10.18

Construct a complete program (*arrays11.dbpro*) to create and display a pack of cards.

The final problem we need to solve is how to shuffle the cards. There are many ways we could tackle this problem. In the approach below we choose two locations in the pack and swap the cards at those locations (see FIG-10.8).

FIG-10.8

Exchanging the
Contents of Two Cells

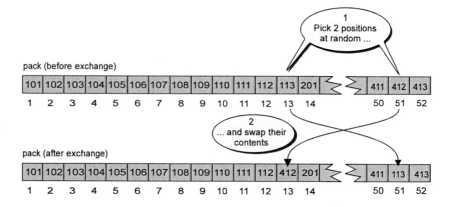

The code required to achieve this

This code should be preceded by a RANDOMIZE TIMER() statement.

```
p1 = RND(51)+1
p2 = RND(51)+1
temp = pack(p1)
pack(p1) = pack(p2)
pack(p2) = temp
```

This operation is then repeated many times with the result that the cards have been rearranged in a random order (i.e. shuffled).

Activity 10.19

Modify your previous program so that the pack is shuffled before its contents are displayed.

Choosing a Set of Unique Values

Perhaps we could get lucky in a lottery by getting a program to generate six numbers. An attempt at doing this is given in LISTING-10.9.

LISTING-10.9

Problems with Duplicated Values

```
REM *** Set up array to hold the numbers ***
DIM lottonumbers(6)

REM *** Seed the random number generator ***
RANDOMIZE TIMER()

REM *** Generate six numbers ***
FOR p = 1 TO 6
   lottonumbers(p) = RND(48)+1
NEXT p

REM *** Display the numbers ***
FOR p = 1 TO 6
    PRINT lottonumbers(p), "   ";
NEXT p

REM *** End program ***
WAIT KEY
END
```

Activity 10.20

Type in the program given in LISTING-10.9 (*arrays12.dbpro*) and test it.

Can you see any problems ? You may have to run the program a few times .

As we see, sometimes we get a number occurring more than once in the list of six values. Obviously, we need a way to stop this happening.

A possible approach is to create a second array with an element for every value that might be generated. So if any number between 1 and 49 can be produced, we'll set up an array containing elements numbered 1 to 49 and then mark off each value generated by changing the matching array element's contents from zero to 1. Before accepting the next generated value, the program checks that the value in question has not already been marked off (see FIG-10.9).

FIG-10.9

Generating a Set of
Unique Values

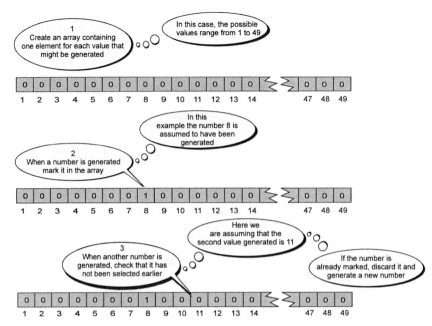

The algorithm required for this task is:

```
Set up the array of possible values
FOR number of values to generate times DO
    Generate a random value
    WHILE value already marked DO
        Generate a new value
    ENDWHILE
    Mark array element corresponding to generated value
ENDFOR
```

The actual DarkBASIC Pro code is given in LISTING-10.10

LISTING-10.10

Avoiding Duplication
Using an Array

```
DIM possiblevalues(49)          'Holds mark for each number generated
DIM lottonumbers(6)             'Holds accepted numbers generated

REM *** Initialise generator***
RANDOMIZE TIMER()

REM *** FOR 6 times DO ***
FOR p = 1 TO 6
   REM *** Generate a number ***
   num = RND(48)+1
   REM *** WHILE that number already used DO ***
   WHILE possiblevalues(num) <> 0
      REM *** Generate another number ***
      num = RND(48)+1
   ENDWHILE
   REM *** Mark the generated number as used ***
   possiblevalues(num) = 1
   REM *** Save the accepted value ***
   lottonumbers(p) = num
NEXT p

REM *** Display the numbers ***
FOR p = 1 TO 6
   PRINT lottonumbers(p), "   ";
NEXT p

REM *** End program ***
WAIT KEY
END
```

Dynamic Arrays

Sometimes it is not possible to know how large an array should be at the time we are writing a program. For example, let's say we need an array to hold the name of each player in a multi-player game. The number of elements needed in the array depends on the number of people who are actually playing on any specific occasion. To handle this situation DarkBASIC Pro allows the size of an array to be set using a variable. Hence, to solve the problems of the players' names we could read in the number of players and then set up an array containing that number of elements (see LISTING-10.11).

LISTING-10.11

Sizing Arrays at Runtime

```
REM *** Find out how many people are playing ***
INPUT "Enter the number of players : ", noofplayers

REM *** Set up an array of that size ***
DIM names$(noofplayers)

REM *** Read in the name of each player ***
FOR p = 1 TO noofplayers
    PRINT "Enter name ",p," : ";
    INPUT names$(p)
NEXT p

REM *** Prove the names have been stored by displaying them ***
PRINT "The names saved are "
FOR p = 1 TO noofplayers
    PRINT names$(p)
NEXT p

REM *** End program ***
WAIT KEY
END
```

The UNDIM Statement

If a program creates a particularly large array with thousands of elements, or has very many arrays, then it will occupy significant amounts of memory. This in turn may slow down the speed at which your program runs. To avoid this it is possible to delete arrays which are no longer required using the UNDIM statement which has the format shown in FIG-10.10.

FIG-10.10

The UNDIM Statement

In the diagram:

name   is the name given to a previously defined array.

Using Arrays in a Game

There are many game situations where an array would be useful. We've already seen one such situation for storing high scores, but any situation where we need a collection of values can often be implemented using an array. Examples include a hand of playing cards, the items carried by a character in a role-playing game or the list of properties owned in Monopoly.

Multi-Dimensional Arrays

Two Dimensional Arrays

Could we represent the game of chess using an array? The problem here is that the chess board has rows and columns while the arrays we have encountered up to now are just one long list of values. Luckily DarkBASIC Pro allows us to created arrays which which have both rows and columns. These are called **two-dimensional** arrays.

To do this we need to start by declaring our array using an extended form of the DIM statement in which the number of rows and columns are specified. For example, the statement

```
DIM grid(3,8)
```

creates a two-dimensional array called *grid* which has 4 rows and 9 columns (see FIG-10.11).

FIG-10.11

Creating a 2D Array

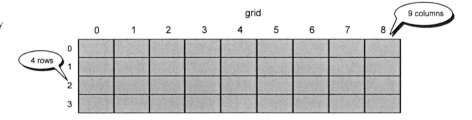

To access a cell in the array we have to give the array name, the row and the column as in the line

```
grid (2,4) = 20
```

which stores the value 20 in the cell at position row 2 column 4 (see FIG-10.12).

FIG-10.12

Accessing a 2D Array.
Row zero and column zero are ignored in this code.

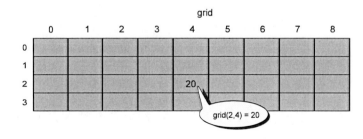

Inputting Values to a 2D Array

To read values into a 2D array we need to use two FOR loops. One of these iterates through the column values (1 to 8 in the example above), while the other loops through the rows (1 to 3 above). The following snippet of code will read a value into every cell of the *grid* array defined earlier:

```
FOR row = 1 TO 3
    FOR column = 1 TO 8
        PRINT "Enter a value for cell (",row,",",column,"): ";
        INPUT grid(row,column)
    NEXT column
NEXT row
```

Activity 10.23

Create a new program (*arrays15.dbpro*) which contains a 2D array called *values*. The array should have 4 rows and 7 columns.
Write code so that a value for each cell is read from the keyboard and then the contents of the array are displayed on the screen.

Even More Dimensions

There's no need to stop at two dimensions, arrays can be created with up to five dimensions. Although we are unlikely to ever need a five-dimensional array, the program in LISTING-10.12 creates a five-dimensional string array which is 2 by 3 by 5 by 4 by 2. It then reads values into the array and finally displays those values on the screen.

LISTING-10.12

Accessing a 5D Array

```
REM *** Set up 5D array ***
DIM list(2,3,5,4,2)
REM *** Read in values ***
FOR d1 = 1 TO 2
    FOR d2 = 1 TO 3
        FOR d3 = 1 TO 5
            FOR d4 = 1 TO 4
                FOR d5 = 1 TO 2
                    CLS
                    PRINT "Enter value for("
                    ,d1,",",d2,",",d3,",",d4,",",d5,"): ";
                    INPUT list(d1,d2,d3,d4,d5)
                NEXT d5
            NEXT d4
        NEXT d3
    NEXT d2
NEXT d1
REM *** Display values ***
FOR d1 = 1 TO 2
    FOR d2 = 1 TO 3
        FOR d3 = 1 TO 5
            FOR d4 = 1 TO 4
                FOR d5 = 1 TO 2
                    PRINT list(d1,d2,d3,d4,d5)
                NEXT d5
            NEXT d4
        NEXT d3
    NEXT d2
NEXT d1
REM *** End program ***
WAIT KEY
END
```

Arrays and Functions

Often we will want to pass an array to a function. For example, we might create a function, *Average()*, which returns the average of a set of numbers. Unfortunately, it is not possible to pass an array as a parameter nor to return an array from a function.

The only way to access a non-local array from within a function is to declare the array as a global one with a statement such as:

```
GLOBAL DIM list(20)
```

The array can then be referenced from anywhere in the program.

Summary

- Arrays can be used to hold a collection of values.

- Every value in an array must be of the same type.

- Arrays are created using the DIM statement.

- The number of elements in an array can be specified as a constant, variable, or expression.

- Using a variable or expression to set the array's size allows that size to be varied each time the program is run.

- Numeric arrays are created with the value zero in every element.

- String arrays are created with empty strings in every element.

- The size of an array can be specified using a variable or expression.

- The space allocated to an array can be freed using the UNDIM statement.

- An array element is accessed by giving the array named followed by the element's subscript value enclosed in parentheses.

- The subscript can be a constant, variable or expression.

- Arrays can have up to five dimensions.

- An array cannot be passed as a parameter to a function.

- An function cannot return an array as a result.

Solutions

Activity 10.1

Start by numbering each line in the algorithm:

```
1.IF
2.    newscore > score1:
3.         score5 := score4
4.         score4 := score3
5.         score3 := score2
6.         score2 := score1
7.         score1 := newscore
8.    newscore > score2:
9.         score5 := score4
10.        score4 := score3
11.        score3 := score2
12.        score2 := newscore
13.   newscore > score3:
14.        score5 := score4
15.        score4 := score3
16.        score3 := newscore
17.   newscore > score4:
18.        score5 := score4
19.        score4 := newscore
20.   newscore > score5:
21.        score5 = newscore
22.ENDIF
```

Create the necessary table:

Instr.	Condition	T/F	Variables					
			newscore	score1	score2	score3	score4	score5
Initial set up			1900	2250	2000	1860	1500	1220
1								
2	newscore > score1	F						
8	newscore > score2	F						
13	newscore > score3	T						
14								1500
15							1860	
16						1900		
22								

Activity 10.2

a)   `DIM list(19)`
b)   `DIM names$(4)`
c)   `DIM weights#(99)`

Activity 10.3

```
numbers(3) = 1500
```

Activity 10.4

a)   `list(15) = 12`
b)   `list(3) = -7`
c)   `list(1) = list(15)+list(3)`
d)   `PRINT list(1)`
e)   `list(15) = list(15)*2`

Activity 10.5

list(15) = 99
list(16) = 5
p = 5
list(5) = 3

Activity 10.6

The modified program is:

```
REM *** Set up nine cell string array ***
DIM cities$(8)
REM *** Read a value into each element ***
FOR c = 1 TO 8
   INPUT "Enter city name : ",cities$(c)
NEXT c
REM *** Display the values entered ***
FOR c = 1 TO 8
   PRINT cities$(c)
NEXT c
REM *** End program ***
WAIT KEY
END
```

Lines that remain unchanged from the original code are in grey.

Activity 10.7

The final version is:

```
REM *** Set up eight cell string array ***
DIM cities$(8)
REM *** Read a value into each element ***
FOR c = 1 TO 8
   PRINT "Enter city name ",c," : ";
   INPUT cities$(c)
NEXT c
REM *** Display the values entered ***
FOR c = 1 TO 8
   PRINT "City number ", c, " is ",
      cities$(c)
NEXT c
REM *** End program ***
WAIT KEY
END
```

Activity 10.8

No solution required.

Activity 10.9

```
REM Set up arrays ***
DIM monthnames$(12)
DIM daysinmonth(12)
REM *** Names of month data ***
DATA "January","February","March"
DATA "April","May","June"
DATA "July","August","September"
DATA "October","November","December"
REM *** Days in each month data ***
DATA 31,28,31,30,31,30,31,31,30,31,30,31
REM *** Place names in array***
FOR c = 1 TO 12
   READ monthnames$(c)
NEXT c
REM *** Place days in array ***
FOR c = 1 TO 12
   READ daysinmonth(c)
NEXT c
REM *** Display moths and days ***
FOR c = 1 TO 12
   PRINT monthnames$(c),"  ",daysinmonth(c)
NEXT c
REM *** End program ***
```

```
WAIT KEY
END
```

Activity 10.10

```
REM *** Set up an 8 element array ***
DIM numbers(8)
REM *** Read a value into each element ***
FOR c = 1 TO 8
    PRINT "Enter number ", c," : ";
    INPUT numbers(c)
NEXT c
REM *** set sum to zero ***
sum = 0
REM *** FOR each element in the array DO ***
FOR p = 1 TO 8
    REM *** Add element's value to sum ***
    sum = sum + numbers(p)
NEXT p
REM *** Calculate average ***
average# = sum / 8
REM *** Display the result ***
PRINT "The average of the numbers is ",
average#
REM *** End program ***
WAIT KEY
END
```

Activity 10.11

```
REM *** Set up a 10 element array ***
DIM numbers(10)
REM *** Read a value into each element ***
FOR c = 1 TO 10
    PRINT "Enter number ", c," : ";
    INPUT numbers(c)
NEXT c
REM *** set largest to numbers(1) ***
largest = numbers(1)
REM *** FOR each element in the array DO ***
FOR p = 2 TO 10
    REM *** IF value is larger, ***
    REM *** change contents of largest ***
    IF numbers(p) > largest
        largest = numbers(p)
    ENDIF
NEXT p
REM *** Display the result ***
PRINT "The largest value is ", largest
REM *** End program ***
WAIT KEY
END
```

Activity 10.12

No solution required

Activity 10.13

```
REM ***Set up topscores array ***
DIM topscores(10)
REM *** Current top score values to be
placed in array ***
DATA
2250,2000,1890,1500,1220,1205,1190,1009,1008,
995
REM *** Place top scores in array***
FOR c = 10 TO 1 STEP -1
    READ topscores(c)
NEXT c
REM *** Get new score ***
INPUT "Enter new score ",newscore
REM *** Display the current top scores ***
```

```
FOR c = 1 TO 10
    PRINT topscores(c), " ";
NEXT c
PRINT
REM *** Search for value greater than new
score ***
p = 10
WHILE topscores(p) >= newscore
    p = p - 1
ENDWHILE
insertposition = p
REM *** Move values between insertposition
and end up ***
FOR c = insertposition TO 2 STEP - 1
    topscores(c-1) = topscores(c)
NEXT c
REM *** Insert new score at the position
created ***
topscores(insertposition) = newscore
REM *** Display the new top scores order
***
FOR c = 1 TO 10
    PRINT topscores(c), " ";
NEXT c
REM *** End program ***
WAIT KEY
END
```

Activity 10.14

No solution required.

Activity 10.15

```
REM *** Months of the year ***
DATA "January", "February", "March"
DATA "April", "May","June"
DATA "July", "August", "September"
DATA "October", "November", "December"

REM *** Place names in array ***
DIM months$(12)
FOR p = 1 TO 12
    READ months$(p)
NEXT p

REM *** Read a number between 1 and 12 ***
INPUT "Enter number (1 - 12) : ", num
WHILE num < 1 OR num > 12
    PRINT "Must be 1 to 12. Re-enter."
    INPUT "Enter number (1 - 12) : ", num
ENDWHILE
PRINT "month number ", num, " is ",
months$(num)
REM *** End program ***
WAIT KEY
END
```

Activity 10.16

a) 8 of Diamonds = 308
b) 2 of Hearts = 202
c) King of Spades = 113

Activity 10.17

```
REM *** Set up arrays for names ***
DIM suits$(4)
DIM cardnames$(13)
REM *** Values for each array ***
DATA "Spades", "Hearts", "Diamonds",
"Clubs"
DATA "Ace","Deuce","Three","Four","Five"
DATA "Six","Seven", "Eight","Nine","Ten"
```

```
DATA "Knave","Queen","King"
REM *** Read in suits ***
FOR p = 1 TO 4
   READ suits$(p)
NEXT p
REM *** Read card names ***
FOR p = 1 TO 13
   READ cardnames$(p)
NEXT p
REM *** Pick a card at random ***
RANDOMIZE TIMER()
card = (RND(3)+1)*100 + RND(12)+1
REM *** Display the card's value ***
suit = card / 100
value = card mod 100
PRINT "Card is ", card ," which is the ",
cardnames$(value)," of ",suits$(suit)
REM *** End program ***
WAIT KEY
END
```

Activity 10.18

```
REM *** Set up arrays for names ***
DIM suits$(4)
DIM cardnames$(13)
REM *** Values for each array ***
DATA "Spades", "Hearts", "Diamonds",
"Clubs"
DATA "Ace","Deuce","Three","Four","Five"
DATA "Six","Seven", "Eight","Nine","Ten"
DATA "Knave","Queen","King"
REM *** Read in suits ***
FOR p = 1 TO 4
   READ suits$(p)
NEXT p
REM *** Read card names ***
FOR p = 1 TO 13
   READ cardnames$(p)
NEXT p
REM *** Set up pack of cards ***
DIM pack(52)
p = 0
FOR suit = 100 TO 400 STEP 100
   FOR card = 1 TO 13
      p = p + 1
      pack(p) = suit + card
   NEXT card
NEXT suit
REM *** Display pack ***
FOR p = 1 TO 52
   suit = pack(p) / 100
   value = pack(p) mod 100
   PRINT "Card is ", pack(p) ,
   " which is the ",cardnames$(value),
   " of ",suits$(suit)
NEXT p
REM *** End program ***
WAIT KEY
END
```

Activity 10.19

```
REM *** Set up arrays for names ***
DIM suits$(4)
DIM cardnames$(13)
REM *** Values for each array ***
DATA "Spades", "Hearts", "Diamonds",
"Clubs"
DATA "Ace","Deuce","Three","Four","Five"
DATA "Six","Seven", "Eight","Nine","Ten"
DATA "Knave","Queen","King"
REM *** Read in suits ***
FOR p = 1 TO 4
   READ suits$(p)
```

```
NEXT p
REM *** Read card names ***
FOR p = 1 TO 13
   READ cardnames$(p)
NEXT p
REM *** Set up pack of cards ***
DIM pack(52)
p = 0
FOR suit = 100 TO 400 STEP 100
   FOR card = 1 TO 13
      p = p + 1
      pack(p) = suit + card
   NEXT card
NEXT suit
REM *** Shuffle cards ***
RANDOMIZE TIMER()
FOR c = 1 TO 1000
   p1 = RND(51)+1
   p2 = RND(51)+1
   temp = pack(p1)
   pack(p1) = pack(p2)
   pack(p2) = temp
NEXT c

REM *** Display pack ***
FOR p = 1 TO 52
   suit = pack(p) / 100
   value = pack(p) mod 100
   PRINT "Card is ", pack(p) ,
   " which is the ", cardnames$(value),
   " of ",suits$(suit)
NEXT p
REM *** End program ***
WAIT KEY
END
```

Activity 10.20

The problem is that the same number may occur more than once.

Activity 10.21

```
DIM possiblevalues(200)
DIM lottonumbers(10)
REM *** Initialise generator***
RANDOMIZE TIMER()
REM *** FOR 10 times DO ***
FOR p = 1 TO 10
   REM *** Generate a number ***
   num = RND(199)+1
   REM *** WHILE number already used DO ***
   WHILE possiblevalues(num) <> 0
      REM *** Generate another number ***
      num = RND(199)+1
   ENDWHILE
   REM *** Mark generated no. as used ***
   possiblevalues(num) = 1
   REM *** Save the accepted value ***
   lottonumbers(p) = num
NEXT p
REM *** Display the numbers ***
FOR p = 1 TO 10
   PRINT lottonumbers(p), " ";
NEXT p
REM *** End program ***
WAIT KEY
END
```

Activity 10.22

No solution required.

Activity 10.23

```
REM *** Set up array ***
DIM values(4,7)
REM *** READ in values ***
FOR row = 1 TO 4
   FOR column = 1 TO 7
      PRINT "Enter value for values("
      ,row,",",column,") ";
      INPUT values(row,column)
   NEXT column
NEXT row
REM *** Display values in array ***
FOR row = 1 TO 4
   FOR column = 1 TO 7
      PRINT values(row,column)," ";
   NEXT column
   PRINT
NEXT row
REM *** End program ***
WAIT KEY
END
```

Game Data

Game Rules

Mini-specs

Program Listing

Screen Layout

Bull and Touch

Introduction

This is another classic paper and pencil game which was adapted to become the commercial game called Mastermind.

The Rules

Player 1 thinks of a 4-digit number using the values 0 to 9. No duplicate digits are allowed.

Player 2 then makes a guess at Player 1's number. If the guess is correct then Player 2 has won. If the guess is not correct, Player 1 responds to the guess by stating:

> ➤ how many digits in the guess are correct and in the correct position - these are known as **bulls**.

> ➤ how many digits in the guess are correct but in the wrong position - these are known as **touches**.

For example, if Player 1 thinks of the number 7136 and Player 2 guesses 3786, then Player 1 would respond with "1 Bull and 2 Touches". We have 1 bull because the 6 in the guess is exactly in the correct position and 2 touches because the 3 and 7 in the guess appear in the original number but at different positions than they appear in the guess.

Player 1 is allowed up to 8 attempts to guess the Player 1's number.

In the computerised version of the game, the machine takes the part of Player 1.

The Screen Layout

Our first ideas on the screen layout can be produced manually using a piece of gridded paper. Remember to mark the coordinates of any item so that the programmer has an easier job of implementing the layout. In this game there are three screen layouts to design. The main one is displayed during the playing of the game; the other two are alternative end-of-game screens declaring a win or lose (see FIG-11.1).

FIG-11.1

The Screen Layouts Design

Game Data

As usual, it is only the main data items we need concern ourselves with. These will be defined as global variables within the program. Any constants are also defined here (see TABLE-11.1).

TABLE-11.1

Game Data Items and Constants

Name	Type/Value	Description
Variables		
number	integer(4)	the number to be guessed
guess	integer(4)	player's guess
bulls	integer	correct digits in correct position
touches	integer	correct digits in wrong position
outat	integer	the y-ordinate for next output
noofguesses	integer	the number of guesses made
Constants		
screenwidth	800	screen width in pixels
screenheight	600	screen height in pixels
fontname	"Arial "	name of font used
fontsize	14	font height in points
fontcolour	RGB(255,128,0)	colour of font
backgroundcolour	RGB(64,128,128)	screen background colour

Game Logic

Our structured English description of the game is as follows:

```
Initialise game
Think of number
Draw initial screen
REPEAT
      Get guess
      Calculate bulls and touches
      Display bulls and touches
UNTIL number guessed OR all 8 attempts are used
Show closing screen
```

Of these statements the following will probably need to be coded as functions:

```
Initialise game
Think of number
Draw initial screen
Get guess
Calculate bulls and touches
Display bulls and touches
Show closing screen
```

Game Documentation

NAME	:	Main
PARAMETERS		
IN	:	None
OUT	:	None
PRE-CONDITION	:	None
DESCRIPTION	:	Plays the game of Bull and Touch. The program produces a random 4 digit number (with no duplicated digits) using the digits 0 to 9. The player attempts to guess the number and the game responds by specifying how many bulls and touches are in the guess.
		continued on next page

	The player continues to guess (and the program responds) until 4 bulls are achieved or until the player has had 8 attempts at the number.	
	If the player guesses the number in 8 or less attempts the *Win* screen appears. This specifies the number of guesses required. If the player loses the *Lose* screen is shown. This displays the number the player was attempting to guess.	
OUTLINE LOGIC	:	Initialise game
		Think of number
		Draw initial screen
		REPEAT
		Get guess
		Calculate bulls and touches
		Display bulls and touches
		UNTIL number guessed OR all 8 attempts are used
		Show closing screen

NAME	:	InitialiseGame
PARAMETERS		
IN	:	None
OUT	:	None
GLOBALS		
READ	:	screenwidth
		screenheight
		fontname
		fontsize
		fontcolour
		backgroundcolour
WRITTEN	:	outat
PRE-CONDITION	:	None
DESCRIPTION	:	This routine sets the screen resolution to *screenwidth* by *screenheight*. The font details are set to *fontname* and *fontsize*. The foreground colour is set to *fontcolour* and the background to *backgroundcolour* The *outat* value is set to 100 and the random number generator is seeded.
OUTLINE LOGIC	:	Set display mode to *screenwidth* x *screenheight*
		Set text font to *fontname*
		Set text size to *fontsize*
		Set foreground colour to *fontcolour*
		Set background colour to *backgroundcolour*
		Set *outat* to 100
		Seed random number generator

NAME	:	ThinkOfNumber
PARAMETERS		
IN	:	None
OUT	:	None
GLOBALS		
READ	:	None
WRITTEN	:	number

continued on next page

<table>
<tr><td>PRE-CONDITION</td><td>:</td><td>None</td></tr>
<tr><td>DESCRIPTION</td><td>:</td><td>Random numeric digits are placed in the elements of number. No digit may be duplicated.</td></tr>
<tr><td>OUTLINE LOGIC</td><td>:</td><td>Create digits array</td></tr>
</table>

PRE-CONDITION	:	None
DESCRIPTION	:	Random numeric digits are placed in the elements of *number*. No digit may be duplicated.
OUTLINE LOGIC	:	Create *digits* array

```
FOR c := 1 TO 4 DO
    REPEAT
        value := RND(9)
    UNTIL digits(value) = 0
    digits(value) := 1
    number(c) := value
ENDFOR
```

Notice that the outline logic of this routine looks more program-like than that of other routines. This is quite acceptable, especially when the algorithm is of a highly technical nature.

NAME	:	DrawInitialScreen
PARAMETERS		
IN	:	None
OUT	:	None
GLOBALS		
READ	:	backgroundcolour
		screenwidth
WRITTEN	:	None
PRE-CONDITION	:	None
DESCRIPTION	:	This routine draws the main screen as shown in the screen design
OUTLINE LOGIC	:	Set screen to *backgroundcolour*
		Move cursor to centre of screen
		Display "B U L L & T O U C H"

NAME	:	GetGuess
PARAMETERS		
IN	:	None
OUT	:	None
GLOBALS		
READ	:	screenheight
WRITTEN	:	noofguesses
		guess
PRE-CONDITION	:	None
DESCRIPTION	:	This routine reads a valid 4-digit numeric guess. Invalid guesses result in an error message and require the player to make a new guess.
OUTLINE LOGIC	:	REPEAT
		Remove any existing text from input area of screen
		Get *readin*
		Validate input
		UNTIL *readin* is valid
		Split *readin* in individual digits and place in *guess* array
		Add 1 to *noofguesses*

As before, accepting input from the keyboard requires a great deal of validation if we are not to allow invalid input to slip through. Looking at the outline logic for *GetGuess* there are two instructions which are probably worthy of being routines in their own right. These are *Validate input* and *Place readin in guess array*.

```
NAME              :   ValidateInput
PARAMETERS
    IN            :   readin : string
    OUT           :   result : integer
GLOBALS
    READ          :   None
    WRITTEN       :   guess
PRE-CONDITION     :   None
DESCRIPTION       :   This routine validates readin. If readin is a valid
                      guess then result is set to 1. readin is valid if it is
                      exactly 4 digits in length; those digits are numeric,
                      and there is no duplicate digits. If readin is invalid,
                      result is set to zero.
OUTLINE LOGIC     :   result := 1
                      IF
                            readin is not exactly 4 digits :
                                result := 0
                            any digits in readin are not numeric:
                                result := 0
                            any digit in readin is duplicated:
                                result := 0
                      ENDIF
```

Although we generally try to name the routines to match the phrases used in the outline logic, in the case of *Place readin in guess array*, we'll give the routine that is going to perform that task the more general name of *SplitStringIntoDigits*.

```
NAME              :   SplitStringIntoDigits
PARAMETERS
    IN            :   readin : string
    OUT           :   None
GLOBALS
    READ          :   None
    WRITTEN       :   guess
PRE-CONDITION     :   readin must be a 4-digit, non-repeating, numeric
                      string
DESCRIPTION       :   The characters in readin are converted to single-digit
                      numbers and placed in the elements of guess.  The
                      first digit is stored in guess(1), the second in
                      guess(2), etc.
OUTLINE LOGIC     :   FOR p := 1 TO 4 DO
                            guess(p) := the numeric value of character p in readin
                      ENDFOR
```

```
NAME              :   CalculateBullsandTouches
PARAMETERS
    IN            :   None
    OUT           :   None
```
continued on next page

```
GLOBALS
   READ            :   None
   WRITTEN         :   bulls
                       touches
PRE-CONDITION     :   None
DESCRIPTION       :   This routine calculates the number of bulls and
                      touches assigned to a guess.
OUTLINE LOGIC     :   Calculate bulls
                      Calculate touches
```

```
NAME              :   CalculateBulls
PARAMETERS
   IN             :   None
   OUT            :   result
GLOBALS
   READ           :   guess
                      number
   WRITTEN        :
PRE-CONDITION     :   None
DESCRIPTION       :   This routine calculates the number of bulls
                      assigned to guess.
OUTLINE LOGIC     :   result := 0
                      FOR p := 1 TO 4 DO
                           IF guess(p) = number(p) THEN
                                Add 1 to result
                           ENDIF
                      ENDFOR
```

```
NAME              :   CalculateTouches
PARAMETERS
   IN             :   None
   OUT            :   result
GLOBALS
   READ           :   guess
                      number
   WRITTEN        :
PRE-CONDITION     :   None
DESCRIPTION       :   This routine calculates the number of touches
                      assigned to guess.
OUTLINE LOGIC     :   result := 0
                      FOR p := 1 TO 4 DO
                           FOR k := 1 TO 4 DO
                                IF guess(p) = number(k) AND p <> k THEN
                                     Add 1 to result
                                ENDIF
                           ENDFOR
                      ENDFOR
```

```
NAME              :   DisplayResult
PARAMETERS
   IN             :   None
```
continued on next page

OUT	:	None
GLOBALS		
READ	:	guess
		bulls
		touches
WRITTEN	:	outat
PRE-CONDITION	:	None
DESCRIPTION	:	This routine displays the guess entered and the number of bulls and touches assigned to the guess. *outat* is updated to move to the next line (+15).
OUTLINE LOGIC	:	Display guess
		Display bulls and touches
		Add 15 to outat

NAME	:	FinishGame
PARAMETERS		
IN	:	None
OUT	:	None
GLOBALS		
READ	:	bulls
WRITTEN	:	None
PRE-CONDITION	:	None
DESCRIPTION	:	This routine displays the WIN screen if the player achieves 4 bulls, otherwise the LOSE screen is displayed.
OUTLINE LOGIC	:	IF 4 bulls achieved THEN
		Display WIN screen
		ELSE
		Display LOSE screen
		ENDIF

NAME	:	WinScreen
PARAMETERS		
IN	:	None
OUT	:	None
GLOBALS		
READ	:	noofguesses
WRITTEN	:	None
PRE-CONDITION	:	None
DESCRIPTION	:	This routine displays "You win!" and the number of guesses made. Output should conform to the layout given in the screen design.
OUTLINE LOGIC	:	Display "YOU WIN!"
		Display " in ", noofguesses," guesses"

NAME	:	LoseScreen
PARAMETERS		
IN	:	None
OUT	:	None
GLOBALS		
READ	:	number

continued on next page

WRITTEN	:	None
PRE-CONDITION	:	None
DESCRIPTION	:	This routine displays "You lose!" and the actual number generated by the computer. Output should conform to the layout given in the screen design.
OUTLINE LOGIC	:	Display "YOU LOSE!"
		Display "the number was ", number

Activity 11.1

From the mini-specs create the complete game of Bull and Touch.

Solutions

```
REM **************************************
REM *** Program   : Bull and Touch     ***
REM *** Version   : 0.1                 ***
REM *** Date      : 11/4/2005           ***
REM *** Author    : A. Stewart          ***
REM *** Language  : DarkBASIC Pro       ***
REM *** Hardware  : PC at least 800 by  ***
REM ***             600 display         ***
REM *** Purpose   : Plays the game of   ***
REM ***             Bull and Touch      ***
REM **************************************

REM *** Global Constants ***
#CONSTANT screenwidth          800
#CONSTANT screenheight         600
#CONSTANT backgroundcolour     RGB(64,128,128)
#CONSTANT fontcolour           RGB(255,128,0)
#CONSTANT fontname             "Arial"
#CONSTANT fontsize             14

REM *** Global Variables ***
GLOBAL DIM number(4)           'Number generated by the computer
GLOBAL DIM guess(4)            'Guess made by the player
GLOBAL bulls                   'Number of bulls in current guess
GLOBAL touches                 'Number of touches in current guess
GLOBAL outat                   'Position for result output
GLOBAL noofguesses             'Total number of guesses made


REM *** Main program ***
InitialiseGame()
ThinkOfNumber()
DrawInitialScreen()
REPEAT
   GetGuess()
   CalculateBTs()
   DisplayResult()
UNTIL bulls = 4 OR noofguesses = 8
FinishGame()
WAIT KEY
END

REM *** Initialise globals, font details, and screen ***
FUNCTION InitialiseGame()
   SET DISPLAY MODE screenwidth, screenheight,16
   SET TEXT FONT fontname
   SET TEXT SIZE fontsize
   INK fontcolour, backgroundcolour
   outat = 100
   RANDOMIZE TIMER()
ENDFUNCTION

REM *** Think of number to be guessed ***
FUNCTION ThinkOfNumber()
   DIM digits(10)
   FOR c = 1 TO 4
      REPEAT
         value = RND(9)
      UNTIL digits(value+1) = 0
      digits(value+1) = 1
      number(c) = value
   NEXT c
ENDFUNCTION
```

```
REM *** Draw start-up screen ***
FUNCTION DrawInitialScreen()
   CLS backgroundcolour
   SET CURSOR screenwidth / 2 -50, 30
   PRINT "B U L L   &   T O U C H"
ENDFUNCTION


REM *** Read player's guess from keyboard ***
FUNCTION GetGuess()
   REM *** Use opaque text mode ***
   SET TEXT OPAQUE
   REPEAT
      REM *** Remove text already at this position ***
      SET CURSOR 10, screenheight-50
      PRINT "                              "
      REM *** Get guess ***
      SET CURSOR 10, screenheight-50
      INPUT "Enter your guess : ", readin$
   UNTIL ValidateInput(readin$) = 1
   REM *** Split input into its component digits ***
   SplitStringIntoDigits(readin$)
   REM *** Return to transparent text ***
   SET TEXT TRANSPARENT
   REM *** Add 1 to number of guesses made ***
   noofguesses = noofguesses + 1
ENDFUNCTION


REM *** Check that input is valid ***
FUNCTION ValidateInput(readin$)
   REM *** If the guess isn't ***
   REM *** exactly 4 digits it's invalid ***
   IF LEN(readin$) <> 4
      EXITFUNCTION 0
   ENDIF
   REM *** Check each digit is numeric ***
   FOR c = 1 TO 4
      REM *** IF non-numeric found, it's invalid ***
      IF MID$(readin$,c) < "0" OR MID$(readin$,c) > "9"
         EXITFUNCTION 0
      ENDIF
   NEXT c
   REM *** Check for duplicates ***
   FOR c = 1 TO 3
      FOR p = c+1 TO 4
         REM *** IF duplicate digit found, it's invalid ***
         IF MID$(readin$,c) = MID$(readin$,p)
            EXITFUNCTION 0
         ENDIF
      NEXT p
   NEXT c
ENDFUNCTION 1


REM *** Turn input into 4 separate digits ***
FUNCTION SplitStringIntoDigits(readin$)
   FOR p = 1 TO 4
      guess(p) = VAL(MID$(readin$,p))
   NEXT p
ENDFUNCTION


REM *** Calculate the number of bulls and touches in guess ***
FUNCTION CalculateBTs()
   bulls = CalculateBulls()
   touches = CalculateTouches()
ENDFUNCTION
```

```
REM *** Calculate number of bulls ***
FUNCTION CalculateBulls()
   result = 0
   FOR p = 1 TO 4
      REM *** IF guess digit p matches number digit p THEN ***
      IF guess(p) = number(p)
         REM *** Add 1 to number of bulls scored ***
         result = result + 1
      ENDIF
   NEXT p
ENDFUNCTION result


REM *** Calculate number of touches ***
FUNCTION CalculateTouches()
   result = 0
   FOR p = 1 TO 4
      FOR k = 1 TO 4
         REM *** IF guess digit p matches any digit in number ***
         REM *** except digit p THEN ***
         IF guess(p) = number(k) AND p <> k
            REM *** Add 1 to the number of touches scored ***
            result = result + 1
         ENDIF
      NEXT k
   NEXT p
ENDFUNCTION result


REM *** Display guess and number of bulls and touches ***
FUNCTION DisplayResult()
   REM *** Move cursor to correct position ***
   SET CURSOR screenwidth/2-40,outat
   REM *** Display guess ***
   FOR p = 1 TO 4
      PRINT guess(p)," ";
   NEXT p
   REM *** Display bulls and touches ***
   PRINT "   ",bulls,"B ",touches,"T"
   REM *** Update output position ***
   outat = outat + 15
ENDFUNCTION


REM *** Display end game screen ***
FUNCTION FinishGame()
   REM *** Wait 1 second ***
   WAIT 1000
   REM *** IF player won THEN ***
   IF bulls = 4
      WinScreen()        `Display winning screen
   ELSE
      LoseScreen()       `Display losing screen
   ENDIF
ENDFUNCTION


REM *** Display winning screen ***
FUNCTION WinScreen()
   CLS backgroundcolour
   SET TEXT SIZE 40
   SET CURSOR screenwidth/2 -60,screenheight/2
   PRINT "YOU WIN!"
   SET CURSOR screenwidth/2 -30,screenheight/2 + 40
   SET TEXT SIZE 20
   PRINT "in ",noofguesses," guesses"
ENDFUNCTION
```

```
REM *** Display losing screen ***
FUNCTION LoseScreen()
   CLS backgroundcolour
   SET TEXT SIZE 40
   CENTER TEXT screenwidth/2,screenheight/2,"YOU LOSE!"
   SET CURSOR screenwidth/2 -70,screenheight/2 + 40
   SET TEXT SIZE 20
   PRINT "the number was ";
   FOR p = 1 TO 4
      PRINT number(p),"";
   NEXT p
   PRINT
ENDFUNCTION
```

12

Advanced Data Types and Operators

Arrays of Records

Bitwise Operators

Dynamic Lists

Increment and Decrement Operators

New Variable Types

Queues

Record Structures

Shift Operators

Stacks

Type Declarations

Using Binary, Hexadecimal and Octal

Data Storage

Introduction

The type of every variable we have used so far has been determined by that variable's name. If it ended with a dollar sign, we had a string variable; a hash symbol at the end meant that we had a variable capable of storing a real number; all others were, by default, integer variables. However, as we will see, DarkBASIC Pro allows variables of many other types as well.

Declaring Variables

Any variable used in a DarkBASIC Pro program can be **declared**. That is, rather than having a variable suddenly appearing for the first time as part of an assignment statement (or an INPUT statement), we can write a line of code stating the variable's name and the type of value it is designed to hold. For example, we can declare *total* as an integer variable using the line:

```
total AS INTEGER
```

But, why should we go to the trouble of adding an extra line in order to declare a variable, when we can quite happily get by without doing so? As a general rule it is considered a good thing to declare your variables. This way we can see the names of every variable in a program or routine by just looking at the section were they are declared. Also we can add a comment beside each variable detailing what that variable is used for (though we should be able to gather that from the name given to the variable). However, there are two other advantages that we derive from declaring our variables.

The first of these is that string and real variables no longer need to end with special characters. For example by including the line

```
name AS STRING
```

in a program, we have created a variable called *name* which does not end with a dollar sign, and yet can hold a string value. This allows us to write a line such as

```
name = "Elizabeth"
```

Secondly, by declaring a variable, many more options are available to use rather than just integer, real and string. The types available are shown in TABLE-12.1.

TABLE-12.1

Data Types

Data Type	Bytes	Range		
BYTE	1	0	to	255
WORD	2	0	to	65536
DWORD	4	0	to	4294967295
INTEGER	4	-2147483648	to	2147483647
DOUBLE INTEGER	8	-9223372036854775808	to	9223372036854775807
FLOAT	4	3.4E +/- 38 (7 digits)		
DOUBLE FLOAT	8	1.7E +/- 308 (15 digits)		
BOOLEAN	1	0	to	255
STRING	NA			

The first three options, BYTE, WORD and DWORD store only **unsigned** integer numbers (no negative numbers), while INTEGER and DOUBLE INTEGER can store both positive and negative integer values.

FLOAT and DOUBLE FLOAT are used for storing real numbers (notice that the term REAL cannot be used when declaring variables). The larger storage space allocated to DOUBLE FLOAT variables means that number can be stored more accurately.

When declaring variables , the general form of the statement is as shown in FIG-12.1

FIG-12.1

Declaring Variables

In the diagram:

variable   is the name to be given to the variable.

data type   is the variable's data type chosen from those given in TABLE-12.1.

Boolean Variables

A Boolean variable is one which is designed to hold just one of two possible values: TRUE or FALSE. However, DarkBASIC Pro implements Booleans as BYTE-styled integer variables which can be assigned any integer value between 0 and 255. If such a Boolean variable contains the value zero, this is taken to be the equivalent of FALSE while every other value (1 to 255) is the equivalent of TRUE. But with a little thought we can use a Boolean variable in the more traditional fashion. By defining the constants

```
#CONSTANT TRUE 1
#CONSTANT FALSE 0
```

we can then set up a Boolean variable

```
letterfound AS BOOLEAN
```

and assign it one of these values, as in the lines:

```
letterfound = TRUE
letterfound = FALSE
```

This approach would allow us to rewrite the Hangman routine *CheckForLetter()* as

```
FUNCTION CheckForLetter()
    letterfound AS BOOLEAN
    letterfound = FALSE
    FOR c = 1 TO LEN(word$)
        IF guess$ = MID$(word$,c)
            letterfound = TRUE
        ENDIF
    NEXT c
    IF letterfound = FALSE
        wrongguesses = wrongguesses + 1
    ENDIF
ENDFUNCTION letterfound
```

When using a Boolean variable in a condition we can omit the test for equality. So rather than write

```
IF letterfound = TRUE
```

we can simplify this to

```
          IF letterfound
```

and

```
          IF letterfound = FALSE
```

can be rewritten as

```
          IF NOT letterfound
```

Activity 12.1

Load up the Hangman game and change the coding for *CheckForLetter()* to use a Boolean variable. Change other lines as required.

Type Definitions

When we need to gather a group of related data values, say the name, address, and age of a game contestant, we can create three separate variables to store this information, as in the lines:

```
     name AS STRING
     address AS STRING
     age AS BYTE
```

But because the three pieces of information all relate to the one person, it would be better to bind them together in some fashion. DarkBASIC Pro allows us to do this by defining a **record**. In fact, the term *record* simply means a collection of related information.

The TYPE Definition

There are two stages to creating a record. Firstly, we must start by defining a blueprint for the structure we require. This is done using a TYPE statement. For the data described above this would be coded as:

```
     TYPE ContestantType
          name AS STRING
          address AS STRING
          age AS BYTE
     ENDTYPE
```

Notice that the keyword TYPE is followed by an identifying name, *ContestantType*. This is the name we wish to give to this record structure design. We can choose any name as long as it conforms to the same rules as naming variables in our programs, but it's a good idea to end the name with *Type* - that way we'll remember that it is not a variable name when we see it used in the program.

The parts that make up a structure are known as **fields**. So the *ContestantType* structure contains fields called *name*, *address*, and *age*. Fields can also be defined without using the AS statement. So it is quite acceptable to write

```
     TYPE ContestantType
          name$
          address$
          age
     ENDTYPE
```

although in the above case *age* will be an integer and not a byte value.

There is no restriction to the number of fields that can be named within a TYPE definition, but it cannot contain arrays. A TYPE definition has the format shown in FIG-12.2.

FIG-12.2

The TYPE Definition

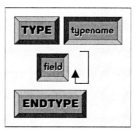

In the diagram:

typename	is the name to be given to the type being defined.
field	is the name and type of a field within the structure.

As many TYPE declarations as required can be placed in a single program.

Activity 12.2

Create new project called *records.dbpro* and add a TYPE definition called *DateType* for a record containing the fields *day, month* and *year,* all of which are of type integer.

Declaring Variables of a Defined Type

Once we have created the TYPE definition, we can then create variables of this type using the AS statement. For example:

```
dob AS DateType
```

The variable *dob* is now created containing all the fields defined in *DateType* (see FIG-12.3).

FIG-12.3

The *dob* Variable

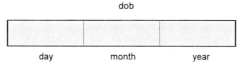

If we need several variables of the same type, we need an AS line for each variable created:

```
dob          AS DateType
anniversary  AS DateType
wifedob      AS DateType
```

The variables constructed in this way are referred to as **records** or **composite variables.**

Activity 12.3

In *records.dbpro*, create two variables, *p1* and *p2* of type *DateType.*

Accessing the Fields in a Composite Variable

When we want to access the fields in a record, we need to start with the variable name followed by a fullstop and then the field name. So, having declared a record variable with the line

```
challenger AS ContestantType
```

we can access that variable's *age* field using the term:

```
challenger.age
```

As long as we use the correct term, then we can do anything with a record's field that we might do with a standard variable. Hence, all of the following are valid statements:

```
challenger.name = "Liz Heron"
INPUT challenger.address
IF challenger.age > 18
    PRINT "Adult"
ENDIF
```

Activity 12.4

In *records.dbpro*, set the fields in *p1* to *the date 22/11/1963.*

Add three more statements so that the values to be held in *p2* can be read from the keyboard.
Add two PRINT statements which display the dates held in *p1* and *p2*.
Turn your code into a complete program and check that it functions as expected.

In most cases, it is invalid to attempt try to access the record as a whole. For example, the line

```
PRINT challenger
```

is not allowed. Instead, the individual fields must be displayed separately:

```
PRINT challenger.name
PRINT challenger.address
PRINT challenger.age
```

The same restriction is true for all other statements - except one. It is allowable to copy the contents of one record into a second record of the same type with just a single statement. For example, if we define two records:

```
champion   AS ContestantType
challenger AS ContestantType
```

and assign values to one of the records:

```
challenger.name = "Liz Heron"
challenger.address = "14 High Street"
challenger.age = 21
```

then we can copy all the values in *challenger* into *champion* with the single line:

```
champion = challenger
```

Nested Record Structures

In the last chapter we created an array of top scores, but this held only the actual scores themselves. In a video game the name of the player associated with each score would also be held. To do this we start with defining a record type:

```
TYPE PlayerType
    name    AS STRING
    score   AS INTEGER
ENDTYPE
```

But if we wanted to store the date on which a high score was achieved, then we could add a date field to this structure:

```
TYPE PlayerType
    name        AS STRING
    score       AS INTEGER
    achieved    AS DateType
ENDTYPE
```

Now we have, within one record structure (*PlayerType*), a field, *achieved*, which is itself a record structure (*DateType*) (see FIG-12.4).

FIG-12.4

A Nested Record
Structure

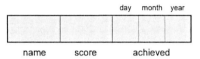

This is known as **nested records**.

If we create a variable of this type:

```
player AS PlayerType
```

we can access the *name* and *score* fields in the usual way:

```
player.name
player.score
```

but the last field, *achieved*, being a record structure in its own right, must be accessed a field at a time:

```
player.achieved.day
player.achieved.month
player.achieved.year
```

Activity 12.5

Define a record structure, *TimeType*, which has two fields: *minutes* and *seconds*, both of which are of type integer.

Define a second record structure, *BestType*, which contains two fields *name* and *time*. *name* is of type string and *time* of type *TimeType*.

Declare a variable, *winner*, of type *BestType* and set its contents to *Jessica McLaren*, *2* minutes *31* seconds.

It is not possible in DarkBASIC Pro to create an array as one of the fields within a record structure.

Arrays of Records

Although we cannot place an array inside a TYPE definition, we can create an array of records:

```
DIM topscores(10) AS PlayerType
```

The array created by this line is shown visually in FIG-12.5.

FIG-12.5

An Array of Records

To keep things simple, we've returned to the original definition of *PlayerType*, without *achieved* field.

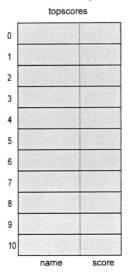

To access a data item in this structure, we start by specifying the array name and element number. This is followed by a full stop and the name of the field to be accessed. So, assuming we're not using element zero, we could set the third entry in the array to *John Farrell*, 2100 with the lines:

```
topscores(3).name = "John Farrell"
topscores(3).score = 2100
```

The effect of the two statements is shown in FIG-12.6.

FIG-12.6

Accessing Records in an Array

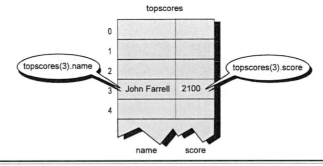

Activity 12.6

Modify *records.dbpro* so that it uses a 3 element array called *topdates* which contains *DateType* records.
Change all references to *p1* and *p2* to *topdates(1)* and *topdates(2)* respectively.

The program in LISTING-12.1 sets up a *topscores* array, reads values into the array from the keyboard, and then displays the array's contents on the screen.

LISTING-12.1

Using an Array of
Records

```
REM *** Define record structure ***
TYPE PlayerType
   name AS STRING
   score AS INTEGER
ENDTYPE

REM *** Declare array ***
DIM topscores(10) AS PlayerType

REM *** Read in a set of values ***
FOR p = 1 TO 10
   INPUT "Enter name : ", topscores(p).name
   INPUT "Enter score : ", topscores(p).score
NEXT p

REM *** Display the information on the screen ***
CLS
FOR p = 1 TO 10
   PRINT topscores(p).name,"  ",topscores(p).score
NEXT p

REM *** End program ***
WAIT KEY
END
```

Activity 12.7

Type in the program given above (*arrayrec.dbpro*).

Before running it, change the array size to 3 (this will save a lot of typing when the time comes to enter the values).

Change the FOR loops to match the new size of the array.

Test the program to check that it performs as expected.

Lists

We saw in an earlier chapter that it was possible to allow the user to specify the number of cells within an array once the program started running. But even this is a limitation, for there are times when it's just not possible to know what size an array must be.

Imagine the situation where we record every move in a game of chess. Each move can be stored in an element of an array, but there's no way of determining what size to make the array since we have no way of knowing how many moves it will take to finish the game.

To solve just such a problem, DarkBASIC Pro allow us to create arrays that can get larger (or smaller) as the program executes. This means that we could create a *moves* array for our chess game with, say, 6 elements, and if that proved to be too small, we could add more elements to the array as and when needed. These dynamically sized arrays are sometimes referred to as **lists** in DarkBASIC Pro.

So, our program would start with the declaration

```
DIM moves(5)    'A 6 element integer array
```

which would set up the initial array (or list) with six elements numbered 0 to 5.

The ARRAY INSERT AT BOTTOM Statement

To add a new element to the end of this array we can use the ARRAY INSERT AT BOTTOM statement. For example, the statement:

```
ARRAY INSERT AT BOTTOM moves(0)
```

will add a seventh element at the end of the array (see FIG-12.7).

FIG-12.7

Adding a Cell to the End of an Array

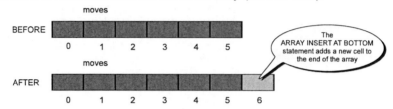

Notice that the statement requires the name of the array followed a zero subscript value enclosed in parentheses. This subscript has no bearing on the operation being performed by the statement.

The same statement can be used to add several cells at a time to the array by extending the command to include the number of cells to be added. Hence, the line

```
ARRAY INSERT AT BOTTOM moves(0),3
```

FIG-12.8

The ARRAY INSERT AT BOTTOM Statement

will add 3 cells to the end of the moves array.

The format for the ARRAY INSERT AT BOTTOM statement is given in FIG-12.8.

In the diagram:

name   is the name of the array to which elements are to be added. The array must have been created previously.

extracells   is a positive integer value specifying the number of cells to be added.
                      If this value is omitted, a single cell will be added to the end of the array.

We'll see how useful this statement can be in the example that follows.

A simple dice game involves a player continuing to throw three dice until 3 sixes are thrown. At that point all the throws made and their grand total are displayed. To store a single throw of the three dice we'll use a record structure defined as:

```
TYPE ThrowType
    dice1 AS BYTE
    dice2 AS BYTE
    dice3 AS BYTE
ENDTYPE
```

To store all of the throws, an array of *ThrowType* records can be used. But again we have the problem of deciding what size of array to create. The player's turn might be over after a single turn if he throws three 6s on the first go, so perhaps we could create just a single element array:

This creates an array
with a single element,
throws(0).

```
DIM throws(0) AS ThrowType
```

This will hold the dice values on the first throw. From then on, every time the dice are thrown. we'll create a new element in the array with the line:

```
ARRAY INSERT AT BOTTOM throws(0)
```

giving us another element in which to store the latest score.

The complete program (see LISTING-12.2) implements the following logic:

```
Create one-element moves array
REPEAT
    Generate dice throw and store in array
    Add a new cell to the end of the array
UNTIL 3 6's thrown
Display all the values thrown
```

LISTING-12.2

Using a List Structure

```
REM *** Define type for dice throw ***
TYPE ThrowType
   dice1 AS BYTE
   dice2 AS BYTE
   dice3 AS BYTE
ENDTYPE
REM *** Seed generator ***
RANDOMIZE TIMER()

REM *** Set up array ***
DIM throws(0) AS ThrowType

REM *** Set thrownumber to count how often dice thrown ***
thrownumber = 0

REM *** Throw 3 dice ***
REPEAT
   REM *** throw the dice placing values in array ***
   throws(thrownumber).dice1 = RND(5) + 1
   throws(thrownumber).dice2 = RND(5) + 1
   throws(thrownumber).dice3 = RND(5) + 1
   REM *** Add 1 to number of times the dice has been thrown ***
   thrownumber = thrownumber + 1
   REM *** Add a new cell to the end of the array ***
   ARRAY INSERT AT BOTTOM throws(0)
UNTIL throws(thrownumber).dice1 + throws(thrownumber).dice2
↳+ throws(thrownumber).dice3 = 18

REM *** Display all throws ***
FOR p = 0 TO thrownumber-1
   PRINT p,"        ",throws(p).dice1," ",throws(p).dice2," ",
   ↳throws(p).dice3
   REM *** Stop every 31 throws so user can see all throws ***
   IF p mod 31 = 0
      WAIT KEY
   ENDIF
NEXT p
REM *** End program ***
WAIT KEY
END
```

The program may take
some time before
producing a result.

Activity 12.8

Type in and test the program in LISTING-12.2 (*lists01.dbpro*).

The ARRAY INSERT AT TOP Statement

We can add elements at the opposite end of an array (that is, at the start of the array) using the ARRAY INSERT AT TOP statement which has the format shown in FIG-12.9.

FIG-12.9

The ARRAY INSERT AT TOP Statement

In the diagram:

name   is the name of the array to which elements are to be added. The array must have been created previously.

extracells   is a positive integer value specifying the number of cells to be added.
                          If this value is omitted, a single cell will be added to the end of the array.

The effect of the statements

```
DIM moves(5)
ARRAY INSERT AT TOP moves(0),3
```

is shown in FIG-12.10. Notice that inserting new cells at the start (top) of the array means that the new cells are numbered from subscript value 0 and that the existing cells are renumbered. The contents of existing cells are unchanged.

FIG-12.10

Adding Cells at the Start of an Array

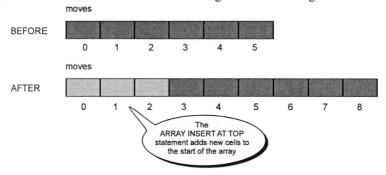

The ARRAY INSERT AT ELEMENT Statement

A final option when adding a cell to an array is to insert it somewhere in the middle of the array. This can be done using the ARRAY INSERT AT ELEMENT statement which has the format shown in FIG-12.11.

FIG-12.11

The ARRAY INSERT AT ELEMENT Statement

In the diagram:

name   is the name of the array to which elements are to be added. The array must have been created previously.

post   is a positive integer value specifying the subscript of the new cell. Its value must lie between 0 and the subscript of the last cell currently in the array.

Note that only a single new cell can be added using this instruction.

The code

```
DIM moves(5)
ARRAY ADD AT ELEMENT moves(0),3
```

has the effect shown in FIG-12.12.

FIG-12.12

Add a Cell in the Middle
of an Array

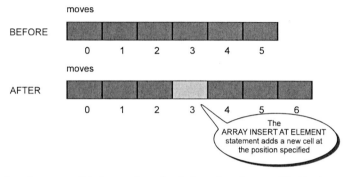

Notice that the new cell is inserted to give it the subscript specified in the statement.

The ARRAY ADD AT ELEMENT statement will not allow you to add a cell at the end of the array. For example, the line

```
ARRAY ADD AT ELEMENT moves(0),6
```

is invalid since the last value, 6, is outside the permitted range of 0 to 5 (the subscript range of the elements currently in the array).

The ARRAY COUNT Statement

The ARRAY COUNT statement can be used to find out the subscript value assigned to the last element in the array. Remember, this is not the number of elements in the array. For example the lines

```
DIM moves(5)             `Six elements - 0 to 5
ARRAY INSERT AT TOP moves(0),3   `Add 3 more elements
PRINT ARRAY COUNT (moves(0))
```

will display the value 8, this being the subscript of the last element in the array after the ARRAY INSERT command is executed.

The ARRAY COUNT statement has the format shown in FIG-12.13.

FIG-12.13

The ARRAY COUNT
Statement

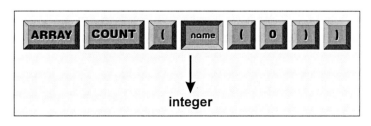

In the diagram:

name   is the name of an existing array.

To find out how many elements are in the array, just add 1 to the value returned by ARRAY COUNT.

The EMPTY ARRAY Statement

Every element in an array can be removed (that is, the array will contain zero elements) by using the EMPTY ARRAY statement which has the format shown in FIG-12.14.

FIG-12.14

The EMPTY ARRAY
Statement

In the diagram:

name   is the name of an existing array whose elements
                                        are to be removed.

The line

```
DIM moves(0)
```

creates an array containing one element, scores(0). This element can be removed from the array using the line

```
EMPTY ARRAY moves(0)
```

The array *moves* continues to exist, but now contains no elements. If we want to store anything in the array, we'll have to use an ARRAY INSERT statement to add elements back into the array.

This isn't as useless a statement as it might appear. When setting up a list structure which we intend to grow dynamically, it's become practice to start with a completely empty (zero elements) structure.

The ARRAY DELETE ELEMENT Statement

Rather than delete all the elements in an array, we can remove a specific element using the ARRAY DELETE ELEMENT statement which has the format shown in FIG-12.15.

FIG-12.15

The ARRAY DELETE
ELEMENT Statement

In the diagram:

name   is the name of an existing array from which
                                        one element is to be removed.

post   is a positive integer value specifying the subscript
                                        of the cell to be removed.
                                        If this value is omitted, the first cell is removed.

The effect of the statement is shown in FIG-12.16 in which element 3 is removed from the *moves* array.

FIG-12.16

The Effect of the ARRAY DELETE ELEMENT Statement

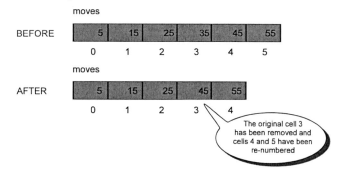

The program in LISTING-12.3 implements the effect shown above.

LISTING-12.3

Removing an Element from an Array

```
REM *** Create array ***
DIM moves(5)

REM *** Fill it with the values 5, 15, 25, etc. ***
FOR c = 0 TO 5
   moves(c) = c*10 + 5
NEXT c

REM *** display its contents ***
FOR c = 0 TO ARRAY COUNT (moves(0))
   PRINT moves(c)," ";
NEXT c
PRINT

REM *** Remove moves(3) ****
ARRAY DELETE ELEMENT moves(0),3

REM *** Display the array again ***
FOR c = 0 TO ARRAY COUNT (moves(0))
   PRINT moves(c), " ";
NEXT c

REM *** End program ***
WAIT KEY
END
```

Activity 12.9

Type in and test the program given in LISTING-12.3 (*lists02.dbpro*).

The NEXT ARRAY INDEX Statement

Normally, we need to specify which element of an array we wish to access. Hence, to access element with subscript 2 of an array named *moves* we would use the expression:

    moves(2)

However, when accessing an array element it is also valid to use the expression

    moves()

But what does such an expression mean? To understand this term we need to realise that DarkBASIC Pro retains a private index for every array we create in a program.

DarkBASIC Pro: Advanced Data Types and Operators

This index contains the number of a specific element in that array. When the array is first created this index is set to zero (see FIG-12.17).

FIG-12.17

An Array's Private Index

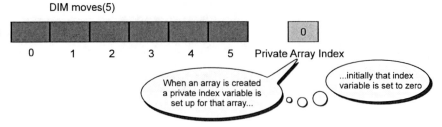

So, when we use a term such as

```
moves()
```

to access an array element, DarkBASIC Pro uses the private array index's value to decide which element of the array we wish to access. So the code

```
REM *** Create array - this sets its private index to zero ***
DIM moves(5)
moves() = 12
```

will store the value 12 in element zero of the array.

Of course, the array index will be of little use to us if it always references element zero of the array. Luckily, we can modify the index using the NEXT ARRAY INDEX statement which adds 1 to the contents of the index (see FIG-12.18).

FIG-12.18

Incrementing the Array Index

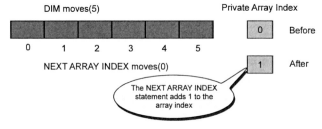

This statement has the format shown in FIG-12.19.

FIG-12.19

The NEXT ARRAY INDEX Statement

In the diagram:

name   is the name of an existing array whose private index is to be incremented.

The code snippet below creates a 6 element array and stores the numbers 0 to 5 in those elements.

```
DIM list(5)
FOR c = 0 TO 5
    list() = c
    NEXT ARRAY INDEX list(0)
NEXT c
```

Notice that the line

```
list() = c
```

accesses the cell specified by the array index and that the line

```
NEXT ARRAY INDEX list(0)
```

increments that index, so that, on the next iteration of the FOR loop, a new cell in the array is accessed.

Activity 12.10

Using the code snippet given earlier, store the values 0 to 5 in the array *list*, and then display the contents of *list* using normal subscripting methods (*list03.dbpro*).

We can combine what we know so far to create a fully dynamic array starting with zero elements and increasing in size, one element at a time, only when a new value needs to be added. The program in LISTING-12.4 demonstrates this technique by simulating 100 dice throws, recording on which throws a six is produced. The program employs the following logic:

```
Create an empty array
FOR 100 times DO
    Throw dice
    IF a six is thrown THEN
        Create a new element in the array
        Store the thrown number in that element
    ENDIF
ENDFOR
Display the total number of sixes thrown
Display contents of the array
```

LISTING-12.4

Using a Fully Dynamic Array

```
REM *** Create an empty array ***
DIM sixthrown(0)
EMPTY ARRAY sixthrown(0)

REM *** Seed generator ***
RANDOMIZE TIMER()

REM *** FOR 100 times DO ***
FOR throw = 1 TO 100
   REM *** Throw dice ***
   dice = RND(5)+1
   REM *** IF it's a six THEN ***
   IF dice = 6
      REM *** Create a new element in sixthrown ***
      ARRAY INSERT AT BOTTOM sixthrown(0)
      REM *** Add save throw number ***
      sixthrown() = throw
   ENDIF
NEXT throw

REM *** Display total sixes and all values saved ***
PRINT "There were ",ARRAY COUNT (sixthrown(0))+1," sixes thrown."
PRINT "These were on the following throws : "
FOR p = 0 TO ARRAY COUNT (sixthrown(0))
   PRINT sixthrown(p)
NEXT p


REM *** End program ***
WAIT KEY
END
```

Activity 12.11

Type in and test the program given in LISTING-12.4 (*list04.dbpro*).

Notice that the NEXT ARRAY INDEX statement is not required. This is because creating a new element in an array causes the array index to move to that new element.

The PREVIOUS ARRAY INDEX Statement

As well as being able to increment an array's index value, it is also possible to decrement it using the PREVIOUS ARRAY INDEX statement which has the format given in FIG-12.20.

FIG-12.20

The PREVIOUS ARRAY INDEX Statement

In the diagram:

name	is the name of an existing array whose array index is to be decremented.

The ARRAY INDEX TO TOP Statement

The array index can be made to reference the first element in the list (that is, element zero) using the ARRAY INDEX TO TOP statement which has the format shown in FIG-12.21.

FIG-12.21

The ARRAY INDEX TO TOP Statement

In the diagram:

name	is the name of an existing array whose array index is to be set to zero.

The ARRAY INDEX TO BOTTOM Statement

The array index can be made to reference the last element in the list using the ARRAY INDEX TO BOTTOM statement which has the format shown in FIG-12.22.

FIG-12.22

The ARRAY INDEX TO BOTTOM Statement

In the diagram:

name	is the name of an existing array whose array index is to be set to reference the last cell in the list.

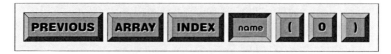

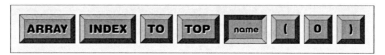

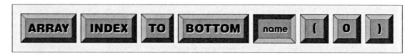

The ARRAY INDEX VALID Statement

If we use the PREVIOUS ARRAY INDEX often enough we'll end up back at the start of the array - with the array index containing the value zero. And if we were to try executing the same statement again, would the array index change to -1?

The answer is , yes it would, and if we tried using NEXT ARRAY INDEX too often it would take on a value larger than the subscript of the last element in the array.

Luckily, we can check that the array index contains a valid value by using the ARRAY INDEX VALID statement which returns 1 if the contents of the array index contains a number between 0 and the subscript of the last element. Zero is returned when this is not the case. The statement has the format shown in FIG-12.23.

FIG-12.23

The ARRAY INDEX
VALID Statement

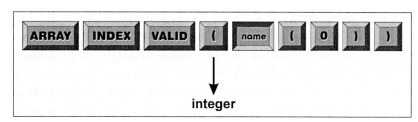

In the diagram:

> *name* is the name of an existing array whose private index is to be examined.

The statement returns 1 if the array index is valid; otherwise zero is returned.

The program in LISTING-12.5 demonstrates the use of the various statements that manipulate the array index value by assigning values to an array and then displaying those values in normal order and reverse order.

LISTING-12.5

using the ARRAY
INDEX Statements

```
REM *** Create an 5 element array ***
DIM list(4)
REM *** Set value to zero ***
value = 0
REM *** Fill it with values ***
WHILE ARRAY INDEX VALID(list(0))
   list() = value
   value = value + 1
   NEXT ARRAY INDEX list(0)
ENDWHILE
REM *** Display array starting at front ***
PRINT "Forward"
ARRAY INDEX TO TOP list(0)
WHILE ARRAY INDEX VALID(list(0))
   PRINT list()," ";
   NEXT ARRAY INDEX list()
ENDWHILE
REM *** Display array starting at back ***
PRINT
PRINT "Backwards"
ARRAY INDEX TO BOTTOM list(0)
WHILE ARRAY INDEX VALID(list(0))
   PRINT list(), " ";
   PREVIOUS ARRAY INDEX list(0)
ENDWHILE
REM *** End program ***
WAIT KEY
END
```

Queues

A **queue** is a special type of list where values may be added only at one end of the list (and nowhere else) and can only be removed from the other end of the list. This is exactly like a queue (line, if you're American) in a self-service canteen. You join the end of the queue and the person at the front is served (and hence removed from the queue) (see FIG-12.24).

FIG-12.24

An Example of a Queue

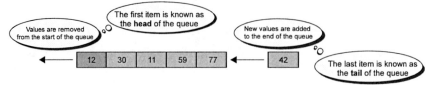

Like most collections of values, we need to be able to add, delete and list the contents of a queue. We'll see how the various queue-related statements work by constructing a set of routines and corresponding test driver. The core of the program is shown in LISTING-12.6.

LISTING-12.6

Using a Queue

```
REM *** Value signifying quit ***
#CONSTANT QUIT 4
REM *** Create global array to hold queue ***
GLOBAL DIM q(0)

REM *** Main section ***
InitialiseQueue()
REPEAT
   DisplayMenu()
   choice = GetChoice(4)
   ExecuteOption(choice)
UNTIL choice = QUIT
REM *** End program ***
END


FUNCTION DisplayMenu()
   PRINT "1 - Add to queue"
   PRINT "2 - Delete head of queue"
   PRINT "3 - Display contents of queue"
   PRINT "4 - QUIT"
ENDFUNCTION

FUNCTION GetChoice(max)
   PRINT "Enter choice 1 - ",max," ";
   INPUT choice
   WHILE choice < 1 OR choice > max
      PRINT "Invalid choice. 1 to ",max," only ";
      INPUT choice
   ENDWHILE
ENDFUNCTION choice

FUNCTION ExecuteOption(choice)
   SELECT choice
      CASE 1
         INPUT "Enter value to be added : ",v
         AddToQueue(v)
      ENDCASE
```

continued on next page

LISTING-12.6
(continued)

Using a Queue - 1

```
            CASE 2
                DeleteFromQueue()
            ENDCASE
            CASE 3
                DisplayQueue()
            ENDCASE
            CASE 4
                PRINT "Program terminating - press any key"
                WAIT KEY
            ENDCASE
        ENDSELECT
    ENDFUNCTION

    REM *** Test stubs ***
    FUNCTION InitialiseQueue()
        PRINT "InitialiseQueue"
    ENDFUNCTION


    FUNCTION AddToQueue(v)
        PRINT "AddToQueue"
    ENDFUNCTION


    FUNCTION DeleteFromQueue()
        PRINT "DeleteFromQueue"
    ENDFUNCTION


    FUNCTION DisplayQueue()
        PRINT "DisplayQueue"
    ENDFUNCTION
```

The queue is created using a standard array declaration:

```
    GLOBAL DIM q(0)
```

The functions which manipulate the queue structure are coded as test stubs for the moment. These will be replaced as we cover the various queue-related statements available.

Activity 12.13

Type in and test the program given in LISTING-12.6 (*queue01.dbpro*).

Another useful operation would be to find out what value is at the front of the queue without affecting the contents of the queue. Modify the program to allow for this option and create a test stub for the new function (call the function *Front()*) which returns the first value in the queue.

HINT: This will require changes to the defined constant, *DisplayMenu()*, *GetChoice()*, *ExecuteOption()*, and the call to *GetChoice()* in the main section.

One of the routines, *InitialiseQueue()*, is designed to make sure that we start with an empty queue. This can be coded with a single line:

```
    FUNCTION InitialiseQueue()
        EMPTY ARRAY q(0)
    ENDFUNCTION
```

The other routine that can be created at this point is *DisplayQueue()* which is coded as:

```
FUNCTION DisplayQueue()
    REM *** FOR each value in the queue ***
    FOR p = 0 TO ARRAY COUNT (q(0))
        REM *** Display it ***
        PRINT q(p)," ";
    NEXT p
    REM *** Move to a new line when complete ***
    PRINT
ENDFUNCTION
```

Activity 12.14

Replace the test stubs for *InitialseQueue()* and *DisplayQueue()* with the code
given.

The ADD TO QUEUE Statement

If we are to implement the *AddToQueue()* function, we need to be able to add cells
to our empty queue. And, although we could use ARRAY INSERT AT BOTTOM,
another statement is available to do this job on a queue - the ADD TO QUEUE
statement which has the format shown in FIG-12.25.

FIG-12.25

The ADD TO QUEUE
Statement

In the diagram:

> *name*   is the name of an existing array to which a single
>   new cell is to be added. The array index will
>   reference this new cell.

If we were to execute the statement

```
ADD TO QUEUE q(0)
```

then the effect on an array which already contains several values is shown in
FIG-12.26.

FIG-12.26

The Effect of
Executing the ADD
TO QUEUE Statement

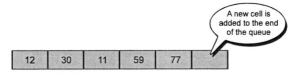

Using this statement, we can create a function to add a value to one end of the queue:

```
FUNCTION AddToQueue(v)
    REM *** Add a new cell to the queue ***
    REM *** Array index will reference this new cell ***
    ADD TO QUEUE q(0)
    REM *** Store value in this new element ***
    q() = v
ENDFUNCTION
```

Activity 12.15

Replace the stub for this routine with the actual code and test the routine,
making sure that values are correctly added to the queue.

The REMOVE FROM QUEUE Statement

The REMOVE FROM QUEUE statement removes the front element (cell zero) of the queue (see FIG-12.27).

FIG-12.27

The Effect of Executing the REMOVE FROM QUEUE Statement

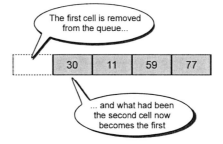

The statement has the format shown in FIG-12.28.

FIG-12.28

The REMOVE FROM QUEUE Statement

In the diagram:

name is the name of an existing queue from which the front element is to be removed. After this operation is complete, the array index will reference the new front element.

With this statement we can write the code for *DeleteFromQueue()* :

```
FUNCTION DeleteFromQueue()
    REM *** Remove head of queue ***
    REMOVE FROM QUEUE q(0)
ENDFUNCTION
```

Activity 12.16

Add the *DeleteFromQueue()* function to your program.

Does the routine correctly remove the front item in the queue?

What happens when you try to remove a value from an empty queue?

Good programming dictates that we shouldn't allow a routine to attempt the impossible, so add a pre-condition check to *DeleteFromQueue()* which makes sure the routine is executed only when the queue is not empty.

The ARRAY INDEX TO QUEUE Statement

The ARRAY INDEX TO QUEUE statement sets the array index to zero, thereby referencing the front of the queue. This statement has the format shown in FIG-12.29.

FIG-12.29

The ARRAY INDEX TO QUEUE Statement

In the diagram:

name	is the name of an existing array whose array index is to be set to zero (the first cell).

Activity 12.17

Use ARRAY INDEX TO QUEUE to create the full code for the *Front()* function. If the queue is empty, *Front()* should return -99.
Test the completed program.

Stacks

A stack is another type of restricted list. This time new values are added at one end of the list and values are removed from the same end. We can think of the structure as a pile of books; each new book is placed on top of the existing pile; when a book is removed, it is the book sitting on top of the pile that is removed first (see FIG-12.30).

FIG-12.30

The Concept of a Stack

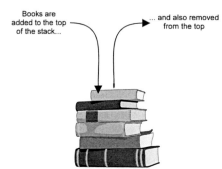

Adding a value to a stack is traditionally known as a **push** operation, while removing a value is known as a **pop** operation. And, since we tend to show stacks as a vertical rather than horizontal collection, the first value in a stack is referred to as the **top** of the stack.

To create a stack we begin by creating an empty array (just as we did when creating a queue).

There are three statements in DarkBASIC Pro specifically used to manipulate stacks once the array holding it has been created. These are described below.

The ADD TO STACK Statement

The ADD TO STACK statement adds a single cell to the top of the stack. This statement has the format shown in FIG-20.31.

FIG-12.31

The ADD TO STACK Statement

In the diagram:

name	is the name of an existing array to which a single new cell is to be added. The array index will reference this new cell.

The effect of this statement is exactly the same as ADD TO QUEUE with a new cell being added to the right-hand end of the array.

DarkBASIC Pro: Advanced Data Types and Operators

The REMOVE FROM STACK Statement

The REMOVE FROM STACK statement removes the top (or last) element of the stack (see FIG-12.32). So if a stack *s* had elements numbered 0 to 3, this statement would remove element 3 from the stack. Notice that this differs from the REMOVE FROM QUEUE operation which would have removed element zero.

FIG-12.32

The REMOVE FROM
STACK Statement

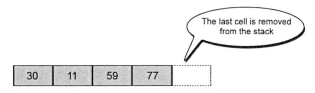

The statement has the format shown in FIG-12.33.

FIG-12.33

The REMOVE FROM
STACK Statement

In the diagram:

name   is the name of an existing stack from which the
                                top element is to be removed. After this
                                operation is complete, the array index will
                                reference the new top element

The ARRAY INDEX TO STACK Statement

The ARRAY INDEX TO STACK statement sets the array index to reference the right-most cell in the array being used as a stack (which contains the latest value to be added). Therefore, if an array *s* contained cells numbered zero to 3, executing the ARRAY INDEX TO STACK with *s* would set the array index to 3.

This statement has the format shown in FIG-12.34.

FIG-12.34

The ARRAY INDEX
TO STACK Statement

In the diagram:

name   is the name of an existing array whose array index
                                is to be set to the subscript value of the
                                right-most cell.

Activity 12.18

Create a new program (*stack01.dbpro*). which performs operations similar to those in LISTING-12.6, but this time using a stack rather than a queue.

The function which adds a value to the stack should be called *Push()*, the function that removes a value should be called *Pop()*, and the function to find the top value in the stack should be called *Top()*.

Summary

- Variables can be specifically declared.

- Declared variables can be of types other than integer, real and string.

- Declared string variables need not have names that end with a dollar ($) symbol.

- Real variables are declared as FLOAT or DOUBLE FLOAT.

- Declared real variables need not have names that end with the # symbol.

- Conceptually Boolean variables should store the values true or false.

- DarkBASIC Pro Boolean variables accept integer values between 0 and 255.

- A DarkBASIC Pro Boolean variable treats the value zero as the equivalent of false - all other values 1 to 255, are treated as true.

- TYPE definitions can be used to create record structures.

- The data items defined within a TYPE are known as fields of the record.

- Fields cannot be arrays.

- Once a TYPE has been defined, variables of that type can be declared.

- Variables of a defined type are known as record variables.

- Fields within a record variable are accessed using the format

        record_variable_name.field_name

- Arrays of a defined type can also be declared.

- To access a field within a record within an array use the format

        array_name[subscript].field_name

Lists

- DarkBASIC Pro uses the term List to describe an array whose size can be modified while a program is running.

- Dynamic lists maintain an array index variable to note which element should be accessed next.

- The element of a list referenced by the array index variable can be accessed using the expression

        array_name()

- New cells an be added at specific positions within a list using one of the following statements

        ARRAY INSERT AT BOTTOM   - array index to left-most new cell
        ARRAY INSERT AT TOP   - array index to right-most new cell
        ARRAY INSERT AT ELEMENT   - array index to new cell

- The ARRAY COUNT Statement is used to find out how many cells are currently held in the specified array.

- Every element of an array can be removed using the EMPTY ARRAY statement.

- Cells in an array can be destroyed using the ARRAY DELETE ELEMENT statement.

- The array index variable can be incremented using the NEXT ARRAY INDEX statement.

- The array index variable can be decremented using the PREVIOUS ARRAY INDEX statement.

- The array index can be made to reference cell 0 using the ARRAY INDEX TO TOP statement.

- The array index can be made to reference the last cell (the cell with the highest subscript) using the ARRAY INDEX TO BOTTOM statement.

- The ARRAY INDEX VALID statement returns 1 if the array index contains a valid reference.

Queues

- Queues are lists in which values are added to the right-hand end of the list and removed from the left-hand end.

- A new value can be added to the end of a queue using the ADD TO QUEUE statement.

- The cell at the front of the queue (cell zero) can be removed using the REMOVE FROM QUEUE statement.

- A queue's array index variable can be set to the front of the queue (to zero) using the ARRAY INDEX TO QUEUE statement.

Stacks

- A stack is a list in which values are added at one end (the top of the stack) and removed from the same end.

- A new value can be added to a stack using the ADD TO STACK statement.

- The cell at the top of the stack (cell zero) can be removed by using the REMOVE FROM STACK statement.

- A stack's array index variable can be set to the top of the stack (the subscript of the right-most cell) using the ARRAY INDEX TO STACK statement.

Data Manipulation

Introduction

Earlier in the book we looked at the basic arithmetic operators such as addition and multiplication. There are, however, several more such operators that either perform more obscure operations or perform those earlier operations in a more processor-efficient manner.

Other Number Systems

Although we spend most of our time working in the decimal number system (properly called the denary number system), computers work in binary, where every possible number is represented as a pattern of 1s and 0s.

If we want to assign a specific binary value to an integer variable, then we can do so by starting our number with a percent (%) sign. For example, the lines

```
value AS BYTE
value = %01000001
```

will store the binary value 01000001 in the variable value. If we are good at converting between number systems, we could have achieved the same effect by writing

```
value AS BYTE
value = 65
```

A specific hexadecimal value can also be assigned by starting with 0X (zero X) as in the line:

```
value = 0XFF
```

The more obscure octal number base is also possible by starting the value with 0C (zero C) as in:

```
value = 0C53
```

The program in LISTING-12.7 uses all four number systems to assign values to four variables. The contents of the variables are then displayed.

LISTING-12.7

Using Different Number Systems

```
REM *** Set up the Variables ***
v1 AS BYTE
v2 AS BYTE
v3 AS BYTE
v4 AS BYTE

REM *** Assign the same value to each ***
REM *** but using a different number base ***
v1 = 65
v2 = %01000001
v3 = 0X41
v4 = 0C101

REM *** Display the contents of each variable ***
PRINT v1
```
continued on next page

LISTING-12.7

(continued)

Using Different Number
Systems

```
PRINT v2
PRINT v3
PRINT v4
REM *** End program ***
WAIT KEY
END
```

Notice that all the variables are displayed in decimal.

Activity 12.19

Type in and test the program given above (*bases01.dbpro*).

Modify the program so that *v2* is displayed in binary and *v3* in hexadecimal.

Incrementing and Decrementing

The INC Statement

Although we can add 1 to a variable with a statement such as

```
count = count + 1
```

a more efficient way to achieve this effect is to use the INC (short for increment) statement which allows us to achieve the same effect with the line

```
INC count
```

When we want to add some other value to a variable, as in the line

```
total = total + score
```

then this can also be done using an extended version of the INC statement:

```
INC total,score
```

The format of the INC statement is shown in FIG-12.35.

FIG-12.35

The INC Statement

In the diagram:

name	is the name of the integer variable that is to be incremented.
value	is an integer value (constant, variable, or expression) which is to be added to *name*. If no value is given, 1 is added to *name*.

The DEC Statement

The DEC operator can be used to subtract 1 (or some other value) from a variable. Therefore, rather than write

```
num = num - 1
```

we can create the same effect with the line

```
DEC num
```

If we need to subtract, say 5, rather than 1, then we would use the line

```
DEC num,5
```

The format of the DEC statement is shown in FIG-12.36.

FIG-12.36

The DEC Statement

In the diagram:

name	is the name of the integer variable that is to be decremented.
value	is an integer value (constant, variable, or expression) which is to be subtracted from *name*. If no value is given, 1 is subtracted from *name*.

Shift Operators

If you have ever sat in a well-organised show and been asked to move all the way along the row, you'll have an idea of what shifting is all about.

Shift operators allow the contents of an integer variable (BYTE, WORD, DWORD, INTEGER, DOUBLE INTEGER) to be moved. For example, in FIG-12.37 we see the contents of a BYTE variable being moved one place to the left or right.

FIG-12.37

The Effects of Shifting
the Contents of a Byte
One Place to the Left or
Right

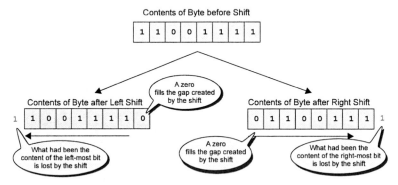

We can see from the diagram that the bit that starts out as the left-most bit falls off the end and is lost. Also, to fill the gap created on the right-hand side of the byte a new digit (a zero) is inserted.

Activity 12.20

Write down the result of the following shifts:

a) 10110001   shifted 2 places to the left
b) 10110001   shifted 3 places to the right

So why would we want to shift the contents of a variable? Well, one reason is that left shifting is a very efficient way of multiplying by powers of 2.

In the decimal system, if we start with a number (say 12) and shift the digits one column to the left (120), we've multiplied the original value by 10; if we shift the original value 2 places to the left (1200), we have multiplied the value by 100.

When we do the same thing to a binary number (say, 00001100) and shift it 1 place to the left (00011000), the original value has been multiplied by 2; a shift of 2 places to the left (00110000) would multiply the original value by 4.

Conversely, a single right shift divides a value by 10 in the decimal system (200 becomes 20) and by 2 in the binary system (00000100 becomes 00000010).

The Shift Left Operator (<<)

If we set up a byte variable containing the value 7 with the lines

```
value AS BYTE
value = 7
```

then we can shift the contents of value one place to the left using the shift-left operator (<<) with the line

```
value = value << 1
```

and hence, since the computer holds everything in binary, double the number held in *value* to 14.

The shift operator is used in an expression which has the form shown in FIG-12.38.

FIG-12.38

The Shift Left Operator

In the diagram

    value   is the integer-type variable, constant or expression whose value is to be left-shifted.

    bits   is an integer value representing the number of places the contents are to be shifted.

For example, the line

```
PRINT %00111010 << 2 '00111010 = 58
```

would display 232 (which is 11101000 in binary)

Activity 12.21

Create a new program (*bits01.dbpro*) which sets a byte variable *num* to 11 and shifts the contents of *num* 1 place to the left. The value held in *num* should be displayed both before and after the shift.

The Shift Right Operator (>>)

By shifting the contents of an integer variable to the right (using the shift-right operator >>) we halve the contents of that variable. Shifting two places results in a quartering of the original value, etc. For example, the lines

```
num2 AS BYTE
num2 = 24
PRINT num2 >> 2
```

will display the value 6 (a quarter of 24). The statement has the format shown in FIG-12.39.

FIG-12.39

The Shift Right Operator

In the diagram

    value   is the integer-type variable, constant or expression whose value is to be right-shifted.

    bits   is an integer value representing the number of places the contents are to be shifted.

Activity 12.22

Modify your last program so that the value in num is shifted one place to the right rather than the left.

Display the value before and after the shift in binary.

Bitwise Boolean Operators

We met the Boolean operators AND, OR and NOT in an earlier chapter. These combined true and false values to give an overall true or false result. But, bitwise Boolean operators work on the individual bits that make up a value, with a binary 1 being treated as the equivalent of true and zero being false.

The Bitwise NOT Operator (..)

The bitwise NOT operator changes all 1s in a value to 0s and changes all 0s to 1s. Therefore if we start with the lines

```
num AS BYTE
result AS BYTE
num = %00001111
```

The value after the NOT operator (i.e. 0) serves no purpose other than to give a second value to the operator. Any value can be used.

then the statement

```
result = num..0
```

uses the bit complement operator (..) to create a binary value whose bits are the exact complement of those in *num* and store the value in *result* (see FIG-12.40).

FIG-12.40

The Effect of the Bitwise NOT Operator

| num | 0 | 0 | 0 | 0 | 1 | 1 | 1 | 1 |

`result = num..`

The value in result is created by complementing each bit in num (1s become 0s; 0s become 1s)

| result | 1 | 1 | 1 | 1 | 0 | 0 | 0 | 0 |

Of course we can do all of this in decimal (or even hexadecimal or octal) and get exactly the same value:

```
num = 15
num = num..0
```

We can even display the contents of *result* in binary with the line

```
PRINT BIN$(num)
```

Since the BIN$() function creates a 32 character result, the display would look better using the line

```
PRINT RIGHT$(BIN$(num),8)
```

An expression using the bitwise NOT operator has the format shown in FIG-12.41.

FIG-12.41

The Bitwise NOT

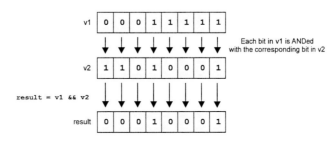

The zero is included simply to satisfy the .. operator which requires two values. The zero has no effect on the result and, in fact, any integer value can be used in its place.

In the diagram:

> *value*   is the integer-type variable, constant or expression whose value is to be complemented.

Activity 12.23

Create a new program (*bits02.dbpro*) which performs the following logic:

```
Create a byte variables s and f
Assigns s the binary value 10101001
Set f = bit complement of s
Display s and f in binary  (8 digits only for each)
```

The Bitwise AND Operator (&&)

The individual bits of two values can be ANDed together using the bitwise AND operator, &&.

The code

```
v1 AS BYTE
v2 AS BYTE
result AS BYTE
v1 = %00011111
v2 = %11010001
result = v1 && v2
PRINT RIGHT$(BIN$(result),8)
```

displays the value 00010001. How this result is derived is shown in FIG-12.42.

FIG-12.42

The Effect of the Bitwise AND Operator

v1	0	0	0	1	1	1	1	1

Each bit in v1 is ANDed with the corresponding bit in v2

v2	1	1	0	1	0	0	0	1

result = v1 && v2

result	0	0	0	1	0	0	0	1

DarkBASIC Pro: Advanced Data Types and Operators

An expression using the bitwise AND operator has the format shown in FIG-12.43.

FIG-12.43

The Bitwise AND
Operator

In the diagram:

value1   value2   are the integer-type values to which the AND
                                     operation is to be applied.

> **Activity 12.24**
>
> Create a new project (*bits03.dbpro*) based on the code above and check that
> the expected results are displayed.

The Bitwise OR Operator (||)

The individual bits of two values can be ORed together using the bitwise OR
operator, ||.

The code

```
v1 AS BYTE
v2 AS BYTE
result AS BYTE
v1 = %00011111
v2 = %11010001
result = v1 || v2
PRINT RIGHT$(BIN$(result),8)
```

displays the value 11011111. How this result is derived is shown in FIG-12.44.

FIG-12.44

The Effect of the Bitwise
OR Operator (||)

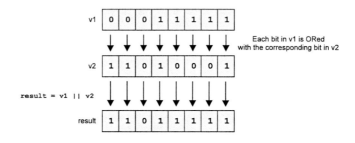

An expression using the bitwise OR operator has the format shown in FIG-12.45.

FIG-12.45

The Bitwise OR Operator

In the diagram:

value1   value2   are the integer-type values to which the OR
                                     operation is to be applied.

> **Activity 12.25**
>
> Modify your last project to OR the two values and check that the expected
> results are displayed.

The Bitwise Exclusive OR Operator (~~)

The exclusive OR operation - sometimes written as XOR - returns a result of 1 if the two bits being compared are different and a 0 if they are the same (see FIG-12.46).

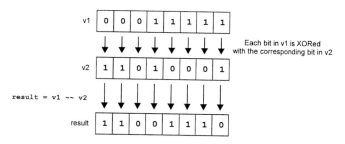

An expression using the bitwise XOR operator has the format shown in FIG-12.47.

In the diagram:

value1 value2   are the integer-type values to which the XOR operation is to be applied.

Activity 12.26

Modify your last project to XOR the two values and check that the expected results are displayed.

Activity 12.27

Work out the results of the following operations:

a)   01100111 ..
b)   01010011 && 10000110
c)   01000011 || 00010000
d)   00100111 ~~ 01001101

A Practical Use For Bitwise Operations

Imagine we are writing an adventure game which contains four locations and 4 items that the player might pick up on his journey. When the player reaches the end of the game, he wins only if he has visited location 1 and possesses item2 and 3.

To finish the game correctly, the program will have to keep track of where the player has been and what he has picked up. Perhaps we could use 8 variables, or an 8-element array to do this. Initially, set everything to zero and then when a place is visited or an item taken, set that variable (array element) to 1. At the end of the game check to see if the appropriate variables are set to 1 and our problem is solved. This approach is fine but can be wasteful of memory, especially if the real game has thousands of locations and hundreds of items.

Another approach is to use a single bit for each piece of information - after all we only need to store a 0 or 1 in each case. Since we need to record 8 pieces of information we can use a single byte. All we have to do is decide the purpose of each bit in that byte (see FIG-12.48).

FIG-12.48

Using Bits to Record Information

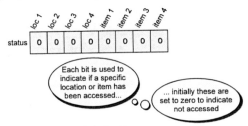

We can create this initial setup with the lines:

```
status AS BYTE
status = 0
```

Now, let's say the player visits location 2 and picks up items 3 and 4, this means we need to change *status* as shown in FIG-12.49).

FIG-12.49

The Recording Locations and Items Accessed

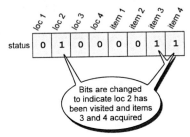

This requires the code:

```
status = %01000011
```

Later, the player visits location 4, so status changes again:

```
status = status || %00010000
```

When we come to the end of the game, we can check if all the criteria for winning have been met by setting up a variable (*win*) to reflect the winning condition (see FIG-12.50).

FIG-12.50

The Win Scenario Recorded in Bits

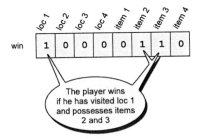

Now, all we have to do is use the bitwise AND operation on *status* and *win* and check that we have the result we need:

```
#CONSTANT win %10000110
result = status && win
IF result = win
    PRINT "You win"
ENDIF
```

The program in LISTING-12.8 demonstrates the code in operation. It uses the following logic:

```
Set up win constant
Set up status variable
Get each location visited
Get each item acquired
Calculate result
IF winning result achieved THEN
    PRINT "Win"
ELSE
    PRINT "Loss"
ENDIF
```

LISTING-12.8

Using the Bitwise AND Operation

```
#CONSTANT win %10000110
status AS BYTE

REM *** Find which locations were visited ***
INPUT "Location 1 visited (Y/N):",reply$
IF LOWER$(reply$)="y"
    status = status || %10000000
ENDIF
INPUT "Location 2 visited (Y/N):",reply$
IF LOWER$(reply$)="y"
    status = status || %01000000
ENDIF
INPUT "Location 3 visited (Y/N):",reply$
IF LOWER$(reply$)="y"
    status = status || %00100000
ENDIF
INPUT "Location 4 visited (Y/N):",reply$
IF LOWER$(reply$)="y"
    status = status || %00010000
ENDIF

REM *** Find which items taken ***
INPUT "Item 1 taken (Y/N):",reply$
IF LOWER$(reply$)="y"
    status = status || %00001000
ENDIF
INPUT "Item 2 taken (Y/N):",reply$
IF LOWER$(reply$)="y"
    status = status || %00000100
ENDIF
INPUT "Item 3 taken (Y/N):",reply$
IF LOWER$(reply$)="y"
    status = status || %00000010
ENDIF
INPUT "Item 4 taken (Y/N):",reply$
IF LOWER$(reply$)="y"
    status = status || %00000001
ENDIF

REM *** check for win ***
result = status && win
IF result = win
    PRINT "win"
ELSE
    PRINT "Lose"
ENDIF

REM *** End program ***
WAIT KEY
END
```

With a bit of imagination we could reduce the code to check for visits to the four locations using the following:

```
value = %10000000
FOR p = 1 TO 4
    PRINT "Location ",p," visited (Y/N):";
    INPUT reply$
    IF LOWER$(reply$)="y"
        status = status || value
    ENDIF
    value = value >> 1
NEXT p
```

Summary

- Integer constants can be specified in binary, hexadecimal or octal.

- Binary constants begin with the % symbol.

- Hexadecimal constants begin with 0X.

- Octal constants begin with 0C.

- The INC statement can be used to add a value to an integer variable.

- The DEC statement can be used to subtract a value from an integer variable.

- Bits within an integer variable can be shifted to the left using the shift left operator (<<).

- Bits within an integer variable can be shifted to the right using the shift right operator (>>).

- The bits of an integer value can be complemented (NOTed) using the bitwise NOT operator (..).

- The bits of two integer values can be ANDed using the bitwise AND operator (&&).

- The bits of two integer values can be ORed using the bitwise OR operator (||).

- The bits of two integer values can be XORed using the bitwise XOR operator (~~).

Solutions

Activity 12.1

```
FUNCTION CheckForLetter()
  letterfound AS BOOLEAN
  letterfound = FALSE
  FOR c = 1 TO LEN(word$)
    IF guess$ = MID$(word$,c)
      letterfound = TRUE
      correctletters = correctletters + 1
    ENDIF
  NEXT c
  IF NOT letterfound
    wrongguesses = wrongguesses + 1
  ENDIF
ENDFUNCTION letterfound
```

Other changes:

Define the constants

```
#CONSTANT TRUE 1
#CONSTANT FALSE 0
```

In the main program the IF statement can be changed to

```
IF letterfound
  DrawLetter()
ELSE
  AddToHangedMan()
ENDIF
```

Activity 12.2

```
REM *** Define record structure ***
TYPE DateType
  day AS INTEGER
  month AS INTEGER
  year AS INTEGER
ENDTYPE
```

Activity 12.3

```
REM *** Define record structure ***
TYPE DateType
  day AS INTEGER
  month AS INTEGER
  year AS INTEGER
ENDTYPE

REM *** Declare variables ***
p1 AS DateType
p2 AS DateType
```

Activity 12.4

```
REM *** Define record structure ***
TYPE DateType
  day AS INTEGER
  month AS INTEGER
  year AS INTEGER
ENDTYPE

REM *** Declare variables ***
p1 AS DateType
p2 AS DateType

REM *** Assign values to p1 ***
p1.day = 22
p1.month = 11
p1.year = 1963
```

```
REM *** Read in values for p2 ***
INPUT "Enter day: ",p2.day
INPUT "Enter month: ",p2.month
INPUT "Enter year: ",p2.year
REM *** Display dates ***
PRINT "Date 1 is ",p1.day,"/",p1.month,
"/",p1.year
PRINT "Date 2 is ",p2.day,"/",p2.month,
"/",p2.year
REM *** End program ***
WAIT KEY
END
```

Activity 12.5

```
TYPE TimeType
  minutes AS INTEGER
  seconds AS INTEGER
ENDTYPE

TYPE BestType
  name AS STRING
  time AS TimeType
ENDTYPE

winner AS BestType

winner.name = "Jessica McLaren"
winner.time.minutes = 2
winner.time.seconds = 31
```

Activity 12.6

```
REM *** Define record structure ***
TYPE DateType
  day AS INTEGER
  month AS INTEGER
  year AS INTEGER
ENDTYPE

REM *** Declare array ***
DIM topdates(2) AS DateType

REM *** Assign values to topdates(1) ***
topdates(1).day = 22
topdates(1).month = 11
topdates(1).year = 1963

REM *** Read in values for topdates(2) ***
INPUT "Enter day: ",topdates(2).day
INPUT "Enter month: ",topdates(2).month
INPUT "Enter year: ",topdates(2).year

REM *** Display dates ***
PRINT "Date 1 is
",topdates(1).day,"/",topdates(1).month,"/"
,topdates(1).year
PRINT "Date 2 is
",topdates(2).day,"/",topdates(2).month,"/"
,topdates(2).year
REM *** End program ***
WAIT KEY
END
```

Activity 12.7

No solution required.

Activity 12.8

No solution required.

Activity 12.9

No solution required.

Activity 12.10

```
REM *** Set up array list ***
DIM list(5)
REM *** Store 0 to 5 in elements 0 to 5 ***
FOR c = 0 TO 5
   list() = c
   NEXT ARRAY INDEX list(0)
NEXT c
REM *** Display contents of list ***
PRINT "list contains the values"
FOR c = 0 TO 5
   PRINT list(c)," ";
NEXT c
REM *** End program ***
WAIT KEY
END
```

Activity 12.11

No solution required.

Activity 12.12

No solution required.

Activity 12.13

```
REM *** Value signifying quit ***
#CONSTANT QUIT 5
REM *** Global array to hold queue ***
DIM q(0)

REM *** Main section ***
InitialiseQueue()
REPEAT
   DisplayMenu()
   choice = GetChoice(5)
   ExecuteOption(choice)
UNTIL choice = QUIT
REM *** End program ***
END

FUNCTION DisplayMenu()
   PRINT "1 - Add value to queue"
   PRINT "2 - Delete head of queue"
   PRINT "3 - List queue"
   PRINT "4 - Show first value in queue"
   PRINT "5 - QUIT"
ENDFUNCTION

FUNCTION GetChoice(max)
   PRINT "Enter choice 1 - ",max," ";
   INPUT choice
   WHILE choice < 1 OR choice > max
      PRINT "Invalid choice. 1 to ",max,
      " only ";
      INPUT choice
   ENDWHILE
ENDFUNCTION choice

FUNCTION ExecuteOption(choice)
   SELECT choice
      CASE 1
         INPUT "Enter value to be added : "
         ,value
         AddToQueue(value)
      ENDCASE
```

```
      CASE 2
         RemoveFromQueue()
      ENDCASE
      CASE 3
         DisplayQueue()
      ENDCASE
      CASE 4
         PRINT "The first value in the
         queue is ", Front()
      ENDCASE
      CASE 5
         PRINT "Program terminated -
         press any key"
         WAIT KEY
      ENDCASE
   ENDSELECT
ENDFUNCTION

FUNCTION InitialiseQueue()
   PRINT "InitialiseQueue"
ENDFUNCTION

FUNCTION AddToQueue(v)
   PRINT "AddToQueue"
ENDFUNCTION

FUNCTION DeleteFromQueue()
   PRINT "RemoveFromQueue"
ENDFUNCTION

FUNCTION DisplayQueue()
   PRINT "DisplayQueue"
ENDFUNCTION

FUNCTION Front()
   PRINT "Front"
ENDFUNCTION -99
```

Function *Front()* is designed to return a value. Eventually, that value will be a copy of the first value in the queue, but for the moment any value can be used. In the code, we've used -99.

Activity 12.14

No solution required.

Activity 12.15

No solution required.

Activity 12.16

DeleteFromQueue() correctly removes the head of the queue.

Attempting to remove the head of an empty queue has no effect.

```
FUNCTION  DeleteFromQueue()
  IF NOT ARRAY INDEX VALID(q(0))
     EXITFUNCTION
  ENDIF
  REM *** Remove head of queue ***
  REMOVE FROM QUEUE q(0)
ENDFUNCTION
```

Activity 12.17

```
FUNCTION Front()
   ARRAY INDEX TO QUEUE q(0)
   IF NOT ARRAY INDEX VALID (q(0))
      result = -99
   ELSE
      result = q()
   ENDIF
ENDFUNCTION result
```

Activity 12.18

```
REM Create an array for stack ***
GLOBAL DIM s(0)

REM *** Start stack with no elements ***
EMPTY ARRAY s(0)

REM *** Main program loop ***
REPEAT
   CLS
   ShowStackMenu()
   option = GetUserOption(4)
   ExecuteOption(option)
UNTIL option = 4
END

FUNCTION Push(v)
   REM *** Add a new cell to the stack ***
   REM *** Array index ref new cell ***
   ADD TO STACK s(0)
   REM *** Store value in new cell ***
   s() = v
ENDFUNCTION

FUNCTION Pop()
   REM *** Array index to top of stack ***
   ARRAY INDEX TO STACK s(0)
   REM *** Save top of stack ... ***
   result = s()
   REM *** ...and then remove from stack ***
   REMOVE FROM STACK s(0)
ENDFUNCTION result

FUNCTION DisplayStack()
   REM *** FOR each value in the stack ***
   REM *** (start with last) ***
   lastposition = ARRAY COUNT(s(0))
   FOR p = lastposition TO 0 STEP -1
      REM *** Display it ***
      PRINT s(p)," ";
   NEXT p
   REM *** New line when complete ***
   PRINT
ENDFUNCTION

FUNCTION ShowStackMenu()
   PRINT "1 - Add to stack"
   PRINT "2 - Remove from stack"
   PRINT "3 - Display contents of stack"
   PRINT "4 - QUIT"
ENDFUNCTION

FUNCTION GetUserOption(max)
   PRINT "Enter choice 1 - ",max," ";
   INPUT choice
   WHILE choice < 1 OR choice > max
      PRINT "Invalid choice. 1 to ",max,
      " only ";
      INPUT choice
   ENDWHILE
ENDFUNCTION choice

FUNCTION ExecuteOption(choice)
   SELECT choice
      CASE 1
```

```
         INPUT "Enter value to be added : ",
         v
         Push(v)
      ENDCASE
      CASE 2
         IF ARRAY INDEX VALID(s(0))
            PRINT " Value removed was ",
            Pop()
         ELSE
            PRINT "Stack already empty"
         ENDIF
         WAIT KEY
      ENDCASE
      CASE 3
         DisplayStack()
         WAIT KEY
      ENDCASE
      CASE 4
         PRINT "Program terminating - press
         any key"
         WAIT KEY
      ENDCASE
   ENDSELECT
ENDFUNCTION
```

Activity 12.19

```
REM *** Set up the Variables ***
v1 AS BYTE
v2 AS BYTE
v3 AS BYTE
v4 AS BYTE
REM *** Assign the same value to each ***
REM *** but using different number base ***
v1 = 65
v2 = %01000001
v3 = 0X41
v4 = 0C101
REM *** Display each variable ***
PRINT v1
PRINT BIN$(v2)
PRINT v3
PRINT HEX$(v4)
REM *** End program ***
WAIT KEY
END
```

Activity 12.20

a) 11000100
b) 00010110

Activity 12.21

```
REM *** Initialise variable ***
num AS BYTE
num = 11
REM *** Display its current value ***
PRINT "Value before shift is ",num
REM *** Shift it 1 place to the left ***
num = num << 1
REM *** Display its new value ***
PRINT "Value after shift is ",num
REM *** End program ***
WAIT KEY
END
```

Activity 12.22

```
REM *** Initialise variable ***
num AS BYTE
num = 11
REM *** Display its current value ***
PRINT "Value before shift is ",num
```

```
REM *** Shift it 1 place to the right ***
num = num >> 1
REM *** Display its new value ***
PRINT "Value after shift is ",num
REM *** End program ***
WAIT KEY
END
```

Activity 12.23

```
REM *** Initialise variables ***
s AS BYTE
f AS BYTE
s = %10101001
REM *** f is complement of s ***
f = s..0
REM *** Display results ***
PRINT "s = ",RIGHT$(BIN$(s),8)
PRINT "f = ",RIGHT$(BIN$(f),8)
REM *** End program ***
WAIT KEY
END
```

Activity 12.24

```
REM *** Initialise variables ***
v1 AS BYTE
v2 AS BYTE
result AS BYTE
v1 = %00011111
v2 = %11010001
REM *** AND v1 and v2 ***
result = v1 && v2
REM *** Display the results ***
PRINT RIGHT$(BIN$(result),8)
REM *** End program ***
WAIT KEY
END
```

Activity 12.25

```
REM *** Initialise variables ***
v1 AS BYTE
v2 AS BYTE
result AS BYTE
v1 = %00011111
v2 = %11010001
REM *** OR v1 and v2 ***
result = v1 || v2
REM *** Display the results ***
PRINT RIGHT$(BIN$(result),8)
REM *** End program ***
WAIT KEY
END
```

Activity 12.26

```
REM *** Initialise variables ***
v1 AS BYTE
v2 AS BYTE
result AS BYTE
v1 = %00011111
v2 = %11010001
REM *** XOR v1 and v2 ***
result = v1 ~~ v2
REM *** Display the results ***
PRINT RIGHT$(BIN$(result),8)
REM *** End program ***
WAIT KEY
END
```

Activity 12.27

a) 10011000
b) 00000010
c) 01010011
d) 01101010

Activity 12.28

No solution required.

Activity 12.29

```
#CONSTANT win %10000110
status AS BYTE
REM *** Find which locations were visited
***
value = %10000000
FOR p = 1 TO 4
    PRINT "Location ",p," visited (Y/N):";
    INPUT reply$
    IF LOWER$(reply$)="y"
        status = status || value
    ENDIF
    value = value >> 1
NEXT p
REM *** Find which items taken ***
FOR p = 1 TO 4
    PRINT "Item ",p," taken (Y/N):";
    INPUT reply$
    IF LOWER$(reply$)="y"
        status = status || value
    ENDIF
    value = value >> 1
NEXT p
REM *** check for win ***
result = status && win
IF result = win
    PRINT "win"
ELSE
    PRINT "Lose"
ENDIF

REM *** End program ***
WAIT KEY
END
```

18

Bitmaps

Copying Sections of a Bitmap

Determining the Dimensions of a Bitmap

How Bitmap Images are Constructed

Image File Formats

Loading and Displaying Bitmaps

Manipulating Bitmaps

Positioning a Bitmap on the Screen

Resizing a Bitmap

Bitmaps Basics

Introduction

Any image we see displayed on a computer screen is actually stored as a set of numbers. These numbers are translated by the computer into a series of coloured dots that form the image on the computer screen.

If we zoom in on part of the image we can see the individual dots that make up the image (see FIG-13.1). These dots are known as **pixels**. This term is derived from the words *picture elements*. The whole image is known as a **bitmap**.

FIG-13.1

Pixels in a Bitmap Image

The simplest images are in black and white with no shades of grey (see FIG-13.2).

FIG-13.2

A Black and White Image

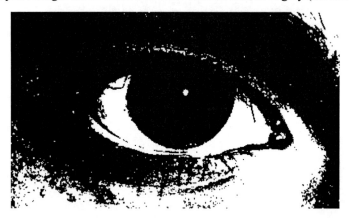

If we could see the series of numbers the computer uses to represent this image, there would be only two values used: 0 and 1. 0 represents a black pixel; 1 a white pixel. So the simple image shown on the left of FIG-13.3 would be stored as the set of numbers given on the right of the figure.

FIG-13.3

An Image and Its Digital Representation

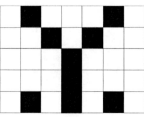

The Visible Image

```
1,0,1,1,1,0,1
1,1,0,1,0,1,1
1,1,1,0,1,1,1
1,1,1,0,1,1,1
1,0,1,0,1,0,1
```

How the Image
is Represented in
Computer Memory

Colour Palette

Not many images are in simple black and white. The next step up is to have a four colour image. This means that each pixel is represented by one of four values: 0,1, 2 or 3. Of course, these will be stored in binary as 00, 01,10 and 11. Exactly which four colours are to be used may vary from image to image and this information is actually held within the image file itself in the form of a **colour palette**. We can think of the colour palette as being a two-column table. The left-hand column represents the code used in the image file, while the right-hand column states which colour that code represents. For example, if a four colour image used the colours red, green, blue, and yellow, the colour palette would be as shown in TABLE-13.1.

TABLE-13.1

A Colour Palette

Code	Colour
0	red
1	green
2	blue
3	yellow

Most images will actually have many more colours. 256 colour, 65536 colour, or even full colour (16.8 million colours) images are the norm.

Full-colour images do not use palettes since the number used to represent a single pixel specifies the actual red, green and blue settings required.

File Size

A two-colour image needs 1 bit of storage for every pixel; while a full colour image needs 3 bytes per pixel (i.e. 24 times more storage space than the equivalent two-colour image).

The more pixels there are in an image the larger the file. So the final storage requirements for an image file are related to its width, height and number of colours.

File Formats

Images may be stored in a large variety of formats. DarkBASIC Pro can display .BMP and .JPG files. These are two of the most popular image formats.

Bitmaps in DarkBASIC Pro

Introduction

DarkBASIC Pro reserves 32 spaces in which bitmap images can be stored. We can think of these as 32 special variables that are always available in every program. Each of these image spaces is assigned a unique number from 0 to 31. A bitmap space grows to accommodate the image placed within it. So if a 600 by 400 pixel image is placed in area 2, then area 2 will grow to 600 by 400. Only area zero differs in that its size always matches the screen resolution. So, if we use a screen resolution of 1280 by 1024, then area zero will automatically match this size. In addition, any bitmap loaded into area zero is automatically displayed on the screen (see FIG-13.4).

FIG-13.4

DarkBASIC Pro's Image
Storage Areas

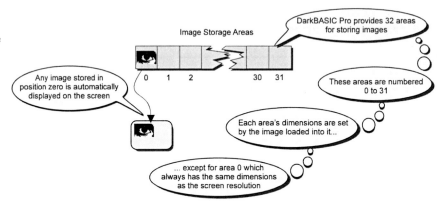

To make use of a bitmap area, that area has to be activated. Area zero, which shows on the screen, is always activated, but other areas can be activated in one of two ways:

 ➢ by loading an image file into that area using the LOAD BITMAP
   statement

 ➢ by using the CREATE BITMAP statement

Each of these methods are explained below.

The LOAD BITMAP Statement

To load a bitmap from a file and place it in one of these reserved spaces we use the LOAD BITMAP command which has the following format shown in FIG-13.5.

FIG-13.5

The LOAD BITMAP
Statement

In the diagram:

filename	is a string giving the name of the file to be loaded. Path information may be included if needed.
imgarea	is an integer representing the area into which the image is to be loaded.

For example, to display the file *flower.bmp,* on the screen we would use the line

```
LOAD BITMAP "flower.bmp",0
```

This assumes the file is stored in the same folder as the DarkBASIC Pro source code.

By loading the bitmap into area zero, it is automatically displayed on the computer screen.

On the other hand, if we use a statement such as

```
LOAD BITMAP "warrior.bmp",1
```

this loads the file *warrior.bmp* into bitmap area 1, but the image will not become visible.

The program shown in LISTING-13.1 will display an image file named *face. bmp.*

LISTING-13.1

Displaying a Bitmap

```
REM *** Display an image on the screen ***
LOAD BITMAP "face.bmp", 0
REM *** End program ***
WAIT KEY
END
```

To load the image into the program's folder use the *Media* button at the bottom right of the screen followed by the *Add* button.

Activity 13.2

Write a program, similar to that given above (*bitmap01.dbpro*), that displays the bitmap image *eyebw.bmp.*
(Make sure the image is in your project directory before you start.)

DarkBASIC Pro assumes that the image to be loaded is in the same directory as your program. If the file can't be found, an error message such as

Runtime error 1003 - Could not load bitmap at line 4

will be displayed (the line number will vary with the position of the LOAD BITMAP instruction in your program).

However, you can load images held in other folders by including path information with the file name. For example, the line

```
LOAD BITMAP "C:\myfolder\myimages\img01.bmp",0
```

will load and display the image *img01.bmp* that is stored on the C: drive in a sub-folder called *myimages* which is, itself, in a folder called *myfolder*.

If you load an image into a position other than zero, the image won't appear on the screen.

Activity 13.3

Change your previous program so that a second file, *eyecol.bmp* is loaded into bitmap area 1.
(The new image shouldn't appear on your screen)

So, why do we need all the extra positions if only an image in position zero can be shown on the computer screen? Well, it takes time to load images from disk and this might delay some programs that rely on quickly changing images. So at the start of the program we can load all the images we need into the areas provided and

DarkBASIC Pro: Bitmaps

then move any image we want to display into position zero. Because the images are held in the computer's memory, images transfer to the screen (area 0) much more rapidly.

The bitmap space activated by the LOAD BITMAP statement is set up to match exactly the dimensions of the image loaded. For example, if we load a bitmap which is 300 pixels wide by 200 pixels high, then the bitmap area will become 300 by 200. We can discover the dimensions of that image by using the BITMAP WIDTH and BITMAP HEIGHT statements.

The BITMAP WIDTH Statement

Once a bitmap area has been set up, we can find its width, in pixels, using the BITMAP WIDTH statement. This statement takes the form shown in FIG-13.6.

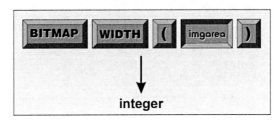

In the diagram:

> *imgarea*   is the integer representing the area into which the image has been loaded. The width of that image is returned.

A typical usage might be

```
LOAD BITMAP "eyecol.bmp", 0
width = BITMAP WIDTH(0)
PRINT "This image is ",width," pixels wide"
```

which will load the image *eyecol.bmp* into bitmap area zero before retrieving and displaying the width of the image.

The BITMAP HEIGHT Statement

The BITMAP HEIGHT statement is identical in format and usage to the BITMAP WIDTH, but returns an image area's height, rather than width. The statement has the format shown in FIG-13.7.

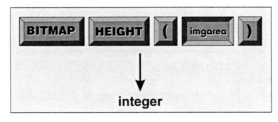

In the diagram:

> *imgarea*   is the integer representing the area into which the image has been loaded.

To find both the width and height of the bitmap file *eyecol.bmp* which has been loaded into area 1, we would use the lines:

```
LOAD BITMAP "eyecol.bmp", 1
width = BITMAP WIDTH(1)
height = BITMAP HEIGHT(1)
```

The BITMAP DEPTH Statement

One last piece of information we can determine about an image area is the number of bits per pixel used to represent colour. This information can be determined using the BITMAP DEPTH statement which has the format shown in FIG-13.8.

FIG-13.8

The BITMAP DEPTH Statement

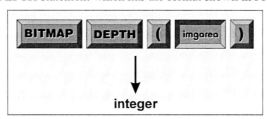

In the diagram:

imgarea   is the integer representing the area into which the image has been loaded.

To determine the dimensions and number of bits per pixel of *eyecol.bmp* we could use the lines:

```
LOAD BITMAP "eyecol.bmp", 1
width = BITMAP WIDTH(1)
height = BITMAP HEIGHT(1)
bits = BITMAP DEPTH(1)
```

By performing the calculation 2^{bits} we can discover the number of colours available in the image. This needs the following line of code:

```
colours = 2^bits
```

The SET CURRENT BITMAP Statement

Once we start dealing with a specific image area, all output will be directed to that area. For example, if we load an image into bitmap area 1 and then output a message with the statements

```
LOAD BITMAP "eyecol.bmp" , 1
PRINT "HELLO"
```

we won't see the word *HELLO* appear on our screen. Instead, the text will have been sent to image area 1.

Activity 13.4

Check out this effect by typing in and running the following program:

```
LOAD BITMAP "eyecol.bmp",1
PRINT "HELLO"
WAIT KEY
END
```

To make sure that the word HELLO is directed to the screen (i.e. bitmap area 0), we need to use the SET CURRENT BITMAP statement which takes the form shown in FIG-13.9.

FIG-13.9

The SET CURRENT
BITMAP Statement

In the diagram:

> *imgarea*   is the integer representing the area into which any subsequent output is to placed.

Using this command forces all subsequent output to be sent to the image area specified. This remains the case until another command involving another image area is executed.

For example, we could force all later output to go to the screen using the line:

```
SET CURRENT BITMAP 0
```

Activity 13.5

Change your previous program so that the PRINT statement causes the word *HELLO* to appear on the screen.

Activity 13.6

Write a program (*bitmap02.dbpro*) which performs the following logic:

Load *eyecol.bmp* into area 1
Determine the width, height and bits per pixel for this image
Change current image area to the screen
Display the width, height and bits per pixel for *eyecol.bmp*

Modify the program to use the file *eyebw.bmp* instead of *eyecol.bmp*.

The CREATE BITMAP Statement

We can also activate an image storage area without loading an image into that area. To do this we use the CREATE BITMAP command. This instruction must be given several values. These are:

➢ the bitmap area number

➢ the required width, in pixels, of the area

➢ the required height, in pixels, of the area

Therefore the statement has the format shown in FIG-13.10.

FIG-13.10

The CREATE BITMAP
Statement

In the diagram:

imgarea	is an integer representing the bitmap area whose dimensions are being set.
width	is an integer value representing the width in pixels to be assigned to the bitmap area.
height	is an integer value representing the height in pixels to be assigned to the bitmap area.

For example, we could set up image area 2 to be 200 pixels wide and 100 pixels high with the statement

```
CREATE BITMAP 2, 200, 100
```

We'll see where we might use this statement in a later example.

The COPY BITMAP Statement

An image can be moved from one storage position to another using the COPY BITMAP command. This statement takes the form shown in FIG-13.11.

FIG-13.11

The COPY BITMAP
Statement

In the diagram:

sourcearea	is an integer value specifying the bitmap area to be copied.
destinationarea	is an integer value specifying the bitmap area which is to receive the copy of the image.

For example, we can move an image from position 1 to position zero (and hence, display the image on the screen) using the command:

```
COPY BITMAP 1, 0
```

In the following program (see LISTING-13.2) we load an image into position 1 and then transfer it to position zero.

LISTING-13.2

Transferring a Bitmap
Between Areas

```
REM *** Load image to area 1, wait, then send to screen ***
LOAD BITMAP "splash.bmp", 1
WAIT KEY
COPY BITMAP 1, 0
REM *** End program ***
WAIT KEY
END
```

Activity 13.7

Add to your previous program (created in Activity 13.6) so that *eyebw.bmp* is moved from position 1 to position zero after the user presses a key.

The next two lines attempt to move an image from area 1 to area 2:

```
LOAD BITMAP "eyecol.bmp",1
```

```
COPY BITMAP 1, 2
```

This will only work if we've remembered to activate bitmap area 2. The earlier example, in LISTING-13.2, worked because we copied our image into area zero which always exists. So to copy *eyecol.bmp* from area 1 to area 2 we need the lines:

```
LOAD BITMAP "eyecol.bmp",1
CREATE BITMAP 2, BITMAP WIDTH (1) ,BITMAP HEIGHT (1)
COPY BITMAP 1,2
```

The FLIP BITMAP Statement

We can turn a bitmap upside down using the FLIP BITMAP command. The number of the bitmap to be flipped must be given. The format for this command is shown in FIG-13.12.

FIG-13.12

The FLIP BITMAP Statement

In the diagram:

imgarea	is an integer representing the bitmap area whose contents are to be flipped.

For example, we can flip the bitmap showing on the screen using the command:

```
FLIP BITMAP 0
```

The program in LISTING-13.3 loads a bitmap, then, when a key is pressed, flips the image.

LISTING-13.3

Flipping a Bitmap

```
REM *** Load bitmap into screen ***
LOAD BITMAP "eyecol.bmp", 0
WAIT KEY

REM *** Flip Image on Screen ***
FLIP BITMAP 0

REM *** End program ***
WAIT KEY
END
```

Activity 13.8

Type in and test the program in LISTING-13.3 (*bitmap03.dbpro*).

Notice that the program flips the whole screen. In the next example, we'll flip the image while it's in area 1 and then load it onto the screen (see LISTING-13.4).

LISTING-13.4

Flipping a Bitmap in Area 1

```
REM *** Load and Flip bitmap ***
LOAD BITMAP "eyecol.bmp", 1
REM *** Flip Image in Area 1 ***
FLIP BITMAP 1
REM *** Copy Area 1 to Screen ***
COPY BITMAP 1, 0

REM *** End program ***
WAIT KEY
END
```

This highlights the difference between flipping area zero and all other image areas: flipping 0 flips the whole screen, flipping other areas flips only the image itself (see FIG-13.13).

FIG-13.13

The Effects of the FLIP BITMAP Statement

FLIP BITMAP 0

Before   After

FLIP BITMAP 1

Before   After

COPY BITMAP 1,0

Screen After Copy

The MIRROR BITMAP Statement

Whereas the FLIP BITMAP command flips an image from top to bottom, the MIRROR BITMAP command flips the image from left to right. The statement has the format shown in FIG-13.14.

FIG-13.14

The MIRROR BITMAP Statement

In the diagram:

    imgarea   is an integer representing the bitmap area whose contents are to be mirrored.

For example, we could mirror the image in area 1 with the line:

```
MIRROR BITMAP 1
```

If you mirror area zero, the whole screen is mirrored, any other position will mirror only the image itself.

The program in LISTING-13.5 gives an example of each approach.

LISTING-13.5

Using the MIRROR BITMAP Statement

```
REM *** Load bitmap to area 1 ***
LOAD BITMAP "eyecol.bmp", 1
REM *** Copy the bitmap to screen ***
COPY BITMAP 1,0
WAIT KEY
REM *** Mirror the image and show it on screen***
MIRROR BITMAP 1
COPY BITMAP 1, 0
WAIT KEY
REM *** Load an image directly to the screen ***
LOAD BITMAP "eyecol.bmp", 0

REM *** and mirror it ***
MIRROR BITMAP 0

REM *** End the program ***
WAIT KEY
END
```

FIG-13.15 highlights the different results of these two approaches.

FIG-13.15

The Effects of the
MIRROR BITMAP
Statement

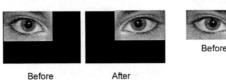 

MIRROR BITMAP 0   MIRROR BITMAP 1   COPY BITMAP 1,0

Before   After   Before   After   Screen After Copy

The BLUR BITMAP Statement

This statement gives an image an out-of-focus look. The degree of blur must also be set. The statement takes the form shown in FIG-13.16.

FIG-13.16

The BLUR BITMAP
Statement

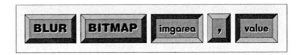

In the diagram:

imgarea	is an integer representing the bitmap area whose contents are to be blurred.
value	is an integer value representing the amount of blur to be applied to the image. This value can range between 1 and 6. 1 represents the minimum blur, 6 the maximum.

The statement

```
BLUR BITMAP 0,6
```

will give maximum blur to the image currently displayed on the screen.

On a large image with a high degree of blurring, this operation may take several seconds.

An example of this statement in use is given in LISTING-13.6.

LISTING-13.6

Using the BLUR
BITMAP Statement

```
REM *** Load bitmap to position 0 ***
LOAD BITMAP "eyecol.bmp", 0
WAIT KEY

REM *** Blur the image ... ***
BLUR BITMAP 0,6

REM *** ... and indicate when the operation is complete ***
PRINT "Done"

REM *** End program ***
WAIT KEY
END
```

Although we can blur an image, It is not possible to unblur an image.

The FADE BITMAP Statement

The FADE BITMAP statement allows the programmer to vary the brightness of a bitmap image. The statement has the format shown in FIG-13.17.

FIG-13.17

The FADE BITMAP Statement

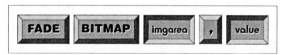

In the diagram:

imgarea	is an integer representing the bitmap area to which the fade operation is to be applied.
value	is an integer value representing the amount of fade to be applied to the image. This value can range between 0 and 100. Using 0 results in a totally black image; 100 gives a normal image with no fading.

The program in LISTING-13.7 performs the following logic:

```
Load eyecol.bmp into bitmap 1
Load eyecol.bmp into bitmap 2
Fade bitmap 1 with a setting of 25
Fade bitmap 2 with a setting of 75
Copy bitmap 1 to bitmap 0
Wait for a key press
Copy bitmap 2 to bitmap 0
Wait for a key press
```

LISTING-13.7

Using the FADE
BITMAP Statement

```
REM *** Load image to position 1 and 2 ***
LOAD BITMAP "eyecol.bmp", 1
LOAD BITMAP "eyecol.bmp", 2

REM *** Fade both images ***
FADE BITMAP 1, 25
FADE BITMAP 2, 75

REM *** Copy first image to screen ***
COPY BITMAP 1, 0
WAIT KEY

REM *** Copy second image to screen ***
COPY BITMAP 2, 0

REM *** End program ***
WAIT KEY
END
```

Activity 13.13

Type in and test the program given above (*bitmap06.dbpro*).

Copying Only Part of a Bitmap

So far we've used the COPY BITMAP command to copy a complete image from one area to another, but it is also possible to copy only part of an image. To do this we need to use a second version of the COPY BITMAP command which has a longer format.

The COPY BITMAP Statement - Version 2

We start by specifying the image area being copied. So if we are copying from image area 1, our statement would begin with

```
COPY BITMAP 1
```

Next we need to specify the section of the image to be copied. This must be a rectangular section and is given by specifying the coordinates of the top-left and bottom-right corners of the area to be copied (see FIG-13.18).

FIG-13.18

The Area of Image to be
Copied

These co-ordinates can be determined by loading the image involved into a paint package and reading off the positions of the corners of the area to be copied.

If we assume our image is currently held in area 1 and the part to be copied corresponds to the figures given in FIG-13.18, then our statement would begin:

```
COPY BITMAP 1,41,180,187,328
```

The next part of the statement specifies the bitmap area where the copy is to be made. If we were copying to area 2, our statement would expand to

```
COPY BITMAP 1,41,180,187,328, 2
```

Finally, the copied section of the image may be placed anywhere within the new image area, so, again, we must give the coordinates of the top-left and bottom-right corners of the spot at which the image is to be placed (see FIG-13.19).

FIG-13.19

The Receiving Area

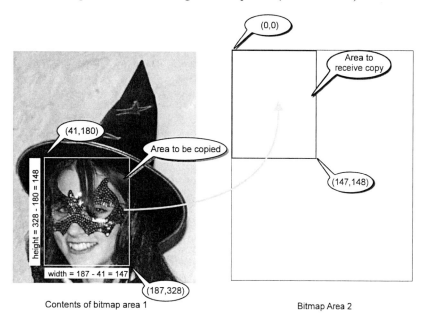

Contents of bitmap area 1   Bitmap Area 2

At last we can finish the command:

```
COPY BITMAP 1,41,180,187,328,2,0,0,147,148
```

The format for this longer version of the COPY BITMAP statement is shown in FIG-13.20.

FIG-13.20

The Extended COPY
BITMAP Statement

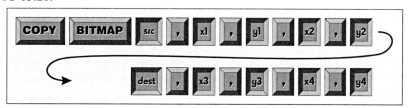

In the diagram:

    src   is an integer value specifying the bitmap area to be copied.

    x1,y1   Are a pair of integer values representing the coordinates of the top-left corner of the area in *src* to be copied.

x2,y2   Are a pair of integer values representing the coordinates of the bottom-right corner of the area in *src* to be copied.

dest   is an integer value specifying the bitmap area which is to receive the copy of the image.

x3,y3   Are a pair of integer values representing the coordinates of the top-left corner of the area in *dest* to receive the bitmap.

x4,y4   Are a pair of integer values representing the coordinates of the bottom-right corner of the area in *dest* to receive the bitmap.

The program in LISTING-13.8 employs the following logic:

Load *witch.bmp* in bitmap area 1
Create bitmap area 2 with the same dimensions as area 1
Copy the selected area from area 1 to area 2
Copy area 2 to the screen (area 0)

LISTING-13.8

Copying Part of a Bitmap

```
REM *** Load image to area 1 ***
LOAD BITMAP "witch.bmp", 1
REM *** Create area 2 same size as area 1 ***
CREATE BITMAP 2, BITMAP WIDTH (1), BITMAP HEIGHT (1)
REM *** Copy part of area 1 to area 2 ***
COPY BITMAP 1,41,180,187,328, 2,0,0,147,148
REM *** Display area 2 on the screen ***
COPY BITMAP 2, 0
REM *** End program ***
WAIT KEY
END
```

Activity 13.14

Type in and test the program in LISTING-13.8 (*bitmap07.dbpro*).

Modify the program so that the section of the image is copied directly to the screen without making use of image 2.

Modify the program again so that the copied section appears in the middle of the screen and not the top-left.

(HINT: You may have to discover the width and height of image area 0.)

The next program (LISTING-13.9) splits a 600 by 600 image into quarters and then moves each quarter to a different position before displaying the re-organised image.

LISTING-13.9

Splitting Up a Bitmap

```
REM *** Load image into area 1 ***
LOAD BITMAP "fox.bmp", 1
REM *** Create new area ***
CREATE BITMAP 2, BITMAP WIDTH (1), BITMAP HEIGHT (1)
```

continued on next page

LISTING-13.9

(continued)

Splitting Up a Bitmap

```
REM *** Copy image quarters to different positions ***
COPY BITMAP 1,0,0,300,300,        2,300,300,600,600
COPY BITMAP 1,300,0,600,300,      2,0,300,300,600
COPY BITMAP 1,0,300,300,600,      2,300,0,600,300
COPY BITMAP 1,300,300,600,600,    2,0,0,300,300
REM *** Display the new image ***
COPY BITMAP 2, 0
REM *** End program ***
WAIT KEY
END
```

Activity 13.15

Type in and test the program above (*bitmap08.dbpro*).

Modify the program so that the image is displayed both before and after it is split up.

Modify the program so that the order of the sections is different.

Zooming

We can make a bitmap (or a section of a bitmap) larger by copying it into an area larger than the one it has come from. For example, if we copy a 300 by 300 section of a picture into a 600 by 600 section, the size of the image will be doubled. The statement below copies a 300x300 section of an image in area 1 to a 600x600 area on the screen:

```
COPY BITMAP 1,0,0,300,300,0,0,0,600,600
```

The program in LISTING-13.10 uses this effect to zoom in on the top-left corner of the image displayed.

LISTING-13.10

Zooming in on a Bitmap

```
REM *** Load image into area 1 ***
SET DISPLAY MODE 800,600,16
LOAD BITMAP "fox.bmp", 1
REM *** Show image on screen ***
COPY BITMAP 1,0
REM *** Wait for key press before continuing ***
WAIT KEY
REM *** Magnify the top-left corner of the image***
COPY BITMAP 1, 0,0,300,300, 0,0,0,600,600
REM *** End program ***
WAIT KEY
END
```

Activity 13.16

Type in and test the program in LISTING-13.10 (*bitmap09.dbpro*).
Replace the second COPY BITMAP statement with the lines

```
FOR p = 300 TO 600 STEP 10
    COPY BITMAP 1, 0,0,300,300,0,0,0,p,p
    WAIT 1
NEXT p
```

Modify the FOR loop so that *p* ranges from 300 to 10 in steps of -10.
How does this effect the display?

DarkBASIC Pro: Bitmaps

The Activity shows that it is also possible to zoom out (make and image smaller) by using a receiving area which is smaller than the original area being copied.

Bitmap Status

There are several commands designed specifically to detect the current status of a bitmap. These are described below.

The BITMAP EXIST Statement

The BITMAP EXIST statement returns 1 if the specified bitmap area contains a bitmap image or has been prepared for an image. The statement has the format shown in FIG-13.21.

FIG-13.21

The BITMAP EXIST Statement

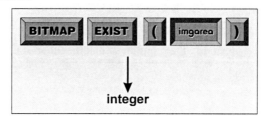

In the diagram:

    imgarea   is an integer representing the bitmap area to be checked.

If the area exists, 1 is returned; otherwise zero is returned.

For example, we could check to see if bitmap area 2 has previously been created using the lines:

```
IF BITMAP EXIST(2)=1
    PRINT "Bitmap area 2 already exists"
ENDIF
```

The BITMAP MIRRORED Statement

The BITMAP MIRRORED statement can be used to determine if a specified bitmap area has been mirrored. The statement has the format shown in FIG-13.22.

FIG-13.22

The BITMAP MIRRORED Statement

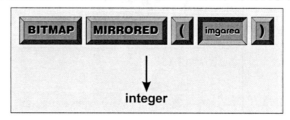

In the diagram:

    imgarea   is an integer representing the bitmap area to be checked.

The statement returns 1 if the BITMAP MIRROR operation has been performed on the specified bitmap area; otherwise zero is returned.

The BITMAP FLIPPED Statement

The BITMAP FLIPPED statement can be used to determine if a specified bitmap area has been flipped. The statement has the format shown in FIG-13.23.

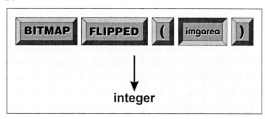

In the diagram:

imgarea   is an integer representing the bitmap area to be checked.

The statement returns 1 if the BITMAP FLIPPED operation has been performed on the specified bitmap area; otherwise zero is returned.

The CURRENT BITMAP Statement

The CURRENT BITMAP statement can be used to determine which bitmap area is currently set to receive output. The statement has the format shown in FIG-13.24.

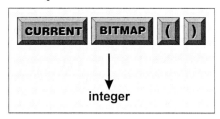

The statement returns the number of the current bitmap. The current bitmap is initially bitmap area 0 (the screen) but changes to match the last bitmap area to be used. It can also be changed using the SET CURRENT BITMAP statement described earlier in this chapter.

For example, we could make sure the screen is the current bitmap area using the lines:

```
IF CURRENT BITMAP() <> 0
    SET CURRENT BITMAP 0
ENDIF
```

The DELETE BITMAP Statement

The contents of a bitmap area can be removed from RAM using the DELETE BITMAP statement which has the format shown in FIG-13.25.

In the diagram:

imgarea   is an integer representing the bitmap area to be deleted.

Placing More than One Image in the Same Area

If we ever need to replace one bitmap with a new one in the same bitmap area, there are a few things we need to watch out for. In the example below (LISTING-13.11), an image, *pheasant.bmp*, is loaded into bitmap area 1 and then copied to the screen. After this a new image is copied to bitmap area 1 and then copied to the screen.

LISTING-13.11

Placing Different Images into the Same Area

```
REM *** Load bitmap into area 1 and copy to screen ***
LOAD BITMAP "pheasant.bmp",1
COPY BITMAP 1,0
WAIT KEY
REM *** Clear the screen ***
SET CURRENT BITMAP 0
CLS
REM *** Load a new image into area 1 and copy to screen ***
LOAD BITMAP "beetle.bmp",1
COPY BITMAP 1,0
REM *** End program ***
WAIT KEY
END
```

Activity 13.17

Use viewer software to look at the two images used by the program above.

Type in and test the program (*bitmap10.dbpro*).

What problems are there with the second image when it appears on the screen?

The problem arises because bitmap area 1 has its dimensions set by the first picture to be loaded, *pheasant.bmp*, which is 120 by 67 pixels. When the second image, *beetle.bmp*, is loaded into the same area, the *pheasant.bmp* image is removed, but the dimensions of the bitmap area remain set at 120 by 67. Because the second image, at 114 by 101 is taller than the dimensions set for the area, not all of the image is visible (see FIG-13.26).

FIG-13.26

Problems When Loading a Second Image into a Bitmap Area

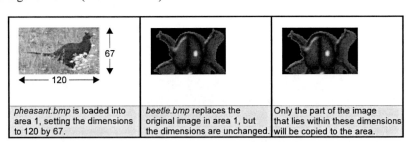

| *pheasant.bmp* is loaded into area 1, setting the dimensions to 120 by 67. | *beetle.bmp* replaces the original image in area 1, but the dimensions are unchanged. | Only the part of the image that lies within these dimensions will be copied to the area. |

We can work round this problem by using the CREATE BITMAP statement to reset the dimensions of the bitmap area before trying to load the second image.

Activity 13.18

In your last program, add the line

```
CREATE BITMAP 1,114,101
```

immediately before loading *beetle.bmp* into area 1.

The problem is slightly different when the screen (area 0) is receiving more than one image. The dimensions of area 0 are set automatically to match those of the screen and are, therefore, not affected by the images loaded there. However, when a smaller image is loaded onto the screen in place of a larger image, we get overlap as shown in FIG-13.27.

FIG-13.27

A Smaller Image Overlaps
the Larger Image

All that is necessary to solve this problem is to clear the screen between each picture with code such as:

```
REM *** View first picture ***
LOAD BITMAP "cherryblossom.bmp",0
WAIT KEY
REM *** Clear the screen ***
CLS
REM *** View second picture ***
LOAD BITMAP "beetle.bmp",0
WAIT KEY
```

Summary

- Bitmaps are images constructed from pixels.

- The colour of each pixel is represented by a binary number

- The more colours an image contains, the more bits are needed to represent each pixels.

- Full colour needs 24 bits (3 bytes) per pixel.

- Images which use less than 24 bits per pixel employ a colour palette to specify the actual colours being used.

- Large bitmaps with many colours create larger files than small images with fewer colours.

- DarkBASIC Pro has 32 reserved areas for holding bitmaps.

- Any bitmap placed in area 0 appears on the screen.

- The dimensions of area 0 automatically match the current screen resolution.

- Other bitmap areas have dimensions that match the images loaded into them.

- A bitmap can be loaded into a bitmap area using the LOAD BITMAP statement.

- A bitmap area's dimensions can also be set using the CREATE BITMAP statement.

- The dimensions of a bitmap can be determined using the BITMAP WIDTH and BITMAP HEIGHT.

- The number of bits per pixel can be determined using BITMAP DEPTH.

- The current bitmap (to which all output is sent) is initially bitmap area 0 (the screen).

- The current bitmap is automatically changed to the last bitmap area used.

- The current bitmap can be changed using the SET CURRENT BITMAP statement.

- The COPY BITMAP allows a bitmap image to be copied from one area to another.

- Bitmap images can be translated using FLIP BITMAP and MIRROR BITMAP.

- Bitmaps can be visually modified using the BLUR BITMAP and FADE BITMAP statements.

- An extended version of the COPY BITMAP statement allows part of a bitmap to be copied.

- By copying part of a bitmap to a larger area, the part of the image copied becomes larger.

- By copying part of a bitmap to a smaller area, the part of the image copied becomes smaller.

- We can check that a bitmap area has been previously activated using the BITMAP EXIST statement.

- We can check if an image has been mirrored or flipped using the BITMAP MIRRORED and BITMAP FLIPPED statements.

- The current bitmap area can be determined using the CURRENT BITMAP statement.

- The image in a specified bitmap area can be deleted using the DELETE BITMAP statement.

- A second image loaded into a bitmap area does not reset the dimensions of that area.

- A second image loaded onto the screen will overlap the image already there.

Solutions

Activity 13.1

Activity 13.2

```
REM *** Display bitmap on screen ***
LOAD BITMAP "eyebw.bmp",0
REM *** End program ***
WAIT KEY
END
```

Activity 13.3

```
REM *** Display bitmap on screen ***
LOAD BITMAP "eyecol.bmp",1
REM *** End program ***
WAIT KEY
END
```

Activity 13.4

No solution required.

Activity 13.5

```
REM *** Display bitmap on screen ***
LOAD BITMAP "eyecol.bmp",1
SET CURRENT BITMAP 0
PRINT "Hello"
REM *** End program ***
WAIT KEY
END
```

Activity 13.6

```
LOAD BITMAP "eyecol.bmp",1
width = BITMAP WIDTH(1)
height = BITMAP HEIGHT(1)
bits = BITMAP DEPTH(1)
SET CURRENT BITMAP 0
PRINT "The image is ",width," wide by ",
height," high"
PRINT "It uses ",bits," bits per pixel"
REM *** End program ***
WAIT KEY
END
```

Change the first line to

```
LOAD BITMAP "eyebw.bmp",1
```

Activity 13.7

```
REM *** Display bitmap on screen ***
LOAD BITMAP "eyebw.bmp",1
width = BITMAP WIDTH(1)
height = BITMAP HEIGHT(1)
bits = BITMAP DEPTH(1)
SET CURRENT BITMAP 0
PRINT "The image is ",width," wide by ",
height," high"
```

```
PRINT "It uses ",bits," bits per pixel"
PRINT "Press any key to view the image "
WAIT KEY
COPY BITMAP 1,0
REM *** End program ***
WAIT KEY
END
```

Activity 13.8

No solution required.

Activity 13.9

Only the image is flipped in the second version rather than the whole screen (as in the first version).

Activity 13.10

No solution required.

Activity 13.11

The time taken to blur the image depends on the size of the image, the degree of blur applied, and the power of your computer - but it can take a few seconds.

The image does become more blurred if the BLUR BITMAP statement is executed for a second time.

Activity 13.12

```
REM *** Load bitmap into area 1 ***
LOAD BITMAP "eyecol.bmp",1
REM *** Blur bitmap ***
BLUR BITMAP 1,6
REM *** Copy bitmap to screen ***
COPY BITMAP 1,0
REM *** End program ***
WAIT KEY
END
```

The process should be faster when carried out in a different area.

Activity 13.13

No solution required.

Activity 13.14

First modification:

```
REM *** Load image to area 1 ***
LOAD BITMAP "witch.bmp", 1
REM *** Copy part of area 1 to screen ***
COPY BITMAP 1,41,180,187,328,0,0,0,147,148
REM *** End program ***
WAIT KEY
END
```

Second modification:

```
REM *** Load image to area 1 ***
LOAD BITMAP "witch.bmp", 1
REM *** Copy part of area 1 to screen ***
```

```
REM *** 147 by 148 section copied ***
COPY BITMAP 1, 41,180,187,328, 0,SCREEN
WIDTH()/2-73,SCREEN HEIGHT()/2-74,
SCREEN WIDTH()/2+73,SCREEN HEIGHT()/2+74
REM *** End program ***
WAIT KEY
END
```

Activity 13.15

```
REM *** Load image into area 1 ***
LOAD BITMAP "fox.bmp", 1
REM *** Show image on screen ***
COPY BITMAP 1,0
WAIT KEY
REM *** Create new area ***
CREATE BITMAP 2,BITMAP WIDTH (1),
BITMAP HEIGHT (1)
REM *** Image 1/4 to different positions ***
COPY BITMAP 1,0,0,300,300, 2,300,300,600,600
COPY BITMAP 1, 300,0,600,300,
2,0,300,300,300
COPY BITMAP 1,0,300,300,600, 2,300,0,600,300
COPY BITMAP 1,300,300,600,600,
2,0,0,300,300
REM *** Display the new image ***
COPY BITMAP 2,0
REM *** End program ***
WAIT KEY
END
```

Activity 13.16

```
REM *** Load image into area 1 ***
SET DISPLAY MODE 800,600,16
LOAD BITMAP "fox.bmp", 1
REM *** Show image on screen ***
COPY BITMAP 1,0
WAIT KEY
REM *** Magnify top-left corner of image***
FOR p = 300 TO 600 STEP 10
    COPY BITMAP 1, 0,0,300,300, 0,0,0,p,p
    WAIT 1
NEXT p
REM *** End program ***
WAIT KEY
END
```

```
REM *** Load image into area 1 ***
SET DISPLAY MODE 800,600,16
LOAD BITMAP "fox.bmp", 1
REM *** Show image on screen ***
COPY BITMAP 1,0
WAIT KEY
REM *** Shrink top-left corner of image***
FOR p = 300 TO 10 STEP -10
    COPY BITMAP 1,0,0,300,300,0,0,0,p,p
    WAIT 1
NEXT p
REM *** End program ***
WAIT KEY
END
```

The area of the image becomes smaller. You may want to modify the WAIT time

Activity 13.17

Not all of the second image is shown.

Activity 13.18

```
REM *** Load bitmap into area 1 ***
LOAD BITMAP "pheasant.bmp",1
REM *** Copy area 1 to the screen ***
COPY BITMAP 1,0
WAIT KEY
REM *** Clear the screen ***
SET CURRENT BITMAP 0
CLS
WAIT KEY
REM *** Reset the dimensions of area 1 ***
CREATE BITMAP 1,114,101
REM *** Load a new image into area 1 ***
LOAD BITMAP "beetle.bmp",1
REM *** Copy area 1 to the screen ***
COPY BITMAP 1,0
REM *** End program ***
WAIT KEY
END
```

14

Video Cards and the Screen

Create a List of Available Screen Resolutions

Create a List of Available Video Cards

Create a Windowed Application

Extract Information from a Checklist

Set Window Features

Showing and Hiding Windows

Video Cards and the Screen

Introduction

When we write visually complex programs, much of the hard work needed to create a stunning display will be carried out by your video card. Since these cards vary in price from a few pounds to several hundred pounds, it should come as no surprise that they vary a great deal in their ability to produce a great image and to perform some of the more complex visual effects (such as fog, lighting and texturing).

Just exactly what your video card and screen is capable of can be determined using several purpose-built DarkBASIC Pro statements which are explained below.

Your Screen

The PERFORM CHECKLIST FOR DISPLAY MODES Statement

The PERFORM CHECKLIST FOR DISPLAY MODES statement will produce a list of screen modes, detailing the resolution and bits per pixel for each mode. This list is just an array of records (see Chapter 12), but with various statements specifically designed to access this list. The statement has the format shown in FIG-14.1.

FIG-14.1

The PERFORM CHECKLIST FOR DISPLAY MODES Statement

Executing this command creates a data structure known as a **checklist**. To gain access to the data placed there we need to use several other commands.

As you'll discover in later chapters, a checklist can be created for other features, such as the drives available on your machine. However, a program can contain only one checklist data structure at a time.

The CHECKLIST QUANTITY Statement

This statement returns the number of entries in the checklist structure and has the format shown in FIG-14.2.

FIG-14.2

The CHECKLIST QUANTITY Statement

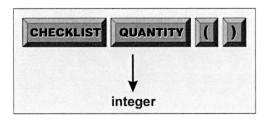

The simple program given in LISTING-14.1 displays how many entries there are in the checklist created by PERFORM CHECKLIST FOR DISPLAY MODES statement.

LISTING-14.1

Finding Out how Many
Entries are in the Checklist

```
REM *** Create a list of display modes ***
PERFORM CHECKLIST FOR DISPLAY MODES
REM *** Display the number of entries in the list ***
size = CHECKLIST QUANTITY()
PRINT "There are ", size, " entries in the list"
REM *** End program ***
WAIT KEY
END
```

Activity 14.1

Type in and test the program above (*screen01.dbpro*).

How many entries are in your list?

The CHECKLIST STRING$ Statement

We can make a copy of an entry in the checklist using the CHECKLIST STRING$ statement, which returns a string containing all of the information at a specified position in the list. This statement has the format shown in FIG-14.3.

FIG-14.3

The CHECKLIST
STRING$ Statement

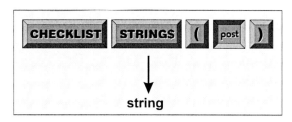

In the diagram:

post   is an integer value representing the position in the list from which the entry is to be extracted. The first entry in the list is at position 1.

LISTING-14.2 extends the previous program to display every entry in the checklist.

LISTING-14.2

Displaying Every Entry in
the Checklist

```
REM *** Create a list of display modes ***
PERFORM CHECKLIST FOR DISPLAY MODES
REM *** Display the number of entries in the list ***
size = CHECKLIST QUANTITY()
PRINT "There are ", size, " entries in the list"
REM *** Display each entry ***
FOR c = 1 TO size
    PRINT CHECKLIST STRING$(c)
NEXT c
REM *** End program ***
WAIT KEY
END
```

Activity 14.2

Modify your own program to match that given above.

Modify the program so that it halts and waits for a key press after every 25 entries displayed.

The string returned by CHECKLIST STRING$ contains the width, height and number of bits per pixel of an available display mode. For example, the line

```
640x400x32
```

tells us that the screen can be used in a mode which is 640 pixels wide, 400 pixels high, and using 32 bits per pixel.

The CHECKLIST VALUE Statement

Rather than extract all three items of information in a checklist entry as a single string, it is possible to extract these values separately. To extract the first item of information (the screen width) in an entry we use the CHECKLIST VALUE A, for the second CHECKLIST VALUE B, the third CHECKLIST VALUE C. Since some checklists have four data items in each entry (as we'll see later), there is also a CHECKLIST VALUE D available.

This statement has the format shown in FIG-14.4.

FIG-14.4

The CHECKLIST
VALUE Statement

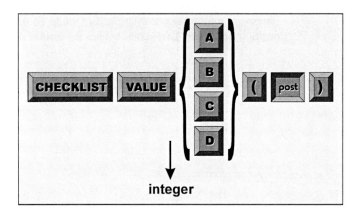

In the diagram:

    post   is an integer value representing the position in the list from which the entry is to be extracted.

The value returned by this statement is an integer.

For example, we could find the screen width setting for the third entry in the checklist by using the statement

```
screenwidth = CHECKLIST VALUE A(3)
```

All three values (width, height, and bits per pixel) of a single entry could be retrieved with lines such as:

```
screenwidth = CHECKLIST VALUE A(5)
screenheight = CHECKLIST VALUE B(5)
bitsperpixel = CHECKLIST VALUE C(5)
```

The EMPTY CHECKLIST Statement

If you have finished with the contents of the checklist, it is best to clear it, thereby saving RAM space. This is done by using the EMPTY CHECKLIST statement which has the format shown in FIG-14.5.

FIG-14.5

The EMPTY
CHECKLIST Statement

The CHECK DISPLAY MODE Statement

Back in Chapter 1 we saw that the SET DISPLAY MODE statement can be used to set the screen resolution. However, the trouble with specifying a screen resolution is that, although your machine may be capable of using the resolution requested, other machines, which could end up running your program, may not. And if someone has just paid out good money for your wonderful game, just to discover it won't run on their machine, they won't be too happy! Luckily, we can check that a machine is capable of displaying a specific resolution by using the CHECK DISPLAY MODE statement. This statement has the format shown in FIG-14.6.

FIG-14.6

The CHECK DISPLAY
MODE

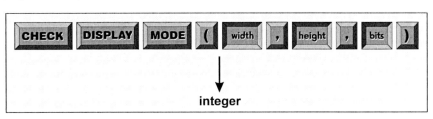

In the diagram:

width	is an integer value representing the width of the screen in pixels.
height	is an integer value representing the height of the screen in pixels.
bits	is an integer value representing the number of bits per pixel.

The statement returns the value 1 if the machine can display the specified resolution; otherwise zero is returned.

The program in LISTING-14.3 checks that the resolution required is available, before switching to that resolution. A message is displayed if the requested resolution is not available.

LISTING-14.3

Checking a Display
Mode is Available

```
REM *** If resolution available, change resolution ***
IF CHECK DISPLAY MODE (1280,1024,16) = 1
   SET DISPLAY MODE 1280,1024,16
ELSE
   PRINT "The requested resolution is not available"
ENDIF

REM *** End program ***
WAIT KEY
END
```

Activity 14.3

Type in and test the program (*screen02.dbpro*).

Modify the width setting to 1380 and check that the error message is displayed.

The settings of the current display mode can be retrieved using three statements we covered back in Chapter 3:

SCREEN WIDTH():integer — This statement returns an integer value representing the width in pixels of the current resolution.

This format used here is

function_name():type returned

SCREEN HEIGHT():integer — This statement returns an integer value representing the height in pixels of the current screen resolution.

SCREEN DEPTH():integer — This statement returns an integer value representing the number of bits per pixel being used by the current screen resolution.

The SCREEN FPS Statement

An important factor in any game that contains movement is how often the screen is updated. This is known as the **frame rate** or **frames per second**(fps) value. To create a realistic game you need to have a frame rate of at least 30 frames per second, otherwise the movement on screen may not appear smooth. The SCREEN FPS statement returns the frame rate achieved by your program. The statement has the format shown in FIG-14.7.

FIG-14.7

The SCREEN FPS Statement

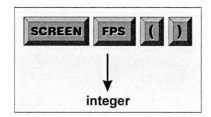

By including a statement such as

```
PRINT SCREEN FPS()
```

in the main loop of your game, you'll see how the frame rate changes as the graphics on screen become more complex. The program in LISTING-14.4 gives an example of this statement in use.

LISTING-14.4

Displaying the Frames Per Second

```
REM *** set display mode ***
SET DISPLAY MODE 1280,1024,16

REM *** Set text opaque ***
SET TEXT OPAQUE

REM *** Draw random lines ... ***
DO
    LINE RND(800),RND(600),RND(800),RND(600)
    SET CURSOR 100,900
    REM *** ... and report frame rate ***
    PRINT SCREEN FPS()
LOOP
REM *** End program ***
WAIT KEY
END
```

The SCREEN INVALID Statement

If you are running more than one program at a time, you can switch to another program by either clicking on its window, or by using Alt-Tab. The SCREEN INVALID statement will return a 1 if another program has been activated while the DarkBASIC Pro game was in the middle of executing. If no switch has been made, then zero is returned. The statement has the format shown in FIG-14.8.

FIG-14.8

The SCREEN INVALID Statement

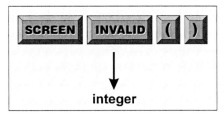

The program in LISTING-14.5 demonstrates the use of this command.

LISTING-14.5

Checking for Another Program Starting Up

```
REM *** set display mode ***
SET DISPLAY MODE 1280,1024,16

REM *** Create an infinite loop ***
DO
    REM *** Draw a line ***
    LINE RND(800),RND(600),RND(800),RND(600)
    REM *** If program switched, display message ***
    IF SCREEN INVALID() = 1
        PRINT "Program was switched"
    ENDIF
LOOP

REM *** End program ***
WAIT KEY
END
```

The results of the last Activity showed that SCREEN INVALID returns 1 when the program is first run. To avoid a message appearing, we could add the line

```
ignore = SCREEN INVALID()
```

before the DO loop.

Your Graphics Card

As well as supplying details about your screen resolution, DarkBASIC Pro can give information about your graphics card. The statements used to obtain these details are listed below.

The PERFORM CHECKLIST FOR GRAPHICS CARDS Statement

FIG-14.9

The PERFORM
CHECKLIST FOR
GRAPHICS CARDS
Statement

Some computers actually have more than one graphics card. You can find out exactly what is available in your computer using the PERFORM CHECKLIST FOR GRAPHICS CARDS statement which has the format shown in FIG-14.9.

Like the PERFORM CHECKLIST FOR DISPLAY MODES statement, this command fills the checklist data structure with relevant information about your graphic card(s). Therefore, you need to use CHECKLIST statements described earlier in this chapter (e.g. CHECKLIST QUANTITY, CHECKLIST STRING$, etc.) to retrieve the information placed in the checklist data structure.

The short program in LISTING-14.7 will display details about all the graphics hardware in your machine.

LISTING-14.7

Displaying Graphics Card
Details

```
REM *** Get graphic card(s) details ***
PERFORM CHECKLIST FOR GRAPHICS CARDS

REM *** Display data about each card ***
PRINT "The machine contains the following cards :"
FOR c = 1 TO CHECKLIST QUANTITY()
   PRINT CHECKLIST STRING$(c)
NEXT c

REM *** End program ***
WAIT KEY
END
```

It would not be appropriate to use the CHECKLIST VALUE statement on this particular checklist since it contains no numeric data.

The SET GRAPHICS CARD Statement

If you do have more than one graphics card, you can choose which one your program is to use by calling the SET GRAPHICS CARD statement which has the format shown in FIG-14.10.

FIG-14.10

The SET GRAPHICS
CARD Statement

In the diagram:

cardname is a string giving the name of the card to be used. This name can be obtained extracting the information previously produced by the PERFORM CHECKLIST FOR GRAPHICS CARDS statement.

For example, we could allow the user to choose which graphics card to use with code such as:

```
PERFORM CHECKLIST FOR GRAPHICS CARDS
PRINT "The machine contains cards :",CHECKLIST QUANTITY(),
" graphics cards"
INPUT "Enter number of card to be used ", cardno
SET GRAPHICS CARD CHECKLIST STRING$(cardno)
```

The CURRENT GRAPHICS CARD$ Statement

If you want to find out the name of the graphics card currently being used by your program, you can use the CURRENT GRAPHICS CARD$ statement. This command has the format shown in FIG-14.11.

FIG-14.11

The CURRENT
GRAPHICS CARD$
Statement

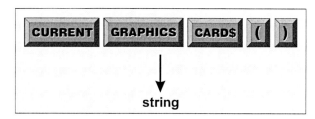

The statement returns a string giving the name of the graphics card currently being used.

The SCREEN TYPE Statement

The term **video accelerator** is used to describe a video card which performs many of the operations required to create a screen display using its own hardware (rather than the power of the computer's own processor). You can check if your own machine has a video accelerator card using the SCREEN TYPE statement which has the format given in FIG-14.12.

FIG-14.12

The SCREEN TYPE
Statement

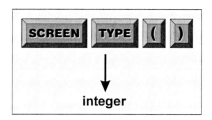

This statement returns the value 1 if a video accelerator is used, and zero if no accelerator is used.

For example, we might write

```
IF SCREEN TYPE() = 0
    PRINT "You have no video accelerator hardware"
ENDIF
```

Activity 14.8

Write a program (*gcard02.dbpro*) which displays a message to indicate if accelerator hardware is present or not.

The SET GAMMA Statement

The SET GAMMA statement is dependent on the abilities of your graphics card, but if it works, you can give an overall tint or shade to everything that appears on your screen. The statement has the format shown in FIG-14.13.

FIG-14.13

The SET GAMMA Statement

In the diagram:

red	is an integer value between 0 and 511 specifying the intensity of the red gamma setting.
green	is an integer value between 0 and 511 specifying the intensity of the red gamma setting.
blue	is an integer value between 0 and 511 specifying the intensity of the red gamma setting.

The default setting for all three colours is 256 which should give no overall effect on the screen.

The program in LISTING-14.8 demonstrates what effect this command has by loading an image and then changing the red gamma setting from 0 in increments of 100 each time a key is pressed.

LISTING-14.8

Adjusting the Gamma Setting

```
REM *** Load image ***
LOAD BITMAP "foliage.jpg",0

REM *** Change red gamma setting 6 times (0 to 500) ***
FOR c = 0 TO 5
   SET GAMMA c*100,255,255
   WAIT KEY
NEXT c

REM *** End program ***
WAIT KEY
END
```

Activity 14.9

Type in and test the program in LISTING-14.8 (*gcard03.dbpro*).

Using a Window

Many games use the full screen since this helps give a feeling of total immersion in the game environment to the player. But some games are better suited to being in a separate window which can be closed and moved like normal applications. The games that come with Microsoft Windows are examples of this approach. DarkBASIC Pro has a set of statements which allows a program to set up and manipulate a window.

The SET WINDOW ON Statement

The first step towards creating a window for your game is to change from full screen to windows mode with the SET WINDOW ON statement which has the format given in FIG-14.14.

FIG-14.14

The SET WINDOW ON
Statement

However, you need to use several more statements before an actual window will appear on your screen.

The SET WINDOW SIZE Statement

This statement allows you to set the width and height of your window and has the format shown in FIG-14.15.

FIG-14.15

The SET WINDOW
SIZE Statement

In the diagram:

width	is an integer value representing the width of the window in pixels.
height	is an integer value representing the height of the window in pixels.

For example, a 500 pixels wide by 300 pixels high window could be created using the line:

```
SET WINDOW SIZE 500, 300
```

The SET WINDOW POSITION Statement

The exact position of the window on the screen is set using the SET WINDOW POSITION statement which has the format given in FIG-14.16.

FIG-14.16

The SET WINDOW
POSITION Statement

In the diagram:

x,y	are integer values giving the coordinates of the top left corner of the window.

For example, we could place the top-left corner of the window at position (12,30) using the statement

```
SET WINDOW POSITION 12,30
```

The SET WINDOW LAYOUT Statement

A few characteristics of the window's appearance can be set using the SET WINDOW LAYOUT statement. This allows us to specify if a title bar and the normal buttons are to be present in the window. The statement has the format shown in FIG-14.17.

In the diagram:

styleflg	is an integer code representing the window style required:

> 1   title bar, minimise, maximise, and close buttons present. The window can be resized by the user.
> 0   title bar and buttons omitted. The window cannot be resized.

barflg	is an integer code which determines if the title bar is present:

> 1   title bar appears even if *styleflg* is set to zero.
> 0   title bar is missing only if *styleflg* is set to zero.

iconno	is an integer code which determines which icon is used if the application is minimised. A value of 1 will result in the default DarkBASIC Pro icon being used.

The combined value of the *styleflg* and *barflg* settings effects the final appearance of the window. All possible combinations are shown in TABLE 14.1 below.

TABLE-14.1

The Combined Effects of
the *styleflg* and *barflg*
Values

styleflg	barflg	Result		
0	0	No title bar;	no buttons;	not resizable
0	1	Title bar;	no buttons;	not resizable
1	0	Title bar;	buttons;	resizable
1	1	Title bar;	buttons;	resizable

The SET WINDOW TITLE Statement

The contents of the window's title bar can be set using the SET WINDOW TITLE statement which has the format shown in FIG-14.18.

FIG-14.18

The SET WINDOW
TITLE Statement

In the diagram:

caption is the string that is to appear in the window's title bar.

For example, we could set the title of the window to *My First Game* using the line

```
SET WINDOW TITLE "My First Game"
```

The program in LISTING-14.8 demonstrates the use of a window by creating a window with a title.

LISTING-14.8

Creating a Window Application

```
REM *** Check desired mode available ***
IF CHECK DISPLAY MODE (1280, 1024, 16) = 1
   SET DISPLAY MODE 1280,1024, 16
ELSE
   REM *** IF not halt program ***
   PRINT "Required display mode not available"
   PRINT "Press a key to terminate the program"
   WAIT KEY
   END
ENDIF
REM *** Use a window ***
SET WINDOW ON

REM *** Set its size to 300 by 200 ***
SET WINDOW SIZE 300,200

REM *** Create a title bar with buttons ***
SET WINDOW LAYOUT 1, 1, 1

REM *** Position window at (100,100) ***
SET WINDOW POSITION 100,100

REM *** Add title ***
SET WINDOW TITLE "My First Game"

REM *** Output to the window ***
PRINT "Hello"

REM *** End program ***
WAIT KEY
END
```

There are two ways to end the program. One is to execute the END statement, the other is to click on the EXIT button on the window's title bar.

Activity 14.10

Type in and test the program above (*window01.dbpro*).

What happens if you remove the WAIT KEY statement at the end of the program?

The HIDE WINDOW Statement

If required, you can make a window invisible by using the HIDE WINDOW statement which has the format shown in FIG-14.19.

FIG-14.19

The HIDE WINDOW Statement

The SHOW WINDOW Statement

FIG-14.20

The SHOW WINDOW
Statement

A hidden window can be made to reappear using the SHOW WINDOW statement which has the format shown in FIG-14.20.

The program in LISTING-14.9 creates a window, which will disappear for 1 second when a key is pressed.

LISTING-14.9

Hiding and Showing a
Window

```
REM *** Set up screen mode ***
SET DISPLAY MODE 1280,1024, 16

REM *** Create the window   ***
SET WINDOW ON
SET WINDOW SIZE 300,200
SET WINDOW LAYOUT 1, 1, 1
SET WINDOW POSITION 100,100

REM *** Wait for key press then hide window ***
WAIT KEY
HIDE WINDOW

REM *** Wait 1 second then reshow window ***
WAIT 1000
SHOW WINDOW

REM *** End program ***
WAIT KEY
END
```

Activity 14.11

Type in and test the program given above (*window02.dbpro*).

Summary

- DarkBASIC Pro can create a data structure known as a checklist.

- A checklist contains a list of options available on the current machine in a specific area.

- Only one checklist can exist at any given time.

- The PERFORM CHECKLIST FOR DISPLAY MODES creates a checklist containing the available screen resolutions.

- The CHECKLIST QUANTITY statement returns the number of entries in the current checklist.

- The CHECKLIST STRING$ returns the entry at a specific position in the checklist.

- When appropriate, the individual parts of a checklist entry can be extracted using the CHECKLIST VALUE statement.

- The EMPTY CHECKLIST statement removes all entries from the checklist.

- The CHECK DISPLAY MODE statement indicates whether a specified display mode is available with the current hardware.

- The SCREEN FPS statement returns the number of frames per second achieved by the program currently executing.

- The SCREEN INVALID statement detects when the user switches to another application.

- PERFORM CHECKLIST FOR GRAPHICS CARDS creates a checklist containing the names of the video cards currently installed.

- SET GRAPHICS CARD allows the graphics card used to be specified.

- CURRENT GRAPHICS CARD$ returns the name of the graphics card currently in use.

- The SCREEN TYPE statement indicates whether a video accelerator is being used.

- The SET GAMMA statement allows the overall tint of the screen output to be adjusted.

- A DarkBASIC Pro application can be made to appear in a window by using a series of WINDOW statements.

- SET WINDOW ON changes the output to a windowed area.

- The dimensions of a window can be set using SET WINDOW SIZE.

- The position of a window can be set using SET WINDOW POSITION.

- The characteristics of a window's title bar can be set using SET WINDOW LAYOUT.

- The text appearing in a window's title bar can be specified using SET WINDOW TITLE.

- A window can be hidden using HIDE WINDOW.

- SHOW WINDOW causes a hidden window to reappear.

Solutions

Activity 14.1

No solution required.

Activity 14.2

```
REM *** Create a list of display modes ***
PERFORM CHECKLIST FOR DISPLAY MODES
REM *** Display the number of entries in
the list ***
size = CHECKLIST QUANTITY()
PRINT "There are ", size, " entries in the
list"
REM *** Display each entry ***
FOR c = 1 TO size
   PRINT CHECKLIST STRING$(c)
   REM *** Wait for key every 25th ***
   IF c mod 25 = 0
      WAIT KEY
   ENDIF
NEXT c
REM *** End program ***
WAIT KEY
END
```

Activity 14.3

No solution required.

Activity 14.4

No solution required.

Activity 14.5

The program displays the message Program was switched when it begins execution.

The message appears for a second time when a switch between applications is made.

Activity 14.6

No solution required.

Activity 14.7

No solution required.

Activity 14.8

```
REM *** Display appropriate message ***
IF SCREEN TYPE() = 0
   PRINT "No accelerator hardware present"
ELSE
   PRINT "Accelerator hardware is installed"
ENDIF
REM *** End program ***
WAIT KEY
END
```

Activity 14.9

No solution required.

Activity 14.10

Removing the WAIT KEY statement at the end of the program allows the program to execute the END statement without waiting for a key press. This means that the application closes automatically without the user being required to press a key or click on the EXIT button.

Activity 14.11

No solution required.

15

Checking that Paths and Files Exist

Closing a File

Copying and Moving Files

Creating Folders

Creating and Reading Pack Files

Deleting a Folder

Executing Another Program from Your Own Program

Extracting Details About a File

Finding Out what Drives are Available

Listing the Contents of a Folder

Loading an Array from a File

Moving Through the Files in a Folder

Random Access of a File

Reading from a File

Renaming Files

Saving an Array to a File

Setting the Current Directory

Files

Introduction

If we intend to hold onto information after a game has been completed, for example, the top ten scores, the name of the current player, or the current state of a game which the player has temporarily stopped playing, then we need to store that information on a backing storage device such as a disk or flash memory.

Luckily, DarkBASIC Pro has a whole set of commands which allow us to do this - and a lot more besides.

Disk Housekeeping Statements

Before seeing how to save information to a file and read it back, we need to look at more mundane tasks such as creating a folder, copying a file, changing the current directory, etc.

For the examples that follow we will assume that the C: drive has the setup shown in FIG-15.1. The main folders and files used in the examples are shown in bold.

FIG-15.1

The C: Drive Setup

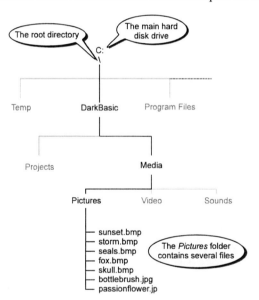

Activity 15.1

Use Windows Explorer to create the *DarkBASIC*, *Media*, and *Pictures* folders as shown in FIG-15.1.

Copy the files named into the *Pictures* folder.

The DRIVELIST Statement

The DRIVELIST statement will display a list of all the drives available on the current system. The format of the statement is given in FIG-15.2.

FIG-15.2

The DRIVELIST
Statement

The three line program below

```
DRIVELIST
WAIT KEY
END
```

is all that is required to display this information.

Activity 15.2

Create a program (*files01.dbpro*) using the code given to display which drives are available on your own machine.

The GET DIR$ Statement

Microsoft Windows always maintains details of which folder it is currently working with. This is known as the **current directory**. We can find out which folder is the current directory using the GET DIR$ statement which returns a string giving this information. The statement has the format shown in FIG-15.3.

FIG-15.3

The GET DIR$ Statement

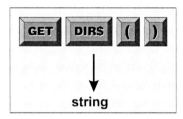

For example, the line

```
PRINT GET DIR$()
```

will display the current directory. This will be the folder in which the running DarkBASIC Pro program is held.

Activity 15.3

Add to your previous program so that the current directory is displayed after the list of drive letters.

The CD Statement

The current directory setting can be moved using the CD statement which allows us to specify a new current directory. The statement has the format shown in FIG-15.4.

FIG-15.4

The CD Statement

In the diagram:

path   is a string specifying the folder which is to become the current directory. Absolute or relative path information can be given.

For example, if we assume the current directory is the *Media* folder (see FIG-15.1) and we want to change to the *Pictures* folder, then we can use the statement

```
CD "C:\DarkBasic\Media\Pictures"
```

which specifies an absolute path, starting with the drive letter. Using this approach the current directory setting is irrelevant. Alternatively, we could change the current directory with the line

```
CD "Pictures"
```

which uses relative path details. That is, it specifies where the new current directory is relative to the existing current directory.

The program in LISTING-15.1 changes the current directory to the *Media* folder using absolute path information and then changes it again to *Pictures* using relative path details.

LISTING-15.1

Using Relative and Absolute Path Addresses

```
REM *** Set Media folder as current directory ***
CD "C:\DarkBasic\Media"
PRINT GET DIR$()

REM *** Set Pictures folder to current directory ***
CD "Pictures"
PRINT GET DIR$()

REM *** End program ***
WAIT KEY
END
```

Activity 15.4

Type in and test the program given in LISTING-15.1 (*files02.dbpro*).

Modify the program so that absolute path details are given in both CD statements.

Use CD "\" to change the current directory to the root of the current drive.

The SET DIR Statement

The SET DIR statement is an alternative to the CD statement and has exactly the same effect. The statement has the format shown in FIG-15.5.

FIG-15.5

The SET DIR Statement

In the diagram:

path   is a string specifying the folder which is to become the current directory. Absolute or relative path information can be given.

The PATH EXIST Statement

Before moving to a new folder, we can check that the path information we are about to use is valid using the PATH EXIST statement. This statement determines if a specified path is valid (that is, if the drive and folders named in the path actually exist). The statement has the format shown in FIG-15.6.

FIG-15.6

The PATH EXIST Statement

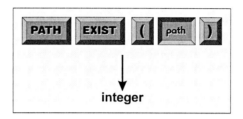

In the diagram:

  path   is a string specifying absolute or relative path information that is to be checked.

The statement returns 1 if the path details are valid; otherwise zero is returned.

The program in LISTING-15.2 allows the user to type in path information and then displays the validity of that path.

LISTING-15.2

Checking that a Path Exists

```
REM *** Get path info ***
INPUT "Enter path : ",path$

REM *** Check if it's valid ***
IF PATH EXIST(path$) = 1
    PRINT "Valid path"
ELSE
    PRINT "Invalid path"
ENDIF

REM *** End program ***
WAIT KEY
END
```

The MAKE DIRECTORY Statement

You can actually create a new folder from within a DarkBASIC Pro program using the MAKE DIRECTORY statement which has the format shown in FIG-15.7.

FIG-15.7

The MAKE
DIRECTORY Statement

In the diagram:

> *folder* is a string giving the name of the folder to be created. Path information may be included in this string. If no path information is given the new folder becomes a sub-folder of the current directory.

The statement will fail if the folder specified already exists.

For example, the line

```
MAKE DIRECTORY "C:\DarkBasic\Media\Video"
```

would create the *Video* subfolder in the *Media* folder (assuming the *Video* folder did not already exist).

Activity 15.7

Use the MAKE DIRECTORY statement to add the *Projects*, *Video* and *Sounds* folders as shown in FIG-15.1.

The DELETE DIRECTORY Statement

An existing folder and its contents can be deleted using the DELETE DIRECTORY statement which has the format given in FIG-15.8.

FIG-15.8

The DELETE
DIRECTORY Statement

In the diagram:

> *folder* is a string giving the name of the folder to be deleted. Path information may be included in this string.

The statement will fail if the folder does not exist.

Activity 15.8

Write a program (*files04.dbpro*) that creates a folder called *DarkTest* as a sub-folder of the *DarkBasic* folder, then sets this as the current directory. Next the program should display the current directory setting and finally delete the *DarkTest* folder.

Is the folder deleted?

Modify the program so that the root directory of C: becomes the current directory before the DELETE DIRECTORY statement is executed.

Is the folder deleted this time?

As we can see from the last Activity, it is not possible to delete the current directory.

The DIR Statement

Once we've moved to the folder we want, we can find out the contents of that folder using the DIR statement. This will list the names of all the files in the current directory and also any sub-folders which the current directory may contain. The format of this statement is given in FIG-15. 9.

FIG-15.9

The DIR Statement

For example the lines:

```
CD "C:\DarkBasic\Media\Videos"
DIR
```

will display all files held in the *Videos* folder.

Activity 15.9

Write a program (*files05.dbpro*) which sets the *Pictures* folder mentioned earlier as the current directory and lists the contents of the folder.

The DELETE FILE Statement

A file can be deleted using the DELETE FILE statement. The file to be deleted can be in the current directory or elsewhere, if path information is supplied. The format of this statement is given in FIG-15.10.

FIG-15.10

The DELETE FILE Statement

In the diagram:

    filename   is a string giving the name of the file to be deleted. Path information may be included, otherwise the file is assumed to be in the current directory.
If the file does not exist or is being used by another program, the command will fail.

Activity 15.10

Create a program to delete the *storm.bmp* file from the *Pictures* folder (*files06.dbpro*).

The COPY FILE Statement

A file can be copied from one folder to another using the COPY FILE statement. After the operation is complete the copied file will exist in both its original folder and the folder to which it has been copied. The format of this statement is given in FIG-15.11.

FIG-15.11

The COPY FILE
Statement

In the diagram:

srcfile   is a string giving the name of the file to be
                                  copied. Path information may be included,
                                  otherwise the file is assumed to be in the
                                  current directory.

destfile   is a string giving the name to be assigned to the
                                  the copied file. Path information may also be
                                  included, otherwise the copy will be placed in
                                  the current directory.

For example, we could copy *storm.bmp* from the *Pictures* folder to the *Video* folder
using the line:

```
COPY FILE "C:\darkbasic\media\pictures\storm.bmp",
"C:\darkbasic\media\video\storm.bmp"
```

Alternatively, we could use relative path information and save some typing:

```
CD "C:\darkbasic\media"
COPY FILE "pictures\skull.bmp","video\skull.bmp"
```

Activity 15.11

Write a program (*files07.dbpro*) which copies the files *Hangman.exe* and
BullandTouch.exe to the *Projects* folder.

The MOVE FILE Statement

A file can be moved from one folder to another using the MOVE FILE statement.
After the operation is complete the moved file will be removed from its original
folder and placed in the new folder specified in the command. The format of this
statement is given in FIG-15.12.

FIG-15.12

The MOVE FILE
Statement

In the diagram:

srcfile   is a string giving the name of the file to be
                                  moved. Path information may be included,
                                  otherwise the file is assumed to be in the
                                  current directory.

destfile   is a string giving the name to be assigned to the
                                  the moved file. Path information may also be
                                  included, otherwise the copy will be placed in
                                  the current directory.

For example, we could move *sunset.bmp* from *Pictures* to the *Video* folder using
the lines:

```
CD "C:\darkbasic\media"
MOVE FILE "pictures\sunset.bmp","video\sunset.bmp"
```

The FILE EXIST Statement

Before trying to copy, move or delete a file we can check to see if the file currently exists using the FILE EXIST statement. The format of this statement is given in FIG-15.13.

FIG-15.13

The FILE EXIST Statement

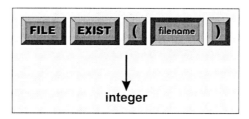

In the diagram:

> *filename*   is a string specifying the name of the file that is to be checked. This string may include path details.

The statement returns 1 if the named file exists; otherwise zero is returned.

For example, we could check to see if *sunset.bmp* exists within the *Pictures* folder using the lines:

```
CD "C:\DarkBasic\Media\Pictures"
IF FILE EXIST ("sunset.bmp")
    PRINT "File sunset.bmp is in the Pictures folder"
ELSE
    PRINT "The file is not in the Pictures folder"
ENDIF
```

The RENAME FILE Statement

A file can be renamed using the RENAME FILE statement. The file must not be open when this statement is executed. The format of this statement is given in FIG-15.14.

FIG-15.14

The RENAME FILE Statement

In the diagram:

> *currentname*   is a string specifying the file's current name. Path information may be included.
>
> *newname*   is a string giving the new name of the file. A file of this name must not already exist in the same folder. This string must not contain path details.

For example, we could rename *sunset.bmp* in the *Pictures* folder as *sunrise.bmp*, using the line:

```
RENAME "C:\DarkBASIC\Media\Pictures\sunset.bmp","sunrise.bmp"
```

The EXECUTE FILE Statement

Files that end with .EXE or .COM are program files capable of being run just like a DarkBASIC Pro program. Using the EXECUTE FILE statement we can execute an existing file from within our current program. Once execution of the file is complete, control returns to the DarkBASIC Pro program. The format of this statement is given in FIG-15.15.

FIG-15.15

The EXECUTE FILE
Statement

In the diagram:

filename	is a string specifying the full name of the file to be executed.
commandline	is a string specifying any values that need to be passed to the program about to be executed.
path	is a string specifying the path to *filename*. If no path is given *filename* is assumed to be in the current folder.
waitflg	is an integer flag value (1 or 0). If the value 1 is given, then the DarkBASIC Pro program containing the EXECUTE FILE statement will pause until *filename* has completed execution. If the value 0 is used, then the DarkBASIC Pro program will continue to execute while *filename* is running.

The program in LISTING-15.3 executes *Hangman.exe* using an EXECUTE FILE statement and also displays the numbers 1 to 100.

LISTING-15.3

Executing Another
Program

```
REM *** Wait for key press before running other program ***
PRINT "Press a key to start playing Hangman"
WAIT KEY
REM *** Load and run Hangman ***
EXECUTE FILE "Hangman.exe", "","C:\DarkBASIC\Projects",1
REM *** Display the numbers 1 to 100 ***
FOR p = 1 TO 100
    PRINT p
    WAIT 100
NEXT p
REM *** End program ***
WAIT KEY
END
```

Activity 15.12

Type in and test the program given in LISTING-15.3 (*files08.dbpro*).

When Hangman is complete, are the numbers 1 to 100 already displayed on the screen?

Modify the program setting the value of *waitflg* to zero. How does this affect the display of the numbers 1 to 100?

The FIND FIRST Statement

The FIND FIRST statement is used to find the first file within a folder. Once found, this file is taken to be the *current file*. We can think of this *current file* reference as something like the array index maintained by a list data structure. The statement has the format shown in FIG-15.16.

FIG-15.16

The FIND FIRST
Statement

This statement will be used in combination with others described below.

The FIND NEXT Statement

The *current file* information can be updated to reference the next file in the current folder using the FIND NEXT statement. This statement has the format shown in FIG-15.17.

FIG-15.17

The FIND NEXT
Statement

The GET FILE NAME$ Statement

The GET FILE NAME$ statement returns the name of the *current file*. The statement has the format shown in FIG-15.18.

FIG-15.18

The GET FILE
NAME$ Statement

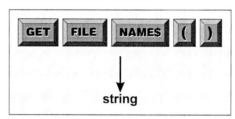

The program in LISTING-15.4 displays the name of the first file in the *Pictures* folder.

LISTING-15.4

Reading a File's Name

```
REM *** Set the Pictures folder as the current folder ***
CD "C:\DarkBasic\Media\Pictures"
REM *** Reference the first file in this folder ***
FIND FIRST
REM *** Display the name of the file ***
PRINT GET FILE NAME$()
REM *** End program ***
WAIT KEY
END
```

Activity 15.13

Type in and test the program in LISTING-15.4 (*files09.dbpro*).

What name is given for the first file?

If the name of the first file is surprising, don't worry. Every folder is created with files named "." and "..". These help the operating system with navigation from folder to folder. By changing the single line FIND FIRST to

```
FIND FIRST
FIND NEXT
FIND NEXT
```

we can bypass these first two files and set the *current file* to the first of the bitmap files.

> **Activity 15.14**
>
> Modify your last program as suggested.
>
> What filename is displayed this time?

The GET FILE DATE$ Statement

The GET FILE DATE$ will return a string giving the date and time on which the *current file* was last updated. The statement has the format shown in FIG-15.19.

FIG-15.19

The GET FILE DATE$
Statement

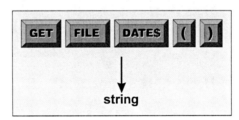

A typical string returned by this function would be:

Tue Apr 19 10:47:31

The GET FILE CREATION$ Statement

The GET FILE CREATION$ statement returns a string specifying the date and time on which *current file* was created. The statement has the format shown in FIG-15.20.

FIG-15.20

The GET FILE
CREATION$ Statement

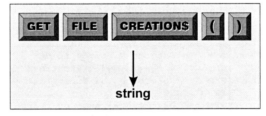

The returned string has the same format as that returned by GET FILE DATE$.

The GET FILE TYPE Statement

Items in a folder may be files or sub-folders. The GET FILE TYPE statement returns an integer specifying which type of file *current file* is. This statement has the format shown in FIG-15.21.

FIG-15.21

The GET FILE TYPE
Statement

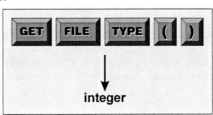

The statement returns a zero to indicate that the *current file* is, in fact, a file; 1 is returned if the current file is a sub-folder; -1 is returned if the current file does not reference a valid file (or sub-folder). This last return value (-1) allows us to move through each file in a folder, stopping when we reach the last file. To do this a program must employ the following logic:

```
Move to the required folder
Move to the first file in the folder
Move to next file
Move to next file
Get file type
WHILE file type NOT -1 DO
        Display file details
        Move to next file
        Get file type
ENDWHILE
```

Activity 15.15

Modify your previous program to match the logic given above and hence display the name, creation date and last written data of each file in the *Pictures* folder.

A variation on this program scans the folder for *.bmp* files and displays them on the screen. The program is given in LISTING-15.5.

LISTING-15.5

Creating a Slide Show

```
REM *** Set screen resolution ***
SET DISPLAY MODE 1280,1024,32

REM *** Set the Pictures folder as the current folder ***
CD "C:\DarkBasic\Media\Pictures"

REM *** Reference the first file in this folder ***
FIND FIRST
FIND NEXT
FIND NEXT
filetype = GET FILE TYPE()

REM *** WHILE a valid file found DO ***
WHILE filetype <> -1
   filename$ = GET FILE NAME$()
   CLS
   IF LOWER$(RIGHT$(filename$,4)) = ".bmp"
      LOAD BITMAP filename$,0
   ELSE
      PRINT "Filename : ", filename$
   ENDIF
   WAIT KEY
   FIND NEXT
   filetype = GET FILE TYPE()
ENDWHILE
PRINT "Scan of folder complete - press any key"

REM *** End program ***
WAIT KEY
END
```

Activity 15.16

Type in and test the program given in LISTING-15.5 (*files10.dbpro*).

Modify the program so that *.jpg* files are also shown.

The FILE SIZE Statement

The FILE SIZE statement returns the size (in bytes) of a specified file. The statement has the format shown in FIG-15.22.

FIG-15.22

The GET FILE SIZE
Statement

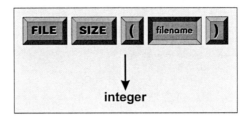

In the diagram:

filename   is a string representing the name of the file
                                whose size is to be returned. This string may
                                contain path information.

Notice that, unlike the last few statements, FILE SIZE does not make use of the
current file setting and that the name of the file to be examined must be given as
part of the statement.

> **Activity 15.17**
>
> By making use of the file name returned by the GET FILE NAME$ statement,
> modify your program *files09.dbpro* to display a file's size along with the other
> information already given.

The WINDIR$ Statement

The WINDIR$ statement will return a string specifying the location of the operating
system. The statement has the format shown in FIG-15.23.

FIG-15.23

The WINDIR$
Statement

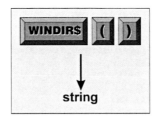

Typically, this statement will return the string:

C:\Windows

The APPNAME$ Statement

The name of the currently executing program (that is, our DarkBASIC Pro project)
can be discovered using the APPNAME$ statement which has the format shown in
FIG-15.24.

FIG-15.24

The APPNAME$
Statement

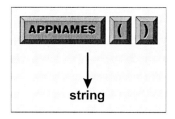

string

A typical example of the string returned by this statement would be:

C:\DarkBasic\Projects\files06\files06.exe

Using Data Files

At last we have all the housekeeping statements out of the way. Now we can concentrate on the main task of being able to store information on a backing storage device and then retrieving that information.

We'll start by finding out how to write data to a file. The basic steps involved consist of the main steps:

Open the file for writing
Output data to the file
Close the file

The OPEN TO WRITE Statement

We need to start by creating the new file in which our data is to be held. This can be done using the OPEN TO WRITE statement which has the format shown in FIG-15.25.

FIG-15.25

The OPEN TO WRITE
Statement

In the diagram:

fileno	is an integer between 1 and 32 specifying which number is to be assigned to this file. No two files can have the same *fileno* value at the same time.
filename	is a string specifying the actual name of the file to be created. This can include path information. If no path information is supplied the file will be created in the current directory.

A typical statement might be:

```
OPEN TO WRITE 1, "C:\DarkBasic\Projects\mydata.dat"
```

This statement actually creates the specified file. If the file already exists then the statement will fail. To safeguard against this we can use the lines:

```
filename$ = "C:\DarkBasic\Projects\mydata.dat"
IF FILE EXIST(filename$)
```

```
        DELETE FILE (filename$)
    ENDIF
    OPEN TO WRITE 1, filename$
```

Remember that Microsoft Windows uses the ending of a file name to decide what type of data is held in that file, so choose your names carefully. For example, it wouldn't be a good idea to end your file name with *.bmp* when you intended to store a set of names and addresses in that file.

The WRITE Statement

There are several statements available for writing to a file, but the most useful is probably the WRITE statement which has the format shown in FIG-15.26.

FIG-15.26

The WRITE Statement

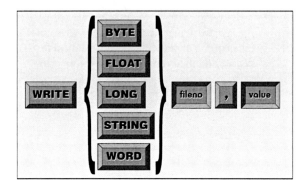

In the diagram:

fileno	is an integer value between 1 and 32 specifying which file is to receive the data being written. This number should have been assigned to the file by an OPEN TO WRITE statement.
value	is the value to be written to the file. *value* should be of the same type chosen earlier in the statement. For example, if the statement starts WRITE STRING, then *value* should be a string.

To write the word *Elizabeth* to the file 1 we would use the statement

```
WRITE STRING 1, "Elizabeth"
```

We can write as much data to a file as we require, but each new data item requires another WRITE statement.

Notice that some variable types (such as Boolean) are not available in the WRITE statement.

The CLOSE FILE Statement

Once we've finished writing data the file must be closed. This frees up RAM space that has been linked to the file and ensures that the last of the data has been written to the file. This is achieved using the CLOSE FILE statement which has the format given in FIG-15.27.

FIG-15.27

The CLOSE FILE
Statement

In the diagram:

> *fileno*   is an integer value between 1 and 32 specifying
> which file is to be closed.
> This number should have been assigned to the file
> by an OPEN TO WRITE statement.

The program in LISTING-15.6 writes the word *Elizabeth* to the file *mydata.dat* in
the *DarkBasic* folder.

LISTING-15.6

Writing to a File

```
REM *** Create the file to be used ***
filename$ = "C:\DarkBasic\Projects\mydata.dat"
IF FILE EXIST(filename$)
    DELETE FILE (filename$)
ENDIF
OPEN TO WRITE 1, filename$

REM *** Write data to file ***
WRITE STRING 1,"Elizabeth"

REM *** Close the file ***
CLOSE FILE 1

REM *** End program ***
PRINT "Data written to file. Press any key."
WAIT KEY
END
```

Activity 15.18

Type in and test the program given above (*files11.dbpro*).

Load the file you have just created (*mydata.dat*) into Notepad.

What contents are displayed?

Modify your program so that the WRITE STRING line is followed by:

```
WRITE BYTE 1,0XFF
WRITE WORD 1,0XABCD
WRITE LONG 1,0X1234
```

Again load the file into Notepad and examine its contents.

The apparent nonsense that appears in Notepad is caused by Notepad's attempt to
turn the bytes held in the file into characters, whereas the new data is actual numeric.

Luckily we can have a more precise look at the contents of our file using the
command line's DEBUG program.

Activity 15.19

From Windows **Start** button select All Programs | Accessories|Command
Prompt.   **continued on next page**

DarkBASIC Pro: File Handling   **395**

Activity 15.19 (continued)

In the Command Prompt window type in the lines
    CD C:\DarkBasic\Projects
    DEBUG mydata.dat

This runs the DEBUG program and loads the file *mydata.dat* into the main memory.

To see the file data, enter D after DEBUG's hyphen prompt.

A description of DEBUG's screen layout is given in FIG-15.28.

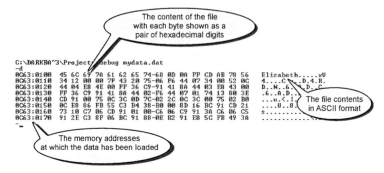

FIG-15.28

The DEBUG Display

The display shows 128 bytes of information. This is much larger than our *mydata.dat* file, the contents of which are shown in FIG-15.29.

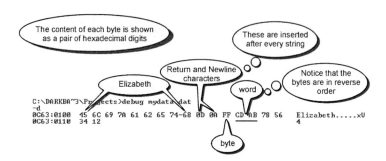

FIG-15.29

The Contents of *mydata.dat*

We can see from this display that strings are written as specified in the WRITE statement but are followed by the RETURN (0D) and newline (0A) characters. This is used to mark the end of the string. The byte value takes up a single byte as might be expected. The word value occupies two bytes, but notice that these are in reverse order, so rather than 12 34 we get 34 12. This reversing of byte order is needed because of the microprocessor architecture. The final long value occupies four bytes, again with the bytes in reverse order.

Activity 15.20

Quit debug by typing Q at the prompt.

Close down the Command Prompt window.

The WRITE FILE Statement

If normal integer values are to be written to a file, rather than use the WRITE BYTE, WRITE WORD or WRITE LONG options of the WRITE statement, we can use the WRITE FILE statement. This statement will write any of these values to the file, always writing four bytes, irrespective of the actual type of data value being written. This statement has the format shown in FIG-15.30.

FIG-15.30

The WRITE FILE Statement

In the diagram:

fileno   is an integer value between 1 and 32 specifying which file is to receive the data being written. This number should have been assigned to the file by an OPEN TO WRITE statement.

value   is the integer value to be written to the file.

A typical code snippet would be:

File 1 requires to be opened for writing by this point in the program.

```
INPUT "Enter number ",v
WRITE FILE 1,v
```

> **Activity 15.21**
>
> Modify your previous program so that the file created by the program is called *mydata2.dat*.
>
> Replace the WRITE statements used to write the three hexadecimal values by WRITE FILE statements.
>
> Use DEBUG to determine how this changes the format of the data written to the file.

DarkBASIC Pro has a complementary set of statements to allow us to read back information we've written to a file. A typical program performing such a task will use the following logic:

```
Open the file for reading
Read data from the file and store it in variable(s)
Close the file
```

The OPEN TO READ Statement

Before reading data from an existing file, that file must be opened for reading using the OPEN TO READ statement which has the format shown in FIG-15.31.

FIG-15.31

The OPEN TO READ Statement

In the diagram:

fileno	is an integer between 1 and 32 specifying which number is to be assigned to this file. No two files can have the same *fileno* value at the same time.
filename	is a string specifying the actual name of the file to be read. The file must already exist. *filename* may include path information. If no path information is supplied, the file will be created in the current directory.

The READ Statement

Once open, data can be copied from the file into program variables using the READ statement. Reading starts from the beginning of the file. The READ statement has the format shown in FIG-15.32.

FIG-15.32

The READ Statement

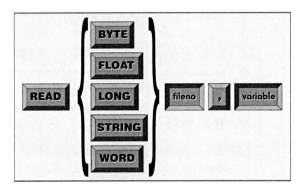

In the diagram:

fileno	is an integer value between 1 and 32 specifying the file to be read. This number should have been assigned to the file by an OPEN TO READ statement.
variable	is the variable to be used to hold the value read. from the file. *variable* must be of an appropriate type for the value being read.

A typical statement might be:

```
READ BYTE 1, v1
```

which would read a single byte from file 1 and store that value in a variable called *v1*.

When writing a program to read from an existing file it is critical that we read the data back in the order that it was written to the file. For example, to read from *mydata.dat*, the program must start by reading a string, then a byte, followed by a word and finally a long integer value. To do otherwise would mean that the READ statements would be accessing file data which would not be in context.

The program in LISTING-15.7 reads back the contents of *mydata.dat* and displays the information read on the screen.

LISTING-15.7

Reading Data from a File

```
REM *** Open the file for reading ***
filename$ = "C:\DarkBasic\Projects\mydata.dat"
OPEN TO READ 1, filename$

REM *** Read data from file ***
READ STRING 1,name$
READ BYTE 1,no1
READ WORD 1,no2
READ LONG 1,no3

REM *** Close the file ***
CLOSE FILE 1

REM *** Display the information read ***
PRINT "The values read were :"
PRINT name$
PRINT HEX$(no1)
PRINT HEX$(no2)
PRINT HEX$(no3)

REM *** End program ***
PRINT "Data read from file. Press any key."
WAIT KEY
END
```

Activity 15.22

Type in and test the program given above (*files12.dbpro*).

Modify the program so that, if *mydata.dat* does not exist, the message "File not found" is displayed and the program terminates.

The READ FILE Statement

If the file to be read contains integer data organised in 4-byte sections (as would be the case when WRITE FILE has been used to create the file data), then we can use the READ FILE statement to read back 4 bytes of data at a time. This statement has the format shown in FIG-15.33.

FIG-15.33

The READ FILE Statement

In the diagram:

fileno	is an integer value between 1 and 32 specifying the file to be read. This number should have been assigned to the file by an OPEN TO READ statement.
variable	is the variable to be used to hold the value read. from the file. *variable* must be of an appropriate type for the value being read.

It's okay to use READ FILE to read a value into a BYTE variable or some other type that occupies less than four bytes, as long as the variable matches the type used when the data was written to the file. For example, if we declare a byte variable *v1*

```
v1 AS BYTE
```

and write the contents of *v1* to a file using the WRITE FILE statement

```
WRITE FILE 1, v1
```

thereby outputting 4 bytes to the file, the data will be correctly retrieved by a later program which uses the lines

```
no1 AS BYTE
       .
       .
       .
READ FILE 1, no1
```

Activity 15.23

Write a program (*files13.dbpro*) to read and display the contents of *mydata2.dat*.

Random Access and File Updating

The SKIP BYTES Statement

As a general rule, when we read from a file we access the data in that file in sequential order. That is to say, we start by reading the first byte, then the second, third, fourth, and so on. However, like skipping tracks on a CD, it is possible to move directly to any part of the file using the SKIP BYTES statement which allows us to skip over a specified number of bytes in a file. Being able to move directly to any part of a file is known as **random access**. However, the SKIP BYTES statement does not allow us to skip backwards and so allows limited random access. The statement has the format shown in FIG-15.34.

FIG-15.34

The SKIP BYTES Statement

In the diagram:

fileno	is an integer value between 1 and 32 specifying the file to be read. This number should have been assigned to the file by an OPEN TO READ statement.
value	is a positive integer specifying the number of bytes to be skipped.

It is not possible to move backwards through a file by using a negative skip size. For example, a line such as

```
SKIP BYTES 1, -8
```

will be ignored.

To make use of this statement, we need to know the precise format of the file. The program in LISTING-15.8 reads the first number in *mydata2.dat* by skipping over the 11 bytes which store the Elizabeth and the RETURN and NEWLINE characters.

LISTING-15.8

Reading Bytes Directly from a File

```
REM *** Specify file to be used ***
filename$ = "C:\DarkBasic\Projects\mydata2.dat"

REM *** Open the file for reading ***
OPEN TO READ 1, filename$

REM *** Skip first 11 bytes then read a value***
SKIP BYTES 1, 11
READ FILE 1,num

REM *** Close the file ***
CLOSE FILE 1

REM *** Display value read ***
PRINT HEX$(num)

REM *** End program ***
WAIT KEY
END
```

Activity 15.24

Type in and test the program in LISTING-15.8 (*files14.dbpro*).

Does the value read back match that written by your earlier program?

Modify the program so that only the third number in the file is read.

The READ BYTE FROM FILE Statement

If we want to read a single byte from anywhere within a file, then we can combine the effect of the SKIP BYTES and READ BYTE statement by using the READ BYTE FROM FILE statement which has the format shown in FIG-15.35.

FIG-15.35

The READ BYTE FROM FILE Statement

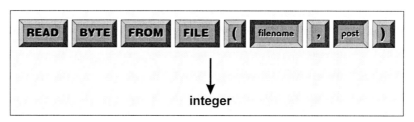

In the diagram:

filename   is a string specified the actual name of the file to be read. The file must already exist.
filename may include path information. If no path information is supplied, the file will be created in the current directory.

post   is a non-negative integer specifying the byte position in the file that is to be accessed. The first byte in the file is byte zero.

Using this statement removes the need to use OPEN TO READ or CLOSE FILE statements since READ BYTE FROM FILE handles these operations automatically.

The program in LISTING-15.9 reads the first and fifth bytes in *mydata2.dat* and displays these values on the screen.

LISTING-15.9

Reading Bytes Directly from a File

```
REM *** Declare byte variables ***
num AS BYTE
num2 AS BYTE

REM ** Read values from file ***
num = READ BYTE FROM FILE("C:\DarkBasic\Projects\mydata2.dat",0)
num2 = READ BYTE FROM FILE("C:\DarkBasic\Projects\mydata2.dat",4)

REM *** Display values read ***
PRINT HEX$(num)
PRINT HEX$(num2)

REM *** End program ***
WAIT KEY
END
```

Activity 15.25

Type in and test the program in LISTING-15.9 (*files15.dbpro*).

What values are displayed by the program?

The WRITE BYTE TO FILE Statement

We can overwrite the existing value of a specific byte within a file using the WRITE BYTE TO FILE statement which has the format shown in FIG-15.36.

FIG-15.36

The WRITE BYTE TO FILE Statement

In the diagram:

filename   is a string specifying the actual name of the file to be accessed. The file must already exist. *filename* may include path information. If no path information is supplied the file will be created in the current directory.

post   is a non-negative integer specifying the byte position in the file that is to be accessed. The first byte in the file is byte zero.

value   is the integer value (0 to 255) to be written to the file.

A typical statement might be

```
WRITE BYTE TO FILE "result.txt",100,0X41
```

which writes the hexadecimal value 41 to the 101st byte in the file *result.txt*.

The program in LISTING-15.10 writes the hexadecimal value AA to byte zero in *mydata2.dat* before reading back the new value and displaying it on the screen.

LISTING-15.10

Using WRITE BYTE TO FILE

```
REM *** Declare byte variable ***
num AS BYTE

REM *** Write to file ***
WRITE BYTE TO FILE "C:\DarkBasic\Projects\mydata2.dat",0,0XAA

REM *** Read byte back from file ***
num = READ BYTE FROM FILE("C:\DarkBasic\Projects\mydata2.dat",0)

REM *** Display value read ***
PRINT HEX$(num)

REM *** End program ***
WAIT KEY
END
```

Activity 15.26

Type in and test the program in LISTING-15.10 (*files16.dbpro*).

Pack Files

DarkBASIC Pro allows us to create a file which contains a collection of other files. The idea is similar to that of a *.zip* file, but no compression of the original data takes place. Such a file is known as a **pack file**.

Pack files are opened and closed in the normal manner. In fact, you can even write standard data values to the file with the normal WRITE and WRITE FILE statements.

The WRITE FILEBLOCK Statement

To copy a whole file to a pack file we use the WRITE FILEBLOCK statement which takes the format shown in FIG-15.37.

FIG-15.37

The WRITE FILEBLOCK Statement

In the diagram:

fileno	is an integer value between 1 and 32 specifying the file to be written. This number should have been assigned to the file by an OPEN TO WRITE statement.
filename	is a string specifying the actual name of the file to be copied into the pack file. The file must already exist. *filename* may include path information. If no path information is supplied the file will be created in the current directory.

The program in LISTING-15.11 copies two images from the *Pictures* folder into a a pack file called *backup.pck* in the *Projects* folder.

LISTING-15.11

Saving Files to a Pack File

```
REM *** Set up file and path name strings ***
filename$ = "C:\DarkBasic\Projects\backup.pck"
path$ = "C:\DarkBasic\Media\Pictures"

REM *** IF pack file already exists, delete it ***
IF FILE EXIST(filename$)
   DELETE FILE (filename$)
ENDIF

REM *** Open pack file for writing ***
OPEN TO WRITE 1,filename$

REM *** Copy files to pack file ***
WRITE FILEBLOCK 1,path$+"\skull.bmp"
WRITE FILEBLOCK 1,path$+"\fox.bmp"

REM *** Close pack file ***
CLOSE FILE 1

REM *** End program ***
PRINT "File copying complete. Press any key"
WAIT KEY
END
```

Activity 15.27

Type in and test LISTING-15.11(*files17.dbpro*).

Modify the program so that *autumn.bmp* in the *Pictures* folder is also copied to the pack file.

The WRITE DIRBLOCK Statement

Rather than save single files to a pack file, we can save a whole directory using a single WRITE DIRBLOCK statement. The WRITE DIRBLOCK statement takes the format shown in FIG-15.38.

FIG-15.38

The WRITE DIRBLOCK Statement

In the diagram:

fileno	is an integer value between 1 and 32 specifying the file to be written. This number should have been assigned to the file by an OPEN TO WRITE statement.
folder	is a string specifying the name of the folder to be copied into the pack file. The folder must already exist.

For example, to copy the *Pictures* folder to a pack file opened with the statement

```
OPEN TO WRITE 1, "C:\DarkBasic\Projects\backup2.pck"
```

we would use the line

```
WRITE DIRBLOCK 1, "C:\DarkBasic\Media\Pictures
```

A full program demonstrating the use of this statement is given in LISTING-15.12.

LISTING-15.12

Backing up a Complete
Directory

```
REM *** Open pack file ***
OPEN TO WRITE 1,"C:\DarkBasic\Projects\backup2.pck"

REM *** Copy folder's contents to pack file ***
WRITE DIRBLOCK 1,"C:\DarkBasic\Media\Pictures"

REM *** Close file ***
CLOSE FILE 1

REM *** End program ***
PRINT "File copying complete. Press any key"
WAIT KEY
END
```

Activity 15.28

Type in and test the program given above (*files18.dbpro*).

Use Windows Explorer to check the size of the pack file created.

The READ FILEBLOCK Statement

Files held in a pack file can be extracted using the READ FILEBLOCK statement. The pack file to be read must be opened and closed in the standard way (OPEN TO READ, CLOSE FILE). The name of the file to be created by extracting from the pack file must be specified. This file will be created as part of the READ FILEBLOCK statement's execution. This statement has the format shown in FIG-15.39.

FIG-15.39

The READ
FILEBLOCK Statement

In the diagram:

fileno	is an integer value between 1 and 32 specifying the pack file to be read. This number should have been assigned to the file by an OPEN TO READ statement.
filename	is a string specifying the name to be assigned to the extracted file. The file must not already exist. *filename* may include path information. If no path information is supplied, the file will be created in the current directory.

The program in LISTING-15.13 extracts a copy of *skull.bmp* and *fox.bmp* from *backup.pck*. The extracted files are named *skullcopy.bmp* and *foxcopy.bmp* and are stored in the *Pictures* folder.

LISTING-15.13

Extracting Individual
Files from a Pack File

```
REM *** Open pack file ***
OPEN TO READ 1,"C:\DarkBasic\Projects\backup.pck"

REM *** Extract first two files ***
READ FILEBLOCK 1,"C:\DarkBasic\Media\Pictures\skullcopy.bmp"
READ FILEBLOCK 1,"C:\DarkBasic\Media\Pictures\foxcopy.bmp"

REM *** Close the pack file ***
CLOSE FILE 1

REM *** End program ***
PRINT "File extraction complete. Press any key"
WAIT KEY
END
```

Notice that it is the programmer's responsibility to know what files are currently
held in the pack file.

Activity 15.29

Type in and test the program given above (*files19.dbpro*).

Use Windows Explorer to check that the extracted files have been saved as
requested.

Modify the program so that *seals.bmp* is also extracted from *backup.pck*.

The READ DIRBLOCK Statement

The READ DIRBLOCK statement is designed to extract the contents of a complete
folder from a pack file. The statement has the format shown in FIG-15.40.

FIG-15.40

The READ DIRBLOCK
Statement

In the diagram:

fileno	is an integer value between 1 and 32 specifying the file to be written. This number should have been assigned to the file by an OPEN TO READ statement.
folder	is a string specifying the name of the folder into which the extracted folder's contents are to be placed. *folder* must already exist.

Previously we archived files in the *Pictures* folder using a WRITE DIRBLOCK
statement, saving the files in *backup2.pck*. We can extract these files into a folder
called *Archive* using the line:

```
READ DIRBLOCK 1,"C:\darkBasic\Archive"
```

The command will be successful only if the *Archive* folder already exists.

The program in LISTING-15.14 demonstrates how this extraction is done.

LISTING-15.14

Extracting the Contents
of a Pack File

```
REM *** Open pack file ***
OPEN TO READ 1,"C:\DarkBasic\Projects\backup2.pck"

REM *** Extract contents of first folder in backup2.pck ***
REM *** into Test folder ***
READ DIRBLOCK 1,"C:\DarkBasic\Test"

REM *** Close pack file ***
CLOSE FILE 1

REM *** End program ***
PRINT "File extraction complete. Press any key"
WAIT KEY
END
```

Activity 15.30

Use Windows Explorer to create a folder called *Test* in the *DarkBasic* directory.

Type in and test the program given above (*files20.dbpro*).

Again using Windows Explorer, check that the contents of the folder saved in *backup2.pck* have been extracted to the *Test* folder.

Notice from this last Activity that the *Pictures* folder is not created as a subfolder of *Test*, only the contents of *Pictures* have been extracted into *Test*.

Creating an Empty File

The MAKE FILE Statement

It is possible to create an empty file using the MAKE FILE statement which has the format shown in FIG-15.41.

FIG-15.41

The MAKE FILE
Statement

In the diagram:

> *filename*　　　　　　　　is a string specifying the actual name of the file to be accessed.
> If *filename* does not exist, it will be created; if *filename* does exist, its current contents will be destroyed.
> *filename* may include path information. If no path information is supplied, the file will be created in the current directory.

For example, we could create a file called *empty.dat* in the *Projects* folder using the line:

```
MAKE FILE "C:\DarkBasic\Projects\empty.dat"
```

If *empty.dat* already existed, its contents would be destroyed by the above statement.

Arrays and Files

The SAVE ARRAY Statement

When the data we want to write to a file is held in an array, rather than write each element of the array separately to the file, we can write the contents of the whole array to the file using a single SAVE ARRAY statement. This statement has the format shown in FIG-15.42.

FIG-15.42

The SAVE ARRAY
Statement

In the diagram:

filename	is a string specifying the actual name of the file to be accessed.
	If *filename* does not exist, it will be created; if *filename* does exist, its current contents will be overwritten.
	filename may include path information. If no path information is supplied the file will be created in the current directory.
name	is the name of the array to be saved.
	The array cannot be an array of a defined type.

For example, if a program held data in an array called *results*, then the contents of that array could be saved to a file called *savedresults.dat* in the *Projects* folder using the line:

```
SAVE ARRAY "C:\DarkBasic\Projects\savedresults.dat",results(0)
```

The program in LISTING-15.15 reads data into an array called *cities$*, displays that information on the screen, and saves the contents of the array to a file called *cities.dat* in the *Projects* folder.

LISTING-15.15

Saving the Contents of
an Array to a File

```
REM *** List of cities ***
DATA "London", "Paris", "Berlin", "Rome"
DATA "Madrid", "Lisbon","Brussels","Amsterdam"
REM *** Set up an eight element string array ***
DIM cities$(8)

REM *** Read a value into each element ***
FOR c = 1 TO 8
   READ cities$(c)
NEXT c
REM *** Display the values entered ***
FOR c = 1 TO 8
   PRINT "City number ", c, " is ",cities$(c)
NEXT c

REM *** Save array contents to cities.dat ***
SAVE ARRAY "C:\DarkBasic\Projects\cities.dat", cities$(0)

REM *** End program ***
PRINT "Data saved to file. Press any key "
WAIT KEY
END
```

Multi-dimensional arrays can also be saved. The program in LISTING-15.16 sets up a 3 row by 9 column array (but ignores row zero and column zero). The array is populated with numeric strings. These values are displayed on screen and saved to a file, *numbers.dat*.

LISTING-15.16

Saving a 2D Array to a File

```
REM *** Set up array ***
DIM numbers$(2,8)

REM *** Assign a value into each element ***
FOR row = 1 TO 2
   FOR col = 1 TO 8
      numbers$(row,col)= STR$(row * col)
   NEXT col
NEXT row

REM *** Display the values entered ***
FOR row = 1 TO 2
   FOR col = 1 TO 8
      PRINT "number ",numbers$(row,col)
   NEXT col
NEXT row

REM *** Save array to file ***
SAVE ARRAY "C:\DarkBasic\Projects\numbers.dat", numbers$(0)

REM *** End program ***
PRINT "Data saved to file. Press any key "
WAIT KEY
END
```

The LOAD ARRAY Statement

To load a file's contents back into an array we use the LOAD ARRAY statement. This statement has the format shown in FIG-15.43.

FIG-15.43

The LOAD ARRAY Statement

In the diagram:

filename	is a string specifying the actual name of the file to be accessed. *filename* may include path information. If no path information is supplied, the file is assumed to be in the current directory.
name	is the name of the array into which data is to be loaded.

Using this statement only makes sense if the array into which the data is to be loaded is the same size and type as the array to which the data was saved in the first place.

The program in LISTING-15.17 loads the data saved earlier by the program in LISTING-15.15.

LISTING 15.17

Loading an Array from a File

```
REM *** this matches the array used when the data was saved ***
DIM names$(8)

REM *** Read the strings from the file ***
LOAD ARRAY "C:\DarkBasic\Projects\cities.dat",names$(0)

REM *** Display the values loaded ***
FOR c = 1 TO 8
   PRINT names$(c)
NEXT c

REM *** End program ***
WAIT KEY
END
```

Activity 15.32

Type in and test the program given above (*files22.dbpro*).

Are the city names correctly retrieved and displayed?

Checklists

There are two checklist statements available which relate to backing storage and files. These are described below.

The PERFORM CHECKLIST FOR DRIVES Statement

The PERFORM CHECKLIST FOR DRIVES statement creates a list of the drives currently available. This statement has the format shown in FIG-15.44.

FIG-15.44

The PERFORM CHECKLIST FOR DRIVES Statement

For example, we could list the drives available with the following code:

```
PERFORM CHECKLIST FOR DRIVES
FOR c = 1 TO CHECKLIST QUANTITY()
   PRINT CHECKLIST STRING$(c)
NEXT c
```

The PERFORM CHECKLIST FOR FILES Statement

The PERFORM CHECKLIST FOR FILES statement creates a checklist containing the names of every file and sub-folder in the current directory. This statement has the format shown in FIG-15.45.

FIG-15.45

The PERFORM CHECKLIST FOR FILES Statement

For example, we could list every file in the *Pictures* folder using the lines:

```
CD "C:\darkbasic\media\pictures"
PERFORM CHECKLIST FOR FILES
FOR c = 1 TO CHECKLIST QUANTITY()
    PRINT CHECKLIST STRING$(c)
NEXT c
```

Summary

- The drives available on your hardware can be listed using DRIVELIST.

- GET DIR$ returns a string giving the name of the current directory.

- The current directory can be changed using the CD or SET DIR statements.

- PATH EXIST returns 1 if a specified path exists.

- A new folder can be created using MAKE DIRECTORY.

- A folder can be deleted using DELETE DIRECTORY.

- The contents of the current directory can be listed using DIR.

- Use DELETE FILE to delete a file.

- Use COPY FILE to copy a file.

- Use MOVE FILE to move a file to a new folder.

- Use RENAME FILE to rename a file.

- Use FILE EXIST to check if a specified file exists.

- Use EXECUTE FILE to execute another program while your own program is running.

- FIND FIRST gives access to the first file (or sub-folder) in the current directory.

- FIND NEXT gives access to the next file (or sub-folder) in the current directly.

- By repeatedly calling FIND NEXT it is possible to access every file in the current directory.

- Details of the file referenced by FIND FIRST or FIND NEXT can be retrieved using the following statements:

```
GET FILE NAME$
GET FILE DATE$
GET FILE CREATION$
GET FILE TYPE
```

- The size of a file can be determined using the FILE SIZE statement.

- The WINDIR$ returns details of the Microsoft Windows directory.

- The APPNAME$ statement returns the name of the DarkBASIC Pro program currently running.

Writing to a Data File

- Use OPEN TO WRITE to prepare the file.

- Use the WRITE statement to write a specific data type to the file. Options are:

    ```
    WRITE BYTE
    WRITE FLOAT
    WRITE LONG
    WRITE STRING
    WRITE WORD
    ```

- The number of bytes written to the file by the WRITE statements varies with the type of value written.

- Use the WRITE FILE statement to write four bytes to the file, irrespective of the type of value actually written.

- Use CLOSE FILE when writing to the file is complete.

Reading from a Data File

- Use OPEN TO READ to prepare the file.

- Use the READ statement to write a specific data type to the file. Options are:

    ```
    READ BYTE
    READ FLOAT
    READ LONG
    READ STRING
    READ WORD
    ```

- The number of bytes read from the file by the READ statements varies with the type of value read.

- Use the READ FILE statement to read four bytes from the file, irrespective of the type of value actually read.

- Use CLOSE FILE when writing to the file is complete.

Random Access

- Any number of bytes in a file can be ignored using the SKIP BYTES statement.

- A Single byte can be read from a file using READ BYTE FROM FILE.

- A single byte can be written to a file using WRITE BYTE TO FILE.

- SKIP BYTES can be used in combination with READ and WRITE statements to randomly access values which occupy more than a single byte.

Pack Files

- A DarkBASIC Pro pack file is similar in concept to a ZIP file.

- A pack file contains a collection of other files.

- Individual files can be written to a pack file using WRITE FILEBLOCK.

- The contents of whole folders can be written to a pack file using WRITE DIRBLOCK.

- An individual file can be extracted from a pack file using READ FILEBLOCK.

- The complete contents of a pack file can be extracted using READ DIRBLOCK.

Arrays and Files

- The contents of an array can be saved to a file using the SAVE ARRAY statement.

- The contents of an array can be loaded from a file using the LOAD ARRAY statement.

Checklists

- A checklist of available drives can be created using the CREATE CHECKLIST FOR DRIVES statement.

- A checklist of files and sub-folders within the current directory can be created using the CREATE CHECKLIST FOR FILES.

- An empty file can be created using the MAKE FILE statement.

Solutions

Activity 15.1

No solution required.

Activity 15.2

```
PRINT "Your computer has the following
drives:"
DRIVELIST
REM *** End program ***
WAIT KEY
END
```

Activity 15.3

```
PRINT "Your computer has the following
drives:"
DRIVELIST
PRINT "The current directory is "; GET
DIR$()
REM *** End program ***
WAIT KEY
END
```

Activity 15.4

```
REM *** Set Media as current directory ***
CD "C:\DarkBasic\Media"
PRINT GET DIR$()
REM *** Set Pictures as current directory***
CD "C:\DarkBasic\Media\Pictures"
PRINT GET DIR$()
REM *** End program ***
WAIT KEY
END
```

Activity 15.5

```
REM *** Set Media as current directory ***
SET DIR "C:\DarkBasic\Media"
PRINT GET DIR$()
REM *** Set Pictures as current directory***
SET DIR "C:\DarkBasic\Media\Pictures"
PRINT GET DIR$()
REM *** End program ***
WAIT KEY
END
```

Activity 15.6

On first run the message *Valid path* should be displayed.

On second run the message *Invalid path* should be displayed.

Activity 15.7

```
REM *** Create Projects folder ***
MAKE DIRECTORY "C:\DarkBasic\Media\Projects"
REM *** Create the Video folder ***
MAKE DIRECTORY "C:\DarkBasic\Media\Video"
REM *** Create the Sounds folder ***
MAKE DIRECTORY "C:\DarkBasic\Media\Sounds"
REM *** End program ***
PRINT "Folders created. Press any key to
end."
WAIT KEY
END
```

Activity 15.8

```
PRINT "Create the folder DarkTest"
MAKE DIRECTORY "C:\DarkBasic\DarkTest"
PRINT "Setting DarkTest as the current
directory"
CD "C:\DarkBasic\DarkTest"
PRINT "The current directory is ",GET DIR$()
PRINT "Deleting folder DarkTest"
DELETE DIRECTORY "C:\DarkBasic\DarkTest"
REM *** End program ***
PRINT "Finished. Press any key."
WAIT KEY
END
```

Although the program runs without error, if you use Windows Explorer to check the disk structure, you'll see that the *DarkTest* folder has not been deleted.

To modify the program, change

```
CD "C:\DarkBasic\DarkTest"
```

to

```
CD "C:\"
```

After modification, the *DarkTest* folder is deleted by the program.

Activity 15.9

```
REM *** Set Pictures as current directory***
CD "C:\DarkBasic\Media\Pictures"
REM *** Display contents of the folder ***
PRINT "The Pictures folder contains : "
DIR
REM *** End program ***
PRINT "Finished. Press any key."
WAIT KEY
END
```

Activity 15.10

```
REM *** Set Pictures as current directory***
CD "C:\DarkBasic\Media\Pictures"
REM *** Display contents of folder ***
PRINT "Contents of folder before any files
are deleted"
DIR
REM *** Delete file ***
DELETE FILE "storm.bmp"
REM *** Display contents of folder ***
PRINT "After delete operation, the folder
now contains"
DIR
REM *** End program ***
PRINT "Finished. Press any key."
WAIT KEY
END
```

Activity 15.11

The exact statements used in the program depend on where your Hangman and Bull and Touch files are held.

```
REM *** Set Projects as current directory***
CD "C:\DarkBasic\Projects"
REM *** Copy the Hangman exe file ***
COPY FILE "C:\DarkBASIC
```

```
Projects\Hangman\Hangman.exe","Hangman.exe"
REM *** Copy Bull and Touch exe file ***
COPY FILE "C:\DarkBasic
Projects\BullandTouch\BullandTouch.exe","Bull
andTouch.exe"
PRINT "The Projects folder now contains:"
DIR
REM *** End program ***
PRINT "Finished. Press any key."
WAIT KEY
END
```

Activity 15.12

On the first run the numbers complete only after the
Hangman game has finished.

On the second run, with waitflg set to zero, the number
continue to display while Hangman is running.

Activity 15.13

The first file list is '.'

Activity 15.14

This time, the file name displayed is "sunset.bmp".

(You may have a different file name listed.)

Activity 15.15

```
REM *** Set Pictures as current folder ***
CD "C:\DarkBasic\Media\Pictures"
REM *** Reference first file in folder ***
FIND FIRST
FIND NEXT
FIND NEXT
REM *** Get current file's type ***
filetype = GET FILE TYPE()
REM *** WHILE not at end of files DO ***
WHILE filetype <> -1
    REM *** Get file details ***
    filename$ = GET FILE NAME$()
    updated$ = GET FILE DATE$()
    created$ = GET FILE CREATION$()
    REM *** Display file details ***
    PRINT "Filename : ",filename$,
    " Created on : ",created$,
    " Last updated : ",updated$
    REM *** Move on to next file ***
    FIND NEXT
    REM *** Get current file's type ***
    filetype = GET FILE TYPE()
ENDWHILE
REM *** End program ***
WAIT KEY
END
```

Activity 15.16

```
REM *** Set screen resolution ***
SET DISPLAY MODE 1280,1024,32
REM *** Set Pictures as current folder ***
CD "C:\DarkBasic\Media\Pictures"
REM *** Reference first file in folder ***
FIND FIRST
FIND NEXT
FIND NEXT
REM *** Get the file's type ***
filetype = GET FILE TYPE()
REM *** WHILE not end of files DO ***
```

```
WHILE filetype <> -1
    REM *** Get the file's name ***
    filename$ = GET FILE NAME$()
    CLS
    REM *** IF file is a BMP or JPG THEN ***
    IF LOWER$(RIGHT$(filename$,4)) = ".bmp"
    OR LOWER$(RIGHT$(filename$,4)) = ".jpg
        REM *** Display it ***
        LOAD BITMAP filename$,0
    ELSE
        REM *** ELSE display its name ***
        PRINT "Filename : ", filename$
    ENDIF
    REM *** Wait for a keypress... ***
    WAIT KEY

    REM *** ... then move to next file ***
    FIND NEXT
    filetype = GET FILE TYPE()
ENDWHILE
REM *** Display finished message ***
PRINT "Scan of folder complete - press any
key"
REM *** End program ***
WAIT KEY
END
```

Activity 15.17

```
REM *** Set Pictures as current folder ***
CD "C:\DarkBasic\Media\Pictures"
REM *** Reference first file in folder ***
FIND FIRST
FIND NEXT
FIND NEXT
REM *** Get current file's type ***
filetype = GET FILE TYPE()
REM *** WHILE not at end of files DO ***
WHILE filetype <> -1
    REM *** Get file details ***
    filename$ = GET FILE NAME$()
    updated$ = GET FILE DATE$()
    created$ = GET FILE CREATION$()
    filesize = FILE SIZE(filename$)
    REM *** Display file details ***
    PRINT "Filename : ", filename$,
    " Created on : ",created$,
    " Last updated : ", updated$,
    " File size : ",filesize," bytes"
    REM *** Move on to next file ***
    FIND NEXT
    REM *** Get current file's type ***
    filetype = GET FILE TYPE()
ENDWHILE
REM *** End program ***
WAIT KEY
END
```

Activity 15.18

The file contains the word *Elizabeth*.

On the second viewing the file contains:

```
Elizabeth
ÿÍ«4
```

The symbols at the end of the file are how Notepad
interprets the hexadecimal values written to the file.

Activity 15.19

DEBUG should produce the following display:

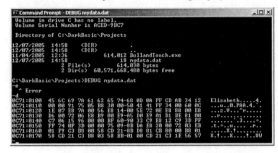

In the hexadecimal area we can see the new values that have been added although the byte order for the values have been reversed.

Activity 15.20

No solution required.

Activity 15.21

The code for the program is now:

```
REM *** Create the file to be used ***
filename$ =
"C:\DarkBasic\Projects\mydata2.dat"
IF FILE EXIST(filename$)
    DELETE FILE (filename$)
ENDIF
OPEN TO WRITE 1, filename$
REM *** Write data to file ***
WRITE STRING 1,"Elizabeth"
WRITE FILE 1, 0XFF
WRITE FILE 1, 0XABCD
WRITE FILE 1, 0X1234
REM *** Close the file ***
CLOSE FILE 1
REM *** End program ***
PRINT "Data written to file. Press any key."
WAIT KEY
END
```

DEBUG produces the following display:

Notice that each numeric value occupies exactly 4 bytes with any bytes that are not used being zero-filled.

Activity 15.22

The modified program is:

```
REM *** Open the file for reading ***
filename$ =
"C:\DarkBasic\Projects\mydata.dat"
```

```
IF NOT FILE EXIST(filename$)
    PRINT "File not found"
    WAIT KEY
    END
ENDIF
OPEN TO READ 1, filename$
REM *** Read data from file ***
READ STRING 1,name$
READ BYTE 1,no1
READ WORD 1,no2
READ LONG 1,no3
REM *** Close the file ***
CLOSE FILE 1
REM *** Display the information read ***
PRINT "The values read were :"
PRINT name$
PRINT HEX$(no1)
PRINT HEX$(no2)
PRINT HEX$(no3)
REM *** End program ***
PRINT "Data read from file. Press any key."
WAIT KEY
END
```

Activity 15.23

```
REM *** Open the file for reading ***
filename$ =
"C:\DarkBasic\Projects\mydata2.dat"
IF NOT FILE EXIST(filename$)
    PRINT "File not found"
    WAIT KEY
    END
ENDIF
OPEN TO READ 1, filename$
REM *** Read data from file ***
READ STRING 1,name$
READ FILE 1,no1
READ FILE 1,no2
READ FILE 1,no3
REM *** Close the file ***
CLOSE FILE 1
REM *** Display the information read ***
PRINT "The values read were :"
PRINT name$
PRINT HEX$(no1)
PRINT HEX$(no2)
PRINT HEX$(no3)
REM *** End program ***
PRINT "Data read from file. Press any key."
WAIT KEY
END
```

Activity 15.24

The value, FF, is read correctly.

The modified version of the program is:

```
REM *** Specify file to be used ***
filename$ =
"C:\DarkBasic\Projects\mydata2.dat"
REM *** Open the file for reading ***
OPEN TO READ 1, filename$
REM *** Skip 19 bytes then read a value***
SKIP BYTES 1, 19
READ FILE 1,num
REM *** Close the file ***
CLOSE FILE 1
REM *** Display value read ***
PRINT HEX$ (num)
REM *** End program ***
WAIT KEY
END
```

Activity 15.25

The values displayed should be 45 (ASCII for *E*) and 61 (ASCII for *a*).

Activity 15.26

No solution required.

Activity 15.27

```
REM *** Set up file & path name strings ***
filename$ =
"C:\DarkBasic\Projects\backup.pck"
path$ = "C:\DarkBasic\Media\Pictures"
REM *** IF pack file exists, delete it ***
IF FILE EXIST(filename$)
    DELETE FILE (filename$)
ENDIF
REM *** Open pack file for writing ***
OPEN TO WRITE 1,filename$
REM *** Copy files to pack file ***
WRITE FILEBLOCK 1,path$+"\skull.bmp"
WRITE FILEBLOCK 1,path$+"\fox.bmp"
WRITE FILEBLOCK 1,path$+"\autumn.bmp"

REM *** Close pack file ***
CLOSE FILE 1

REM *** End program ***
PRINT "File copying complete. Press any
key"
WAIT KEY
END
```

Activity 15.28

No solution required.

Activity 15.29

```
REM *** Open pack file ***
OPEN TO READ
1,"C:\DarkBasic\Projects\backup.pck"
REM *** Extract first two files ***
READ FILEBLOCK 1,
"C:\DarkBasic\Media\Pictures\skullcopy.bmp"
READ FILEBLOCK 1,
"C:\DarkBasic\Media\Pictures\foxcopy.bmp"
READ FILEBLOCK 1,
"C:\DarkBasic\Media\Pictures\sealscopy.bmp
REM *** Close the pack file ***
CLOSE FILE 1
REM *** End program ***
PRINT "File extraction complete. Press any
key"
WAIT KEY
END
```

Activity 15.30

No solution required.

Activity 15.31

The blank line at the beginning of the file represents the contents of *cities$(0)*. Remember, every array has an element zero. If this element is not used it will be empty.

Activity 15.32

The names are correctly retrieved and displayed.

16

Handling Music Files

Playing a MIDI and MP3 Files

Setting the Playing Speed

Setting the Volume

Playing a CD

Handling Music Files

Introduction

DarkBASIC Pro has a set of statements specifically for handling **MIDI** and **MP3** files. These instructions are described here.

There are separate instructions for handling **WAV** and other sound formats which are described in a later chapter.

MIDI files contain sets of instructions which are processed by your sound card. Although MIDI files are very small in comparison to other types of sound files, they are limited to playing the effects available from your sound card. Typically this means they are used for instrumental music. The MIDI format cannot be used to record live sounds or vocals.

MP3 files are simply compressed sound files. Compression means that the files are smaller than normal sound files but have a lower sound quality. However, any type of sound can be stored in an MP3 file.

The files you use in your program must already exist and can be created with various music and sound editing packages. A discussion of these packages is outside the scope of this book.

Like a music file, sound files must be loaded before being played, looped or deleted. Their volume and speed can also be adjusted.

Playing a Sound File

When a MIDI or MP3 file is first loaded from disk it must be assigned an identifying integer value. From that point on, this value is used to identify the music file.

The LOAD MUSIC Statement

Before using a MIDI or MP3 file, it must be loaded using the LOAD MUSIC statement which has the format shown in FIG-16.1.

FIG-16.1

The LOAD MUSIC Statement

In the diagram:

filename	is the name of the file to be loaded. It is best if the file has been previously copied to your directory using the Media|Add option.
mscnum	is an integer representing the area in which the file is to be stored. Any positive integer value can be used.

A typical example of using this statement would be:

```
LOAD MUSIC "greensleeves.mid", 1
```

If the requested file is not found or cannot be loaded for some reason, then the program will terminate.

The PLAY MUSIC Statement

Once the music file has been loaded it can be played using the PLAY MUSIC statement which has the format shown in FIG-16.2.

FIG-16.2

The PLAY MUSIC Statement

In the diagram:

    mscnum   is an integer representing the number assigned to a previously loaded music file.

LISTING-16.1 gives a simple example of how the statement might be used.

LISTING-16.1

Playing a MIDI File

```
REM *** Load music ***
LOAD MUSIC "greensleeves.mid", 1

REM *** Play music ***
PLAY MUSIC 1

REM *** End program ***
WAIT KEY
END
```

Activity 16.1

Type in and test the program given in LISTING-16.1 (*music01.dbpro*).

Make sure you've copied the required music file to your folder.

The music file will play through completely but any other statements in your program will be executed at the same time.

Activity 16.2

To demonstrate that the other lines of a program continue to be executed while a sound file is playing, add the following lines to your program:

```
FOR p = 1 TO 100
    PRINT p
    WAIT 100
NEXT p
```

The lines should be added immediately after the PLAY MUSIC statement.

Run the program and check that the numbers are displayed as the music plays.

The LOOP MUSIC Statement

Whereas the PLAY MUSIC statement plays the music file only once, the LOOP MUSIC statement will replay the music continuously. The format for this statement is given in FIG-16.3.

FIG-16.3

The LOOP MUSIC
Statement

In the diagram:

  mscnum   is an integer representing the number assigned
              to a previously loaded music file.

Activity 16.3

Modify your previous program so that your music is played continuously.

The PAUSE MUSIC Statement

It is possible to pause a music file using the PAUSE MUSIC statement, which has
the format shown in FIG-16.4.

FIG-16.4

The PAUSE MUSIC
Statement

In the diagram:

  mscnum   is an integer representing the number assigned
              to a previously loaded music file.

We could, therefore, pause the music assigned the music number 1 with the line

```
PAUSE MUSIC 1
```

This assumes, of course, that the music assigned the value 1 is currently playing.

The RESUME MUSIC Statement

A paused music file can be resumed using the RESUME MUSIC statement, which
has the format shown in FIG-16.5.

FIG-16.5

The RESUME MUSIC
Statement

In the diagram:

  mscnum   is an integer value previously assigned to the
              music file.

Of course, we should only use this statement on a music file that has previously
been paused. So, assuming we have previously paused music with the statement

```
PAUSE MUSIC 1
```

then we could resume the music using the line

```
RESUME MUSIC 1
```

Paused music resumes at the same spot where it was paused.

The program in LISTING-16.2 pauses the playing music when any key is pressed and resumes it when a second key is pressed. Pressing a third key terminates the program.

LISTING-16.2

Pausing and Resuming
Music

```
REM *** Load music ***
LOAD MUSIC "demo.mp3", 1
REM *** Play music continuously ***
LOOP MUSIC 1

REM *** Pause when key is pressed ***
WAIT KEY
PAUSE MUSIC 1

REM *** Resume when key is pressed ***
WAIT KEY
RESUME MUSIC 1

REM *** End program ***
WAIT KEY
END
```

Activity 16.4

Type in and test the program given above (*music02.dbpro*).

The STOP MUSIC Statement

Rather than just pause a music file, we can stop it altogether using the STOP MUSIC statement which has the format shown in FIG-16.6.

FIG-16.6

The STOP MUSIC
Statement

In the diagram:

mscnum   is an integer previously assigned to the music file.

For example, the line

```
STOP MUSIC 1
```

will terminate the playing of the music file assigned the value 1.

However, the music file can still be restarted using the RESUME MUSIC statement. However, when resuming after a STOP MUSIC statement, play starts at the beginning of the music, rather than where it was stopped.

The SET MUSIC SPEED Statement

The speed at which a music file plays can be changed using the SET MUSIC SPEED statement which has the format shown in FIG-16.7.

FIG-16.7

The SET MUSIC
SPEED Statement

In the diagram:

mscnum   is the integer value previously assigned to the music file.

speedperc   is an integer value representing the percentage of the normal speed that the music file is to play at. Use a value of 100 for normal speed.

To play the music file at half speed we would use the line

```
SET MUSIC 1, 50
```

whereas double speed would be achieved with the line

```
SET MUSIC 1, 200
```

Activity 16.5

Create a program (*music03.dbpro*) which plays the file *demo1.mp3*. When a key is pressed, the sound should change to half normal speed. On the second key press, set the speed to double normal speed. After a final key press, the play speed should return to normal.

The SET MUSIC VOLUME Statement

This statement is designed to modify the volume of a playing music file and has the format shown in FIG-16.8.

FIG-16.8

The SET MUSIC VOLUME Statement

In the diagram:

mscnum   is the integer value previously assigned to the music file.

volperc   is an integer value representing the percentage of the normal volume that the music file is to play at. The value given can range between 0 (silent) and 200 (double normal volume).

For example, to play music item 1 at half normal volume we would use the line:

```
SET MUSIC VOLUME 1, 50
```

The DELETE MUSIC Statement

A loaded music file occupies RAM space, so when you're finished with the music it is best to delete it. This will free up the RAM space that is holding the music file. This is done using the DELETE MUSIC statement which has the format shown in FIG-16.9.

FIG-16.9

The DELETE MUSIC Statement

In the diagram:

mscnum   is the integer value previously assigned to the
                                  music file.

To delete music item 1 we would use the line:

```
DELETE MUSIC 1
```

Retrieving Music File Data

Several statements exist in DarkBASIC Pro which allow information about
currently loaded music files to be retrieved. For example, we can find out whether
it is playing, stopped or paused, etc. The statements that supply us with this
information are described below.

The MUSIC EXIST Statement

We can find out if a specific number has been assigned to a music file by using the
MUSIC EXIST statement. This statement returns the value 1 if the specified number
has been assigned to a music file, otherwise zero is returned. The statement has the
format shown in FIG-16.10.

FIG-16.10

The MUSIC EXIST
Statement

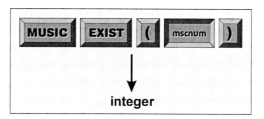

In the diagram:

mscnum   is the integer value being checked for an assigned
                                  music file.

A typical example of how the statement might be used is:

```
IF MUSIC EXIST(3) = 1
    PRINT "Music item 3 is loaded"
ELSE
    PRINT "Music item 3 is not loaded"
ENDIF
```

The MUSIC PLAYING Statement

This statement returns 1 if the music file is currently playing, otherwise zero is
returned. The statement has the format shown in FIG-16.11.

FIG-16.11

The MUSIC PLAYING
Statement

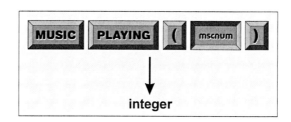

In the diagram:

    mscnum   is the integer value previously assigned to the music file.

The value 1 is returned if the music file is currently playing, otherwise zero is returned. Playing may have been initiated by either a PLAY MUSIC or LOOP MUSIC statement.

The MUSIC LOOPING Statement

The MUSIC LOOPING statement can be used to determine if a specified music item is currently playing in a loop. The statement has the format shown in FIG-16.12.

FIG-16.12

The MUSIC LOOPING
Statement

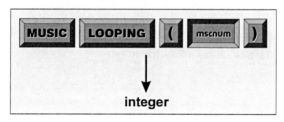

In the diagram:

    mscnum   is the integer value previously assigned to the music file.

A value of 1 is only returned if the music file is playing because of a LOOP MUSIC statement. A playing music file initiated using the PLAY MUSIC statement will return zero as will a music item in any other state (paused, stopped, etc.).

For example, we could start a music item looping using the lines:

```
IF NOT MUSIC LOOPING(1)
    LOOP MUSIC 1
ENDIF
```

The MUSIC PAUSED Statement

The MUSIC PAUSED statement can be used to determine if a specified music item is currently paused. The statement has the format shown in FIG-16.13.

FIG-16.13

The MUSIC PAUSED
Statement

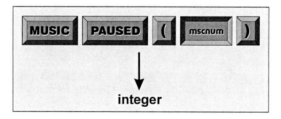

In the diagram:

    mscnum   is the integer value previously assigned to the music file.

This statement returns 1 if the music file is currently paused, otherwise zero is returned.

The program in LISTING-16.3 displays the state of a music file.

LISTING-16.3

Checking the State of a Music Item

```
REM *** Load music file ***
LOAD MUSIC "greensleeves.mid", 1

REM *** Play music file continuously ***
LOOP MUSIC 1

REM *** Get music file's status ***
playing = MUSIC PLAYING(1)
looping = MUSIC LOOPING(1)
paused = MUSIC PAUSED(1)

REM *** Display details ***
IF playing = 1
    PRINT "MUSIC is playing"
ENDIF
IF looping = 1
    PRINT "MUSIC is looping"
ENDIF
IF paused = 1
    PRINT "MUSIC is paused"
ENDIF

REM *** End program ***
WAIT KEY
END
```

Activity 16.6

Type in and test the program given above (*music04.dbpro*).

1) Change the line
```
    LOOP MUSIC 1
```
   to
```
    PLAY MUSIC 1
```

   How does this affect the messages displayed?

2) Add the lines
```
    WAIT KEY
    PAUSE MUSIC 1
```
   after the PLAY MUSIC 1 statement.

   How do the messages change?

3) Change the line
```
    PAUSE MUSIC 1
```
   to
```
    STOP MUSIC 1
```

   Are the messages changed?

The MUSIC VOLUME Statement

The MUSIC VOLUME statement returns the volume setting for the specified music item. The statement's format is shown in FIG-16.14.

FIG-16.14

The MUSIC VOLUME
Statement

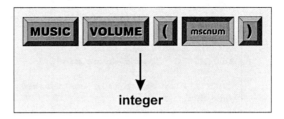

In the diagram:

  mscnum   is the integer value previously assigned to the
               music file.

The value returned by this statement will be zero where the sound has been turned off, 50 for music at half normal volume, 100 for normal volume and 200 for twice normal volume. In fact, the value returned will match that used in the last SET MUSIC VOLUME statement applied to the specified music item.

A typical statement would be:

```
volume = MUSIC VOLUME(1)
```

The MUSIC SPEED Statement

The MUSIC SPEED statement returns the speed setting for the specified music item. The statement's format is shown in FIG-16.15.

FIG-16.15

The MUSIC SPEED
Statement

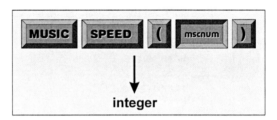

In the diagram:

  mscnum   is the integer value previously assigned to the
               music file.

A music item playing at half normal speed will return 50; full speed returns 100; double speed returns 200. The value returned will match the last SET MUSIC SPEED statement executed for this music item.

A typical statement would be:

```
IF MUSIC SPEED(1) > 100
    SET MUSIC SPEED 1, 100
ENDIF
```

Activity 16.7

Modify your previous program to display the speed and volume settings of the playing music file.

Playing Multiple Music Files

It's possible to play two or more music files at the same time by loading multiple music files. For example, we could load two music files with the lines:

```
LOAD MUSIC "demo.mp3",1
LOAD MUSIC "onestop.mid",2
```

These can then be played at the same time using the lines

```
PLAY MUSIC 1
PLAY MUSIC 2
```

The program in LISTING-16.4 demonstrates two music files being played. The first file starts playing right away, but the second file starts playing after a key is pressed.

LISTING-16.4

Playing Multiple Music Items

```
REM *** Load music files ***
LOAD MUSIC "demo.mp3", 1
LOAD MUSIC "greensleeves.mid",2

REM *** Play first music file continuously ***
LOOP MUSIC 1

REM *** Wait for key press, then start second file playing ***
WAIT KEY
LOOP MUSIC 2

REM *** End program ***
WAIT KEY
END
```

Activity 16.8

Type in and test the program given above (*music05.dbpro*).

Summary

- The LOAD MUSIC statement can be used to prepare a MIDI or MP3 file for playing.

- For a single playing of a loaded music file use PLAY MUSIC.

- To have the file played repeatedly use LOOP MUSIC.

- PAUSE MUSIC halts a playing music file.

- RESUME MUSIC continues the music after it has been paused. Playing resumes at the point in the music where it was paused.

- STOP MUSIC terminates a playing music file.

- SET MUSIC SPEED sets the speed at which a music file plays.

- SET MUSIC VOLUME sets the volume at which a music file plays.

- DELETE MUSIC removes a music file from RAM.

- MUSIC EXIST returns 1 if the specified music file is loaded.

- MUSIC PLAYING returns 1 if the specified music file is currently playing.

- MUSIC LOOPING returns 1 if the specified music file is currently looping.

- MUSIC PAUSED returns 1 if the specified music file is currently paused.

- MUSIC VOLUME returns the current volume setting for a specified music file.

- MUSIC SPEED returns the current speed setting for a specified music file.

- More than one music file can be played at the same time.

Playing CDs

Introduction

DarkBASIC Pro has a few statements specifically designed to handle the loading and playing of music CDs.

CD Control Statements

The LOAD CDMUSIC Statement

If you are going to play music stored on a CD, then, rather than use the standard LOAD MUSIC statement, you need to use LOAD CDMUSIC instead. This has the format shown in FIG-16.16.

FIG-16.16

The LOAD CDMUSIC
Statement

In the diagram:

> *trackno*   is an integer number representing the track to be loaded. To load the first track on a CD, *trackno* would have the value 1.

> *mscnum*   is an integer value to be assigned to the music.

A typical statement would be

```
LOAD CDMUSIC 2,1
```

which loads track 2 of the CD and assigns it the value 1.

To operate correctly, you must place a CD in your CDROM drive before running your DarkBASIC Pro program. If you have more than one CD or DVD drive, the disc must be placed in the drive with the lowest letter (e.g. drive D: rather than E:).

Once loaded, the normal PLAY MUSIC statement can be used to start the CD playing. Other statements such as LOOP MUSIC and PAUSE MUSIC can also be used once the CD track has been loaded, but some statements such as SET MUSIC SPEED do not function.

The program in LISTING-16.5 demonstrates loading and playing a track from a CD.

LISTING-16.5

Playing a CD

```
REM *** Load CD track 2 and assign it the value 1 ***
LOAD CDMUSIC 2, 1

REM *** Play CD track ***
PLAY MUSIC 1

REM *** End program ***
WAIT KEY
END
```

The GET NUMBER OF CD TRACKS Statement

Most music CDs contain several tracks. You can find out how many tracks are on the currently loaded CD using the GET NUMBER OF CD TRACKS statement, which has the format shown in FIG-16.17.

FIG-16.17

The GET NUMBER OF CD TRACKS Statement

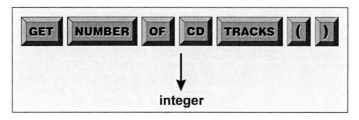

For example, we can display the number of tracks using the statement:

```
PRINT "This CD contains ", GET NUMBER OF CD TRACKS()," tracks"
```

The next program (see LISTING-16.6) displays the number of tracks on a CD and then allows the user to choose which track is to be played.

LISTING-16.6

Picking a Track from a CD

```
REM *** Get and display number of tracks ***
noOfTracks = GET NUMBER OF CD TRACKS()
PRINT "Your CD contains ", noOfTracks," tracks"

REM *** Get user to choose track ***
INPUT "Enter the track you wish to play : ", trackno
WHILE trackno < 1 OR trackno > noOfTracks
    PRINT "You must enter a value between 1 and ",noOfTracks
    INPUT "Choose a track : ", trackno
ENDWHILE

REM *** Load chosen track ***
LOAD CDMUSIC trackno, 1

REM *** Play CD track ***
PLAY MUSIC 1

REM *** End program ***
PRINT "Press any key to quit"
WAIT KEY
END
```

Some games are controlled by the human players and the computer is used as a tool to offer features which would otherwise be difficult to achieve manually. An example of such a game is given in the next Activity.

Activity 16.11

In this Activity we are going to write a program which chooses a track at random from the loaded CD and then plays the track for 10 seconds. The player then has to verbally guess the name of the track being played. (The program is not involved in checking the player's answer). The program requires the following logic:

Seed random number generator
Get the number of tracks on the loaded CD
Generate a random value between 1 and the number of tracks
Select the track corresponding to the random value
Play the track for 10 seconds (Sleep the program for 10 seconds and then stop the music playing)
Prompt user for guess

Modify the program so that the computer picks another track at random every time a key is pressed.

Name the program *music08.dbpro*.

Summary

- When playing a CD, make sure it is placed in the CD or DVD drive with the lowest letter.

- CD tracks are loaded using the LOAD CDMUSIC statement.

- Once loaded, some of the other music statements can be applied to the CD track. For example, PAUSE MUSIC, RESUME MUSIC and STOP MUSIC.

- Some basic music statements cannot be applied to a CD track. For example, SET MUSIC SPEED and SET MUSIC VOLUME.

- The number of tracks on a CD can be determined using the GET NUMBER OF CD TRACKS statement.

Solutions

Activity 16.1

No solution required.

Activity 16.2

No solution required.

Activity 16.3

```
REM *** Load music ***
LOAD MUSIC "greensleeves.mid", 1
REM *** Loop music ***
LOOP MUSIC 1
REM *** Keep the program busy ***
FOR p = 1 TO 100
    PRINT p
    WAIT 100
NEXT p
REM *** End program ***
WAIT KEY
END
```

Activity 16.4

No solution required.

Activity 16.5

```
REM *** Load music ***
LOAD MUSIC "demo1.mp3", 1
REM *** Play music ***
PLAY MUSIC 1
REM *** Half speed when key is pressed ***
WAIT KEY
SET MUSIC SPEED 1,50
REM *** Double speed ***
WAIT KEY
SET MUSIC SPEED 1,200
REM *** Normal speed ***
WAIT KEY
SET MUSIC SPEED 1,100
REM *** End program ***
WAIT KEY
END
```

Activity 16.6

1) After the first change, the message displayed is:
   MUSIC is playing

2) After the second change, the message is:
   MUSIC is paused

3) After the third change, no message appears.

Activity 16.7

```
REM *** Load music file ***
LOAD MUSIC "demo.mp3", 1
REM *** Play music file continuously ***
LOOP MUSIC 1
REM *** Get music file's status ***
playing = MUSIC PLAYING(1)
looping = MUSIC LOOPING(1)

paused = MUSIC PAUSED(1)
REM *** Display details ***
```

```
IF playing = 1
    PRINT "MUSIC is playing"
ENDIF
IF looping = 1
    PRINT "MUSIC is looping"
ENDIF
IF paused = 1
    PRINT "MUSIC is paused"
ENDIF
REM *** Display speed and volume ***
PRINT "Volume : ",MUSIC VOLUME (1)
PRINT "Speed : ", MUSIC SPEED(1)
REM *** End program ***
WAIT KEY
END
```

This will display speed and volume values of 100. You might want to try setting the volume and speed to other values and check that these new values are reported by the PRINT statements.

Activity 16.8

No solution required.

Activity 16.9

```
REM *** Load CD track 3 ***
LOAD CDMUSIC 3, 1
REM *** Play CD track ***
PLAY MUSIC 1
REM *** End program ***
WAIT KEY
END
```

Activity 16.10

No solution required.

Activity 16.11

The final version is:

```
REM *** Seed random number generator ***
RANDOMIZE TIMER()
REM *** Get the number of tracks on CD ***
tracks = GET NUMBER OF CD TRACKS()
DO
  REM *** Select track at random ***
  trackselected = RND(tracks-1)+1
  REM *** Load selected track ***
  LOAD CDMUSIC trackselected ,1
  REM *** Play track for 10 seconds ***
  PRINT "Playing music ..."
  PLAY MUSIC 1
  WAIT 10000
  STOP MUSIC 1
  DELETE MUSIC 1
  REM *** Prompt for guess ***
  CLS
  PRINT "Guess the track title."
  PRINT "Press any key to continue"
  WAIT KEY
LOOP
REM *** End program ***
WAIT KEY
END
```

Version 1 omits the DO and LOOP keywords.

17

Displaying Video Files

Loading and Playing a Video

Pausing and Restarting a Video

Playing a DVD

Positioning a Video on Screen

Resizing a Video

Retrieving Video Information

Setting Video Speed

Setting Video Volume

Stopping a Video

Displaying Video Files

Introduction

When a video is recorded on a computer, the way in which it is stored is known as the **video file format**. Different formats have different characteristics, but the two main considerations are the quality of the image produced when the file is played, and the size of the file. As a general rule, to reduce the size of a file we need to reduce the quality of the video image.

Many different video file formats exist and the main types can be identified by the file name extension. If you look through the files on your computer, chances are you'll find video files with *.mpg* (or *.mpeg*) and *.avi* extensions and possibly others.

To play a video file on your computer, software must decode the binary values in the file and reconstruct the video image on the screen. To achieve this the software must recognise the file format. If it doesn't, then you won't be able to see the video.

DarkBASIC Pro has a set of commands for loading and playing video files. These commands allow video file formats such as MPEG, AVI and Quicktime to be played as part of your program. Strangely enough, these same instructions can be used for playing certain types of sound-only files as well. We'll discuss this at the end of the chapter.

Any such media files that you intend to use in your program must already exist. Various programs are available to allow you to create such files, but a description of these is outside the scope of this text.

The Internet can supply you with samples of such media files if you have none of your own. Remember to check on copyright issues if you ever use other people's files in any game you intend to distribute amongst others.

The next section explains how the video handling instructions available in DarkBASIC Pro are used.

Playing Video Files

DarkBASIC Pro reserves 32 positions for sound and video files. These are numbered 1 to 32. When a file is first loaded from disk it must be placed within one of these areas.

The LOAD ANIMATION Statement

Before using an animation or sound file, it must be loaded using the LOAD ANIMATION statement which has the format shown in FIG-17.1.

FIG-17.1

The LOAD ANIMATION Statement

In the diagram:

    filename   is a string giving the name of the file to be loaded.

It is best if the file has been previously copied to your directory using the Media|Add option.

varea is an integer representing the area in which the file is to be stored. This should be between 1 and 32. Only one file can be stored in each area.

A typical example of using this statement would be:

```
LOAD ANIMATION "spaceship.avi", 1
```

If the requested file is not found or cannot be loaded for some reason, then your program will terminate.

The PLAY ANIMATION Statement

FIG-17.2

The PLAY
ANIMATION Statement

Once the video has been loaded, it can be displayed on the computer screen using the PLAY ANIMATION statement. This statement can be used in several forms, as shown in FIG-17.2.

In the diagram:

varea is the integer value previously assigned to the video in the LOAD ANIMATION statement.

bmparea is an integer value representing the bitmap area into which the video is to be placed. If no *bmparea* value is given, the current bitmap area is used. When this option is included, values for *x1,y1, x2* and *y2* must also be given.

x1,y1 are the coordinates of the top-left corner of the area in which the video is to play. If no values are given for x1 and y1, then the video's top-left corner is at position (0,0)

x2,y2 are the coordinates of the bottom-right corner of the area in which the video is to play. If no values are given, then the coordinates of the bottom-right corner are determined by the width and height of the video recording.

In the statement's simplest form, only the video storage area needs to be specified. Hence, if you've loaded a file into storage area 1, then that file can be played using the statement:

```
PLAY ANIMATION 1
```

The video will play through completely, but subsequent statements in your program will be executed at the same time.

LISTING-17.1 gives a simple example of how the statement might be used.

LISTING-17.1

Playing a Video

```
REM *** Load video ***
LOAD ANIMATION "va01.avi", 1

REM *** Play video ***
PLAY ANIMATION 1

REM *** End program ***
WAIT KEY
END
```

Activity 17.1

Type in and test the program given in LISTING-17.1 (*video01.dbpro*).

Make sure you've copied the required media file to your folder.

There's more to playing a video than meets the eye. In fact, there are two main stages involved. First the video must be loaded from file to a video storage area. As we've seen already, this is done using the LOAD ANIMATION statement. The second stage is to copy the information in the video area onto a bitmap area. This is done automatically when the PLAY ANIMATION statement is used.

By default, the video is loaded into the current bitmap area and, unless you've been using BITMAP statements at an earlier point in the program, the current bitmap area will be bitmap storage area 0 - the screen.

If the video loads to any bitmap area other than zero, it won't be visible but you'll still hear it! This is demonstrated in LISTING-17.2.

LISTING-17.2

Loading a Video into a Different Bitmap Area

```
REM *** Load video ***
LOAD ANIMATION "vm01.mpg", 1

REM *** Set up a bitmap area ***
CREATE BITMAP 1,400,400

REM *** And make it the current area ***
SET CURRENT BITMAP 1

REM *** Now try playing the video ***
PLAY ANIMATION 1

REM *** End program ***
WAIT KEY
END
```

Activity 17.2

Type in and test the program given above (*video02.dbpro*).

Check that the video does not appear.

The video will automatically be positioned at the top-left corner of the screen, but it is possible to place it elsewhere by using an extended form of the PLAY ANIMATION statement which allows the position of the top-left corner of the video to be specified.

For example, to place the top-left corner 150 pixels in and 50 pixels down we would use the statement:

```
PLAY ANIMATION 1, 150,50
```

The video will play at its normal width and height, but again, we can control this by adding more options to the PLAY ANIMATION statement, specifying the position of the bottom-right corner of the video. For example, the line

```
PLAY ANIMATION 1, 150, 50, 220, 100
```

plays the video within the rectangular area defined by the corners (150,50), (220, 100). This causes the dimensions of the playing video to change to fit the area specified in the PLAY ANIMATION command.

A final option in the PLAY ANIMATION statement is that you can specify exactly which bitmap storage area is to hold the video. You must make sure the bitmap area has already been created or the screen area will be used. For example, we could place the video in bitmap area 3 using the command:

```
PLAY ANIMATION 1, 3, 150, 50, 220, 100
```

Notice that when specifying a bitmap area you also need to specify the position of the video (i.e. values for *x1,y1, x2,y2*).

The LOOP ANIMATION Statement

FIG-17.3

The LOOP
ANIMATION Statement

Whereas the PLAY ANIMATION statement plays a video only once, the LOOP ANIMATION statement will replay the video continuously. The format for the LOOP ANIMATION statement is shown in FIG-17.3.

In the diagram:

varea	is the integer value previously assigned to the video in the LOAD ANIMATION statement.
bmparea	is an integer value representing the bitmap area into which the video is to be placed. If no *bmparea* value is given, the current bitmap

area is used. When this option is included, values for *x1,y1, x2* and *y2* must also be given.

x1,y1   are the coordinates of the top-left corner of the area in which the video is to play. If no values are given for x1 and y1, then the video's top-left corner is at position (0,0)

x2,y2   are the coordinates of the bottom-right corner of the area in which the video is to play. If no values are given, then the coordinates of the bottom-right corner are determined by the width and height of the video recording.

The simplest option is shown in the statement

```
LOOP ANIMATION 1
```

which will repeatedly play the video loaded into video storage area 1.

To loop the video in a specific area of the screen we would use a statement such as:

```
LOOP ANIMATION 1, 0, 150, 50, 220, 100
```

This will load the animation into bitmap area 0 within the rectangular area (150,50), (220,100).

Note from the format given above that this statement does not allow for as many options as the PLAY ANIMATION statement. For example, you cannot give the top-left corner coordinates without also including the bottom-right position.

Activity 17.6

Modify project *video01.dbpro* so that your video is played continuously.

The PAUSE ANIMATION Statement

It is possible to pause a playing animation using the PAUSE ANIMATION statement, which has the format shown in FIG-17.4.

FIG-17.4

The PAUSE
ANIMATION Statement

In the diagram:

varea   is an integer value representing the storage area holding the video.

We could, therefore, pause the video in area 1 with the line

```
PAUSE ANIMATION 1
```

This assumes, of course, that the video in that area is currently playing.

The RESUME ANIMATION Statement

A paused video can be resumed using the RESUME ANIMATION statement, which has the format shown in FIG-17.5.

FIG-17.5

The RESUME
ANIMATION Statement

In the diagram:

varea   is an integer value representing the storage area
                                            holding the video.

Of course, we should only use this statement on a video that has previously been paused. So, assuming we have previously paused a video with the statement

```
PAUSE ANIMATION 1
```

then we could resume the video using the line

```
RESUME ANIMATION 1
```

The program in LISTING-17.3 pauses the video when any key is pressed and resumes playing when a second key is pressed.

LISTING-17.3

Pausing and Resuming a
Video

```
REM *** Load video ***
LOAD ANIMATION "vm01.mpg", 1

REM *** Play video continuously ***
LOOP ANIMATION 1,0,200,300,270,350

REM *** Pause when key is pressed ***
WAIT KEY
PAUSE ANIMATION 1

REM *** Resume when key is pressed ***
WAIT KEY
RESUME ANIMATION 1

REM *** End program ***
WAIT KEY
END
```

Activity 17.7

Type in and test the program given above (*video3.dbpro*).

The STOP ANIMATION Statement

Rather than just pause a video, we can stop it altogether using the STOP ANIMATION statement which has the format shown in FIG-17.6.

FIG-17.6

The STOP
ANIMATION Statement

In the diagram:

varea   is an integer value representing the storage area
                                            holding the video.

For example, the line

```
STOP ANIMATION 1
```

will terminate the playing of the video stored in area 1.

However, the video can still be resumed using the RESUME ANIMATION statement. So, in effect, there's no difference between the PAUSE ANIMATION and STOP ANIMATION statements.

The PLACE ANIMATION Statement

A playing animation can be moved about the screen or resized using the PLACE ANIMATION statement, which takes the format as shown in FIG-17.7.

FIG-17.7

The PLACE
ANIMATION
Statement

In the diagram:

varea	is an integer value representing the storage area holding the video.
x1,y1	are the coordinates of the top-left corner of the video.
x2,y2	are the coordinates of the bottom-right corner of the video.

For example, we could move the video stored in area 1 to occupy the screen area (50,50), (120,100) with the statement

```
PLACE ANIMATION 1, 50,50,120,100
```

or we could make the video occupy all of an 800 by 600 screen with the line

```
PLACE ANIMATION 1, 0,0,799,599
```

The program in LISTING-17.4 positions the loaded video randomly each time a key is pressed.

LISTING-17.4

Repositioning a Video

```
REM *** Load video ***
LOAD ANIMATION "vm01.mpg", 1

REM *** Play video continuously ***
LOOP ANIMATION 1,0,200,300,270,350

REM *** Seed random number generator ***
RANDOMIZE TIMER()

REM *** Move video when key is pressed ***
WAIT KEY
x1 = RND(100)
y1 = RND(100)


                                    Continued on next page
```

LISTING-17.4
(continued)

Repositioning a Video

```
PLACE ANIMATION 1, x1,y1 ,x1+70, y1+50

REM *** Move video when key is pressed ***
WAIT KEY
x1 = RND(100)
y1 = RND(100)
PLACE ANIMATION 1, x1,y1 ,x1+70, y1+50

REM *** Move video when key is pressed ***
WAIT KEY
x1 = RND(100)
y1 = RND(100)
PLACE ANIMATION 1, x1,y1 ,x1+70, y1+50

REM *** End program ***
WAIT KEY
END
```

Activity 17.8

Type in and test the program given above (*video4*.dbpro).

What happens when the video is moved?

As you can see from the result of the last Activity, the video image is not cleared from its old position when it is moved elsewhere. To rectify this we can add a CLS (clear screen) command each time the video moves. This should be added immediately after each of the WAIT KEY statements.

Activity 17.9

Update your program so that the video is cleared from its old position each time it is moved.

The SET ANIMATION SPEED Statement

The speed at which a video plays can be changed using the SET ANIMATION SPEED statement which has the format shown in FIG-17.8.

FIG-17.8

The SET ANIMATION SPEED Statement

In the diagram:

> *varea*   is an integer value representing the storage area holding the video.

> *spdperc*   is an integer value representing the percentage of the normal speed at which the video is to play.

To play the video at half speed, we would use the line

```
SET ANIMATION SPEED 1, 50
```

whereas double speed would be achieved with the line

```
SET ANIMATION SPEED 1, 200
```

The SET ANIMATION VOLUME Statement

This statement is designed to modify the volume of a playing video's soundtrack and has the format shown in FIG-17.9.

FIG-17.9

The SET ANIMATION VOLUME Statement

In the diagram:

varea   is an integer value representing the storage area holding the video.

volperc   is an integer value representing the percentage of the normal volume at which the video is to play (0 to 200).

The DELETE ANIMATION Statement

A loaded video occupies RAM space, so when you're finished with a video it is best to delete it. This will free up the RAM space and video storage area that is holding the video. This is done using the DELETE ANIMATION statement which has the format shown in FIG-17.10.

FIG-17.10

The DELETE ANIMATION Statement

In the diagram:

varea   is an integer value representing the storage area holding the video to be deleted.

Even though a video has been deleted, the last frame played will still be visible on the screen (assuming it was loaded into bitmap area 0), so you'll need to follow up with a CLS statement to clear the screen.

Retrieving Video Data

Several statements exist in DarkBASIC which allow information about currently loaded videos to be retrieved. For example, we can find out the position and dimensions of a video, whether it is playing or paused, etc. The statements that supply us with this information are described below.

The ANIMATION EXIST Statement

We can find out if a video storage area contains a video image by using the

ANIMATION EXIST statement. This statement returns the value 1 if the specified video has been loaded, otherwise zero is returned. The statement has the format given in FIG-17.11.

FIG-17.11

The ANIMATION EXIST Statement

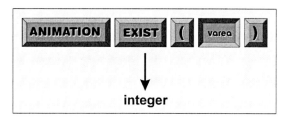

In the diagram:

varea　　　　　　　　　　is an integer value representing the storage area which may be holding the video.

Typical examples of how the statement might be used are

```
loaded = ANIMATION EXIST(1)
```

and

```
IF ANIMATION EXIST(3) = 1
    PRINT "Animation loaded"
ELSE
    PRINT "Animation not loaded"
ENDIF
```

The ANIMATION POSITION Statement

This statement has two variations. These are used to return the x-ordinate or y-ordinate of the top-left corner of the specified video. The format of the statement is shown in FIG-17.12.

FIG-17.12

The ANIMATION POSITION Statement

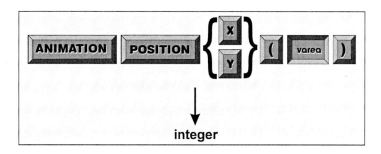

In the diagram:

varea　　　　　　　　　　is an integer value representing the storage area holding the video.

For example, we could determine the coordinates of the top-left corner of video 1 using the lines:

```
x = ANIMATION POSITION X(1)
y = ANIMATION POSITION Y(1)
```

The ANIMATION WIDTH Statement

This statement returns the width of the specified video in pixels. The format of the statement is given in FIG-17.13.

FIG-17.13

The ANIMATION
WIDTH Statement

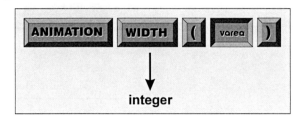

In the diagram:

    varea   is an integer value representing the storage area holding the video.

The ANIMATION HEIGHT Statement

This statement returns the height of the specified video in pixels. The format of the statement is shown in FIG-17.14.

FIG-17.14

The ANIMATION
HEIGHT Statement

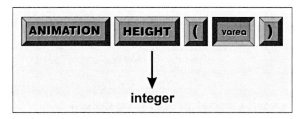

In the diagram:

    varea   is an integer value representing the storage area holding the video.

The program in LISTING-17.5 loads a video and then displays the coordinates and dimensions of the video.

LISTING-17.5

Determining the Position
and Dimensions of a
Video

```
REM *** Load video ***
LOAD ANIMATION "vm01.mpg", 1

REM *** Play video continuously ***
LOOP ANIMATION 1,0,50,50,120,100

REM *** Get video's details ***
x = ANIMATION POSITION X(1)
y = ANIMATION POSITION Y(1)
width = ANIMATION WIDTH(1)
height = ANIMATION HEIGHT(1)

REM *** Display details ***
PRINT "Top-left at : (",x,",",y,")"
PRINT "Width  : ",width
PRINT "Height : ",height

REM *** End program ***
WAIT KEY
END
```

We can also discover if the video is playing, paused or looping using the following statements.

The ANIMATION PLAYING Statement

This statement returns 1 if the video is currently playing, otherwise zero is returned. The statement has the format shown in FIG-17.15.

FIG-17.15

The ANIMATION
PLAYING Statement

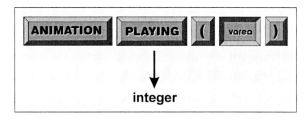

In the diagram:

varea   is an integer value representing the storage area holding the video.

The value 1 is returned if the video is currently playing because of either a PLAY ANIMATION or LOOP ANIMATION statement.

The ANIMATION LOOPING Statement

This statement returns 1 if the video is currently looping, otherwise zero is returned. The statement has the format shown in FIG-17.16.

FIG-17.16

The ANIMATION
LOOPING Statement

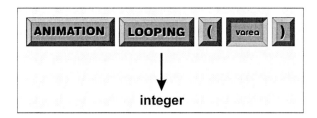

In the diagram:

varea   is an integer value representing the storage area holding the video.

A value of 1 is only returned if the video is playing because of a LOOP ANIMATION statement. A playing video initiated using the PLAY ANIMATION statement will return zero.

The ANIMATION PAUSED Statement

This statement returns 1 if the video is currently paused, otherwise zero is returned. The statement has the format shown in FIG-17.17.

FIG-17.17

The ANIMATION
PAUSED Statement

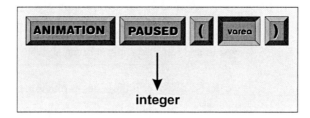

In the diagram:

    varea   is an integer value representing the storage area
                                   holding the video.

The program in LISTING-17.6 displays the state of the playing video, stating if it
is playing, looping, or paused.

LISTING-17.6

Determining the Playing
State of a Video

```
REM *** Load video ***
LOAD ANIMATION "vm01.mpg", 1

REM *** Play video continuously ***
LOOP ANIMATION 1,0,150,150,220,200

REM *** Get video's status ***
playing = ANIMATION PLAYING(1)
looping = ANIMATION LOOPING(1)
paused = ANIMATION PAUSED(1)

REM *** Display details ***
IF playing = 1
    PRINT "Animation is playing"
ENDIF
IF looping = 1
    PRINT "Animation is looping"
ENDIF
IF paused = 1
    PRINT "Animation is paused"
ENDIF

REM *** End program ***
WAIT KEY
END
```

Activity 17.12

Type in and test the program given above (*video6.dbpro*).

1) Change the line
      LOOP ANIMATION 1
   to
      PLAY ANIMATION 1

   How does this affect the messages displayed?

2) Add the lines
      WAIT KEY
      PAUSE ANIMATION 1

   after the PLAY ANIMATION 1 statement.

   How do the messages change?   **continued on next page**

There are two last facts we can discover about a video by using DarkBASIC Pro statements. These are; its volume level, and speed.

The ANIMATION VOLUME Statement

This statement returns the volume setting for the specified animation. The statement's format is shown in FIG-17.18.

FIG-17.18

The ANIMATION
VOLUME Statement

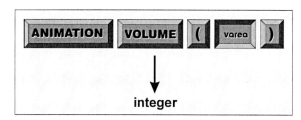

In the diagram:

    varea   is an integer value representing the storage area holding the video.

A typical statement would be:

```
volume = ANIMATION VOLUME(1)
```

A video playing at default volume would return the value 100.

The ANIMATION SPEED Statement

This statement returns the speed setting for the specified animation. The statement's format is shown in FIG-17.19.

FIG-17.19

The ANIMATION
SPEED Statement

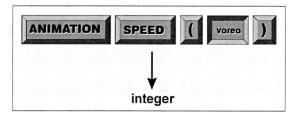

In the diagram:

    varea   is an integer value representing the storage area holding the video.

A typical statement would be:

```
speed = ANIMATION SPEED(1)
```

A video playing at default speed would return the value 100.

> **Activity 17.13**
>
> Modify your previous program to display the speed and volume settings of the playing video.

Playing Multiple Videos

It's possible to play two or more videos at the same time simply by creating more than one video area. This allows you to play the same video multiple times, or to display completely different videos.

The program in LISTING-17.7 displays two different videos simultaneously.

LISTING-17.7

Playing More than One Video Simultaneously

```
REM *** Load both videos ***
LOAD ANIMATION "vm01.mpg", 1
LOAD ANIMATION "va01.avi",2

REM *** Play both videos continuously ***
LOOP ANIMATION 1,0,150,150,220,200
LOOP ANIMATION 2,0,300,300,370,350

REM *** End program ***
WAIT KEY
END
```

> **Activity 17.14**
>
> Type in and test the program given above (*video7.dbpro*).

Playing Sound

The ANIMATION statements can actually be used to load and play sound files which cannot be handled by the other music and sound statements available in DarkBASIC Pro.

The program in LISTING-17.8 demonstrates how to load and play a an *.au* file.

LISTING-17.8

Using the Animation Statements to Play a Sound File

```
REM *** Load sound file ***
LOAD ANIMATION "spacemusic.au",1
REM *** Play sound ***
PLAY ANIMATION 1
REM *** End program ***
WAIT KEY
END
```

Summary

- DarkBASIC Pro's animation statements can be used to play video or sound files.

- The LOAD ANIMATION statement loads a video (or sound) file and allocates it to one of 32 reserved areas.

- The PLAY ANIMATION statement plays a loaded video.

- The video is loaded into a bitmap area for playing.

- The position of the video on the screen can be specified.

- By specifying a position, the size of the video can be adjusted.

- PLAY ANIMATION plays the video once only.

- The LOOP ANIMATION statement can be used to play a video repeatedly.

- The video can be paused using PAUSE ANIMATION.

- A video can restart from the point in the video at which it was paused using the RESUME ANIMATION statement.

- A video can be stopped using the STOP ANIMATION statement.

- A playing video can be repositioned on the screen using the PLACE ANIMATION statement.

- The video's play speed can be set using SET ANIMATION SPEED.

- The video's volume can be set using SET ANIMATION VOLUME.

- The space occupied by a video can be freed using the DELETE ANIMATION statement.

- The ANIMATION EXIST statement returns 1 if the specified animation is currently loaded; otherwise zero is returned.

- By using ANIMATION POSITION X and ANIMATION POSITION Y, the coordinates of the top-left corner of the video can be discovered.

- ANIMATION WIDTH returns the width of a video in pixels.

- ANIMATION HEIGHT returns the height of a video in pixels.

- ANIMATION PLAYING returns 1 if the specified video is currently playing or looping.

- ANIMATION LOOPING returns 1 if the specified video is in looping mode.

- ANIMATION PAUSED returns 1 if the specified video is currently paused.

- ANIMATION VOLUME returns the current volume setting of the specified video.

- ANIMATION SPEED returns the current speed setting of the specified video.

- Several videos can be played at the same time.

Playing DVDs

Introduction

DarkBASIC Pro has a few statements specifically designed to handle the loading and playing of DVDs. These are described below.

DVD Handling Statements

The LOAD DVD ANIMATION Statement

If you are going to play a DVD, then, rather than use the standard LOAD ANIMATION statement, you need to use LOAD DVD ANIMATION instead. This has the format shown in FIG-17.20.

FIG-17.20

The LOAD DVD ANIMATION Statement

In the diagram:

> *varea*   is an integer value representing the storage area holding the video.

Of course, you can only play a DVD if your computer has a DVD drive.

Notice that no filename is required. You need simply to have a DVD in your DVD drive.

A typical statement would be

```
LOAD DVD ANIMATION 1
```

Once loaded, the normal PLAY ANIMATION statement can be used to start the DVD playing. Unfortunately, if you need to interact with the DVD's on-disk menu where things such as a Play Movie option must be clicked, then you're going to run into a major stumbling block, because there is no way to select an option from such a menu through your program.

The TOTAL DVD CHAPTERS Statement

A DVD can be divided into several titles (each different item being a title). In turn, each title can be split into several chapters. For most DVDs there will only be one title (the main movie) and this will have several chapters (they may even be listed on the inside of the DVD cover).

The number of chapters in a specified title is returned by the TOTAL DVD CHAPTERS statement which takes the format shown in FIG-17.21.

FIG-17.21

The TOTAL DVD CHAPTERS Statement

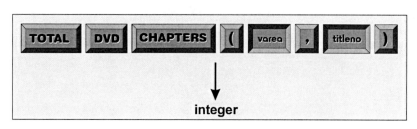

In the diagram:

  varea   is an integer value representing the storage area holding the video.

  titleno   is an integer representing the DVD title number. Normally this will be 1.

If you have a DVD loaded in your DVD drive, then we can determine the number of chapters in title 1 by first loading the DVD

```
LOAD DVD ANIMATION 1
```

and then calling the TOTAL DVD CHAPTERS statement:

```
PRINT "This DVD contains ", TOTAL DVD CHAPTERS(1,1)
```

The SET DVD CHAPTER Statement

We should be able to set the DVD to a specific chapter in a given title using the SET DVD CHAPTER statement which has the format shown in FIG-17.22.

FIG-17.22

The SET DVD
CHAPTER Statement

In the diagram:

  varea   is an integer value representing the storage area holding the video.

  titleno   is an integer representing the DVD title number. Normally this will be 1.

  chapno   is an integer representing the chapter required.

A Sample Program

The program in LISTING-17.9 will play any loaded DVD. Unfortunately, it won't take you any further than the main menu.

LISTING-17.9

Playing a DVD

```
REM *** Set screen resolution ***
SET DISPLAY MODE 1280,1024,32
REM *** Load DVD ***
LOAD DVD ANIMATION 1
REM *** Start playing DVD ***
PLAY ANIMATION 1
REM *** End program ***
WAIT KEY
END
```

> **Activity 17.15**
>
> If you have a DVD drive, insert a DVD and test the program given in LISTING-17.8

Summary

- To play a DVD use LOAD DVD ANIMATION followed by PLAY ANIMATION.

- Use TOTAL DVD CHAPTERS to discover how many chapters are in a DVD.

- Set the part of the DVD to be played using the SET DVD CHAPTER statement.

Solutions

Activity 17.1

No solution required.

Activity 17.2

No solution required.

Activity 17.3

```
REM *** Load video ***
LOAD ANIMATION "va01.avi", 1

REM *** Play video ***
PLAY ANIMATION 1,100,80

REM *** End program ***
WAIT KEY
END
```

Activity 17.4

```
REM *** Load video ***
LOAD ANIMATION "va01.avi", 1

REM *** Play video ***
PLAY ANIMATION 1,100,80,170,120

REM *** End program ***
WAIT KEY
END
```

Activity 17.5

```
REM *** Load video ***
LOAD ANIMATION "vm01.mpg", 1
REM *** Set up a bitmap area ***
CREATE BITMAP 1,400,400
REM *** And make it the current area ***
SET CURRENT BITMAP 1
REM *** Now try playing the video ***
PLAY ANIMATION 1,0,100,80,170,120
REM *** End program ***
WAIT KEY
END
```

Activity 17.6

```
REM *** Load video ***
LOAD ANIMATION "va01.avi", 1

REM *** Play video ***
LOOP ANIMATION 1,0,100,80,170,120

REM *** End program ***
WAIT KEY
END
```

Activity 17.7

No solution required.

Activity 17.8

The last frame played at the previous position persists on the screen when the video is moved.

Activity 17.9

```
REM *** Load video ***
LOAD ANIMATION "vm01.mpg", 1
REM *** Play video continuously ***
PLAY ANIMATION 1,0,200,300,270,350
REM *** Seed random number generator ***
RANDOMIZE TIMER()
REM *** Move video when key is pressed ***
WAIT KEY
x1 = RND(100)
y1 = RND(100)
CLS
PLACE ANIMATION 1, x1,y1 ,x1+70, y1+50
REM *** Move video when key is pressed ***
WAIT KEY
x1 = RND(100)
y1 = RND(100)
CLS
PLACE ANIMATION 1, x1,y1 ,x1+70, y1+50
REM *** Move video when key is pressed ***
WAIT KEY
x1 = RND(100)
y1 = RND(100)
CLS
PLACE ANIMATION 1, x1,y1 ,x1+70, y1+50
REM *** End program ***
WAIT KEY
END
```

Activity 17.10

```
REM *** Load video ***
LOAD ANIMATION "vm01.mpg", 1
REM *** Play video continuously ***
PLAY ANIMATION 1,0,200,300,270,350
REM *** Seed random number generator ***
RANDOMIZE TIMER()
REM *** Move video when key is pressed ***
WAIT KEY
x1 = RND(100)
y1 = RND(100)
CLS
PLACE ANIMATION 1, x1,y1 ,x1+70, y1+50
SET ANIMATION SPEED 1, 50
REM *** Move video when key is pressed ***
WAIT KEY
x1 = RND(100)
y1 = RND(100)
CLS
PLACE ANIMATION 1, x1,y1 ,x1+70, y1+50
SET ANIMATION SPEED 1, 200
REM *** Move video when key is pressed ***
WAIT KEY
x1 = RND(100)
y1 = RND(100)
CLS
PLACE ANIMATION 1, x1,y1 ,x1+70, y1+50
SET ANIMATION SPEED 1, 100
REM *** End program ***
WAIT KEY
END
```

Activity 17.11

No solution required.

Activity 17.12

1) When using LOOP, the messages
    Animation is playing
  and *Animation is looping*
  are both displayed.

   When using PLAY, only
    Animation is playing
  is displayed.

2) When the PAUSE statement is added the messages
  displayed become
    Animation is playing
  and *Animation is paused*

3) When STOP replaces PAUSE, no messages are
  displayed.

Activity 17.13

The WAIT KEY and STOP ANIMATION statements
added by Activity 17.12 have been removed.

```
REM *** Load video ***
LOAD ANIMATION "vm01.mpg", 1
REM *** Play video continuously ***
PLAY ANIMATION 1,0,150,150,220,200
REM *** Get video's status ***
playing = ANIMATION PLAYING(1)
looping = ANIMATION LOOPING(1)
paused = ANIMATION PAUSED(1)
volume = ANIMATION VOLUME(1)
speed = ANIMATION SPEED(1)
REM *** Display details ***
IF playing = 1
    PRINT "Animation is playing"
ENDIF
IF looping = 1
    PRINT "Animation is looping"
ENDIF
IF paused = 1
    PRINT "Animation is paused"
ENDIF
PRINT "Volume setting is ", volume
PRINT "Speed setting is   ",speed
REM *** End program ***
WAIT KEY
END
```

Activity 17.14

No solution required.

Activity 17.15

No solution required.

18

Accessing the Keyboard

Accessing the Keyboard Buffer

Checking for Control Key Presses

Reading from the Keyboard with Pausing the Program

Retrieving Scan Codes

Accessing the Keyboard

Introduction

We've already met a few statements such as INPUT and WAIT KEY which allow us to interact with the keyboard, but there are several more commands available that give us even greater control over keyboard input - something we need in order to create interactive games. These statements are explained below.

Reading a Key

The INPUT and WAIT KEY statements both halt execution of a program while waiting for a key to be pressed on the keyboard. However, in an interactive game, this is the last thing we want. Imagine playing a game like Space Invaders , which is controlled from the keyboard, and having the program stop every time input from the keyboard is accepted.

An interactive game has to keep moving. If a key is pressed the game reacts to that key press, but if no key is pressed the game continues as normal.

The INKEY$ Statement

This effect can be achieved in DarkBASIC Pro by using the INKEY$ statement. If a key has been pressed when the INKEY$ statement is executed, a string containing the value of that key is returned by the statement, but if no key has been pressed, then an empty string is returned. In either case, the program does not stop and wait for input, it simply moves on to the next statement in the program. This statement has the format shown in FIG-18.1.

FIG-18.1

The INKEY$ Statement

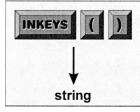

The program in LISTING-18.1 gives a simple demonstration of the effect of this statement by displaying any key pressed or, when no key is being pressed, a full stop.

LISTING-18.1

Using INKEY$

```
DO
    REM *** Read any key that has been pressed ***
    char$ = INKEY$()
    REM *** IF no key pressed, display full stop ***
    IF char$=""
        PRINT "."
    ELSE
        REM *** ELSE display key pressed ***
        PRINT char$
    ENDIF
LOOP

REM *** End program ***
WAIT KEY
END
```

You should have noticed that the keyboard can be checked many times in a single second. Even when you press and release a key quickly, often the program will have managed to execute the INKEY$ several times while the key is down and hence a single key press can result in the character being displayed several times.

The program in LISTING-18.2 demonstrates the use of this statement by controlling the movement of a character on the screen. The character 'o' moves horizontally across the screen, reversing direction when it reaches the edges of the screen. However, pressing 'z' at any time will make the character move left while pressing 'x' will move the character to the right.

LISTING-18.2

Controlling the movement of a Character on Screen.

```
REM *** Set screen resolution ***
SET DISPLAY MODE 800,600,32
REM *** Initialise variables ***
x = 1                           'Horizontal position of character
movex = 1                       'Amount moved along on each turn
DO
   REM *** Output letter o in white at position (x,200) ***
   INK RGB(255,255,255),0
   SET CURSOR x,200
   PRINT "o";
   REM *** Wait 5 milliseconds ***
   WAIT 5
   REM *** Hide character (re-output in black) ***
   INK 0,0
   SET CURSOR x,200
   PRINT "o";
   REM *** Calculate next position for character ***
   x = x + movex
   REM *** IF char at left or right edge, reverse direction ***
   IF x < 1 OR x > 800
      movex = -move
   ENDIF
   REM *** IF z pressed, move left ***
   IF LOWER$(INKEY$()) = "z"
      movex = -1
   ELSE
       REM *** IF x pressed, move right ***
       IF LOWER$(INKEY$()) = "x"
          movex = 1
       ENDIF
   ENDIF
LOOP

REM *** End program ***
WAIT KEY
END
```

Checking the Arrow Keys

We can specifically check for the up, down, left and right arrow keys being pressed using the statements described below.

The UPKEY Statement

The UPKEY statement allows us to check if the up-arrow key is currently being pressed. This statement has the format shown in FIG-18.2.

FIG-18.2

The UPKEY Statement

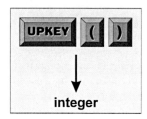

The UPKEY statement will return the value 1 if that up-arrow key is being pressed at the instant this statement is executed; otherwise zero is returned.

Typically, we would use UPKEY within an IF statement as in the lines

```
IF  UPKEY() = 1
    movey = -1
ENDIF
```

The DOWNKEY Statement

If the down-arrow key is currently being pressed, the DOWNKEY statement will return the value 1. If that key is not being pressed, then zero is returned. This statement has the format shown in FIG-18.3.

FIG-18.3

The DOWNKEY
Statement

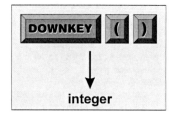

We could change the vertical direction of movement using the lines

```
IF  UPKEY() = 1
    movey = -1
ELSE
    IF DOWNKEY() = 1
        movey = 1
    ENDIF
ENDIF
```

The LEFTKEY Statement

If the left-arrow key is currently being pressed, the LEFTKEY statement will return the value 1. If that key is not being pressed, then zero is returned. This statement has the format shown in FIG-18.4.

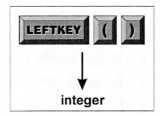

The RIGHTKEY Statement

If the right-arrow key is currently being pressed, the RIGHTKEY statement will return the value 1. If that key is not being pressed, then zero is returned. This statement has the format shown in FIG-18.5.

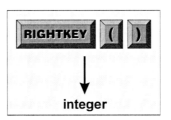

Activity 18.4

Modify your previous program so that the up and down arrow keys are used to control the vertical movement of the character.

Modify the program again so that movement speeds up if the same arrow key is pressed repeatedly.

Checking For Other Special Keys

As well as checking for the arrow keys being pressed, there are similar commands which allow us to check for the CTRL, ESC, SHIFT, RETURN and SPACE keys being pressed. Each command returns 1 if the key in question is being pressed and returns zero if the key is untouched. Since these statements are similar in format to the arrow key statements they are not dealt with separately. The details of each statement is given in TABLE-18.1.

Statement	Return Value
CONTROLKEY()	1 if a Ctrl key is being pressed
ESCAPEKEY()	1 if Esc key is being pressed
RETURNKEY()	1 if Enter key is being pressed
SHIFTKEY()	1 if Shift key is being pressed
SPACEKEY()	1 if space key is being pressed

In fact, a program will detect if more than one of these keys is pressed at the same time - but you have to program for this.

Activity 18.5

In your previous program, replace the

```
IF UPKEY() = 1
    dec movey
```

with the lines

```
IF UPKEY() = 1
    IF SHIFTKEY() = 1
        dec movey,5
    ELSE
        dec movey,1
    ENDIF
```

How does this affect the operation of the program?

Scan Codes

You already know that the characters held in the computer are stored using a coding system known as ASCII. But this translation into ASCII code is done by the computer itself, your keyboard actually transmits different values when you press a key on the keyboard.

The SCANCODE Statement

Just exactly what code is being transmitted from the keyboard can be determined using the SCANCODE statement which has the format shown in FIG-18.6:

FIG-18.6

The SCANCODE
Statement

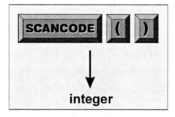

This statement returns an integer representing the code of the key currently being pressed. If no key is being pressed when this statement is executed, the value zero is returned.

The program in LISTING-18.3 prints the scan code of every key pressed.

LISTING-18.3

Displaying Scan Codes

```
DO
    REM *** Clear screen ***
    CLS
    REM *** IF key pressed, display the scancode ***
    key = SCANCODE()
    IF key <> 0
        PRINT key
    ENDIF
LOOP
```

As you will have noticed from the last Activity, scan code values are determined only by which key is being pressed, so there is no difference between the code returned by an uppercase or lowercase letter.

The problem with SCANCODE is that it cannot tell you when several keys are being pressed at the same time, since it only returns the value of the first of these keys to be hit.

The KEYSTATE Statement

If we want to know if a particular key has been pressed (the A key, for example), then we can use the KEYSTATE statement which returns a 1 if the key with the specified scancode is currently pressed down; otherwise zero is returned. This statement has the format shown in FIG-18.7.

FIG-18.7

The KEYSTATE
Statement

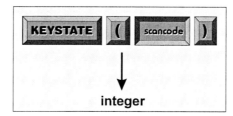

In the diagram:

    scancode   is an integer value representing the scan code returned by the key being tested.

For example we could check if the A key (which has a scancode value of 30) is pressed using the statement

```
IF KEYSTATE(30) = 1
    PRINT "The A key is currently being pressed"
ENDIF
```

The power of the KEYSTATE statement is that it can be used to check if several keys are pressed at the same time. This is a common requirement for many games.

The program in LISTING-18.4 reports on the state of keys Z, X, C and V using the KEYSTATE statement to detect which combination of these keys is currently being pressed.

LISTING-18.4

Detecting Several Simultaneous Key Presses

```
DO
   REM *** Clear the screen **
   CLS
   REM *** IF Z pressed, display "Z" ***
   IF KEYSTATE(44) = 1
      PRINT "Z";
   ENDIF
   REM *** IF X pressed, display "X" ***
   IF KEYSTATE(45) = 1
      PRINT "X";
   ENDIF
   REM *** IF C pressed, display "C" ***
   IF KEYSTATE(46) = 1
      PRINT "C";
   ENDIF
   REM *** IF V pressed, display "V" ***
   IF KEYSTATE(47) = 1
      PRINT "V";
   ENDIF
LOOP
REM *** End program ***
END
```

Activity 18.7

Type in and test the program given in LISTING-18.4 (*keys04.dbpro*).

Modify the program to check for the 1, 2, decimal point, and Enter keys on the numeric pad.

In a games program, one routine will often do the job of detecting which keys have been pressed while an entirely different routine will cause the game screen to react to those key presses. In these circumstances we need some way of recording which keys have been pressed so that this information can be passed from one routine to the other.

Like most things in programming, there are several ways of tackling this problem. One approach would be to create a string containing the character of each key pressed, as shown in LISTING-18.5.

LISTING-18.5

Using a String to Record which Keys Have been Pressed

```
REM *** Main loop ***
DO
   keyspressed$ = ReadKeyboard$()
   HandleGame(keyspressed$)
LOOP
END


FUNCTION ReadKeyboard$()
   REM *** Clear string ***
   keyspressed$=""
   REM *** IF Z pressed, display "Z" ***
   IF KEYSTATE(44) = 1
      keyspressed$ = keyspressed$+"Z";
   ENDIF
   REM *** IF X pressed, display "X" ***
   IF KEYSTATE(45) = 1
```

continued on next page

LISTING-18.5
(continued)

Using a String to Record
which Keys Have been
Pressed

```
        keyspressed$ = keyspressed$+"X"
    ENDIF
    REM *** IF C pressed, display "C" ***
    IF KEYSTATE(46) = 1
        keyspressed$ = keyspressed$+"C"
    ENDIF
    REM *** IF V pressed, display "V" ***
    IF KEYSTATE(47) = 1
        keyspressed$ = keyspressed$+"V"
    ENDIF
ENDFUNCTION keyspressed$


FUNCTION HandleGame(keyspressed$)
    REM *** Create code that reacts to keys pressed ***
    CLS
    PRINT keyspressed$
ENDFUNCTION
```

Activity 18.8

Type in and test the program in LISTING-18.5 (*keys05.dbpro*).

Modify the program so that the *HandleGame()* function only displays the
number of keys that are being simultaneously pressed.

This approach is quite good, but we're going to get into difficulties when we want
to record keys such as *Shift* and *Enter* which don't represent any characters which
can easily be added to a string.

A second method of recording key presses is to use the individual bits within a
variable as yes/no checkboxes uses to indicate if individual keys have been pressed.

Let's assume we want to check for the keys Z, X, C, and V being pressed. We can
set up a byte variable (*keyspressed*) and use 4 bits within that variable to record
what keys are pressed (see FIG-18.8).

FIG-18.8

Using Bits to Record Key
Presses

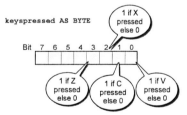

We can see this in practice in LISTING-18.6 which has the same basic structure as
the previous listing, but with the string replaced by a single byte.

LISTING-18.6

Using a Byte to Record
Key Presses

```
REM *** Main loop ***
DO
    keyspressed = ReadKeyboard()
    HandleGame(keyspressed)
LOOP
END

FUNCTION ReadKeyboard()
    REM *** Declare byte ***
    keyspressed AS BYTE
    REM *** IF Z pressed, set bit 3 ***
```

continued on next page

LISTING-18.6
(continued)

Using a Byte to Record
Key Presses

```
      IF KEYSTATE(44) = 1
         keyspressed = keyspressed || %1000
      ENDIF
      REM *** IF X pressed, set bit 2 ***
      IF KEYSTATE(45) = 1
         keyspressed = keyspressed || %0100
      ENDIF
      REM *** IF C pressed, set bit 1 ***
      IF KEYSTATE(46) = 1
         keyspressed = keyspressed || %0010
      ENDIF
      REM *** IF V pressed, set bit 0 ***
      IF KEYSTATE(47) = 1
         keyspressed = keyspressed || 0001
      ENDIF
ENDFUNCTION keyspressed



FUNCTION HandleGame(keyspressed)
   REM *** Create code that reacts to keys pressed ***
   CLS
   REM *** IF bit 3 set, display "Z" ***
   IF keyspressed && %1000
      PRINT "Z";
   ENDIF
   REM *** IF bit 2 set, display "X" ***
   IF keyspressed && %0100
      PRINT "X";
   ENDIF
   REM *** IF bit 1 set, display "C" ***
   IF keyspressed && %0010
      PRINT "C";
   ENDIF
   REM *** IF bit 0 set, display "V" ***
   IF keyspressed && %0001
      PRINT "V";
   ENDIF
ENDFUNCTION
```

Activity 18.9

Modify your previous program to match the code above and test the program.

The ENTRY$ Statement

Have you ever noticed that you can enter text at the keyboard while the computer
is busy doing something else? Then, when the machine is ready, the text you've
entered will suddenly appear on the screen. The computer does this by interrupting
whatever it is doing when you hit a key and taking the time to store the ASCII value
of that key hit in an area of RAM known as the **keyboard buffer**. You can find
out exactly what's in that buffer area without actually removing it from the buffer
using the ENTRY$ statement which has the format shown in FIG-18.9.

FIG-18.9

The ENTRY$
Statement

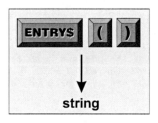

This function returns a string containing the characters currently held in the buffer area.

The program in LISTING-18.7 demonstrates the use of this statement by waiting for 5 seconds (during which time you should enter some characters at the keyboard) and then displaying what is in the buffer area.

LISTING-18.7

Using the ENTRY$ Statement

```
REM *** Give the user time to type ***
PRINT "Press keys now!"
WAIT 5000

REM *** Copy what was typed from the keyboard buffer ***
text$= ENTRY$()

REM *** Display the data retrieved ***
PRINT text$

REM *** end program ***
WAIT KEY
END
```

Activity 18.10

Type in and test the program given above (*keys06.dbpro*).

The CLEAR ENTRY BUFFER Statement

You can clear the keyboard buffer area at any time using the CLEAR ENTRY BUFFER statement which has the format shown in FIG-18.10.

FIG-18.10

The CLEAR ENTRY BUFFER Statement

Activity 18.11

In your previous program, add the lines

```
RANDOMIZE TIMER()
IF RND(1) = 0
    CLEAR ENTRY BUFFER
    PRINT "Buffer cleared"
ELSE
    PRINT "Buffer untouched"
ENDIF
```

immediately before the line

```
text$ = ENTRY$
```

Try out the program a few times and check that the buffer is correctly cleared on occasion.

The SUSPEND FOR KEY Statement

This has exactly the same effect as the WAIT KEY statement, halting the execution of the program until a key is pressed. The format of the statement is given in FIG-18.11.

FIG-18.11

The SUSPEND FOR
KEY Statement

Summary

- The INKEY$ statement will return the value of any key currently being pressed.

- Various statements can be used to detect if a control key is currently being pressed. These statements are:

  ```
  UPKEY
  DOWNKEY
  LEFTKEY
  RIGHTKEY
  CONTROLKEY
  ESCAPEKEY
  RETURNKEY
  SHIFTKEY
  SPACEKEY
  ```

- The scan code returned by a key press can be accessed using the SCANCODE statement.

- The state of a key specified by its scan code can be determined using the KEYSTATE statement.

- The KEYSTATE command can be used to detect when several keys have been pressed at the same time.

- Which keys have been pressed can be recorded as a string or by setting individual bits within a variable.

- The ENTRY$ statement returns the set of characters currently held in the keyboard buffer area.

- The CLEAR ENTRY BUFFER statement deletes all characters from the keyboard buffer area.

- The SUSPEND FOR KEY statement halts a program until a key is pressed.

Solutions

Activity 18.1

```
DO
  REM *** Read any key pressed ***
    char$ = INKEY$()
  REM *** IF no key pressed, display . ***
    IF char$=""
        PRINT "."
    ELSE
      REM *** ELSE display key pressed ***
        PRINT char$
    ENDIF
    WAIT 10
LOOP

REM *** End program ***
WAIT KEY
END
```

Activity 18.2

A WAIT time of around 100 will probably be okay.

Activity 18.3

```
SET DISPLAY MODE 800,600,32
y = 1
movey = 1
DO
    INK RGB(255,255,255),0
    SET CURSOR 400,y
    PRINT "o";
    WAIT 5
    INK 0,0
    SET CURSOR 400,y
    PRINT "o";
    y = y + movey
    IF y < 1 OR y > 600
        movey = -movey
    ENDIF
    IF LOWER$(INKEY$()) = "q"
        movey = -1
    ELSE
        IF LOWER$(INKEY$()) = "a"
            movey = 1
        ENDIF
    ENDIF
LOOP
```

Activity 18.4

```
SET DISPLAY MODE 800,600,32
y = 1
movey = 1
DO
    INK RGB(255,255,255),0
    SET CURSOR 400,y
    PRINT "o";
    WAIT 5
    INK 0,0
    SET CURSOR 400,y
    PRINT "o";
    y = y + movey
    IF y < 1 OR y > 600
        movey = -movey
    ENDIF
    IF UPKEY()= 1
        movey = -1
    ELSE
        IF DOWNKEY() = 1
            movey = 1
```

```
        ENDIF
    ENDIF
LOOP


SET DISPLAY MODE 800,600,32
y = 1
movey = 1
DO
    INK RGB(255,255,255),0
    SET CURSOR 400,y
    PRINT "o";
    WAIT 5
    INK 0,0
    SET CURSOR 400,y
    PRINT "o";
    y = y + movey
    IF y < 1 OR y > 600
        move = -movey
    ENDIF
    IF UPKEY() = 1
        dec movey
    ELSE
        IF DOWNKEY() = 1
            inc movey
        ENDIF
    ENDIF
LOOP
```

Activity 18.5

```
SET DISPLAY MODE 800,600,32
y = 1
movey = 1
DO
    INK RGB(255,255,255),0
    SET CURSOR 400,y
    PRINT "o";
    WAIT 5
    INK 0,0
    SET CURSOR 400,y
    PRINT "o";
    y = y + movey
    IF y < 1 OR y > 600
        movey = -movey
    ENDIF
    IF UPKEY()= 1
        IF SHIFTKEY() = 1
            DEC movey,5
        ELSE
            DEC movey
        ENDIF
    ELSE
        IF DOWNKEY() = 1
         INC  movey
        ENDIF
    ENDIF
LOOP
```

The 'o' moves faster when the Shift key is pressed.

Activity 18.6

1) The A key gives a scan code of 30.

2) The caps Lock key gives a scan code of 58 , but setting caps lock has no effect on the value the scan code generated by the A key.

3) The scan codes are :

$z = 44$ $x = 45$ $c = 46$ $v = 47$
$1 = 79$ $2 = 80$ $. = 83$ Enter $= 156$

4) $1 = 79$; $2 = 80$; $. = 83$, Enter $= 156$

5) The 1 keys produce different scan codes.

6) Only the scan code of the first key to be hit is returned.

Activity 18.7

```
DO
    REM *** Clear the screen **
    CLS
    REM *** IF 1 pressed, display "1" ***
    IF KEYSTATE(79) = 1
        PRINT "1";
    ENDIF
    REM *** IF 2 pressed, display "2" ***
    IF KEYSTATE(80) = 1
        PRINT "2";
    ENDIF
    REM *** IF . pressed, display "." ***
    IF KEYSTATE(83) = 1
        PRINT ".";
    ENDIF
    REM *** IF V pressed, display "Enter" ***
    IF KEYSTATE(156) = 1
        PRINT "Enter";
    ENDIF
LOOP
REM *** End program ***
END
```

Activity 18.8

```
REM *** Main loop ***
DO
    keyspressed$ = ReadKeyboard$()
    HandleGame(keyspressed$)
LOOP
END

FUNCTION ReadKeyboard$()
    REM *** Clear string ***
    keyspressed$=""
    REM *** IF Z pressed, display "Z" ***
    IF KEYSTATE(44) = 1
        keyspressed$ = keyspressed$+"Z";
    ENDIF
    REM *** IF X pressed, display "X" ***
    IF KEYSTATE(45) = 1
        keyspressed$ = keyspressed$+"X"
    ENDIF
    REM *** IF C pressed, display "C" ***
    IF KEYSTATE(46) = 1
        keyspressed$ = keyspressed$+"C"
    ENDIF
    REM *** IF V pressed, display "V" ***
    IF KEYSTATE(47) = 1
        keyspressed$ = keyspressed$+"V"
    ENDIF
ENDFUNCTION keyspressed$

FUNCTION HandleGame(keyspressed$)
    REM *** Create code that reacts to the
keys that have been pressed ***
    CLS
    PRINT "keys pressed : ",LEN(keyspressed$)
ENDFUNCTION
```

Activity 18.9

No solution required.

Activity 18.10

No solution required.

Activity 18.11

```
REM *** Give the user time to type ***
PRINT "Press keys now!"
WAIT 5000
REM *** Empty buffer 50% of time ***
    RANDOMIZE TIMER()
    IF RND(1) = 0
        CLEAR ENTRY BUFFER
        PRINT "Buffer cleared"
    ELSE
        PRINT "Buffer untouched"
    ENDIF
REM *** Copy what's left in buffer ***
text$= ENTRY$()
REM *** Display the data retrieved ***
PRINT text$
REM *** end program ***
WAIT KEY
END
```

19

Mathematical Functions

ABS, EXP, INT and SQRT Statements

Calculating Angles using ACOS and ASIN

Cartesian Coordinates

e Constant

Hyperbolic Functions

Quadrants

Restraining Angles to 360° using WRAPVALUE

Screen Coordinates

TAN and ATAN Functions

Unary Circles and the COS and SIN Functions

Mathematical Functions

Introduction

DarkBASIC Pro comes with a few built-in mathematical functions. Many of these, as we will discover later, are of fundamental importance when creating games that involve moving objects on screen. Below is a description of those functions and some of their underlying principles.

Coordinates

In 2D coordinate geometry objects are positioned by specifying x,y **Cartesian coordinates** (see FIG-19.1).

FIG-19.1

The Cartesian Coordinate System

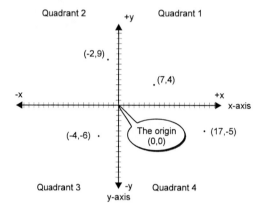

From FIG-19.1 we can see that the **origin** is the position where the two axes cross and that the axes split the area into four **quadrants**:

- ➢ quadrant 1: both x and y values are positive

- ➢ quadrant 2: x values are negative and y values positive

- ➢ quadrant 3: both x and y values are negative

- ➢ quadrant 4: x values are positive and y values negative

However, on a computer screen the y axis has been turned upside down so that positive y values are at the bottom while negative y values are at the top (see FIG-19.2).

FIG-19.2

The Screen's Coordinate System

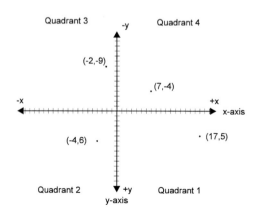

This modification changes the position of the four quadrants. From this point on we'll use the screen coordinate system since that's the one we need to use when creating games.

Mathematical Functions in DarkBASIC Pro

The COS Statement

If we draw a line starting at the origin which is exactly one unit in length at an angle of 30° to the x-axis, then we create the setup shown in FIG-19.3.

FIG-19.3

Rotating a Line 1 Unit Long by 30°

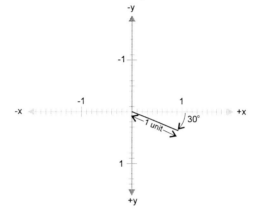

We know that one end of the line has the coordinates (0,0), but what are the coordinates of the other end?

We'll start by examining the x ordinate. From FIG-19.4 we can see that the x ordinate of the end point changes as we rotate the line to 70° from the x-axis.

FIG-19.4

How the x Ordinate Reduces as the Line Rotates to 70°

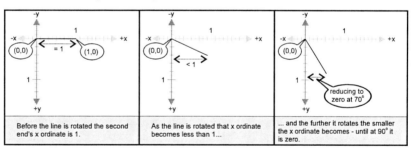

Before the line is rotated the second end's x ordinate is 1.

As the line is rotated that x ordinate becomes less than 1...

... and the further it rotates the smaller the x ordinate becomes - until at 90° it is zero.

Activity 19.1

What would be the x-ordinate of the line if it was rotated

    a) 45°
    b) 90°

Although it is easy enough to work out the x ordinate when the line lies along one of the axes, things are a bit more difficult when some other angle of rotation is involved. Luckily for us, someone worked all the x ordinates for every possible angle several hundred years ago and called it the **cosine** of the angle (often shortened to **cos**).

So, if we draw a line starting at the origin which is 1 unit in length and rotate by an angle of theta (θ), then the x-ordinate for the other end of that line is given by the expression cosine θ.

If we rotate our line by more than 90° it moves into quadrant 2 and the x-ordinate will become negative. As we pass 180° and move into quadrant 3, the x-ordinate remains negative, but after 270°, the x-ordinate is once again positive.

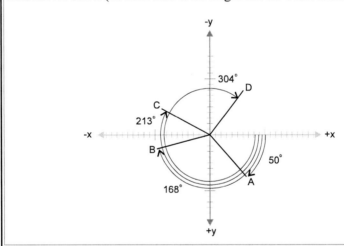
DarkBASIC Pro performs this calculation using the COS statement which has the format shown in FIG-19.5.

FIG-19.5

The COS Statement

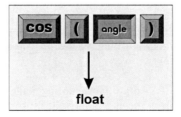

In the diagram:

angle   is a real number specifying the angle through
                                 which the line has been rotated. This is measured
                                 in a clockwise direction starting from the positive
                                 x-axis.

The real value returned by the function gives the x-ordinate of one end of the rotated
line (the other end being at the origin).

The angle through which the line has been rotated may also be measured in an
anti-clockwise direction, but is then specified as a negative value (see FIG-19.6).

FIG-19.6

Angles Measured in an
Anti-Clockwise Direction are
Expressed as a Negative
Value

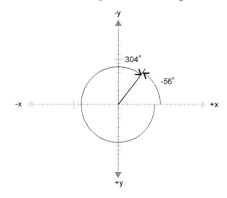

This means that the expressions

`COS(304)`

and

`COS(-56)`

both return the same value.

The SIN Statement

To determine the y-ordinate of our one unit line, we use the SIN statement which
has the format shown in FIG-19.7.

FIG-19.7

The SIN Statement

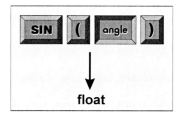

In the diagram:

angle   is a real number specifying the angle through
                                 which the line has been rotated. This is measured
                                 in a clockwise direction starting from the positive
                                 x-axis.

The real value returned by the function gives the y-ordinate of one end of the rotated line (the other end being at the origin).

Activity 19.4

Using *Calculator*, write down the y-ordinates of the four lines shown in Activity 19.3.

Dealing with Longer Lines

It's all very well to calculate the end point of a line which is one unit in length, but what of lines that are 2, 4 or 7.5 units long?

Actually, the calculation required is quite simple: if the line is twice as long, the coordinates of its end point are twice the value of those for a one unit line. If the line is four times longer, then the coordinate values are four times as large.

All of this can be simplified to:

x-ordinate = length of line * cos θ
y-ordinate = length of line * sin θ

Activity 19.5

If a line is drawn from the origin and is 3.7 units in length, what are the coordinates of its end point after it has been rotated by 191.5°?

The SQRT Statement

If we started by knowing the end points of a line, could we work out the length of the line? Well, if we take a second look at what's going on when we calculate the value of a sine or cosine (see FIG-19.8), we can see how this calculation can be done.

FIG-19.8

Calculating the Length of a Line

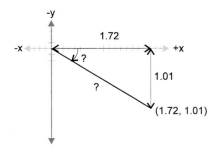

From the diagram we can see that the end point coordinates actually represent the lengths of two sides of a right-angled triangle, so the length of the third side (the line we've drawn and the hypotenuse of the triangle) is given as:

$$\text{length of line} = \sqrt{\text{x-ord}^2 + \text{y-ord}^2}$$

Calculating the square of a value can be done with a line such as

```
xord * xord
```

or

```
xord^2
```

but to calculate the square root, although we might use

```
result ^ 0.5
```

DarkBASIC Pro provides a SQRT statement which has the format shown in FIG-19.9.

FIG-19.9

The SQRT Statement

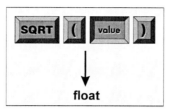

In the diagram:

value   is the real value whose square root is to be found. This cannot be a negative value.

So, the length of our line could be calculated as

```
hyp = SQRT(xord*xord + yord*yord)
```

The ACOS Statement

Although we've found the length of the line, how are we to calculate the angle of rotation.

Also written as $\cos^{-1}$

The **arc-cosine** (or **acos**) function in mathematics will perform the invert operation to that of cosine. Whereas the cosine takes an angle and returns the x-ordinate of the end point, the arc-cosine operation takes the end point and returns the angle.

DarkBASIC Pro's ACOS statement has the format shown in FIG-19.10.

FIG-19.10

The ACOS Statement

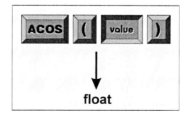

In the diagram:

value   is a real number representing the x-ordinate of a line which is one unit in length.

The value returned by the statement represents the angle of rotation of the line in degrees.

But what if the line isn't one unit in length? We already know that for lines of length greater than 1 the following equation holds:

x-ordinate = length of line * cos θ

So, applying a little reverse engineering to this we get

$$\cos \theta = \text{x-ordinate} / \text{length of line}$$

and therefore

$$\theta = \text{acos}(\text{x-ordinate} / \text{length of line})$$

Activity 19.6

A line of length 15 has one end at the position (0,0) and the other at (9,12). Use *Calculator* to find out the angle of rotation of the line.

(HINT: Select the *Inv* check box and then click COS to get the acos function.)

The ASIN Statement

The arcsine operation returns the degree of rotation using the y-ordinate. In DarkBASIC Pro this operation is performed by the ASIN statement which has the format shown in FIG-19.11.

FIG-19.11

The ASIN Statement

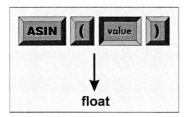

In the diagram:

    value   is a real number representing the y-ordinate of a line which is one unit in length.

Activity 19.7

Using the same line as described in the previous Activity, check that the angle of rotation is the same as before when calculated using the y-ordinate and the arcsine operation.

The TAN Statement

The **tangent** operation returns the gradient (steepness) of the line when given the angle of rotation. Perhaps you've seen a road sign beside a steep hill which read something like 1: 10, meaning that the hill rises 1 metre for every 10 metres travelled (see FIG-19.12). Such a hill is referred to as having a "1 in 10" gradient.

FIG-19.12

The Gradient of a Slope

A 1 in 10 Gradient

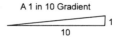

More modern signs give the gradient as a percentage. For example a hill that rises 1 metre in 12 would have a gradient of 8.3% (1/12 *100).

The value returned by the tangent operation is the ratio of the y-ordinate divided by the x-ordinate.

In DarkBASIC Pro the TAN statement has the format shown in FIG-19.13.

FIG-19.13

The TAN Statement

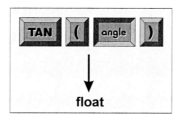

In the diagram:

angle   is a real number specifying the angle through which the line has been rotated. This is measured in a clockwise direction starting from the positive x-axis.

The ATAN Statement

The arctangent operation is the inverse of the tangent operation, returning the angle of rotation when given the gradient value. DarkBASIC Pro implements this operation using the ATAN statement, whose format is given in FIG-19.14.

FIG-19.14

The ATAN Statement

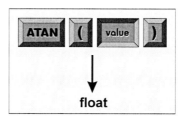

In the diagram:

value   is a real number representing the ratio y-ordinate / x-ordinate.

The statement returns the angle of rotation required to obtain the specified ratio.

The program in LISTING-19.1 rotates a 100 unit line, fixed at (0,0) between an angle of zero and 90° in increments of 1°. Each time the line is drawn its gradient is also displayed.

LISTING-19.1

Rotating a Line

```
REM *** Constants for line size and colours ***
#CONSTANT black = RGB(0,0,0)
#CONSTANT white = RGB(255,255,255)
#CONSTANT linesize = 100

REM *** Set display mode ***
SET DISPLAY MODE 1280, 1024,32

REM *** Set end of line coordinates ***
xord# = linesize
yord# = 0

REM *** Draw line ***
LINE 0,0,xord#,yord#
```

continued on next page

LISTING-19.1
(continued)

Rotating a Line

```
REM *** Rotate line ***
FOR angle = 0 TO 90
   REM *** Erase old line ***
   INK black, black
   LINE 0,0,xord#,yord#
   REM *** Draw new line ***
   INK white,black
   xord# = linesize * COS(angle)
   yord# = linesize * SIN(angle)
   LINE 0,0,xord#,yord#
   REM *** Display gradient ***
   SET TEXT OPAQUE
   SET CURSOR 200,200
   PRINT "                                         "
   PRINT "Line gradient : ",TAN(angle)*100, "%"
   WAIT 100
NEXT angle
REM *** End program ***
WAIT KEY
END
```

Activity 19.8

Type in and test the program given in LISTING-19.1 (*rotate01.dbpro*).

So far all our discussions have been based on the premise that any line has one end positioned at the origin, but this is too restrictive. How can we move a line to some other position and still make use of the SIN and COS functions to rotate that line?

The solution is quite simple. Decide where you would like the line to be moved to and then adjust all your coordinates by that amount. For example, in the last program we rotated our line about the origin, to change the position of the line to 600,500 we could add the lines

```
#CONSTANT xadjust 600
#CONSTANT yadjust 500
```

to the start of the program and then change the statement

```
LINE 0,0,xord#,yord#
```

to

```
LINE xadjust, yadjust, xord#+xadjust, yord#+yadjust
```

and the line will be positioned at the centre of the screen (assuming you are in a 1280 by 1024 display mode).

Activity 19.9

Make the adjustments given above to your program and check that the rotating line has moved to the centre of the screen.

Modify the program again so that the line rotates a full 360°.

We could use this code to represent the second hand of a clock, but clock hands start from a vertical position (12 o'clock) rather than the horizontal position used in the example. To achieve this effect we need the rotation to start at 270°.

If we try using code such as

```
startingangle = 270
FOR degrees = 0 TO 360 DO
    angle = startingangle + degrees
```

angle will range from 270 to 630.

For example, when angle reaches a value of 390, this is really just the same as an angle of 30 (see FIG-19.15).

FIG-19.15

Restraining an Angle to the Range 0 to 360

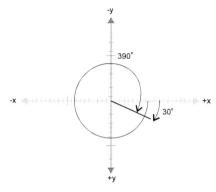

The WRAPVALUE Statement

DarkBASIC Pro's WRAPVALUE statement takes an angle and returns a value which always lies in the range 0 to 360. For example, given the value 390 it would return 30. The format for this statement is shown in FIG-19.16.

FIG-19.16

The WRAPVALUE Statement

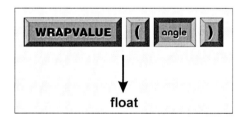

In the diagram:

angle	is a real value representing the angle which is to be reduced to the equivalent angle in the range 0 to 360. If *angle* is already in this range, then the returned value is an exact copy of *angle*.

Activity 19.10

Modify your previous project to move the line through a full 360° starting at the 12 o'clock position.

Other Mathematical Functions

The ABS Statement

There are occasions when we want the value of a number without worrying about whether this is a positive or negative number. For example, we know that the COS function gives the x-ordinate of a point. Sometimes this will be a negative value, sometimes positive (depending on which quadrant the point lies in). We also saw that this value represents the length of one side of a right angled triangle (see FIG-19.8). But when treating the value as the length of a line, most of the time we won't care about the values sign. After all, if the x-ordinate is 0.7 or -0.7, the line is still 0.7 units in length. The ABS statement takes a numeric value and returns the positive form of that number. Hence, ABS(0.7) returns 0.7 and ABS(-0.7) also returns 0.7.

The format for the ABS statement is given in FIG-19.17.

FIG-19.17

The ABS Statement

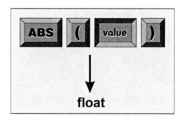

In the diagram:

    value   is a real value.

The absolute value of *value* will be returned by the statement.

The INT Statement

The INT statement returns the largest integer part of a real number. The format for this statement is shown in FIG-19.18.

FIG-19.18

The INT Statement

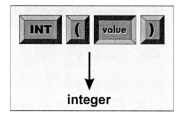

In the diagram:

    value   is a real value.

The largest integer value not greater than *value* will be returned by the statement.

For example, the expression

    `INT(7.9)`

returns the value 7.

Activity 19.11

What values are returned by the following expressions?

  a) `INT (6.1)`   b) `INT(6.0)`   c) `INT(-7.9)`

The EXP Statement

There are probably two fixed values that crop up in mathematics more than any others. These are **pi** (3.14159265) and **e** (2.71828). The EXP statement raises *e* to a specified power. The format for this statement is given in FIG-19.19.

FIG-19.19

The EXP Statement

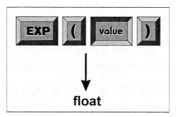

In the diagram:

    value   is a real value.

The value e^{value} will be returned by the statement.

There's no immediately obvious need for using this function in a games program, but, in fact, if you are programming real-world games you may well need this statement to implement physical laws you wish to apply to objects in your game.

The HCOS Statement

The HCOS statement calculates the hyperbolic cosine (shortened to **cosh** in mathematical circles) of a value. Despite its name, this doesn't have much to do with the cosine function described earlier and is likely to be used in very specialised cases only. The format for the statement is shown in FIG-19.20.

FIG-19.20

The HCOS Statement

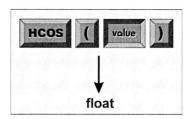

In the diagram:

    value   is a real number.

The statement returns the result of the following calculation: $0.5(e^{value} + e^{-value})$

The HSIN Statement

The hyperbolic sine function (sinh) is another specialised mathematical operation of limited use. DarkBASIC Pro implements this function using the HSIN statement which has the format shown in FIG-19.21.

FIG-19.21

The HSIN Statement

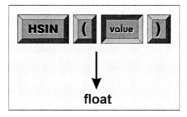

In the diagram:

value   is a real number.

The statement returns the result of the following calculation: $0.5(e^{value} - e^{-value})$

The HTAN Statement

The final hyperbolic function, hyperbolic tangent, is implemented in DarkBASIC Pro by the HTAN statement which has the format shown in FIG-19.22.

FIG-19.22

The HTAN Statement

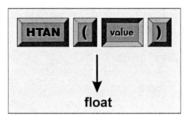

In the diagram:

value   is a real number.

The statement returns the result of the following calculation: $sinh / cosh$, or, if you prefer: $(e^{2value} - 1) / (e^{2value} + 1)$

Summary

- The Cartesian coordinate system specifies a position using an (x,y) value pair.

- Space is divided into four quadrants.

- The screen coordinate system uses an inverted y-axis.

- In mathematics, angles of rotation are measured in an anticlockwise direction measured from a line along the positive section of the x-axis.

- On screen angles are measured in a clockwise direction measured from a line along the positive section of the x-axis.

- When a line one unit in length is drawn from the origin and rotated by angle θ, then the end point of the line is given by the coordinates $(COS(\theta), SIN(\theta))$.

- If the line drawn from the origin is h units in length and rotated by angle of θ degrees, then the coordinates of the end of the line are given as $(hCOS(\theta), hSIN(\theta))$

- If we know the end point of a line and its angle of rotation, then we can calculate the length of the line using the formula:

  $SQRT(x\text{-}ord^2 + y\text{-}ord^2)$

- If a rotated unary line ends at (x-ord, y-ord), then the angle of rotation of that line can be determined by either of the following

  angle = ACOS(x-ord)

$$\text{angle} = \text{ASIN}(y\text{-ord})$$

- A line that has been rotated by θ degrees has a gradient calculated by the formula:

  $$\text{grad} = \text{TAN}(\theta)$$

- A line with a gradient g has been rotated by an angle given by the formula:

  $$\text{angle} = \text{ATAN}(g)$$

- The WRAPVALUE statement takes an angle of any value and returns the equivalent angle in the range 0 to 360 degrees.

- The ABS statement returns the absolute value of a specified number.

- The INT statement returns the largest integer not greater than a specified real value.

- The EXP statement takes a value, v, and returns the result of the calculation

  $$e^v$$

- The HCOS statement takes a value, v, and returns the result of the calculation

  $$0.5(e^v + e^{-v})$$

- The HSIN statement takes a value, v, and returns the result of the calculation

  $$0.5(e^v - e^{-v})$$

- The HTAN statement takes a value, v, and returns the result of the calculation

  $$\text{HSIN}(v) / \text{HCOS}(v)$$

Solutions

Activity 19.1

a) 0.5
b) 0

Activity 19.2

a) 1
b) 0
c) 0.866
d) 0.342

Activity 19.3

The x-ordinate of each line is :

A 0.643
B -0.978
C -0.839
D 0.559

Activity 19.4

The y-ordinate of each line is :

A 0.766
B 0.208
C -0.545
D -0.829

Activity 19.5

The coordinates of the line are:

```
(3.7cos(191.5),3.7sin(191.5))
= (-3.626,-0.738)
```

Activity 19.6

The angle is calculated as ACOS(9/15) which gives a result of 53.130

Activity 19.7

the expression ASIN(12/15) gives the same result as ACOS(9/15).

Activity 19.8

No solution required.

Activity 19.9

```
REM *** Line and colour constants ***
#CONSTANT black = RGB(0,0,0)
#CONSTANT white = RGB(255,255,255)
#CONSTANT linesize = 100
#CONSTANT xadjust = 600
#CONSTANT yadjust = 500
REM *** Set display mode ***
SET DISPLAY MODE 1280, 1024,32
REM *** Set end of line coordinates***
xord# = linesize
```

```
yord# = 0
REM *** Draw line ***
LINE xadjust,yadjust,xord#+xadjust,
  yord#+yadjust
REM *** Rotate line ***
FOR angle = 0 TO 360
  REM *** Erase old line ***
  INK black, black
  LINE xadjust,yadjust,xord#+xadjust,
    yord#+yadjust
  REM *** Draw new line ***
  INK white,black
  xord# = linesize * COS(angle)
  yord# = linesize * SIN(angle)
  LINE xadjust,yadjust,xord#+xadjust,
    yord#+yadjust
  REM *** Display gradient ***
  SET TEXT OPAQUE
  SET CURSOR 200,200
  PRINT "                             "
  PRINT "Line gradient : ",TAN(angle)*100,
    "%"
  WAIT 100
NEXT angle
REM *** End program ***
WAIT KEY
END
```

Activity 19.10

```
#CONSTANT black = RGB(0,0,0)
#CONSTANT white = RGB(255,255,255)
#CONSTANT linesize = 100
#CONSTANT xadjust = 600
#CONSTANT yadjust = 500
#CONSTANT startangle = 270
REM *** Set display mode ***
SET DISPLAY MODE 1280, 1024,32
REM *** Set end of line coordinates***
xord# = 0
yord# = -linesize
REM *** Draw line ***
LINE xadjust,yadjust,xord#+xadjust,
  yord#+yadjust
REM *** Rotate line ***
FOR degrees = 0 TO 360
  angle = startangle + degrees
  REM *** Erase old line ***
  INK black, black
  LINE xadjust,yadjust,xord#+xadjust,
    yord#+yadjust
  REM *** Draw new line ***
  INK white,black
  xord# = linesize * COS(angle)
  yord# = linesize * SIN(angle)
  LINE xadjust,yadjust,xord#+xadjust,
    yord#+yadjust
  REM *** Display gradient ***
  SET TEXT OPAQUE
  SET CURSOR 200,200
  PRINT "                             "
  PRINT "Line gradient : ",TAN(angle)*100,
    "%"
  WAIT 100
NEXT degrees
REM *** End program ***
WAIT KEY
END
```

Activity 19.11

a) 6   b) 6   c) -7

Copying an Image from a Bitmap

Loading and Displaying an Image

Setting the Transparency Colour

Images

Introduction

In the next chapter we will be examining the **sprite** commands available in DarkBASIC Pro. A sprite is simply a graphical shape which can be moved and manipulated in ways not possible with bitmaps. However, in order to use a sprite we must first load the graphic to be used by the sprite into an **image** object. From here it is then transferred to a sprite. Images can also be transferred to a 3D object to add texture to that object.

The term **image** has a special meaning in DarkBASIC Pro and should not be confused with bitmaps.

Below are the statements available for loading and manipulating image objects.

Image Handling Statements

The LOAD IMAGE Statement

We need to start by loading the picture file into an image area. This process is similar to that already seen when loading music files. The simplest LOAD IMAGE statement has the format shown in FIG-20.1.

FIG-20.1

The LOAD IMAGE Statement

In the diagram:

filename   is a string giving the name of the file to be loaded. It is best that you have previously added the file to your project using the **Media|Add** option.

imgno   is a positive integer value specifying the value to be assigned to the image.

The LOAD IMAGE statement can handle any of the bitmap image formats as listed below:

BMP
JPG
PNG
TGA
DDS
DIB

TGA, DDS and PNG files will retain their alpha channel information allowing transparent areas within the image.

To load the file *eye.bmp* into image area 1, we would use the statement

```
LOAD IMAGE "eye.bmp", 1
```

A longer version of the LOAD IMAGE statement exists, but we'll postpone examining that until the chapter on 3D graphics.

The PASTE IMAGE Statement

If you do want to see an image on screen, then you can use the PASTE IMAGE statement. This statement also contains an option to have black parts of the image become transparent when displayed. The statement has the format shown in FIG-20.2.

FIG-20.2

The PASTE IMAGE
Statement

In the diagram:

imgno	is an integer specifying the value assigned to the image. This value will have been assigned in the LOAD IMAGE statement.
x,y	is the position for the top-left corner of the image on the screen.
transflg	0 - black areas of the image are shown as black. 1 - black areas of the image are transparent. If this option is omitted, black areas show up as black.

In LISTING 20.1 the program loads an image and displays it at position (200,200) of the screen.

LISTING-20.1

Displaying an Image
Object

```
REM *** Set screen resolution ***
SET DISPLAY MODE 1280,1024,32

REM *** Create a green screen ***
CLS RGB(0,255,0)

REM *** Load image from file ***
LOAD IMAGE "crosshairs.bmp",1

REM *** Paste image to screen ***
PASTE IMAGE 1,200,200

REM *** End program ***
WAIT KEY
END
```

Activity 20.1

Type in and test the program (*images01.dbpro*).

Modify the program so that black pixels in the image become transparent.

In fact, the image is always pasted to the current bitmap area. By default this is the screen (bitmap area zero), but if you've been using the SET CURRENT BITMAP instruction in your program, this may have changed. If you want to see the image on the screen, make sure the current bitmap area is set to zero.

The SET IMAGE COLORKEY Statement

Although black is the colour that is normally rendered as transparent, it is possible to set a different colour using the SET IMAGE COLORKEY statement. This statement should be executed before any images are loaded. The colour specified will then become transparent if the PASTE IMAGE statement has its transparency value set to 1. This statement has the format shown in FIG-20.3.

FIG-20.3

The SET IMAGE
COLORKEY Statement

In the diagram:

red	is an integer value between 0 and 255 representing the intensity of the red component in the transparent colour.
green	is an integer value between 0 and 255 representing the intensity of the green component in the transparent colour.
blue	is an integer value between 0 and 255 representing the intensity of the blue component in the transparent colour.

Using this command sets the transparency colour for every image.

The program in LISTING-20.2 sets yellow as the transparent colour before loading and displaying an image. The screen background colour is green.

LISTING-20.2

Changing the Transparent
Colour

```
REM *** Set screen resolution ***
SET DISPLAY MODE 1280,1024,32
REM *** Set green background ***
CLS RGB(0,255,0)

REM *** Set yellow as the transparent colour for all images ***
SET IMAGE COLORKEY 255,255,0

REM *** Load image ***
LOAD IMAGE "crosshairs.bmp",1

REM *** Paste image to screen ***
PASTE IMAGE 1, 200,200, 1

REM *** End program ***
WAIT KEY
END
```

Activity 20.2

Type in and test the program (*images02.dbpro*).

Change the transparent colour to red.

The SAVE IMAGE Statement

It is possible to save a loaded image back to disk using the SAVE IMAGE statement. which takes the format shown in FIG-20.4.

FIG-20.4

The SAVE IMAGE
Statement

In the diagram:

filename	is a string representing the name to be given to the file that will be created by this operation. A file of this name must not already exist or the operation will fail. When specifying the file extension (.BMP, JPG, etc.) use the same format as the original file from which the image was loaded.
imgno	is an integer representing the image to be saved. This image must have been loaded previously.

The program in LISTING 20.3 loads an image, displays it on the screen then saves it to a file.

LISTING-20.3

Saving an Image Object
to a File

```
REM *** Set screen resolution ***
SET DISPLAY MODE 1280,1024,32
REM *** Load image ***
LOAD IMAGE "crosshairs.bmp",1

REM *** Display image on screen ***
PASTE IMAGE 1,0,0,1

REM *** Save image back to a file ***
SAVE IMAGE "crosscopy.bmp",1

REM *** End program ***
WAIT KEY
END
```

Activity 20.3

Type in and test the program given above (*images03.dbpro*).

Open up Windows Explorer and view the saved file as an image.

Is it an exact copy of the original file?

The DELETE IMAGE Statement

If an image is no longer required (that is if you are no longer using it in a sprite or as a texture for a 3D object), it may be deleted. This will free up RAM space and may increase the speed of your program. To do this, use the DELETE IMAGE statement which has the format shown in FIG-20.5.

FIG-20.5

The DELETE IMAGE
Statement

In the diagram:

imgno	is an integer representing the image to be deleted.

The GET IMAGE Statement

An alternative way of acquiring an image is to create it from a section of an existing bit map. To do this we first load a picture file into a bitmap area (using LOAD BITMAP) and then copy a section of that bitmap into an image area. This last stage is done using the GET IMAGE statement which has the format shown in FIG-20.6.

FIG-20.6

The GET IMAGE
Statement

In the diagram:

imgno	is an integer representing the image area used to store the image.
x1,y1	is an integer pair representing the coordinates of the top-left corner of the area in the bitmap to be copied.
x2,y2	is an integer pair representing the coordinates of the bottom-right corner of the area in the bitmap to be copied.

A longer version of the GET IMAGE statement exists and this will be covered in Volume 2.

Notice that the bitmap area from which the copy is to be made is not mentioned in this statement. This is because the copy is always taken from the current bitmap area. By default this is bitmap area zero (the screen) but can be changed using the SET CURRENT BITMAP statement.

The program in LISTING-20.4 loads bitmap area 1 with a picture and transfers the top-left corner of the picture to an image. The contents of the image are then displayed on screen.

LISTING-20.4

Creating an Image from a Bitmap

```
REM *** Set screen resolution ***
SET DISPLAY MODE 1280,1024,32

REM *** Load file into bitmap area 1 **
LOAD BITMAP "waves.jpg",1

REM *** Set bitmap area 1 as the current bitmap ***
SET CURRENT BITMAP 1

REM *** Copy a section of the bitmap  ***
GET IMAGE 1,480,590,830,814

REM *** Set the current bitmap area to the screen ***
SET CURRENT BITMAP 0
REM *** Paste the image to the current bitmap area ***
PASTE IMAGE 1, 0,0,1

REM *** End program ***
WAIT KEY
END
```

Activity 20.4

Type in and test the program given in LISTING-20.4 (*images04.dbpro*).

Change the area captured from bitmap 1 to (848,70), (1238,690).

The IMAGE EXIST Statement

It is possible to check that an image area does actually contain a valid image using the IMAGE EXIST statement which has the format shown in FIG-20.7.

FIG-20.7

The IMAGE EXIST
Statement

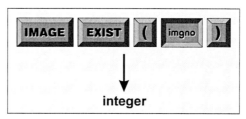

In the diagram:

imgno   is an integer representing the image area being checked.

The statement returns the value 1 if the image number specified does contain a valid image, otherwise zero is returned.

A typical use for this statement is shown in the lines below:

```
IF IMAGE EXIST(2) = 1
    PRINT "Image area 2 contains a valid image"
ENDIF
```

Summary

- An image object is used to hold a picture file.

- Every image object must be assigned an integer value.

- Images are created primarily for use with sprite objects and 3D objects.

- An image object is loaded from a picture file using the LOAD IMAGE statement.

- An image can be displayed on the screen using the PASTE IMAGE statement.

- An image displayed on the screen can have a specified colour become transparent.

- By default, black is the colour which may be set as transparent.

- The transparency colour can be changed using SET IMAGE COLORKEY.

- An image can be saved to a file using the SAVE IMAGE statement.

- An image can be deleted from memory using DELETE IMAGE.

- Part of an existing bitmap object can be copied into an image object using the GET IMAGE statement.

- To check if an image of a specified number exists, use IMAGE EXIST.

Solutions

Activity 20.1

```
REM *** Set screen resolution ***
SET DISPLAY MODE 1280,1024,32

REM *** Create a green screen ***
CLS RGB(0,255,0)

REM *** Load image from file ***
LOAD IMAGE "crosshairs.bmp",1

REM *** Paste image to screen ***
PASTE IMAGE 1,200,200,1

REM *** End program ***
WAIT KEY
END
```

Activity 20.2

```
REM *** Set screen resolution ***
SET DISPLAY MODE 1280,1024,32
REM *** Create a green screen ***
CLS RGB(0,255,0)
REM *** Set red as transparent colour ***
SET IMAGE COLORKEY 255,0,0
REM *** Load image from file ***
LOAD IMAGE "crosshairs.bmp",1
REM *** Paste image to screen ***
PASTE IMAGE 1,200,200,1
REM *** End program ***
WAIT KEY
END
```

Activity 20.3

The file should be an exact copy of the original picture.

Activity 20.4

```
REM *** Set screen resolution ***
SET DISPLAY MODE 1280,1024,32
REM *** Load file into bitmap area 1 ***
LOAD BITMAP "waves.jpg",1
REM *** Bitmap area 1 as current bitmap ***
SET CURRENT BITMAP 1
REM *** Copy a section of the bitmap ***
GET IMAGE 1,848,70,1238,690
REM *** Set current bitmap to the screen ***
SET CURRENT BITMAP 0
REM *** Paste the image to screen ***
PASTE IMAGE 1, 0,0,1
REM *** End program ***
WAIT KEY
END
```

21

Sprites 1

Controlling a Sprite's Movement

Creating a Sprite

Creating a Sprite with a Transparent Background

Giving a Sprite a Velocity

Mirroring and Flipping a Sprite

Positioning a Sprite

Rotating a Sprite

Setting a Sprite's Origin

Sprite Rebound

Creating and Moving Sprites

Introduction

A **sprite** is an object designed to contain an image. We've already seen that an image can be displayed and manipulated in DarkBASIC Pro using the BITMAP or IMAGE commands. However, if we want to use an image such as a spaceship or a ball as part of a game, it may be more useful to load that image as a sprite.

Programming commands are available to allow manipulation of a sprite in ways that are not possible with other types of screen images.

Loading a Sprite Image

We cannot load an image file directly into a sprite. Instead we must begin by loading the image file into an image object. For example, we can load the *arrow.bmp* file into image 1 using the statement:

```
LOAD IMAGE "arrow.bmp", 1
```

This assumes that the file *arrow.bmp* is in the current folder on your disk.

From here the image can then be loaded into a sprite.

The SPRITE Statement

The SPRITE statement copies an image into a sprite component. The sprite is then displayed at a specified position on the screen. This statement has the format shown in FIG-21.1.

In the diagram:

FIG-21.1

The SPRITE Statement

spriteno	is the integer value to be assigned to the sprite.
x,y	is a pair of integer values specifying the position on the screen at which the sprite is to be placed. The position is given in pixels.
imgno	is the integer value specifying the image to be loaded into the sprite. A picture should already have been loaded into this image.

To assign image object 1 to sprite number 1 and display it at position (100,200) on the screen we would use the line:

```
SPRITE 1,100,200,1
```

The resulting display is shown in FIG-21.2.

FIG-21.2

Creating and Positioning
a Sprite

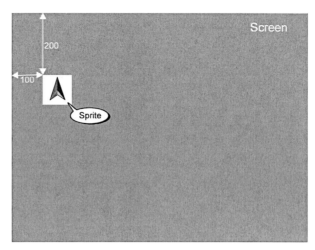

Of course, this will only work if the LOAD IMAGE statement given earlier has
already been executed by the program.

Activity 21.1

What statement would be required to load image 1 to sprite 5 and display the
sprite at position (150,50)?

The program in LISTING-21.1 demonstrates the use of the SPRITE statement.

LISTING-21.1

Displaying a Sprite

```
REM *** Set screen resolution ***
SET DISPLAY MODE 1280,1024,32

REM *** Load image and transfer to sprite ***
LOAD IMAGE "arrow.bmp", 1
SPRITE 1,100,200,1

REM *** End program ***
WAIT KEY
END
```

Activity 21.2

Type in and test the program given above (*sprites01.dbpro*).

The arrow sprite is 32 pixels wide by 32 pixels high, so when we request the sprite
to be placed a position (100,200), just exactly which part of the sprite will be placed
at that position? From FIG-21.2 above we can see that it is the top-left corner of the
sprite that is placed at (100,200). To understand why this is we need to know a little
more about how the coordinate system works.

We already know that the screen has its own coordinate system with the origin (0,0)
at the top-left of the screen, but each sprite we place on that screen has its own local
coordinate system with the sprite's origin at the top-left corner of the sprite (see
FIG-21.3).

So the statement

```
SPRITE 1,100,200,1
```

should be read as

Transfer image 1 to sprite 1 and draw sprite 1 on the screen with the sprite's origin at screen coordinates (100,200).

FIG-21.3

Screen Coordinates and
Sprite Coordinates

Translating a Sprite

It is possible to move the sprite to a new position by simply using the SPRITE statement again, but this time with different coordinates. For example, the line

```
SPRITE 1,150,20,1
```

will move the arrow from its original position to the location (150,20).

Activity 21.3

In your previous program, add the following lines

```
REM *** Move arrow ***
WAIT KEY
SPRITE 1,150,20,1
```

immediately before the REM *** End program *** line.

Test your program and check that the arrow moves after you press a key.

This is probably the commonest method used for moving a sprite, but other methods are available.

The PASTE SPRITE Statement

A second way to move a sprite is to use the PASTE SPRITE which allows an existing sprite to be moved to any position on the screen. The statement has the format shown in FIG-21.4.

FIG-21.4

The PASTE SPRITE
Statement

In the diagram:

spriteno   is the integer number of the sprite to be moved.

x,y   specifies the position on the screen for the top left corner of the sprite.

For example, we can move sprite 1 to the location (450,230) using the statement

```
PASTE SPRITE 1, 420, 230
```

The program in LISTING-21.2 moves a sprite to 10 random positions with a one second delay between each move.

LISTING-21.2

Repositioning a Sprite

```
REM *** Set screen resolution ***
SET DISPLAY MODE 1280,1024,32

REM *** Seed randomiser ***
RANDOMIZE TIMER()

REM*** Load image and transfer to sprite ***
LOAD IMAGE "arrow.bmp", 1
SPRITE 1,100,200,1

REM *** Reposition sprite randomly ***
FOR c = 1 TO 10
    PASTE SPRITE 1, RND(600),RND(500)
    WAIT 1000
NEXT c

REM *** End program ***
WAIT KEY
END
```

Activity 21.4

Type in and test the program given above (*sprites02.dbpro*).

Modify the program so that the sprite is moved 20 times with a half second delay between each move.

The MOVE SPRITE Statement

A final way to move a sprite is to use the MOVE SPRITE statement which takes the format shown in FIG-21.5.

FIG-21.5

The MOVE SPRITE Statement

In the diagram:

spriteno   is the integer number of the sprite to be moved.

distance   is a real number representing the distance the sprite is to be moved. The distance is given in pixels, so if the value used contains a fraction, automatic rounding to the nearest integer will occur.

Movement can only be in an up/down direction - no sideways movement is possible. By assigning a positive value to *distance,* movement is in an upward direction; negative values cause a downward movement.

For example, the statement

```
MOVE SPRITE 1, 50.3
```

will move sprite 1 up 50 pixels (being rounded to the nearest integer)while the statement

```
MOVE SPRITE 1, -25.0
```

will move the sprite down 25 pixels.

The program in LISTING-21.3 moves the arrow sprite up 30 pixels, and then, after a key press, down 15 pixels.

LISTING-21.3

Moving a Sprite

```
REM *** Set screen resolution ***
SET DISPLAY MODE 1280,1024,32

REM *** Load image and transfer to sprite ***
LOAD IMAGE "arrow.bmp", 1
SPRITE 1,100,200,1

REM *** Move sprite up ***
WAIT KEY
MOVE SPRITE 1, 30
REM *** Move sprite down ***
WAIT KEY
MOVE SPRITE 1, -15

REM *** End program ***
WAIT KEY
END
```

Activity 21.5

Type in and test the program in LISTING-21.3 (*sprites03.dbpro*).

Modify the program so that the arrow is first moved up by 100 units and then down by 250 units.

The ROTATE SPRITE Statement

A sprite may be rotated to a specified angle using the ROTATE SPRITE statement. This statement has the format shown in FIG-21.6.

FIG-21.6

The ROTATE SPRITE Statement

In the diagram:

spriteno   is the integer number of the sprite to be rotated.

angle   is a real number representing the absolute angle (in degrees) to which the sprite is to be turned. The angle is measured from the positive x-axis in a clockwise direction.

We could rotate sprite 1 to 90° using the statement

```
ROTATE SPRITE 1, 90.0
```

FIG-21.7 shows the effect of rotating the arrow sprite 90° starting from the position of (100,200).

FIG-21.7

Rotating a Sprite

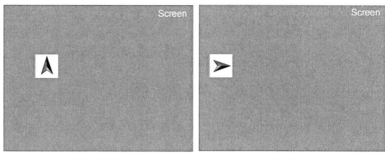

Before Rotation   After Rotation

A close examination of the before and after screen dumps given in FIG-21.7 shows that not only has the sprite been rotated, but it also appears to have moved position on the screen. This is because the sprite rotates about its own origin (the top-left corner of the sprite). The effect of this is shown in FIG-21.8.

FIG-21.8

How a Sprite Rotates

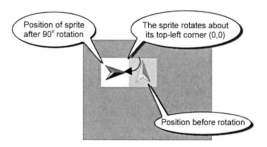

We can see exactly how this works by running the next program (LISTING-21.4) which rotates the arrow sprite through a full 360°, one degree at a time.

LISTING-21.4

Rotating a Sprite
Incrementally

```
REM *** Set screen resolution ***
SET DISPLAY MODE 1280,1024,32

REM *** Load image and transfer to sprite ***
LOAD IMAGE "arrow.bmp", 1
SPRITE 1,100,200,1

REM *** Rotate sprite in increments ***
FOR angle = 0 TO 360
    ROTATE SPRITE 1, angle
    WAIT 10
NEXT angle

REM *** End program ***
WAIT KEY
END
```

Activity 21.6

Type in and test the program in LISTING-21.3 (*sprites04.dbpro*).

Rotating a sprite has a knock-on effect on the MOVE SPRITE statement. Once rotated, the direction in which the sprite travels in response to a MOVE SPRITE command changes. After a 90° rotation, instead of moving up or down, the sprite will now move to left or right. The program in LISTING-21.5 demonstrates this by first moving a sprite up and down and then, after rotating the sprite, moving it right and left.

LISTING-21.5

Moving a Sprite that has been Rotated

```
REM *** Set screen resolution ***
SET DISPLAY MODE 1280, 1024, 32
REM *** Load image & transfer to sprite ***
LOAD IMAGE "arrow.bmp", 1
SPRITE 1,100,200,1

REM *** Move sprite up and down ***
WAIT KEY
MOVE SPRITE 1, 21
WAIT KEY
MOVE SPRITE 1, -21

REM *** Rotate sprite by 90 degrees ***
WAIT KEY
ROTATE SPRITE 1, 90

REM *** Move sprite right and left ***
WAIT KEY
MOVE SPRITE 1, 40
WAIT KEY
MOVE SPRITE 1, -40

REM *** End program ***
WAIT KEY
END
```

Activity 21.7

Type in and test the program given in LISTING-21.5 (*sprites05.dbpro*).

Change the rotation of the sprite from 90° to 45°. How does this effect the movement of the sprite?

How MOVE SPRITE Operates

At first glance, the effect of the MOVE SPRITE command may seem strange, but, in fact, it is quite consistent. If we consider a sprite to have a leading edge which, when initially created, is at the top of the sprite, rotating the sprite moves that leading edge (see FIG-21.9).

FIG-21.9

How Rotating a Sprite Affects the Direction in which it Moves

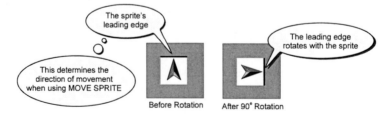

The sprite always moves perpendicular to the leading edge, hence, the line

```
MOVE SPRITE 1, 40.0
```

moves the unrotated sprite in a different direction from the rotated one (see FIG-21.10).

FIG-21.10

The Direction of
Movement

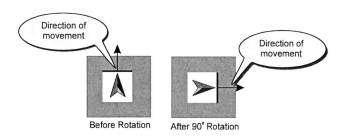

Before Rotation   After 90° Rotation

Using a negative value for the distance moved, as in the line

```
MOVE SPRITE 1, -40.0
```

will cause the sprite to move in the opposite direction.

Notice that the direction of travel is 270° ahead (or 90° behind) the angle of rotation of the sprite. That is to say, that when a sprite is first placed on the screen, its direction of movement is at an angle of 270° from the positive x-axis, but having rotated the sprite by 90°, the direction of movement is then 0° (90 + 270). Because of this, it is sometimes easier to think of a sprite's rotation angle as being measured from the negative y-axis (see FIG-21.11).

FIG-21.11

Measure a Sprite's
Rotation from the
Negative y-axis

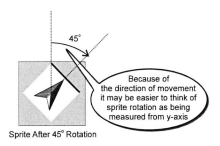

Sprite After 45° Rotation

Moving a Sprite's Origin

The OFFSET SPRITE Statement

Although a sprite's origin is initially taken as the top-left corner, that origin can be moved to a different position using the OFFSET SPRITE statement which has the format shown in FIG-21.12.

FIG-21.12

The OFFSET SPRITE
Statement

In the diagram:

spriteno	is the integer number of the sprite whose origin is to be moved.
xoffset	is an integer value specifying how far the origin is to be moved in the *x* direction. The value is specified in pixels.
yoffset	is an integer value specifying how far the origin is to be moved in the *y* direction. The value is specified in pixels.

In the case of the arrow sprite used earlier, this 64 by 64 pixel sprite could have its origin moved to the centre of the image using the statement

```
OFFSET SPRITE 1,32,32
```

The effect of this statement is shown visually in FIG-21.13.

FIG-21.13

Move a Sprite's Origin

Initial Situation   OFFSET SPRITE 1,32,32

Moving the origin of a sprite affects the positioning of the sprite on screen and the results produced by other operations on the sprite. The program in LISTING-21.6 creates a sprite, waits for a key press and then moves the sprite's origin.

LISTING-21.6

Changing a Sprite's Origin

```
REM *** Set screen resolution ***
SET DISPLAY MODE 1280,1024,32
REM *** Load image and transfer to sprite ***
LOAD IMAGE "arrow.bmp", 1
SPRITE 1,100,200,1
REM *** Wait for key press then move origin ***
WAIT KEY
OFFSET SPRITE 1,32,32
REM *** End program ***
WAIT KEY
END
```

Activity 21.8

Type in and test the program given in LISTING-21.6 (*sprites06.dbpro*).

What affect does changing the origin have on the position of the sprite on the screen.

From the above Activity we saw that moving the sprite's origin caused the position of the sprite on the screen to change too. Remember that the line

```
SPRITE 1,100,200,1
```

is a request to place the sprite's origin at screen position (100,200). Since the sprite's origin has moved when the OFFSET SPRITE statement was executed, the program redraws the sprite so that its new origin is placed at (100,200). And, since a sprite rotates about its origin, the OFFSET SPRITE statement also modifies the effect of ROTATE SPRITE.

Activity 21.9

Modify the program *sprites05.dbpro* so that the sprite's origin is offset by 32 pixels along both the x and y axes before the FOR loop is executed. How is the rotation affected by this change?

A sprite's origin can be offset by amounts larger than the size of the sprite itself. In LISTING-21.7 we position the arrow sprite in the centre of the screen, offset its origin by 300 pixels in the x-axis and 200 in the y-axis and then rotate the sprite about its new origin.

LISTING-21.7

Rotating an Offset Sprite

```
REM *** Set screen resolution ***
SET DISPLAY MODE 1280,1024,32

REM *** Load image and transfer to sprite ***
LOAD IMAGE "arrow.bmp", 1
SPRITE 1,640,512,1
REM *** Wait for key press then move origin ***
WAIT KEY
OFFSET SPRITE 1,300,200

REM *** Rotate sprite ***
FOR angle = 0 TO 360
   ROTATE SPRITE 1, angle
   WAIT 10
NEXT angle

REM *** End program ***
WAIT KEY
END
```

Activity 21.10

Type in and test the program given in LISTING-21.7 (*sprites07.dbpro*).

Sprite Reflection

The MIRROR SPRITE Statement

A sprite can be reflected about an imaginary vertical line drawn through the centre of the sprite using the MIRROR SPRITE statement. This statement takes the format shown in FIG-21.14.

FIG-21.14

The MIRROR SPRITE Statement

In the diagram:

    spriteno   is the integer number of the sprite to be reflected about its central y-axis.

A typical statement would be

```
MIRROR SPRITE 1
```

The visual effect of such a statement is shown in FIG-21.15.

FIG-21.15

The Effect of Using MIRROR SPRITE

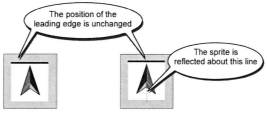

Sprite Before Reflection   Sprite After Reflection

Notice that the position of the leading edge is unchanged, so any subsequent call to MOVE SPRITE will still move the sprite in an up/down direction. Also the position of the sprite is unaffected by this statement.

The FLIP SPRITE Statement

A sprite can also be reflected about an imaginary horizontal line using the statement FLIP SPRITE which has the format shown in FIG-21.16.

FIG-21.16

The FLIP SPRITE Statement

In the diagram:

spriteno　　　　　　　　is the integer value of the sprite to be reflected about its central x-axis.

A typical statement would be

```
FLIP SPRITE 1
```

The visual effect of such a statement is shown in FIG-21.17.

FIG-21.17

The Effect of Using FLIP SPRITE

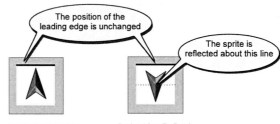

The position of the leading edge is unchanged

The sprite is reflected about this line

Sprite Before Reflection　　　　Sprite After Reflection

Again, the position of the leading edge is unaffected by this command.

The program in LISTING-21.8 demonstrates the use of the MIRROR SPRITE and FLIP SPRITE statements.

LISTING-21.8

Using MIRROR SPRITE and FLIP SPRITE

```
REM *** Set screen resolution ***
SET DISPLAY MODE 1280,1024,32

REM *** Load image & transfer to sprite ***
LOAD IMAGE "arrow.bmp", 1
SPRITE 1,100,200,1

REM *** Mirror sprite ***
WAIT KEY
MIRROR SPRITE 1

REM *** Move sprite ***
WAIT KEY
MOVE SPRITE 1,60

REM *** Flip sprite ***
WAIT KEY
FLIP SPRITE 1

REM *** Move sprite ***
WAIT KEY
MOVE SPRITE 1,60

REM *** End program ***
WAIT KEY
END
```

Reflecting a Tilted Sprite

If we tilt a sprite, for example, by rotating it through 45°, then the line of reflection also rotates and hence affects how the sprite is reflected when using a MIRROR or FLIP statement. FIG-21.18 shows the effect of reflecting a rotated sprite.

FIG-21.18

Reflecting a Tilted Sprite

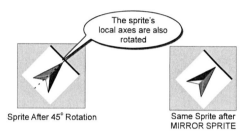

Sprite After 45° Rotation   Same Sprite after MIRROR SPRITE

Sprite Background Transparency

You will have noticed that all the sprites we have used have a white background. It is much more likely that any game we write will require a sprite to blend with the screen background. In other words, the sprite's own background needs to be transparent.

Luckily, DarkBASIC Pro will assume that any black pixels in the sprite's image are to be treated as transparent when the sprite is displayed. All we have to do is make sure we create our images with a black background.

A second version of the *arrow.bmp* image has been created with a black background. This second image is called *arrowtrans. bmp*. The two images are shown in FIG-21.19.

FIG-21.19

A Black Background can become Transparent when Displayed

Sprite with White Background   Sprite with Black Background

If you are creating your own sprites, there are a few points you should watch out for:

➢ Since anything which is black will end up transparent, make sure black is only used in the background.

> ➢ When creating the sprite image in your paint program, make sure anti-aliasing has been switched off, otherwise you'll get an unwanted border effect round the edge of your image.

Activity 21.13

Modify your previous program to use the *arrowtrans. bmp* image rather than *arrow.bmp*.

Giving the User Control of a Sprite

We can allow the user to control the movement of a sprite by reading a value from the keyboard and using that value to decide in which direction to move the sprite.

Vertical Movement

In the next program (LISTING-21.9) the user can move the sprite up by hitting the apostrophe (') key , and down by hitting the forward slash (/) key. The program loops to allow the user to move the sprite as often as required.

LISTING-21.9

User-Controlled Vertical Movement

```
REM *** Set screen resolution ***
SET DISPLAY MODE 1280,1024,32
REM *** Load image; transfer to sprite ***
LOAD IMAGE "arrowtrans.bmp", 1
SPRITE 1,100,200,1

REM *** Main loop ***
DO
    REM *** Read a key ***
    ch$ = INKEY$()
    REM *** IF it's ' move arrow up ***
    IF ch$ = "'"
        MOVE SPRITE 1,1
    ELSE
        REM *** IF it's / move arrow down ***
        IF ch$ = "/"
            MOVE SPRITE 1,-1
        ENDIF
    ENDIF
LOOP

REM *** End program ***
END
```

Activity 21.14

Type in and test the program given in LISTING-21.9 (*sprites10.dbpro*).

Modify the program so that the sprite moves at twice the speed of the original program.

Horizontal Movement

Since the MOVE SPRITE command always moves the sprite at right angles to the leading edge, by default a sprite can only move vertically (up and down). But if we rotate the sprite through 90° , the leading edge moves to a vertical position and MOVE SPRITE then causes horizontal movement (right and left).

In the next program (LISTING-21.10), the transparent arrow sprite is first rotated through 90° and then moved horizontally under user control. Movement is achieved by using the x (right) and z (left) keys.

LISTING-21.10

User-Controlled
Horizontal Movement

```
REM *** Set screen resolution ***
SET DISPLAY MODE 1280,1024,32

REM *** Load image and transfer to sprite ***
LOAD IMAGE "arrowtrans.bmp", 1
SPRITE 1,100,200,1

REM *** Rotate sprite through 90 degrees ***
ROTATE SPRITE 1,90

REM *** Main Loop ***
DO
   REM *** Read a key ***
   ch$ = INKEY$()
   REM *** IF it's x move arrow right ***
   IF ch$ = "x"
      MOVE SPRITE 1,1
   ELSE
      REM *** IF it's z move arrow left ***
      IF ch$ = "z"
         MOVE SPRITE 1,-1
      ENDIF
   ENDIF
LOOP

REM *** End program ***
END
```

Activity 21.15

Type in and test the program given above (*sprites11.dbpro*).

Modify the program to use scan codes to check for key presses.

Modify the program again so that the sprite is at an angle of 45°.

Rotational Movement

To control the rotation of a sprite we can use the ROTATE SPRITE statement. Because this command requires an absolute angle, we need to store the current angle of rotation in a variable. In LISTING-21.11 hitting the "a" key causes the angle to decrease so that the sprite rotates anticlockwise and the "s" key causes it to increase thereby rotating the sprite clockwise. Since we'll want the sprite to rotate about its centre, the OFFSET SPRITE statement is used to move the sprite's origin to the centre.

LISTING-21.11

Rotational Movement

```
REM *** Set screen resolution ***
SET DISPLAY MODE 1280,1024,32

REM *** Load image and transfer to sprite ***
LOAD IMAGE "arrowtrans.bmp", 1
SPRITE 1,100,200,1

REM *** Move sprite origin to centre ***
OFFSET SPRITE 1,32,32
```

continued on next page

LISTING-21.11
(continued)

Rotational Movement

```
REM *** Set the angle ***
angle = 0

REM *** Main Loop ***
DO
   REM *** Read a key ***
   key = SCANCODE()
   REM *** IF it's "a" decrease angle ***
   IF key = 30
      DEC angle
   ELSE
      REM *** IF it's "s" increase angle ***
      IF key = 31
         INC angle
      ENDIF
   ENDIF
   ROTATE SPRITE 1, angle
LOOP

REM *** End program ***
END
```

Activity 21.16

Type in and test the program given in LISTING-21.11 (*sprites12.dbpro*).

Activity 21.17

Create a new program (*sprites13.dbpro*) which combines rotation ("a" and "s") with forward and backward movement ("x" and "z") to move the sprite.

Free Movement

With free movement we allow the sprite to move anywhere on the screen. Many games achieve this by using a mouse or joystick, but for the moment we'll stick to the keyboard (other methods are given in later chapters).

The simplest way to achieve free movement of a sprite is to use the SPRITE statement rather than MOVE SPRITE since the latter requires the sprite to be rotated before it can move in the required direction.

Using SPRITE allows us to move the sprite to any position on the screen. However, since the SPRITE command requires the exact coordinates of where the sprite is to be placed, we'll need to keep a record of the sprite's position at all times.

The program that follows (LISTING-21.12) uses the *f* and *c* keys to move the sprite up and down, while using the *z* and *x* keys to move the sprite left and right. The program employs the following logic:

```
Load image
Set (x,y) value to the centre of the screen
Load sprite at position (x,y)
Offset its origin to the sprite's centre
DO
    Read a key
    IF
        key = "f":
            y := y - 5
        key = "c":
            y := y + 5
        key = "z":
```

```
                                     x := x -5
                             key = "x":
                                     x := x + 5
                     ENDIF
                     Move sprite to (x,y)
              LOOP
```

LISTING-21.12

Free Movement of a
Sprite

```
REM *** Set screen resolution ***
SET DISPLAY MODE 1280,1024,32

REM *** Load image; transfer to sprite ***
LOAD IMAGE "arrowtrans.bmp", 1

REM *** Set the position ***
x = 640
y = 512

REM *** Load sprite ***
SPRITE 1,x,y,1

REM *** Move sprite origin to centre ***
OFFSET SPRITE 1,32,32

REM *** Main Loop ***
DO
   REM *** Read a key ***
   key = SCANCODE()
   SELECT key
      CASE 33   ` up (f)
         DEC y,5
      ENDCASE
      CASE 46   ` down (c)
         INC y,5
      ENDCASE
      CASE 44   ` left (z)
         DEC x,5
      ENDCASE
      CASE 45   ` right (x)
         INC x,5
      ENDCASE
   ENDSELECT
   REM *** Move sprite ***
   SPRITE 1,x,y,1
LOOP
REM *** End program ***
END
```

Activity 21.18

Type in and test the program given in LISTING-21.12 (*sprites14.dbpro*).

How far can the sprites be moved?

Restricting Sprite Movement

In most games we'll want to restrict the area of the screen through which a sprite
can move. To do this we need to check that the sprite's coordinates stay within
certain limits.

For example, in our last program we could get the sprite to disappear off the top of
the screen by holding down the *z* key. Since pressing the *z* key causes the line

```
DEC y,5
```

to be executed, we eventually get a *y* value of less than zero and the sprite begins to disappear off the top of the screen. To stop this happening we need to change the code to read

```
IF y >= 5
    DEC y,5
ENDIF
```

which will stop *y* becoming less than zero.

Activity 21.19

Modify your previous program so that the sprite cannot disappear at the top of the screen.

Modify the code which moves the sprite in the other three directions to ensure that the sprite remains on screen at all times.

Storing the Position of the Sprite in a Record

In the program above, the position of a sprite is recorded in the two variables, *x* and *y*. But since these two values belong together, we could bind them more tightly to each other by creating them within a record structure. To do this we start by defining that structure:

```
TYPE PositionType
    x AS INTEGER
    y AS INTEGER
ENDTYPE
```

and then declaring a variable of this type:

```
post as PositionType
```

This variable can then hold the coordinates of the sprite:

```
post.x = 640
post.y = 512
```

Activity 21.20

Modify your last program to use a record structure (as defined above) to hold the position of the sprite.

Velocity

In the programs we've created so far, the sprite stops moving when we stop pressing a key. But many games use sprites which continue to move in a given direction once set in motion; pressing a key may change the speed or direction of that movement.

We can achieve this effect by assigning a **velocity** to a sprite. Velocity gives us information about the speed and direction of travel.

In FIG-21.20 we see three spheres (A, B, and C), each with an arrowed line indicating the velocity (that is, speed and direction) of that sphere. The longer a line, the faster the sphere is moving; the direction in which the line points tells us the

DarkBASIC Pro: Sprites 1

FIG-21.20

Objects and their
Velocities

direction in which the sphere is travelling.

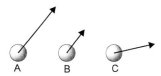

In a program we can store the velocity of an object by recording two pieces of information:

➢ the distance moved in the x direction within one unit of time

➢ the distance moved in the y direction within one unit of time

For example in FIG-21.21 we can see how to represent the three velocities given earlier in FIG-21.20.

FIG-21.21

Velocity is Recorded as
Distance along the x and
y axes

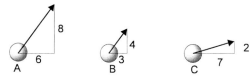

So that the direction is correctly recorded, it is important to add a sign to the x and y values. On a computer system, where the origin is at the top-left corner of the screen, y ordinates increase as we move down the screen. Taking this into account, the velocity of the three balls shown in FIG-21.20 should be recorded as shown in FIG-21.22.

FIG-21.22

Velocity Components
are Signed

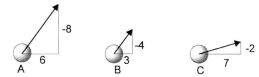

When writing down a velocity, we'll show the x and y values in square brackets. This will allow us to tell the difference between a point, with values in parentheses, and a velocity. For example, we would express the velocity A in FIG-21.22 as

$A = [6,-8]$

Activity 21.21

The velocity of a ball is set to one of four possible values (V_1, V_2, V_3, V_4). The possible velocities are shown in the diagram below.

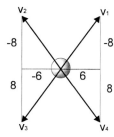

Write down the x and y values for each velocity.

Velocity, like a position, could be defined as a record structure, but this time we'll use real values rather than integers:

```
TYPE VelocityType
    xoffset AS FLOAT
    yoffset AS FLOAT
ENDTYPE
```

A variable of this type can now be used to record a velocity:

```
v1 AS VelocityType

v1.xoffset = 6
v1.yoffset = -8
```

The program in LISTING-21.13 demonstrates the use of this technique to move a ball with a fixed velocity across the screen.

LISTING-21.13

An Sprite with a Velocity

```
REM *** Set up Data types used ***
TYPE PositionType
   x AS INTEGER
   y AS INTEGER
ENDTYPE

TYPE VelocityType
   xoffset AS FLOAT
   yoffset AS FLOAT
ENDTYPE

REM *** Set screen resolution ***
SET DISPLAY MODE 1280,1024,32
screenwidth = 1280
screenheight = 1024

REM *** Load ball image ***
LOAD IMAGE "ball.bmp",1

REM *** Position and velocity variables ***
post AS PositionType
velocity AS VelocityType

REM *** Set position ***
post.x = 640
post.y = 512

REM *** Set Velocity ***
velocity.xoffset = 6
velocity.yoffset = -8

REM *** Set up sprite and move origin to centre ***
SPRITE 1, post.x,post.y,1
OFFSET SPRITE 1,16,16

REM *** Main loop ***
DO
   REM *** Update position of ball ***
   INC post.x,velocity.xoffset
   INC post.y,velocity.yoffset
   REM *** Redraw ball ***
   SPRITE 1,post.x,post.y,1
   WAIT 10
LOOP

REM *** End program ***
END
```

We still need to prevent the ball from disappearing off the edge of the screen. Of course, as before, we can check if the sprite is near the edge of the screen with a statement such as

```
IF post.x <8 OR post.x> screenwidth - 8
```

But, when the ball does reach the edge, we need to change its velocity so that it is deflected off that edge. The situation is similar to a snooker ball bouncing off the edge of the table. FIG-21.23 shows how a ball's velocity changes depending on the angle at which it hits the edge of the snooker table.

FIG-21.23

How a Round Object is Deflected by an Edge

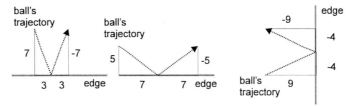

From the examples you can see that an object bounces off a smooth edge with a velocity which has the *y* component changed when the bottom (or top) wall is hit, and with a changed *x* component when a side wall is hit. Only the sign of the component changes, its absolute value remains unchanged.

To incorporate this into our program we need to produce code to implement the following logic:

```
IF the ball reaches the left or right limit THEN
        Change the sign of the velocity's x component
ENDIF
IF the ball reaches the top or bottom limit THEN
        Change the sign of the velocity's y component
ENDIF
```

This is coded as:

```
IF post.x < 8 OR post.x > screenwidth - 8
    velocity.xoffset = - velocity.xoffset
ENDIF
IF post.y < 8 OR post.y > screenheight - 8
    velocity.yoffset = -velocity.yoffset
ENDIF
```

Since the path of the ball is predictable, it won't make for an interesting game, so we could modify the velocity slightly by a random amount each time the ball hits the right or left edges by changing the line

```
velocity.xoffset = - velocity.xoffset
```

to

```
velocity.xoffset = -(velocity.xoffset + RND(2)-1)
```

which will add -1, 0, or 1 to the *xoffset* value. A similar statement should be used to add a slight randomness to the velocity when the top and bottom edges are reached.

Activity 21.24

Modify your program to add a random factor to both the *xoffset* and *yoffset* values.

There's a second way to measure velocity and that is to give the speed at which an object is travelling and the direction of travel. FIG-21.24 shows an example of how a ball's velocity would be represented using this approach.

FIG-21.24

Velocity as Speed and Direction

Notice that the angle is measured in a clockwise direction starting from the "12 o'clock" position. This has been chosen to tie in with the measurement used when rotating a sprite.

When using this approach in a program we can start by defining a new velocity structure:

```
TYPE VelocityType2
    speed AS FLOAT
    angle AS FLOAT
ENDTYPE
```

To move a sprite using such a structure, we need to employ a combination of ROTATE SPRITE and MOVE SPRITE as shown in LISTING-21.14.

LISTING-21.14

Using a Structure to Record Velocity

```
REM *** Set screen resolution ***
SET DISPLAY MODE 1280,1024,32

REM *** Load ball image ***
LOAD IMAGE "ball.bmp",1

TYPE VelocityType2
    speed AS FLOAT
    angle AS FLOAT
ENDTYPE

REM *** Velocity variable ***
velocity AS VelocityType2

REM *** Set Velocity ***
velocity.speed = 3
velocity.angle = 12

REM *** Set up sprite and move origin to centre ***
SPRITE 1,640,512,1
OFFSET SPRITE 1,16,16
```

continued on next page

LISTING-21.14
(continued)

Using a Structure to
Record Velocity

```
REM *** Rotate sprite to match velocity ***
ROTATE SPRITE 1, velocity.angle

REM *** Main loop ***
DO
   REM *** Move sprite at specified speed ***
   MOVE SPRITE 1,velocity.speed
   WAIT 10
LOOP

REM *** End program ***
END
```

Activity 21.25

Type in and test the program given in LISTING-21.14(*sprites16.dbpro*).

Modify the program so that a random angle between 0 and 360 is chosen and that the speed is set to a random value between 1 and 10.

When the edge of the screen is reached, the velocity must change, but this time we need to specify that change in terms of an angle. In FIG-21.25 we can see how the angle between the object and the edge is affected as the object collides with that edge.

FIG-21.25

How a Round Object is
Deflected Off an Edge

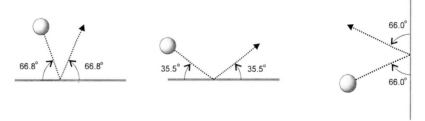

The diagram shows that the angle at which the ball approaches an edge matches the angle of departure. But this is the angle between edge and trajectory, not the angle of rotation of the sprite which is what we require for the program code.

Let's see how that angle changes by considering the sprite's velocity angle when a top or bottom edge is hit, as shown in FIG-21.26.

FIG-21.26

Measuring a Sprite's
Deflection for a Top
and Bottom Edge

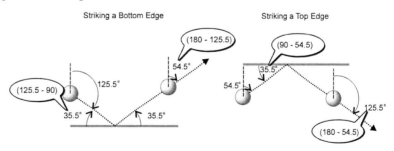

We can see from the results that, after a bottom edge is hit, the sprite's angle of rotation changes to *180 - its rotation on approach*. When a top edge is hit, the same formula applies:

new angle of rotation = 180 - the original angle of rotation.

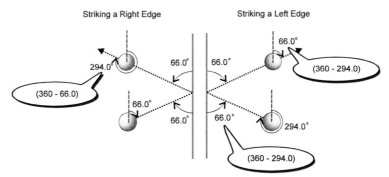
When we hit a left or right edge (as shown in FIG-21.27) the calculation is slightly different.

FIG-21.27

Measuring a Sprite's Deflection for a Right and Left Edge

This time the sprite's angle of rotation after collision is given by the expression

    360 - the approach angle

for both a left and right edge collision.

The trouble with using speed and direction to denote velocity is that we haven't recorded the actual position of the sprite, and without that we have no way of knowing when the sprite reaches the edge of the screen. To detect this, we'll need to convert every move (given as a speed and angle) into an x and y displacement. We need some maths to do the conversion, since the speed represents the hypotenuse of a right-angle triangle with the x and y offsets being the other two sides (see FIG-21.28).

FIG-21.28

How the x and y Offsets relate to the Direction and Speed

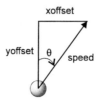

If this were a normal triangle we could use the following formulae to calculate the *xoffset* and *yoffset* values:

    xoffset = speed * $\cos\theta$
    yoffset = speed * $\sin\theta$

Unfortunately, we have to take into account that the offsets are sometimes negative values. To do this we must allow θ to range all the way from 0° to 360°. Also the sprite measures rotation from a vertical position while the mathematical functions measure from a horizontal origin (see FIG-21. 29).

FIG-21.29

Direction of Travel and Maths Functions Measure Angles from Different Starting Points

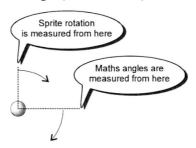

This means that a sprite which has not been rotated is considered to be at an angle of 270° when calculating sines, cosines and other mathematical functions (see FIG-21.30).

FIG-21.30

A Sprite's Initial Angle of Rotation as Measured from the Traditional Starting Position

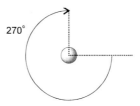

Angles can also be measured in an anti-clockwise direction and this gives a negative value as shown in FIG-21.31.

FIG-21.31

A Sprite's Angle Measured in an Anti-Clockwise Direction

We can see from the two diagrams above that 270° is exactly the same as -90°.

This means that the formulae for calculating the x and y offset values become:

    xoffset = speed * cos (sprite's rotation angle + 270)
    yoffset = speed * sin (sprite's rotation angle + 270)

or, alternatively

    xoffset = speed * cos (sprite's rotation angle -90)
    yoffset = speed * sin (sprite's rotation angle -90)

For the moment we'll use positive angle measurements only.

Now, if a sprite is rotated by 120° then the above calculation (sprite's rotation angle + 270) will give a value of 390°. But this is really just the same as a rotation of 30° (see FIG-21.32), so we need to make sure the angle always lies in the range 0 to 360.

FIG-21.32

Restraining the Angle of Rotation to a Range of 0 to 360

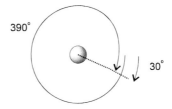

Luckily, we have the WRAPVALUE statement that we met back in Chapter 19. At last we have the formula we need to calculate the *xoffset* and *yoffset* values when only the speed and direction of the sprite is known. These are:

```
xoffset = speed * COS(WRAPVALUE(angle+270))
yoffset = speed * SIN(WRAPVALUE(angle+270))
```

In the next program (LISTING-21.15) the arrow sprite is placed in the centre of the screen, rotated by 60° and given a speed of 7 units. The position of the sprite is determined by calculating the offset values using the formulae given above.

```
IF post.y < 16 OR post.y > 1008
    velocity.angle = WRAPVALUE(180 - velocity.angle)
ENDIF
IF post.x < 16 OR post.x > 1264
    velocity.angle = WRAPVALUE(360 - velocity.angle)
ENDIF
```

LISTING-21.15

Dealing with Deflection as an Angle

```
REM *** Define required data types ***
TYPE VelocityType2
    speed AS FLOAT
    angle AS FLOAT
ENDTYPE

TYPE PositionType
   x AS FLOAT
   y AS FLOAT
ENDTYPE

velocity AS VelocityType2
post AS PositionType

REM *** Set screen resolution ***
SET DISPLAY MODE 1280,1024,32

REM *** Set up sprite with origin at centre ***
LOAD IMAGE "arrowtrans.bmp",1
SPRITE 1,640,512,1
OFFSET SPRITE 1,32,32

REM *** Set sprite speed and angle ***
velocity.speed = 7
velocity.angle = 60

REM *** Record sprite position ***
post.x = 640
post.y = 512

REM *** Rotate sprite ***
ROTATE SPRITE 1, velocity.angle

REM *** Main loop ***
DO
   MOVE SPRITE 1, velocity.speed
   REM *** Calculate new position ***
   post.x = post.x + velocity.speed *
               ↳COS(WRAPVALUE(velocity.angle+270))
   post.y = post.y + velocity.speed *
               ↳SIN(WRAPVALUE(velocity.angle+270))
   SET CURSOR 0,900
   PRINT "x: ",post.x
   PRINT " y : ",post.y
   PRINT "angle : ",velocity.angle
   REM *** Check for top or bottom edge hit ***
   IF post.y < 16 OR post.y > 1008
```

continued on next page

LISTING-21.15
(continued)

Dealing with Deflection as
an Angle

```
        velocity.angle = WRAPVALUE(180 - velocity.angle)
    ENDIF
    REM *** Check for side hit ***
    IF post.x < 16 OR post.x > 1264
        velocity.angle = WRAPVALUE(360 - velocity.angle)
    ENDIF
    ROTATE SPRITE 1,velocity.angle
LOOP

REM *** End program ***
END
```

Activity 21.27

Type in and test the program given in LISTING-21.15 (*sprites17.dbpro*).

Sprites and the PRINT Statement

When a program uses sprites, the screen is automatically redrawn several times per second. When doing this, the program examines all the bitmaps, images and sprites that are currently on the screen and redraws them. However, a problem arises if you want to display text using the PRINT statement at the same time as using sprites. We can see what that problem is by running the short program in LISTING-21.16.

LISTING-21.16

Using the PRINT
Statement with Sprites

```
REM *** Set screen resolution ***
SET DISPLAY MODE 1280,1024,32

REM *** Create sprite ***
LOAD IMAGE "ball.bmp",1
SPRITE 1,640,512,1

REM *** Display text ***
PRINT "Hello"

REM *** End program ***
WAIT KEY
END
```

Activity 21.28

Type in and test the program given above (*sprites18.dbpro*).

If we want the text to remain on the screen, then we must place the PRINT statement within a loop structure such as

```
DO
    PRINT "Hello"
LOOP
```

However, this code would cause the word *Hello* to be displayed on a new line each time the PRINT statement is executed. To avoid this, we could include a SET CURSOR statement:

```
DO
    SET CURSOR 100,100
    PRINT "Hello"
LOOP
```

In a more dynamic program, other statements would appear within the DO..LOOP structure. For example, statements to move the sprite.

Summary

- The image from which a sprite is formed must first be loaded into an image object.

- The SPRITE statement creates a sprite from an image object.

- The SPRITE statement can also be used to reposition a sprite on the screen.

- The PASTE SPRITE statement can also be used to reposition an existing sprite.

- A sprite's origin is initially at the top-left of the sprite.

- A sprite's origin can be moved using the OFFSET SPRITE statement.

- A sprite can be rotated about it's origin using the ROTATE SPRITE statement.

- A sprite's angle of rotation is measured in degrees from a "12 o'clock" baseline in a clockwise direction.

- The MOVE SPRITE statement moves a sprite along a line which is determined by the sprite's angle of rotation.

- MIRROR SPRITE reflects a sprite about its y-axis.

- FLIP SPRITE reflects a sprite about its x-axis.

- By default, any black portions of a sprite will appear transparent on screen.

- By using the SPRITE, ROTATE SPRITE and MOVE SPRITE commands in response to key presses, the user can be given control of sprite movement.

- A moving sprite can have its velocity recorded as a pair of values.

- A velocity can be recorded as *xoffset* and *yoffset* values or as direction and speed values.

- A uniform object rebounds from a flat edge at the same angle as the approach.

Solutions

Activity 21.1

```
SPRITE 5,150,50,1
```

Activity 21.2

No solution required.

Activity 21.3

```
REM *** Set screen resolution ***
SET DISPLAY MODE 1280,1024,32
REM *** Load image; transfer to sprite ***
LOAD IMAGE "arrow.bmp", 1
SPRITE 1,100,200,1
REM *** Move arrow ***
WAIT KEY
SPRITE 1,150,20,1
REM *** End program ***
WAIT KEY
END
```

Activity 21.4

```
REM *** Set screen resolution ***
SET DISPLAY MODE 1280,1024,32
REM *** Seed randomiser ***
RANDOMIZE TIMER()
REM *** Load image;transfer to sprite ***
LOAD IMAGE "arrow.bmp", 1
SPRITE 1,100,200,1
REM *** Reposition sprite randomly ***
FOR c = 1 TO 20
   PASTE SPRITE 1, RND(600),RND(500)
   WAIT 500
NEXT c
REM *** End program ***
WAIT KEY
END
```

Activity 21.5

```
REM *** Set screen resolution ***
SET DISPLAY MODE 1280,1024,32
REM *** Seed randomiser ***
RANDOMIZE TIMER()
REM *** Load image; transfer to sprite ***
LOAD IMAGE "arrow.bmp", 1
SPRITE 1,100,200,1
REM *** Move sprite up  ***
WAIT KEY
MOVE SPRITE 1,100
REM *** Move sprite down ***
WAIT KEY
MOVE SPRITE 1,-250
REM *** End program ***
WAIT KEY
END
```

Activity 21.6

No solution required.

Activity 21.7

```
REM *** Set screen resolution ***
SET DISPLAY MODE 1280,1024,32
REM *** Load image; transfer to sprite ***
LOAD IMAGE "arrow.bmp", 1
```

```
SPRITE 1,100,200,1
REM *** Move sprite up ***
WAIT KEY
MOVE SPRITE 1,21
REM *** Move sprite down ***
WAIT KEY
MOVE SPRITE 1,-21
REM *** Rotate sprite by 45 degrees ***
WAIT KEY
ROTATE SPRITE 1,45
REM *** Move sprite right ***
WAIT KEY
MOVE SPRITE 1,40
REM *** Move sprite left ***
WAIT KEY
MOVE SPRITE 1,-40
REM *** End program ***
WAIT KEY
END
```

When rotation is changed to 45°, the sprite moves diagonally.

Activity 21.8

The sprite's position moves slightly since the new origin (in the middle of the sprite) is placed at position (100,200).

Activity 21.9

```
REM *** Set screen resolution ***
SET DISPLAY MODE 1280,1024,32
REM *** Load image; transfer to sprite ***
LOAD IMAGE "arrow.bmp", 1
SPRITE 1,100,200,1
REM *** Move sprite's origin ***
OFFSET SPRITE 1,32,32
REM *** Rotate sprite in increments ***
FOR angle = 0 TO 360
   ROTATE SPRITE 1,angle
   WAIT 10
NEXT angle
REM *** End program ***
WAIT KEY
END
```

The sprite now rotates about its centre rather than about the top-left corner.

Activity 21.10

No solution required.

Activity 21.11

```
REM *** Set screen resolution ***
SET DISPLAY MODE 1280, 1024, 32
REM *** Load image; transfer to sprite ***
LOAD IMAGE "arrow.bmp", 1
SPRITE 1,100,200,1
REM *** Flip sprite ***
WAIT KEY
FLIP SPRITE 1
REM *** Move sprite ***
WAIT KEY
MOVE SPRITE 1,60
REM *** Mirror sprite ***
WAIT KEY
MIRROR SPRITE 1
```

```
REM *** Move sprite ***
WAIT KEY
MOVE SPRITE 1, 60
REM *** End program ***
WAIT KEY
END
```

The change makes no difference to the movement of the sprite.

Activity 21.12

```
REM *** Set screen resolution ***
SET DISPLAY MODE 1280,1024,32
REM *** Load image; transfer to sprite ***
LOAD IMAGE "arrow.bmp",1
SPRITE 1,100,200,1
REM *** Move origin to centre ***
OFFSET SPRITE 1,32,32
REM *** Rotate sprite ***
WAIT KEY
ROTATE SPRITE 1,60
REM *** Flip sprite ***
WAIT KEY
FLIP SPRITE 1
REM *** End program ***
WAIT KEY
END
```

Activity 21.13

```
REM *** Set screen resolution ***
SET DISPLAY MODE 1280,1024,32
REM *** Load image; transfer to sprite ***
LOAD IMAGE "arrowtrans.bmp",1
SPRITE 1,100,200,1
REM *** Move origin to centre ***
OFFSET SPRITE 1,32,32
REM *** Rotate sprite ***
WAIT KEY
ROTATE SPRITE 1,60
REM *** Flip sprite ***
WAIT KEY
FLIP SPRITE 1
REM *** End program ***
WAIT KEY
END
```

Activity 21.14

```
REM *** Set screen resolution ***
SET DISPLAY MODE 1280,1024,32
REM *** Load image; transfer to sprite ***
LOAD IMAGE "arrowtrans.bmp", 1
SPRITE 1,100,200,1
REM *** Main loop ***
DO
   REM *** Read a key ***
   ch$ = INKEY$()
   REM *** IF it's ' move arrow up ***
   IF ch$ = "'"
      MOVE SPRITE 1,2
   ELSE
      REM *** IF it's / move arrow down ***
      IF ch$ = "/"
         MOVE SPRITE 1,-2
      ENDIF
   ENDIF
LOOP
REM *** End program ***
END
```

Activity 21.15

```
REM *** Set screen resolution ***
SET DISPLAY MODE 1280,1024,32
REM *** Load image; transfer to sprite ***
LOAD IMAGE "arrowtrans.bmp", 1
SPRITE 1,100,200,1
REM *** Rotate sprite through 45 degrees ***
ROTATE SPRITE 1,45
REM *** Main Loop ***
DO
   REM *** Read a key ***
   key = SCANCODE()
   REM *** IF it's x move arrow right ***
   IF key = 45
      MOVE SPRITE 1,1
   ELSE
      REM *** IF it's z move arrow left ***
      IF key = 44
         MOVE SPRITE 1,-1.0
      ENDIF
   ENDIF
LOOP
REM *** End program ***
END
```

You should notice that sprite movement is much smoother when using the SCANCODE approach.

Activity 21.16

No solution required.

Activity 21.17

```
REM *** Set screen resolution ***
SET DISPLAY MODE 1280,1024,32
REM *** Load image; transfer to sprite ***
LOAD IMAGE "arrowtrans.bmp", 1
SPRITE 1,100,200,1
REM *** Move sprite origin to centre ***
OFFSET SPRITE 1,32,32
REM *** Set the angle ***
angle = 0
REM *** Main Loop ***
DO
   REM *** Set movement ***
   move = 0
   REM *** Read a key and respond ***
   key = SCANCODE()
   SELECT key
      CASE 30 `*** a: decrease angle ***
         DEC angle
      ENDCASE
      CASE 31 `*** s: increase angle ***
         INC angle
      ENDCASE
      CASE 44 ` z:*** Move back ***
         move = -5
      ENDCASE
      CASE 45 `*** x: Move forward ***
         move = 5
      ENDCASE
   ENDSELECT
   REM *** Rotate/Move sprite ***
   ROTATE SPRITE 1, angle
   MOVE SPRITE 1, move
LOOP
REM *** End program ***
END
```

Activity 21.18

The sprite can be moved to any position - even off screen.

Activity 21.19

```
REM *** Set screen resolution ***
SET DISPLAY MODE 1280,1024,32
REM *** Set up width and height values ***
screenwidth = 1280
screenheight = 1024
REM *** Load image; transfer to sprite ***
LOAD IMAGE "arrowtrans.bmp", 1
REM *** Set the position ***
x = 640
y = 512
REM *** Load sprite ***
SPRITE 1,x,y,1
REM *** Move sprite origin to centre ***
OFFSET SPRITE 1,32,32
REM *** Main Loop ***
DO
    REM *** Read a key ***
    key = SCANCODE()
    SELECT key
        CASE 33  ` up (f)
            IF y >= 5
                DEC y,5
            ENDIF
        ENDCASE
        CASE 46  ` down (c)
            IF y < screenheight-5
                INC y,5
            ENDIF
        ENDCASE
        CASE 44  ` left (z)
            IF x >= 5
                DEC x,5
            ENDIF
        ENDCASE
        CASE 45  ` right (x)
            IF x < screenwidth - 5
                INC x,5
            ENDIF
        ENDCASE
    ENDSELECT
    REM *** Move sprite ***
    SPRITE 1,x,y,1
LOOP
REM *** End program ***
END
```

Activity 21.20

```
REM *** Define type ***
TYPE PositionType
    x  AS INTEGER
    y  AS INTEGER
ENDTYPE
REM *** Variable for sprite's location ***
post AS PositionType
REM *** Set screen resolution ***
SET DISPLAY MODE 1280,1024,32
REM *** Set up width and height values ***
screenwidth = 1280
screenheight = 1024
REM *** Load image; transfer to sprite ***
LOAD IMAGE "arrowtrans.bmp", 1
REM *** Set the position ***
post.x = 640
post.y = 512
REM *** Load sprite ***
SPRITE 1,post.x,post.y,1
REM *** Move sprite origin to centre ***
OFFSET SPRITE 1,32,32
REM *** Main Loop ***
DO
    REM *** Read a key ***
    key = SCANCODE()
    SELECT key
        CASE 33  ` up (f)
```

```
            IF post.y >= 5
                DEC post.y,5
            ENDIF
        ENDCASE
        CASE 46  ` down (c)
            IF post.y < screenheight-5
                INC post.y,5
            ENDIF
        ENDCASE
        CASE 44  ` left (z)
            IF post.x >= 5
                DEC post.x,5
            ENDIF
        ENDCASE
        CASE 45  ` right (x)
            IF post.x < screenwidth-5
                INC post.x,5
            ENDIF
        ENDCASE
    ENDSELECT
    SPRITE 1,post.x,post.y,1
LOOP
REM *** End program ***
END
```

Activity 21.21

$v_1 = [6,-8]$
$v_2 = [-6,-8]$
$v_3 = [-6,8]$
$v_4 = [6,8]$

Activity 21.22

No solution required.

Activity 21.23

```
REM *** Set up Data types used ***
TYPE PositionType
    x AS INTEGER
    y AS INTEGER
ENDTYPE
TYPE VelocityType
    xoffset AS FLOAT
    yoffset AS FLOAT
ENDTYPE
REM *** Set screen resolution ***
SET DISPLAY MODE 1280,1024,32
screenwidth = 1280
screenheight = 1024
REM *** Load ball image ***
LOAD IMAGE "ball.bmp",1
REM *** Position and velocity variables ***
post AS PositionType
velocity AS VelocityType
REM *** Set position ***
post.x = 640
post.y = 512
REM *** Set Velocity ***
velocity.xoffset = 6
velocity.yoffset = -8
REM *** Create sprite;origin to centre ***
SPRITE 1,post.x,post.y,1
OFFSET SPRITE 1,16,16
REM *** Main loop ***
DO
    REM *** Update position of ball ***
    IF post.x < 8 OR post.x >
    screenwidth - 8
        velocity.xoffset = - velocity.xoffset
    ENDIF
    IF post.y < 8 OR post.y >
    screenheight - 8
```

```
        velocity.yoffset = - velocity.yoffset
    ENDIF
    INC post.x,velocity.xoffset
    INC post.y,velocity.yoffset
    REM *** Redraw ball ***
    SPRITE 1,post.x,post.y,1
    WAIT 10
LOOP
REM *** End program ***
END
```

Activity 21.24

```
REM *** Set up Data types used ***
TYPE PositionType
    x AS INTEGER
    y AS INTEGER
ENDTYPE
TYPE VelocityType
    xoffset AS FLOAT
    yoffset AS FLOAT
ENDTYPE
REM *** Seed random number generator ***
RANDOMIZE TIMER()
REM *** Set screen resolution ***
SET DISPLAY MODE 1280, 1024,32
screenwidth = 1280
screenheight = 1024
REM *** Load ball image ***
LOAD IMAGE "ball.bmp",1
REM *** Position and velocity variables ***
post AS PositionType
velocity AS VelocityType
REM *** Set position ***
post.x = 640
post.y = 512
REM *** Set Velocity ***
velocity.xoffset = 6
velocity.yoffset = -8
REM *** Set up sprite and move origin to
centre ***
SPRITE 1, position.x,position.y,1
OFFSET SPRITE 1, 16,16
REM *** Main loop ***
DO
    REM *** Update position of ball ***
    IF post.x < 8 OR
    post.x > screenwidth - 8
        velocity.xoffset =
          -(velocity.xoffset + RND(2)-1)
    ENDIF
    IF post.y < 8 OR
    post.y > screenheight - 8
        velocity.yoffset =
          -(velocity.yoffset + RND(2)-1)
    ENDIF
    INC post.x,velocity.xoffset
    INC post.y,velocity.yoffset
    REM *** Redraw ball ***
    SPRITE 1,post.x,post.y,1
    WAIT 10
LOOP
REM *** End program ***
END
```

Activity 21.25

```
REM *** Seed random number generator ***
RANDOMIZE TIMER()
REM *** Set screen resolution ***
SET DISPLAY MODE 1280, 1024,32
REM *** Load ball image ***
LOAD IMAGE "ball1.bmp",1
TYPE VelocityType2
    speed AS FLOAT
    angle AS FLOAT
```

```
ENDTYPE
REM *** Velocity variable ***
velocity AS VelocityType2
REM *** Set Velocity ***
velocity.speed = RND(9)+1
velocity.angle = RND(360)
REM *** Set up sprite and move origin ***
SPRITE 1, 640,512,1
OFFSET SPRITE 1, 16,16
REM *** Rotate sprite to direction ***
ROTATE SPRITE 1, velocity.angle
REM *** Main loop ***
DO
    REM *** Move sprite at spec'd speed ***
    MOVE SPRITE 1,velocity.speed
    WAIT 10
LOOP
REM *** End program ***
END
```

Activity 21.26

a = 35.5
b = 305.5
c = -54.5
d = 35.5
e = 234.5
f = -125.5

Activity 21.27

No solution required.

Activity 21.28

The word *Hello* appears briefly and then disappears.

Activity 21.29

```
REM *** Set screen resolution ***
SET DISPLAY MODE 1280, 1024, 32
REM *** Create sprite ***
LOAD IMAGE "ball.bmp",1
SPRITE 1, 640,512,1
REM *** Display text ***
DO
    SET CURSOR 100,100
    PRINT "Hello"
LOOP
REM *** End program ***
WAIT KEY
END
```

The word *Hello* no longer disappears from the screen.

Cloning Sprites

Creating a Scrolling Background

Diffuse Settings

Reshaping Sprites

Setting Sprite Transparency

Setting the Screen Background

Showing and Hiding Sprites

Sprite Priority

Changing a Sprite's Appearance

Introduction

We now know how to create and move a sprite, but there are many more commands which allow us to control and manipulate sprites. These commands are introduced in this section.

Resizing Sprites

By default the size of a sprite is determined by the size of the image that is loaded into the sprite. Hence, in our previous examples, sprites have been 64 by 64 pixels or 32 by 32 pixels simply because that has been the size of the images they contained. However, we can scale the size of a sprite using two statements.

The SCALE SPRITE Statement

We can magnify or shrink a sprite using the SCALE SPRITE statement. This statement has the format shown in FIG-22.1.

FIG-22.1

The SCALE SPRITE Statement

In the diagram:

  spriteno   is the integer value of the sprite to be scaled.

  percentage   is an integer value giving the new size of the sprite
                        as a percentage of the original's size.
                        (e.g. 200 - double size, 50 - half size)

To double the size of sprite 1 we would use the statement:

```
SCALE SPRITE 1, 200
```

The program in LISTING-22.1 first doubles, then halves the size of a ball sprite. Each change in size is initiated by a key press.

LISTING-22.1

Scaling a Sprite

```
REM *** Set screen resolution ***
SET DISPLAY MODE 1280,1024,32

REM *** Load image and transfer to sprite ***
LOAD IMAGE "ball.bmp", 1
SPRITE 1,100,200,1

REM *** Make sprite larger ***
WAIT KEY
SCALE SPRITE 1,200
REM *** Make sprite smaller ***
WAIT KEY
SCALE SPRITE 1,50

REM *** End program ***
WAIT KEY
END
```

Notice that the scaling factor is always based on the sprite's original size. Hence the line SCALE SPRITE 1, 50 does not shrink the sprite back to its original size, but to half that of the original.

Activity 22.1

Type in and test the program given above (*sprites201.dbpro*).

One use of this command is to give the impression that the sprite is either moving away from the user (shrinking) or heading towards the user (growing). The program in LISTING-22.2 shows the ball moving towards the user. The main work of the program is done by a FOR loop which changes the sprite's scale each time the loop is iterated.

LISTING-22.2

Moving a Sprite Towards the Viewer

```
REM *** Set screen resolution ***
SET DISPLAY MODE 1280,1024,32
REM *** Load image and transfer to sprite ***
LOAD IMAGE "ball.bmp", 1
SPRITE 1,100,200,1

REM *** Make sprite larger ***
FOR c = 1 TO 100
    SCALE SPRITE 1,(50+c*2)
    WAIT 10
NEXT c

REM *** End program ***
WAIT KEY
END
```

Activity 22.2

Type in and test the program given above (*sprites202.dbpro*).

Modify the program so that the ball moves away from the user rather than towards him.

Notice that, as the sprite becomes much larger than the image size, the individual pixels become obtrusive.

The STRETCH SPRITE Statement

A limitation of the SCALE SPRITE commands is that both the width and height of the sprite are changed by the same amount. However, there will be times when you may wish to change only one dimension of the sprite. To do that we need to use the STRETCH SPRITE statement which takes the form shown in FIG-22.2.

FIG-22.2

The STRETCH SPRITE Statement

In the diagram:

spriteno	is the integer value of the sprite to be stretched.
wperc	is a real value representing the new width of the sprite as a percentage of its original width.

| | *hperc* | is the new height of the sprite as a percentage of its original height. |

We could half the height of a 64 x 64 sprite without affecting its width using the

```
STRETCH SPRITE 1,100,50
```

To return the sprite to its original dimensions we would then use the line

```
STRETCH SPRITE 100,100
```

The SIZE SPRITE Statement

The SIZE SPRITE statement performs an identical function to the STRETCH SPRITE command, but uses a different unit of measurement for the width and height parameters. The SIZE SPRITE statement takes the form shown in FIG-22.3.

FIG-22.3

The SIZE SPRITE Statement

In the diagram:

	spriteno	is the number of the sprite to be scaled.
	xsize	is an integer value specifying the new height of the sprite in pixels.
	ysize	is an integer value specifying the new width of the sprite in pixels.

We could half the height of a 64 x 64 sprite without affecting its width using the line:

```
SIZE SPRITE 1,64,32
```

Changing Transparency and Colour Brightness

The SET SPRITE ALPHA Statement

The SET SPRITE ALPHA command allows us to make the whole sprite transparent. The degree of transparency can be set from opaque (normal) to completely invisible. This statement has the format shown in FIG-22.4.

FIG-22.4

The SET SPRITE ALPHA Statement

In the diagram:

| | *spriteno* | is the number of the sprite to be modified. |
| | *alphavalue* | is an integer value. This value is assigned to the sprite's alpha channel setting. (0 - invisible; 255 - opaque) |

For example, in the following code (see LISTING-22.3) two ring sprites are created, one is normal, the other has an alpha channel setting of 150.

LISTING-22.3

Setting a Sprite's
Transparency

```
REM *** Set screen resolution ***
SET DISPLAY MODE 1280,1024,32

REM *** Load image ... ***
LOAD IMAGE "ring.bmp",1

REM ... and copy into two sprites ***
SPRITE 1,100,100,1
SPRITE 2,160,100,1

REM *** Make first sprite translucent ***
WAIT KEY
SET SPRITE ALPHA 1,150

REM *** End program ***
WAIT KEY
END
```

Activity 22.3

Type in and test the program in LISTING-22.3 (*sprites203.dbpro*).

Vary the alpha settings for sprite 1 and observe the effects of these changes.

The SET SPRITE DIFFUSE Statement

The SET SPRITE DIFFUSE statement allows you to modify the strength of the individual red, green and blue components that make up a sprite's image. For example, you might want to change the tint of a sprite to red to show that it is in danger. This statement takes the format shown in FIG-22.5.

FIG-22.5

The SET SPRITE
DIFFUSE Statement

In the diagram:

spriteno	is the number of the sprite to be tinted.
red	is an integer value representing the emphasis to be given to the red component of the sprite. (0 - colour off; 255 - colour at full)
green	is an integer value representing the emphasis to be given to the green component of the sprite. (0 - colour off; 255 - colour at full)
blue	is an integer value representing the emphasis to be given to the blue component of the sprite. (0 - colour off; 255 - colour at full)

The program in LISTING-22.4 displays two identical sprites and then varies the diffuse settings in the first sprite.

LISTING-22.4

Changing the Diffuse Settings of a Sprite

```
REM *** Set screen resolution ***
SET DISPLAY MODE 1280,1024,32

REM *** Load image ... ***
LOAD IMAGE "flag.bmp", 1

REM ... and copy into two sprites ***
SPRITE 1,100,100,1
SPRITE 2,300,100,1

REM *** Change diffuse settings of each colour of sprite 1 ***
WAIT KEY
FOR diffuse = 0 TO 255
   SET SPRITE DIFFUSE 1,diffuse,255-diffuse,diffuse
   WAIT 10
NEXT diffuse

REM *** End program ***
WAIT KEY
END
```

Activity 22.4

Type in and test the program in LISTING-22.4 (*sprites204.dbpro*).

Modify the program so that *pheasant.bmp* is used in place of *flag.bmp*.

Modify the SET SPRITE DIFFUSE statement so that all three colours start with a diffuse setting of 0 and end with a value of 255.

Showing and Hiding Sprites

The HIDE SPRITE Statement

By default, a sprite is visible on the screen, but we can make any sprite invisible by using the HIDE SPRITE command, which has the format shown in FIG-22.6.

FIG-22.6

The HIDE SPRITE Statement

In the diagram:

    spriteno   is the number of the sprite to be hidden.

For example, the statement

```
HIDE SPRITE 1
```

would cause the image of sprite 1 to disappear from the screen.

Activity 22.5

Modify *sprites204.dbpro* so that sprite 1 is hidden after the FOR loop is complete.

The SHOW SPRITE Statement

Any sprite which has been hidden (using the HIDE SPRITE statement) can be displayed again using the SHOW SPRITE statement, which takes the form shown in FIG-22.7.

FIG-22.7

The SHOW SPRITE
Statement

In the diagram:

    spriteno   is the number of the sprite to be reshown

Activity 22.6

Modify *sprites204.dbpro* again so that sprite 1 reappears after the user presses a key.

The HIDE ALL SPRITES Statement

If there are several sprites on the screen and you need all of them to be hidden, then the HIDE ALL SPRITES statement can be used. This takes the format shown in FIG-22.8.

FIG-22.8

The HIDE ALL SPRITES
Statement

The SHOW ALL SPRITES Statement

Similarly, we can display every sprite using the SHOW ALL SPRITES statement which uses the format shown in FIG-22.9.

FIG-22.9

The SHOW ALL
SPRITES Statement

Duplicating a Sprite

The CLONE SPRITE Statement

Obviously we can create a new sprite that contains the same image as an existing sprite using the SPRITE statement, but if we want to make an exact copy of a sprite that has already been rotated, stretched, or had some other change made to it since it was created, then we need to use the CLONE SPRITE statement. This statement creates an exact copy of a specified sprite, retaining all the current settings (rotation, transparency, etc.) of the sprite being copied. The statement has the format shown in FIG-22.10.

FIG-22.10

The CLONE SPRITE
Statement

In the diagram:

origspriteno   is the number of the sprite to be copied.

newspriteno   is the integer value to be assigned to the duplicate sprite that is being created.

The new sprite is created at exactly the same position on the screen as the sprite being copied so, most of the time, we'll want to move the copy. Once created, changes to either sprite, the original or copy, affects the specified sprite only.

The program in LISTING-22.5 demonstrates the duplication of an existing sprite. The new sprite is then moved to a new position.

LISTING-22.5

Cloning a Sprite

```
REM *** Set screen resolution ***
SET DISPLAY MODE 1280,1024,32

REM *** Create first sprite ***
LOAD IMAGE "arrowtrans.bmp",1
SPRITE 1,600,500,1

REM *** Rotate and shrink sprite ***
WAIT KEY
OFFSET SPRITE 1,32,32
ROTATE SPRITE 1,45
SCALE SPRITE 1,75

REM *** Duplicate sprite ***
WAIT KEY
CLONE SPRITE 1,2

REM *** Move new sprite ***
WAIT KEY
MOVE SPRITE 2,100

REM *** End program ***
WAIT KEY
END
```

Activity 22.7

Type in and test the program given above (*sprites205.dbpro*).

Modify the program to create a second copy of the original sprite, rotate it by 90° and move it 200 pixels.

Summary

- A sprite can be resized using the SCALE SPRITE statement.

- A sprite can be reshaped using the STRETCH SPRITE or SIZE SPRITE statements.

- The transparency of a sprite can be altered using the SET SPRITE ALPHA statement.

- The diffuse setting of the primary colours in a sprite can be modified using the SET SPRITE DIFFUSE statement.

- Individual sprites can be made invisible using the HIDE SPRITE statement and reshown with the SHOW SPRITE statement.

- All sprites can be made invisible using the HIDE ALL SPRITES and visible using the SHOW ALL SPRITES statement.

- A sprite can be duplicated using the CLONE SPRITE statement.

- A duplicated sprite retains the current settings of the sprite being copied.

- Subsequent changes to the original sprite or the duplicate sprite effects the specified sprite only.

Adding a Background

Introduction

Possibly, by this time you have grown a bit bored with the blue screen background that appears in every program that uses a sprite. Luckily, there are a few ways in which we can make the background a little more interesting. These techniques and the statements they use are explained below.

Ways to Change the Background

The COLOR BACKDROP Statement

The COLOR BACKDROP statement allows us to specify the colour of the screen background when using sprites. The statement has the format shown in FIG-22.11.

FIG-22.11

The COLOR
BACKDROP Statement

In the diagram:

> *colour*　　　　　　　　is an integer value representing the new background colour.

To set the background colour to black we would use the statement

```
COLOR BACKGROUND 0
```

but for other colours we would probably use an RGB statement, as in the line

```
COLOR BACKGROUND RGB(255,255,0)
```

The BACKDROP ON Statement

There's another stage in changing the background: we need to activate the new background we've set up. This is done using the BACKDROP ON statement which has the format shown in FIG-22.12.

FIG-22.12

The BACKDROP ON
Statement

The next program (see LISTING-22.6) displays the arrow sprite on a black background.

LISTING-22.6

Changing the Screen
Background

```
REM *** Set screen resolution ***
SET DISPLAY MODE 1280,1024,32

REM *** Create first sprite ***
LOAD IMAGE "arrowtrans.bmp",1
SPRITE 1,600,500,1
```

LISTING-22.6
(continued)

Changing the Screen
Background

```
REM *** Change background to black ***
WAIT KEY
COLOR BACKDROP 0
BACKDROP ON

REM *** End program ***
WAIT KEY
END
```

Activity 22.8

Type in and test the program given in LISTING-22.6 (*sprites206.dbpro*).

Change the background colour to yellow.

The BACKDROP OFF Statement

We can revert to the normal blue background by using the BACKDROP OFF statement which has the format shown in FIG-22.13.

FIG-22.13

The BACKDROP OFF
Statement

Activity 22.9

Modify your last program so that the background reverts to its blue colour after a key press.

Using a Sprite as a Background

A second way to create a more interesting background is to use a sprite. Of course it has to be rather a large one!

We can see an example of this in LISTING-22.7.

LISTING-22.7

Using a Large Sprite as
the Background

```
REM *** Set screen resolution ***
SET DISPLAY MODE 1280,1024,32

REM *** Load large image as background ***
LOAD IMAGE "background1.bmp",2
SPRITE 1001,0,0,2

REM *** Create first sprite ***
LOAD IMAGE "arrowtrans.bmp",1
SPRITE 1,600,500,1

REM *** End program ***
WAIT KEY
END
```

Activity 22.10

Type in and test the program given in LISTING-22.7 (*sprites207.dbpro*).

Modify the program to use your own background image.

DarkBASIC Pro: Sprites 2

Sprite Order

In your last program, the arrow sprite appears in front of the background sprite. Which sprite is "in front" is determined by the order in which sprites are created, with the last sprite to be created being at the front.

Activity 22.11

Modify your last program so that the arrow sprite is created first.

How does this affect what is displayed on the screen?

Return the program to its original state.

By taking care about the order in which sprites are placed, we can make one sprite pass behind another. This technique is demonstrated in LISTING-22.8 where the arrow sprite passes behind a tree sprite.

LISTING-22.8

Demonstrating Sprite Order

```
REM *** Set screen resolution ***
SET DISPLAY MODE 1280,1024,32

REM *** Load large image as background ***
LOAD IMAGE "background1.bmp",2
SPRITE 1001,0,0,2

REM *** Create first sprite ***
LOAD IMAGE "arrowtrans.bmp",1
SPRITE 1,600,500,1

LOAD IMAGE "tree.bmp",3
SPRITE 501,100,250,3

REM *** Move arrow past tree ***
FOR x = 600 TO 50 STEP -10
   SPRITE 1,x,500,1
   WAIT 20
NEXT x

REM *** End program ***
WAIT KEY
END
```

Activity 22.12

Type in and test the program in LISTING-22.15 (*sprites208.dbpro*).

The SET SPRITE PRIORITY Statement

The order in which sprites are drawn is known as **sprite priority**. The default is, as we saw in the last program, that sprites are drawn in the order in which they are created. But this can be changed. For example, we can force the sprite which is created first to be drawn last, and hence come to the front of the screen. This is done using the SET SPRITE PRIORITY statement, which has the format shown in FIG-22.14.

FIG-22.14

The SET SPRITE PRIORITY Statement

In the diagram:

spriteno	is the number of the sprite whose priority is to be set.
priority	is an integer value specifying the priority to be given to the sprite. By default, all sprites have a priority of zero. The sprite with the highest priority is drawn last.

For example, if a program contained three sprites numbered 1, 2, and 3, we could ensure that sprite 2 was drawn last using the line

```
SET SPRITE PRIORITY 2,1
```

Activity 22.13

Modify your last program so that, by using the SET SPRITE PRIORITY statement, the arrow sprite moves in front of the tree rather than behind it.

The SET SPRITE TEXTURE COORD Statement

The image placed in a sprite is also known as the sprite's texture.

A sprite and the image it contains are, by default, perfectly aligned. That is to say, that the top left corner of the image becomes the top left corner of the sprite. But it is possible to change this using the SET SPRITE TEXTURE COORD statement.

We can think of the link between the image and the sprite as being similar to sticking a photograph onto a piece of cardboard. Normally, the four corners all match up (see FIG-22.15).

FIG-22.15

Linking an Image to a Sprite

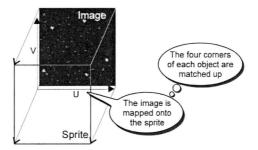

The four corners of the sprite are numbered 0 to 3 and the coordinates of the image are (0.0,0.0) for the top-left corner and (1.0,1.0) for the bottom right (see FIG-22.16). The image coordinates, rather than being measured along x and y axes are measured against U and V axes.

FIG-22.16

Default Image/Sprite Mapping

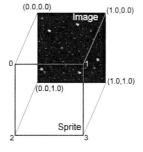

Using the SET SPRITE TEXTURE COORD statement we can explicitly state

which part of the image is to map to each corner of the sprite. For example we can define the default mapping of sprite 1 using the lines:

```
SET SPRITE TEXTURE COORD 1,0,0.0,0.0
SET SPRITE TEXTURE COORD 1,1,1.0,0.0
SET SPRITE TEXTURE COORD 1,2,0.0,1.0
SET SPRITE TEXTURE COORD 1,3,1.0,1.0
```

FIG-22.17

The SET SPRITE
TEXTURE Statement

The SET SPRITE TEXTURE COORD statement has the format shown in FIG-22.17.

In the diagram:

spriteno   is the number of the sprite whose texture
                         mapping is to be changed.

corner   is an integer value in the range 0 to 3 specifying
                         which corner of the sprite is being given a new
                         mapping value.

Uvalue, Vvalue   is a pair of real values representing the part of the
                         image to be mapped to that corner.

In the next program (see LISTING-22.9) we see the effect of changing the mapping of the sprite's texture by changing each corner in turn. Initially, the image uses its default mapping to the sprite, then the top left corner of the sprite is mapped to the middle of the image (0.5,0.5), after that each corner is remapped using a displacement from its normal setting of 0.5 in both directions.

LISTING-22.9

Changing the Texture
Mapping of a Sprite

```
REM *** Set screen resolution ***
SET DISPLAY MODE 1280,1024,32

REM *** Create sprite ***
LOAD IMAGE "FourSquare.bmp",1
SPRITE 1001,0,0,1

REM *** Change sprite texture mapping one corner at a time ***
WAIT KEY
SET SPRITE TEXTURE COORD 1001,0,0.5,0.5
WAIT KEY
SET SPRITE TEXTURE COORD 1001,1,1.5,0.5
WAIT KEY
SET SPRITE TEXTURE COORD 1001,2,0.5,1.5
WAIT KEY
SET SPRITE TEXTURE COORD 1001,3,1.5,1.5

REM *** End program ***
WAIT KEY
END
```

Activity 22.14

Type in and test the program in LISTING-22.9 (*sprites209.dbpro*).

Try modifying the U,V values used and see what affect this has on the image displayed.

We can take this one step further and continually change the mapping. This gives us a scrolling effect within the sprite as demonstrated in LISTING-22.10.

LISTING-22.10

Scrolling the Image on a Sprite

```
REM *** Set screen resolution ***
SET DISPLAY MODE 1280,1024,32

REM *** Create sprite ***
LOAD IMAGE "FourSquare.bmp",1
SPRITE 1001,0,0,1
Voffset# = 0
DO
    SET SPRITE TEXTURE COORD 1001,0,0.0,Voffset#
    SET SPRITE TEXTURE COORD 1001,1,1.0,Voffset#
    SET SPRITE TEXTURE COORD 1001,2,0.0,1+Voffset#
    SET SPRITE TEXTURE COORD 1001,3,1.0,1+Voffset#
    Voffset# = Voffset# +0.01
    WAIT 10
LOOP

REM *** End program ***
WAIT KEY
END
```

Activity 22.15

Type in and test LISTING-22.10 (*sprites210.dbpro*).

There is no point in making the offset larger than 1.0 since that represents the whole image (remember (1.0,1.0) is the bottom right corner) so rather than let the value of *Voffset#* get too large we should add the lines

```
IF Voffset# > 1
    Voffset# = Voffset# - 1
ENDIF
```

in the DO loop of our code.

Activity 22.16

Modify your previous program to incorporate the IF statement given above.

Change the program again so that the image in the sprite scrolls horizontally rather than vertically.

By using a very large sprite (the size of the screen resolution) we can create a scrolling background.

Activity 22.17

Create a new program (*sprites211.dbpro*) which contains two sprites. Sprite 1001 contains the *background.bmp* image and sprite 1 contains the *arrowtrans.bmp* image.

Modify the texture of sprite 1001 so that its scrolls vertically in the background.

Allow sprite 1 to be rotated using the z (anticlockwise) and x (clockwise) keys.

The SET SPRITE Statement

As a sprite is moved on the screen it automatically erases itself from its old position and redraws itself at the new position. Should we want to, we can stop the sprite from erasing itself from the old position using the SET SPRITE statement. The effect of this can be to leave a trail of duplicate copies of the sprite (or part of the sprite).

This command can be used for a second, and apparently unrelated purpose of making a sprite's background opaque. While the black areas in a sprite are normally transparent, the SET SPRITE statement can be used to switch this effect off, making the black area opaque.

The SET SPRITE statement has the format shown in FIG-22.18.

FIG-22.18

The SET SPRITE Statement

In the diagram:

spriteno	is the number of the sprite whose properties are to be changed.
saveflg	is 0 or 1. 0 - background not saved. 1 - background saved.
transflg	is 0 or 1. 0 - all colours within the sprite are visible. 1 - any black pixels in the sprite are transparent.

The program in LISTING-22.11 switches off the restore feature of the arrow sprite, so, as it moves across the screen, the arrow is not erased from its previous position, leaving a trail as it moves.

LISTING-22.11

Sprite Trails

```
REM *** Set display mode ***
SET DISPLAY MODE 1280,1024,32

REM *** Load image used in sprite ***
LOAD IMAGE "arrowtrans.bmp",1

REM *** Disable restoration of background ***
SET SPRITE 1,0,1

REM *** Move sprite across the screen ***
FOR x = 300 to 800 step 10
   SPRITE 1,x,512,1
   WAIT 1
NEXT x

REM *** End program ***
WAIT KEY
END
```

Activity 22.18

Type in and test the program given in LISTING-22.11 (*sprites212.dbpro*).

It is a bit different if the sprite passes in front of another sprite. Now the trail will disappear since every sprite is redrawn automatically each time the screen is refreshed and this will clear any trail that might have appeared over the background sprite. You can see this effect in the next Activity.

Activity 22.19

In your last program, add the lines

```
LOAD IMAGE "cherryblossom.bmp",2
SPRITE 2,400,400,2
```

immediately after the SET DISPLAY MODE statement.

Run the program and observe how the trail is absent when the arrow passes over the background sprite.

Summary

- The screen colour displayed when using sprites can be specified using the COLOR BACKDROP statement.

- To activate the new screen colour use BACKDROP ON.

- To return to the default screen background use BACKDROP OFF.

- A screen-sized sprite can be used to create an image background.

- By default, sprites are drawn in the order they are added, so the last sprite to be added appears to be "in front" of all other images.

- The order in which sprites are drawn can be changed by setting a sprite's priority.

- Use SET SPRITE PRIORITY to set a sprite's priority.

- Sprite's with a higher priority value are drawn last.

- The images used by sprites have their own coordinate system.

- The axes of a sprite image are labelled U and V in place of x and y.

- Irrespective of a sprite image's actual size, its top left corner has the coordinates (0.0,0.0) and the bottom-right (1.0,1.0)

- The four corners of a sprite are labelled 0,1,2, and 3 in the order top-left, top-right, bottom-left, bottom-right.

- By default, a sprite's image maps (0,0) to corner 0, (1,0) to corner 1, (0,1) to corner 2, and (1,1) to corner 3.

- How an image is mapped to a sprite can be modified using the SET SPRITE TEXTURE COORD statement.

- The SET SPRITE statement is used to determine if the background over which a sprite moves is saved.

Retrieving Data About Sprites

Introduction

There are many functions in DarkBASIC Pro designed to return data about sprite positions and settings. These are described below.

Sprite Data Retrieval Statements

The SPRITE EXIST Statement

The SPRITE EXIST statement returns 1 if a sprite of the specified number currently exists. The statement has the format shown in FIG-22.19.

FIG-22.19

The SPRITE EXIST Statement

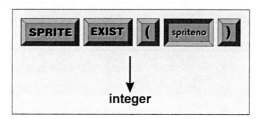

In the diagram:

spriteno   is the number of the sprite to be checked.

The statement returns 1 if the specified sprite exists, otherwise zero is returned.

The SPRITE X Statement

The SPRITE X statement returns the *x* ordinate of the specified sprites's position on the screen as measured from the sprite's origin. The statement has the format shown in FIG-22.20.

FIG-22.20

The SPRITE X Statement

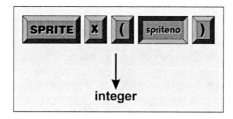

In the diagram:

spriteno   is the number of the sprite whose x ordinate is to be returned.

The SPRITE Y Statement

The SPRITE Y statement returns the *y* ordinate of the specified sprites's position on the screen as measured from the sprite's origin. The statement has the format shown in FIG-22.21.

FIG-22.21

The SPRITE Y Statement

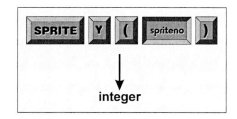

In the diagram:

spriteno   is the number of the sprite whose *y* ordinate is
                          to be returned.

Activity 22.20

In the previous chapter we had to store the position of a sprite so we could
detect when it hit the edge of the screen (see LISTING-20.14).

Modify the program you created (*sprites14.dbpro*) so that the position of the
sprite is determined using the SPRITE X and SPRITE Y statements.

The SPRITE ANGLE Statement

The angle to which a sprite has been rotated can be determined using the SPRITE
ANGLE statement. This has the format shown in FIG-22.22.

FIG-22.22

The SPRITE ANGLE
Statement

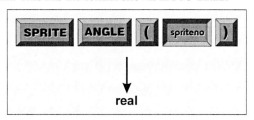

In the diagram:

spriteno   is the number of the sprite whose angle of rotation
                          is to be returned.

The SPRITE OFFSET X Statement

The number of pixels by which a sprite's origin has been offset along the x-axis can
be discovered using the SPRITE OFFSET X statement which takes the format
shown in FIG-22.23.

FIG-22.23

The SPRITE OFFSET X
Statement

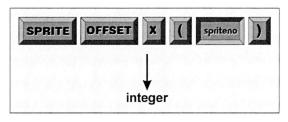

In the diagram:

spriteno   is the number of the sprite whose *x* offset is to be
                          returned.

The SPRITE OFFSET Y Statement

The number of pixels by which a sprite's origin has been offset along the y-axis can be discovered using the SPRITE OFFSET Y statement which takes the format shown in FIG-22.24.

FIG-22.24

The SPRITE OFFSET Y
Statement

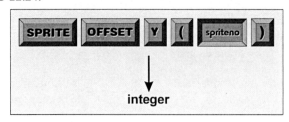

In the diagram:

    spriteno   is the number of the sprite whose *y* offset is to be returned.

The SPRITE SCALE X Statement

The degree to which a sprite's width has been changed can be determined using the SPRITE SCALE X statement. The figure returned is a percentage of the original size. Therefore if the sprite's width is unchanged, a value of 100 is returned. If halved in width, 50 is returned; while a doubled width would return 200. The format of this statement is given in FIG-22.25.

FIG-22.25

The SPRITE SCALE X
Statement

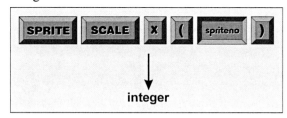

In the diagram:

    spriteno   is the number of the sprite whose width setting is to be returned.

The SPRITE SCALE Y Statement

The degree to which a sprite's height has been changed can be determined using the SPRITE SCALE Y statement. The figure returned is a percentage of the original size. The format of this statement is given in FIG-22.26.

FIG-22.26

The SPRITE SCALE Y
Statement

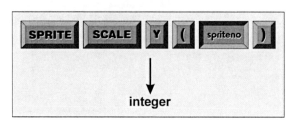

In the diagram:

    spriteno   is the number of the sprite whose height setting is to be returned.

The SPRITE WIDTH Statement

If you want to find out the width of a sprite in pixels, rather than as a percentage of its original width, then we can use the SPRITE WIDTH statement which has the format shown in FIG-22.27.

FIG-22.27

The SPRITE WIDTH
Statement

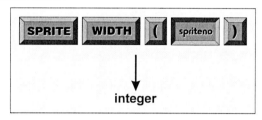

In the diagram:

spriteno   is the number of the sprite whose width is to be returned.

The SPRITE HEIGHT Statement

To find the height of a sprite in pixels we can use the SPRITE HEIGHT statement which has the format shown in FIG-22.28.

FIG-22.28

The SPRITE HEIGHT
Statement

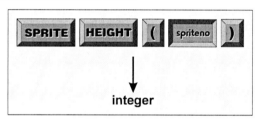

In the diagram:

spriteno   is the number of the sprite whose height is to be returned.

The SPRITE MIRRORED Statement

We can determine if a sprite has been mirrored using the SPRITE MIRRORED statement. The statement returns 1 if the sprite is mirrored, otherwise zero is returned. The format of the statement is given in FIG-22.29.

FIG-22.29

The SPRITE
MIRRORED Statement

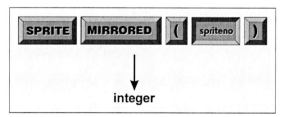

In the diagram:

spriteno   is the number of the sprite to be tested for having been mirrored.

The SPRITE FLIPPED Statement

We can determine if a sprite has been flipped using the SPRITE FLIPPED statement. The statement returns 1 if the sprite is flipped, otherwise zero is returned. The format of the statement is given in FIG-22.30.

FIG-22.30

The SPRITE FLIPPED Statement

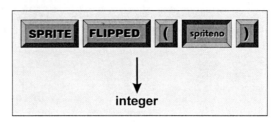

In the diagram:

  spriteno   is the number of the sprite to be tested for having been flipped.

The SPRITE VISIBLE Statement

We can determine if a sprite is currently visible using the SPRITE VISIBLE statement. The statement returns 1 if the sprite is visible, and zero if the sprite is hidden. The format of the statement is given in FIG-22.31.

FIG-22.31

The SPRITE VISIBLE Statement

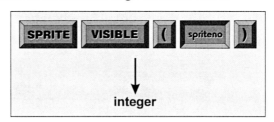

In the diagram:

  spriteno   is the number of the sprite whose visibility is to be checked.

The SPRITE ALPHA Statement

The current alpha setting of a sprite (as set by the SET SPRITE ALPHA statement) can be discovered using the SPRITE ALPHA statement. The alpha setting lies between (0 and 255). The format of the statement is given in FIG-22.32.

FIG-22.32

The SPRITE ALPHA Statement

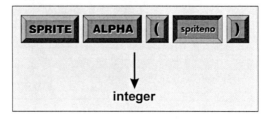

In the diagram:

  spriteno   is the number of the sprite whose alpha value is to be retrieved.

The SPRITE RED Statement

The current diffuse setting of the red component in a sprite can be accessed using the SPRITE RED statement which has the format shown in FIG-22.33.

FIG-22.33

The SPRITE RED
Statement

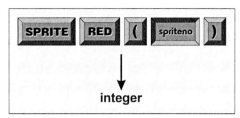

In the diagram:

>   *spriteno*   is the number of the sprite whose diffuse red
>   value is to be retrieved.

The value returned by this statement lies in the range 0 to 255.

The SPRITE GREEN Statement

The current diffuse setting of the green component in a sprite can be accessed using the SPRITE GREEN statement which has the format shown in FIG-22.34.

FIG-22.34

The SPRITE GREEN
Statement

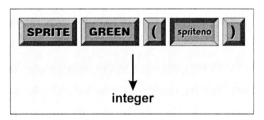

In the diagram:

>   *spriteno*   is the number of the sprite whose diffuse green
>   value is to be retrieved.

The value returned by this statement lies in the range 0 to 255.

The SPRITE BLUE Statement

The current diffuse setting of the blue component in a sprite can be accessed using the SPRITE BLUE statement which has the format shown in FIG-22.35.

FIG-22.35

The SPRITE BLUE
Statement

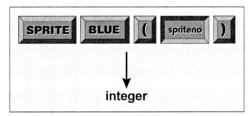

In the diagram:

>   *spriteno*   is the number of the sprite whose diffuse blue
>   value is to be retrieved.

The value returned by this statement lies in the range 0 to 255.

Summary

- We can check that a sprite exists using SPRITE EXIST.

- Use SPRITE X and SPRITE Y to find the coordinates of a sprite's origin.

- SPRITE ANGLE returns the angle of rotation of a specified sprite.

- The offset coordinates of a sprite's origin can be found using SPRITE OFFSET X and SPRITE OFFSET Y.

- The scaling applied to a sprite can be determined using SPRITE SCALE X and SPRITE SCALE Y.

- The dimensions of a sprite (in pixels) can be found using SPRITE WIDTH and SPRITE HEIGHT.

- SPRITE MIRRORED returns 1 if the specified sprite has been reflected about the y-axis.

- SPRITE FLIPPED returns 1 if the specified sprite has been reflected about the x-axis.

- SPRITE VISIBLE returns 1 if the specified sprite is visible.

- SPRITE ALPHA returns the alpha setting for a specified sprite.

- The diffuse settings of a sprite's primary colours can be found using SPRITE RED, SPRITE GREEN and SPRITE BLUE.

Sprite Collision

Introduction

Most 2D games involve collisions between sprites; a ball hits a bat, a missile hits an enemy craft. DarkBASIC Pro contains a couple of statements specifically to detect these collisions.

Dealing With Sprite Collisions

The SPRITE HIT Statement

We can check if two sprites have collided using the SPRITE HIT statement. The statement has the format shown in FIG-22.36.

FIG-22.36

The SPRITE HIT
Statement

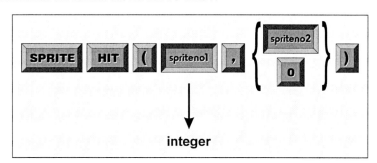

In the diagram:

spriteno1	is an integer value specifying the first sprite to be checked for collision.
spriteno2	is an integer value specifying the second sprite to be checked. When this option is used, the command returns 1 if *spriteno1* and *spriteno2* have collided, otherwise zero is returned.
0	the value zero is used when we want to check if *spriteno1* has collided with any other sprite. If *spriteno1* has collided with another sprite, the number of that sprite is returned; if *spriteno1* has not collided with any sprite, zero is returned.

For example, we can check if sprite 1 has collided with sprite 2 using the line:

```
IF SPRITE HIT(1,2) = 1
```

Using the second version of the statement, we could check if sprite 1 has collided with any other sprite using the line:

```
IF SPRITE HIT(1,0) > 0
```

In the next program (LISTING-22.12) a ball sprite moves towards a bat sprite. When the ball hits the bat, the collision is detected and the ball bounces off the bat.

LISTING-22.12

Detecting Sprite Collisions

```
REM *** Define constants for each sprite ***
#CONSTANT ball 1
#CONSTANT bat 2
REM *** Set screen resolution and background ***
SET DISPLAY MODE 1280,1024,32
COLOR BACKDROP RGB(0,0,255)
BACKDROP ON

REM *** Set up ball and bat ***
LOAD IMAGE "ball.bmp",1
SPRITE ball,640,512,1
LOAD IMAGE "paddle.bmp",2
SPRITE bat,640,900,2

REM *** Main loop ***
move = -5
DO
   MOVE SPRITE ball,move
   REM *** IF the sprites collide, move ball up ***
   IF SPRITE HIT(bat,ball)
      move = -move
   ENDIF
   WAIT 1
LOOP
END
```

NOTE: The sprites have been assigned names using the #CONSTANT statement.

This makes code much easier to read when several sprites are used.

Activity 22.21

Type in and test the program given in LISTING-22.12 (*sprites213.dbpro*).

Is there anything unusual about the collision?

As you saw when running this program, the collision seems to be detected before the sprites have actually touched. In fact, this isn't the case: the transparent parts of the sprites have come into contact with each other and this has caused the SPRITE HIT statement to return a 1. We can check this out by turning off sprite transparency.

Activity 22.22

Add the lines

```
REM *** Switch off sprite transparency ***
SET SPRITE ball,0,0
SET SPRITE bat,0,0
```

before the main loop in your previous program.

Run the program and check when collision occurs.

FIG-22.37 highlights the problem with collision detection.

FIG-22.37

Sprites Collide When
Any Two Parts Overlap

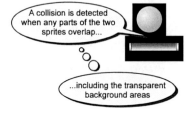

A collision is detected when any parts of the two sprites overlap...

...including the transparent background areas

To create a more realistic collision we must make sure that the black background area within the original image used by the sprite is kept to a minimum.

> **Activity 22.23**
>
> In your previous program, replace the pictures used within the sprites to *ballB.bmp* and *paddleB.bmp*. Both of these images have had the background area reduced to a minimum.
>
> How does this change affect the collision on the screen?

The SPRITE COLLISION Statement

The SPRITE COLLISION statement performs the same function as the SPRITE HIT statement. This statement has the format shown in FIG-22.38.

FIG-22.38

The SPRITE COLLISION Statement

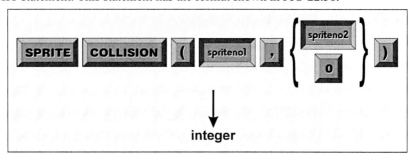

In the diagram:

spriteno1	is an integer value specifying the first sprite to be checked for collision.
spriteno2	is an integer value specifying the second sprite to be checked. When this option is used, the command returns 1 if *spriteno1* and *spriteno2* have collided, otherwise zero is returned.
0	the value zero is used when we want to check if *spriteno1* has collided with any other sprite. If *spriteno1* has collided with another sprite, the number of that sprite is returned; if *spriteno1* has not collided with any sprite, zero is returned.

A Basic Bat and Ball Game

One of the earliest ever video games was Pong. This consisted of a bat and a ball. The player had to keep the ball in play by deflecting it with the bat when it approached one edge of the screen. This basic idea is implemented in the program given in LISTING-22.13.

Data structures are defined within the program for velocity and position. Global variables are then created for the bat and ball to hold this information.

The program contains three main routines which are described informally below:

InitialiseGame	This routine sets up the screen, loads the sprites, and initialises the main variables in the program.

HandleBall	This routine handles movement of the ball. It checks for edges being hit and for the ball striking the bat.
HandleBat	This routine handles the movement of the bat. It checks for the Z and X keys being pressed and moves the bat accordingly (Z - left; X - right)

The game finishes when the ball disappears off the bottom of the screen.

LISTING-22.13

A Bat and Ball Game

```
REM *** Define constants for the sprites ***
#CONSTANT ball 1
#CONSTANT bat 2

REM *** Define required data type ***
TYPE VelocityType
   speed AS INTEGER
   angle AS INTEGER
ENDTYPE

TYPE PositionType
   x AS INTEGER
   y AS INTEGER
ENDTYPE

REM *** Create global variables for each sprite's data ***
GLOBAL ballvelocity AS VelocityType
GLOBAL ballposition AS PositionType
GLOBAL batposition AS PositionType


REM *** The main program logic ***
InitialiseGame()
REM *** Main loop ***
REPEAT
   HandleBall()
   HandleBat()
UNTIL ballposition.y > 1040
END

FUNCTION InitialiseGame()
   REM *** Set sprite speed and angle ***
   ballvelocity.speed = 7
   ballvelocity.angle = 60
   REM *** Set screen resolution ***
   SET DISPLAY MODE 1280,1024,32
   REM *** Set up ball with origin at centre ***
   LOAD IMAGE "ballB.bmp",1,1
   SPRITE ball,640,512,1
   OFFSET SPRITE ball, 16,16
   REM *** Rotate sprite ***
   ROTATE SPRITE ball, ballvelocity.angle
   REM *** Set up bat ***
   LOAD IMAGE "paddleB.bmp",2,1
   SPRITE bat,640,900,2
   STRETCH SPRITE bat,200,120
ENDFUNCTION

FUNCTION HandleBall()
   REM *** Handle ball ***
   MOVE SPRITE ball, ballvelocity.speed
   REM *** Check for top or bottom edge hit ***
   ballposition.x = SPRITE X(ball)
   ballposition.y = SPRITE Y(ball)
```

continued on next page

DarkBASIC Pro: Sprites 2

LISTING-22.13
(continued)

A Bat and Ball Game

```
        IF ballposition.y < 16
            ballvelocity.angle = WRAPVALUE(180 - ballvelocity.angle)
        ENDIF
        REM *** Check for side hit ***
        IF ballposition.x < 16 OR ballposition.x > 1264
            ballvelocity.angle = WRAPVALUE(360 - ballvelocity.angle)
        ENDIF
        REM *** Check for bat hit ***
        IF SPRITE HIT(bat,ball)
            ballvelocity.angle = WRAPVALUE(180 - ballvelocity.angle)
        ENDIF
        REM *** Rotate sprite to new angle ***
        ROTATE SPRITE ball,ballvelocity.angle
    ENDFUNCTION

    FUNCTION HandleBat()
        REM *** Check for key ***
        keycode = SCANCODE()
        REM *** Get position of bat ***
        batposition.x = SPRITE X(bat)
        batposition.y = SPRITE Y(bat)
        REM *** Update bat position ***
        IF keycode = 44 AND batposition.x > 8   'Z
            DEC batposition.x,10
        ELSE
            IF keycode = 45 AND batposition.x < 1180 `X
                INC batposition.x,10
            ENDIF
        ENDIF
        REM *** Redraw sprite ***
        SPRITE bat, batposition.x, batposition.y, 2
    ENDFUNCTION
```

Activity 22.24

Type in and test the program given in LISTING-22.13 (*sprites214.dbpro*).

Modify the program so that the speed of the ball increases by 1 each time the ball hits the bat.

Modify the program again so that it displays the game's duration (mins:secs).

Firing Projectiles

Another situation in which we have to detect collisions is when projectiles are fired. The classic example of this is Space Invaders which appeared in the late 1970's. The basic idea is not that different from the bat and ball. One sprite (the weapon) initiates a "fire" command. A new sprite (the projectile) is then created beside the weapon and travels in a straight line away from the weapon. When the projectile travels off the edge of the screen, its sprite is destroyed. To keep things simple, a second projectile cannot be created while the first is still visible.

The DELETE SPRITE Statement

A sprite can be removed from RAM using the DELETE SPRITE statement which has the format shown in FIG-22.39

FIG-22.39

The DELETE SPRITE Statement

In the diagram:

spriteno   is an integer specifying the sprite to be deleted.

The Missile Game

The program in LISTING-22.14 demonstrates the basic concepts.

Constants are defined to name the sprites and for the terms TRUE and FALSE (used by a Boolean variable). Data structures are defined to hold position and velocity. A Boolean variable, *missileexists*, is set to *true* while a missile is visible on the screen.

Like the last program it contains three routines:

InitialiseGame   This routine sets up the screen, loads the sprites, and initialises the main variables in the program.

HandlePlane   This routine handles movement of the weapon (a plane). It checks for the Z and X keys being pressed and moves the plane accordingly (Z - left; X - right) In addition, it checks for a missile being fired (by pressing the space bar).

HandleMissile   This routine handles the movement of the missile. Once the missile reaches the top of the screen it disappears.

The main logic of the program is very simple and can be described in structured English as:

```
Initialise game
REPEAT
    Handle plane
    IF a missile has been fired THEN
        Handle missile
    ENDIF
UNTIL false
```

LISTING-22.14

Firing Missiles

```
REM *** Define required data type ***
#CONSTANT plane    1
#CONSTANT missile 2
#CONSTANT TRUE     1
#CONSTANT FALSE    0
REM *** Define required data types ***
TYPE VelocityType
    speed AS INTEGER
    angle AS INTEGER
ENDTYPE

TYPE PositionType
    x AS INTEGER
    y AS INTEGER
ENDTYPE

REM *** Set up main variables ***
GLOBAL missilevelocity AS VelocityType
GLOBAL planeposition AS PositionType
GLOBAL missileexists AS BOOLEAN
```

continued on the next page

LISTING-22.14

(continued)

Firing Missiles

```
REM *** Main program logic ***
InitialiseGame()
DO
  HandlePlane()
  IF missileexists
     HandleMissile()
   ENDIF
LOOP
END

FUNCTION InitialiseGame()
   REM *** Set up missile velocity ***
   missilevelocity.speed = 15
   missilevelocity.angle = 0
   REM *** Set screen resolution ***
   SET DISPLAY MODE 1280,1024,32
   REM *** Set backdrop colour ***
   COLOR BACKDROP RGB(64,64,255)
   BACKDROP ON
   REM *** Set up plane sprite***
   LOAD IMAGE "plane.bmp",1
   SPRITE plane,640,900,1
   REM *** Load image to be used for missile ***
   LOAD IMAGE "missile.bmp",2
   REM *** No missile exists at start of game ***
   missileexists = FALSE
ENDFUNCTION

FUNCTION HandleMissile()
   MOVE SPRITE missile, missilevelocity.speed
   IF SPRITE Y (missile) < 0
      missileexists = FALSE
      DELETE SPRITE missile
   ENDIF
ENDFUNCTION

FUNCTION HandlePlane()
   REM *** Find plane's position ***
   planeposition.x = SPRITE X(plane)
   planeposition.y = SPRITE Y(plane)
   REM *** Check for keyboard hit ***
   keycode = SCANCODE()
   REM *** React to key pressed ***
   SELECT keycode
      CASE 44   'Z (left)
         IF planeposition.x > 8
            DEC planeposition.x,10
         ENDIF
      ENDCASE
      CASE 45   'X (right)
         IF planeposition.x < 1180 'X
            INC planeposition.x,10
         ENDIF
      ENDCASE
      CASE 57 'space (fire missile)
         REM *** IF missile does not already exist ***
         IF NOT missileexists
            REM *** Create missile sprite at top of plane ***
            missileexists = TRUE
            SPRITE missile,planeposition.x+SPRITE WIDTH(plane)/2,
               planeposition.y,2
         ENDIF
      ENDCASE
   ENDSELECT
   REM *** Move the plane sprite to its new position ***
   SPRITE plane,planeposition.x,planeposition.y,1
ENDFUNCTION
```

Extending the Game

If we're going to fire weapons, then we'd best have something to fire at. Next we'll introduce an enemy - a beetle. To update the program we need to add new constants and variables:

```
#CONSTANT beetle 3
GLOBAL beetlevelocity AS VelocityType
GLOBAL beetleposition AS PositionType
```

In *InitialiseGame()* we'll create the beetle sprite and set its velocity with the lines:

```
REM *** Set the beetle's velocity ***
beetlevelocity.speed = 12
beetlevelocity.angle = 0

REM *** Load beetle ***
LOAD IMAGE "beetle.bmp",3
SPRITE beetle,1100,100,3
```

The main logic needs to be changed to include a routine to handle the beetle:

```
InitialiseGame()
DO
    HandleBeetle()
    HandlePlane()
    IF SPRITE EXIST(missile)
        HandleMissile()
    ENDIF
LOOP
```

The new routine, *HandleBeetle()*, has the following code:

```
FUNCTION HandleBeetle()
    REM *** Find beetle's position ***
    beetleposition.x = SPRITE X(beetle)
    beetleposition.y = SPRITE Y(beetle)
    IF beetleposition.x < 20
        beetlevelocity.speed = -beetlevelocity.speed
    ENDIF
    IF beetleposition.x > 1100
        beetlevelocity.speed = -beetlevelocity.speed
    ENDIF
    INC beetleposition.x, beetlevelocity.speed
    SPRITE beetle,beetleposition.x,beetleposition.y,3
ENDFUNCTION
```

Activity 22.27

Add the lines given above to *sprites215.dbpro* and test the updated program.

Next, we need to detect and react to a collision between the beetle and the missile. This can be added to the *HandleMissile()* routine. The updated version is given below.

```
FUNCTION HandleMissile()
    MOVE SPRITE missile, missilevelocity.speed
    IF SPRITE HIT(missile,beetle)
        DELETE SPRITE beetle
        DELETE SPRITE missile
    ELSE
        IF SPRITE Y (missile) < 0
            DELETE SPRITE missile
        ENDIF
    ENDIF
ENDFUNCTION
```

We must be careful not to try moving the beetle once it has been destroyed. To handle this we can either change the main program from

```
HandleBeetle()
```

to

```
IF SPRITE EXIST(beetle)
    HandleBeetle()
ENDIF
```

or we can update *HandleBeetle()* to start with the lines

```
IF NOT SPRITE EXIST(beetle)
    EXITFUNCTION
ENDIF
```

Which option you choose is really up to you. Since the beetle will be there for most of the game, and to keep the main section of the program as simple as possible, we'll use the second option here. One last touch would be to make the beetle explode when it is hit. To do this we'll write a new routine which loads a different graphic into the beetle sprite when it is hit. The image will then expand, giving a simple explosion effect, before finally being deleted. Two statements which might be useful in such a situation are described below.

The SET SPRITE IMAGE Statement

The image shown in a sprite can be changed using the SET SPRITE IMAGE statement which has the format shown in FIG-22.40.

FIG-22.40

The SET SPRITE
IMAGE Statement

It is likely that, rather than use this technique of swapping the image held in a sprite, it will be more useful to use an animated sprite to create the same effect. Animated sprites are explained in the next chapter.

In the diagram:

spriteno	is an integer value representing the sprite whose image is to be changed.
imgno	is an integer value representing a previously loaded image which is to become the new content of the sprite.

The SPRITE IMAGE Statement

We can discover which image is currently associated with a sprite by using the SPRITE IMAGE statement which has the format shown in FIG-22.41.

FIG-22.41

The SPRITE IMAGE
Statement

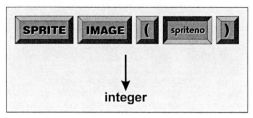

In the diagram:

> *spriteno*   is an integer value representing the sprite whose image is to be returned.

The value returned is that of the image currently being used by the specified sprite.

We need a constant for the new image, and code to load this image must be added to *InitialiseGame()*. The new lines are:

```
#CONSTANT explosion    4
LOAD IMAGE "explode.bmp",explosion
```

The routine to perform the explosion effect is given below:

```
FUNCTION Explode()
    IF NOT SPRITE EXIST(beetle)
        EXITFUNCTION
    ENDIF
    SET SPRITE IMAGE beetle,explosion
    FOR c = 60 TO 180 STEP 30
        SCALE SPRITE beetle,c
        WAIT 1
    NEXT c
    DELETE SPRITE beetle
ENDFUNCTION
```

Since we're now deleting the beetle within the *HandleBeetle()* function, the existing line that performs the same operation in *HandleMissile()* can be removed. The latest version of the program is given in LISTING-22.15.

LISTING-22.15

Firing Missiles Updated

```
REM *** Define constants ***
#CONSTANT plane        1
#CONSTANT missile      2
#CONSTANT beetle       3
#CONSTANT explosion    4
REM *** Define required data type ***
TYPE VelocityType
    speed AS INTEGER
    angle AS INTEGER
ENDTYPE
TYPE PositionType
    x AS INTEGER
    y AS INTEGER
ENDTYPE
REM *** Set up main variables ***
GLOBAL missilevelocity AS VelocityType
GLOBAL beetlevelocity AS VelocityType
GLOBAL planeposition AS PositionType
GLOBAL beetleposition AS PositionType
```
continued on next page

LISTING-22.15

(continued)

Firing Missiles Updated

```
REM *** Main program logic ***
InitialiseGame()
DO
    HandleBeetle()
    HandlePlane()
    IF SPRITE EXIST(missile)
        HandleMissile()
    ENDIF
LOOP
END


FUNCTION InitialiseGame()
    REM *** Set up missile velocity ***
    missilevelocity.speed = 15
    missilevelocity.angle = -1      'Not used
    REM *** Set up beetle's velocity ***
    beetlevelocity.speed = 12
    beetlevelocity.angle = -1        'Not used
    REM *** Set screen resolution ***
    SET DISPLAY MODE 1280, 1024, 32
    REM *** Set backdrop colour ***
    COLOR BACKDROP RGB(64,64,255)
    BACKDROP ON
    REM *** Set up plane sprite***
    LOAD IMAGE "plane.bmp",plane
    SPRITE plane,640,900,plane
    REM *** Load image to be used for missile ***
    LOAD IMAGE "missile.bmp",missile
    REM *** Load beetle ***
    LOAD IMAGE "beetle.bmp",beetle
    SPRITE beetle,1100,100,beetle
    LOAD IMAGE "explode.bmp",explosion
ENDFUNCTION

FUNCTION HandleMissile()
    REM *** Move the missile ***
    MOVE SPRITE missile, missilevelocity.speed
    REM *** IF missile hits beetle, create explosion ... ***
    REM *** and remove missile ***
    IF SPRITE HIT(missile,beetle)
        Explode()
        DELETE SPRITE missile
    ELSE
        REM *** IF missile has moved off top remove it ***
        IF SPRITE Y (missile) < 0
            DELETE SPRITE missile
        ENDIF
    ENDIF
ENDFUNCTION

FUNCTION HandlePlane()
    REM *** Find plane's position ***
    planeposition.x = SPRITE X(plane)
    planeposition.y = SPRITE Y(plane)
    REM *** Check for keyboard hit ***
    keycode = SCANCODE()
    REM *** React to key pressed ***
    SELECT keycode
        CASE 44   'Z (left)
            IF planeposition.x > 8
                DEC planeposition.x,10
            ENDIF
        ENDCASE
        CASE 45   'X (right)
```

continued on next page

LISTING-22.15
(continued)

Firing Missiles Updated

```
                IF planeposition.x < 1180 'X
                    INC planeposition.x,10
                ENDIF
            ENDCASE
            CASE 57 'space (fire missile)
                REM *** IF missile does not already exist ***
                IF NOT SPRITE EXIST(missile)
                    REM *** Create missile sprite at top of plane ***
                    SPRITE missile,planeposition.x +
                    ⤷SPRITE WIDTH(plane)/2,planeposition.y,missile
                ENDIF
            ENDCASE
        ENDSELECT
        REM *** Move the plane sprite to its new position ***
        SPRITE plane,planeposition.x,planeposition.y,plane
    ENDFUNCTION

    FUNCTION HandleBeetle()
        REM *** IF beetle doesn't exist, exit this routine ***
        IF NOT SPRITE EXIST(beetle)
            EXITFUNCTION
        ENDIF
        REM *** Find beetle's position ***
        beetleposition.x = SPRITE X(beetle)
        beetleposition.y = SPRITE Y(beetle)
        REM *** IF beetle hit edge of screen, reverse its direction ***
        IF beetleposition.x < 20
            IF beetlevelocity.speed < 0
                beetlevelocity.speed = -beetlevelocity.speed
            ENDIF
        ENDIF
        IF beetleposition.x > 1100
            IF beetlevelocity.speed > 0
                beetlevelocity.speed = -beetlevelocity.speed
            ENDIF
        ENDIF
        REM *** Update beetle's position ***
        INC beetleposition.x,beetlevelocity.speed
        SPRITE beetle,beetleposition.x,beetleposition.y,beetle
    ENDFUNCTION

    FUNCTION Explode()
        REM *** Change beetle image to explosion image ***
        SET SPRITE IMAGE beetle, explosion
        REM *** Expand exploding image ***
        FOR c = 60 TO 180 STEP 30
            SCALE SPRITE beetle,c
            WAIT 1
        NEXT c
        REM *** Delete beetle sprite ***
        DELETE SPRITE beetle
    ENDFUNCTION
```

Activity 22.28

Update your program to match that in LISTING-22.15.

Updating the Screen

By default, the computer screen is updated (refreshed) many times per second. If several objects are changing - for example, planes and beetles moving, missiles exploding - the computer can struggle trying to keep up with all the changes. This can lead to a flicker effect on the screen. To avoid this we can take control of screen updating using the various DarkBASIC Pro SYNC statements explained next.

The SYNC ON Statement

The SYNC ON statement switches off automatic screen updating. Once this statement has been executed, the program must explicitly state that the screen is to be updated. The SYNC ON statement has the format shown in FIG-22.42.

FIG-22.42

The SYNC ON Statement

The SYNC Statement

The SYNC statement updates the screen's contents. This statement must be used when a previous SYNC ON statement has been executed. Every time we need the screen's contents to change another SYNC statement must be executed. The format for this statement is given in FIG-22.43.

FIG-22.43

The SYNC Statement

The program in LISTING-22.16 demonstrates the use of SYNC ON and SYNC.

LISTING-22.16

Using SYNC ON and SYNC

```
REM *** Set screen resolution ***
SET DISPLAY MODE 1280,1024,32

REM *** Set backdrop colour ***
COLOR BACKDROP RGB(255,0,0)
BACKDROP ON

REM *** LOAD sprite ***
LOAD IMAGE "popcorn.bmp",1,1
SPRITE 1,640,50,1

REM *** Switch synchronisation on ***
SYNC ON

REM *** Move the sprite ***
FOR y = 50 TO 1000 STEP 10
    SPRITE 1, 640,y,1
    REM *** Update screen ***
    SYNC
NEXT Y

REM *** End program ***
WAIT KEY
END
```

Activity 22.29

Type in and test the program in LISTING-22.16 (*sprites216.dbpro*).

Modify the program by removing the SYNC statement. How is the screen display affected by this change?

The SYNC OFF Statement

The SYNC OFF statement returns screen updating to automatic, thereby eliminating the need to use SYNC. The format of this statement is shown in FIG-22.44.

FIG-22.44

the SYNC OFF Statement

The SYNC RATE Statement

The SYNC OFF statement defaults to refreshing the screen no more than 40 times per second (also described as a frame rate of 40 frames per second). However, it is possible to set a higher frame rate in conjunction with the SYNC ON statement. The SYNC RATE statement allows you to request a frame rate of between 1 and 1000 frames per second. This statement has the format shown in FIG-22.45.

FIG-22.45

The SYNC RATE
Statement

In the diagram:

    framerate   is an integer value in the range 1 to 1000 specifying the maximum frames per second refresh rate for the screen.

Even when a frame rate is specified, it may not be possible to achieve that rate due to the number of calculations required within your code, or because of limitations of the computer's hardware. The SYNC RATE should be used in conjunction with the SYNC ON and SYNC statements.

The FASTSYNC Statement

Because your program is running under Microsoft Windows, the processor continually leaves your program to check on what's happening elsewhere in the system. For example, if you have a DarkBASIC Pro game running in one window, the computer must still react to the user clicking some option in a second window.

By replacing the SYNC statement with a FASTSYNC statement, this checking is ignored during screen updating and can, as a result, help your program run just that little bit faster. The FASTSYNC statement has the format shown in FIG-22.46.

FIG-22.46

The FASTSYNC
Statement

Activity 22.30

Update your previous program by restoring the SYNC statement and adding the lines

The SCREEN FPS
statement was covered in
Chapter 14.

```
SET CURSOR 20,200
PRINT "FPS  : ", SCREEN FPS()
```

at the end of the FOR loop.

Check the frame rate achieved.

Replace SYNC with FASTSYNC. Does this make a difference?

Summary

- Collision between two sprites can be detected using either the SPRITE HIT or SPRITE COLLISION statements.

- Use DELETE SPRITE to remove a sprite from RAM.

- Use SET SPRITE IMAGE to change the image displayed in a sprite.

- Use SPRITE IMAGE to discover the image number of the image current used by a sprite.

- Screen updating can be handled by the program by using the SYNC ON statement followed by a SYNC statement every time the screen has to be redrawn.

- The SYNC OFF statement returns a program to automatic screen refreshing.

- The SYNC RATE statement can be used to set a maximum refresh rate.

- The FASTSYNC statement can be used to reduce the overheads caused by Microsoft Windows' event handling routines.

Solutions

Activity 22.1

No solution required.

Activity 22.2

```
REM *** Set screen resolution ***
SET DISPLAY MODE 1280, 1024, 32
REM *** Load image; transfer to sprite ***
LOAD IMAGE "ball1.bmp", 1
SPRITE 1,100,200,1
REM *** Make sprite smaller ***
FOR c = 100 TO 1 STEP -1
   SCALE SPRITE 1, (50+c*2)
   WAIT 10
NEXT c
REM *** End program ***
WAIT KEY
END
```

Activity 22.3

No solution required.

Activity 22.4

```
REM *** Set screen resolution ***
SET DISPLAY MODE 1280, 1024, 32
REM *** Load image ... ***
LOAD IMAGE "pheasant.bmp", 1
REM ... and copy into two sprites ***
SPRITE 1,100,100,1
SPRITE 2,300,100,1
REM *** Change diffuse settings ***
WAIT KEY
FOR diffuse = 0 TO 255
   SET SPRITE DIFFUSE 1,diffuse,diffuse,
   diffuse
   WAIT 10
NEXT diffuse
REM *** End program ***
WAIT KEY
END
```

Activity 22.5

```
REM *** Set screen resolution ***
SET DISPLAY MODE 1280, 1024, 32
REM *** Load image ... ***
LOAD IMAGE "pheasant.bmp", 1
REM ... and copy into two sprites ***
SPRITE 1,100,100,1
SPRITE 2,300,100,1
REM *** Change diffuse settings ***
WAIT KEY
FOR diffuse = 0 TO 255
   SET SPRITE DIFFUSE 1,diffuse,diffuse,
   diffuse
   WAIT 10
NEXT diffuse
REM *** Hide sprite 1 ***
HIDE SPRITE 1
REM *** End program ***
WAIT KEY
END
```

Activity 22.6

```
REM *** Set screen resolution ***
SET DISPLAY MODE 1280, 1024, 32
```

```
REM *** Load image ... ***
LOAD IMAGE "pheasant.bmp", 1
REM ... and copy into two sprites ***
SPRITE 1,100,100,1
SPRITE 2,300,100,1
REM *** Change diffuse settings ***
WAIT KEY
FOR diffuse = 0 TO 255
   SET SPRITE DIFFUSE 1,diffuse,diffuse,
   diffuse
   WAIT 10
NEXT diffuse
REM *** Hide sprite 1 ***
HIDE SPRITE 1
REM *** Reshow sprite ***
WAIT KEY
SHOW SPRITE 1
REM *** End program ***
WAIT KEY
END
```

Activity 22.7

```
REM *** Set screen resolution ***
SET DISPLAY MODE 1280, 1024, 32
REM *** Create first sprite ***
LOAD IMAGE "arrowtrans.bmp",1
SPRITE 1,600,500,1
REM *** Rotate and shrink sprite ***
WAIT KEY
OFFSET SPRITE 1, 32,32
ROTATE SPRITE 1, 45
SCALE SPRITE 1, 75
REM *** Duplicate sprite ***
WAIT KEY
CLONE SPRITE 1, 2
REM *** Move new sprite ***
WAIT KEY
MOVE SPRITE 2, 100
REM *** Create a second copy ***
WAIT KEY
CLONE SPRITE 1, 3
ROTATE SPRITE 3,90
WAIT KEY
MOVE SPRITE 3, 200
REM *** End program ***
WAIT KEY
END
```

Activity 22.8

```
REM *** Set screen resolution ***
SET DISPLAY MODE 1280, 1024, 32
REM *** Create first sprite ***
LOAD IMAGE "arrowtrans.bmp",1
SPRITE 1,600,500,1
COLOR BACKDROP RGB(255,255,0)
BACKDROP ON
REM *** End program ***
WAIT KEY
END
```

Activity 22.9

```
REM *** Set screen resolution ***
SET DISPLAY MODE 1280, 1024, 32
REM *** Create first sprite ***
LOAD IMAGE "arrowtrans.bmp",1
SPRITE 1,600,500,1
COLOR BACKDROP RGB(255,255,0)
BACKDROP ON
REM *** Revert to default background ***
```

```
WAIT KEY
BACKDROP OFF
REM *** End program ***
WAIT KEY
END
```

Activity 22.10

No solution required.

Activity 22.11

```
REM *** Set screen resolution ***
SET DISPLAY MODE 1280, 1024, 32
REM *** Create first sprite ***
LOAD IMAGE "arrowtrans.bmp",1
SPRITE 1,600,500,1
REM *** Load large image as background
***
LOAD IMAGE "background1.bmp",2
SPRITE 1001,0,0,2
REM *** End program ***
WAIT KEY
END
```

The arrow sprite is now hidden by the background sprite.

Activity 22.12

No solution required.

Activity 22.13

```
REM *** Set screen resolution ***
SET DISPLAY MODE 1280, 1024, 32
REM *** Load large image as background
***
LOAD IMAGE "background1.bmp",2
SPRITE 1001,0,0,2
REM *** Create first sprite ***
LOAD IMAGE "arrowtrans.bmp",1
SPRITE 1,600,500,1
LOAD IMAGE "tree.bmp",3
SPRITE 501,100,250,3
REM *** Make sure arrow is drawn last ***
SET SPRITE PRIORITY 1,1
REM *** Move arrow past tree ***
FOR x = 600 TO 50 STEP -10
    SPRITE 1,x,500,1
    WAIT 20
NEXT x
REM *** End program ***
WAIT KEY
END
```

Activity 22.14

No solution required.

Activity 22.15

No solution required.

Activity 22.16

```
REM *** Set screen resolution ***
SET DISPLAY MODE 1280, 1024, 32
REM *** Create sprite ***
LOAD IMAGE "FourSquare.bmp",1
SPRITE 1001,0,0,1
```

```
Voffset# = 0
DO
    SET SPRITE TEXTURE COORD 1001,
    0,0.0,Voffset#
    SET SPRITE TEXTURE COORD 1001,
    1,1.0,Voffset#

    SET SPRITE TEXTURE COORD 1001,
    2,0.0,1+Voffset#
    SET SPRITE TEXTURE COORD 1001,
    3,1.0,1+Voffset#
    Voffset# = Voffset# +0.01
    IF Voffset# > 1
        Voffset# = Voffset# - 1
    ENDIF
    WAIT 10
LOOP
REM *** End program ***
WAIT KEY
END
```

Activity 22.16

```
REM *** Set screen resolution ***
SET DISPLAY MODE 1280, 1024, 32
REM *** Create sprite ***
LOAD IMAGE "FourSquare.bmp",1
SPRITE 1001,0,0,1
Uoffset# = 0
DO
    SET SPRITE TEXTURE COORD 1001,
    0,Uoffset#,0.0
    SET SPRITE TEXTURE COORD 1001,
    1,1+Uoffset#,0.0
    SET SPRITE TEXTURE COORD 1001,
    2,Uoffset#,1.0
    SET SPRITE TEXTURE COORD 1001,
    3,1+Uoffset#,1.0
    Uoffset# = Uoffset# +0.01
    IF Uoffset# > 1
        Uoffset# = Uoffset# - 1
    ENDIF
    WAIT 10
LOOP
REM *** End program ***
WAIT KEY
END
```

Activity 22.17

```
REM *** Set screen resolution ***
SET DISPLAY MODE 1280, 1024, 32
REM *** Create background sprite ***
LOAD IMAGE "background1.bmp",1
SPRITE 1001,0,0,1
REM *** Create arrow sprite ***
LOAD IMAGE "arrowtrans.bmp",2
SPRITE 1, 640, 512,2
OFFSET SPRITE 1, 32,32
REM *** Set angle of rotation to zero ***
angle = 0
REM *** Create vertical offset variable ***
Voffset# = 0
DO
    REM *** Scroll background vertically ***
    SET SPRITE TEXTURE COORD 1001,
    0,0.0,Voffset#
    SET SPRITE TEXTURE COORD 1001,
    1,1.0,Voffset#
    SET SPRITE TEXTURE COORD 1001,
    2,0.0,1+Voffset#
    SET SPRITE TEXTURE COORD 1001,
    3,1.0,1+Voffset#
    Voffset# = Voffset# +0.01
    IF Voffset# > 1
        Voffset# = Voffset# - 1
```

```
    ENDIF
    REM *** Read key and change angle ***
    key = SCANCODE()
    IF key = 44
        angle = WRAPVALUE (angle - 5)
    ENDIF
    IF key = 45
        angle = WRAPVALUE (angle + 5)
    ENDIF
    ROTATE SPRITE 1,angle
LOOP
REM *** End program ***
WAIT KEY
END
```

Activity 22.18

No solution required.

Activity 22.19

No solution required.

Activity 22.20

```
TYPE VelocityType2
    speed AS FLOAT
    angle AS FLOAT
ENDTYPE
velocity AS VelocityType2
REM *** Set screen resolution ***
SET DISPLAY MODE 1280, 1024, 32
REM *** Set up sprite at screen centre ***
LOAD IMAGE "arrowtrans.bmp",1
SPRITE 1,640,512,1
OFFSET SPRITE 1, 32,32
REM *** Set sprite speed and angle ***
velocity.speed = 7
velocity.angle = 60
REM *** Rotate sprite ***
ROTATE SPRITE 1, velocity.angle
REM *** Main loop ***
DO
    MOVE SPRITE 1, velocity.speed
    SET CURSOR 0,900
    PRINT "x: ",SPRITE X(1)
    PRINT "y : ",SPRITE Y(1)
    PRINT "angle : ",velocity.angle
    REM *** Check for top or bottom hit ***
    IF SPRITE Y(1) < 16 OR SPRITE Y(1) >
1008
        velocity.angle =
        WRAPVALUE(180 - velocity.angle)
    ENDIF
    REM *** Check for side hit ***
    IF SPRITE X(1) < 16 OR SPRITE X(1) >
1264
        velocity.angle =
        WRAPVALUE(360 - velocity.angle)
    ENDIF
    ROTATE SPRITE 1,velocity.angle
LOOP
REM *** End program ***
END
```

Activity 22.21

The ball seems to bounce back before it has actually hit the bat.

Activity 22.22

Collision occurs when any part of the sprite (including the transparent black area) comes into contact with any part of another sprite.

Activity 22.23

The reduced background in each sprite means that the collision is detected as the visible areas collide.

Activity 22.24

```
REM *** Define constants for sprites ***
#CONSTANT ball 1
#CONSTANT bat 2
REM *** Define required data type ***
TYPE VelocityType
    speed AS INTEGER
    angle AS INTEGER
ENDTYPE
TYPE PositionType
    x AS INTEGER
    y AS INTEGER
ENDTYPE
REM *** Global variable for each sprite
***
GLOBAL ballvelocity AS VelocityType
GLOBAL ballposition AS PositionType
GLOBAL batposition AS PositionType
REM *** Starting time ***
GLOBAL starttime
REM *** The main program logic ***
InitialiseGame()
REM *** Main loop ***
REPEAT
    HandleBall()
    HandleBat()
    DisplayTime()
UNTIL ballposition.y > 1040
REM *** End program ***
END

FUNCTION InitialiseGame()
    REM *** Set sprite speed and angle ***
    ballvelocity.speed = 7
    ballvelocity.angle = 60
    REM *** Set screen resolution ***
    SET DISPLAY MODE 1280, 1024, 32
    REM *** Set up ball ***
    LOAD IMAGE "ballB.bmp",1,1
    SPRITE ball,640,512,1
    OFFSET SPRITE ball, 16,16
    REM *** Rotate sprite ***
    ROTATE SPRITE ball, ballvelocity.angle
    REM *** Set up bat ***
    LOAD IMAGE "paddleB.bmp",2,1
    SPRITE bat,640,900,2
    STRETCH SPRITE bat,200,120
    REM *** Record start time ***
    starttime = TIMER()
ENDFUNCTION

FUNCTION HandleBall()
    REM *** Handle ball ***
    MOVE SPRITE ball, ballvelocity.speed
    REM *** Check for top/bottom edge ***
    ballposition.x = SPRITE X(ball)
    ballposition.y = SPRITE Y(ball)
    IF ballposition.y < 16
        ballvelocity.angle =
        WRAPVALUE(180 - ballvelocity.angle)
    ENDIF
    REM *** Check for side hit ***
    IF ballposition.x < 16 OR
    ballposition.x > 1264
        ballvelocity.angle =
```

```
            WRAPVALUE(360 - ballvelocity.angle)
        ENDIF
        IF SPRITE HIT(bat,ball)
            ballvelocity.angle =
            WRAPVALUE(180 - ballvelocity.angle)
            INC ballvelocity.speed
        ENDIF
        ROTATE SPRITE ball,ballvelocity.angle
    ENDFUNCTION

    FUNCTION HandleBat()
        REM *** Handle bat ***
        keycode = SCANCODE()
        batposition.x = SPRITE X(bat)
        batposition.y = SPRITE Y(bat)
        IF keycode = 44 AND batposition.x > 8
            DEC batposition.x,10
        ELSE
            IF keycode = 45 AND batposition.x
            < 1180
                INC batposition.x,10
            ENDIF
        ENDIF
        SPRITE bat, batposition.x,
        batposition.y, 2
    ENDFUNCTION

    FUNCTION DisplayTime()
        time = TIMER()-starttime
        seconds = time/1000
        timemins = seconds / 60
        timesecs = seconds mod 60
        SET CURSOR 10,10
        PRINT "                    "
        SET CURSOR 10,10
        PRINT "TIME : ",timemins,":",timesecs
    ENDFUNCTION
```

Activity 22.25

If you look at the plane image, you'll see that the plane itself isn't centred in the image. Since the missile is launched from the midpoint of the image width, it is slightly over from the centre of the plane.

No. Because the program uses SCANCODE to determine key presses, it can't detect two keys being pressed at the same time.

Activity 22.26

```
REM *** Define required data type ***
#CONSTANT plane 1
#CONSTANT missile 2
TYPE VelocityType
    speed AS INTEGER
    angle AS INTEGER
ENDTYPE
TYPE PositionType
    x AS INTEGER
    y AS INTEGER
ENDTYPE
GLOBAL missilevelocity AS VelocityType
GLOBAL planeposition AS PositionType

InitialiseGame()
REM *** Main loop ***
DO
    HandlePlane()
    IF SPRITE EXIST(missile)
        HandleMissile()
    ENDIF
LOOP
END
```

```
FUNCTION InitialiseGame()
    REM *** Set up missile velocity ***
    missilevelocity.speed = 15
    missilevelocity.angle = 0
    REM *** Set screen resolution ***
    SET DISPLAY MODE 1280, 1024, 32
    REM *** Set backdrop colour ***
    COLOR BACKDROP RGB(64,64,255)
    BACKDROP ON
    REM *** Set up plane sprite***
    LOAD IMAGE "plane.bmp",1,1
    SPRITE plane,640,900,1
    REM *** Load image for missile ***
    LOAD IMAGE "missile.bmp",2
ENDFUNCTION

FUNCTION HandleMissile()
    MOVE SPRITE missile,
missilevelocity.speed
    IF SPRITE Y (missile) < 0
        DELETE SPRITE missile
    ENDIF
ENDFUNCTION

FUNCTION HandlePlane()
    REM *** Find plane's position ***
    planeposition.x = SPRITE X(plane)
    planeposition.y = SPRITE Y(plane)
    REM *** Check for keyboard hit ***
    keycode = SCANCODE()
    REM *** React to key pressed ***
    SELECT keycode
        CASE 44 `Z (left)
            IF planeposition.x > 8
                DEC planeposition.x,10
            ENDIF
        ENDCASE
        CASE 45 `X (right)
            IF planeposition.x < 1180 `X
                INC planeposition.x,10
            ENDIF
        ENDCASE
        CASE 57 `space (fire missile)
            REM *** IF no missile exists ***
            IF NOT SPRITE EXIST(missile)
                REM *** Create missile ***
                SPRITE missile,planeposition.x
                + SPRITE WIDTH(plane)/2,
                planeposition.y,2
            ENDIF
        ENDCASE
    ENDSELECT
    REM *** Move plane to new position ***
    SPRITE plane, planeposition.x,
    planeposition.y, 1
ENDFUNCTION
```

As well as the changes highlighted, several lines have been removed from the original code.

Activity 22.27

```
REM *** Define required data type ***
#CONSTANT plane    1
#CONSTANT missile 2
#CONSTANT beetle   3
#CONSTANT TRUE 1
#CONSTANT FALSE 0
TYPE VelocityType
    speed AS INTEGER
    angle AS INTEGER
ENDTYPE
TYPE PositionType
    x AS INTEGER
    y AS INTEGER
ENDTYPE
GLOBAL missilevelocity AS VelocityType
```

```
GLOBAL planeposition AS PositionType
GLOBAL beetlevelocity AS VelocityType
GLOBAL beetleposition AS PositionType

InitialiseGame()
REM *** Main loop ***
DO
    HandleBeetle()
    HandlePlane()
    IF SPRITE EXIST(missile)
        HandleMissile()
    ENDIF
LOOP
END

FUNCTION InitialiseGame()
    REM *** Set up missile velocity ***
    missilevelocity.speed = 15
    missilevelocity.angle = 0
    REM *** Set the beetle's velocity ***
    beetlevelocity.speed = 12
    beetlevelocity.angle = 0
    REM *** Set screen resolution ***
    SET DISPLAY MODE 1280, 1024, 32
    REM *** Set backdrop colour ***
    COLOR BACKDROP RGB(64,64,255)
    BACKDROP ON
    REM *** Set up plane sprite***
    LOAD IMAGE "plane.bmp",1,1
    SPRITE plane,640,900,1
    REM *** Load image for missile ***
    LOAD IMAGE "missile.bmp",2
    REM *** Set up beetle sprite ***
    LOAD IMAGE "beetle.bmp",3
    SPRITE beetle,1100,100,3
    LOAD IMAGE "explode.bmp",4
ENDFUNCTION

FUNCTION HandleMissile()
    MOVE SPRITE missile,
missilevelocity.speed
    IF SPRITE Y(missile) < 0
        DELETE SPRITE missile
    ENDIF
ENDFUNCTION

FUNCTION HandlePlane()
    REM *** Find plane's position ***
    planeposition.x = SPRITE X(plane)
    planeposition.y = SPRITE Y(plane)
    REM *** Check for keyboard hit ***
    keycode = SCANCODE()
    REM *** React to key pressed ***
    SELECT keycode
        CASE 44 `Z (left)
            IF planeposition.x > 8
                DEC planeposition.x,10
            ENDIF
        ENDCASE
        CASE 45 `X (right)
            IF planeposition.x < 1180 `X
                INC planeposition.x,10
            ENDIF
        ENDCASE
        CASE 57 `space (fire missile)
            REM *** IF missile doesn't exist
***
            IF NOT SPRITE EXIST(missile)
                REM *** Create missile ***
                SPRITE missile,planeposition.x
                + SPRITE WIDTH(plane)/2,
                planeposition.y,2
            ENDIF
        ENDCASE
    ENDSELECT
    REM *** Move plane to new position ***
    SPRITE plane, planeposition.x,
planeposition.y, 1
```

```
ENDFUNCTION

FUNCTION HandleBeetle()
    REM *** Find beetle's position ***
    beetleposition.x = SPRITE X(beetle)
    beetleposition.y = SPRITE Y(beetle)
    IF beetleposition.x < 20
        beetlevelocity.speed =
        -beetlevelocity.speed
    ENDIF
    IF beetleposition.x > 1100
        beetlevelocity.speed =
        -beetlevelocity.speed
    ENDIF
    INC beetleposition.x,
    beetlevelocity.speed
    SPRITE beetle,beetleposition.x,
    beetleposition.y,3
ENDFUNCTION
```

Activity 22.28

No solution required.

Activity 22.29

Without the SYNC statement the screen is not updated
and remains blank.

Activity 22.30

In fact, for such a simple program, you're unlikely to see
any difference between the use of SYNC and
FASTSYNC.

DarkBASIC Pro: Sprites 2

Controlling Multiple Sprites

Creating an Animated Sprite

Playing an Animated Sprite

Setting the Sprite Frame

Using Animated Sprites to Create a 3D Effect

Animated Sprites

Introduction

There are many situations where we need a sprite to consist of more than a single image. For example, we might use a sprite to represent a playing card, in which case we need the sprite to contain two images, one for the front of the card, another for the back. A sprite that is created containing more than a single image is known as an **animated sprite**. The images that make up the animated sprite are known as **frames**.

An animated sprite of a man walking would contain several images that show the arms and legs in varying positions, so that, when the images are displayed one after the other in quick succession, we'd get the effect of someone walking. However, like the card example, animated sprites are not always used to literally create an animation in the traditional sense of the word.

As you might expect, DarkBASIC Pro has a set of statements designed specifically to deal with animated sprites. However, some preparation needs to be done before we can use such a sprite in a program. First we need to create the set of equal-sized images that are to make up our animation (these will become the frames of the animation). Once this is done, these images must be combined into a single image (just like a film strip).

The images can be saved in a single line, or over several rows. FIG-23.1 shows two different ways of laying out the images required for a six-sided dice.

FIG-23.1

Possible Layouts for a Dice Image

Layout 1 (6 by 1)   Layout 2 (3 by 2)

Creation of such graphics should be done in a paint package such as Paint Shop Pro or Photoshop.

Setting Up the Sprite

The CREATE ANIMATED SPRITE Statement

FIG-23.2

The CREATE ANIMATED SPRITE Statement

When creating an animated sprite, rather than use LOAD IMAGE, we use the CREATE ANIMATED SPRITE statement. This command creates the animated sprite, names the file containing the image and details how the image is laid out. Loading a picture into an animated sprite also creates an image object which has to be assigned an image number. The statement has the format shown in FIG-23.2.

In the diagram:

   spriteno   is the number to be allocated to the sprite being created.

filename	is a string giving the name of the file containing the image being used. This string may include path information.
columns	is an integer value giving the number of frames in a single row.
rows	is an integer value giving the number of rows in the picture.
imgno	is the image number to be assigned to the image created by this statement.

If we assume our dice pictures (shown in FIG-23.1) are named *dice61.bmp* and *dice32.bmp* respectively, and are held in the same directory as the project being created, then we could load these images into sprites 1 and 2 using the lines:

```
CREATE ANIMATED SPRITE 1,"dice61.bmp",6,1,11
CREATE ANIMATED SPRITE 2,"dice32.bmp",3,2,12
```

These lines would also create image objects numbered 11 and 12.

The CREATE ANIMATED SPRITE statement does not cause the sprite to appear on the screen. To do that, we need to use the normal SPRITE statement. For example, to display the dice in sprite 1, we would use the line

```
SPRITE 1,640,500,11
```

The program in LISTING-23.1 demonstrates the basic idea.

LISTING-23.1

Displaying an Animated Sprite

```
REM *** set up a name for the sprite ***
#CONSTANT dice 1

REM *** Set screen resolution ***
SET DISPLAY MODE 1280,1024,32

REM *** Load animated sprite ***
CREATE ANIMATED SPRITE dice,"dice61.bmp",6,1,1
REM *** Display sprite ***
SPRITE dice,640,500,1

REM *** End program ***
WAIT KEY
END
```

Activity 23.1

Type in and test the program in LISTING-23.1 (*sprites301.dbpro*).

Which frame in the sprite is displayed?

The SET SPRITE FRAME Statement

In earlier versions of DarkBASIC Pro, the first frame of an animated sprite was identified as frame zero.

The first frame in an animated sprite is identified as frame 1. As we saw in the last Activity, it's frame 1 that is displayed by default. However, we can control which frame is being shown using the SET SPRITE FRAME statement which has the format shown in FIG-23.3.

FIG-23.3

The SET SPRITE
FRAME Statement

In the diagram:

spriteno	is the number of the animated sprite whose frame is to be set.
frame	is an integer value specifying which frame of the sprite is to be displayed. The value should lie between 1 and the number of frames in the sprite.

Activity 23.2

In your previous program, add the lines

```
FOR frame = 1 TO 6
    SET SPRITE FRAME dice,frame
    WAIT KEY
NEXT frame
```

before the last REM statement.

Modify your program to use the second dice image (*dice32.bmp*) instead of *dice61.bmp*.

If you are using a version of DarkBASIC Pro that identifies the first frame as frame zero, either add a blank first frame to the images you use or adjust the frame number in your code. In this example, the FOR loop would be modified to run from 0

Activity 23.3

Create a new program (*sprites302.dbpro*) which randomly sets a dice to a value between 1 and 6.

Create a second sprite within the program using the file *0to9.bmp*. This is a 10 frame image (10 by 1) which contains images of the digits 0 to 9. The new sprite should be displayed in the top-left corner of the screen and made to show the same value as appears on the dice. Place the main logic of the program in a DO LOOP structure.

The SPRITE FRAME Statement

We can find out which frame is currently being displayed within an animated sprite using the SPRITE FRAME statement. This statement has the format shown in FIG-23.4.

FIG-23.4

The SPRITE FRAME
Statement

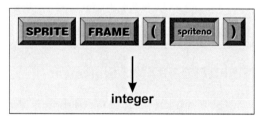

In the diagram:

spriteno	is the number of the animated sprite whose frame is to returned

For example, if the line

```
SET SPRITE FRAME dice, 3
```

is followed later by the line

```
framenum = SPRITE FRAME(dice)
```

then the variable *framenum* would be set to 3.

A Simple Dice Game

Back in Chapter 5 we introduced a simple dice game where we threw two dice until at least one dice showed a 1. In the next program (see LISTING-23.2), we're going to recreate this game using sprites.

FIG-23.5 shows the screen layouts which appear in the game and the images used.

FIG-23.5

The Screen Layouts and Sprites Used in the Game

Main Screen

End Screen

Images Used

Notice that sprites are being used for all of the text that is to appear on the screen. This is because of the problems that occur when trying to display text using the PRINT statement.

Since two dice and two numeric digits are used in the score, duplicate sprites are created using the CLONE SPRITE statement.

The program contains the following constants which are used to identify the sprites:

```
#CONSTANT dice1        1
#CONSTANT dice2        2
#CONSTANT units        3
#CONSTANT tens         4
#CONSTANT headingmsg   5
#CONSTANT scoremsg     6
#CONSTANT throwmsg     7
#CONSTANT finalmsg     8
```

and global variables to hold the main data:

```
GLOBAL dice1value AS INTEGER    'throw on first dice
GLOBAL dice2value AS INTEGER    'throw on second dice
GLOBAL score AS INTEGER         'total score
```

There are five routines in the program:

InitialiseGame   This routine initialises the global variables, loads up the sprites and sets up the main screen layout.

ThrowDice   This routine generates new values for the dice and updates the frame being shown by the dice sprites.

NoOnes   This routine returns 1 if neither dice is showing a 1; otherwise zero is returned.

UpdateScore   This routine updates the *score* variable and the sprites which display the score.

FinishGame   This routine displays an end-of-game message and the final score.

The overall logic of the game is:

```
Initialise game
Throw dice
WHILE no 1's are thrown DO
    Update score
    Throw dice
ENDWHILE
Finish game
```

LISTING-23.2

The Dice Game

```
REM *** Sprite names ***
#CONSTANT dice1      1
#CONSTANT dice2      2
#CONSTANT units      3
#CONSTANT tens       4
#CONSTANT headingmsg 5
#CONSTANT scoremsg   6
#CONSTANT throwmsg   7
#CONSTANT finalmsg   8

REM *** Main data items ***
GLOBAL dice1value AS INTEGER   'throw on first dice
GLOBAL dice2value AS INTEGER   'throw on second dice
GLOBAL score AS INTEGER        'total score

REM *** Main Logic ***
InitialiseGame()
ThrowDice()
WHILE NoOnes()
   UpdateScore()
   ThrowDice()
ENDWHILE
FinishGame()
END


FUNCTION InitialiseGame()
   REM *** Seed random number generator ***
   RANDOMIZE TIMER()
   REM *** Set number of throws and score to zero ***
   throws = 0
   score = 0
   REM *** Set screen resolution ***
   SET DISPLAY MODE 1280,1024,32
   REM *** Load game heading ***
```
continued on next page

LISTING-23.2
(continued)

The Dice Game

```
    LOAD IMAGE "diceHeading.bmp",5
    SPRITE headingmsg,470,50,5
    REM *** Load score message ***
    LOAD IMAGE "diceScore.bmp",6
    SPRITE scoremsg,1020,105,6
    REM *** Set up score digits ***
    CREATE ANIMATED SPRITE units, "0to9.bmp",10,1,3
    CLONE SPRITE units, tens
    SPRITE tens,1100,100,3
    SPRITE units,1125,100,3
    REM *** Set up dice ***
    CREATE ANIMATED SPRITE dice1,"dice61.bmp",6,1,1
    CLONE SPRITE dice1,dice2
    SPRITE dice1,550,500,1
    SPRITE dice2,650,500,1
    REM *** Set up message to roll dice ... ***
    LOAD IMAGE "diceThrow.bmp",7
    SPRITE throwmsg,470,800,7
    REM *** ... but hide it ***
    HIDE SPRITE throwmsg
    REM *** Load and hide game over message ***
    LOAD IMAGE "diceOver.bmp",8
    SPRITE finalmsg,530,500,8
    HIDE SPRITE finalmsg
ENDFUNCTION

FUNCTION ThrowDice()
    REM *** Display prompt ***
    SHOW SPRITE throwmsg
    WAIT KEY
    REM *** Hide message ***
    HIDE SPRITE throwmsg
    WAIT 500
    REM *** throw dice ***
    dice1value = RND(5)+1
    dice2value = RND(5)+1
    SET SPRITE FRAME dice1,dice1value
    SET SPRITE FRAME dice2,dice2value
    WAIT 500
ENDFUNCTION

FUNCTION NoOnes()
    REM *** IF either dice is a 1, return zero ***
    IF dice1value =1 OR dice2value = 1
        result = 0
    ELSE
        result = 1
    ENDIF
ENDFUNCTION result

FUNCTION UpdateScore()
    REM *** Add dice values to score ***
    score = score + dice1value + dice2value
    REM *** Update the score sprites ***
    tensvalue = score / 10
    unitsvalue = score mod 10
    SET SPRITE FRAME tens,(tensvalue+1)
    SET SPRITE FRAME units,(unitsvalue + 1)
    REM *** Make score blink ***
    HIDE SPRITE tens
    HIDE SPRITE units
    WAIT 500
    SHOW SPRITE tens
    SHOW SPRITE units
    REM *** Wait before going on ***
    WAIT 1000
ENDFUNCTION
```

continued on next page

LISTING-23.2
(continued)

The Dice Game

```
FUNCTION FinishGame()
    REM *** Hide all sprites ... ***
    HIDE ALL SPRITES
    REM *** ... then show final message and score ***
    SHOW SPRITE finalmsg
    SPRITE tens,610,600,3
    SPRITE units,640,600,3
    SHOW SPRITE tens
    SHOW sprite units
    REM *** Wait before exiting game ***
    WAIT 4000
ENDFUNCTION
```

Activity 23.4

Type in and test the program in LISTING-23.2 (*sprites303.dbpro*).

Modify the program so that the main screen also displays the number of throws taken. (Use a sprite containing *throws.bmp* to display the word *throws*.)

Creating a Sprite that Really is Animated

So far our animated sprites haven't really been animated in the traditional sense of the word. But if you create an image containing the correct pictures, and make the frames in the sprite change quickly enough, you can create the genuine article.

The DarkBASIC Pro software has just the image we need in one of its examples. If you've done a standard installation of DarkBASIC Pro, then the file you need is at *C:\Program Files\Dark Basic Software\Help\Examples\sprite*. The file itself is called *animspr.bmp* and is shown in FIG-23.6 below.

FIG-23.6

An Image Designed to be Animated

With *animspr.bmp* copied into the current project folder, we can load it into a sprite using the lines:

```
CREATE ANIMATED SPRITE 1, "animspr.bmp",4,4,1
SPRITE 1,640,500,1
```

The PLAY SPRITE Statement

When we intend to display the frames of an animated sprite in quick succession, we can use the PLAY SPRITE statement which displays a selected sequence of frames from the sprite with a specified delay between each frame's appearance. This

FIG-23.7

statement has the format shown in FIG-23.7.

In the diagram:

spriteno	is the number of the animated sprite to be played.
startframe	is an integer value specifying the first frame to be played.
finishframe	is an integer value specifying the last frame to be played.
delay	is an integer value representing the delay in milliseconds between the display of each frame.

For example, we could play all 16 frames of the sprite created above, with a 20 millisecond delay between each frame, using the line

```
PLAY SPRITE 1, 1, 16, 20
```

A complete example of the animation effect is shown in LISTING-23.3.

LISTING-23.3

Playing an Animated Sprite

```
REM *** Set screen resolution ***
SET DISPLAY MODE 1280,1024,32
REM *** Create and position the animated sprite ***
CREATE ANIMATED SPRITE 1,"animspr.bmp",4,4,1
SPRITE 1,640,500,1
REM *** Play sprite ***
DO
    PLAY SPRITE 1,1,16,20
LOOP
REM *** End program ***
END
```

Activity 23.5

Type in and test the program given in LISTING-23.3 (*sprites304.dbpro*).

Modify the delay between frames value in PLAY LOOP and see how this affects the display.

Changing the Transparent Colour

As we know, any black area within a sprite is, by default, made transparent on the screen. However, the asteroid contains black areas which we don't want to become transparent. We can get round this problem by using the SET IMAGE COLORKEY statement to change which colour is to be made transparent. In the case of the asteroid image, we've made the background colour magenta - a colour that does not appear in the asteroid itself. We can then make magenta the transparent colour using the line:

The SET IMAGE
COLORKEY was
described in Chapter 19.

```
SET IMAGE COLORKEY 255,0,255
```

Of course, this does mean that every other sprite we use in this program must have a magenta background if we want that background to be transparent.

Activity 23.6

Modify your last program by adding the SET IMAGE COLORKEY statement given above. The statement should be placed immediately before the CREATE ANIMATED SPRITE command.

Moving the Sprite

We now have a stationary animated sprite. The next obvious step is to have the sprite move across the screen while its frames are being played. To do this we need to do is add the line

```
MOVE SPRITE 1,10
```

at the start of the DO loop.

Activity 23.7

Add the above line to your program and check out the resulting display.

In some games, when a sprite moves off the edge of the screen it reappears at the opposite edge (this is known as **screen wrapping**). We'll modify our program so it performs the same trick. First we'll change the sprite's origin to the centre of the image with the line:

```
OFFSET SPRITE 1,SPRITE WIDTH(1)/2,SPRITE HEIGHT(1)/2
```

This makes the movement look a little better. Now we'll check for the sprite moving off the top of the screen and bring it back on at the bottom using the lines

```
IF SPRITE Y(1) < 0
    SPRITE 1,SPRITE X(1),1260,1
ENDIF
```

The latest version of the program is shown in LISTING-23.4.

LISTING-23.4

Wrapping a Moving Sprite

```
REM *** Set screen resolution ***
SET DISPLAY MODE 1280,1024,32
REM *** Make magenta the transparent colour in all images ***
SET IMAGE COLORKEY 255,0,255
REM *** Create and position the animated sprite ***
CREATE ANIMATED SPRITE 1,"animspr.bmp",4,4,1
SPRITE 1,640,500,1
REM *** Reposition sprite's origin at centre of sprite ***
OFFSET SPRITE 1, SPRITE WIDTH(1)/2, SPRITE HEIGHT(1)/2
DO
    REM *** Move sprite ***
    MOVE SPRITE 1,10
    REM *** If its at top, move to bottom ***
    IF SPRITE Y(1) < 0
        SPRITE 1,SPRITE X(1),1260,1
    ENDIF
    REM *** Play sprite ***
    PLAY SPRITE 1,1,16,40
LOOP
REM *** End program ***
END
```

Varying the Velocity

We can change the flight path of the asteroid by starting it on one of the four edges of the screen and then rotating it by a random amount. Since we want the asteroid to travel inwards, the angle of rotation must be within fixed limits for each side (see FIG-23.8.

FIG-23.8

How the Angle Range
Changes With the Start
Position

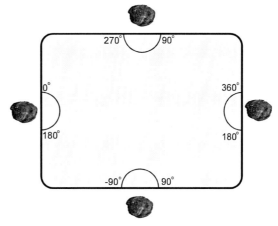

From this we can see that an asteroid entering from the top of the screen should be rotated by an angle of between 90° and 270° to ensure it will start by moving into the screen area. Since we don't want the asteroid to always enter at the exact centre of the side chosen, we need to use another random value to set the x ordinate (top and bottom sides) or the y ordinate (left and right sides). All of this can be coded with the following lines:

```
REM *** Choose which side the asteroid is to enter at ***
side = RND(3)
REM *** Select random coords and angle for the side chosen ***
SELECT side
    CASE 0    'Top of screen
        x = RND(SCREEN WIDTH())
        y = 0
        angle = RND(180)+90
    ENDCASE
    CASE 1    'Right side
        x = SCREEN WIDTH()
        y = RND(SCREEN HEIGHT())
        angle = RND(180)+180
    ENDCASE
    CASE 2    'Bottom of screen
        x = RND(SCREEN WIDTH())
        y = SCREEN HEIGHT()
        angle = RND(180) - 90
    ENDCASE
    CASE 3    'Left of screen
        x = 0
        y = RND(SCREEN HEIGHT())
        angle = RND(180)
    ENDCASE
ENDSELECT
REM *** Rotate and position sprite ***
ROTATE SPRITE 1, angle
SPRITE 1, x, y, 1
```

Now we'll have to check for the sprite moving off the screen on any side too. This needs the following code:

```
IF SPRITE Y(1) < 0                          `Top
    SPRITE 1,SPRITE X(1),SCREEN HEIGHT(),1
ENDIF
IF SPRITE Y(1) > SCREEN HEIGHT()      `Bottom
    SPRITE 1,SPRITE X(1),0,1
ENDIF
IF SPRITE X(1) < 0                          `Left
    SPRITE 1,SCREEN WIDTH(),SPRITE Y(1),1
ENDIF
IF SPRITE X(1) > SCREEN WIDTH()        `Right
    SPRITE 1,0,SPRITE Y(1),1
ENDIF
```

Activity 23.9

Use the code given to modify your program so that the asteroid takes a
random trajectory.

Multiple Asteroids

The program in LISTING-23.5 uses 10 asteroids rather than just one. It uses a
constant to define the sprite number of the first asteroid:

```
#CONSTANT firstasteroid    51
```

The first asteroid is then prepared using the lines

```
REM *** Load sprite and set origin ***
CREATE ANIMATED SPRITE firstasteroid, "animspr.bmp",4,4,1
OFFSET SPRITE firstasteroid, SPRITE WIDTH(firstasteroid)/2,
⮡SPRITE HEIGHT(firstasteroid)/2
```

and cloned nine times with the code:

```
FOR spriteno = firstasteroid+1 TO firstasteroid + 9
    CLONE SPRITE firstasteroid,spriteno
NEXT spriteno
```

Positioning and moving the asteroids uses the same logic as before, but this time
that logic is placed inside a FOR loop with each iteration handling a different sprite.
In addition, the code has been split into routines to make it easier to follow.

LISTING-23.5

Using Multiple Asteroids

```
REM *** First asteroid's sprite number ***
#CONSTANT firstasteroid 51


InitialiseGame()
CreateAsteroids()
StartPositionsForAsteroids()
DO
   HandleAsteroids()
LOOP
END




                                    continued on next page
```

LISTING-23.5

(continued)

Using Multiple Asteroids

```
FUNCTION InitialiseGame()
   REM *** Seed random number generator ***
   RANDOMIZE TIMER()
   REM *** Set screen resolution ***
   SET DISPLAY MODE 1280,1024,32
   REM *** Make magenta the transparent colour ***
   SET IMAGE COLORKEY 255,0,255
ENDFUNCTION

FUNCTION CreateAsteroids()
   REM *** Load sprite and set origin ***
   CREATE ANIMATED SPRITE firstasteroid,"animspr.bmp",4,4,1
   OFFSET SPRITE firstasteroid, SPRITE WIDTH(firstasteroid)/2,
   ⮑SPRITE HEIGHT(firstasteroid)/2
   REM *** Create 9 other copies ***
   FOR spriteno = firstasteroid + 1 TO firstasteroid + 9
      CLONE SPRITE firstasteroid,spriteno
   NEXT spriteno
ENDFUNCTION

FUNCTION StartPositionsForAsteroids()
   REM *** FOR each asteroid DO ***
   FOR spriteno = firstasteroid TO firstasteroid + 9
      REM *** Choose the side of screen where it will start ***
      side = RND(3)
      REM *** Set coordinates and rotation based on side ***
      SELECT side
         CASE 0   'Top of screen
               x = RND(SCREEN WIDTH())
               y = 0
               angle = RND(180)+90
         ENDCASE
         CASE 1   'Right side
               x = SCREEN WIDTH()
               y = RND(SCREEN HEIGHT())
               angle = RND(180)+180
         ENDCASE
         CASE 2    'Bottom of screen
               x = RND(SCREEN WIDTH())
               y = SCREEN HEIGHT()
               angle = RND(180) - 90
         ENDCASE
         CASE 3   'Left of screen
               x = 0
               y = RND(SCREEN HEIGHT())
               angle = RND(180)
         ENDCASE
      ENDSELECT
      REM *** Rotate sprite and move to start position ***
      ROTATE SPRITE spriteno,angle
      SPRITE spriteno, x, y, 1
   NEXT spriteno
ENDFUNCTION

FUNCTION HandleAsteroids
   REM *** FOR each asteroid DO ***
   FOR spriteno = firstasteroid TO firstasteroid + 9
      REM *** Move the sprite ***
      MOVE SPRITE spriteno, 10
      REM *** IF it goes off the edge wrap it round ***
      IF SPRITE Y(spriteno) < 0
         SPRITE spriteno,SPRITE X(spriteno),SCREEN HEIGHT(),1
      ENDIF
      IF SPRITE Y(spriteno) > SCREEN HEIGHT()
         SPRITE spriteno,SPRITE X(spriteno),0,1
      ENDIF
```

continued on next page

LISTING-23.5
(continued)

Using Multiple Asteroids

```
        IF SPRITE X(spriteno) < 0
            SPRITE spriteno,SCREEN WIDTH(),SPRITE Y(spriteno),1
        ENDIF
        IF SPRITE X(spriteno) > SCREEN WIDTH()
            SPRITE spriteno,0,SPRITE Y(spriteno),1
        ENDIF
        REM *** Run through the frames in the sprite ***
        PLAY SPRITE spriteno,1,16,40
    NEXT spriteno
ENDFUNCTION
```

Activity 23.10

Type in and test the program given above (*sprites305.dbpro*).

Controlling the Spaceship

The next stage is to create a missile-firing spaceship which sits in the centre of the screen. We'll do this as a separate program for the moment, just to keep things simple. There are quite a few new techniques in this program, so we'll build two separate versions, working through it a routine at a time. The main logic for the program is:

```
Initialise game
DO
     Handle keyboard
     Handle ship
     Handle missile
LOOP
```

The *HandleKeyboard()* Function

Each of the main statements can be turned into routines. What's involved in Initialise game isn't too obvious at this stage, so we'll start with Handle keyboard.

This routine needs to detect the *z*, *x* and *spacebar* keys being pressed on the keyboard. If *z* is pressed, the spaceship should rotate 5° anti-clockwise; if *x* is pressed, then the spaceship needs to rotate 5° clockwise; when the space bar is pressed a new missile should be created. Since key presses control more than one sprite, we'll make the routine record what keys have been pressed and then pass this information on to the other routines. These other routines can then handle the sprites accordingly.

We'll record the keys pressed by setting individual bits within a byte using the following setup:

Key pressed	Bit set
z	0
x	1
space	2

The byte can be set up in a global variable with the line:

```
GLOBAL keyspressed AS BYTE
```

The code for the routine is shown overleaf:

```
FUNCTION HandleKeyboard()
    REM *** Clear byte ***
    keyspressed = 0
    REM *** IF z pressed set bit 0 ***
    IF KEYSTATE(44) = 1
        keyspressed = keyspressed || %001
    ELSE
        REM *** IF x pressed, set bit 1
        IF KEYSTATE(45)= 1
            keyspressed = keyspressed || %010
        ENDIF
    ENDIF
    REM *** IF space pressed, set bit 2  ***
    IF KEYSTATE(57) = 1
        keyspressed = keyspressed || %100
    ENDIF
ENDFUNCTION
```

We can try out this routine by creating a test handler as shown below:

```
GLOBAL keyspressed AS BYTE
REM *** Test driver for HandleKeyboard() ***
REM *** Set screen resolution ***
SET DISPLAY MODE 1280,1024,32
DO
    REM *** Call routine being tested ***
    HandleKeyboard()
    REM *** Display key pressed data ***
    CLS
    PRINT "Keys pressed ";
    IF (keyspressed && %001) > 0
        PRINT "z";
    ENDIF
    IF (keyspressed && %010) > 0
        PRINT "x";
    ENDIF
    IF (keyspressed && %100) > 0
        PRINT "space";
    ENDIF
LOOP
END
```

Activity 23.11

Create a complete program containing *HandleKeyboard()* and its test driver
(*sprites306.dbpro*).

Modify the driver so that the numeric value of *keyspressed* is also displayed.

The *HandleShip()* Function

With the *HandleKeyboard()* function operating correctly we can move on to
HandleShip().

The ship reacts to the key presses, by rotating left, rotating right, or launching a
missile. This can be coded as follows:

```
FUNCTION HandleShip()
    REM *** If z, decrease angle of rotation ***
    IF (keyspressed && %001) > 0
        angle = WRAPVALUE(angle-5);
    ENDIF
    REM *** IF x, increase angle of rotation ***
```

```
            IF (keyspressed && %010) > 0
                angle = WRAPVALUE(angle+5)
            ENDIF
            REM *** IF space, launch missile ***
            IF (keyspressed && %100) > 0
                LaunchMissile()
            ENDIF
            REM *** Update ship's rotation ***
            ROTATE SPRITE ship, angle
        ENDFUNCTION
```

From this we can see that we need a global variable to hold the ship's angle of
rotation (*angle*), that we need access to the ship's sprite, identified using the constant
(*ship*), and a new routine to launch a missile (*LaunchMissile()*).

The constant and variable are created with the lines:

```
#CONSTANT ship 1
GLOBAL angle AS INTEGER
```

The new routine can be created as a test stub for the moment:

```
FUNCTION LaunchMissile()
    PRINT "Launch missile"
ENDFUNCTION
```

We also need code to create the ship sprite. Since this is the sort of thing done at
the start of a program, we now have some code which can be placed in
InitialiseGame():

ship.bmp contains an image
with a magenta background.
This matches the background
colour used by *animspr.bmp*.

The image number assigned to
ship.bmp is 2 since 1 is
already used by *animspr.bmp*
which will eventually be
incorporated in this program.

```
FUNCTION InitialiseGame()
    REM *** Set screen resolution ***
    SET DISPLAY MODE 1280,1024,32
    REM *** Make magenta the transparent colour ***
    SET IMAGE COLORKEY 255,0,255
    REM *** Load ship sprite ***
    LOAD IMAGE "ship.bmp",2
    SPRITE ship, SCREEN WIDTH()/2, SCREEN HEIGHT()/2,2
    REM *** Centre origin of sprite ***
    OFFSET SPRITE ship,SPRITE WIDTH(ship)/2,SPRITE HEIGHT(ship)/2
ENDFUNCTION
```

The complete program so far is shown in LISTING-23.6.

LISTING-23.6

Adding the *HandleShip()*
Routine

```
#CONSTANT ship      1
GLOBAL keyspressed AS BYTE
GLOBAL angle AS INTEGER
REM *** Test driver for HandleShip() ***
InitialiseGame()
DO
   HandleKeyboard()
   REM *** Call routine being tested ***
   HandleShip()
LOOP
END

FUNCTION InitialiseGame()
   REM *** Set screen resolution ***
   SET DISPLAY MODE 1280,1024,32
   REM *** Make magenta the transparent colour ***
   SET IMAGE COLORKEY 255,0,255
   REM *** Load ship sprite ***
   LOAD IMAGE "ship.bmp",2
```

continued on next page

LISTING-23.6
(continued)

Adding the *HandleShip()*
Routine

```
     SPRITE ship, SCREEN WIDTH()/2, SCREEN HEIGHT()/2,2
     REM *** Centre origin of sprite ***
     OFFSET SPRITE ship, SPRITE WIDTH(ship)/2, SPRITE HEIGHT(ship)/2
ENDFUNCTION

FUNCTION HandleKeyboard()
   REM *** Clear byte ***
   keyspressed = 0
   REM *** IF z pressed set bit 0 ***
   IF KEYSTATE(44) = 1
      keyspressed = keyspressed || %001
   ELSE
      REM *** IF x pressed, set bit 1
      IF KEYSTATE(45)= 1
         keyspressed = keyspressed || %010
      ENDIF
   ENDIF
   REM *** IF space pressed, set bit 2  ***
   IF KEYSTATE(57) = 1
      keyspressed = keyspressed || %100
   ENDIF
ENDFUNCTION

FUNCTION HandleShip()
   REM *** If z, decrease angle of rotation ***
   IF (keyspressed && %001) > 0
      angle = WRAPVALUE(angle-5)
   ENDIF
   REM *** IF x, increase angle of rotation ***
   IF (keyspressed && %010) > 0
      angle = WRAPVALUE(angle+5)
   ENDIF
   REM *** IF space, launch missile ***
   IF (keyspressed && %100) > 0
      LaunchMissile()
   ENDIF
   REM *** Update ship's rotation ***
   ROTATE SPRITE ship, angle
ENDFUNCTION

FUNCTION LaunchMissile()
   PRINT "LaunchMissile()"
ENDFUNCTION
```

Activity 23.12

Update your program to match the code in LISTING-23.6.

Does the ship rotate correctly? Is the *LaunchMissile()* routine called when the space bar is pressed?

In the game, a missile can only be created if at least one second has passed since the last missile was created. If we record the time when a new missile is created in the *LaunchMissile()* function using the line

```
    lastfired = TIMER()
```

then we can update the IF statement used to call the *LaunchMissile()* function from

```
    IF (keyspressed && %100) > 0
```
to
```
    IF (keyspressed && %100) > 0 AND TIMER() - lastfired > 1000
```

which will ensure that missiles cannot be created too rapidly.

The variable *lastfired* needs to be declared as a GLOBAL and intialised in the *InitialiseGame()* function with the line

```
lastfired = TIMER()
```

Activity 23.13

Make the changes described above to your program.

A one second delay between missile firings will be too large a delay, change the time gap to 100 milliseconds.

The *LaunchMissile()* Function

It is time to replace the *LaunchMissile()* stub with the actual code for the routine.

This routine is designed to create the missile sprite. Movement of the missile is then handled by another routine, *HandleMissile()* which we will code later. Since the missile is fired from the ship, the missile's position and orientation needs to match that of the ship. The other problem we have is deciding what value to assign to the missile sprite. Unlike the ship, there may be several missiles and each must be assigned a unique integer value. However, once a missile is destroyed its value may be reused when another missile is created. The basic logic required by this routine is:

```
Create a missile sprite
Rotate the missile to match the rotation of the ship
Position the missile at the front of the ship
Record when the missile was created
```

We'll need to load the image used by the missile sprite. Since this is a one-off task, it should be done in *InitialiseGame()* using the line:

```
LOAD IMAGE "missile.bmp",3
```

We need to record two pieces of information about the missile's sprite number:

➤ The number assigned to the first missile

➤ The number assigned to the next missile to created

For the first of these we can use a constant; for the second, a global variable:

```
#CONSTANT firstmissile      101
GLOBAL missileno AS INTEGER
```

At the start of the program, these two values will be equal:

```
missileno = firstmissile
```

This last line belongs in *InitialiseGame()*.

Now we can code our new routine:

```
FUNCTION LaunchMissile()
    REM *** Create a new missile sprite ***
    REM *** Match new missile position with front of ship ***
```

```
            SPRITE missileno, SPRITE X(ship), SPRITE Y(ship),3
            OFFSET SPRITE missileno, SPRITE WIDTH(missileno)/2,
            ↳SPRITE HEIGHT(missileno)/2
            ROTATE SPRITE missileno, SPRITE ANGLE(ship)
            MOVE SPRITE missileno, 30
            REM *** Record the time this missile was fired ***
            lastfired = TIMER()
            REM *** Add to missileno ***
            INC missileno
        ENDFUNCTION
```

Activity 23.14

Update your program with the new code described above.

If we leave the *LaunchMissile()* code as it is, then the player will be able to create an unlimited number of missiles and the value of *missileno* could become very large. To stop this we'll limit the number of missiles that can be active at any time to 10 and keep the value of *missileno* in the range *firstmissile* to *firstmissile* + 9. To achieve this we'll need to increment *missileno* using the line:

```
missileno = missileno mod 10 + firstmissile
```

Activity 23.15

If *missileno* has the value 110 before the above line is executed, what value will it have after that line is executed?

Since we will be reusing sprite numbers, we need to make sure that a sprite of the same number does not already exist before we attempt to create a new sprite. So *LaunchMissile()* needs to start with the lines:

```
IF SPRITE EXIST(missileno)
    EXITFUNCTION
ENDIF
```

With these changes, the new code for *LaunchMissile()* becomes:

```
FUNCTION LaunchMissile()
    REM *** IF missile exists, exit routine ***
    IF SPRITE EXIST(missileno)
        EXITFUNCTION
    ENDIF
    REM *** Create a new missile sprite ***
    REM *** Match new missile position with front of ship ***
    SPRITE missileno, SPRITE X(ship), SPRITE Y(ship),3
    OFFSET SPRITE missileno, SPRITE WIDTH(missileno)/2,
    ↳SPRITE HEIGHT(missileno)/2
    ROTATE SPRITE missileno,SPRITE ANGLE(ship)
    MOVE SPRITE missileno, 30
    REM *** Record the time this missile was fired ***
    lastfired = TIMER()
    REM *** Add to missileno ***
    missileno = missileno mod 10 + firstmissile
ENDFUNCTION
```

Activity 23.16

Modify your program to match this code. How many missiles can be created?

At the moment missiles are never deleted, so we run out of unique sprite numbers after 10 missiles are created, but later we'll make sure missiles are destroyed when they have travelled a fixed distance from the ship or when an asteroid is hit.

The *HandleMissiles()* Routine

The last routine we need here, *HandleMissiles()*, must cycle through each missile sprite number, and if that sprite exists, move it a fixed amount along its path. In the code given we've moved each missile by 15 pixels every time the function is called. The code for this routine is:

```
FUNCTION HandleMissiles()
    REM *** FOR each possible missile DO ***
    FOR spriteno = firstmissile TO firstmissile + 9
        REM *** IF it exists, move it ***
        IF SPRITE EXIST(spriteno)
            MOVE SPRITE spriteno, 15
        ENDIF
    NEXT spriteno
ENDFUNCTION
```

We can incorporate this new routine into our program by changing the main logic to read:

```
REM *** Main section ***
InitialiseGame()
DO
    HandleKeyboard()
    HandleShip()
    HandleMissiles()
LOOP
END
```

Activity 23.17

Change your program as described and make sure the missiles move correctly.

We've now got a working program, but it would be good if we could fire more missiles after the first 10 had disappeared off the screen. In the next change we're going to allow the missiles 40 moves (a distance of 600 pixels) before they disappear. When that happens, the sprite number can be reused to make a new missile.

To achieve this goal we'll need to keep track of how many moves each of the 10 missiles has made, and to do that we'll use an array:

```
GLOBAL DIM missilemoves (9)    'Moves made by each missile
```

How many times missile 101 has moved will be recorded in *missilemoves(0)*, the moves made by missile 102 in *missilemoves(1)*, etc.

Initially, at the start of the game, the array elements will contain zero:

```
FOR c = 0 TO 9
    missilemoves(c) = 0
NEXT c
```

DarkBASIC Pro doesn't really need this code since array elements are automatically set to zero. However, most other languages won't be that obliging, so we'll keep the code just in case we ever try to convert the program to some other language!

Whenever a missile moves, the contents of the appropriate cell of the array need to be incremented. If the number of moves for a missile reaches 40, then that missile is destroyed. This involves rewriting *HandleMissiles()* to use the following logic:

```
FOR each possible missile DO
    IF the missile exists THEN
        Move the missile
        Add 1 to the number of moves made by that missile
        IF the number of moves is 40 or above THEN
            Destroy the missile
            Reset the move count for that missile to zero
        ENDIF
    ENDIF
ENDFOR
```

This is implemented using the following code:

```
FUNCTION HandleMissiles()
    REM *** FOR each possible missile ***
    FOR spriteno = firstmissile TO firstmissile + 9
        REM *** IF it exists, move it and add 1 to moves ***
        IF SPRITE EXIST(spriteno)
            MOVE SPRITE spriteno, 15
            REM *** Calculate array element used by this sprite ***
            post = spriteno - firstmissile
            INC missilemoves(post)
            REM *** If sprite made 40 moves, destroy it ***
            REM *** and set moves back to zero ***
            IF missilemoves(post) >= 40
                DELETE SPRITE spriteno
                missilemoves(post) = 0
            ENDIF
        ENDIF
    NEXT spriteno
ENDFUNCTION
```

Activity 23.18

Update your program to incorporate these changes and make sure an unlimited number of missiles can be created so long as there are no more than 10 on screen.

Adding the Asteroids

Now it's time to add the two sections of our game together to create the final product.

Activity 23.19

Copy the following routines from s*prites305.dbpro* into *sprites306.dpro*.
   CreateAsteroids()
   StartPositionsForAsteroids()
   HandleAsteroids()
Place calls to *CreateAsteroids()* and *StartPositionForAsteroids()* in the *InitialiseGame()* function.
Modify the main section to call *HandleAsteroids()* after the call to *HandleMissiles()*.

Now we have to destroy the asteroids when the missiles hit them. This is done in the *HandleMissiles()* function. Since a missile could hit any of the asteroids we need to use the line

```
spritehit = SPRITE HIT(spriteno,0)
```

to return the sprite number of anything hit by the missile. If nothing is hit, zero is returned. This is followed by code to destroy the asteroid and missile as well as reset the missile's move count to zero:

We're using the condition *spritehit > 1* so that the missile cannot hit the ship (sprite 1).

```
IF spritehit > 1
    DELETE SPRITE spritehit
    DELETE SPRITE spriteno
    post = spriteno - firstmissile
    missilemoves(post) = 0
```

The remaining code, that is, updating the missile sprites moves, is only executed if the missile wasn't destroyed, so much of our previous code must now appear in the ELSE section of this new IF statement. The final code for the routine is:

```
FUNCTION HandleMissiles()
    REM *** FOR each possible missile DO ***
    FOR spriteno = firstmissile + 1 TO firstmissile + 10
        REM *** IF it exists THEN ***
        IF SPRITE EXIST(spriteno)
            REM *** move it ***
            MOVE SPRITE spriteno, 15
            REM *** IF missile hits asteroid, destroy both ***
            spritehit = SPRITE HIT(spriteno,0)
            IF spritehit > 1
                DELETE SPRITE spritehit
                DELETE SPRITE spriteno
                post = spriteno - firstmissile
                missilemoves(post) = 0
            ELSE
                REM *** Add update no. of moves ***
                post = spriteno - firstmissile
                INC missilemoves(post)
                REM *** IF 40 or more moves, destroy it ***
                IF missilemoves(post) >= 40
                    DELETE SPRITE spriteno
                    REM *** and reset moves to zero ***
                    missilemoves(post) = 0
                ENDIF
            ENDIF
        ENDIF
    NEXT spriteno
ENDFUNCTION
```

The *HandleAsteroid()* function assumes that all 10 asteroids exist. Since that is no longer always true we have to check for the asteroid's existence before trying to move it. The new code for the routine is:

```
FUNCTION HandleAsteroids()
    REM *** FOR each asteroid DO ***
    FOR spriteno = 1 TO 10
        IF SPRITE EXIST (spriteno)
            REM *** Move the sprite ***
            MOVE SPRITE spriteno, 10
            REM *** IF it goes off the edge wrap it round ***
            IF SPRITE Y(spriteno) < 0
                SPRITE spriteno, SPRITE X(spriteno),
                SCREEN HEIGHT(),1
            ENDIF
            IF SPRITE Y(spriteno) > SCREEN HEIGHT()
                SPRITE spriteno, SPRITE X(spriteno),0,1
            ENDIF
            IF SPRITE X(spriteno) < 0
                SPRITE spriteno, SCREEN WIDTH(),
                SPRITE Y(spriteno),1
            ENDIF
            IF SPRITE X(spriteno) > SCREEN WIDTH()
```

```
                    SPRITE spriteno, 0,SPRITE Y(spriteno),1
            ENDIF
            REM *** Run through the frames in the sprite ***
            PLAY SPRITE spriteno,1,16,40
        ENDIF
    NEXT spriteno
ENDFUNCTION
```

A screen shot of the final game is shown in FIG-23.9.

FIG-23.9

A Screen Shot of the
Completed Game

Activity 23.20

Add the asteroid routines and the changes described to create the final
program.

The game is probably too easy. How could we adjust the code to make the
game more challenging?

Summary

- An animated sprite consists of two or more frames.

- The frames of an animated sprite are initially held in a single picture file.

- An animated sprite is created using the CREATE ANIMATED SPRITE
  statement.

- When an animated sprite is created, the picture specified is split into the set of
  frames that make up the animation.

- To display an animated sprite, use the normal SPRITE statement.

- Initially, an animated sprite displays the first frame (frame 1) of its frame
  sequence.

- The SET SPRITE FRAME statement is used to display any single frame of an
  animated sprite.

- The SPRITE FRAME statement returns the number of the frame currently being displayed by a specified sprite.

- The PLAY SPRITE statement can be used to cycle through all or some of the frames within a specified sprite.

Solutions

Activity 23.1

The first frame of the sprite is visible.

Activity 23.2

```
REM *** set up a name for the sprite ***
#CONSTANT dice 1
REM *** Set screen resolution ***
SET DISPLAY MODE 1280,1024,32
REM *** Load animated sprite ***
CREATE ANIMATED SPRITE dice, "dice32.bmp",
3,2,1
REM *** Display sprite ***
SPRITE dice,640,500,1
FOR frame = 1 TO 6
    SET SPRITE FRAME dice, frame
    WAIT KEY
NEXT frame
REM *** End program ***
WAIT KEY
END
```

Activity 23.3

```
REM *** set up a name for each sprite ***
#CONSTANT dice    1
#CONSTANT digit   2
REM *** Seed random number generator ***
RANDOMIZE TIMER()
REM *** Set screen resolution ***
SET DISPLAY MODE 1280,1024,32
REM *** Load dice sprite ***
CREATE ANIMATED SPRITE dice,
"dice32.bmp",3,2,1
REM *** Load digits sprite ***
CREATE ANIMATED SPRITE digit,
"0to9.bmp",10,1,2
DO
    REM *** Display dice ***
    SPRITE dice,640,500,1
    dicevalue = RND(5)+1
    SET SPRITE FRAME dice,dicevalue
    SPRITE digit, 10,12,2
    SET SPRITE FRAME digit, dicevalue+1
    REM *** Wait for key press ***
    WAIT KEY
LOOP
REM *** End program ***
END
```

Activity 23.4

```
REM *** Sprite names ***
#CONSTANT dice1          1
#CONSTANT dice2          2
#CONSTANT units          3
#CONSTANT tens           4
#CONSTANT headingmsg     5
#CONSTANT scoremsg       6
#CONSTANT throwmsg       7
#CONSTANT finalmsg       8
#CONSTANT throwsmademsg  9
#CONSTANT throwunits     10
#CONSTANT throwtens      11
REM *** Main data items ***
GLOBAL dice1value AS INTEGER  `throw on
first dice
GLOBAL dice2value AS INTEGER  `throw on
second dice
GLOBAL score AS INTEGER       `total score
GLOBAL throws AS INTEGER       `throws taken
```

```
REM *** Main Logic ***
InitialiseGame()
ThrowDice()
WHILE NoOnes()
    UpdateScore()
    UpdateThrows()
    ThrowDice()
ENDWHILE
FinishGame()
END

FUNCTION InitialiseGame()
    REM *** Seed random number generator ***
    RANDOMIZE TIMER()
    REM *** Set throws and score to zero ***
    throws = 0
    score = 0
    REM *** Set screen resolution ***
    SET DISPLAY MODE 1280,1024,32
    REM *** Load game heading ***
    LOAD IMAGE "diceHeading.bmp",5
    SPRITE headingmsg,470,50,5
    REM *** Load score message ***
    LOAD IMAGE "diceScore.bmp",6
    SPRITE scoremsg,1020,105,6
    REM *** Set up score digits ***
    CREATE ANIMATED SPRITE units,
    "0to9.bmp",10,1,3
    CLONE SPRITE units, tens
    SPRITE tens,1100,100,3
    SPRITE units,1125,100,3
    REM *** Set up dice ***
    CREATE ANIMATED SPRITE dice1,
    "dice61.bmp",6,1,1
    CLONE SPRITE dice1, dice2
    SPRITE dice1,550,500,1
    SPRITE dice2,650,500,1
    REM *** Set up roll dice message... ***
    LOAD IMAGE "diceThrow.bmp",7
    SPRITE throwmsg,470,800,7
    REM *** ... but hide it ***
    HIDE SPRITE throwmsg
    REM *** Load & hide gameover message ***
    LOAD IMAGE "diceover.bmp",8
    SPRITE finalmsg,530,500,8
    HIDE SPRITE finalmsg
    REM *** Set up number of throws ***
    LOAD IMAGE "throws.bmp",9
    SPRITE throwsmademsg, 1020,155,9
    REM *** Set up throws digits ***
    CLONE SPRITE units, throwunits
    CLONE SPRITE units, throwtens
    SPRITE throwtens, 1100,150,3
    SPRITE throwunits, 1125,150,3
ENDFUNCTION

FUNCTION ThrowDice()
    REM *** Display prompt ***
    SHOW SPRITE throwmsg
    WAIT KEY
    REM *** Hide message ***
    HIDE SPRITE throwmsg
    WAIT 500
    REM *** throw dice ***
    dice1value = RND(5)+1
    dice2value = RND(5)+1
    SET SPRITE FRAME dice1,dice1value
    SET SPRITE FRAME dice2,dice2value
    WAIT 500
ENDFUNCTION

FUNCTION NoOnes()
    REM *** IF either dice 1, return 0 ***
    IF dice1value =1 OR dice2value = 1
        result = 0
```

```
        ELSE
            result = 1
        ENDIF
ENDFUNCTION result

FUNCTION UpdateScore()
    REM *** Add dice values to score ***
    score = score + dice1value + dice2value
    REM *** Update the score sprites ***
    tensvalue = score / 10
    unitsvalue = score mod 10
    SET SPRITE FRAME tens, (tensvalue+1)
    SET SPRITE FRAME units, (unitsvalue + 1)
    REM *** Make score blink ***
    HIDE SPRITE tens
    HIDE SPRITE units
    WAIT 500
    SHOW SPRITE tens
    SHOW SPRITE units
    REM *** Wait before going on ***
    WAIT 1000
ENDFUNCTION

FUNCTION FinishGame()
    REM *** Hide all sprites ***
    HIDE ALL SPRITES
    REM *** Show end message & score ***
    SHOW SPRITE finalmsg
    SPRITE tens,610,600,3
    SPRITE units,640,600,3
    SHOW SPRITE tens
    SHOW sprite units
    REM *** Wait before exiting game ***
    WAIT 4000
ENDFUNCTION

FUNCTION UpdateThrows()
    REM *** Add 1 to throws made ***
    INC throws
    tensvalue = throws / 10
    unitsvalue = throws mod 10
    SET SPRITE FRAME throwtens, (tensvalue+1)
    SET SPRITE FRAME throwunits,
    (unitsvalue + 1)
    REM *** Make score blink ***
    HIDE SPRITE throwtens
    HIDE SPRITE throwunits
    WAIT 500
    SHOW SPRITE throwtens
    SHOW SPRITE throwunits
    REM *** Wait before going on ***
    WAIT 1000
ENDFUNCTION
```

Activity 23.5

No solution required.

Activity 23.6

```
REM *** Set screen resolution ***
SET DISPLAY MODE 1280, 1024, 32
REM *** Transparent colour to magenta ***
SET IMAGE COLORKEY 255,0,255
REM *** Create & place animated sprite ***
CREATE ANIMATED SPRITE 1,
"animspr.bmp",4,4,1
SPRITE 1,640,500,1
REM *** Play sprite ***
DO
    PLAY SPRITE 1,1,16,20
LOOP
REM *** End program ***
END
```

Activity 23.7

```
REM *** Set screen resolution ***
SET DISPLAY MODE 1280, 1024, 32
REM *** Transparent colour to magenta ***
SET IMAGE COLORKEY 255,0,255
REM *** Create & place animated sprite ***
SET IMAGE COLORKEY 255,0,255
CREATE ANIMATED SPRITE 1,
"animspr.bmp",4,4,1
SPRITE 1,640,500,1
REM *** Play sprite ***
DO
    MOVE SPRITE 1,10
    PLAY SPRITE 1,1,16,20
LOOP
REM *** End program ***
END
```

Activity 23.8

No solution required.

Activity 23.9

```
REM *** Set screen resolution ***
SET DISPLAY MODE 1280, 1024, 32
REM *** Transparent colour to magenta ***
SET IMAGE COLORKEY 255,0,255
REM *** Create & place animated sprite ***
CREATE ANIMATED SPRITE 1,
"animspr.bmp",4,4,1
SPRITE 1,640,500,1
REM *** Sprite's origin to centre ***
OFFSET SPRITE 1, SPRITE WIDTH(1)/2, SPRITE
HEIGHT(1)/2
REM *** Seed random number generator ***
RANDOMIZE TIMER()
REM *** Position sprite ***
side = RND(3)
SELECT side
    CASE 0  `Top of screen
        x = RND(SCREEN WIDTH())
        y = 0
        angle = RND(180)+90
    ENDCASE
    CASE 1  `Right side
        x = SCREEN WIDTH()
        y = RND(SCREEN HEIGHT())
        angle = RND(180)+180
    ENDCASE
    CASE 2  `Bottom of screen
        x = RND(SCREEN WIDTH())
        y = SCREEN HEIGHT()
        angle = RND(180) - 90
    ENDCASE
    CASE 3  `Left of screen
        x = 0
        y = RND(SCREEN HEIGHT())
        angle = RND(180)
    ENDCASE
ENDSELECT
ROTATE SPRITE 1, angle
SPRITE 1, x, y, 1
DO
    REM *** Move sprite ***
    MOVE SPRITE 1, 10
    REM *** If off screen, wrap it ***
    IF SPRITE Y(1) < 0
        SPRITE 1, SPRITE X(1),
        SCREEN HEIGHT(),1
    ENDIF
    IF SPRITE Y(1) > SCREEN HEIGHT()
        SPRITE 1, SPRITE X(1),0,1
    ENDIF
```

```
        IF SPRITE X(1) < 0
            SPRITE 1, SCREEN WIDTH(),
            SPRITE Y(1),1
        ENDIF
        IF SPRITE X(1) > SCREEN WIDTH()
            SPRITE 1,0,SPRITE Y(1),1
        ENDIF
        REM *** Play sprite ***
        PLAY SPRITE 1,1,16,20
    LOOP
    END
```

Activity 23.10

No solution required.

Activity 23.11

```
    GLOBAL keyspressed AS BYTE

    REM *** Test driver for HandleKeyboard()
    ***
    REM *** Set screen resolution ***
    SET DISPLAY MODE 1280, 1024, 32
    DO
        REM *** Call routine being tested ***
        HandleKeyboard()
        REM *** Display key pressed data ***
        CLS
        REM *** Display value of keyspressed ***
        PRINT "keyspressed = ",keyspressed
        PRINT "Keys pressed ";
        IF (keyspressed && %001) > 0
            PRINT "z";
        ENDIF
        IF (keyspressed && %010) > 0
            PRINT "x";
        ENDIF
        IF (keyspressed && %100) > 0
            PRINT "space";
        ENDIF
    LOOP
    END

    FUNCTION HandleKeyboard()
        REM *** Clear byte ***
        keyspressed = 0
        REM *** IF z pressed set bit 0 ***
        IF KEYSTATE(44) = 1
            keyspressed = keyspressed || %001
        ELSE
            REM *** IF x pressed, set bit 1
            IF KEYSTATE(45)= 1
                keyspressed = keyspressed || %010
            ENDIF
        ENDIF
        REM *** IF space pressed, set bit 2  ***
        IF KEYSTATE(57) = 1
            keyspressed = keyspressed || %100
        ENDIF
    ENDFUNCTION
```

Activity 23.12

The ship rotates as expected. The *CreateMissile()* function is called when the space bar is pressed.

Activity 23.13

```
    #CONSTANT ship     1
    GLOBAL keyspressed AS BYTE
    GLOBAL angle AS INTEGER
    GLOBAL lastfired AS INTEGER
```

```
    REM *** Test driver for HandleShip() ***
    InitialiseGame()
    DO
        HandleKeyboard()
        REM *** Call routine being tested ***
        HandleShip()
    LOOP
    END

    FUNCTION InitialiseGame()
        REM *** Set screen resolution ***
        SET DISPLAY MODE 1280, 1024, 32
        REM *** Make background magenta ***
        SET IMAGE COLORKEY 255, 0, 255
        REM *** Load ship sprite ***
        LOAD IMAGE "ship.bmp",2
        SPRITE ship, SCREEN WIDTH()/2,
        SCREEN HEIGHT()/2,2
        OFFSET SPRITE ship,SPRITE WIDTH(ship)/2,
        SPRITE HEIGHT(ship)/2
        lastfired = TIMER()
    ENDFUNCTION

    FUNCTION HandleKeyboard()
        REM *** Clear byte ***
        keyspressed = 0
        REM *** IF z pressed set bit 0 ***
        IF KEYSTATE(44) = 1
            keyspressed = keyspressed || %001
        ELSE
            REM *** IF x pressed, set bit 1
            IF KEYSTATE(45)= 1
                keyspressed = keyspressed || %010
            ENDIF
        ENDIF
        REM *** IF space pressed, set bit 2  ***
        IF KEYSTATE(57) = 1
            keyspressed = keyspressed || %100
        ENDIF
    ENDFUNCTION

    FUNCTION HandleShip()
        REM *** If z, decrease angle ***
        IF (keyspressed && %001) > 0
            angle = WRAPVALUE(angle-5);
        ENDIF
        REM *** IF x, increase angle ***
        IF (keyspressed && %010) > 0
            angle = WRAPVALUE(angle+5)
        ENDIF
        REM *** IF space, launch missile ***
        IF (keyspressed && %100) > 0 AND
        TIMER() - lastfired > 100
            LaunchMissile()
        ENDIF
        REM *** Update ship's rotation ***
        ROTATE SPRITE ship, angle
    ENDFUNCTION

    FUNCTION LaunchMissile()
        PRINT "LaunchMissile()"
        lastfired = TIMER()
    ENDFUNCTION
```

Activity 23.14

```
    #CONSTANT ship          1
    #CONSTANT firstmissile   101

    GLOBAL keyspressed AS BYTE
    GLOBAL angle AS INTEGER
    GLOBAL lastfired AS INTEGER
    GLOBAL missileno  AS INTEGER

    REM *** Test driver for LaunchMissile() ***
    InitialiseGame()
    DO
```

```
      HandleKeyboard()
      REM *** Call routine being tested ***
      HandleShip()
   LOOP
   END

   FUNCTION InitialiseGame()
      REM *** Set screen resolution ***
      SET DISPLAY MODE 1280, 1024, 32
      REM *** Make background magenta ***
      SET IMAGE COLORKEY 255,0,255
      REM *** Load ship sprite ***
      LOAD IMAGE "ship.bmp",2
      SPRITE ship, SCREEN WIDTH()/2,
      SCREEN HEIGHT()/2,2
      OFFSET SPRITE ship, SPRITE WIDTH(ship)/2,
      SPRITE HEIGHT(ship)/2
      lastfired = TIMER()
      LOAD IMAGE "missilemag.bmp",3
      missileno = firstmissile
   ENDFUNCTION

   FUNCTION HandleKeyboard()
      REM *** Clear byte ***
      keyspressed = 0
      REM *** IF z pressed set bit 0 ***
      IF KEYSTATE(44) = 1
         keyspressed = keyspressed || %001
      ELSE
         REM *** IF x pressed, set bit 1 ***
         IF KEYSTATE(45)= 1
            keyspressed = keyspressed || %010
         ENDIF
      ENDIF
      REM *** IF space pressed, set bit 2  ***
      IF KEYSTATE(57) = 1
         keyspressed = keyspressed || %100
      ENDIF
   ENDFUNCTION

   FUNCTION HandleShip()
      REM *** If z, decrease angle ***
      IF (keyspressed && %001) > 0
         angle = WRAPVALUE(angle-5);
      ENDIF
      REM *** IF x, increase angle ***
      IF (keyspressed && %010) > 0
         angle = WRAPVALUE(angle+5)
      ENDIF
      REM *** IF space, launch missile ***
      IF (keyspressed && %100) > 0 AND TIMER()
- lastfired > 100
         LaunchMissile()
      ENDIF
      REM *** Update ship's rotation ***
      ROTATE SPRITE ship, angle
   ENDFUNCTION

   FUNCTION LaunchMissile()
      REM *** Create a new missile sprite ***
      REM *** Match new missile position with
front of ship ***
      SPRITE missileno, SPRITE X(ship), SPRITE
Y(ship),3
      OFFSET SPRITE missileno, SPRITE
WIDTH(missileno)/2, SPRITE
HEIGHT(missileno)/2
ROTATE SPRITE missileno,SPRITE ANGLE(ship)
      MOVE SPRITE missileno, 30
      REM *** Record the time this missile was
fired ***
      lastfired = TIMER()
      REM *** Add to missileno ***
      INC missileno
   ENDFUNCTION
```

Activity 23.15

missileno will be 101.

Activity 23.16

Exactly 10 missiles can be created when the modified program is run.

Activity 23.17

```
   #CONSTANT ship               1
   #CONSTANT firstmissile      101
   GLOBAL keyspressed AS BYTE
   GLOBAL angle AS INTEGER
   GLOBAL lastfired AS INTEGER
   GLOBAL missileno  AS INTEGER

   REM *** Main logic ***
   InitialiseGame()
   DO
      HandleKeyboard()
      HandleShip()
      HandleMissiles()
   LOOP
   END

   FUNCTION InitialiseGame()
      REM *** Set screen resolution ***
      SET DISPLAY MODE 1280, 1024, 32
      REM *** Make background magenta ***
      SET IMAGE COLORKEY 255,0,255
      REM *** Load ship sprite ***
      LOAD IMAGE "ship.bmp",2
      SPRITE ship, SCREEN WIDTH()/2,
      SCREEN HEIGHT()/2,2
      OFFSET SPRITE ship, SPRITE
WIDTH(ship)/2,
      SPRITE HEIGHT(ship)/2
      lastfired = TIMER()
      LOAD IMAGE "missilemag.bmp",3
      missileno = firstmissile
   ENDFUNCTION

   FUNCTION HandleKeyboard()
      REM *** Clear byte ***
      keyspressed = 0
      REM *** IF z pressed set bit 0 ***
      IF KEYSTATE(44) = 1
         keyspressed = keyspressed || %001
      ELSE
         REM *** IF x pressed, set bit 1 ***
         IF KEYSTATE(45)= 1
            keyspressed = keyspressed || %010
         ENDIF
      ENDIF
      REM *** IF space pressed, set bit 2  ***
      IF KEYSTATE(57) = 1
         keyspressed = keyspressed || %100
      ENDIF
   ENDFUNCTION

   FUNCTION HandleShip()
      REM *** If z, decrease angle ***
      IF (keyspressed && %001) > 0
         angle = WRAPVALUE(angle-5);
      ENDIF
      REM *** IF x, increase angle ***
      IF (keyspressed && %010) > 0
         angle = WRAPVALUE(angle+5)
      ENDIF
      REM *** IF space, launch missile ***
      IF (keyspressed && %100) > 0 AND
      TIMER() - lastfired > 100
```

```
        LaunchMissile()
    ENDIF
    REM *** Update ship's rotation ***
    ROTATE SPRITE ship, angle
ENDFUNCTION


FUNCTION LaunchMissile()
    REM *** IF missile exists, exit ***
    IF SPRITE EXIST(missileno)
        EXITFUNCTION
    ENDIF
    REM *** Create a new missile sprite ***
    REM *** Match missile post. with ship ***
    SPRITE missileno, SPRITE X(ship),
    SPRITE Y(ship),3
    OFFSET SPRITE missileno,
    SPRITE WIDTH(missileno)/2,
    SPRITE HEIGHT(missileno)/2
    ROTATE SPRITE missileno,
    SPRITE ANGLE(ship)
    MOVE SPRITE missileno, 30
    REM *** Record time missile was fired ***
    lastfired = TIMER()
    REM *** Add to missileno ***
    missileno = missileno mod 10 +
    firstmissile
ENDFUNCTION


FUNCTION HandleMissiles()
    REM *** FOR each possible missile DO ***
    FOR spriteno = firstmissile TO
    firstmissile + 9
        REM *** IF it exists, move it ***
        IF SPRITE EXIST(spriteno)
            MOVE SPRITE spriteno, 15
        ENDIF
    NEXT spriteno
ENDFUNCTION
```

Activity 23.18

```
#CONSTANT ship           1
#CONSTANT firstmissile   101
GLOBAL keyspressed AS BYTE
GLOBAL angle AS INTEGER
GLOBAL lastfired AS INTEGER
GLOBAL missileno  AS INTEGER
GLOBAL DIM missilemoves(9)
REM *** Main logic ***
InitialiseGame()
DO
    HandleKeyboard()
    HandleShip()
    HandleMissiles()
LOOP
END


FUNCTION InitialiseGame()
    REM *** Set screen resolution ***
    SET DISPLAY MODE 1280, 1024, 32
    REM *** Make background magenta ***
    SET IMAGE COLORKEY 255,0,255
    REM *** Load ship sprite ***
    LOAD IMAGE "ship.bmp",2
    SPRITE ship, SCREEN WIDTH()/2,
    SCREEN HEIGHT()/2,2
    OFFSET SPRITE ship, SPRITE WIDTH(ship)/2,
    SPRITE HEIGHT(ship)/2
    lastfired = TIMER()
    LOAD IMAGE "missilemag.bmp",3
    missileno = firstmissile
    REM *** Set all missile moves to zero ***
    FOR c = 0 TO 9
        missilemoves(c) = 0
    NEXT c
ENDFUNCTION
```

```
FUNCTION HandleKeyboard()
    REM *** Clear byte ***
    keyspressed = 0
    REM *** IF z pressed set bit 0 ***
    IF KEYSTATE(44) = 1
        keyspressed = keyspressed || %001
    ELSE
        REM *** IF x pressed, set bit 1
        IF KEYSTATE(45)= 1
            keyspressed = keyspressed || %010
        ENDIF
    ENDIF
    REM *** IF space pressed, set bit 2  ***
    IF KEYSTATE(57) = 1
        keyspressed = keyspressed || %100
    ENDIF
ENDFUNCTION


FUNCTION HandleShip()
    REM *** If z, decrease angle ***
    IF (keyspressed && %001) > 0
        angle = WRAPVALUE(angle-5);
    ENDIF
    REM *** IF x, increase angle ***
    IF (keyspressed && %010) > 0
        angle = WRAPVALUE(angle+5)
    ENDIF
    REM *** IF space, launch missile ***
    IF (keyspressed && %100) > 0 AND
    TIMER() - lastfired > 100
        LaunchMissile()
    ENDIF
    REM *** Update ship's rotation ***
    ROTATE SPRITE ship, angle
ENDFUNCTION


FUNCTION LaunchMissile()
    REM *** IF missile exists, exit ***
    IF SPRITE EXIST(missileno)
        EXITFUNCTION
    ENDIF
    REM *** Create a new missile sprite ***
    REM *** Match missile post. with ship ***
    SPRITE missileno, SPRITE X(ship),
    SPRITE Y(ship),3
    OFFSET SPRITE missileno,
    SPRITE WIDTH(missileno)/2,
    SPRITE HEIGHT(missileno)/2
    ROTATE SPRITE missileno,
    SPRITE ANGLE(ship)
    MOVE SPRITE missileno, 30
    REM *** Record time missile was fired ***
    lastfired = TIMER()
    REM *** Add to missileno ***
    missileno = missileno mod 10 +
    firstmissile
ENDFUNCTION


FUNCTION HandleMissiles()
    REM *** FOR each possible missile DO ***
    FOR spriteno = firstmissile TO
    firstmissile + 9
    REM *** IF it exists THEN ***
        IF SPRITE EXIST(spriteno)
            REM *** Move the sprite ***
            MOVE SPRITE spriteno, 15
            REM *** Add 1 to missiles moves ***
            post = spriteno - firstmissile
            INC missilemoves(post)
            REM *** If 40 moves, destroy it ***
            REM *** and set moves to zero ***
            IF missilemoves(post) >= 40
                DELETE SPRITE spriteno
                missilemoves(post) = 0
            ENDIF
        ENDIF
    NEXT spriteno
ENDFUNCTION
```

DarkBASIC Pro: Animated Spites   **599**

Activity 23.19

```
#CONSTANT firstasteroid    51
#CONSTANT ship             1
#CONSTANT firstmissile     101

GLOBAL keyspressed AS BYTE
GLOBAL angle AS INTEGER
GLOBAL lastfired AS INTEGER
GLOBAL missileno  AS INTEGER
GLOBAL DIM missilemoves(9)
REM *** Test driver for HandleShip() ***
InitialiseGame()
DO
   HandleKeyboard()
   HandleShip()
   HandleMissiles()
   HandleAsteroids()
LOOP
END

FUNCTION InitialiseGame()
   REM *** Set screen resolution ***
   SET DISPLAY MODE 1280, 1024, 32
   REM *** Make background magenta ***
   SET IMAGE COLORKEY 255,0,255
   REM *** Load ship sprite ***
   LOAD IMAGE "ship.bmp",2
   SPRITE ship, SCREEN WIDTH()/2,
   SCREEN HEIGHT()/2,2
   OFFSET SPRITE ship,
   SPRITE WIDTH(ship)/2,
   SPRITE HEIGHT(ship)/2
   lastfired = TIMER()
   LOAD IMAGE "missilemag.bmp",3
   missileno = firstmissile
   REM *** Set all missile moves to zero ***
   FOR c = 0 TO 9
      missilemoves(c) = 0
   NEXT c
   REM *** Seed random number generator ***
   RANDOMIZE TIMER()
   REM *** Create asteroids ***
   CreateAsteroids()
   REM *** Asteroids to start positions ***
   StartPositionsForAsteroids()
ENDFUNCTION

FUNCTION HandleKeyboard()
   REM *** Clear byte ***
   keyspressed = 0
   REM *** IF z pressed set bit 0 ***
   IF KEYSTATE(44) = 1
      keyspressed = keyspressed || %001
   ELSE
      REM *** IF x pressed, set bit 1 ***
      IF KEYSTATE(45)= 1
         keyspressed = keyspressed || %010
      ENDIF
   ENDIF
   REM *** IF space pressed, set bit 2 ***
   IF KEYSTATE(57) = 1
      keyspressed = keyspressed || %100
   ENDIF
ENDFUNCTION

FUNCTION HandleShip()
   REM *** If z, decrease angle ***
   IF (keyspressed && %001) > 0
      angle = WRAPVALUE(angle-5);
   ENDIF

   REM *** IF x, increase angle ***
   IF (keyspressed && %010) > 0
      angle = WRAPVALUE(angle+5)
   ENDIF
   REM *** IF space, launch missile ***
   IF (keyspressed && %100) > 0 AND
```

```
      TIMER() - lastfired > 100
      LaunchMissile()
   ENDIF
   REM *** Update ship's rotation ***
   ROTATE SPRITE ship, angle
ENDFUNCTION

FUNCTION LaunchMissile()
   REM *** IF missile exists, exit ***
   IF SPRITE EXIST(missileno)
      EXITFUNCTION
   ENDIF
   REM *** Create a new missile sprite ***
   REM *** Match missile post. with ship ***
   SPRITE missileno, SPRITE X(ship),
   SPRITE Y(ship),3
   OFFSET SPRITE missileno,
   SPRITE WIDTH(missileno)/2,
   SPRITE HEIGHT(missileno)/2
   ROTATE SPRITE missileno,
   SPRITE ANGLE(ship)
   MOVE SPRITE missileno, 30
   REM *** Record the time missile fired ***
   lastfired = TIMER()
   REM *** Add to missileno ***
   missileno = missileno mod 10 +
   firstmissile
ENDFUNCTION

FUNCTION HandleMissiles()
   REM *** FOR each possible missile DO ***
   FOR spriteno = firstmissile TO
   firstmissile + 9
      REM *** IF it exists, THEN ***
      IF SPRITE EXIST(spriteno)
         REM *** Move the sprite ***
         MOVE SPRITE spriteno, 15
         REM *** Add 1 to missiles moves ***
         post = spriteno - firstmissile
         INC missilemoves(post)
         REM *** If 40 moves, destroy it ***
         REM *** and set moves to zero ***
         IF missilemoves(post) >= 40
            DELETE SPRITE spriteno
            missilemoves(post) = 0
         ENDIF
      ENDIF
   NEXT spriteno
ENDFUNCTION

FUNCTION CreateAsteroids()
   REM *** Load sprite and set origin ***
   CREATE ANIMATED SPRITE firstasteroid,
   "animspr.bmp",4,4,1
   OFFSET SPRITE firstasteroid,
   SPRITE WIDTH(firstasteroid)/2,
   SPRITE HEIGHT(firstasteroid)/2
   REM *** Create 9 other copies ***
   FOR spriteno = firstasteroid+1 TO
   firstasteroid + 9
      CLONE SPRITE firstasteroid , spriteno
   NEXT spriteno
ENDFUNCTION

FUNCTION StartPositionsForAsteroids()
   REM *** FOR each asteroid DO ***
   FOR spriteno = firstasteroid TO
   firstasteroid + 9
      REM *** Choose entry point  ***
      side = RND(3)
      REM *** Set coords & angle ***
      SELECT side
         CASE 0 `Top of screen
            x = RND(SCREEN WIDTH())
            y = 0
            angle = RND(180)+90
         ENDCASE
         CASE 1 `Right side
```

600   **DarkBASIC Pro: Animated Spites**

```
            x = SCREEN WIDTH()
            y = RND(SCREEN HEIGHT())
            angle = RND(180)+180
        ENDCASE
        CASE 2 `Bottom of screen
            x = RND(SCREEN WIDTH())
            y = SCREEN HEIGHT()
            angle = RND(180) - 90
        ENDCASE
        CASE 3 `Left of screen
            x = 0
            y = RND(SCREEN HEIGHT())
            angle = RND(180)
        ENDCASE
    ENDSELECT
    REM *** Position sprite ***
    ROTATE SPRITE spriteno, angle
    SPRITE spriteno, x, y, 1
  NEXT spriteno
ENDFUNCTION

FUNCTION HandleAsteroids()
  REM *** FOR each asteroid DO ***
  FOR spriteno = firstasteroid TO
  firstasteroid + 9
    REM *** Move the sprite ***
    MOVE SPRITE spriteno, 10
    REM *** IF off edge, wrap it round
***
    IF SPRITE Y(spriteno) < 0
        SPRITE spriteno,
        SPRITE X(spriteno),
        SCREEN HEIGHT(),1
    ENDIF
    IF SPRITE Y(spriteno) > SCREEN
HEIGHT()
        SPRITE spriteno,
        SPRITE X(spriteno),0,1
    ENDIF
    IF SPRITE X(spriteno) < 0
        SPRITE spriteno,
        SCREEN WIDTH(),SPRITE
Y(spriteno),1
    ENDIF
    IF SPRITE X(spriteno) > SCREEN
WIDTH()
        SPRITE spriteno, 0,
        SPRITE Y(spriteno),1
    ENDIF
    REM *** Play sprite frames ***
    PLAY SPRITE spriteno,1,16,40
  NEXT spriteno
ENDFUNCTION
```

Activity 23.20

```
#CONSTANT firstasteroid    51
#CONSTANT ship              1
#CONSTANT firstmissile    101

GLOBAL keyspressed AS BYTE
GLOBAL angle AS INTEGER
GLOBAL lastfired AS INTEGER
GLOBAL missileno  AS INTEGER
GLOBAL DIM missilemoves(9)
REM *** Test driver for HandleShip() ***
InitialiseGame()
DO
   HandleKeyboard()
   HandleShip()
   HandleMissiles()
   HandleAsteroids()
LOOP
END

FUNCTION InitialiseGame()
   REM *** Set screen resolution ***
```

```
    SET DISPLAY MODE 1280, 1024, 32
    REM *** Make background magenta ***
    SET IMAGE COLORKEY 255,0,255
    REM *** Load ship sprite ***
    LOAD IMAGE "ship.bmp",2
    SPRITE ship, SCREEN WIDTH()/2,
    SCREEN HEIGHT()/2,2
    OFFSET SPRITE ship,
    SPRITE WIDTH(ship)/2,
    SPRITE HEIGHT(ship)/2
    lastfired = TIMER()
    LOAD IMAGE "missilemag.bmp",3
    missileno = firstmissile
    REM *** Set all missile moves to zero
***
    FOR c = 0 TO 9
        missilemoves(c) = 0
    NEXT c
    REM *** Seed random number generator ***
    RANDOMIZE TIMER()
    REM *** Create asteroids ***
    CreateAsteroids()
    REM *** Asteroids to start positions ***
    StartPositionsForAsteroids()
ENDFUNCTION

FUNCTION HandleKeyboard()
    REM *** Clear byte ***
    keyspressed = 0
    REM *** IF z pressed set bit 0 ***
    IF KEYSTATE(44) = 1
        keyspressed = keyspressed || %001
    ELSE
        REM *** IF x pressed, set bit 1 ***
        IF KEYSTATE(45)= 1
            keyspressed = keyspressed || %010
        ENDIF
    ENDIF
    REM *** IF space pressed, set bit 2  ***
    IF KEYSTATE(57) = 1
        keyspressed = keyspressed || %100
    ENDIF
ENDFUNCTION

FUNCTION HandleShip()
    REM *** If z, decrease angle ***
    IF (keyspressed && %001) > 0
        angle = WRAPVALUE(angle-5);
    ENDIF
    REM *** IF x, increase angle ***
    IF (keyspressed && %010) > 0
        angle = WRAPVALUE(angle+5)
    ENDIF
    REM *** IF space, launch missile ***
    IF (keyspressed && %100) > 0 AND
    TIMER() - lastfired > 100
        LaunchMissile()
    ENDIF
    REM *** Update ship's rotation ***
    ROTATE SPRITE ship, angle
ENDFUNCTION

FUNCTION LaunchMissile()
    REM *** IF missile exists, exit ***
    IF SPRITE EXIST(missileno)
        EXITFUNCTION
    ENDIF
    REM *** Create a new missile sprite ***
    REM *** Match missile post. to ship ***
    SPRITE missileno, SPRITE X(ship),
    SPRITE Y(ship),3
    OFFSET SPRITE missileno,
    SPRITE WIDTH(missileno)/2,
    SPRITE HEIGHT(missileno)/2
    ROTATE SPRITE missileno,
    SPRITE ANGLE(ship)
    MOVE SPRITE missileno, 30
    REM *** Record time missile fired ***
```

```
      lastfired = TIMER()
      REM *** Add to missileno ***
      missileno = missileno mod 10 +
      firstmissile
ENDFUNCTION

FUNCTION HandleMissiles()
   REM *** FOR each possible missile DO ***
   FOR spriteno = firstmissile TO
   firstmissile + 9
      REM *** IF it exists, THEN ***
      IF SPRITE EXIST(spriteno)
         REM *** Move the sprite ***
         MOVE SPRITE spriteno, 15
         REM *** IF missile hits asteroid,
         REM *** destroy both ***
         spritehit = SPRITE HIT(spriteno,0)
         IF spritehit > 1
            DELETE SPRITE spritehit
            DELETE SPRITE spriteno
            post = spriteno - firstmissile
            missilemoves(post) = 0
         ELSE
            REM *** Incr. missiles moves ***
            post = spriteno - firstmissile
            INC missilemoves(post)
            REM *** If 40 moves, destroy ***
            REM *** and set moves to 0 ***
            IF missilemoves(post) >= 40
               DELETE SPRITE spriteno
               missilemoves(post) = 0
            ENDIF
         ENDIF
      ENDIF
   NEXT spriteno
ENDFUNCTION

FUNCTION CreateAsteroids()
   REM *** Load sprite and set origin ***
   CREATE ANIMATED SPRITE firstasteroid,
   "animspr.bmp",4,4,1
   OFFSET SPRITE firstasteroid,
   SPRITE WIDTH(firstasteroid)/2,
   SPRITE HEIGHT(firstasteroid)/2
   REM *** Create 9 other copies ***
   FOR spriteno = firstasteroid+1 TO
   firstasteroid + 9
      CLONE SPRITE firstasteroid , spriteno
   NEXT spriteno
ENDFUNCTION

FUNCTION StartPositionsForAsteroids()
   REM *** FOR each asteroid DO ***
   FOR spriteno = firstasteroid TO
   firstasteroid + 9
      REM *** Choose entry point  ***
      side = RND(3)
      REM *** Set coords & angle ***
      SELECT side
         CASE 0 `Top of screen
            x = RND(SCREEN WIDTH())
            y = 0
            angle = RND(180)+90
         ENDCASE
         CASE 1 `Right side
            x = SCREEN WIDTH()
            y = RND(SCREEN HEIGHT())
            angle = RND(180)+180
         ENDCASE
         CASE 2 `Bottom of screen
            x = RND(SCREEN WIDTH())
            y = SCREEN HEIGHT()
            angle = RND(180) - 90
         ENDCASE
         CASE 3 `Left of screen
            x = 0
            y = RND(SCREEN HEIGHT())
            angle = RND(180)
```

```
         ENDCASE
      ENDSELECT
      REM *** Position sprite ***
      ROTATE SPRITE spriteno, angle
      SPRITE spriteno, x, y, 1
   NEXT spriteno
ENDFUNCTION

FUNCTION HandleAsteroids()
   REM *** FOR each asteroid DO ***
   FOR spriteno = firstasteroid TO
   firstasteroid + 9
      IF SPRITE EXIST(spriteno)
         REM *** Move the sprite ***
         MOVE SPRITE spriteno, 10
         REM *** IF off edge, wrap round ***
         IF SPRITE Y(spriteno) < 0
            SPRITE spriteno,
            SPRITE X(spriteno),
            SCREEN HEIGHT(),1
         ENDIF
         IF SPRITE Y(spriteno) >
         SCREEN HEIGHT()
            SPRITE spriteno,
            SPRITE X(spriteno),0,1
         ENDIF
         IF SPRITE X(spriteno) < 0
            SPRITE spriteno,
            SCREEN WIDTH(),SPRITE Y(spriteno)
            ,1
         ENDIF
         IF SPRITE X(spriteno)>SCREEN WIDTH()
            SPRITE spriteno, 0,
            SPRITE Y(spriteno),1
         ENDIF
         REM *** Play sprite frames ***
         PLAY SPRITE spriteno,1,16,40
      ENDIF
   NEXT spriteno
ENDFUNCTION
```

To make the game more difficult we could make the delay
between missile launches longer; reduce the number of
missiles on screen ; decrease the size of the asteroids;
increase the number of asteroids. But the most obvious
thing to do is to have the ship destroyed if it is hit by an
asteroid!

24

Sound

Creating 3D Sound

Loading and Playing Mono and Stereo WAV Files

Positioning a 3D sound

Positioning the Listener

Rotating the Listener

Setting Sound Speed

Setting Sound Volume

Mono and Stereo Sound

Introduction

Don't confuse sound files with music files. The set of instructions for handling sound files is much more extensive than that for music (which we looked at in Chapter 15). The position of a sound can be moved around in 3-dimensional space, giving the listener a total surround-sound experience. Even the apparent position of the listener can be moved.

DarkBASIC Pro sound commands only handle WAV files. To play other file types use either the MUSIC or ANIMATION commands.

WAV files can be recorded in mono (1 track) or stereo (2 tracks). Stereo sound has the advantage of retaining spatial information about sound sources, but creates files twice the size of the equivalent mono file. The commands given below apply equally to each type of recording.

The Basics of Loading and Playing Sounds

The LOAD SOUND Statement

Before using a WAV file, it must be loaded using the LOAD SOUND statement which has the format shown in FIG-24.1.

FIG-24.1

The LOAD SOUND
Statement

In the diagram:

filename	is a string specifying the name of the file to be loaded. It is best if the file has been previously copied to your directory using the **Media|Add** option. However, path information can be included in the string.
sndno	is an integer value by which the sound is identified within the program. Any positive integer value can be used, although no two sounds can use the same value at the same time.

A typical example of using this statement would be:

```
LOAD SOUND "help.wav", 1
```

If the requested file is not found or cannot be loaded for some reason, then your program will terminate.

The PLAY SOUND Statement

Once the sound file has been loaded, it can be played using the PLAY SOUND statement. In its simplest form we need only state the sound number of the file we want to play. For example, assuming we've loaded a sound file and assigned it the number 1, we can play that sound with the statement:

```
PLAY SOUND 1
```

The PLAY SOUND statement causes the sound file to start playing, but subsequent statements in your program will continue to be executed while the sound plays.

LISTING-24.1 gives a simple example of how to play a sound file.

LISTING-24.1

Playing a Sound File

```
REM *** Load sound ***
LOAD SOUND "welcome.wav", 1
WAIT 500
REM *** Play sound ***
PLAY SOUND 1
REM *** End program ***
WAIT KEY
END
```

The WAIT 500 statement gives the program time to complete the LOAD instruction before attempting to play the file. Without this, it is possible that the first part of the sound will be missing when it is played.

Activity 24.1

Type in and test the program given in LISTING-24.1 (*sounds01.dbpro*).

Make sure you've copied the required sound file to your folder and that sound is enabled on your computer.

Sound files need not be played from the start. Instead, by using an extended version of the PLAY SOUND statement, you can specify how many bytes into the file playing should begin. So, if we don't want to play the first 10000 bytes (bytes 0 to 9999) of the sound file, we could use the statement:

```
PLAY SOUND 1, 10000
```

You'll probably have to play about with the byte value until you get the starting point you want.

The complete format of the PLAY SOUND statement is given in FIG-24.2.

FIG-24.2

The PLAY SOUND Statement

In the diagram:

sndno	is the integer previously assigned to the sound file to be played.
startbyte	is an integer representing the number of bytes into the file at which playing is to start. If omitted, a value of zero is assumed.

Activity 24.2

Modify your last program so that it begins playing at byte 20000.

The LOOP SOUND Statement

Whereas the PLAY SOUND statement plays the sound file only once, the LOOP SOUND statement will replay the sound continuously. Again, there is more than one option when using this statement. The simplest of these is to state only the sound number. For example, the line

```
LOOP SOUND 1
```

will play sound 1 over and over again.

A second option is to specify a start byte in the file, as in the line:

```
LOOP SOUND 1,11000
```

This causes the first 11000 bytes of the file to be omitted on every play.

The next option allows us to stop the sound before the end of the file is reached. Typically, we might write

```
LOOP SOUND 1,11000,50000
```

This time, only the sound which occupies bytes 11000 to 50000 will be played during each loop.

If you want the first playing to start at a different position, you can add a final parameter, as in the line:

```
LOOP SOUND 1,11000,50000,30000
```

Now bytes 30000 to 50000 will play the first time round and subsequently it will be bytes 11000 to 50000 that play.

FIG-24.3

The LOOP SOUND Statement

The complete format of the LOOP SOUND statement is given in FIG-24.3.

In the diagram:

sndno	is the integer previously assigned to the sound file to be looped.
startbyte	is an integer representing the number of bytes into the file at which playing is to start on each iteration.
endbyte	is an integer representing the number of bytes into the file at which playing is to cease.
firsttimebyte	is an integer representing the number of bytes into the file at which playing is to begin on the first play only. *firsttimebyte* should have a value between *startbyte* and *endbyte*.

> **Activity 24.3**
>
> Modify your previous program so that the complete sound file is played continuously.
>
> Modify the file again so that it plays bytes 20000 to 50000 only.

The PAUSE SOUND Statement

It is possible to pause a playing sound file using the PAUSE SOUND statement, which has the format shown in FIG-24.4.

FIG-24.4

The PAUSE SOUND
Statement

In the diagram:

>   *sndno*   is an integer giving the number of the sound to be paused.

We could, therefore, pause the sound assigned sound number 1 with the line:

```
PAUSE SOUND 1
```

This assumes, of course, that the sound 1 is currently playing.

The RESUME SOUND Statement

A paused sound file can be resumed using the RESUME SOUND statement, which has the format shown in FIG-24.5.

FIG-24.5

The RESUME SOUND
Statement

In the diagram:

>   *sndno*   is an integer giving the number of the sound to be resumed.

Of course, we should only use this statement on a sound file that has previously been paused. So, assuming we have a paused sound with the statement

```
PAUSE SOUND 1
```

then we could resume the sound using the line

```
RESUME SOUND 1
```

The sound resumes from exactly the point in the file where it paused.

The program in LISTING-24.3 pauses the playing sound when any key is pressed and resumes it when a second key is pressed. Pressing a third key terminates the program.

LISTING-24.2

Pausing and Resuming a
Playing Sound

```
REM *** Load sound ***
LOAD SOUND "demo.wav", 1
WAIT 500
REM *** Play sound continuously ***
LOOP SOUND 1

REM *** Pause when key is pressed ***
WAIT KEY
PAUSE SOUND 1

REM *** Resume when key is pressed ***
WAIT KEY
RESUME SOUND 1

REM *** End program ***
WAIT KEY
END
```

Activity 24.4

Type in and test the program given above (*sounds02.dbpro*).

Does the sound resume looping?

The STOP SOUND Statement

Rather than just pause a sound file, we can stop it altogether using the STOP SOUND statement, which has the format shown in FIG-24.6.

FIG-24.6

The STOP SOUND
Statement

In the diagram:

sndno   is an integer giving the number of the sound to be stopped.

For example, the line

```
STOP SOUND 1
```

will terminate the playing of sound 1.

However, the sound file can still be resumed using the RESUME SOUND statement. But, when resuming a stopped sound, play starts from the beginning of the file.

The SET SOUND SPEED Statement

By changing the speed of a sound, we can make an everyday sound resemble a clap of thunder (when the sound is slowed down) or like a high-pitched squeak (when it's speeded up).

The speed at which a sound file plays can be changed using the SET SOUND SPEED statement. The format of this statement is shown in FIG-24.7.

FIG-24.7

The SET SOUND
SPEED Statement

In the diagram:

sndno   is an integer giving the number of the sound whose speed is to be set.

freq   is an integer value representing the upper frequency to be produced when the file is playing. This value must lie in the range 100 to 100,000.

A frequency value may seem a rather strange way to set the speed of a sound file, but a bit of trial and error will soon get the effect you want. Most files will sound normal with a frequency setting of 22,000, with 11,000 giving half speed and 44,000 giving double speed.

To play sound 1 at half speed we would use the lines:

```
SET SOUND SPEED 1, 11000
PLAY SOUND 1
```

Activity 24.5

Modify your previous program so that the sound file is at half speed when it is first played and double speed when it is resumed.

The SET SOUND VOLUME Statement

The SET SOUND VOLUME statement is designed to modify the volume of a sound and has the format shown in FIG-24.8.

FIG-24.8

The SET SOUND
VOLUME Statement

In the diagram:

sndno   is an integer giving the number of the sound whose volume is to be set.

perc   is an integer value representing the new volume as a percentage of the original volume. This value must lie in the range 0 (silent) to 100 (normal).

Because of the percentage values allowed, it is not possible to increase the volume of the sound from its normal level, only decrease it.

For example, we could reduce the volume of a sound with the statements

```
SET SOUND VOLUME 1, 90
PLAY SOUND 1
```

The CLONE SOUND Statement

If required, you can assign as second sound number to an already loaded sound file. This allows the second sound file to be played independently from the first, but does not require a second copy of the sound file to be held in RAM and thereby saves memory space.

A copy of an existing sound file is made using the CLONE SOUND statement which has the format shown in FIG-24.9.

FIG-24.9

The CLONE SOUND Statement

In the diagram:

    newsndno   is the additional integer value to be assigned to the new sound object.

    origsndno   is the integer value specifying which existing sound object is to be copied into the new sound object.

The program in LISTING-24.3 assigns two values to a sound file and then plays both sound objects with a one second delay between each.

LISTING-24.3

Cloning a Sound

```
REM *** Load sound file ***
LOAD SOUND "sample.wav", 1

REM *** Assign a second value to the sound ***
CLONE SOUND 2,1

REM *** Start playing the sound using its first value ***
PLAY SOUND 1

REM *** Wait 1 second ***
SLEEP 1000

REM *** Play the sound using its second value ***
PLAY SOUND 2

REM *** End program ***
WAIT KEY
END
```

Activity 24.6

Type in and test the program given above (*sounds03.dbpro*).

The DELETE SOUND Statement

A loaded sound file occupies RAM space, so when you're finished with the sound it is best to delete it - thereby freeing up the RAM space that is holding the sound file. The DELETE SOUND statement has the format shown in FIG-24.10.

FIG-24.10

The DELETE SOUND Statement

In the diagram:

    sndno   is the number of the existing sound object to be deleted.

Note that the sound object is not deleted if a clone exists. To remove the sound from RAM the original sound object and all of its clones must be deleted.

Recording Sound

It is also possible to make a DarkBASIC Pro program record sound if you have a microphone attached to your sound card.

The RECORD SOUND Statement

To record a sound use the RECORD SOUND statement. The statement defaults to a 5 second recording, but by entering duration information, a recording of any (reasonable) length can be made. The format for the RECORD SOUND statement is given in FIG-24.11.

FIG-24.11

The RECORD SOUND
Statement

In the diagram:

sndno   is the integer value to be assigned to the recording.

duration   is an integer representing duration of the
                           recording in milliseconds.

So, the command

```
RECORD SOUND 1
```

should create sound object 1 from a 5 second recording from the microphone - but it's not quite that easy!

The RECORD SOUND statement only works if you've already used that sound number to load a file. So, the line

```
RECORD SOUND 1
```

will give us an error unless we have previously loaded a file (even though you're not going to use that file) using the sample sound number. For example:

```
LOAD "sample.wav",1
RECORD SOUND 1
```

To make a 10 second recording and assign it to sound number 3, we could use the statements

```
LOAD "mysound.wav",3
RECORD SOUND 3, 10000
```

The program will continue to execute other statements in your program while the recording is being made. Normally, you won't want this to happen, so the RECORD SOUND statement should be followed by a WAIT KEY statement or a WAIT milliseconds statement (in which the number of milliseconds matches, or is slightly greater than, the length of the recording).

The STOP RECORDING SOUND Statement

If you want to stop a recording before the specified duration has elapsed, then you can use the STOP RECORDING SOUND statement which has the format shown in FIG-24.12.

FIG-24.12

The STOP
RECORDING SOUND
Statement

The program in LISTING-24.4 records from the microphone for up to 10 seconds, but stops early if a key is pressed. When the recording is complete, it is replayed.

LISTING-24.4

Recording a Sound

```
REM *** Load a sound file for sound number being used   ***
REM *** We won't use this file, but the sound number    ***
REM *** needs to be loaded first, otherwise RECORD SOUND ***
REM *** won't work                                       ***
LOAD SOUND "sample.wav",1

REM *** Start recording - 10 seconds ***
PRINT "Speak now "
RECORD SOUND 1,10000

REM *** Stop recording after 10 secs or key pressed ***
WAIT KEY
STOP RECORDING SOUND

REM *** Play back the recorded sound ***
PRINT "Replaying now..."
SLEEP 500
PLAY SOUND 1

REM *** End program ***
WAIT KEY
END
```

Activity 24.7

Plug a microphone into your system. Check that it is operating correctly (Try **Accessories|Entertainment|Sound Recorder**)

Type in the program given above (*sounds04.dbpro*) and test that it operates correctly.

The SAVE SOUND Statement

Your recorded sound can be saved to a file using the SAVE SOUND statement which has the format shown in FIG-24.13.

FIG-24.13

The SAVE SOUND
Statement

In the diagram:

> *filename*   is a string giving the file name to be used when saving the sound data. This string may include path information. The named file should not already exist.

> *sndno*   is the integer value previously assigned to the sound that is to be saved.

We could save a recorded sound (with sound number 1) to a file named *speech.wav* in the current folder with the line:

```
SAVE SOUND "speech.wav",1
```

> **Activity 24.8**
>
> Modify your previous program so that the recorded sound is saved to *speech.wav* after it has been replayed.
>
> What happens if you try to run this program a second time?

Retrieving Sound File Data

Several statements exist in DarkBASIC Pro which allow information about currently loaded sound files to be retrieved. For example, we can find out whether a sound object is playing, stopped, paused, etc. The statements that supply us with this information are described below.

The SOUND EXIST Statement

We can find out if a specific number has been assigned to a sound file by using the SOUND EXIST statement. This statement returns the value 1 if the specified number has been assigned to a sound file, otherwise zero is returned. The statement has the format shown in FIG-24.14.

FIG-24.14

The SOUND EXIST Statement

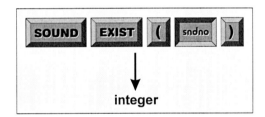

In the diagram:

    sndno   is the number of the sound object being checked.

Typical examples of how the statement might be used are:

```
loaded = SOUND EXIST(1)
```

and

```
IF SOUND EXIST(3) = 1
    PRINT "SOUND file loaded in 3"
ELSE
    PRINT "SOUND file not loaded in 3"
ENDIF
```

The SOUND PLAYING Statement

This statement returns 1 if the sound file is currently playing, otherwise zero is returned. The statement has the format shown in FIG-24.15.

FIG-24.15

The SOUND PLAYING
Statement

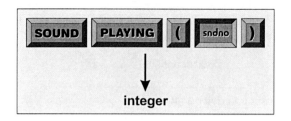

In the diagram:

> *sndno*   is the number of the sound object being tested.

The value 1 is returned if the sound file is currently playing because of either a PLAY SOUND or LOOP SOUND statement.

The SOUND LOOPING Statement

The SOUND LOOPING statement returns 1 if the sound file is currently looping, otherwise zero is returned. The statement has the format shown in FIG-24.16.

FIG-24.16

The SOUND LOOPING
Statement

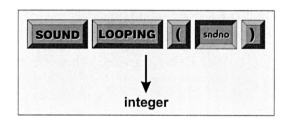

In the diagram:

> *sndno*   is the number of the sound object being tested.

A value of 1 is only returned if the sound file is playing because of a LOOP SOUND statement. A playing sound file initiated using the PLAY SOUND statement will return zero.

The SOUND PAUSED Statement

The SOUND PAUSED statement returns 1 if the sound file is currently paused, otherwise zero is returned. The statement has the format shown in FIG-24.17.

FIG-24.17

The SOUND PAUSED
Statement

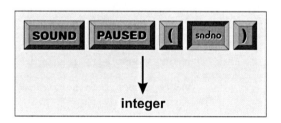

In the diagram:

> *sndno*   is the number of the sound object being tested.

The program in LISTING-24.5 displays the state of the playing sound file.

LISTING-24.5

Displaying the State of a
Sound File

```
REM *** Load sound file ***
LOAD SOUND "demo2.wav", 1
WAIT 500

REM *** Play sound file continuously ***
LOOP SOUND 1

REM *** Get sound file's status ***
playing = SOUND PLAYING(1)
looping = SOUND LOOPING(1)
paused = SOUND PAUSED(1)

REM *** Display details ***
IF playing = 1
   PRINT "SOUND is playing"
ENDIF
IF looping = 1
   PRINT "SOUND is looping"
ENDIF
IF paused = 1
   PRINT "SOUND is paused"
ENDIF

REM *** End program ***
WAIT KEY
END
```

Activity 24.9

Type in and test the program given above (*sounds05.dbpro*).

1) Change the line

```
      LOOP SOUND 1
```
   to
```
      PLAY SOUND 1
```

   How does this affect the messages displayed?

2) Add the lines

```
      WAIT KEY
      PAUSE SOUND 1
```
   after the
```
      PLAY SOUND 1  statement.
```

   How do the messages change?

3) Change the line

```
      PAUSE SOUND 1
```
   to
```
      STOP SOUND 1
```

   Are the messages changed?

The SOUND VOLUME Statement

This statement returns the volume setting for the specified sound. The statement's format is shown in FIG-24.18

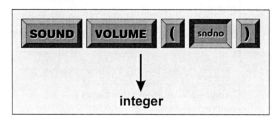

In the diagram:

    sndno   is the number of the sound object being interrogated.

A typical statement to determine the current volume setting for sound 1 would be:

```
volume = SOUND VOLUME(1)
```

A sound file playing at default volume would return the value 100.

The SOUND SPEED Statement

This statement returns the speed setting for the specified sound. The statement's format is shown in FIG-24.19.

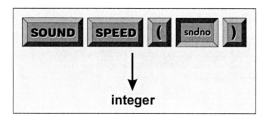

In the diagram:

    sndno   is the number of the sound object being interrogated.

A typical statement to determine the current speed setting for sound 1 would be:

```
speed = SOUND SPEED(1)
```

A sound file playing at default speed would return the value 100.

Activity 24.10

Modify your previous program to display the speed and volume settings of the playing sound file.

Activity 24.11

Modify the final version of the asteroids project you created in the last chapter to play a sound when a missile is fired and an asteroid is hit.

Moving a Sound

When stereo sound was first introduced, a favourite demonstration of its effects was to have a train rush past the listener. You could here it move from the left, through the centre and off to the right. In its day, it was very impressive!

The SET SOUND PAN Statement

We can create a similar effect, making a sound appear as if its coming from anywhere between our two speakers using the SET SOUND PAN statement. The statement has the format shown in FIG-24.20.

FIG-24.20

The SET SOUND PAN Statement

In the diagram:

sndno   is the number of the sound object to be panned.

panvalue   is an integer value between -10,000 and + 10,000. A value of -10,000 will make the sound come exclusively from the left speaker, zero places the sound at the centre position between the speakers, and 10,000 places the sound by the right speaker.

In LISTING-24.6 a sound is panned while it plays.

LISTING-24.6

Panning a Sound File

```
REM *** Load sound ***
LOAD SOUND "welcome.wav", 1

REM *** Play sound ***
WAIT 500
PLAY SOUND 1
REM *** Change pan setting while sound playing ***
FOR c = -10000 TO 10000 STEP 1000
   SET SOUND PAN 1,c
   WAIT 100
NEXT c

REM *** End program ***
WAIT KEY
END
```

Activity 24.12

Type in and test the program in LISTING-24.7 (*sounds06.dbpro*).

Reverse the FOR loop (making it go from 10,000 to -10,000). How does this affect the sound output?

The SOUND PAN Statement

We can determine the current pan setting using the SOUND PAN statement. This has the format shown in FIG-24.21.

FIG-24.21

The SOUND PAN
Statement

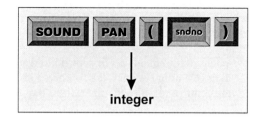

In the diagram:

    sndno   is the number of the sound object to be tested.

The value returned will be an integer in the range -10,000 to +10,000 and will match the value assigned by the last SET SOUND PAN statement for this object. If a SET SOUND PAN has not been performed on the object, then a value of zero will be returned.

Playing Multiple Sound Files

It's possible to play two or more sound files at the same time by loading multiple sound files. For example, we could load two sound files with the lines:

```
LOAD SOUND "demo1.wav",1
LOAD SOUND "demo2.wav",2
```

These can then be played at the same time using the lines

```
PLAY SOUND 1
PLAY SOUND 2
```

The program in LISTING-24.7 demonstrates two sound files being played. The first file starts playing right away, but the second file starts playing after a key is pressed.

LISTING-24.7

Playing Multiple Sound
Files

```
REM *** Load sound files ***
LOAD SOUND "demo1.wav",1
LOAD SOUND "demo2.wav",2

REM *** Play first sound file continuously ***
LOOP SOUND 1

REM *** Wait for key press, then start second file playing ***
WAIT KEY
LOOP SOUND 2

REM *** End program ***
WAIT KEY
END
```

Activity 24.13

Type in and test the program given above (*sounds07.dbpro*).

Summary

- The SOUND statements are designed to *.wav* files only.

- Use LOAD SOUND to load a sound file into RAM.

- Use PLAY SOUND to play a sound file once only.

- Use LOOP SOUND to play a sound file repeatedly.

- Use PAUSE SOUND to pause a sound file which is currently playing.

- Use RESUME SOUND to resume a sound file which has been paused.

- Use STOP SOUND to halt a playing sound file.

- Use SET SOUND SPEED to set the highest frequency (and hence the speed) of a sound file.

- Use SET SOUND VOLUME to set the volume of a sound file when it is played.

- Use CLONE SOUND to make an independent copy of a loaded sound file.

- Use DELETE SOUND to remove a sound from RAM.

- Use RECORD SOUND to initiate a sound recording.

- Use STOP RECORDING SOUND to stop the current recording.

- Use SAVE SOUND to save a sound file currently held in RAM to backing store.

- SOUND EXIST returns 1 if the specified sound file is currently in RAM.

- SOUND PLAYING returns 1 if the specified sound file is currently playing or looping.

- SOUND LOOPING returns 1 if the specified sound file is currently looping.

- SOUND PAUSED returns 1 if the specified sound file is currently paused.

- SOUND VOLUME returns the volume setting of a specified sound file.

- SOUND SPEED returns the current maximum frequency of a specified sound file.

- Use SET SOUND PAN to set the balance between the two front speakers.

- SOUND PAN returns the current balance setting of a specified sound file.

- Several sound files can be played simultaneously.

3D Sound Effects

Introduction

DarkBASIC Pro contains an additional set of commands specifically for handling 3D sound effects. A 3D sound can appear to the listener to originate from anywhere in space - to the side, front, back, above, or below the listener.

The 3D effect is not recorded within the sound file, but is created by manipulating the balance, delay and loudness of the speakers connected to your sound card. A good sound card will allow you to use a 5.1 speaker system (with five speakers and a sub-woofer). The speakers should be positioned as shown in FIG-24.22. The position of the sub-woofer, which generates the very low frequency noises, is not important since our brain cannot detect the direction of such low frequency sounds.

FIG-24.22

A Suitable Setup for 3D Sound

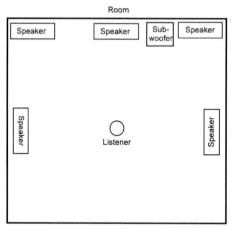

If we image we're floating in the centre of a room, then sounds can come from our left or right (i.e. anywhere along the x-axis), above or below us (i.e. anywhere along the y-axis), and anywhere in front or behind us (i.e. the z-axis). The concept is shown in FIG-24.23.

FIG-24.23

Our Listening Position in 3D Space

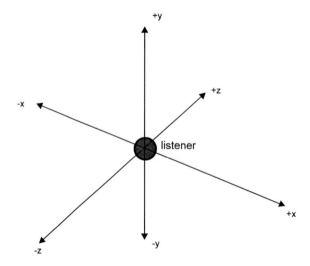

Notice that your head is placed at the origin, where all three axes meet. To our left is the -x part of the x-axis and in front of us is the +z part of the z-axis.

Loading and Playing 3D Sounds

The LOAD 3DSOUND Statement

Although the sounds used are in every way normal mono WAV files, if you intend to create a 3D effect with such a file, it must be loaded using the LOAD 3DSOUND statement which has the following format shown in FIG-24.24.

FIG-24.24

The LOAD 3DSOUND Statement

In the diagram:

filename   is a string specifying the name of the file to be loaded. It is best if the file has been previously copied to your directory using the **Media|Add** option. The file must be a mono WAV file.

sndno   is an integer representing the value by which the sound object created is identified within the program.

A typical example of using this statement would be:

```
LOAD 3DSOUND "help.wav", 1
```

If the requested file is not found or cannot be loaded for some reason, then your program will terminate.

You can play the sound using the normal PLAY SOUND or LOOP SOUND. The sound file will be played at equal volume through all speakers and should give the impression that the sound originates from inside your head.

Activity 24.14

Find out what effects are produced on your own system by executing the following program (*sounds3D.dbpro*):

```
LOAD 3DSOUND "laser.wav",1
WAIT 500
LOOP SOUND 1
WAIT KEY
END
```

The POSITION SOUND Statement

We can move the position from which the sound is coming using the POSITION SOUND statement. This statement allows you to specify the 3D coordinates at which the sound is to be placed and has the format shown in FIG-24.25.

FIG-24.25

The POSITION SOUND Statement

In the diagram:

sndno   is the number previously assigned to the 3D
                                   sound.

x,y,z   are three real numbers representing the 3D
                                   coordinates of the sound's new position.
                                   Typically, values for these parameters should be
                                   given in 100's.

For example, we could place a sound at position (100,300,50) (see FIG-24.26) using
the statement:

```
POSITION SOUND 1,100,300,50
```

FIG-24.26

Positioning a Sound

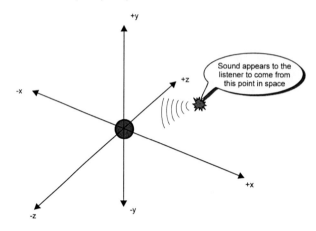

Activity 24.15

Modify your previous program to add the code

```
FOR x = -300 TO 300 STEP 100
    FOR y = -300 TO 300 STEP 100
        FOR z = -300 TO 300 STEP 100
            POSITION SOUND 1, x, y, z
            WAIT 1000
        NEXT z
    NEXT y
NEXT x
```

This should be placed immediately after the LOOP SOUND statement.

Controlling the Listener

The POSITION LISTENER Statement

Not only can a sound be positioned, but the apparent position of the listener can
also be moved. Of course, rather than physically move the listener, the effect is
achieved by adjusting the output from the speakers to give the impression that the
listener has moved to a new position. The effect is achieved using the POSITION
LISTENER statement which has the format shown in FIG-24.27.

FIG-24.27

The POSITION
LISTENER Statement

In the diagram:

x,y,z   are three real numbers representing the 3D
                                               coordinates to which the listener is to be moved.

For example, we might move the listener forward using the statement:

```
POSITION LISTENER 0,0,200
```

The ROTATE LISTENER Statement

Even though a listener's position is moved, the listener continues to face in a forward
direction (towards +z). However, by using the ROTATE LISTENER, we can rotate
the listener by 360° around any axis we wish.

Imagine you are sitting in a swivel chair listening to a piece of music. You can turn
the chair to the left or right (technically, this is called **rotation about the y-axis**).
You can also tilt the chair forwards or backwards - to a limited extent (**rotation
about the x-axis**). A final option is to lean your body over to the left or right
(**rotation about the z-axis**). The format for this statement is given in FIG-24.28.

FIG-24.28

The ROTATE
LISTENER Statement

In the diagram:

x,y,z   are three real numbers representing the degrees
                                               of rotation about each axis. These values should
                                               all lie in the range 0 to 360.

For example, we can make the listener do the equivalent of swivelling his chair to
face backwards with the line

```
ROTATE LISTENER, 0,180,0
```

The SCALE LISTENER Statement

The SCALE LISTENER statement does the equivalent of turning down the
listener's hearing sensitivity. In effect this can be used to turn down the volume on
all sounds that are playing or to be played. The statement has the format shown in
FIG-24.29.

FIG-24.29

The SCALE
LISTENER Statement

In the diagram:

factor   is a real value representing the scaling factor.
                                               This value should lie between 0.0 and 1.0, with
                                               1.0 being the default, normal value.

Retrieving Data on 3D Sounds and the Listener

Another batch of statements is available to retrieve the various settings of both 3D sounds and the listener. These are described below.

The SOUND POSITION X Statement

The x ordinate of a 3D sound can be determined using the SOUND POSITION X statement which has the format shown in FIG-24.30.

FIG-24.30

The SOUND POSITION
X Statement

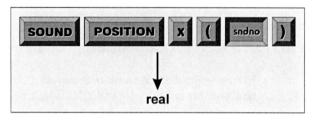

In the diagram:

    sndno   is the number of the existing 3D sound object whose x ordinate is to be returned.

The SOUND POSITION Y Statement

The y ordinate of a 3D sound can be determined using the SOUND POSITION Y statement which has the format shown in FIG-24.31.

FIG-24.31

The SOUND POSITION
Y Statement

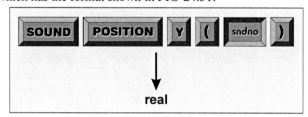

In the diagram:

    sndno   is the number of the existing 3D sound object whose y ordinate is to be returned.

The SOUND POSITION Z Statement

The z ordinate of a 3D sound can be determined using the SOUND POSITION Z statement which has the format shown in FIG-24.32.

FIG-24.32

The SOUND POSITION
Z Statement

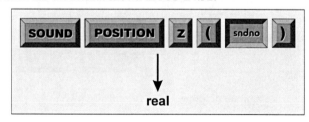

In the diagram:

    sndno   is the number of the existing 3D sound object whose z ordinate is to be returned.

The LISTENER POSITION X Statement

The x ordinate of the listener can be discovered using the LISTENER POSITION X statement whose format is shown in FIG-24.33.

FIG-24.33

The LISTENER POSITION X Statement

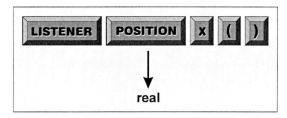

The LISTENER POSITION Y Statement

The y ordinate of the listener can be discovered using the LISTENER POSITION Y statement whose format is shown in FIG-24.34.

FIG-24.34

The LISTENER POSITION Y Statement

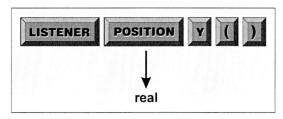

The LISTENER POSITION Z Statement

The z ordinate of the listener can be discovered using the LISTENER POSITION Z statement whose format is shown in FIG-24.35.

FIG-24.35

The LISTENER POSITION Z Statement

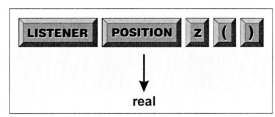

The LISTENER ANGLE X Statement

The angle to which the listener has been rotated about the x-axis (i.e. forward or backward) can be retrieved using the LISTENER ANGLE X statement which has the format shown in FIG-24.36.

FIG-24.36

The LISTENER ANGLE X Statement

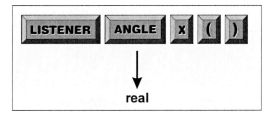

The LISTENER ANGLE Y Statement

The angle to which the listener has been rotated about the y-axis can be retrieved using the LISTENER ANGLE Y statement which has the format shown in FIG-24.37.

FIG-24.37

The LISTENER
ANGLE Y Statement

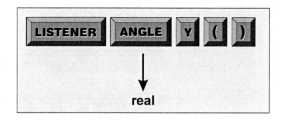

The LISTENER ANGLE Z Statement

The angle to which the listener has been rotated about the z-axis can be retrieved using the LISTENER ANGLE Z statement which has the format shown in FIG-24.38.

FIG-24.38

The LISTENER
ANGLE Z Statement

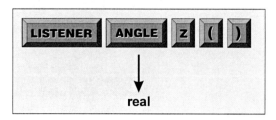

Summary

- A 3D sound can appear to originate from anywhere in space - left, right, in front, behind, below, or above the listener.

- A computer setup needs an appropriate sound card and speaker setup to create 3D sounds.

- The sound file used for 3D sound should be a mono file. The position of the sound within space (that is, the 3D effect) is created by the sound card and speakers.

- Use LOAD 3DSOUND to load a sound file to be used for 3D sound.

- Use POSITION SOUND to specify from where in space a sound should appear to originate.

- Use POSITION LISTENER to place the listener at any point in space.

- Use ROTATE LISTENER to rotate the listener's position.

- Use SCALE LISTENER to adjust the listeners hearing sensitivity.

- SOUND POSITION X returns the x-ordinate of a specified sound's position.

- SOUND POSITION Y returns the y-ordinate of a specified sound's position.

- SOUND POSITION Z returns the z-ordinate of a specified sound's position.

- LISTENER POSITION X returns the x-ordinate of the listener's position.

- LISTENER POSITION Y returns the y-ordinate of the listener's position.

- LISTENER POSITION Z returns the z-ordinate of the listener's position.

- LISTENER ANGLE X returns the listener's angle of rotation about the x-axis.

- LISTENER ANGLE Y returns the listener's angle of rotation about the y-axis.

- LISTENER ANGLE Z returns the listener's angle of rotation about the z-axis.

Solutions

Activity 24.1

No solution required.

Activity 24.2

```
REM *** Load sound ***
LOAD SOUND "welcome.wav", 1
WAIT 500
REM *** Play sound ***
PLAY SOUND 1,20000
REM *** End program ***
WAIT KEY
END
```

Activity 24.3

```
REM *** Load sound ***
LOAD SOUND "welcome.wav", 1
WAIT 500
REM *** Loop sound ***
LOOP SOUND 1,20000,50000
REM *** End program ***
WAIT KEY
END
```

Activity 24.4

The sound resumes playing at the point it was paused but does not loop.

Activity 24.5

```
REM *** Load sound ***
LOAD SOUND "demo.wav", 1
WAIT 500
REM *** Play at half speed ***
SET SOUND SPEED 1,11000
REM *** Play sound continuously ***
LOOP SOUND 1
REM *** Pause when key is pressed ***
WAIT KEY
PAUSE SOUND 1
REM *** Resume when key is pressed ***
WAIT KEY
REM *** Set to double speed ***
SET SOUND SPEED 1,44000
RESUME SOUND 1
REM *** End program ***
WAIT KEY
END
```

Activity 24.6

No solution required.

Activity 24.7

No solution required.

Activity 24.8

```
REM *** Specify file ***
LOAD SOUND "sample.wav",1
REM *** Start recording - 10 seconds ***
PRINT "Speak now "
RECORD SOUND 1,10000
```

```
REM *** Stop after 10s or key pressed ***

WAIT KEY
STOP RECORDING SOUND
REM *** Play back the recorded sound ***
PRINT "Replaying now..."
SLEEP 500
PLAY SOUND 1
REM *** Save the sound ***
PRINT "Saving recording to file"
SAVE SOUND "speech.wav",1
REM *** End program ***
WAIT KEY
END
```

A second attempt will fail since the file *speech.wav* already exists this time round.

Activity 24.9

1) The message displayed is:
   SOUND is playing

2) The message displayed is
   SOUND is paused

3) No messages are displayed.

Activity 24.10

```
REM *** Load sound file ***
LOAD SOUND "demo2.wav", 1
REM *** Play sound file ***
PLAY SOUND 1
WAIT KEY
STOP SOUND 1
REM *** Get sound file's status ***
playing = SOUND PLAYING(1)
looping = SOUND LOOPING(1)
paused = SOUND PAUSED(1)
REM *** Display details ***
IF playing = 1
    PRINT "SOUND is playing"
ENDIF
IF looping = 1
    PRINT "SOUND is looping"
ENDIF
IF paused = 1
    PRINT "SOUND is paused"
ENDIF
PRINT "Volume setting : ",SOUND VOLUME(1)
PRINT "Speed setting  : ",SOUND SPEED(1)
REM *** End program ***
WAIT KEY
END
```

Activity 24.11

The changes required are:

Add constants to identify the sound objects:

```
#CONSTANT firstasteroid     51
#CONSTANT ship               1
#CONSTANT firstmissile     101
#CONSTANT launchsound        1
#CONSTANT hitsound           2
```

Create the sound objects in *InitialiseGame()*:

```
FUNCTION InitialiseGame()
    REM *** Set screen resolution ***
    SET DISPLAY MODE 1280, 1024, 32
    REM *** Magenta transparent ***
    SET IMAGE COLORKEY 255,0,255
    REM *** Load ship sprite ***
    LOAD IMAGE "ship.bmp",2
    SPRITE ship, SCREEN WIDTH()/2,
    SCREEN HEIGHT()/2,2
    OFFSET SPRITE ship,
    SPRITE WIDTH(ship)/2,
    SPRITE HEIGHT(ship)/2
    lastfired = TIMER()
    LOAD IMAGE "missilemag.bmp",3
    missileno = firstmissile
    REM *** Set all missile moves to zero ***
    FOR c = 0 TO 9
        missilemoves(c) = 0
    NEXT c
    REM *** Seed random number generator ***
    RANDOMIZE TIMER()
    REM *** Load sound objects ***
    LOAD SOUND "launch.wav",launchsound
    LOAD SOUND "explode.wav",hitsound
    REM *** Create asteroids ***
    CreateAsteroids()
    REM *** position asteroids ***
    StartPositionsForAsteroids()
ENDFUNCTION
```

Play the sound when a missile is launched:

```
FUNCTION LaunchMissile()
    REM *** IF missile exists, exit ***
    IF SPRITE EXIST(missileno)
        EXITFUNCTION
    ENDIF
    REM *** Create a new missile sprite ***
    REM *** Match position with ship ***
    SPRITE missileno, SPRITE X(ship),
    SPRITE Y(ship),3
    OFFSET SPRITE missileno,
    SPRITE WIDTH(missileno)/2,
    SPRITE HEIGHT(missileno)/2
    ROTATE SPRITE missileno,
    SPRITE ANGLE(ship)
    MOVE SPRITE missileno, 30
    REM *** Play launch sound ***
    PLAY SOUND launchsound
    REM *** Record time missile was fired ***
    lastfired = TIMER()
    REM *** Add to missileno ***
    missileno = missileno mod 10 +
firstmissile
ENDFUNCTION
```

Play sound when asteroid is hit:

```
FUNCTION HandleMissiles()
    REM *** FOR each possible missile DO ***
    FOR spriteno = firstmissile TO
    firstmissile + 9
        REM *** IF it exists, THEN ***
        IF SPRITE EXIST(spriteno)
            REM *** Move the sprite ***
            MOVE SPRITE spriteno, 15
            REM *** IF missile hits THEN ***
            spritehit = SPRITE HIT(spriteno,0)
            IF spritehit > 1
                REM *** Play hit sound ***
                PLAY SOUND hitsound
                REM *** Delete sprites hit ***
                DELETE SPRITE spritehit
                DELETE SPRITE spriteno
```

```
                REM *** Zeroise move count ***
                post = spriteno - firstmissile
                missilemoves(post)=0
            ELSE
                REM *** Inc missile moves ***
                post = spriteno - firstmissile
                INC missilemoves(post)
                REM *** IF 40 moves, destroy ***
                IF missilemoves(post) >= 40
                    DELETE SPRITE spriteno
                    missilemoves(post) = 0
                ENDIF
            ENDIF
        ENDIF
    NEXT spriteno
ENDFUNCTION
```

Activity 24.12

Reversing the FOR loop causes the sound to travel from right to left.

Activity 24.13

No solution required.

Activity 24.14

No solution required.

Activity 24.15

```
LOAD 3DSOUND "laser.wav"
WAIT 500
LOOP SOUND 1
FOR x = -300 TO 300 STEP 100
    FOR y = -300 TO 300 STEP 100
        FOR z = -300 TO 300 STEP 100
            POSITION SOUND 1, x, y, z
            WAIT 1000
        NEXT z
    NEXT y
NEXT x
WAIT KEY
END
```

25

2D Vectors

2D Vector Arithmetic

Creating a 2D Vector Object

Using a 2D Vector to Store Velocity

Vectors in Mathematics and Geometry

2D Vectors

Introduction

When placing a sprite on the screen, its position is always specified using two values: the x-ordinate and y-ordinate. In past examples we've either used two separate variables to hold this information, as in the code

```
x# = 4.6
y# = 1.7
```

or we've designed an appropriate record structure

```
TYPE PositionType
    x   AS FLOAT
    y   AS FLOAT
ENDTYPE
```

and used a variable of this type to store the position:

```
point AS PositionType
point.x = 4.6
point.y = 1.7
```

We've also used a similar structure for storing velocity when describing it in terms of an x-offset and a y-offset.

Another option available to us when storing the coordinates or a velocity is to use a DarkBASIC Pro's 2D vector object (see FIG-25.1). This is really nothing more than a variable that can hold two values at the same time; a bit like the record structure which we created above.

FIG-25.1

The Format of a 2D Vector Object

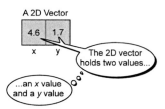

A Mathematical Description of Vectors

To a mathematician, single values (such as 12, or -3) are known as **scalar** values. The term **vector** is used to denote a list of values, a 2D vector containing exactly two numbers. The values in a vector are shown in square brackets - for example, [4.6,1.7]. Vectors written horizontally, as in the previous example, are known as **row vectors** while vectors written vertically

$$\begin{bmatrix} 4.6 \\ 1.7 \end{bmatrix}$$

are known as **column vectors**.

A vector may be assigned an identifying name. Mathematicians will normally use a lowercase letter (i.e. **a** = [4.6,1.7]). To differentiate between scalar identifiers (as in b = 12) and vector identifiers, the latter are normally printed in bold, **a**.

The individual components of a 2D vector are referred to using the vector name and

x and y subscripts. Therefore, if $\mathbf{a} = [4.6, 1.7]$ then

$$a_x = 4.6$$
$$a_y = 1.7$$

In a graphical context, the term vector refers to a directed line that has both **magnitude** and **direction** (see FIG-25.2).

FIG-25.2

Visualisation of a Vector

The diagram assumes the positive y-axis is towards the bottom of the diagram.

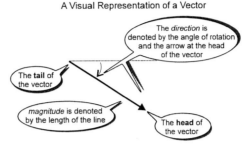

A Visual Representation of a Vector

Although, as we saw in Chapter 18, velocity (which is really just a vector) can be described in two ways (as a distance and an angle, or as x and y offset values), vectors always use the x and y offset approach. So if vector $\mathbf{a}$ is [4.6,1.7] then this represents the vector shown in FIG-25.3.

FIG-25.3

How Vectors are Specified

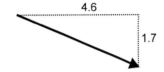

Since a vector holds x and y offsets, determining the equivalent magnitude and direction requires two simple calculations. The magnitude of vector $\mathbf{a}$ (written as $\|\mathbf{a}\|$) being the hypotenuse of a right-angled triangle, can be calculated as follows

$$\|\mathbf{a}\| = \sqrt{a_x^2 + a_y^2}$$

The direction, or angle, of the vector can be derived from the equation

$$\text{direction} = \text{atan}(a_y \,/\, a_x)$$

Activity 25.1

Calculate, to one decimal place, the magnitude and direction for the vector [4.6, 1.7].

Vectors in DarkBASIC Pro

So why should we use a vector in our programs rather than define a record structure? The answer is simply that DarkBASIC Pro provides us with several statements specifically designed to manipulate vectors. If we don't use vectors, then we'd have to write our own code for these operations.

Creating a 2D Vector

The MAKE VECTOR2 Statement

Unlike real, integer or string variables, vector variables have to be explicitly created. And rather than being assigned a name, vector objects are assigned a number (just like sprites, images and sounds).

To create a 2D vector object we use the MAKE VECTOR2 statement which has the form shown in FIG-25.4.

FIG-25.4

The MAKE VECTOR2
Statement

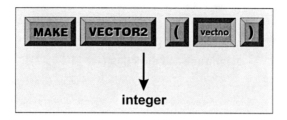

In the diagram:

vectno	is the integer value to be assigned to the 2D vector object that is to be created. Each 2D vector must have its own unique number.

In addition, this statement returns a value of 1 when the 2D vector has been successfully created; if the operation is unsuccessful, zero is returned. It is possible that the operation might fail if you tried to assign the same value to more than one vector, or if the system runs out of RAM space.

A typical statement creating a 2D vector might be

```
result = MAKE VECTOR2(1)
```

which will attempt to create a 2D vector data item which is assigned the identifying value 1. The variable *result* is assigned the value returned by this operation. We could check to make sure the vector has been created with code such as

```
IF result = 0
    PRINT "2D vector creation failed"
    END
ENDIF
```

but most of the time we don't bother with the check, and just assume the vector was created without a problem.

As we saw with images and sprites, a better approach to creating a 2D vector is to start by creating a constant to be associated with the vector:

```
#CONSTANT firstvector  1
```

and then use this variable when creating the 2D vector:

```
result = MAKE VECTOR2(firstvector)
```

Now we can use the term *firstvector* when referring to the vector data structure that has been created, rather than the meaningless value 1.

The SET VECTOR2 Statement

With the data structure created, we'll now want to store values in it. To do this we need to use the SET VECTOR2 statement which has the format shown in FIG-25.5.

FIG-25.5

The SET VECTOR2
Statement

In the diagram:

vectno   is the integer value previously assigned to the 2D vector.

xvalue   is the real number to be assigned to the x part of the 2D vector
                data structure.

yvalue   is the real number to be assigned to the y part of the 2D vector
                data structure.

To store the coordinates (100.5, 53.8) in our vector we would use the statement

```
SET VECTOR firstvector,100.5,53.8
```

The X VECTOR2 Statement

Should we want to retrieve the values we've stored in our 2D vector structure we
need to use the X VECTOR2 statement to retrieve the x element of the structure.
This statement has the format shown in FIG-25.6.

FIG-25.6

The X VECTOR2
Statement

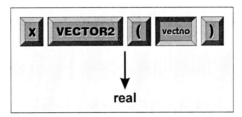

In the diagram:

vectno   is the integer value previously assigned to the 2D
                                    vector.

So we could retrieve the x value stored in the vector identified using *firstvector* with
the line:

```
xord# = X VECTOR2(firstvector)
```

The Y VECTOR2 Statement

To retrieve the y component of our vector we use the Y VECTOR 2 statement which
has the format shown in FIG-25.7.

FIG-25.7

The X VECTOR2
Statement

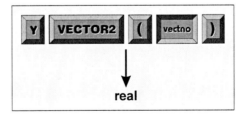

In the diagram:

vectno   is the integer value previously assigned to the 2D
                                    vector.

So we could retrieve the y value stored in the vector identified using *firstvector* with the line:

```
yord# = Y VECTOR2(firstvector)
```

LISTING-25.1 demonstrates the use of the statement given so far by creating, assigning, and retrieving the contents of a 2D vector.

LISTING-25.1

Using 2D Vectors

```
REM *** Create identifying constant for vector***
#CONSTANT firstvector   1

REM *** Create 2D vector ***
result = MAKE VECTOR2(firstvector)

REM *** Store (10.6,25.3) in vector ***
SET VECTOR2 firstvector,10.6,25.3

REM *** Retrieve the values in the vector ***
xord# = X VECTOR2(firstvector)
yord# = Y VECTOR2(firstvector)

REM *** Display retrieved values ***
PRINT xord#,"   ",yord#

REM *** End program ***
WAIT KEY
END
```

Activity 25.2

Type in and test the program given above (*vector01.dbpro*).

Change the values stored to -25.9, 87.0 and check that the correct results are displayed.

The DELETE VECTOR2 Statement

When you have no more use for a vector in your program it should be deleted. This will free up RAM space. To delete the vector we use the DELETE VECTOR2 statement which has the format shown in FIG-25.8.

FIG-25.8

The DELETE VECTOR2
Statement

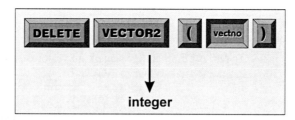

In the diagram:

> *vectno*   is the integer value identifying the 2D vector to be deleted.

Like MAKE VECTOR2, this statement returns a value indicating the success of the operation. 1 is returned if the operation succeeds; otherwise zero is returned.

Typically, we might write

```
result = DELETE VECTOR2(firstvector)
```

The COPY VECTOR2 Statement

If we want to make a copy of an existing 2D vector we can use the COPY VECTOR2 statement which has the format given in FIG-25.9.

FIG-25.9

The COPY VECTOR2 Statement

In the diagram:

> *destvectno*   is an integer value identifying the existing vector to which the data is to be copied.

> *srcvectno*   is an integer value previously assigned to a 2D vector.   This is the vector from which the data is to be copied.

Assuming we had two vectors (1 and 2), then the contents of vector 1 could be copied to vector 2 using the line

```
COPY VECTOR2 2,1
```

The program in LISTING-25.2 demonstrates how to copy the contents of one vector to another.

LISTING-25.2

Copying a 2D Vector

```
REM *** Identifiers for both vectors ***
#CONSTANT firstvector     1
#CONSTANT secondvector    2

REM *** Create two vectors ***
result = MAKE VECTOR2(firstvector)
result = MAKE VECTOR2(secondvector)

REM *** Assign values to both vectors ***
SET VECTOR2 firstvector,10.6,25.3
SET VECTOR2 secondvector,1,2

REM *** Copy contents of first vector to second vector ***
COPY VECTOR2 secondvector, firstvector

REM *** Retrieve the values in the second vector ***
xord# = X VECTOR2(secondvector)
yord# = Y VECTOR2(secondvector)

REM *** and print them ***
PRINT xord#,"  ",yord#

REM *** End program ***
WAIT KEY
END
```

The MULTIPLY VECTOR2 Statement

The contents of a vector can be multiplied by a specified figure using the MULTIPLY VECTOR2 statement which has the format shown in FIG-25.10.

In the diagram:

vectno   is the integer value previously assigned to the 2D vector.

multiplier   is a real value specifying the amount by which the contents of the vector is to be multiplied.

The result of this operation is calculated as follows:

```
vectno.x = vectno.x * multiplier
vectno.y = vectno.y * multiplier
```

For example, the code

```
result = MAKE VECTOR2 (1)
SET VECTOR2 1,10,5
MULTIPLY VECTOR2 1,3
```

would result in the vector's x value being 30 and its y value 15.

The SCALE VECTOR2 Statement

The SCALE VECTOR2 statement is similar to the MULTIPLE VECTOR2 statement, but this time the result is stored in a second vector, the first remaining unchanged. The statement has the format shown in FIG-25.11.

In the diagram:

destvectno   is the integer value previously assigned to the 2D vector which is to contain the result.

srcvectno   is the integer value previously assigned to the 2D vector which is to have its values multiplied.

multiplier   is a real value by which the contents of *srcvectno* is to be multiplied.

The contents of vector *destvectno* is calculated as follows:

```
destvectno.x = srcvectno.x * multiplier
destvectno.y = srcvectno.y * multiplier
```

The DIVIDE VECTOR2 Statement

The contents of a vector can be divided by a specified value using the DIVIDE VECTOR2 statement which has the format shown in FIG-25.12.

FIG-25.12

The DIVIDE VECTOR2
Statement

In the diagram:

vectno	is the integer value previously assigned to the 2D vector.
divisor	is the real value by which the contents of the vector is to be divided.

The result is calculated as follows:

```
vectno.x = vectno.x / dividend
vectno.y = vectno.y / dividend
```

The LENGTH VECTOR2 Statement

We can use the LENGTH VECTOR2 statement to determine the magnitude of a vector. This statement has the format shown in FIG-25.13.

FIG-25.13

The LENGTH
VECTOR2 Statement

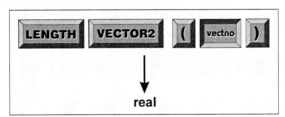

In the diagram:

vectno	is the integer value previously assigned to the 2D vector whose hypotenuse is to be calculated.

This statement will return the value of $\|vectno\|$.

The program in LISTING-25.3 demonstrates the use of this statement.

LISTING-25.3

Calculating the
Magnitude of a Vector

```
REM *** Set up identifier for vector ***
#CONSTANT firstvector = 1

REM *** Create vector ***
result = MAKE VECTOR2(firstvector)

REM *** Assign lengths to the vector ***
SET VECTOR2 firstvector,3,4

REM *** Calculate and display the vector's magnitude ***
PRINT "Magnitude : ",LENGTH VECTOR2 (firstvector)

REM *** end program ***
WAIT KEY
END
```

The second component of the velocity, direction (or angle), can be determined using the formula:

angle = atan(vectno.y / vectno.x)

The SQUARED LENGTH VECTOR2 Statement

The sum of the squares of the two values held in a 2D vector (i.e. the value magntiude^2) can be obtained using the SQUARED LENGTH VECTOR2 statement which has the format shown in FIG-25.14.

FIG-25.14

The SQUARED
LENGTH VECTOR2
Statement

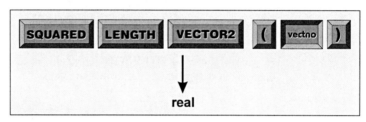

In the diagram:

vectno   is the integer value previously assigned to the 2D vector.

The statement returns the value $\|a\|^2$ calculated as

vectno.x^2 + vectno.y^2

Hence if *vectno.x* = 10 and *vectno.y* = 5, the value returned would be 125 ($10^2 + 5^2$).

The ADD VECTOR2 Statement

The values in two vectors can be added and the result stored in a third vector using the ADD VECTOR2 statement which has the format shown in FIG-25.15.

FIG-25.15

The ADD VECTOR2
Statement

In the diagram:

destvectno   is an integer value previously assigned to the vector which is to contain the sum of the other two vectors.

vectno1, vectno2   are integers previously assigned to the vectors whose values are to be added.

The result of this statement is calculated as follows:

```
destvectno.x = vectno1.x + vectno2.x
destvectno.y = vectno1.y + vectno2.y
```

The program in LISTING-25.4 demonstrates the use of the ADD VECTOR2 statement by summing two vectors and displaying the result.

LISTING-25.4

The ADD VECTOR2 Statement

```
REM *** Set up identifiers for vectors ***
#CONSTANT firstvector = 1
#CONSTANT secondvector = 2
#CONSTANT sumvector = 3

REM *** Create vectors ***
result = MAKE VECTOR2(firstvector)
result = MAKE VECTOR2(secondvector)
result = MAKE VECTOR2(sumvector)

REM *** Assign values to the first two vectors ***
SET VECTOR2 firstvector,10.6,25.3
SET VECTOR2 secondvector,1,2

REM *** Add the two vectors ***
ADD VECTOR2 sumvector,secondvector,firstvector

REM *** Print the result from the third vector ***
xord# = X VECTOR2(sumvector)
yord# = Y VECTOR2(sumvector)
PRINT xord#,"  ",yord#

REM *** end program ***
WAIT KEY
END
```

Activity 25.7

Type in and test the program given above (*vector04.dbpro*).

Imagine a spacecraft moving along a fixed path without any external influences to change its velocity. The spacecraft then rotates about its own axes. This maneuver won't affect the craft's velocity: it may now be travelling sideways, but it is still travelling with the same velocity. The main engine of the craft is now switched on giving thrust in a new direction. The craft's new velocity is determined by adding together the ship's original velocity and the thrust velocity (see FIG-25.16).

FIG-25.16

Adding Two Vectors

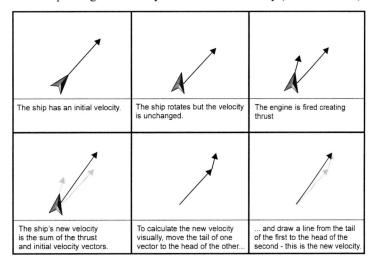

The ship has an initial velocity.	The ship rotates but the velocity is unchanged.	The engine is fired creating thrust
The ship's new velocity is the sum of the thrust and initial velocity vectors.	To calculate the new velocity visually, move the tail of one vector to the head of the other...	... and draw a line from the tail of the first to the head of the second - this is the new velocity.

In the program in LISTING-25.5 we see this theory put into practice. A spacecraft is positioned in the middle of the screen. It may be rotated using the z and x keys and its engines fired using the Enter key.

LISTING-25.5

The ADD VECTOR2
Statement

```
REM *** Set ship's sprite id ***
#CONSTANT ship      1
REM *** Set ship's vector id ***
#CONSTANT shipvector  1
REM *** Set the thrust's vector id
#CONSTANT thrust    2

REM *** Create a variable to store which keys have been pressed
***
GLOBAL keyspressed AS INTEGER
REM *** Create variable ship's angle ***
GLOBAL shipsorientation AS FLOAT


REM *** Main section ***
InitialiseGame()
DO
   HandleKeyboard()
   HandleShip()
LOOP
END



FUNCTION InitialiseGame()
   REM *** Set up data ***
   REM *** Create vector to hold ship's velocity ***
   result = MAKE VECTOR2(shipvector)
   SET VECTOR2 shipvector,0,0
   REM *** Create vector to hold thrust velocity ***
   result = MAKE VECTOR2(thrust)
   SET VECTOR2 thrust,0,0
   REM *** Set up screen ***
   REM *** Set screen resolution ***
   SET DISPLAY MODE 1280, 1024, 32
   REM *** Create a black background ***
   COLOR BACKDROP 0
   BACKDROP ON
   REM *** Set magenta as the transparent colour ***
   SET IMAGE COLORKEY 255,0,255
   REM *** Load animated sprite ***
   CREATE ANIMATED SPRITE ship,"ship02.bmp",3,1,1
   REM *** Move its origin to centre ***
   OFFSET SPRITE ship,SPRITE WIDTH(ship)/2,SPRITE HEIGHT(ship)/2
   REM *** Draw ship ***
   SPRITE ship,640,500,1
ENDFUNCTION



FUNCTION HandleKeyboard()
   REM *** No keys pressed ***
   keyspressed = 0
   REM *** IF z pressed set bit 0
   IF KEYSTATE(44) = 1
      keyspressed = 1
   ELSE
      REM *** IF x pressed set bit 1
      IF KEYSTATE(45) = 1
         keyspressed = 2
      ENDIF
   ENDIF
```

continued on next page

LISTING-25.5
(continued)

The ADD VECTOR2
Statement

```
        REM *** IF ENTER pressed, set bit 2 ***
        IF KEYSTATE(28) = 1
            keyspressed = keyspressed + 4
        ENDIF
ENDFUNCTION


FUNCTION HandleShip()
    REM *** IF bit 0 set rotate ship left ***
    IF (keyspressed && 1) > 0
        DEC shipsorientation,5
    ENDIF
    REM *** IF bit 1 set, rotate ship right ***
    IF (keyspressed && 2) > 0
        INC shipsorientation,5
    ENDIF
    REM *** IF bit 2 set THEN ***
    IF (keyspressed && 4 )> 0
        REM *** Calculate thrust vector ***
        thrustxoffset# = COS(shipsorientation+270)
        thrustyoffset# = SIN(shipsorientation+270)
        SET VECTOR2 thrust,thrustxoffset#,thrustyoffset#
        REM *** Add thrust to current velocity vector ***
        ADD VECTOR2 shipvector,shipvector,thrust
        REM *** Show engine firing on sprite ***
        PLAY SPRITE ship,2,3,20
    ELSE
        REM *** IF ENTER not pressed, show normal ship ***
        SET SPRITE FRAME ship,1
    ENDIF
    REM *** Rotate sprite to latest angle ***
    ROTATE SPRITE ship, shipsorientation
    REM *** Move the sprite an amount equal to the velocity ***
    SPRITE ship,SPRITE X(ship)+ X VECTOR2(shipvector),
    ⮑SPRITE Y(ship)+Y VECTOR2(shipvector),1
ENDFUNCTION
```

Activity 25.8

Type in and test the program given in LISTING-25.4 (*vector05.dbpro*).

The SUBTRACT VECTOR2 Statement

The values in two vectors can be subtracted and the result stored in a third vector using the SUBTRACT VECTOR2 statement which has the format shown in FIG-25.17.

FIG-25.17

The SUBTRACT
VECTOR2 Statement

In the diagram:

destvectno	is an integer value previously assigned to the vector which is to contain the difference of the other two vectors.
vectno1, vectno2	are integers previously assigned to the vectors whose values are to be subtracted.

The result produced by the SUBTRACT VECTOR2 statement is calculated as follows:

```
destvectno.x = vectno1.x - vectno2.x
destvectno.y = vectno1.y - vectno2.y
```

If we assume vector1 and vector2 are used to hold the coordinates of two points rather than a velocity, then the SUBTRACT VECTOR2 can be used to calculate the vector between these two points (see FIG-25.18).

FIG-25.18

Calculating the Vector between Two Points

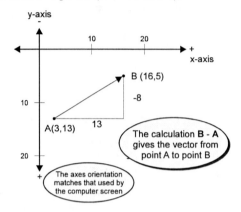

And, if we simply want to find the distance between the two points (v1 and v2) we can do this using the expression

This assumes that v1,v2 and v3 are vector identifiers.

```
SUBTRACT VECTOR2 v3,v1,v2
distance = LENGTH VECTOR2 v1
```

The DOT PRODUCT VECTOR2 Statement

When two vectors (**a** and **b**) are multiplied together, this is written as **a.b**, the dot being used to indicate multiplication. The multiplication returns a single value which is calculated as:

$$a_x b_x + a_y b_y$$

It turns out that this value is always equal to

$$\|a\| \|b\| \cos\theta$$

where θ is the angle between the two vectors (see FIG-25.19).

FIG-25.19

The Angle between Two Vectors

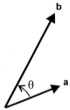

With a bit of algebraic manipulation we can rewrite this as:

$$\theta = \operatorname{acos}\left(\frac{a.b}{\|a\| \|b\|}\right)$$

It is this operation that the DOT PRODUCT VECTOR2 statement performs. The operation gets its name from the dot used between the vectors to signify multiplication. The DOT PRODUCT VECTOR2 statement has the format shown in FIG-25.20.

FIG-25.20

The DOT PRODUCT
VECTOR2 Statement

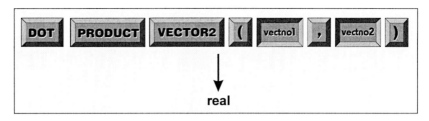

In the diagram:

vectno1,vectno2 are integers previously assigned to the vectors whose values are to be multiplied together.

The program in LISTING-25.6 uses the DOT PRODUCT VECTOR2 statement to work out the angle between two vectors.

LISTING-25.6

Calculating the Angle
between Two Vectors

```
REM *** Set up identifiers for vectors ***
#CONSTANT firstvector   1
#CONSTANT secondvector   2

REM *** Create vectors ***
result = MAKE VECTOR2(firstvector)
result = MAKE VECTOR2(secondvector)

REM *** Assign values to the two vectors ***
SET VECTOR2 firstvector,2,3
SET VECTOR2 secondvector,5,7

REM *** Calculate angle between vectors ***
dotproduct# = DOT PRODUCT VECTOR2 (firstvector, secondvector)
magproduct# = LENGTH VECTOR2(firstvector)*
                LENGTH VECTOR2(secondvector)
angle# = ACOS(dotproduct#/magproduct#)

REM *** display angle ***
PRINT "The angle between the two vectors is ", angle#

REM *** end program ***
WAIT KEY
END
```

Activity 25.9

Type in and try out the program given above (*vectors06.dbpro*).

Change the values held in the vector referenced by *firstvector* to (12,-9) and check that the displayed result is as you expect.

The IS EQUAL VECTOR2 Statement

We can check if two vectors are exactly equal (that is, if $a_x = b_x$ and $a_y = b_y$) using the IS EQUAL VECTOR2 statement which has the format shown in FIG-25.21.

FIG-25.21

The IS EQUAL
VECTOR2 Statement

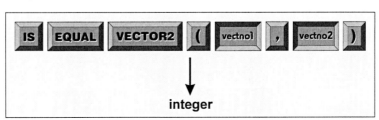

In the diagram:

vectno1,vectno2   are integers previously assigned to the vectors
                                 whose values are to be compared.

The statement returns 1 if the two vectors are exactly equal, otherwise zero is
returned.

For example, assuming *vect1* and *vect2* have been created as follows

```
REM *** Create identifiers for each vector ***
#CONSTANT vect1    1
#CONSTANT vect2    2

REM *** Create vectors ***
result = MAKE VECTOR2(vect1)
result = MAKE VECTOR2(vect2)

REM *** Assign values to each vector ***
SET VECTOR2 vect1,3,4
SET VECTOR2 vect2,3,4
```

then we could check that both vectors contain identical values using the lines

```
IF IS EQUAL VECTOR2(vect1, vect2) = 1
    PRINT "The two vectors are equal"
ELSE
    PRINT "The two vectors are not equal"
ENDIF
```

The MAXIMIZE VECTOR2 Statement

The MAXIMIZE VECTOR2 statement returns a vector constructed by extracting
the larger x and y values from two other vectors (see FIG-25.22).

FIG-25.22

How MAXIMIZE
VECTOR2 Operates

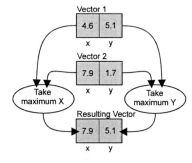

The statement has the format shown in FIG-25.23.

FIG-25.23

The MAXIMIZE
VECTOR2 Statement

In the diagram:

destvectno   is an integer value previously assigned to the
                                 vector which is to contain the larger values from
                                 vectno1 and *vectno2*.

vectno1,vectno2   are integers previously assigned to the vectors
                                 from which the result is to be extracted.

The program in LISTING-25.7 demonstrates the use of this statement.

LISTING-25.7

Demonstrating the
MINIMIZE VECTOR2
Statement

```
REM *** Set up identifiers for vectors ***
#CONSTANT firstvector     1
#CONSTANT secondvector    2
#CONSTANT resultvector    3

REM *** Create vectors ***
result = MAKE VECTOR2(firstvector)
result = MAKE VECTOR2(secondvector)
result = MAKE VECTOR2(resultvector)

REM *** Assign values to the first two vectors ***
SET VECTOR2 firstvector,9,4
SET VECTOR2 secondvector,5,7

REM *** Extract maximum values ***
MAXIMIZE VECTOR2 resultvector, firstvector,secondvector

REM *** Print the result from the third vector ***
xord# = X VECTOR2(resultvector)
yord# = Y VECTOR2(resultvector)
PRINT xord#,"  ",yord#

REM *** End program ***
WAIT KEY
END
```

Activity 25.10

Type in and test the program above (*vector07.dbpro*).

Change the contents of *firstvector* to (-2,11) and *secondvector* to (0,9).

What values are displayed when you run the program, this time?

The MINIMIZE VECTOR2 Statement

The MINIMIZE VECTOR2 statement returns a vector constructed by extracting the smaller x and y values from two other vectors (see FIG-25.24).

FIG-25.24

How MINIMIZE
VECTOR2 Operates

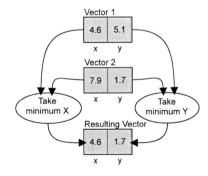

The statement has the format shown in FIG-25.25.

FIG-25.25

The MINIMIZE
VECTOR2 Statement

In the diagram:

destvectno   is an integer value previously assigned to the vector which is to contain the smaller values from *vectno1* and *vectno2*.

vectno1, vectno2   are integers previously assigned to the vectors from which the result is to be extracted.

Summary

In Mathematics

- A single value is known as a scalar value.

- A list of values is known as a vector.

- A 2D vector is a list of two numbers.

- The values in a vector are shown enclosed in square brackets.

- A row vector is a vector where its values are shown horizontally.

- A column vector is a vector where its values are shown vertically.

- A vector identifier is shown in bold.

- If a 2D vector is named **a**, then the values it contains are identified as $\mathbf{a}_x$ and $\mathbf{a}_y$.

In Geometry

- A vector has a magnitude and direction.

- A vector is represented visually as an arrowed line.

- The length of the line represents the magnitude of the vector. For a vector, **a**, this is represented algebraically as $\|\mathbf{a}\|$.

- The angle of the line represents the direction of the vector.

- The values within a vector represent the x and y offset of the vector line.

- The magnitude of a vector, **a**, can be calculated as $\text{SQRT}(\mathbf{a}_x{}^2 + \mathbf{a}_y{}^2)$.

- The direction of a vector, **a**, can be calculated as $\text{ATAN}(\mathbf{a}_x / \mathbf{a}_y)$.

In DarkBASIC Pro

- A 2D vector is created using the MAKE VECTOR2D statement.

- Use SET VECTOR2 to assign values to a 2D vector.

- Use X VECTOR2 to retrieve the x component of a 2D vector.

- Use Y VECTOR2 to retrieve the y component of a 2D vector.

- Use DELETE VECTOR2 to remove a 2D vector from RAM.

- Use COPY VECTOR2 to copy a value from one 2D vector to another.

- Use MULTIPLY VECTOR2 to multiply a 2D vector by a second 2D vector.

- Use SCALE VECTOR2 to scale a vector by a scalar value.

- Use DIVIDE VECTOR2 to divide a 2D vector by a scalar value.

- Use LENGTH VECTOR2 to determine the magnitude of a vector.

- Use SQUARED LENGTH VECTOR2 to determine the square of the magnitude of a vector.

- Use ADD VECTOR2 to assign the sum of two 2D vectors to a third 2D vector.

- Use SUBTRACT VECTOR2 to assign the difference between two 2D vectors to a third 2D vector.

- Use DOT PRODUCT VECTOR2 to multiply the components of two 2D vectors.

- Use IS EQUAL VECTOR2 to determine if two 2D vectors are equal.

- Use MAXIMIZE VECTOR2 to assign the maximum components of two 2D vectors to a third 2D vector.

- Use MINIMIZE VECTOR2 to assign the minimum components of two 2D vectors to a third 2D vector.

Solutions

Activity 25.1

magnitude = 4.9 (1 dp)
direction = 20.3 (1 dp)

Activity 25.2

The values displayed may differ slightly due to rounding errors.

Activity 25.3

```
REM *** Constant for vector***
#CONSTANT firstvector 1
REM *** Create 2D vector ***
result = MAKE VECTOR2(firstvector)
REM *** Store (10.6,25.3) in vector ***
SET VECTOR2 firstvector, -25.9, 87.0
REM *** Retrieve values in the vector ***
xord# = X VECTOR2(firstvector)
yord# = Y VECTOR2(firstvector)
result = DELETE VECTOR2 (firstvector)
REM *** Display retrieved values ***
PRINT xord#," ",yord#
REM *** End program ***
WAIT KEY
END
```

Activity 25.4

No solution required.

Activity 25.5

No solution required.

Activity 25.6

```
REM *** Set up identifier for vector ***
firstvector = 1
REM *** Create vector ***
result = MAKE VECTOR2(firstvector)
REM *** Assign lengths to the vector ***
SET VECTOR2 firstvector, 3, 4
REM *** Display vector's magnitude ***
PRINT "Magnitude : ",
LENGTH VECTOR2 (firstvector)
REM *** Display vector's direction ***
x# = X VECTOR2(firstvector)
y# = Y VECTOR2(firstvector)
angle# = ATAN(y#/x#)
PRINT "Angle : ",angle#
REM *** end program ***
WAIT KEY
END
```

Activity 25.7

No solution required.

Activity 25.8

No solution required.

Activity 25.9

The new vector value should produce a result of 91.33° between the vectors.

Activity 25.10

The result displayed using the new vector values should be 0,11.

How to Create a Two-Player Game

Using Record Structures to Hold Game Data

Creating a Two-Player Game

Introduction

In this chapter we're going to make use of what we've learned about sprites and vectors to create a simple two-player real-time shooting game.

The Rules of the Game

Winning

This game is a duel between two opposing spacecraft. The winner of the game is the first person who destroys the opponent's ship.

Basic Play

Each player controls a spacecraft. The spacecraft can be rotated and moved by firing thruster engines. Since the ship is in interstellar space, its velocity remains unchanged unless the engines are fired again. Each ship can launch a missile which will exist until it hits the enemy craft or until it has travelled a set distance. No more than one missile from each ship can exist at any time.

Controls

A single keyboard is used to control both ships. The control keys are shown in TABLE-26.1.

TABLE-26.1

Game Control Keys

Key	Function
Player 1	
z	Rotate craft left
x	Rotate craft right
c	Fire engines
v	Launch missile
Player 2	
1	Rotate craft left
2	Rotate craft right
. (decimal point)	Fire engines
Enter	Launch missile

Player 2's keys are on the numeric pad on the right-hand side of the keyboard (see FIG-26.1).

FIG-26.1

The Keyboard Layout

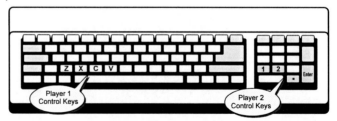

The Screen Layout

The basic game displays only a single screen layout shown in FIG-26.2.

FIG-26.2

The Initial Screen Layout

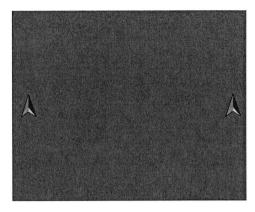

The game uses screen wrapping, so if a spacecraft moves off one edge, it will reappear at the opposite edge. This is not true of missiles, which are deleted when they move off screen.

Game Data

We need to maintain data about each spacecraft and the missiles that they launch. The data required of a missile is:

spriteno	an integer value specifying the missile sprite's number.
trajectory	an integer value identifying a 2D vector holding the velocity of the missile.
moves	an integer value specifying the number of times the missile has moved since launch. It will be destroyed after a specified number of moves.

This data structure is defined in DarkBASIC Pro with the following code:

```
TYPE MissileType
    spriteno        AS INTEGER
    trajectory      AS INTEGER
    moves           AS INTEGER
ENDTYPE
```

The data required by a spacecraft is:

spriteno	an integer value specifying the ship's sprite number.
velocity	an integer value identifying the 2D vector holding the current velocity of the ship.
angle	a real value specifying the ship's angle of rotation (measured clockwise from the 12 o'clock position).
missile	a **MissileType** value giving details of any missile launched by the ship.

This structure is defined in DarkBASIC Pro as follows:

```
TYPE ShipType
    spriteno        AS INTEGER
    velocity        AS INTEGER
    angle           AS FLOAT
    missile         AS MissileType
ENDTYPE
```

Two global variables of *ShipType* are required by the game; one for each ship:

```
GLOBAL leftship   AS ShipType
GLOBAL rightship  AS ShipType
```

The constants used by the program are shown in TABLE-26.2.

TABLE-26.2

Named Constants

Name	Value	Description
leftshipid	1	Used as left ship's sprite number.
rightshipid	2	Used as right ship's sprite number.
maximumshipspeed	30	The maximum speed a ship can achieve.
missilespeed	15	The launch speed of a missile.
screenheight	1024	The screen height.
screenwidth	1280	The screen width.

The values shown in TABLE-26.3 are used for image, sprite and 2D vector identities.

TABLE-26.3

Sprite IDs

Value	File	Description
Images		
1	ship02.bmp	Spacecraft
2	missilemag.bmp	Missile
Sprites		
1		Left ship
2		Right ship
11		Left ship missile
12		Right ship missile
2D Vectors		
1		Left ship velocity
2		Right ship velocity
5		Temporary vector used in *HandleShip()* to hold engine thrust
11		Left ship missile trajectory
12		Right ship missile trajectory
31		Temporary vector used to basic missile thrust in *CreateMissile()*

Game Logic

As always, the overall game logic can be described quite briefly in structured English:

```
Initialise the game
REPEAT
    Get keys pressed
    Handle the left ship
    Handle the right ship
    Handle any missiles fired
UNTIL one ship is destroyed
Display the Game Over screen
```

Game Documentation

The mini-specs for each routine are given overleaf:

NAME	:	Main
PARAMETERS		
IN	:	None
OUT	:	None
PRE-CONDITION	:	None
DESCRIPTION	:	This game places two spacecraft on the screen. Each spacecraft can be turned and moved using the keyboard. Each craft can fire a missile. When one craft is hit by a missile, the game ends.

OUTLINE LOGIC	:	Initialise the game
		REPEAT
		    Get keys pressed
		    Handle the left ship
		    Handle the right ship
		    Handle any missiles fired
		UNTIL one ship is destroyed
		Display the Game Over screen

NAME	:	InitialiseGame
PARAMETERS		
IN	:	None
OUT	:	None
GLOBALS		
READ	:	None
WRITTEN	:	leftship : ShipType rightship : ShipType
PRE-CONDITION	:	None
DESCRIPTION	:	This routine creates the initial screen layout, and initialises the global variables *leftship* and *rightship*.
OUTLINE LOGIC	:	Set up initial screen layout Initialise the fields in leftship and rightship and create sprites

NAME	:	SetUpScreen
PARAMETERS		
IN	:	None
OUT	:	None
GLOBALS		
READ	:	None
WRITTEN	:	None
PRE-CONDITION	:	None
DESCRIPTION	:	Sets the screen resolution and creates a black background.
OUTLINE LOGIC	:	Set screen resolution Create a black background

NAME	:	InitialiseShipsData
PARAMETERS		
IN	:	None
OUT	:	None

continued on next page

```
GLOBALS
    READ            :   None
    WRITTEN         :   leftship : ShipType
                        rightship : ShipType
PRE-CONDITION       :   None
DESCRIPTION         :   This routine initialises the data fields for both ships.
                        It also creates and positions the ship sprites.
OUTLINE LOGIC       :   Initialise leftship fields
                        Load leftship's animated sprite
                        Move the leftship sprite's origin to centre of sprite
                        Position leftship sprite at (100, screenheight/2)
                        Create vector for leftship's velocity
                        Initialise rightship fields
                        Create rightship sprite from clone of leftship sprite
                        Position rightship sprite at (screenwidth-100, screenheight/2)
                        Create vector for rightship's velocity
```

```
NAME                :   HandleKeyboard
PARAMETERS
    IN              :   None
    OUT             :   keyspressed : Integer
GLOBALS
    READ            :   None
    WRITTEN         :   None
PRE-CONDITION       :   None
DESCRIPTION         :   This routine sets individual bits in keyspressed
                        according to which keys have been pressed:
                            Key         Bit
                            z           0
                            x           1
                            c           2
                            v           3
                            1           4
                            2           5
                            .           6
                            Enter       7
OUTLINE LOGIC       :   Set keyspressed to zero
                        IF
                            z pressed:      Set bit 0 of keyspressed
                            x pressed:      Set bit 1 of keyspressed
                            c pressed:      Set bit 2 of keyspressed
                            v pressed       Set bit 3 of keyspressed
                            1 pressed:      Set bit 4 of keyspressed
                            2 pressed:      Set bit 5 of keyspressed
                            . pressed:      Set bit 6 of keyspressed
                            Enter pressed:  Set bit 7 of keyspressed
                        ENDIF
```

Notice that *keypressed* is a parameter of *HandleKeyboard* and not a global variable as it has been in previous examples.

```
NAME               :   HandleShip
PARAMETERS
   IN              :   ship : ShipType
                       keyspressed : Integer
   OUT             :   shipangle
GLOBALS
   READ            :   None
   WRITTEN         :   None
PRE-CONDITION      :   None
DESCRIPTION        :   ship values and sprite are updated. What changes are
                       made depends on the value of keyspressed:


                       Bit set              Action
                          0         Ship's angle decreased by 5°.
                          1         Ship's angle increased by 5°.
                          2         Ship's current velocity changed.
                                    by engine thrust. Flames displayed
                                    on ship's sprite.
                          3         Missile fired (only if ship has no
                                    other missile at this time).

OUTLINE LOGIC   :   IF
                         bit 0 set:
                              Subtract 5 from ship.angle
                         bit 1 set:
                              Add 5 to ship.angle
                         bit 2 set:
                              Calculate engine thrust vector
                              Add engine thrust vector to ship.velocity
                              IF ship's speed is too fast THEN
                                     Slow it down to maximumshipspeed
                              ENDIF
                              Play flame frames on ship's sprite
                         bit 3 set:
                              IF ship does not have a current missile THEN
                                     Create missile
                              ENDIF
                    ENDIF
                    Set ship's sprite frame back to no-flames
                    Bring ship back on screen if necessary
                    Position ship's sprite
                    Set shipangle to ship.angle
```

The important point to grasp about *Handleship* is that, rather than write two separate routines to handle the left and right ships, the task can be performed by this single routine as long as we tell it which ship is to be dealt with each time the routine is called. This is done by the *ship* parameter.

One restriction of a function is that it cannot return a record structure. This is a bit of a problem since we need to update the ship's angle of rotation each time this routine is called. We get round this problem by returning the new angle of rotation as a single integer value and then assign this value to the *angle* field in the appropriate ship's record.

NAME	:	CreateMissile
PARAMETERS		
IN	:	ship : ShipType
OUT	:	None
GLOBALS		
READ	:	None
WRITTEN	:	None
PRE-CONDITION	:	Missile does not already exist
DESCRIPTION	:	This routine creates a missile at the front of ship. The missile's final velocity is a combination of its launch velocity and the ship's velocity. The missile's sprite is placed on the screen.
OUTLINE LOGIC:		Determine the missile's basic velocity based on *ship.angle*
		Determine the missile's actual trajectory as missile's basic velocity + *ship.velocity*
		Create missile sprite
		Rotate and position sprite to front of ship

NAME	:	HandleMissiles
PARAMETERS		
IN	:	None
OUT	:	kill: Integer
GLOBALS		
READ	:	None
WRITTEN	:	leftship : ShipType
		rightship : ShipType
PRE-CONDITION	:	None
DESCRIPTION	:	This routine moves any missiles on the screen. It also checks to see if a ship has been hit by the missile. *kill* is set to zero if no ship is hit, 1 if the *leftship* is hit and 2 if *rightship* is hit.

OUTLINE LOGIC:

```
Set kill to zero
IF leftship missile exists THEN
      Move the missile
      IF missile hits rightship THEN
            Delete missile and rightship
            Set kill to 2
      ELSE
            Add 1 to moves made by missile
            IF missile moved more than 30 times THEN
                  Destroy missile
                  Reset missile moves to zero
            ENDIF
      ENDIF
ENDIF
IF rightship missile exists THEN
      Move the missile
      IF missile hits leftship THEN
            Delete missile and leftship
            Set kill to 1
      ELSE
            Add 1 to moves made by missile
```

continued on next page

```
                                    IF missile moved more than 30 times THEN
                                        Destroy missile
                                        Reset missile moves to zero
                                    ENDIF
                                ENDIF
                            ENDIF
```

NAME	:	WrapShip
PARAMETERS		
IN	:	ship : ShipType
OUT	:	None
GLOBALS		
READ	:	None
WRITTEN	:	None
PRE-CONDITION	:	None
DESCRIPTION	:	This routine checks to see if ship has moved off the edge of the screen and if so, brings it back on at the opposite edge.
OUTLINE LOGIC:		IF

```
                            IF
                                ship moved off left      : bring on at right
                                ship moved off right     : bring on at left
                                ship moved off top       : bring on at bottom
                                ship moved off bottom: bring on at top
                            ENDIF
```

NAME	:	GameOver
PARAMETERS		
IN	:	kill : Integer
OUT	:	None
GLOBALS		
READ	:	None
WRITTEN	:	None
PRE-CONDITION	:	None
DESCRIPTION	:	This routine displays an end screen message. The *kill* parameter will be 1 if the left ship has been destroyed; 2 if the right ship has been destroyed. The end screen produced can be varied according to the value of *kill*.
OUTLINE LOGIC	:	Clear screen
		Display message

Activity 26.1

The *GameOver* routine should include screen layouts showing the programmer exactly what should be displayed on the screen by this routine. Design your own layouts giving two alternative displays depending on which player has won.

Coding the Program

Our best approach here will be top-down programming, so we'll start with the constants, globals and main section. The code for this is shown overleaf:

```
REM *** Declare constants ***
#CONSTANT leftshipid          1
#CONSTANT rightshipid         2
#CONSTANT maximumshipspeed    30
#CONSTANT missilespeed        15
#CONSTANT screenheight        1024
#CONSTANT screenwidth         1280
REM *** Define types ***
TYPE MissileType
    spriteno       AS INTEGER
    trajectory     AS INTEGER
    moves          AS INTEGER
ENDTYPE

TYPE ShipType
    spriteno       AS INTEGER       'Ship's sprite number
    velocity       AS INTEGER       'Ship's velocity vector number
    angle          AS FLOAT         'Angle of rotation of the ship
    missile        AS MissileType   'Ship's missile sprite number
ENDTYPE

REM *** Declare globals ***
GLOBAL leftship   AS ShipType
GLOBAL rightship  AS ShipType


REM *** Main program logic ***
InitialiseGame()
REPEAT
    keyspressed = HandleKeyboard()
    leftship.angle = HandleShip(leftship,keyspressed)
    rightship.angle = Handleship(rightship,keyspressed >> 4)
    kill = HandleMissiles()
UNTIL kill <> 0
GameOver(kill)
END
```

Activity 26.2

Type in the code given above (*duel01.dbpro*)

Add in test stubs for each of the functions called.

Run the program and make sure each routine is called as expected.

Adding *InitialiseGame()*

Since there is so much to do when setting up the game, the *InitialiseGame()* function simply calls other routines to do the various sections of the work:

```
FUNCTION InitialiseGame()
    SetUpScreen()
    InitialiseShipsData()
    PrepareSprites()
ENDFUNCTION
```

Activity 26.3

Replace the stub for *InitialiseGame()* with the code given above.

Add new stubs for the routines called by *InitialiseGame()*.

The code for *SetUpScreen()* sets the screen resolution and the backdrop colour:

```
FUNCTION SetUpScreen()
    REM *** Set screen resolution ***
    SET DISPLAY MODE screenwidth,screenheight, 32
    REM *** Create a black background ***
    COLOR BACKDROP 0
    BACKDROP ON
ENDFUNCTION
```

The code for *InitialiseShipsData()* initialises the fields within the *leftship* and *rightship* records:

```
FUNCTION InitialiseShipsData()
    REM *** Initialise left ship variable ***
    leftship.spriteno = leftshipid
    leftship.velocity = leftshipid
    leftship.angle = 0
    leftship.missile.spriteno = leftshipid + 10
    leftship.missile.trajectory = leftshipid + 10
    leftship.missile.moves = 0
    REM *** Create ship's velocity vector ***
    result = MAKE VECTOR2(leftship.velocity)
    SET VECTOR2 leftship.velocity,0,0

    REM *** Initialise right ship variable***
    rightship.spriteno = rightshipid
    rightship.velocity = rightshipid
    rightship.angle = 0
    rightship.missile.spriteno = rightshipid + 10
    rightship.missile.trajectory = rightshipid + 10
    rightship.missile.moves = 0
    REM *** Create ship's velocity vector ***
    result = MAKE VECTOR2(rightship.velocity)
    SET VECTOR2 rightship.velocity,0,0
ENDFUNCTION
```

PrepareSprites() sets magenta as the transparent colour, loads the ship image and uses this to create a sprite for the left and right ships. In addition, the missile image is loaded ready for use by any missile sprite that is created during the game:

```
FUNCTION PrepareSprites()
    REM *** Set transparent colour to magenta ***
    SET IMAGE COLORKEY 255,0,255

    REM *** Load left ship's animated sprite ***
    CREATE ANIMATED SPRITE leftship.spriteno,"ship02.bmp",3,1,1
    REM *** Move its origin to centre ***
    OFFSET SPRITE leftship.spriteno,SPRITE WIDTH
    ↪(leftship.spriteno)/2,
    SPRITE HEIGHT(leftship.spriteno)/2
    REM *** Position left ship ***
    SPRITE leftship.spriteno,100,SCREEN HEIGHT()/2,1

    REM *** Load right ship's animated sprite ***
    CLONE SPRITE leftship.spriteno,rightship.spriteno
    REM *** Position right ship ***
    SPRITE rightship.spriteno,SCREEN WIDTH()-100,
    ↪SCREEN HEIGHT()/2,2

    REM *** Load image used by missiles ***
    LOAD IMAGE "missilemag.bmp",2
ENDFUNCTION FUNCTION
```

Adding *HandleKeyboard()*

Now we need to add the code for *HandleKeyboard()*:

```
FUNCTION HandleKeyboard()
    REM *** No keys pressed ***
    keyspressed = 0
    REM *** IF z pressed set bit 0 ***
    IF KEYSTATE(44) = 1
        keyspressed = keyspressed || %1
    ENDIF
    REM *** IF x pressed set bit 1 ***
    IF KEYSTATE(45) = 1
        keyspressed = keyspressed || %10
    ENDIF
    REM *** IF c pressed, set bit 2 ***
    IF KEYSTATE(46) = 1
        keyspressed = keyspressed || %100
    ENDIF
    REM *** IF v pressed, set bit 3 ***
    IF KEYSTATE(47) = 1
        keyspressed = keyspressed || %1000
    ENDIF
    REM *** IF 1 pressed, set bit 4 ***
    IF KEYSTATE(79) = 1
        keyspressed = keyspressed || %10000
    ENDIF
    REM *** IF 2 pressed, set bit 5 ***
    IF KEYSTATE(80) = 1
        keyspressed = keyspressed || %100000
    ENDIF
    REM *** IF . pressed, set bit 6 ***
    IF KEYSTATE(83) = 1
        keyspressed = keyspressed || %1000000
    ENDIF
    REM *** IF Enter pressed, set bit 7 ***
    IF KEYSTATE(156) = 1
        keyspressed = keyspressed || %10000000
    ENDIF
ENDFUNCTION keyspressed
```

Adding *HandleShip()*

The *HandleShip()* function starts with the line:

```
FUNCTION HandleShip(ship AS ShipType, keyspressed)
```

By passing the ship's details to the routine, we can make this one routine handle the left ship when passed *leftship* as a parameter and, when called for a second time, handle the right ship by passing *rightship* as a parameter.

Activity 26.6

A detailed description of the logic for *HandleShip()* is given below. Change these comments into the equivalent code and hence add the *HandleShip()* function to your program.

```
IF keyspressed bit 0 set THEN
       Subtract 5 to ship.angle   (keep within 0 to 360)
ENDIF
IF keyspressed bit 1 set THEN
       Add 5 to ship.angle        (keep within 0 to 360)
ENDIF
IF keyspressed bit 2 set THEN
       Calculate enginethrustxoffset as COS(ship.angle+270)
       Calculate enginethrustyoffset as SIN(ship.angle+270)
       Create thrust vector
       Set thrust vector to enginethrustxoffset, enginethrustyoffset
       Add thrust vector to the ship.velocity vector
       IF speed of ship > maximumshipspeed THEN
             Reduce speed of ship to maximumshipspeed
       ENDIF
       Play engine firing frames of ship.spriteno
ELSE
       Set ship.spriteno sprite to first frame
ENDIF
IF keyspressed bit 3 set AND ship.missile.spriteno sprite does not exist THEN
       CreateMissile(ship)
ENDIF
Rotate ship.spriteno sprite to ship.angle
Move ship.spriteno sprite by ship.velocity vector amount
WrapShip(ship)
```

The lines CreateMissile(ship) and WrapShip(ship) are function calls. Include test stubs for these functions.

Next, we'll replace the newest test stubs, *CreateMissile()* and *WrapShip()* with their actual code. This is relatively easy since they are very similar to routines we created in a previous chapter.

```
FUNCTION CreateMissile(ship AS ShipType)
    REM *** IF missile already exists, exit routine ***
    IF SPRITE EXIST(ship.missile.spriteno)
        EXITFUNCTION
    ENDIF
    REM *** Missile's basic velocity based on ship's angle***
    launchvector = 31
    result = MAKE VECTOR2(launchvector)
    launchmissileX# = COS(ship.angle+270)*15
    launchmissileY# = SIN(ship.angle+270)*15
    SET VECTOR2 launchvector,launchmissileX#,launchmissileY#
    REM ***Missile's path is basic velocity + ship's velocity***
    result = MAKE VECTOR2(ship.missile.trajectory)
    ADD VECTOR2 ship.missile.trajectory,ship.velocity,launchvector
    REM *** Rotate and position sprite to front of ship ***
    SPRITE ship.missile.spriteno, SPRITE X(ship.spriteno),
    ⤷SPRITE Y(ship.spriteno),2
    ROTATE SPRITE ship.missile.spriteno,
```

```
                    ⤷SPRITE ANGLE(ship.spriteno)
                MOVE SPRITE ship.missile.spriteno,50
                REM *** Delete the basic velocity vector used earlier ***
                result = DELETE VECTOR2 (launchvector)
            ENDFUNCTION

            FUNCTION WrapShip(ship AS ShipType)
                REM *** IF off left edge, bring back on right edge ***
                IF SPRITE X(ship.spriteno) < 0
                    SPRITE ship.spriteno,SCREEN WIDTH(),
                    ⤷SPRITE Y(ship.spriteno),ship.spriteno
                ELSE
                    REM *** IF off right edge, bring back at left ***
                    IF SPRITE X(ship.spriteno) > SCREEN WIDTH()
                        SPRITE ship.spriteno,0,SPRITE Y(ship.spriteno),
                        ⤷ship.spriteno
                    ELSE
                        REM *** IF off top, bring on at bottom ***
                        IF SPRITE Y(ship.spriteno) < 0
                            SPRITE ship.spriteno,SPRITE X(ship.spriteno),
                            ⤷SCREEN HEIGHT(),ship.spriteno
                        ELSE
                            REM *** IF off bottom, bring back at top ***
                            IF SPRITE Y(ship.spriteno) > SCREEN HEIGHT()
                                SPRITE ship.spriteno,SPRITE X(ship.spriteno)
                                ⤷,0,ship.spriteno
                            ENDIF
                        ENDIF
                    ENDIF
                ENDIF
            ENDFUNCTION
```

Activity 26.7

Replace the stubs for *CreateMissile()* and *WrapShip()* with the code given.

Adding *HandleMissiles()*

The final routine required in the main loop handles any missiles created and checks for a missile hitting a ship. The function returns 1 if a ship is hit, otherwise zero is returned. The code for this routine is:

```
            FUNCTION HandleMissiles()
                kill = 0
                REM *** IF the left ship's missile exists THEN ***
                IF SPRITE EXIST(leftship.missile.spriteno)
                    REM *** Move missile on screen ***
                    MOVE SPRITE leftship.missile.spriteno,
                    ⤷LENGTH VECTOR2 (leftship.missile.trajectory)
                    REM *** IF missile hits ship ***
                    IF SPRITE HIT(leftship.missile.spriteno,
                    ⤷rightship.spriteno) > 0
                        REM *** Delete missile and rightship ***
                        DELETE SPRITE leftship.missile.spriteno
                        result = DELETE VECTOR2(leftship.missile.trajectory)
                        leftship.missile.moves = 0
                        DELETE SPRITE rightship.spriteno
                        kill = rightship.spriteno
                    ELSE
                        REM *** Increment the number of moves made ***
                        INC leftship.missile.moves
                        REM *** IF more than 30 moves, destroy missile ***
                        IF leftship.missile.moves > 30
                            DELETE SPRITE leftship.missile.spriteno
```

```
                         result = DELETE VECTOR2
                         ↳(leftship.missile.trajectory)
                         leftship.missile.moves = 0
                     ENDIF
                 ENDIF
             ENDIF
             IF SPRITE EXIST(rightship.missile.spriteno)
                 MOVE SPRITE rightship.missile.spriteno,
                 ↳LENGTH VECTOR2(rightship.missile.trajectory)
                 IF SPRITE HIT(rightship.missile.spriteno,
                 ↳leftship.spriteno) > 0
                     REM *** Delete missile and rightship ***
                     DELETE SPRITE rightship.missile.spriteno
                     result = DELETE VECTOR2(rightship.missile.trajectory)
                     rightship.missile.moves = 0
                     DELETE SPRITE leftship.spriteno
                     kill = leftship.spriteno
                 ELSE
                     INC rightship.missile.moves
                     IF rightship.missile.moves > 30
                         DELETE SPRITE rightship.missile.spriteno
                         result = DELETE VECTOR2(rightship.missile.
                         ↳trajectory)
                         rightship.missile.moves = 0
                     ENDIF
                 ENDIF
             ENDIF
         ENDFUNCTION kill
```

Activity 26.8

Add *HandleMissiles()* to your program.

Adding *GameOver()*

The final routine of all is *GameOver()* which displays a final message before the program terminates.

Activity 26.9

Implement the *GameOver()* so that it displays the screen layout you designed back in Activity 26.1.

Add an 8 second delay at the end of the routine to give the players sufficient time to view the end screen before the program terminates.

A complete listing of the final program is given overleaf.

Space Duel - A Program Listing

```
REM ****************************************
REM *** Program   : Space Duel         ***
REM *** Version   : 0.1                ***
REM *** Date      : 27/8/2005          ***
REM *** Author    : A. Stewart         ***
REM *** Language  : DarkBASIC Pro       ***
REM *** Hardware  : PC at least 1280 by ***
REM ***              1024 display       ***
REM *** Purpose   : A two-player space  ***
REM ***              shooting game       ***
REM ****************************************

REM *** Declare constants ***
#CONSTANT leftshipid            1
#CONSTANT rightshipid           2
#CONSTANT maximumshipspeed      30
#CONSTANT missilespeed          15
#CONSTANT screenheight          1024
#CONSTANT screenwidth           1280

REM *** Define types ***
TYPE MissileType
   spriteno    AS INTEGER
   trajectory  AS INTEGER
   moves       AS INTEGER
ENDTYPE

TYPE ShipType
   spriteno    AS INTEGER    `Ship's sprite number
   velocity    AS INTEGER    `Ship's velocity vector number
   angle       AS FLOAT      `Angle of rotation of the ship
   missile     AS MissileType `Ship's missile sprite number
ENDTYPE

REM *** Declare globals ***
GLOBAL leftship AS ShipType
GLOBAL rightship AS ShipType




REM *** Main program logic ***
InitialiseGame()
REPEAT
   keyspressed = HandleKeyboard()
   leftship.angle = HandleShip(leftship,keyspressed)
   rightship.angle = Handleship(rightship, keyspressed >> 4)
   kill = HandleMissiles()
UNTIL kill <> 0
GameOver()
END




FUNCTION InitialiseGame()
   SetUpScreen()
   InitialiseShipsData()
   PrepareSprites()
ENDFUNCTION
```

continued on next page

```
FUNCTION SetUpScreen()
   REM *** Set screen resolution ***
   SET DISPLAY MODE screenwidth,screenheight,32
   REM *** Create a black background ***
   COLOR BACKDROP 0
   BACKDROP ON
ENDFUNCTION

FUNCTION InitialiseShipsData()
   REM *** Initialise left ship variable ***
   leftship.spriteno = leftshipid
   leftship.velocity = leftshipid
   leftship.angle = 0
   leftship.missile.spriteno = leftshipid+10
   leftship.missile.trajectory = leftshipid+10
   leftship.missile.moves = 0
   REM *** Create ship's velocity vector ***
   result = MAKE VECTOR2(leftship.velocity)
   SET VECTOR2 leftship.velocity,0,0

   REM *** Initialise right ship variable***
   rightship.spriteno = rightshipid
   rightship.velocity = rightshipid
   rightship.angle = 0
   rightship.missile.spriteno = rightshipid+10
   rightship.missile.trajectory = rightshipid+10
   rightship.missile.moves = 0
   REM *** Create ship's velocity vector ***
   result = MAKE VECTOR2(rightship.velocity)
   SET VECTOR2 rightship.velocity,0,0
ENDFUNCTION

FUNCTION PrepareSprites()
   REM *** Set transparent colour to magenta ***
   SET IMAGE COLORKEY 255,0,255
   REM *** Load left ship's animated sprite ***
   CREATE ANIMATED SPRITE leftship.spriteno,"ship02.bmp",3,1,1
   REM *** Move its origin to centre ***
   OFFSET SPRITE leftship.spriteno,
   ↳SPRITE WIDTH(leftship.spriteno)/2,
   ↳SPRITE HEIGHT(leftship.spriteno)/2
   REM *** Position left ship ***
   SPRITE leftship.spriteno,100, SCREEN HEIGHT()/2,1

   REM *** Load right ship's animated sprite ***
   CLONE SPRITE leftship.spriteno,rightship.spriteno
   REM *** Position right ship ***
   SPRITE rightship.spriteno,SCREEN WIDTH()-100,
   ↳SCREEN HEIGHT()/2, 2

   REM *** Load image used by missiles ***
   LOAD IMAGE "missilemag.bmp",2
ENDFUNCTION

FUNCTION HandleKeyboard()
   REM *** No keys pressed ***
   keyspressed = 0
   REM *** IF z pressed set bit 0 ***
   IF KEYSTATE(44) = 1
      keyspressed = keyspressed || %1
   ENDIF
   REM *** IF x pressed set bit 1 ***
   IF KEYSTATE(45) = 1
      keyspressed = keyspressed || %10
   ENDIF
```

continued on next page

```
            REM *** IF c pressed, set bit 2 ***
            IF KEYSTATE(46) = 1
               keyspressed = keyspressed || %100
            ENDIF
            REM *** IF v pressed, set bit 3 ***
            IF KEYSTATE(47) = 1
               keyspressed = keyspressed || %1000
            ENDIF
            REM *** IF 1 pressed, set bit 4 ***
            IF KEYSTATE(79) = 1
               keyspressed = keyspressed || %10000
            ENDIF
            REM *** IF 2 pressed, set bit 5 ***
            IF KEYSTATE(80) = 1
               keyspressed = keyspressed || %100000
            ENDIF
            REM *** IF . pressed, set bit 6 ***
            IF KEYSTATE(83) = 1
               keyspressed = keyspressed || %1000000
            ENDIF
            REM *** IF Enter pressed, set bit 7 ***
            IF KEYSTATE(156) = 1
               keyspressed = keyspressed || %10000000
            ENDIF
ENDFUNCTION keyspressed

FUNCTION HandleShip(ship AS ShipType, keyspressed)
            REM *** IF bit 0 set, rotate ship left ***
            IF (keyspressed && 1) > 0
               ship.angle = WRAPVALUE(ship.angle-5)
            ENDIF
            REM *** IF bit 1 set, rotate ship right ***
            IF (keyspressed && 2) > 0
               ship.angle = WRAPVALUE(ship.angle+5)
            ENDIF
            REM *** IF bit 2 set THEN ***
            IF (keyspressed && 4 )> 0
               REM *** Calculate thrust vector ***
               thrustxoffset# = COS(ship.angle+270)
               thrustyoffset# = SIN(ship.angle+270)
               thrustvector = 2
               result = MAKE VECTOR2(thrustvector)
               SET VECTOR2 thrustvector, thrustxoffset#, thrustyoffset#
               REM *** Add thrust to current velocity vector ***
               ADD VECTOR2 ship.velocity, ship.velocity, thrustvector
               REM *** Reduce speed if too fast **
               IF LENGTH VECTOR2(ship.velocity) > maximumshipspeed
                  MULTIPLY VECTOR2 ship.velocity,
                  ⮡maximumshipspeed/LENGTH VECTOR2(ship.velocity)
               ENDIF
               REM *** Show engine firing on sprite ***
               PLAY SPRITE ship.spriteno,2,3,20
            ELSE
               REM *** IF ENTER not pressed, show normal ship ***
               SET SPRITE FRAME ship.spriteno,1
            ENDIF
            REM *** IF bit 3 set AND missile doesn't exist, fire ***
            IF (keyspressed && 8) > 0 AND
            ⮡(NOT SPRITE EXIST(ship.missile.spriteno))
               CreateMissile(ship)
            ENDIF
            REM *** Rotate sprite to latest angle ***
            ROTATE SPRITE ship.spriteno, ship.angle
```

continued on next page

```
    REM *** Move the sprite an amount equal to the velocity ***
    SPRITE ship.spriteno, SPRITE X(ship.spriteno)+
    ↳X VECTOR2(ship.velocity), SPRITE Y(ship.spriteno)+
    ↳Y VECTOR2(ship.velocity),1
    WrapShip(ship)
ENDFUNCTION ship.angle

FUNCTION CreateMissile(ship AS ShipType)
    REM *** IF missile already exists, exit routine ***
    IF SPRITE EXIST(ship.missile.spriteno)
        EXITFUNCTION
    ENDIF
    REM *** Create missile's direction based on ship's angle ***
    launchvector = 31
    result = MAKE VECTOR2(launchvector)
    launchmissileX# = COS(ship.angle+270)*15
    launchmissileY# = SIN(ship.angle+270)*15
    SET VECTOR2 launchvector,launchmissileX#,launchmissileY#
    REM *** Missile's path is basic velocity + ship's velocity ***
    result = MAKE VECTOR2(ship.missile.trajectory)
    ADD VECTOR2 ship.missile.trajectory,ship.velocity,launchvector
    REM *** Rotate and position sprite to front of ship ***
    SPRITE ship.missile.spriteno,SPRITE X(ship.spriteno),
    ↳SPRITE Y(ship.spriteno),2
    OFFSET SPRITE ship.missile.spriteno,
    ↳SPRITE WIDTH(ship.missile.spriteno)/2,
    ↳SPRITE HEIGHT(ship.missile.spriteno)/2
    ROTATE SPRITE ship.missile.spriteno,
    ↳SPRITE ANGLE(ship.spriteno)
    MOVE SPRITE ship.missile.spriteno, 50
    REM *** Delete the basic velocity vector used earlier ***
    result = DELETE VECTOR2 (launchvector)
ENDFUNCTION

FUNCTION WrapShip(ship AS ShipType)
    REM *** IF moved off left edge, bring back on right edge ***
    IF SPRITE X(ship.spriteno) < 0
        SPRITE ship.spriteno, SCREEN WIDTH(),
        ↳SPRITE Y(ship.spriteno),ship.spriteno
    ELSE
        REM *** IF moved off right edge, bring back at left ***
        IF SPRITE X(ship.spriteno) > SCREEN WIDTH()
            SPRITE ship.spriteno, 0,
            ↳SPRITE Y(ship.spriteno),ship.spriteno
        ELSE
            REM *** IF moved off top, bring on at bottom ***
            IF SPRITE Y(ship.spriteno) < 0
                SPRITE ship.spriteno,SPRITE X(ship.spriteno),
                ↳SCREEN HEIGHT(),ship.spriteno
            ELSE
                REM *** IF moved off at bottom, bring back at top ***
                IF SPRITE Y(ship.spriteno) > SCREEN HEIGHT()
                    SPRITE ship.spriteno,SPRITE X(ship.spriteno),
                    ↳0,ship.spriteno
                ENDIF
            ENDIF
        ENDIF
    ENDIF
ENDFUNCTION

FUNCTION HandleMissiles()
    kill = 0
    REM *** IF the left ship's missile exists THEN ***
    IF SPRITE EXIST(leftship.missile.spriteno)
```

continued on next page

```
        REM *** Move missile on screen ***
        MOVE SPRITE leftship.missile.spriteno,
        ⤷LENGTH VECTOR2 (leftship.missile.trajectory)
        REM *** IF missile hits ship ***
        IF SPRITE HIT(leftship.missile.spriteno,rightship.spriteno)
        ⤷> 0
            REM *** Delete missile and rightship ***
            DELETE SPRITE leftship.missile.spriteno
            result = DELETE VECTOR2 (leftship.missile.trajectory)
            leftship.missile.moves = 0
            DELETE SPRITE rightship.spriteno
            kill = rightship.spriteno
        ELSE
            REM *** Increment the number of moves made ***
            INC leftship.missile.moves
            REM *** IF more than 30 moves, destroy missile ***
            IF leftship.missile.moves > 30
                DELETE SPRITE leftship.missile.spriteno
                result = DELETE VECTOR2(leftship.missile.trajectory)
                leftship.missile.moves = 0
            ENDIF
        ENDIF
    ENDIF
    IF SPRITE EXIST(rightship.missile.spriteno)
        MOVE SPRITE rightship.missile.spriteno,
        ⤷LENGTH VECTOR2(rightship.missile.trajectory)
        IF SPRITE HIT(rightship.missile.spriteno,leftship.spriteno)
        ⤷> 0
            REM *** Delete missile and rightship ***
            DELETE SPRITE rightship.missile.spriteno
            result = DELETE VECTOR2 (rightship.missile.trajectory)
            rightship.missile.moves = 0
            DELETE SPRITE leftship.spriteno
            kill = leftship.spriteno
        ELSE
            INC rightship.missile.moves
            IF rightship.missile.moves > 30
                DELETE SPRITE rightship.missile.spriteno
                result=DELETE VECTOR2(rightship.missile.trajectory)
                rightship.missile.moves = 0
            ENDIF
        ENDIF
    ENDIF
ENDFUNCTION kill

FUNCTION GameOver(kill)
    REM *** Hide any sprite still on screen ***
    HIDE ALL SPRITES
    REM *** Create a new sprite ***
    CREATE ANIMATED SPRITE 3,"ship02.bmp",3,1,1
    OFFSET SPRITE 3, SPRITE WIDTH(3)/2, SPRITE HEIGHT(3)/2
    SPRITE 3,640,480,1
    REM *** Set sprite's angle to zero ***
    angle = 0
    REM *** Set font details ***
    SET TEXT FONT "Arial Black"
    SET TEXT SIZE 40
    REM *** Record start time ***
    starttime = TIMER()
    REPEAT
        REM *** Display screen title ***
        SET CURSOR 550,100
        PRINT "Game Over"
        REM *** Rotate ship ***
        ROTATE SPRITE 3, angle
```

continued on next page

```
        angle = WRAPVALUE(angle+5)
        REM *** Display winner details ***
        SET CURSOR 510,900
        IF kill = 2
            PRINT "Left ship wins"
        ELSE
            PRINT "Right ship wins"
        ENDIF
    UNTIL TIMER() - starttime > 8000
ENDFUNCTION
```

Solutions

Activity 26.1

No solution required.

Activity 26.2

```
REM *** Set up constants ***
#CONSTANT leftshipid          1
#CONSTANT rightshipid         2
#CONSTANT maximumshipspeed    30
#CONSTANT missilespeed        15
#CONSTANT screenheight        1024
#CONSTANT screenwidth         1280

REM *** Define types used ***
TYPE MissileType
    spriteno    AS INTEGER
    trajectory  AS INTEGER
    moves       AS INTEGER
ENDTYPE

TYPE ShipType
    spriteno    AS INTEGER
    velocity    AS INTEGER
    angle       AS FLOAT
    missile     AS MissileType
ENDTYPE

REM *** Declare globals ***
GLOBAL leftship AS ShipType
GLOBAL rightship AS ShipType

REM *** Main program logic ***
InitialiseGame()
REPEAT
    keyspressed = HandleKeyboard()
    leftship.angle =
    HandleShip(leftship,keyspressed)
    rightship.angle =
    Handleship(rightship,keyspressed >> 4)
    kill = HandleMissiles()
UNTIL kill <> 0
GameOver(kill)
WAIT KEY
END


REM *** Test stubs ***

FUNCTION InitialiseGame()
    PRINT "InitialiseGame"
ENDFUNCTION

FUNCTION HandleKeyboard()
    PRINT "HandleKeyboard"
ENDFUNCTION 1

FUNCTION HandleShip(ship AS ShipType,
keyspressed)
    PRINT "HandleShip"
ENDFUNCTION 1

FUNCTION HandleMissiles()
    PRINT "HandleMissiles"
ENDFUNCTION 1

FUNCTION GameOver(kill)
  PRINT "GameOver"
ENDFUNCTION
```

A final WAIT KEY statement has been added before the END statement so that the output produced can be viewed. This statement will be removed after testing is complete.

Notice that most test stubs need to return a dummy value.

Activity 26.3

```
REM *** Declare constants ***
#CONSTANT leftshipid          1
#CONSTANT rightshipid         2
#CONSTANT maximumshipspeed    30
#CONSTANT missilespeed        15
#CONSTANT screenheight        1024
#CONSTANT screenwidth         1280

REM *** Define types ***
TYPE MissileType
    spriteno    AS INTEGER
    trajectory  AS INTEGER
    moves       AS INTEGER
ENDTYPE

TYPE ShipType
    spriteno    AS INTEGER
    velocity    AS INTEGER
    angle       AS FLOAT
    missile     AS MissileType
ENDTYPE

REM *** Declare globals ***
GLOBAL leftship AS ShipType
GLOBAL rightship AS ShipType

REM *** Main program logic ***
InitialiseGame()
REPEAT
    keyspressed = HandleKeyboard()
    leftship.angle =
HandleShip(leftship,keyspressed)
    rightship.angle = Handleship(rightship,
keyspressed >> 4)
    kill = HandleMissiles()
UNTIL kill <> 0
GameOver(kill)
WAIT KEY
END

FUNCTION InitialiseGame()
    SetUpScreen()
    InitialiseShipsData()
    PrepareSprites()
ENDFUNCTION

REM *** Test stubs ***

FUNCTION HandleKeyboard()
    PRINT "HandleKeyboard"
ENDFUNCTION 1

FUNCTION HandleShip(ship AS ShipType,
keyspressed)
    PRINT "HandleShip"
ENDFUNCTION 1

FUNCTION HandleMissiles()
    PRINT "HandleMissiles"
ENDFUNCTION 1

FUNCTION GameOver(kill)
    PRINT "GameOver"
ENDFUNCTION

FUNCTION SetUpScreen()
    PRINT "SetUpScreen"
ENDFUNCTION
```

```
FUNCTION InitialiseShipsData()
   PRINT "InitialiseShipsData"
ENDFUNCTION

FUNCTION PrepareSprites()
  PRINT "PrepareSprites"
ENDFUNCTION
```

Activity 26.4

```
REM *** Declare constants ***
#CONSTANT leftshipid          1
#CONSTANT rightshipid         2
#CONSTANT maximumshipspeed    30
#CONSTANT missilespeed        15
#CONSTANT screenheight        1024
#CONSTANT screenwidth         1280

REM *** Define types ***
TYPE MissileType
    spriteno    AS INTEGER
    trajectory  AS INTEGER
    moves       AS INTEGER
ENDTYPE

TYPE ShipType
    spriteno    AS INTEGER
    velocity    AS INTEGER
    angle       AS FLOAT
    missile     AS MissileType
ENDTYPE

REM *** Declare globals ***
GLOBAL leftship AS ShipType
GLOBAL rightship AS ShipType

REM *** Main program logic ***
InitialiseGame()
REPEAT
    keyspressed = HandleKeyboard()
    leftship.angle =
    HandleShip(leftship,keyspressed)
    rightship.angle =
    Handleship(rightship, keyspressed >> 4)
    kill = HandleMissiles()
UNTIL kill <> 0
GameOver(kill)
WAIT KEY
END


FUNCTION InitialiseGame()
    SetUpScreen()
    InitialiseShipsData()
    PrepareSprites()
ENDFUNCTION

FUNCTION SetUpScreen()
    REM *** Set screen resolution ***
    SET DISPLAY MODE screenwidth,
    screenheight, 32
    REM *** Create a black background ***
    COLOR BACKDROP 0
    BACKDROP ON
ENDFUNCTION

FUNCTION PrepareSprites()
    REM *** Transparent colour to magenta ***
    SET IMAGE COLORKEY 255,0,255
    REM *** Load left ship's sprite ***
    CREATE ANIMATED SPRITE leftship.spriteno,
    "ship02.bmp",3,1,1
    REM *** Move its origin to centre ***
    OFFSET SPRITE leftship.spriteno,
    SPRITE WIDTH(leftship.spriteno)/2,
    SPRITE HEIGHT(leftship.spriteno)/2
    REM *** Position left ship ***
```

```
    SPRITE leftship.spriteno,100,
    SCREEN HEIGHT()/2,1
    REM *** Load right ship's sprite ***
    CLONE SPRITE leftship.spriteno,
    rightship.spriteno
    REM *** Position right ship ***
    SPRITE rightship.spriteno,
    SCREEN WIDTH()-100,SCREEN HEIGHT()/2, 2

    REM *** Load image used by missiles ***
    LOAD IMAGE "missilemag.bmp",2
ENDFUNCTION

FUNCTION InitialiseShipsData()
    REM *** Initialise left ship variable ***
    leftship.spriteno = leftshipid
    leftship.velocity = leftshipid
    leftship.angle = 0
    leftship.missile.spriteno =
    leftshipid+10
    leftship.missile.trajectory =
    leftshipid+10
    leftship.missile.moves = 0
     REM *** Create ship's vector ***
    result = MAKE VECTOR2(leftship.velocity)
    SET VECTOR2 leftship.velocity,0,0
    REM *** Initialise right ship variable***
    rightship.spriteno = rightshipid
    rightship.velocity = rightshipid
    rightship.angle = 0
    rightship.missile.spriteno =
    rightshipid + 10
    rightship.missile.trajectory =
    rightshipid + 10
    rightship.missile.moves = 0
    REM *** Create ship's vector ***
    result =
    MAKE VECTOR2(rightship.velocity)
    SET VECTOR2 rightship.velocity,0,0
ENDFUNCTION

REM *** Test stubs ***

FUNCTION HandleKeyboard()
    PRINT "HandleKeyboard"
ENDFUNCTION 1

FUNCTION HandleShip(ship AS ShipType,
keyspressed)
    PRINT "HandleShip"
ENDFUNCTION 1

FUNCTION HandleMissiles()
    PRINT "HandleMissiles"
ENDFUNCTION 1

FUNCTION GameOver(kill)
    PRINT "GameOver"
ENDFUNCTION
```

Activity 26.5

```
REM *** Declare constants ***
#CONSTANT leftshipid          1
#CONSTANT rightshipid         2
#CONSTANT maximumshipspeed    30
#CONSTANT missilespeed        15
#CONSTANT screenheight        1024
#CONSTANT screenwidth         1280

REM *** Define types ***
TYPE MissileType
    spriteno    AS INTEGER
    trajectory  AS INTEGER
    moves       AS INTEGER
ENDTYPE
```

```
        TYPE ShipType
            spriteno     AS INTEGER
            velocity     AS INTEGER
            angle        AS FLOAT
            missile      AS MissileType
        ENDTYPE

        REM *** Declare globals ***
        GLOBAL leftship AS ShipType
        GLOBAL rightship AS ShipType

        REM *** Main program logic ***
        InitialiseGame()
        REPEAT
            keyspressed = HandleKeyboard()
            SET CURSOR 100,100
            PRINT RIGHT$(BIN$(keyspressed),8)
            leftship.angle =
            HandleShip(leftship,keyspressed)
            rightship.angle =
            Handleship(rightship, keyspressed >> 4)
            kill = HandleMissiles()
        UNTIL kill <> 0
        GameOver(kill)
        WAIT KEY
        END


        FUNCTION InitialiseGame()
            SetUpScreen()
            InitialiseShipsData()
            PrepareSprites()
        ENDFUNCTION

        FUNCTION SetUpScreen()
            REM *** Set screen resolution ***
            SET DISPLAY MODE screenwidth,
            screenheight, 32
            REM *** Create a black background ***
            COLOR BACKDROP 0
            BACKDROP ON
        ENDFUNCTION

        FUNCTION PrepareSprites()
            REM *** Transparent colour to magenta
        ***
            SET IMAGE COLORKEY 255,0,255
            REM *** Load left ship's sprite ***
            CREATE ANIMATED SPRITE
        leftship.spriteno,
            "ship02.bmp",3,1,1
            REM *** Move its origin to centre ***
            OFFSET SPRITE leftship.spriteno,
            SPRITE WIDTH(leftship.spriteno)/2,
            SPRITE HEIGHT(leftship.spriteno)/2
            REM *** Position left ship ***
            SPRITE leftship.spriteno,100,
            SCREEN HEIGHT()/2,1
            REM *** Load right ship's sprite ***
            CLONE SPRITE leftship.spriteno,
            rightship.spriteno
            REM *** Position right ship ***
            SPRITE rightship.spriteno,
            SCREEN WIDTH()-100,SCREEN HEIGHT()/2, 2
            REM *** Load image used by missiles ***
            LOAD IMAGE "missilemag.bmp",2
        ENDFUNCTION

        FUNCTION InitialiseShipsData()
            REM *** Initialise left ship variable
        ***
            leftship.spriteno = leftshipid
            leftship.velocity = leftshipid
            leftship.angle = 0
            leftship.missile.spriteno =
            leftshipid+10
            leftship.missile.trajectory =
            leftshipid+10
```

```
            leftship.missile.moves = 0
             REM *** Create ship's vector ***
            result = MAKE VECTOR2(leftship.velocity)
            SET VECTOR2 leftship.velocity,0,0
            REM *** Initialise right ship
        variable***
            rightship.spriteno = rightshipid
            rightship.velocity = rightshipid
            rightship.angle = 0
            rightship.missile.spriteno =
            rightshipid + 10
            rightship.missile.trajectory =
            rightshipid + 10
            rightship.missile.moves = 0
            REM *** Create ship's vector ***
            result =
            MAKE VECTOR2(rightship.velocity)
            SET VECTOR2 rightship.velocity,0,0
        ENDFUNCTION

        FUNCTION HandleKeyboard()
            REM *** No keys pressed ***
            keyspressed = 0
            REM *** IF z pressed set bit 0 ***
            IF KEYSTATE(44) = 1
                keyspressed = keyspressed || %1
            ENDIF
            REM *** IF x pressed set bit 1 ***
            IF KEYSTATE(45) = 1
                keyspressed = keyspressed || %10
            ENDIF
            REM *** IF c pressed, set bit 2 ***
            IF KEYSTATE(46) = 1
                keyspressed = keyspressed || %100
            ENDIF
            REM *** IF v pressed, set bit 3 ***
            IF KEYSTATE(47) = 1
                keyspressed = keyspressed || %1000
            ENDIF
            REM *** IF 1 pressed, set bit 4 ***
            IF KEYSTATE(79) = 1
                keyspressed = keyspressed || %10000
            ENDIF
            REM *** IF 2 pressed, set bit 5 ***
            IF KEYSTATE(80) = 1
                keyspressed = keyspressed || %100000
            ENDIF
            REM *** IF . pressed, set bit 6 ***
            IF KEYSTATE(83) = 1
                keyspressed = keyspressed || %1000000
            ENDIF
            REM *** IF Enter pressed, set bit 7 ***
            IF KEYSTATE(156) = 1
                keyspressed = keyspressed ||
        %10000000
            ENDIF
        ENDFUNCTION keyspressed


        REM *** Test stubs ***

        FUNCTION HandleShip(ship AS ShipType,
        keyspressed)
            PRINT "HandleShip"
        ENDFUNCTION 1

        FUNCTION HandleMissiles()
            PRINT "HandleMissiles"
        ENDFUNCTION 0

        FUNCTION GameOver(kill)
            PRINT "GameOver"
        ENDFUNCTION
```

Activity 26.6

```
REM *** Declare constants ***
#CONSTANT leftshipid          1
#CONSTANT rightshipid         2
#CONSTANT maximumshipspeed    30
#CONSTANT missilespeed        15
#CONSTANT screenheight        1024
#CONSTANT screenwidth         1280

REM *** Define types ***
TYPE MissileType
    spriteno    AS INTEGER
    trajectory  AS INTEGER
    moves       AS INTEGER
ENDTYPE

TYPE ShipType
    spriteno    AS INTEGER
    velocity    AS INTEGER
    angle       AS FLOAT
    missile     AS MissileType
ENDTYPE

REM *** Declare globals ***
GLOBAL leftship AS ShipType
GLOBAL rightship AS ShipType

REM *** Main program logic ***
InitialiseGame()
REPEAT
    keyspressed = HandleKeyboard()
    leftship.angle =
    HandleShip(leftship,keyspressed)
    rightship.angle =
    Handlship(rightship, keyspressed >> 4)
    kill = HandleMissiles()
UNTIL kill <> 0
GameOver(kill)
WAIT KEY
END


FUNCTION InitialiseGame()
    SetUpScreen()
    InitialiseShipsData()
    PrepareSprites()
ENDFUNCTION

FUNCTION SetUpScreen()
    REM *** Set screen resolution ***
    SET DISPLAY MODE screenwidth,
    screenheight, 32
    REM *** Create a black background ***
    COLOR BACKDROP 0
    BACKDROP ON
ENDFUNCTION

FUNCTION PrepareSprites()
    REM *** Transparent colour to magenta ***
    SET IMAGE COLORKEY 255,0,255
    REM *** Load left ship's sprite ***
    CREATE ANIMATED SPRITE leftship.spriteno,
    "ship02.bmp",3,1,1
    REM *** Move its origin to centre ***
    OFFSET SPRITE leftship.spriteno,
    SPRITE WIDTH(leftship.spriteno)/2,
    SPRITE HEIGHT(leftship.spriteno)/2
    REM *** Position left ship ***
    SPRITE leftship.spriteno,100,
    SCREEN HEIGHT()/2,1
    REM *** Load right ship's sprite ***
    CLONE SPRITE leftship.spriteno,
    rightship.spriteno
    REM *** Position right ship ***
    SPRITE rightship.spriteno,
    SCREEN WIDTH()-100,SCREEN HEIGHT()/2, 2
    REM *** Load image used by missiles ***
```

```
    LOAD IMAGE "missilemag.bmp",2
ENDFUNCTION

FUNCTION InitialiseShipsData()
    REM *** Initialise left ship variable ***
    leftship.spriteno = leftshipid
    leftship.velocity = leftshipid
    leftship.angle = 0
    leftship.missile.spriteno =
    leftshipid+10
    leftship.missile.trajectory =
    leftshipid+10
    leftship.missile.moves = 0
    REM *** Create ship's vector ***
    result = MAKE VECTOR2(leftship.velocity)
    SET VECTOR2 leftship.velocity,0,0
    REM *** Initialise right ship variable***
    rightship.spriteno = rightshipid
    rightship.velocity = rightshipid
    rightship.angle = 0
    rightship.missile.spriteno =
    rightshipid + 10
    rightship.missile.trajectory =
    rightshipid + 10
    rightship.missile.moves = 0
    REM *** Create ship's vector ***
    result =
    MAKE VECTOR2(rightship.velocity)
    SET VECTOR2 rightship.velocity,0,0
ENDFUNCTION

FUNCTION HandleKeyboard()
    REM *** No keys pressed ***
    keyspressed = 0
    REM *** IF z pressed set bit 0 ***
    IF KEYSTATE(44) = 1
        keyspressed = keyspressed || %1
    ENDIF
    REM *** IF x pressed set bit 1 ***
    IF KEYSTATE(45) = 1
        keyspressed = keyspressed || %10
    ENDIF
    REM *** IF c pressed, set bit 2 ***
    IF KEYSTATE(46) = 1
        keyspressed = keyspressed || %100
    ENDIF
    REM *** IF v pressed, set bit 3 ***
    IF KEYSTATE(47) = 1
        keyspressed = keyspressed || %1000
    ENDIF
    REM *** IF 1 pressed, set bit 4 ***
    IF KEYSTATE(79) = 1
        keyspressed = keyspressed || %10000
    ENDIF
    REM *** IF 2 pressed, set bit 5 ***
    IF KEYSTATE(80) = 1
        keyspressed = keyspressed || %100000
    ENDIF
    REM *** IF . pressed, set bit 6 ***
    IF KEYSTATE(83) = 1
        keyspressed = keyspressed || %1000000
    ENDIF
    REM *** IF Enter pressed, set bit 7 ***
    IF KEYSTATE(156) = 1
        keyspressed = keyspressed || %10000000
    ENDIF
ENDFUNCTION keyspressed

FUNCTION HandleShip(ship AS ShipType,
keyspressed)
    REM *** IF bit 0, add to angle ***
    IF (keyspressed && 1) > 0
        ship.angle = WRAPVALUE(ship.angle-5)
    ENDIF
    REM *** IF bit 1, subtract from angle ***
    IF (keyspressed && 2) > 0
        ship.angle = WRAPVALUE(ship.angle+5)
    ENDIF
```

```
    REM *** IF bit 2 THEN ***
    IF (keyspressed && 4 )> 0
       REM *** Calculate thrust vector ***
       thrustxoffset# = COS(ship.angle+270)
       thrustyoffset# = SIN(ship.angle+270)
       thrustvector = 5
       result = MAKE VECTOR2(thrustvector)
       SET VECTOR2 thrustvector,
       thrustxoffset#, thrustyoffset#
       REM *** Add thrust to velocity ***
       ADD VECTOR2 ship.velocity,
       ship.velocity, thrustvector
       REM *** Reduce speed if too fast ***

       IF LENGTH VECTOR2(ship.velocity) >
       maximumshipspeed
          MULTIPLY VECTOR2 ship.velocity,
          maximumshipspeed/
          LENGTH VECTOR2(ship.velocity)
       ENDIF
       REM *** Show engine firing ***
       PLAY SPRITE ship.spriteno,2,3,20
    ELSE
       REM *** Show normal ship ***
       SET SPRITE FRAME ship.spriteno,1
    ENDIF
    REM *** IF bit 3 AND missile does not
    currently exist, fire missile ***
    IF (keyspressed && 8) > 0 AND
    (NOT SPRITE EXIST(ship.missile.spriteno))
       CreateMissile(ship)
    ENDIF
    REM *** Rotate sprite to latest angle ***
    ROTATE SPRITE ship.spriteno, ship.angle
    REM *** Move sprite velocity amount ***
    SPRITE ship.spriteno,
    SPRITE X(ship.spriteno)+
    X VECTOR2(ship.velocity),
    SPRITE Y(ship.spriteno)+
    Y VECTOR2(ship.velocity),1
    WrapShip(ship)
ENDFUNCTION ship.angle

REM *** Test stubs ***

FUNCTION CreateMissile(ship AS ShipType)
    PRINT "CreateMissile"
ENDFUNCTION

FUNCTION WrapShip(ship AS ShipType)
    PRINT "WrapShip"
ENDFUNCTION

FUNCTION HandleMissiles()
    PRINT "HandleMissiles"
ENDFUNCTION 0

FUNCTION GameOver(kill)
    PRINT "GameOver"
ENDFUNCTION
```

Activity 26.7

No solution required.

Activity 26.8

No solution required.

Activity 26.9

No solution required.

27

Using the Mouse

Controlling the Mouse

Introduction

Many computer games use a mouse rather than the keyboard to accept input from players. It should therefore be no surprise that DarkBASIC Pro has several statements which allow you to control the mouse.

Waiting for a Mouse Click

The WAIT MOUSE Statement

Many of our programs have used the WAIT KEY statement which pauses the program's execution, waiting for a key to be pressed. We can achieve the same effect, but this time reactivating the program when a mouse button is pressed with the WAIT MOUSE statement. This command has the format shown in FIG-27.1.

FIG-27.1

The WAIT MOUSE Statement

The SUSPEND FOR MOUSE Statement

Exactly the same effect can be achieved using the SUSPEND FOR MOUSE statement which has the format shown in FIG-27.2.

FIG-27.2

The SUSPEND FOR MOUSE Statement

The program in LISTING-27.1 displays a message on the screen, but only terminates when a mouse button is pressed.

LISTING-27.1

Waiting for the Mouse

```
PRINT "Hello world"
WAIT MOUSE
END
```

Activity 27.1

Type in and test the program above (*mouse01.dbpro*).

Modify the program substituting SUSPEND FOR MOUSE for the WAIT MOUSE statement.

Both commands given above will halt your program and wait for the mouse button to be clicked.

The MOUSECLICK Statement

There will be times when we will want a program to react when the mouse button is pressed. In fact, we'll probably want to know exactly which button on the mouse has been pressed. Both these requirements are handled by the MOUSECLICK

FIG-27.3

The MOUSECLICK
Statement

statement which has the format shown in FIG-27.3.

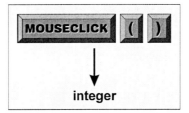

integer

The value returned by this statement depends on which mouse button has been pressed. The actual values returned are shown in TABLE 27.1.

TABLE-27.1

Values Returned by the
MOUSECLICK Statement

Mouse Button	Value
Left	1
Right	2
Centre	4
Fourth	8

Notice that the command allows for up to 4 buttons on the mouse. If you have a wheel in the centre of your mouse, it is treated as button 3. It's unusual to have a fourth button.

If more than one button is pressed at the same time, the value returned is the sum of the button values. For example, pressing the left and right buttons together returns the value 3.

Like INKEY\$, the MOUSECLICK statement does not cause the program to pause awaiting input. If no mouse button is pressed at the time this statement is executed, then a value of zero is returned, and execution moves on to the next statement in the program.

The program in LISTING-27.1 moves a sprite (in the shape of a bug) in a straight line. The bug's direction changes when a mouse button is clicked.

LISTING-27.2

Controlling a Sprite
using the Mouse

```
REM *** Set screen resolution ***
SET DISPLAY MODE 1280,1024,32

REM *** Load image of bug ***
LOAD IMAGE "bug01.bmp",1

REM *** Position sprite ***
x = 600
y = 500
SPRITE 1,x,y,1

REM *** Make sprite's origin its centre ***
OFFSET SPRITE 1,32,32

REM *** Main loop ***
DO
   REM *** Move sprite ***
   MOVE SPRITE 1,1
   REM *** Check for mouse click ***
   mousevalue = MOUSECLICK()
   REM *** Change bug direction depending on mouse button ***
   SELECT mousevalue
      CASE 1    `Left button - rotate 90
         ROTATE SPRITE 1,90
      ENDCASE
```

continued on next page

LISTING-27.2
(continued)

Controlling a Sprite
using the Mouse

```
        CASE 2   `Right button rotate 180
           ROTATE SPRITE 1,180
        ENDCASE
        CASE 4   `Centre button rotate 270 degrees
           ROTATE SPRITE 1,270
        ENDCASE
   ENDSELECT
LOOP

REM *** End program ***
WAIT KEY
END
```

Activity 27.2

Type in and test the program given above (*mouse02.dbpro*).

Modify the program so that the sprite rotates to 0° if the left and right mouse buttons are pressed at the same time.

The Mouse Pointer

Sometimes the normal mouse cursor (the pointing arrow) remains on the screen, but often another shape will be used, or the mouse pointer may disappear altogether.

The HIDE MOUSE Statement

To make the mouse pointer disappear from the screen, we use the HIDE MOUSE statement which has the format shown in FIG-27.4.

FIG-27.4

The HIDE MOUSE
Statement

The SHOW MOUSE Statement

To make a hidden mouse pointer reappear we use the SHOW MOUSE statement. Its format is shown in FIG-27.5.

FIG-27.5

The SHOW MOUSE
Statement

The program in LISTING-27.3 makes the mouse pointer disappear when a mouse button is clicked, and then reappear when a second click is detected.

LISTING-27.3

Hiding the Mouse Pointer

```
REM *** Hide mouse pointer when mouse clicked **
WAIT MOUSE
HIDE MOUSE

REM *** Show mouse after next click ***
WAIT MOUSE
SHOW MOUSE

REM *** End program on mouse click ***
WAIT MOUSE
END
```

The POSITION MOUSE Statement

Normally, the mouse pointer on the screen is moved by the player dragging the mouse, but it can also be moved by the program itself using the POSITION MOUSE statement, which has the format shown in FIG-27.6.

FIG-27.6

The POSITION MOUSE
Statement

In the diagram:

    x,y   are integer values specifying the new position of the mouse pointer.

The program in LISTING-27.4 moves the mouse to the the top-left corner of the screen when the mouse is clicked. A second click terminates the program.

LISTING-27.4

Using POSITION
MOUSE

```
WAIT MOUSE
POSITION MOUSE 0,0
WAIT MOUSE
END
```

The CHANGE MOUSE Statement

Normally, the mouse pointer on the screen appears as an arrow, but it is possible to change this shape using the CHANGE MOUSE statement. This command has the format shown in FIG-27.7.

FIG-27.7

The CHANGE MOUSE
Statement

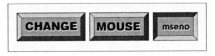

In the diagram:

    mseno   is an integer value representing which mouse image is to be displayed.

By default, *mseno* can take one of only two values (0 or 1). 0 represents the default arrow shape, while 1 is the hourglass shape.

These are the only two mouse pointer images built into your program.

The program in LISTING-27.5 changes the cursor to the hourglass image in response to a mouse click. The image changes back to the arrow on a second click, and a third click terminates the program.

LISTING-27.5

Changing the Mouse
Pointer Shape

```
REM *** Change to hourglass ***
WAIT MOUSE
CHANGE MOUSE 1

REM *** Change back to arrow ***
WAIT MOUSE
CHANGE MOUSE 0

REM *** End program ***
WAIT MOUSE
END
```

Activity 27.5

Type in the above program (*mouse05.dbpro*) and check that it works correctly.

It is possible to use other images as our mouse pointer, but these must first be loaded into our project folder. Unlike normal images, DarkBASIC Pro won't do the copying for us. We have to Use Windows Explorer to copy the files we want into our project folder.

There are a wealth of existing cursor images which come with Microsoft Windows XP. You'll find these cursor files in the folder C:\WINDOWS\CURSORS. The files you're interested in have a *.cur* file extension.

FIG-27.8

Adding Cursor Images

Once the cursor files have been copied we can return to DarkBASIC Pro. Start by making sure that the Project Manager window is showing (it's usually on the right hand side of your screen). Click on the blue CURSORS button near the bottom right of the Project Manager window. Now click the *Add* button and add each of the cursors you require in your program. FIG-27.8 shows a typical display after two cursors have been added.

By adding our own cursor, we remove the default arrow and hourglass cursors. So, despite the fact that the cursors are numbered from 1 in the Project Manager window, the first cursor shown there becomes cursor zero in your program.

Activity 27.6

From the folder *C:\Windows\Cursors*, copy the files *harrow.cur* and *pen_i.cur* to the folder containing your previous program (*mouse05.dbpro*).

Reload *mouse05.dbpro* into the DarkBASIC Pro editor.

Click on the *Cursors* button of the Project Manager.

Use the *Add* option to add the two cursor files to your project.

Run the program.

Which cursors appeared when the program was run?

If you want to retain the arrow and hourglass cursor, just add these as the first two cursors in your project.

Reading the Mouse Position

The exact position of the mouse pointer on the screen can be determined using the two statements described below.

The MOUSEX Statement

The MOUSEX statement returns the x-ordinate of the mouse pointer and has the format shown in FIG-27.9.

FIG-27.9

The MOUSEX Statement

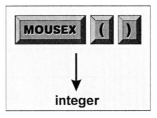

For example, we could return the x-ordinate of the mouse pointer when the mouse button is clicked with the statements

```
WAIT MOUSE
x = MOUSEX()
```

The MOUSEY Statement

This statement returns the y-ordinate of the mouse pointer and has the format shown in FIG-27.10.

FIG-27.10

The MOUSEY Statement

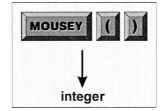

The program in LISTING-27.6 continually displays the mouse position. Press ESC to terminate the program.

LISTING-27.6

Retrieving the Mouse's Position

```
REM *** Set Screen display ***
SET DISPLAY MODE 1280,1024,32
REM *** Set text background opaque ***
SET TEXT OPAQUE

DO
   REM *** Remove old display ***
   SET CURSOR 100,100
   PRINT "                    "
   REM *** Read mouse coordinates ***
   x = MOUSEX()
   y = MOUSEY()
   REM *** Display on screen ***
   SET CURSOR 100,100
   PRINT "X :",x,"  Y :",y
LOOP

REM *** End program ***
WAIT MOUSE
END
```

Mouse Speed

If you are working with an application such as a paint program, chances are you'll move the mouse quite slowly. On the other hand, playing an action game will probably mean the mouse is being moved fairly rapidly.

One way for a program to find out how quickly the mouse is being moved is to read the position of the mouse, and then, after a slight delay, read its position again. The larger the difference between the two readings, the faster the mouse is being moved.

Luckily, we don't have to make this calculation - DarkBASIC Pro has commands to do the job for us, returning details of how quickly the mouse is moving in both the x and y directions.

The MOUSEMOVEX Statement

This statement returns a real number representing the speed at which the mouse is moving in the x direction. The statement takes the form shown in FIG-27.11.

FIG-27.11

The MOUSEMOVEX
Statement

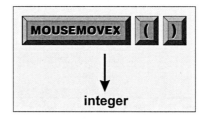

A typical statement using this command might be:

```
xspeed = MOUSEMOVEX()
```

The value returned will be positive if movement is left-to-right (increasing x value) and negative if the movement is right-to-left (decreasing x value).

The MOUSEMOVEY Statement

This statement returns a real number representing the speed at which the mouse is moving in the y direction. The statement takes the form shown in FIG-27.12.

The value returned will be positive if movement is up-to-down (increasing y value) and negative if the movement is down-to-up (decreasing y value).

FIG-27.12

The MOUSEMOVEY
Statement

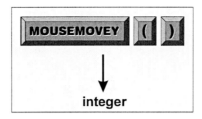

integer

The program in LISTING-27.7 demonstrates the use of the last two statements by displaying the changing mouse speeds.

LISTING-27.7

Detect Mouse Speed

```
REM *** Set screen resolution ***
SET DISPLAY MODE 1280,1024,32

REM *** Set text background opaque ***
SET TEXT OPAQUE
DO
   REM *** Remove old display ***
   SET CURSOR 100,100
   PRINT "                                "
   REM *** Read mouse speeds ***
   xspeed = MOUSEMOVEX()
   yspeed = MOUSEMOVEY()
   REM *** Display on screen ***
   SET CURSOR 100,100
   PRINT "X speed :",xspeed,"    Y speed :",yspeed
LOOP

REM *** End program ***
WAIT KEY
END
```

Activity 27.8

Type in and test the program given in LISTING-27.6 (save as *mouse07.dbpro*).

The Mouse Wheel

Most modern mice have a wheel between the left and right buttons. Although this can be clicked in the same way as the more traditional buttons, it can also be rotated. Information about the wheel's rotation can be accessed.

The MOUSEZ Statement

When a program begins execution, the mouse wheel is assumed to be at position zero. The MOUSEZ statement can be used to determine the amount of wheel rotation that has occurred after the program has begun execution. This statement has the format shown in FIG-27.13.

FIG-27.13

The MOUSEZ Statement

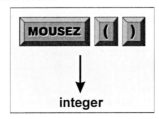

integer

As the user rotates the wheel away from themselves (towards the front of the mouse) the integer number returned grows larger; rotation in the opposite direction causes the value returned to grow smaller. Both positive and negative values may be returned by this statement.

The program in LISTING-27.8 demonstrates the MOUSEZ statement in use.

LISTING-27.8

Detecting Mouse Wheel Movement

```
REM *** Set screen resolution ***
SET DISPLAY MODE 1280,1024,32

REM *** Set text background opaque ***
SET TEXT OPAQUE

REM *** Main loop ***
DO
   REM *** Remove old display ***
   SET CURSOR 100,100
   PRINT "                                    "
   REM *** Read mouse wheel ***
   wheelsetting = MOUSEZ()
   REM *** Display on screen ***
   SET CURSOR 100,100
   PRINT "wheel :",wheelsetting
LOOP

REM *** End program ***
WAIT KEY
END
```

Activity 27.9

Type in and test the program above (*mouse08.dbpro*).

The MOUSEMOVEZ Statement

The speed at which the mouse wheel is being turned can be determined using the MOUSEMOVEZ statement. This has the format shown in FIG-27.14.

FIG-27.14

The MOUSEMOVEZ Statement

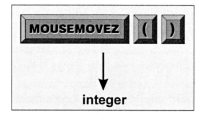

Speeds can be positive (when the wheel is turned towards the front of the mouse) or negative (when turned towards the back of the mouse).

The program in LISTING-27.9 demonstrates the use of this statement by continually displaying the wheel speed reading. Notice a small delay has been added at the end of the loop to give you time to see the display!

LISTING-27.9

Detecting Mouse Wheel Speed

```
REM *** Set Screen display ***
SET DISPLAY MODE 1280,1024,32
REM *** Set text background opaque ***
SET TEXT OPAQUE
DO
   REM *** Remove old display ***
   SET CURSOR 100,100
   PRINT "                          "
```

continued on next page

LISTING-27.9
(continued)

Detecting Mouse Wheel
Speed

```
    REM *** Read mouse wheel speed ***
    wheelspeed = MOUSEMOVEZ()
    REM *** Display on screen ***
    SET CURSOR 100,100
    PRINT "wheel speed :",wheelspeed
    WAIT 50
LOOP

REM *** End program ***
WAIT KEY
END
```

Activity 27.10

Type in and test the program above (*mouse09.dbpro*).

Summary

- The WAIT MOUSE statement causes a program to halt until a mouse button is pressed.

- The SUSPEND FOR MOUSE statement has the same effect as the WAIT MOUSE statement.

- The MOUSECLICK statement returns an integer value indicting which mouse button(s) have been pressed.

- The HIDE MOUSE statement causes the screen mouse pointer to become invisible screen.

- The SHOW MOUSE causes the screen mouse pointer to become visible.

- The POSITION MOUSE statement allows the mouse pointer to be positioned at any point on the screen.

- The CHANGE MOUSE statement allows the image used for the mouse pointer to be changed.

- There are two default mouse pointer images: the arrow and hourglass.

- To use new mouse pointer images, these must be copied into the current project folder and then added to the project.

- The exact position of the mouse pointer can be determined using the MOUSEX and MOUSEY statements.

- The speed at which the mouse is being moved can be determined using the MOUSEMOVEX and MOUSEMOVEY statements.

- The position of the mouse wheel can be determined using the MOUSEZ statement.

- The speed at which the mouse wheel is being moved can be determined using the MOUSEMOVEZ statement.

Mouse Handling Techniques

Rollovers

We've seen it on almost every web page, in every program; the mouse moves over an image and the image reacts by changing colour, getting larger, or changing to 3D. This is the rollover effect.

By using a 2-framed sprite and some mouse handling statements, we can achieve the same effect in our DarkBASIC Pro programs.

In the program in LISTING-27.10 a glowing LED effect is achieved using a 2-framed sprite. Frame 1 shows an image of the LED in the off-state; while frame 2 shows the LED in on-state. Initially, the LED is off, but when the mouse pointer moves over it, the LED switches to on. It returns to off as soon as the mouse pointer moves away. The program uses the following logic:

```
Show LED (off)
DO
    Get mouse coordinates
    IF mouse over LED THEN
        Switch LED to ON
    ELSE
        Switch LED to OFF
    ENDIF
LOOP
```

LISTING-27.10

Detecting when the Mouse is over a Sprite

```
REM *** Set screen resolution ***
SET DISPLAY MODE 1280,1024,32

REM *** Load animated sprite ***
CREATE ANIMATED SPRITE 1, "glow.bmp",2,1,1
SPRITE 1,640,512,1

DO
   REM *** Get mouse coordinates ***
   x = MOUSEX()
   y = MOUSEY()
   REM *** IF mouse on sprite, set ON ***
   IF x >= 640 AND x <= 671 AND y >=512 AND y <= 543
      SET SPRITE FRAME 1,2
   ELSE
      REM *** ELSE set OFF ***
      SET SPRITE FRAME 1,1
   ENDIF
LOOP
END
```

Activity 27.11

Type in and test the program in LISTING-27.10 (*mouse10.dbpro*).

It is the IF statement

```
IF x >= 640 AND x <= 671 AND y >=512 AND y <= 543
```

which determines if the mouse pointer is over the LED sprite. The values used in the IF statement are dependent on the position (640,512) and size (32 by 32) of the sprite.

A Second Approach

A second way of tackling the same problem is to create a single pixel invisible sprite
and position it at the head of the mouse pointer. Whenever the mouse pointer moves
the invisible sprite moves also. Now we can detect when the mouse pointer has
moved over some other sprite simply by checking for a sprite collision - the invisible
sprite and the one it has moved over.

The program in LISTING-27.11 uses the following logic to achieve the rollover
effect:

```
Load one pixel sprite
Hide the sprite
Load LED sprite
DO
      Move hidden pixel to mouse pointer position
      IF sprite collision THEN
            Switch LED to ON
      ELSE
            Switch LED to OFF
      ENDIF
LOOP
```

LISTING-27.11

Using SPRITE HIT to
Create a Rollover Effect

```
REM *** Set screen resolution ***
SET DISPLAY MODE 1280,1024,32

REM *** Load and hide 1 pixel sprite ***
LOAD IMAGE "1pixel.bmp",1
SPRITE 1,1,1,1
HIDE SPRITE 1

REM *** Load animated sprite ***
CREATE ANIMATED SPRITE 2, "squareLED.bmp",2,1,2
SPRITE 2,100,100,2

DO
   REM *** Get mouse coordinates ***
   x = MOUSEX()
   y = MOUSEY()
   SPRITE 1,x,y,1
   REM *** IF mouse on sprite, set ON ***
   IF SPRITE HIT(1,2)> 0
      SET SPRITE FRAME 2,2
   ELSE
      REM *** ELSE set OFF ***
      SET SPRITE FRAME 2,1
   ENDIF
LOOP
END
```

It's easy to see the advantages of this second approach: there's no longer any need
to worry about the position or size of the sprite involved in the rollover.

We can even deal with several sprites reacting to rollover, as shown in the next program (see LISTING-27.12). The main change is that we need a FOR loop to check each sprite in turn for rollover.

```
REM *** Set screen resolution ***
SET DISPLAY MODE 1280,1024,32

REM *** Load and hide 1 pixel sprite ***
LOAD IMAGE "1pixel.bmp",1
SPRITE 1,1,1,1
HIDE SPRITE 1

REM *** Load animated sprite ***
CREATE ANIMATED SPRITE 2, "squareLED.bmp",2,1,2

REM *** Clone sprite ***
FOR spriteno = 3 TO 5
   CLONE SPRITE 2, spriteno
NEXT spriteno

REM *** Position each sprite ***
FOR spriteno = 2 TO 5
   SPRITE spriteno,100,100+spriteno*40,2
NEXT spriteno

DO
   REM *** Get mouse coordinates ***
   x = MOUSEX()
   y = MOUSEY()
   SPRITE 1,x,y,1
   REM *** Test each visible sprite for rollover ***
   FOR spriteno = 2 TO 5
      REM *** IF mouse on sprite, set ON ***
      IF SPRITE HIT(1,spriteno)> 0
         SET SPRITE FRAME spriteno,2
      ELSE
         REM *** ELSE set OFF ***
         SET SPRITE FRAME spriteno,1
      ENDIF
   NEXT spriteno
LOOP

END
```

Activity 27.14

Type in and test the program given above (*mouse11.dbpro*).

Clicking On-Screen Buttons

Basic Concept

Another common use of the mouse is to click on a button. We can create a button image in much the same way as the rollover images used earlier. Often a button will use three images: a standard image, a mouse over image, and a button clicked image. An example is shown in FIG-27.15.

The program in LISTING-27.13 demonstrates how to change which frame of the button is showing as the mouse moves over and clicks on the button.

LISTING-27.13

```
REM *** Set screen resolution ***
SET DISPLAY MODE 1280,1024,32
REM *** Load and hide 1 pixel sprite ***
LOAD IMAGE "1pixel.bmp",1
SPRITE 1,1,1,1
HIDE SPRITE 1
REM *** Load animated sprite ***
CREATE ANIMATED SPRITE 2, "button1.bmp",3,1,1
SPRITE 2,100,100,2
DO
   REM *** Get mouse coordinates ***
   x = MOUSEX()
   y = MOUSEY()
   SPRITE 1,x,y,1
   REM *** IF mouse on sprite, set ON ***
   IF SPRITE HIT(1,2)> 0
      IF MOUSECLICK() > 0
         SET SPRITE FRAME 2,3
      ELSE
         SET SPRITE FRAME 2,2
      ENDIF
   ELSE
      REM *** ELSE set OFF ***
      SET SPRITE FRAME 2,1
   ENDIF
LOOP
END
```

Activity 27.15

Type in and test the program in LISTING-27.13 (*mouse12.dbpro*).

Reacting to a Button Click

Most of the time we'll need to react to a screen button being pressed. Sometimes this will simply mean that a variable needs to change value, as in the next program where several buttons give us a choice of background colours (see LISTING-27.14).

LISTING-27.14

Changing Backdrop
Colour Using On-Screen
Buttons

```
REM *** Set screen resolution ***
SET DISPLAY MODE 1280,1024,32

REM *** Set backdrop black ***
COLOR BACKDROP 0
BACKDROP ON

REM *** Load and hide 1 pixel sprite ***
LOAD IMAGE "1pixel.bmp",1
SPRITE 1,1,1,1
HIDE SPRITE 1

REM *** Load buttons ***
DATA "butred.bmp","butblue.bmp","butgreen.bmp"
FOR c = 2 TO 4
   READ filename$
   CREATE ANIMATED SPRITE c,filename$,3,1,c
   SPRITE c,100,100+c*40,c
NEXT c

DO
   REM *** Get mouse coordinates ***
   x = MOUSEX()
   y = MOUSEY()
   SPRITE 1,x,y,1
```

continued on next page

LISTING-27.14
(continued)

Changing Backdrop
Colour Using On-Screen

```
   REM *** Check for each button ***
   FOR c = 2 TO 4
      REM *** IF mouse over button ***
      IF SPRITE HIT(1,c) > 0
         REM *** A mouse button pressed ***
         IF MOUSECLICK() > 0
            REM *** Show frame 3 ***
            SET SPRITE FRAME c,3
            REM *** Change background colour ***
            ChangeColour(c)
         ELSE
            REM *** If mouse button not clicked ***
            REM *** show frame 2 ***
            SET SPRITE FRAME c,2
         ENDIF
      ELSE
         REM *** If mouse not over button ***
         REM *** show frame 1 ***
         SET SPRITE FRAME c,1
      ENDIF
   NEXT c
LOOP
END


FUNCTION ChangeColour(button)
   SELECT button
      CASE 2
         colour = RGB(255,0,0)
      ENDCASE
      CASE 3
         colour = RGB(0,0,255)
      ENDCASE
      CASE 4
         colour = RGB(0,255,0)
      ENDCASE
   ENDSELECT
   COLOR BACKDROP colour
ENDFUNCTION
```

Some of the techniques used are worth highlighting. For example, the buttons have
been set up using the code:

```
REM *** Load buttons ***
DATA "butred.bmp","butblue.bmp","butgreen.bmp"
FOR c = 2 TO 4
    READ filename$
    CREATE ANIMATED SPRITE c,filename$,3,1,c
    SPRITE c,100,100+c*40,c
NEXT c
```

By storing the file names in a DATA statement we can use a loop structure to load
and place each of the button sprites.

The main part of the code checks to see if the mouse is over a button

```
IF SPRITE HIT(1,c) > 0
```

and if a mouse button is being pressed

```
IF MOUSECLICK() > 0
```

before changing the frame shown and executing a function which changes the
backdrop colour:

```
REM *** Show frame 3 ***
SET SPRITE FRAME c,3
REM *** Change background colour ***
ChangeColour(c)
```

Notice that the routine is passed the number of the button pressed. The routine then sets the backdrop colour in accordance with the value passed to it.

> **Activity 27.16**
>
> Type in and test the program given in LISTING-27.14 (*mouse13.dbpro*).

Controlling Program Flow

A second use of a button is to control program flow. For example, a button labelled *New Game*, will, when clicked, take the player back to the code that initialises the game. In the next example, we have added a splash screen to the *Space Duel* game. Only by clicking on the *Start* button of the splash screen will the game begin. The splash screen is controlled by the *ShowSplashScreen()* function given below:

Splash screen is the term used for the introductory screen that often appears at the start of a game or other software.

```
FUNCTION ShowSplashScreen()
    REM *** Load mouse tip sprite ***
    LOAD IMAGE "1pixel.bmp",4
    SPRITE 4,0,0,4
    HIDE SPRITE 4
    REM *** Load splash screen as sprite ***
    LOAD IMAGE "splashduel.bmp",5
    SPRITE 5,0,0,5
    REM *** Load start button sprite ***
    CREATE ANIMATED SPRITE 6,"button1.bmp",3,1,6
    SPRITE 6,620,900,6
    REM *** Start button not pressed ***
    pressed = 0
    REPEAT
        REM *** Get mouse position ***
        x = MOUSEX()
        y = MOUSEY()
        SPRITE 4,x,y,4
        REM *** IF mouse over start button ***
        IF SPRITE HIT(4,6)>0
            REM *** IF mouse clicked over start button ***
            IF MOUSECLICK() > 0
                REM *** Change button to frame 3 ***
                SET SPRITE FRAME 6,3
                REM *** Record start clicked ***
                pressed = 1
            ELSE
                REM ***IF mouse not clicked, set to frame 2 ***
                SET SPRITE FRAME 6,2
            ENDIF
        ELSE
            REM *** If mouse not over start, use frame 1 ***
            SET SPRITE FRAME 6,1
        ENDIF
    UNTIL pressed = 1
    REM *** Wait so frame 3 has time to show ***
    WAIT 500
    REM *** Delete all sprites used here ***
    DELETE SPRITE 4
    DELETE SPRITE 5
    DELETE SPRITE 6
    REM *** Hide mouse pointer during game ***
    HIDE MOUSE
ENDFUNCTION
```

This time the mouse is handled in a REPEAT..UNTIL structure rather than a DO..LOOP since we want to exit the loop when the *Start* button is pressed.

We detect when that has happened using the variable *pressed*, which is initially set to zero and changes to 1 when the *Start* button is clicked.

After the loop, all sprites are deleted and the mouse pointer hidden during the main game.

All that is needed now is that *InitialiseGame()*'s code changes to call this new routine:

```
FUNCTION InitialiseGame()
    SetUpScreen()
    ShowSplashScreen()
    InitialiseShipsData()
    PrepareSprites()
ENDFUNCTION
```

Activity 27.17

Update your *Space Duel* game to include the splash screen as described earlier.

Summary

- A rollover effect can be achieved by placing an invisible sprite at the position of the mouse pointer and checking for a collision with another sprite. The other sprite's frame is changed when the hit occurs.

- On-screen buttons are pressed when a collision occurs between the hidden mouse pointer sprite and the on-screen button sprite at the same time as a mouse button click.

Solutions

Activity 27.1

```
PRINT "Hello world"
SUSPEND FOR MOUSE
END
```

Activity 27.2

```
REM *** Set screen resolution ***
SET DISPLAY MODE 1280,1024,32
REM *** Load image of bug ***
LOAD IMAGE "bug01.bmp",1
REM *** Position sprite ***
x = 600
y = 500
SPRITE 1,x,y,1
REM *** Make sprite's origin its centre ***
OFFSET SPRITE 1,32,32
REM *** Main loop ***
DO
    REM *** Move sprite ***
    MOVE SPRITE 1,1
    REM *** Check for mouse click ***
    mousevalue = MOUSECLICK()
    REM *** Change bug direction ***
    SELECT mousevalue
        CASE 1    `Left button - rotate 90
            ROTATE SPRITE 1,90
        ENDCASE
        CASE 2    `Right button rotate 180
            ROTATE SPRITE 1,180
        ENDCASE
        CASE 3    `Left&right rotate to zero
            ROTATE SPRITE 1,0
        ENDCASE
        CASE 4    `Centre button rotate 270
            ROTATE SPRITE 1,270
        ENDCASE
    ENDSELECT
LOOP
REM *** End program ***
WAIT KEY
END
```

Activity 27.3

No solution required.

Activity 27.4

No solution required.

Activity 27.5

No solution required.

Activity 27.6

The mouse pointer initially shows as the hand and then changes to the pen.

Activity 27.7

Use the *Settings* button to choose a Windowed application.

The mouse coordinates are measured from the top-left corner of the window in which the application appears - not from the top-left corner of the screen.

Activity 27.8

No solution required.

Activity 27.9

No solution required.

Activity 27.10

No solution required.

Activity 27.11

No solution required.

Activity 27.12

```
REM *** Set screen resolution ***
SET DISPLAY MODE 1280,1024,32
REM *** Load animated sprite ***
CREATE ANIMATED SPRITE 1, "squareLED.bmp",
2,1,1
SPRITE 1,100,100,1
DO
    REM *** Get mouse coordinates ***
    x = MOUSEX()
    y = MOUSEY()
    REM *** IF mouse on sprite, set ON ***
    IF x >= 100 AND x <= 149 AND y >= 100
    AND y <= 129
        SET SPRITE FRAME 1,2
    ELSE
        REM *** ELSE set OFF ***
        SET SPRITE FRAME 1,1
    ENDIF
LOOP
END
```

Activity 27.13

No solution required.

Activity 27.14

No solution required.

Activity 27.15

No solution required.

Activity 27.16

No solution required.

Activity 27.17

No solution required.

How to Create a Mouse-Driven Game

The Game of Pelmanism

Rules

Pelmanism is a card-based memory game. Normally it is played by two or more players, but this computer-based version is for one player only.

The game uses a number of paired cards. In this particular case 16 cards (8 pairs). The cards are shuffled and then placed face down on the playing surface. The cards are arranged in organised rows and columns.

The player then turns over any two cards. If the pair of cards match, they are retained by the player. If the cards do not match, they are placed face down once again. In a multiplayer game, the next player would then repeat the process of choosing a pair of cards. For our single player game, the player simply takes another turn. When all cards have been removed, the game is over.

In the single player game, the player begins with a score of 48 and this score is reduced by one every time a card is turned over.

Activity 28.1

Write a structured English algorithm for the single player version of the game. Begin with the line:

> Shuffle cards

and end with

> Display final score

The Screen Layout

The main screen layout is shown in FIG-28.1.

FIG-28.1

The Screen Layout for Pelmanism

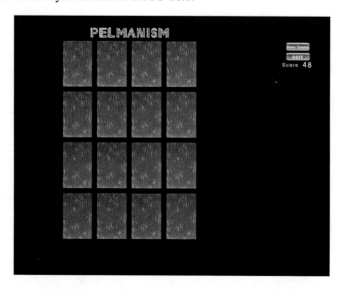

Game Data

Constants

The majority of constants are sprite (and image) numbers, but constants are also defined for TRUE and FALSE (used to assign values to a Boolean variable) and for the orientation of a card. The full list is shown in TABLE-28.1.

TABLE-28.1

Named Constants

Name	Value	Description
scoretext	17	Score text sprite id.
tens	18	Tens digit sprite id.
units	19	Units digit sprite id.
heading	20	Heading text sprite id
mousetip	21	Mouse tip sprite id.
newgamebutton	22	New game button sprite id.
quitbutton	23	Quit game button sprite id.
TRUE	1	*True* value for Boolean assignment.
FALSE	0	*False* value for Boolean assignment.
FACEDOWN	1	*Face down* value for card orientation.
FACEUP	2	*Face up* value for card orientation.

Structures Defined

The value and orientation of a single card is defined in a structure as:

```
TYPE CardType
    value AS INTEGER        `Card value
    orientation AS INTEGER  `Card orientation
ENDTYPE
```

The details of all 16 cards are recorded in an array.

On each turn the player flips over two cards, placing them face-up. Exactly how many cards have been flipped at any moment during a turn (0, 1, or 2), and the positions of those cards are stored in the structure defined as:

```
TYPE TurnType
    firstcard   AS INTEGER  `Position in array of first card
    secondcard  AS INTEGER  `Position in array of second card
    cardsturned AS INTEGER  `Number of cards turned up this round
ENDTYPE
```

Global Variables

Global variables are required to store the card array and turn details. A third global variable records the player's score. To make sure there is a gap between mouse clicks, the time of the latest click is recorded and no new click is allowed for at least 300 milliseconds. Finally, a *quit* variable is initialised to FALSE and set to TRUE when the player clicks on the *Quit* button. The full list of global variables is given in TABLE-28.2.

TABLE-28.2

Global Variables

Name	Type/Value	Description
carddata	CardType(16)	Details of each card.
playerturn	TurnType	Details of current round.
score	integer	Player's score.
quit	Boolean	TRUE when game to terminate.
lastclick	integer	Time of last mouse click.

Game Logic

The implementation of the game will employ the mouse to allow the user to select cards or start a new game. Because of this, the main game logic will simply be:

```
Initialise game
REPEAT
    Handle mouse
UNTIL player quits
Show end screen
```

The Program Code

Getting Started

Since the primary purpose of this chapter is to demonstrate how to create a mouse-driven game, we'll keep the formal documentation of the program to a minimum and just spend time looking at any new techniques that are used here.

From what has been given so far, we can start our coding as follows:

```
REM *** Sprite numbers ***
#CONSTANT scoretext      17
#CONSTANT tens           18
#CONSTANT units          19
#CONSTANT heading        20
#CONSTANT mousetip       21
#CONSTANT newgamebutton 22
#CONSTANT quitbutton     23
REM *** Named constants ***
#CONSTANT TRUE           1
#CONSTANT FALSE          0
#CONSTANT FACEDOWN       1
#CONSTANT FACEUP         2

REM *** Type definition for card data ***
TYPE CardType
    value AS INTEGER         `Card value
    orientation AS INTEGER   `Card orientation
ENDTYPE

TYPE TurnType
    firstcard   AS INTEGER   `Position in array of first card
    secondcard  AS INTEGER   `Position in array of second card
    cardsturned AS INTEGER   `Number of cards turned up this round
ENDTYPE

REM *** Main variables ***
GLOBAL DIM carddata(16) AS CardType    `Details about all 16 cards
GLOBAL playerturn AS TurnType          `Details of player's turn
GLOBAL lastclick AS INTEGER            `Time of last mouse click
GLOBAL score AS INTEGER                `Player's score
GLOBAL quit AS BOOLEAN                 `True when player to quit

REM *** Main section ***
InitialiseGame()
REPEAT
    HandleMouse()
UNTIL quit = TRUE
REM *** End program ***
GameOver()
END
```

Adding *InitialiseGame()*

InitialiseGame() consists of two main sections: initialising the data used in the game and setting up the screen. These jobs are done by other routines. All the code required is given below:

```
FUNCTION InitialiseGame()
    InitialiseData()
    SetUpScreen()
ENDFUNCTION

FUNCTION InitialiseData()
    REM *** Seed random generator ***
    RANDOMIZE TIMER()

    REM *** Set quit to false ***
    quit = FALSE

    Rem *** Create pack of cards ***
    CreateCards()

    REM *** Shuffle cards ***
    ShuffleCards()

    REM *** Set player's turn ***
    playerturn.firstcard = 0
    playerturn.secondcard = 0
    playerturn.cardsturned = 0

    REM *** Set score to 48 ***
    score = 48

    REM *** last time mouse clicked ***
    lastclick = 0
ENDFUNCTION

FUNCTION SetUpScreen()
    REM *** Set screen resolution ***
    SET DISPLAY MODE 1280,1024,32
    REM *** Create black backdrop ***
    COLOR BACKDROP 0
    BACKDROP ON

    REM *** Place game title ***
    LOAD IMAGE "pelmanism.bmp",heading
    SPRITE heading,300,30,heading

    REM *** Place the cards ***
    SetOutCards()

    REM *** Place new game button ***
    CREATE ANIMATED SPRITE newgamebutton,"newgame.bmp",1,2,
    ⮡newgamebutton
    SPRITE newgamebutton,1100,100,newgamebutton

    REM *** Place QUIT button ***
    CREATE ANIMATED SPRITE quitbutton,"quit.bmp",1,2,quitbutton
    SPRITE quitbutton,1100,140,quitbutton

    REM *** Display score ***
    SetupScore()

    REM *** Create hidden sprite at mouse tip ***
    LOAD IMAGE "mousetip.bmp",21
    SPRITE mousetip, 0,0,21
    HIDE SPRITE mousetip
ENDFUNCTION
```

Even this isn't the end of adding the code for *InitialiseGame()*: if you look carefully you'll see that both *InitialiseData()* and *SetUpScreen()* both call yet more functions!

The code for these is given below:

```
FUNCTION CreateCards()
    REM ** Set card value and orientation ***
    FOR card = 0 TO 15
        carddata(card+1).value = card / 2 + 1
        carddata(card+1).orientation = FACEDOWN
    NEXT card
ENDFUNCTION


FUNCTION ShuffleCards()
    temp AS CardType
    REM *** FOR 500 times DO ***
    FOR c = 1 TO 500
        REM *** Choose two cards at random ... ***
        card1 = RND(15)+1
        card2 = RND(15)+1

        REM *** ... and swap their positions in the pack ***
        temp = carddata(card1)
        carddata(card1) = carddata(card2)
        carddata(card2) = temp
    NEXT c
ENDFUNCTION


FUNCTION SetOutCards()
    REM*** Lay out cards on screen ***
    FOR c = 1 TO 16
        REM *** Calculate row and column for card ***
        row = (c-1) / 4
        column = (c-1) mod 4

        REM *** Create an animated sprite for each card ***
        filename$ = "card" + STR$(carddata(c).value)+".jpg"
        CREATE ANIMATED SPRITE c,filename$,2,1,c

        REM *** Place card at correct position ***
        SPRITE c,column*140+200,row*200+100,c

        REM *** Face down ***
        SET SPRITE FRAME c,carddata(c).orientation
    NEXT c
ENDFUNCTION


FUNCTION SetupScore()
    REM *** Position the text ***
    LOAD IMAGE "score.bmp",score
    SPRITE score,1080,180,score

    REM *** Create both digits of the score ***
    CREATE ANIMATED SPRITE units,"0TO9.bmp",10,1,units
    CLONE SPRITE units, tens
    SPRITE tens,1160,175,tens
    SPRITE units,1180,175,units

    REM *** Set score to 48 ***
    SET SPRITE FRAME tens,4+1
    SET SPRITE FRAME units, 8+1
ENDFUNCTION
```

Make sure you copy all the images used into the new project folder.

Adding *HandleMouse()*

The *HandleMouse()* routine is at the core of this program and shows how to tackle mouse-driven games.

The player can activate a response from the game only by using the mouse. If the mouse point moves over either button it will change from black and white to colour. All other responses involve moving and clicking the mouse. When over a face-down card, that card should be turned over; when a button is clicked, a new game should be started (the *New Game* button) or the game should terminate (the *Quit* button)

To achieve this, the *HandleMouse()* function uses the following logic:

```
Move mousetip sprite to position of mouse pointer
Check for button rollover
Check for sprite clicked
IF
    card clicked:
        Handle card
    New game button clicked:
        Start new game
    Quit button clicked:
        Set quit to true
ENDIF
```

The code for the routine is:

```
FUNCTION HandleMouse()
    REM *** Move mousetip sprite to mouse pointer ***
    SPRITE mousetip,MOUSEX(),MOUSEY(),21

    REM *** Check for mouse over one of the buttons ***
    CheckForButtonRollover()

    REM *** Get id of sprite hit (if any) ***
    spritehit = CheckForSpriteClicked()

    REM *** IF no sprite clicked, exit routine ***
    IF spritehit = 0
        EXITFUNCTION
    ENDIF

    REM *** IF card clicked, handle card ****
    IF  spritehit <= 16
        HandleCardClick(spritehit)
    ENDIF

    REM *** IF new button hit start new game ***
    IF spritehit = newgamebutton
        StartNewGame()
    ENDIF
```

```
            REM *** IF quit button hit, set quit indicator ***
            IF spritehit = quitbutton
                quit = TRUE
            ENDIF
        ENDFUNCTION
```

Most of the routines called are quite short:

```
        FUNCTION CheckForButtonRollover()
            REM *** Check for sprite hit ***
            spritehit = SPRITE HIT(mousetip,0)

            REM *** IF new game rollover change to frame 2 ***
            IF spritehit = newgamebutton
                SET SPRITE FRAME newgamebutton,2
            ELSE
                REM *** Otherwise, frame 1 ***
                SET SPRITE FRAME newgamebutton,1
            ENDIF

            REM *** IF quit rollover, change to frame 2 ***
            IF spritehit = quitbutton
                SET SPRITE FRAME quitbutton,2
            ELSE
                REM *** Otherwise, frame 1 ***
                SET SPRITE FRAME quitbutton,1
            ENDIF
        ENDFUNCTION


        FUNCTION CheckForSpriteClicked()
            REM *** Check for sprite hit ***
            clicked = SPRITE HIT(mousetip,0)

            REM *** IF hit & mouse clicked after 300 msecs ***
            IF clicked <> 0 AND MOUSECLICK() AND TIMER()-lastclick > 300
                REM *** Set return value to sprite number ***
                result = clicked
                REM *** Reset time since last mouse click ***
                lastclick = TIMER()
            ELSE
                REM *** IF no sprite clicked return zero ***
                result = 0
            ENDIF
        ENDFUNCTION result


        FUNCTION StartNewGame()
            REM *** Delete all existing sprites ***
            FOR c = 1 TO 23
                IF SPRITE EXIST(c)
                    DELETE SPRITE c
                ENDIF
            NEXT c

            REM *** Set up a new game ***
            InitialiseGame()
        ENDFUNCTION
```

But the main routine called by *HandleMouse()* is *HandleCardClick()*. This routine must turn over cards and when the second card is flipped check to see if it matches the first card. If we have a match, the two cards are deleted, otherwise the cards must be returned to the face-down position. Also, the score must be reduced every time a card is turned over. The logic for this routine is:

```
                    IF the card clicked is face up THEN
                        Exit function
                    ENDIF
                    Decrement the score
                    IF
                        first card of round:
                            Turn over card
                            Record which card has been turned
                        second card turned:
                            Turn over card
                            Record which card has been turned
                            IF first and second cards match THEN
                                Delete both cards
                            ELSE
                                Turn both cards face down again
                            ENDIF
                    ENDIF
```

This is coded as:

```
FUNCTION HandleCardClick()
    REM *** IF card already face up, exit routine ***
    IF carddata(card).orientation = FACEUP
        EXITFUNCTION
    ENDIF
    REM *** Reduce score ***
    DecrementScore()
        SELECT playerturn.cardsturned
        CASE 0      `First card turned
            REM *** Turn card face up ***
            carddata(card).orientation = FACEUP
            SET SPRITE FRAME card,carddata(card).orientation

            REM *** Record which card was turned ***
            playerturn.firstcard = card

            REM *** Record number of cards turned ***
            INC playerturn.cardsturned
        ENDCASE
        CASE 1       `Second card
            REM *** Turn card face up
            carddata(card).orientation = FACEUP
            SET SPRITE FRAME card,carddata(card).orientation

            REM *** record which card was turned ***
            playerturn.secondcard = card

            REM *** IF the two cards match, delete them ***
            IF carddata(playerturn.firstcard).value =
            ⤷carddata(playerturn.secondcard).value
                WAIT 1000
                DELETE SPRITE playerturn.firstcard
                DELETE SPRITE playerturn.secondcard
            ELSE
                REM *** ELSE, turn the cards back over ***
                WAIT 3000
                carddata(playerturn.firstcard).orientation =
                ⤷FACEDOWN
                SET SPRITE FRAME playerturn.firstcard,
                ⤷carddata(playerturn.firstcard).orientation
                carddata(playerturn.secondcard).orientation =
                ⤷FACEDOWN
                SET SPRITE FRAME playerturn.secondcard,
                ⤷carddata(playerturn.secondcard).orientation
            ENDIF
            REM *** No cards turned over ***
            playerturn.cardsturned = 0
        ENDCASE
```

```
        ENDSELECT
    ENDFUNCTION
```

The only routine called is *DecrementScore()* which is coded as:

```
FUNCTION DecrementScore()
    REM *** IF score is less than 1, exit ***
    IF score < 1
        EXITFUNCTION
    ENDIF

    REM *** Decrease score ***
    DEC score

    REM *** Update score on screen ***
    SET SPRITE FRAME tens, score/10 + 1
    SET SPRITE FRAME units, score mod 10 + 1
ENDFUNCTION
```

Activity 28.2

Add the extra routines to your program and check that the program plays the game as expected.

Adding *GameOver()*

The final routine of the game simply displays the message *Game Over* and is coded as:

```
FUNCTION GameOver()
    REM *** Hide any sprite currently on the screen ***
    HIDE ALL SPRITES

    REM *** Set up font and size ***
    SET TEXT FONT "Arial bold"
    SET TEXT SIZE 40

    REM *** Display message for a few seconds ***
    FOR c = 1 TO 100
        SET CURSOR 500,500
        PRINT "GAME OVER"
        WAIT 10
    NEXT c
ENDFUNCTION
```

Activity 28.3

Complete your game and make sure it is operating correctly.

A complete listing of the game is given overleaf.

Pelmanism - Program Listing

```
REM ****************************************
REM *** Program   :   Pelmanism        ***
REM *** Version   :   0.1              ***
REM *** Date      :   3/9/2005         ***
REM *** Author    :   A. Stewart       ***
REM *** Hardware  :   PC 1280 by 1024  ***
REM *** Purpose   :   Single player game ***
REM ****                of Pelmanism    ***
REM ****************************************

REM *** Global constants ***

REM *** Sprite numbers ***
#CONSTANT scoretext      17
#CONSTANT tens           18
#CONSTANT units          19
#CONSTANT heading        20
#CONSTANT mousetip       21
#CONSTANT newgamebutton  22
#CONSTANT quitbutton     23

REM *** Named constants ***
#CONSTANT TRUE        1
#CONSTANT FALSE       0
#CONSTANT FACEDOWN    1
#CONSTANT FACEUP      2


REM *** Type definition for card data ***
TYPE CardType
    value AS INTEGER         `Card value
    orientation AS INTEGER `Card orientation (1 = face down; 2
face up)
ENDTYPE

TYPE TurnType
    firstcard   AS INTEGER  `Position in array of first card
    secondcard  AS INTEGER  `Position in array of second card
    cardsturned AS INTEGER  `Number of cards turned up this round
ENDTYPE


REM *** Main variables ***
GLOBAL DIM carddata(16) AS CardType  `Details about all 16 cards
GLOBAL lastclick AS INTEGER        `Time of last mouse click over
card
GLOBAL playerturn AS TurnType
GLOBAL score AS INTEGER            `Player's score
GLOBAL quit AS BOOLEAN             `True when player wants to quit




REM *** Main section ***
InitialiseGame()
REPEAT
    HandleMouse()
UNTIL quit = TRUE
REM *** End program ***
GameOver()
END
```

continued on next page

```
FUNCTION InitialiseGame()
   InitialiseData()
   SetUpScreen()
ENDFUNCTION



FUNCTION InitialiseData()
   REM *** Seed random generator ***
   RANDOMIZE TIMER()

   REM *** Set quit to false ***
   quit = FALSE

   Rem *** Create pack of cards ***
   CreateCards()

   REM *** Shuffle cards ***
   ShuffleCards()

   REM *** Set player's turn ***
   playerturn.firstcard = 0
   playerturn.secondcard = 0
   playerturn.cardsturned = 0

   REM *** Set score to 48 ***
   score = 48

   REM *** last time mouse clicked ***
   lastclick = 0
ENDFUNCTION



FUNCTION SetUpScreen()
   REM *** Set screen resolution ***
   SET DISPLAY MODE 1280,1024,32
   REM *** Create black backdrop ***
   COLOR BACKDROP 0
   BACKDROP ON

   REM *** Place game title ***
   LOAD IMAGE "pelmanism.bmp",heading
   SPRITE heading,300,30,heading

   REM *** Place the cards ***
   SetOutCards()

   REM *** Place new game button ***
   CREATE ANIMATED SPRITE newgamebutton,"newgame.bmp",1,2,
   ⇓newgamebutton
   SPRITE newgamebutton,1100,100,newgamebutton

   REM *** Place QUIT button ***
   CREATE ANIMATED SPRITE quitbutton,"quit.bmp",1,2,quitbutton
   SPRITE quitbutton,1100,140,quitbutton

   REM *** Display score ***
   SetupScore()

   REM *** Create hidden sprite at mouse tip ***
   LOAD IMAGE "mousetip.bmp",21
   SPRITE mousetip, 0,0,21
   HIDE SPRITE mousetip
ENDFUNCTION
```

continued on next page

```
FUNCTION CreateCards()
   REM ** Set card value and orientation ***
   FOR card = 0 TO 15
      carddata(card+1).value = card / 2 + 1
      carddata(card+1).orientation = FACEDOWN
   NEXT card
ENDFUNCTION



FUNCTION ShuffleCards()
   temp AS CardType
   REM *** FOR 500 times DO ***
   FOR c = 1 TO 500
      REM *** Choose two cards at random ... ***
      card1 = RND(15)+1
      card2 = RND(15)+1

      REM *** ... and swap their positions in the pack ***
      temp = carddata(card1)
      carddata(card1) = carddata(card2)
      carddata(card2) = temp
   NEXT c
ENDFUNCTION



FUNCTION SetOutCards()
   REM *** Lay out cards on screen ***
   FOR c = 1 TO 16
       REM *** Calculate row and column for card ***
      row = (c-1) / 4
      column = (c-1) mod 4

      REM *** Create an animated sprite for each card ***
      filename$ = "card" + STR$(carddata(c).value)+".jpg"
      CREATE ANIMATED SPRITE c,filename$,2,1,c

      REM *** Place card at correct position ***
      SPRITE c,column*140+200,row*200+100,c

      REM *** Face down ***
      SET SPRITE FRAME c,carddata(c).orientation
   NEXT c
ENDFUNCTION



FUNCTION SetupScore()
   REM *** Position the text ***
   LOAD IMAGE "score.bmp",score
   SPRITE score,1080,180,score

   REM *** Create both digits of the score ***
   CREATE ANIMATED SPRITE units,"0TO9.bmp",10,1,units
   CLONE SPRITE units, tens
   SPRITE tens,1160,175,tens
   SPRITE units,1180,175,units

   REM *** Set score to 48 ***
   SET SPRITE FRAME tens,4+1
   SET SPRITE FRAME units, 8+1
ENDFUNCTION
```

continued on next page

```
FUNCTION HandleMouse()
   REM *** Move mousetip sprite to mouse pointer ***
   SPRITE mousetip,MOUSEX(),MOUSEY(),21
   CheckForButtonRollover()

   REM *** Get sprite hit (if any) ***
   spritehit = CheckForSpriteClicked()

   REM *** IF no sprite clicked, exit routine ***
   IF spritehit = 0
      EXITFUNCTION
   ENDIF

   REM *** IF card clicked, handle card ****
   IF  spritehit <= 16
      HandleCardClick(spritehit)
   ENDIF

   REM *** IF new button hit start new game ***
   IF spritehit = newgamebutton
      StartNewGame()
   ENDIF

   REM *** IF quit button hit, set quit indicator ***
   IF spritehit = quitbutton
      quit = TRUE
   ENDIF
ENDFUNCTION

FUNCTION CheckForButtonRollover()
   REM *** Check for sprite hit ***
   spritehit = SPRITE HIT(mousetip,0)

   REM *** IF new game rollover change to frame 2 ***
   IF spritehit = newgamebutton
      SET SPRITE FRAME newgamebutton,2
   ELSE
      REM *** Otherwise, frame 1 ***
      SET SPRITE FRAME newgamebutton,1
   ENDIF

   REM *** IF quit rollover, change to frame 2 ***
   IF spritehit = quitbutton
      SET SPRITE FRAME quitbutton,2
   ELSE
      REM *** Otherwise, frame 1 ***
      SET SPRITE FRAME quitbutton,1
   ENDIF
ENDFUNCTION

FUNCTION CheckForSpriteClicked()
   REM *** Check for sprite hit ***
   clicked = SPRITE HIT(mousetip,0)

   REM *** IF hit and mouse clicked after 300 msecs ***
   IF clicked <> 0 AND MOUSECLICK() AND TIMER()-lastclick > 300
      REM *** Set return value to sprite number ***
      result = clicked
      REM *** Reset time since last mouse click ***
      lastclick = TIMER()
   ELSE
      REM *** IF no sprite clicked return zero ***
      result = 0
   ENDIF
ENDFUNCTION result
```

continued on next page

```
FUNCTION StartNewGame()
    REM *** Delete all existing sprites ***
    FOR c = 1 TO 23
        IF SPRITE EXIST(c)
            DELETE SPRITE c
        ENDIF
    NEXT c

    REM *** Set up a new game ***
    InitialiseGame()
ENDFUNCTION


FUNCTION HandleCardClick(card)
    REM *** IF card already face up, exit routine ***
        IF carddata(card).orientation = FACEUP
            EXITFUNCTION
        ENDIF

        REM *** Reduce score ***
        DecrementScore()

        SELECT playerturn.cardsturned
            CASE 0      `First card turned
                REM *** Turn card face up ***
                carddata(card).orientation = 2
                SET SPRITE FRAME card,carddata(card).orientation

                REM *** Record which card was turned ***
                playerturn.firstcard = card

                REM *** Record number of cards turned ***
                INC playerturn.cardsturned
            ENDCASE
            CASE 1      `Second card
                REM *** Turn card face up
                carddata(card).orientation = 2
                SET SPRITE FRAME card,carddata(card).orientation

                REM *** record which card was turned ***
                playerturn.secondcard = card

                REM *** IF the two cards match, delete them ***
                IF carddata(playerturn.firstcard).value =
                ⤷carddata(playerturn.secondcard).value
                    WAIT 1000
                    DELETE SPRITE playerturn.firstcard
                    DELETE SPRITE playerturn.secondcard
                ELSE
                    REM *** ELSE, turn the cards back over ***
                    WAIT 3000
                    carddata(playerturn.firstcard).orientation = 1
                    SET SPRITE FRAME playerturn.firstcard,
                    ⤷carddata(playerturn.firstcard).orientation
                    carddata(playerturn.secondcard).orientation = 1
                    SET SPRITE FRAME playerturn.secondcard,
                    ⤷carddata(playerturn.secondcard).orientation
                ENDIF
                REM *** No cards turned over ***
                playerturn.cardsturned = 0
            ENDCASE
        ENDSELECT
    ENDFUNCTION
ENDFUNCTION
```

continued on next page

```
FUNCTION DecrementScore()
    REM *** IF score is less than 1, exit ***
    IF score < 1
        EXITFUNCTION
    ENDIF

    REM *** Decrease score ***
    DEC score

    REM *** Update score on screen ***
    SET SPRITE FRAME tens, score/10 + 1
    SET SPRITE FRAME units, score mod 10 + 1
ENDFUNCTION



FUNCTION GameOver()
    REM *** Hide any sprite currently on the screen ***
    HIDE ALL SPRITES

    REM *** Set up font and size ***
    SET TEXT FONT "Arial bold"
    SET TEXT SIZE 40

    REM *** Display message for a few seconds ***
    FOR c = 1 TO 100
        SET CURSOR 500,500
        PRINT "GAME OVER"
        WAIT 10
    NEXT c
ENDFUNCTION
```

Solutions

Activity 28.1

```
Shuffle cards
Lay cards out face down in a 4x4 grid
Set score to 48
REPEAT
  Pick a card and turn face up
  Pick a card and turn face up
  Reduce score by 2
  IF cards match THEN
     Retain cards
  ELSE
     Return cards to face-down position
  ENDIF
UNTIL all cards have been retained
Display final score
```

Activity 28.2

No solution required.

Activity 28.3

No solution required.

Checking for a Joystick

Controlling Sprite Movement using a Joystick

Detecting Joystick Movement

Detecting Joystick Button Presses

Reading Joystick Slider, Twist and HAT Values

Simulating a Third Dimension in a Game

Using Feedback Effects

Using a Joystick

Introduction

Some games use a joystick as the main control device. Often the player finds a joystick has a much more natural feel, especially if he is controlling a flying vehicle or the sights of a gun. The other advantage of a more advanced joystick is that it gives feedback. Under computer control we can make the joystick shake, or become harder to move. Obviously, this feature can be used by the programmer to give the player an added feeling of realism.

The remainder of this chapter explains the commands available from within DarkBASIC Pro for using a joystick; if you don't have one, just skip this chapter until you have installed the necessary hardware.

Checking the System for a Joystick

Of course, unlike a keyboard and mouse, which we can assume are attached to everyone's computer, it is much less likely that your player has a joystick, so we need to check for it. If a joystick is found, we need to check out if it accepts feedback signals which allow the computer to control joystick movement.

The PERFORM CHECKLIST FOR CONTROL DEVICES Statement

This statement creates a list of all the devices attached to the user's computer and has the format shown in FIG-29.1.

FIG-29.1

The PERFORM
CHECKLIST FOR
CONTROL DEVICES
Statement

After executing this statement you need to use the CHECKLIST commands to find out what entries have been made. The program in LISTING-29.1 demonstrates how this is done.

LISTING-29.1

Checking for Control
Devices

```
REM *** Create list of devices ***
PERFORM CHECKLIST FOR CONTROL DEVICES

REM *** Display each entry in the list ***
FOR c = 1 TO CHECKLIST QUANTITY()
   PRINT CHECKLIST STRING$(c)
NEXT c

REM *** End program ***
WAIT KEY
END
```

Activity 29.1
Type in and test the program above (*joy01.dbpro*).

Notice that normal devices, such as the keyboard and mouse, do not appear in the list.

If you do have a joystick attached, you can find out if it has feedback capabilities by using the CHECKLIST VALUE A statement. This will return a 1 for force-feedback joysticks and 0 for normal joysticks.

Activity 29.2

Modify your previous program to display the feedback abilities of the joystick.

We can divide the instructions available into two main categories: those to read data from the joystick and those to create feedback in the joystick. We'll start with the first group, so even if you're not using a feedback stick, you can still test this first group of statements.

Reading the Position of the Joystick

The JOYSTICK Direction Statement

There are four variations of the JOYSTICK movement statement which returns the direction in which the joystick is being moved. The format of the statement is shown in FIG-29.2.

FIG-29.2

The JOYSTICK
Movement Statement

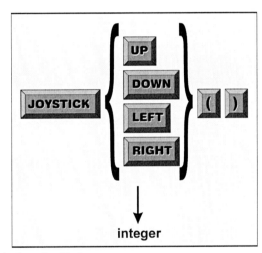

Each variation is described below:

JOYSTICK UP()   this option will return a value of 1 if the joystick is being pushed forward (up); otherwise zero is returned.

JOYSTICK DOWN()   this option will return a value of 1 if the joystick is being pulled backwards (down); otherwise zero is returned.

JOYSTICK LEFT()   this option will return a value of 1 if the joystick is being pushed to the left; otherwise zero is returned.

JOYSTICK RIGHT()   this option will return a value of 1 if the joystick is being pushed to the right; otherwise zero is returned.

It is possible for the joystick to return 1 for more than two of these functions at the same time. For example, if the joystick is being pushed to the right and up at the same time, then JOYSTICK UP and JOYSTICK RIGHT would both return 1. The program in LISTING-29.2 uses a crosshairs sprite which is moved using the joystick.

LISTING-29.2

Detecting Joystick Movement

```
REM *** Set screen resolution ***
SET DISPLAY MODE 1280,1024,32
REM *** Set sprite coordinates ***
xord = 500
yord = 400
REM *** Load image ***
LOAD IMAGE "crosshairs.bmp",1
SPRITE 1,xord,yord,1
REM *** Main loop ***
DO
   REM *** Get joystick reading ***
   IF JOYSTICK LEFT() = 1
      DEC xord,5
   ENDIF
   IF JOYSTICK RIGHT() = 1
      INC xord,5
   ENDIF
   IF JOYSTICK UP() = 1
      DEC yord,5
   ENDIF
   IF JOYSTICK DOWN() = 1
      INC yord,5
   ENDIF
   REM *** Move sprite to new position ***
   SPRITE 1, xord,yord,1
LOOP
REM *** End program ***
END
```

Activity 29.3

Type in and test the program given above (*joy02.dbpro*).

What problems arise, if any?

The JOYSTICK Position Statement

Rather than just detect the direction in which the joystick is being moved, we can actually determine how far to the left, right, back, or forward the stick is being pushed using another JOYSTICK statement which takes the format shown in FIG-29.3.

FIG-29.3

The JOYSTICK Coordinates Statement

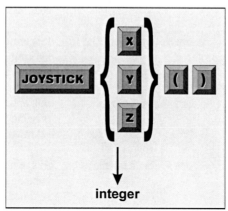

Each variation of this statement is described below:

JOYSTICK X()   this option will return an integer x-ordinate which specifies how far to the left or right the joystick is being pushed. The value returned ranges from -1000 (extreme left) to + 1000 (extreme right).

JOYSTICK Y()   this option will return an integer y-ordinate which specifies how far forward or backward the joystick is being pushed. The value returned ranges from -1000 (fully forward) to + 1000 (fully back).

JOYSTICK Z()   this option will return an integer z-ordinate. Not every joystick returns a z-value. Those that do, often achieve this with a separate control.

The program in LISTING-29.3 uses the JOYSTICK X() and JOYSTICK Y() instructions to position the crosshairs sprite.

LISTING-29.3

Measuring the Joystick's Position Accurately

```
REM *** Set display mode ***
SET DISPLAY MODE 1280,1024,32

REM *** Set up sprite ***
LOAD IMAGE "crosshairs.bmp",1
SPRITE 1,500,400,1

REM *** main loop ***
DO
    REM *** Move sprite to joystick coordinates ***
    SPRITE 1, JOYSTICK X(), JOYSTICK Y(), 1
LOOP

REM *** End program ***
END
```

Activity 29.4

Type in and test the program shown above (*joy03.dbpro*).

How far can the crosshairs be moved?

Since the joystick reading is translated exactly into screen coordinates, the crosshairs can move off the screen on two sides and can reach the edge of the other two.

Assuming we want to keep the crosshairs on screen, we need to adjust our program so that the joystick readings convert to better on-screen values.

The first change we can make is to modify the value from the joystick so that it is in the range 0 to 2000 rather than -1000 to 1000 which can be achieved by the expression

```
JOYSTICK X() + 1000
```

A player might reasonably expect the crosshairs to be at the left-hand edge of the screen when the joystick is pushed fully to the left, and to be at the right-hand edge when the joystick is pushed fully to the right. On the screen this represents a movement by the crosshairs sprite of 1280 pixels (assuming we're using a 1280 by 1024 screen resolution). For the joystick, the movement signifies a change from a reading of -1000 to +1000 - a range of 2000. That is,

> a movement of 2000 joystick X units = a sprite movement of 1280 pixels

and therefore,

> 1 joystick X unit   = 1280/2000 pixels
>   = 0.640 pixels

The values used in this Activity assume screen dimensions of 1280 by 1024.

But we can't be sure that everyone is going to be playing the game in this resolution, so we have to make the program more general using the formulae:

> 1 joystick X unit = screen width / 2000 pixels

> 1 joystick Y unit = screen height / 2000 pixels

The code for the final version of the program is shown in LISTING-29.4.

LISTING-29.4

Adjusting Joystick Readings to Match the Screen's Resolution

```
REM *** Set screen resolution ***
SET DISPLAY MODE 1280,1024,32

REM *** Set up sprite ***
LOAD IMAGE "crosshairs.bmp",1
SPRITE 1,500,400,1

REM *** All calculations from middle of sprite ***
imagewidth = SPRITE WIDTH(1)
imageheight = SPRITE HEIGHT(1)
OFFSET SPRITE 1,imagewidth/2,imageheight/2
```

continued on next page

```
REM *** Calculate joystick to pixel ratio ***
width = SCREEN WIDTH()
height = SCREEN HEIGHT()
Xunit# = width/2000
Yunit# = height/2000
REM *** Main loop ***
DO
    REM *** Move sprite using joystick ***
    SPRITE 1,(JOYSTICK X()+1000)*Xunit#,(JOYSTICK Y()+1000)*
    ⮑Yunit#, 1
LOOP
END
```

Activity 29.8

Modify *joy03.dbpro* to match LISTING-29.4.

Joystick Controls

The JOYSTICK FIRE Statement

Joysticks also have one or more buttons. DarkBASIC Pro contains a JOYSTICK FIRE statement used to check if any of these buttons are being pressed. The statement has the format shown in FIG-29.4.

FIG-29.4

The JOYSTICK FIRE
Statement

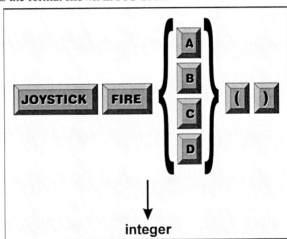

Each variation of this statement is described below:

JOYSTICK FIRE A()   this option is used to detect if button A on the joystick is being pressed. The statement returns the integer value 1 if button A is being pressed, otherwise zero is returned.

JOYSTICK FIRE B()   this option is used to detect if button B on the joystick is being pressed. The statement returns the integer value 1 if button B is being pressed, otherwise zero is returned.

JOYSTICK FIRE C()   this option is used to detect if button C on the joystick is being pressed. The statement returns the integer value 1 if button C is being pressed, otherwise zero is returned.

```
JOYSTICK FIRE D()
```
this option is used to detect if button D on the joystick is being pressed. The statement returns the integer value 1 if button D is being pressed, otherwise zero is returned.

Activity 29.9

Write a program (*joy04.dbpro*) constructed from the following logic:

```
Set screen resolution
Set text opaque
DO
      Move cursor to (100,100)
      IF joystick button A pressed THEN
            Display "Pressed"
      ELSE
            Display "          "
      ENDIF
LOOP
```

By running the above program, check out which button on your joystick is identified as button A.

Activity 29.10

Modify your *joy04.dbpro* program by adding three more IF statements, to check out each of the other JOYSTICK FIRE statements.

The JOYSTICK FIRE X Statement

Rather than use four different statements to check for button presses, there's a single statement that will do the same job. This is the JOYSTICK FIRE X statement which takes a parameter which specifies the identity of the button to be checked. This statement has the format shown in FIG-29.5.

FIG-29.5

The JOYSTICK FIRE X Statement

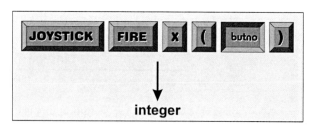

In the diagram:

butno   is an integer identifying which button is to be checked. *butno* can have any value between 0 and 32 - with zero being equivalent to button A.

Activity 29.11

Replace the JOYSTICK FIRE statements in your last program with a single JOYSTICK FIRE X statement which performs the same task.

The JOYSTICK SLIDER Statement

If your joystick has a slider control, this can be checked using the JOYSTICK SLIDER statement. Up to four sliders can be read. These are identified using the letters A, B, C and D. The statement has the format shown in FIG-29.6.

FIG-29.6

The JOYSTICK SLIDER Statement

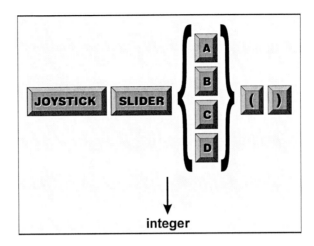

The value returned will lie between 0 and 65767. Most joysticks have a single slider, A.

The program in LISTING-29.5 shows the current settings for slider A, B, C and D.

LISTING-29.5

Reading the Joystick's Slider Setting

```
REM *** Set display mode ***
SET DISPLAY MODE 1280,1024,32

REM *** Set up sprite ***
SET TEXT OPAQUE

REM *** main loop ***
DO
    REM *** Position cursor ***
    SET CURSOR 100,100
    PRINT "               "
    SET CURSOR 100,100
    PRINT JOYSTICK SLIDER A()
    WAIT 1
LOOP

REM *** End program ***
END
```

Activity 29.12

Type in and test the program given above (*joy05.dbpro*).

What is the smallest change in value that can be achieved when moving the slider control?

The JOYSTICK TWIST Statement

If the joystick performs a rotational twist movement, the amount of twist can be read using the JOYSTICK TWIST statement which has the format shown in FIG-29.7.

FIG-29.7

The JOYSTICK TWIST
Statement

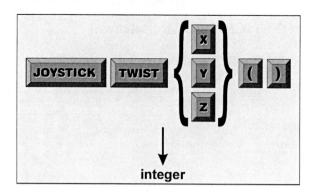

The value returned will be between 0 and 65535.

A typical joystick can be physically twisted 45° to the right or left of centre. When twisted fully to the left, the JOYSTICK TWIST Z() statement will return the value zero; twisted fully to the right gives a value of 65535.

The program in LISTING-29.6 shows a real-time reading of the x, y and z twist settings.

LISTING-29.6

Using the JOYSTICK
TWIST Statement

```
REM *** Set display mode ***
SET DISPLAY MODE 1280,1024,32

REM *** Set up sprite ***
SET TEXT OPAQUE

REM *** main loop ***
DO
   REM *** Position cursor ***
   SET CURSOR 100,100
   REM *** Erase any previous output ***
   PRINT "                      "

   REM *** Reposition cursor ***
   SET CURSOR 100,100
   REM *** Display joystick readings ***
   PRINT "X:",JOYSTICK TWIST X()," Y:",JOYSTICK TWIST Y(),
   ⤷" Z:",JOYSTICK TWIST Z()

   REM *** Delay before looping ***
   WAIT 1
LOOP

REM *** End program ***
END
```

Activity 29.13

Type in and test the program above (*joy06.dbpro*).

Which axes return a non-zero value?

The JOYSTICK HAT ANGLE Statement

The value of a HAT controller can be read using the JOYSTICK HAT ANGLE statement which has the format shown in FIG-29.8.

FIG-29.8

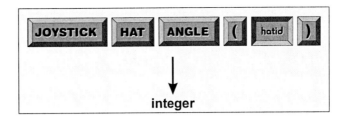

The JOYSTICK HAT
ANGLE Statement

In the diagram:

hatid   is an integer value identifying the HAT controller
                                         to be read. This can be any value between 0 and 3.

The value returned by this statement depends on the state of the HAT controller. If
it is untouched, the value -1 is returned. Pushed to the north the value zero is
returned; east returns 9000; south 18000; west 27000. Some HAT controllers also
offer mid-way positions. For example, a north-east position returns 4500. See
FIG-29.9 for all possible values.

FIG-29.9

HAT Controller Return
Values

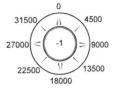

HAT Controller

Most joysticks have a single HAT controller (controller zero). The program in
LISTING-29.7 displays the value returned by HAT controller zero.

LISTING-29.7

Reading the HAT
Controller Value

```
REM *** Set display mode ***
SET DISPLAY MODE 1280,1024,32

REM *** Set up sprite ***
SET TEXT OPAQUE

REM *** main loop ***
DO
   REM *** Display HAT value ***
   SET CURSOR 100,100
   PRINT "                           "
   SET CURSOR 100,100
   PRINT "HAT Controller :",JOYSTICK HAT ANGLE(0)
   WAIT 1
LOOP

REM *** End program ***
END
```

Activity 29.14

Type in and test the program in LISTING-29.7 (*joy07.dbpro*).

Feedback Effects

The commands that follow will only operate if your joystick is capable of reacting
to feedback signals. Check its user manual to see if this facility is available and
make sure that the correct joystick drivers have been installed. If your joystick does
not have this ability the commands will have no effect.

Most of the statements take a magnitude value of between zero and 100 to specify the force of the feedback, with 100 being the largest effect.

The FORCE Direction Statement

The joystick itself can be forced to move in a particular direction. If the player is holding the stick when the feedback occurs, then he will feel the stick attempt to move in the direction specified. There are four options in the FORCE UP statement, each producing movement in a different direction. The statement has the format shown in FIG-29.10.

FIG-29.10

The FORCE Direction Statement

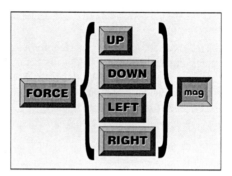

In the diagram:

UP, DOWN, LEFT, RIGHT

Use one of these option to determine the direction in which the joystick is to be moved.

mag

is an integer value representing the strength of the movement. Zero has no effect; 100 is the maximum effect.

The program in LISTING-29.8 forces the joystick in a different direction depending on which joystick button has been pressed.

LISTING-29.8

Using the FORCE Direction Statement

```
REM *** Set display mode ***
SET DISPLAY MODE 1280,1024,32

REM *** main loop ***
DO
   IF JOYSTICK FIRE A()
      FORCE UP 100
   ENDIF
   IF JOYSTICK FIRE B()
      FORCE DOWN 100
   ENDIF
LOOP

REM *** End program ***
END
```

Activity 29.15

Type in and test the program given in LISTING-29.8 (*joy08.dbpro*).

Modify the program so that buttons C and D push the joystick to the left and right respectively.

The FORCE ANGLE Statement

Whereas the FORCE direction statement can only move the joystick in one of four directions, the FORCE ANGLE statement can move the stick to any specified angle for a given amount of time at a given strength. The statement has the format shown in FIG-29.11.

FIG-29.11

The FORCE ANGLE Statement

In the diagram:

mag	is an integer value representing the strength of the movement. Zero has no effect; 100 is the maximum effect.
angle	is a real number representing the angle of the movement.
time	is an integer value representing the duration of the effect in milliseconds. Use zero for a continuous effect.

For example, the statement

```
FORCE ANGLE 100,180.0,500
```

will push the stick forward with maximum force for half a second. The stick's movement would be in the same direction as that produced by a FORCE UP statement.

The program in LISTING-29.9 executes a FORCE ANGLE statement whenever button A is pressed on the joystick.

LISTING-29.9

Using the FORCE ANGLE Statement

```
REM *** Set display mode ***
SET DISPLAY MODE 1280,1024,32

REM *** main loop ***
DO
    IF JOYSTICK FIRE A()
        FORCE ANGLE 100,45,500
    ENDIF
LOOP

REM *** End program ***
END
```

Activity 29.16

Type in and test the program in LISTING-29.9 (*joy09.dbpro*).

Modify the angle, force and duration values specified in the FORCE ANGLE statement and observe what effects these changes have on the reaction of the joystick.

In the final version of your program set the magnitude value to 100 and duration to zero.

The FORCE NO EFFECT Statement

If we have set a feedback effect for continuous duration, then we need to execute the FORCE NO EFFECT statement to end that previous effect. This statement has the format shown in FIG-29.12.

FIG-29.12

The FORCE NO
EFFECT Statement

Activity 29.17

Modify your last program so that the FORCE ANGLE effect is terminated when button B is pressed.

The FORCE AUTO CENTER Statement

This statement forces the stick back to the central position (using the ON option) or cancels this effect (using the OFF option). If the player is holding the stick when this statement is executed, he will feel it attempt to move back to the central position. The statement has the format shown in FIG-29.13.

FIG-29.13

The FORCE AUTO
CENTER Statement

In the diagram:

ON   the centring effect is activated.

OFF   The centring effect of any previous FORCE
                               AUTO CENTER ON statement is cancelled.

The FORCE WATER EFFECT Statement

The FORCE WATER EFFECT statement makes the stick more resistant to movement (a bit like trying to walk through deep water - hence the name). The statement has the format shown in FIG-29.14.

FIG-29.14

The FORCE WATER
EFFECT Statement

In the diagram:

mag   is an integer value representing the strength of
                               the resistance. Zero has no effect; 100 is the
                               maximum effect.

time   is an integer value representing the duration of
                               the effect in milliseconds. Use zero for a
                               continuous effect.

This effect is only apparent if the player is attempting to move the stick. A simple example of the WATER EFFECT is given in LISTING-29.10.

LISTING-29.10

Using the WATER
EFFECT Statement

```
REM *** Set display mode ***
SET DISPLAY MODE 1280,1024,32

REM *** Get ready ***
PRINT "Begin moving the joystick"
WAIT 1000
PRINT "Effects start in 2 seconds"
WAIT 2000

REM *** The FORCE WATER EFFECT ***
CLS
PRINT "FORCE WATER"
WAIT 300
FORCE WATER EFFECT 100,10000

REM *** End program ***
WAIT KEY
END
```

Activity 29.18

Type in and test the program given in LISTING-29.10 (*joy10.dbpro*).

Notice the subtle effect of the FORCE WATER statement and how the stick reverts to normal after 10 seconds.

We need to be careful when using effects which are meant to last for a specific amount of time. Although the joystick should react for the amount of time specified, the program continues to execute other statements while the effect is being performed. If one of these other statements should terminate the program or change the effect being felt, then the original effect will not last for the allotted time.

Activity 29.19

Remove the WAIT KEY statement from your previous program and find out how this changes the effects felt by the player.

The exact delay given in the WAIT statement will be dependent on the duration of the effect.

As we can see from the results of the last Activity, the program executes the END statement before the FORCE WATER EFFECT has time to be effective. This won't be a problem if the effect appears in the middle of a long program, but we may want to add a delaying statement such as WAIT 10000 after a timed joystick effect.

The FORCE CHAINSAW Statement

The FORCE CHAINSAW statement forces the whole joystick device to vibrate. The effect can be anything form a gentle shiver to a tooth-loosening judder. The statement has the format shown in FIG-29.15.

FIG-29.15

The FORCE
CHAINSAW Statement

In the diagram:

> *mag*   is an integer value representing the strength of the recoil. Zero has no effect; 100 is the maximum effect.

<table>
<tr><td>

time

</td><td>

is an integer value representing the duration of the effect in milliseconds. Use zero for a continuous effect.

</td></tr>
</table>

Like, FORCE WATER EFFECT, FORCE CHAINSAW will only activate the joystick correctly if it has sufficient time to execute the command to completion.

Activity 29.20

Write a program (*joy11.dbpro*) which causes the chainsaw effect to execute at full magnitude for 5 seconds.

The FORCE SHOOT Statement

The FORCE SHOOT statement forces the stick to recoil, as a gun would in reaction to being fired. The statement has the format shown in FIG-29.16.

FIG-29.16

The FORCE SHOOT Statement

In the diagram:

<table>
<tr><td>

mag

</td><td>

is an integer value representing the strength of the recoil. Zero has no effect; 100 is the maximum effect.

</td></tr>
<tr><td>

time

</td><td>

is an integer value representing the duration of the effect in milliseconds. Use zero for a continuous effect.

</td></tr>
</table>

The recoil effect works best if it is activated for a short duration in response to some other event, such as pressing a button on the joystick. The program in LISTING-29.11 demonstrates the effect which we might want to achieve when simulating gun-fire.

LISTING-29.11

Simulating Gunfire Recoil

```
REM *** Set display mode ***
SET DISPLAY MODE 1280,1024,32

REM *** Main loop ***
DO
   REM *** IF button 1 pressed, create recoil ***
   IF JOYSTICK FIRE A() = 1
      FORCE SHOOT 100,50
   ENDIF
LOOP

REM *** End program ***
END
```

Activity 29.21

Type in and test LISTING-29.11 (*joy12.dbpro*).

Modify the program so that sound file *laser.wav* is played when button A on the joystick is pressed.

The FORCE IMPACT Statement

This statement simulates being hit. We might use this statement to create the effect of a character being hit by a bullet or car crashing into a barrier. The statement has the format shown in FIG-29.17.

FIG-29.17

The FORCE IMPACT
Statement

In the diagram:

mag   is an integer value representing the strength of the recoil. Zero has no effect; 100 is the maximum effect.

time   is an integer value representing the duration of the effect in milliseconds. Use zero for a continuous effect.

Activity 29.22

Create a program (*joy13.dbpro*) similar to that given in LISTING-29.11 to demonstrate the use of the FORCE IMPACT statement.

Summary

- Use PERFORM CHECKLIST FOR CONTROL DEVICES to detect the presence of a joystick.

- Use the JOYSTICK movement statement to detect the direction of movement of the joystick.

- Use the JOYSTICK position statement to get an exact reading of joystick movement.

- Use JOYSTICK FIRE to detect joystick button presses.

- Use JOYSTICK SLIDER to read the position of a joystick slider.

- Use JOYSTICK TWIST to read the degree of twist applied to the joystick.

- Use JOYSTICK HAT ANGLE to read the position of the joystick's HAT controller.

- Force feedback statements can only be applied to a joystick with feedback capabilities.

- Make sure the correct joystick drivers have been installed before using force feedback statements.

- Use the FORCE direction statement to force the joystick to move in a specified direction.

- Use FORCE ANGLE to force the joystick to move to a specific angle.

- Use FORCE NO EFFECT to switch off a long-lasting effect that has been applied to the joystick.

- Use FORCE AUTO CENTER to force the joystick back to the centre position.

- Use FORCE WATER EFFECT to create a resistance to movement in the joystick.

- Use FORCE CHAINSAW to create a vibration in the joystick.

- Use FORCE SHOOT to create a recoil effect in the joystick.

- Use FORCE IMPACT to create a jolt effect in the joystick.

A Joystick-Based Game

Introduction

This game not only controls the movement of a sprite using a joystick, but also simulates a 3D environment by making a sprite missile reduce in size as it travels away from it launch position.

The Rules Of the Game

The game involves controlling a crosshair sight and launching a missile at an alien craft which is some distance off. When the alien craft has been hit 5 times it explodes and the game is over.

The Screen Layout

The only layout used in the game is shown in FIG-29.18.

FIG-29.18

Game Screenshot

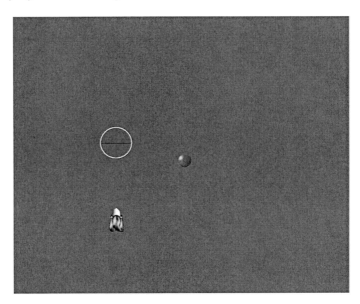

The screen shows the crosshairs, missile, and alien space craft

The Data

A record structure is defined for the velocity of the alien ship:

```
REM *** Define Velocity structure ***
TYPE VelocityType
    xoffset
    yoffset
ENDTYPE
```

Three constants are defined for the sprites and corresponding images. Two more constants are used for sound file IDs. All of these are given in TABLE-29.1.

TABLE-29.1

Constants Declared

Name	Value	Description
crosshairs	1	crosshairs sprite id.
alien	2	alien sprite id.
missile	3	missile sprite id.
launch	1	missile launch sound id.
explode	2	alien explosion sound id

Global variables are used to store the pixel to joystick movement ratios, the alien's velocity, the number of moves made by the missile, the distance between the missiles launch position and its final position, and the missile sprite's dimensions. These are listed in TABLE-29.2.

TABLE-29.2

Global Variables Used

Name	Type/Value	Description
xpixels#	real	Joystick/pixel ratio x-axis.
ypixels#	real	Joystick/pixel ratio y-axis.
missilemoves	integer	Number of times missile has moved.
verticaldistance	integer	Initial distance from missile to crosshairs.
missilewidth#	real	Missile sprite width.
missileheight#	real	Missile sprite height.
alienvelocity	VelocityType	Velocity of alien ship.

Media Used

The sprites used are shown in FIG-29.19.

FIG-29.19

The Sprites used in the Program

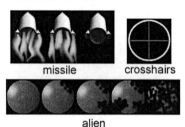

missile   crosshairs

alien

Notice that two of the sprites contain frames.

The first two missile frames are used when the missile is first launched, the third frame is displayed once the missile has reached the half way mark in its journey. This last frame gives the impression that the missile's engines have been switch off.

The alien spacecraft has five frames, starting with an intact craft and moving through various stages of damage until final destruction is depicted in the final frame.

Two sound files are used. *launch.wav*, plays when the missile is fired, and *explode.wav* plays when the alien has been destroyed.

The Program Code

The program starts by declaring types, constants and globals:

```
REM *** Define Velocity structure ***
TYPE VelocityType
    xoffset
    yoffset
ENDTYPE
```

```
REM *** Named Constants ***

REM *** Sprite and image values ***
#CONSTANT crosshairs    1
#CONSTANT alien         2
#CONSTANT missile       3

REM *** Sounds id values ***
#CONSTANT launch        1
#CONSTANT explode       2

REM Global variables ***
GLOBAL xpixels#                 `joystick/pixel ratio x-axis
GLOBAL ypixels#                 `joystick/pixel ratio y-axis
GLOBAL missilemoves = 0         `No. of times missile moved
GLOBAL verticaldistance         `Initial distance from missile to
                                `crosshairs
GLOBAL missilewidth#            `Missile sprite width
GLOBAL missileheight#           `Missile sprite height
GLOBAL alienvelocity AS VelocityType `velocity of alien craft
```

The main logic comes next. As usual, this is nothing more than calls to other routines
and terminates when the alien sprite has been destroyed.

```
InitialiseGame()
REM *** main loop ***
REPEAT
   HandleJoystick()
   HandleAlien()
   HandleMissile()
UNTIL NOT SPRITE EXIST(alien)
REM *** End program ***
WAIT 4000
END
```

Adding *InitialiseGame()*

Again, there are no surprises here. This routine sets the screen resolution, loads the
media files used, creates the main sprite and hides the mouse pointer. Since setting
up the alien requires image, sprites and a velocity to be handled, this is done by a
call to a helper routine named *CreateAlien()*.

```
FUNCTION InitialiseGame()
   REM *** Set Screen resolution ***
   SET DISPLAY MODE 1280,1024,32
   COLOR BACKDROP 0
   BACKDROP ON
   REM *** Calculate joystick/sprite movement ***
   xpixels# = 1280/2000.0
   ypixels# = 1024/2000.0
   REM *** Load Sound files ***
   LOAD SOUND "launch.wav",launch
   LOAD SOUND "explode.wav",explode
   REM *** Create sprites ***
   REM *** Load crosshairs image ***
   LOAD IMAGE "crosshairs.bmp",crosshairs
   SPRITE crosshairs,640,900,crosshairs
   SET SPRITE PRIORITY crosshairs,1
   REM *** Offset crosshairs sprite ***
   OFFSET SPRITE crosshairs, SPRITE WIDTH(1)/2, SPRITE HEIGHT(1)/2
   REM *** Create alien sprite ***
   CreateAlien()
   REM *** Hide the mouse pointer ***
   HIDE MOUSE
ENDFUNCTION
```

Adding *CreateAlien()*

The *CreateAlien()* routine loads the animated sprite used to display the alien. Initially, frame 1 of this sprite is displayed. A random downward velocity is also created for the alien.

```
FUNCTION CreateAlien()
   RANDOMIZE TIMER()
   REM *** Create, position, and size alien sprite ***
   CREATE ANIMATED SPRITE alien,"alien.bmp",5,1,alien
   SPRITE alien,640,20,alien
   SIZE SPRITE alien,50,50
   OFFSET SPRITE alien, SPRITE WIDTH(2)/2, SPRITE HEIGHT(2)/2
   REM *** Give alien sprite a velocity ***
   alienvelocity.xoffset = RND(5)
   alienvelocity.yoffset = RND(10)+1
ENDFUNCTION
```

Adding *HandleJoystick()*

There are two events which need to be handled by this routine: joystick movement which controls the crosshairs sprite, and pressing the joystick button which launches a missile (assuming a missile is not currently on screen).

```
FUNCTION HandleJoystick()
   REM *** Move crosshairs to joystick coordinates ***
   SPRITE crosshairs,(JOYSTICK X()+1000)*xpixels#,
     (JOYSTICK Y()+1000)*ypixels#,1
   IF JOYSTICK FIRE A() = 1 AND (NOT SPRITE EXIST(3))
      PLAY SOUND launch
      FORCE SHOOT 50,5
      CreateMissile()
   ENDIF
ENDFUNCTION
```

Adding *CreateMissile()*

CreateMissile() is called by *HandleJoystick()* and creates a new missile at the bottom of the screen vertically under the centre of the crosshairs. It also calculates the distance from the missile's starting position to its end position at the centre of the crosshairs. The initial dimensions of the missile are also recorded - these are used in another routine to shrink the sprite.

```
FUNCTION CreateMissile()
   REM *** Create missile sprite ***
   CREATE ANIMATED SPRITE missile,"missile2.bmp",3,1,missile
   SPRITE missile,SPRITE X(1),900,missile
   PLAY SPRITE missile,1,2,10
   REM *** Calculate amount of vertical distance ***
   verticaldistance = 900 - SPRITE Y(1)
   REM *** Record width and height of sprite ***
   missilewidth# = SPRITE WIDTH(3)
   missileheight# = SPRITE HEIGHT(3)
ENDFUNCTION
```

Adding *HandleAlien()*

The *HandleAlien()* routine moves the alien ship by an amount specified by *alienvelocity* and calls *WrapAlien()* to handle the alien sprite moving off screen.

```
FUNCTION HandleAlien()
   REM *** Move alien ***
   SPRITE alien,SPRITE X(2)+alienvelocity.xoffset,SPRITE Y(2) +
   ↳alienvelocity.yoffset,alien
   REM *** Check for and handle off screen situation ***
   WrapAlien()
ENDFUNCTION
```

Adding *WrapAlien()*

The *WrapAlien()* routine checks for the sprite moving off an edge of the screen and, when this occurs, brings the sprite back on at the opposite edge.

```
FUNCTION WrapAlien()
   IF SPRITE X(2) > 1280
      SPRITE alien,0,SPRITE Y(2),alien
   ENDIF
   IF SPRITE X(2) < 0
      SPRITE alien,1280,SPRITE Y(2),alien
   ENDIF
   IF SPRITE Y(2) > 1024
      SPRITE alien,SPRITE X(2),0,alien
   ENDIF
   IF SPRITE Y(2) < 0
      SPRITE alien,SPRITE X(2),1024,alien
   ENDIF
ENDFUNCTION
```

Adding *HandleMissile()*

The longest routine in the program is *HandleMissile()*. If a missile exists, this routine moves the missile towards the crosshairs position destroying the missile after 15 moves. During the first 8 moves the engines of the missile are shown firing, after that the missile engines shut down.

Each move reduces the size of the missile - this gives the impression that the missile is moving away from the player.

When the missile has made 15 moves, the routine checks for a collision between the missile and alien sprites. Any earlier collision between the two sprites is ignored because the missile is not deemed to have travelled far enough *inwards* to have made contact with the alien ship.

If the alien ship is hit, its sprite frame is changed to show damage. After five hits the ship explodes. Visually this is done by expanding and fading the sprite while playing the explode sound.

```
FUNCTION HandleMissile()
   REM *** IF missile exists, move 1/15 of total distance ***
   IF SPRITE EXIST(missile)
      MOVE SPRITE missile, verticaldistance / 15
      REM *** IF first 7 moves, show engine blast ***
      IF missilemoves < 8
         PLAY SPRITE missile,1,2,10
      ENDIF
      REM *** IF 8th move, switch off engines ***
      IF missilemoves = 8
         SET SPRITE FRAME missile,3
      ENDIF
      REM *** Reduce size of missile ***
      missilewidth# = missilewidth# - missilewidth#/15
```

```
              missileheight# = missileheight# - missileheight#/15
              SIZE SPRITE missile,missilewidth#,missileheight#
              OFFSET SPRITE missile, SPRITE WIDTH(3)/2, 0
              REM *** Increment number of moves ***
              INC missilemoves
              REM *** IF more than 15 moves THEN ***
              IF missilemoves > 15
                  REM *** Check for hit on alien
                  hit = SPRITE HIT(alien,missile)
                  REM *** Delete missile and reset moves ***
                  missilemoves = 0
                  DELETE SPRITE missile
                  REM *** IF alien hit THEN ***
                  IF hit = 1
                      REM *** Move alien sprite to next frame ***
                      displayframe = SPRITE FRAME(alien) + 1
                      SET SPRITE FRAME alien,displayframe
                      REM *** IF 5th frame, destroy alien ***
                      IF displayframe = 5
                          PLAY SOUND explode
                          REM *** Show alien exploding ***
                          FOR c = 50 TO 250 STEP 10
                              SIZE SPRITE alien,c,c
                              OFFSET SPRITE alien,SPRITE WIDTH(2)/2,
                              ⮩SPRITE HEIGHT(2)/2
                              SET SPRITE ALPHA alien, 300-c
                              WAIT 1
                          NEXT c
                          DELETE SPRITE alien
                      ENDIF
                  ENDIF
              ENDIF
          ENDIF
ENDFUNCTION
```

Activity 29.23

From the coding given on the previous pages, create a program (*joy14.dbpro*) to test the game described.

Solutions

Activity 29.1

No solution required.

Activity 29.2

```
REM *** Create list of devices ***
PERFORM CHECKLIST FOR CONTROL DEVICES
REM *** Display each entry in the list ***
FOR c = 1 TO CHECKLIST QUANTITY()
    PRINT CHECKLIST STRING$(c)
NEXT c
REM *** Assume joystick 1st device ***
IF CHECKLIST VALUE A(1) = 1
    PRINT "Joystick has force feedback"
ELSE
    PRINT "Joystick has no force feedback"
ENDIF
REM *** End program ***
WAIT KEY
END
```

This code only works if a joystick is connected as the first device in the check list.

Activity 29.3

It may be difficult with some joysticks to activate a single direction at a time.

Activity 29.4

Assuming your screen is set to 1280 by 1024, the crosshairs can be moved off the left and top edges of the screen but will not reach the right and bottom edges.

Activity 29.5

```
REM *** Set display mode ***
SET DISPLAY MODE 1280,1024,32
REM *** Set up sprite ***
LOAD IMAGE "crosshairs.bmp",1
SPRITE 1,500,400,1
REM *** Offset sprite to its centre ***
OFFSET SPRITE 1, SPRITE WIDTH(1)/2,
SPRITE HEIGHT(1)/2
REM *** main loop ***
DO
    REM *** Move sprite to joyst'k coords ***
    SPRITE 1,JOYSTICK X()+1000,
    JOYSTICK Y()+1000,1
LOOP
REM *** End program ***
END
```

Activity 29.6

1 joystick Y unit   = 1024/2000 pixels
                           = 0.512 pixels

Activity 29.7

```
REM *** Set display mode ***
SET DISPLAY MODE 1280,1024,32
REM *** Set up sprite ***
LOAD IMAGE "crosshairs.bmp",1
SPRITE 1,500,400,1
```

```
REM *** Calculate screen/joystick ratios ***
width = SCREEN WIDTH()
height = SCREEN HEIGHT()
Xunits# = width/2000.0
Yunits# = height/2000.0
REM *** Offset sprite to its centre ***
OFFSET SPRITE 1, SPRITE WIDTH(1)/2,
SPRITE HEIGHT(1)/2
REM *** main loop ***
DO
    REM *** Move sprite to joyst'k coords ***
    SPRITE 1,(JOYSTICK X()+1000)*Xunits,
    (JOYSTICK Y()+1000)*Yunits,1
LOOP
REM *** End program ***
END
```

Activity 29.8

No solution required.

Activity 29.9

```
REM *** Set display mode ***
SET DISPLAY MODE 1280, 1024, 32
REM *** Set up sprite ***
SET TEXT OPAQUE
REM *** main loop ***
DO
    REM *** Position cursor ***
    SET CURSOR 100,100
    IF JOYSTICK FIRE A()= 1
        PRINT "Pressed"
    ELSE
        PRINT "        "
    ENDIF
LOOP
REM *** End program ***
END
```

Activity 29.10

```
REM *** Set display mode ***
SET DISPLAY MODE 1280, 1024, 32
REM *** Set up sprite ***
SET TEXT OPAQUE
REM *** main loop ***
DO
    REM *** Position cursor ***
    SET CURSOR 100,100
    IF JOYSTICK FIRE A()= 1
        PRINT "Pressed"
    ELSE
        PRINT "        "
    ENDIF
    REM *** Position cursor ***
    SET CURSOR 100,150
    IF JOYSTICK FIRE B()= 1
        PRINT "Pressed"
    ELSE
        PRINT "        "
    ENDIF
    REM *** Position cursor ***
    SET CURSOR 100,200
    IF JOYSTICK FIRE C()= 1
        PRINT "Pressed"
    ELSE
        PRINT "        "
    ENDIF
    REM *** Position cursor ***
    SET CURSOR 100,150
    IF JOYSTICK FIRE D()= 1
```

```
        PRINT "Pressed"
    ELSE
        PRINT "                    "
    ENDIF
LOOP
REM *** End program ***
END
```

Activity 29.11

```
REM *** Set display mode ***
SET DISPLAY MODE 1280, 1024, 32
REM *** Set up sprite ***
SET TEXT OPAQUE
REM *** main loop ***
DO
    FOR button = 1 TO 4
        REM *** Position cursor ***
        SET CURSOR 100,button*50 + 150
        IF JOYSTICK FIRE X(button)= 1
            PRINT "Pressed"
        ELSE
            PRINT "                    "
        ENDIF
    NEXT button
LOOP
REM *** End program ***
END
```

Activity 29.12

The smallest change in value may vary between joysticks.

Activity 29.13

In the joystick used, only the Z axis returned a non-zero value.

Activity 29.14

No solution required.

Activity 29.15

```
REM *** Set display mode ***
SET DISPLAY MODE 1280,1024,32
REM *** main loop ***
DO
    IF JOYSTICK FIRE A()
        FORCE UP 100
    ENDIF
    IF JOYSTICK FIRE B()
        FORCE DOWN 100
    ENDIF
    IF JOYSTICK FIRE C()
        FORCE LEFT 100
    ENDIF
    IF JOYSTICK FIRE D()
        FORCE RIGHT 100
    ENDIF
LOOP
REM *** End program ***
END
```

Activity 29.16

No solution required.

Activity 29.17

```
REM *** Set display mode ***
```

```
SET DISPLAY MODE 1280,1024,32
REM *** main loop ***
DO
    IF JOYSTICK FIRE A()
        FORCE ANGLE 100,12,0
    ENDIF
    IF JOYSTICK FIRE B()
        FORCE NO EFFECT
    ENDIF
LOOP
REM *** End program ***
END
```

Activity 29.18

No solution required.

Activity 29.19

By removing the WAIT KEY statement, the FORCE WATER EFFECT has no time to activate before the program is terminated.

Activity 29.20

```
REM *** Set display mode ***
SET DISPLAY MODE 1280,1024,32
REM *** Get ready ***
PRINT "Begin moving the joystick"
WAIT 1000
PRINT "Effects start in 2 seconds"
WAIT 2000
REM *** The CHAINSAW EFFECT ***
CLS
PRINT "CHAINSAW"
WAIT 300
FORCE CHAINSAW 100,5000
REM *** End program ***
WAIT KEY
END
```

Activity 29.21

```
REM *** Set display mode ***
SET DISPLAY MODE 1280,1024,32
REM *** Load sound file ***
LOAD SOUND "laser.wav",1
REM *** Main loop ***
DO
    REM *** IF A pressed, create recoil ***
    IF JOYSTICK FIRE A() = 1
        FORCE SHOOT 100, 50
        PLAY SOUND 1
    ENDIF
LOOP
REM *** End program ***
END
```

Activity 29.22

```
REM *** Set display mode ***
SET DISPLAY MODE 1280,1024,32
REM *** Main loop ***
DO
    REM *** IF A pressed, create recoil ***
    IF JOYSTICK FIRE A() = 1
        FORCE IMPACT 100, 50
    ENDIF
LOOP
REM *** End program ***
END
```

```
REM *** Define Velocity structure ***
TYPE VelocityType
   xoffset
   yoffset
ENDTYPE
REM *** Named Constants ***

REM *** Sprite and image values ***
#CONSTANT crosshairs    1
#CONSTANT alien         2
#CONSTANT missile       3

REM *** Sounds id values ***
#CONSTANT launch        1
#CONSTANT explode       2

REM Global variables ***
GLOBAL xpixels# `joystick/pixel ratio x-axis
GLOBAL ypixels# `joystick/pixel ratio y-axis
GLOBAL missilemoves = 0
                    `No. of times missile moved
GLOBAL verticaldistance `Initial distance
             `from missile to crosshairs
GLOBAL missilewidth# `Missile sprite width
GLOBAL missileheight# `Missile sprite height
GLOBAL alienvelocity AS VelocityType
                    `velocity of alien craft

InitialiseGame()
REM *** main loop ***
REPEAT
   HandleJoystick()
   HandleAlien()
   HandleMissile()
UNTIL NOT SPRITE EXIST(alien)
REM *** End program ***
WAIT 4000
END

FUNCTION InitialiseGame()
   REM *** Set Screen resolution ***
   SET DISPLAY MODE 1280,1024,32
   COLOR BACKDROP 0
   BACKDROP ON
   REM *** Joystick/sprite movement ***
   xpixels# = 1280/2000.0
   ypixels# = 1024/2000.0
   REM *** Load Sound files ***
   LOAD SOUND "launch.wav",launch
   LOAD SOUND "explode.wav",explode
   REM *** Create sprites ***
   REM *** Load crosshairs image ***
   LOAD IMAGE "crosshairs.bmp",crosshairs
   SPRITE crosshairs,640,900,crosshairs
   SET SPRITE PRIORITY crosshairs,1
   REM *** Offset crosshairs sprite ***
   OFFSET SPRITE crosshairs,
   ⮡SPRITE WIDTH(1)/2, SPRITE HEIGHT(1)/2
   REM *** Create alien sprite ***
   CreateAlien()
   REM *** Hide the mouse pointer ***
   HIDE MOUSE
ENDFUNCTION

FUNCTION CreateAlien()
   RANDOMIZE TIMER()
   REM *** Position and size alien ***
   CREATE ANIMATED SPRITE alien,"alien.bmp"
   ⮡,5,1,alien
   SPRITE alien,640,20,alien
   SIZE SPRITE alien,50,50
   OFFSET SPRITE alien, SPRITE WIDTH(2)/2,
   ⮡SPRITE HEIGHT(2)/2
   REM *** Give alien sprite a velocity ***
   alienvelocity.xoffset = RND(5)
```

```
   alienvelocity.yoffset = RND(10)+1
ENDFUNCTION

FUNCTION HandleJoystick()
   REM *** Crosshairs to joystick coords ***
   SPRITE crosshairs,(JOYSTICK X()+1000)*
   ⮡xpixels#,(JOYSTICK Y()+1000)*ypixels#,1
   IF JOYSTICK FIRE A() = 1 AND
   ⮡(NOT SPRITE EXIST(3))
      PLAY SOUND launch
      FORCE SHOOT 50,5
      CreateMissile()
   ENDIF
ENDFUNCTION

FUNCTION CreateMissile()
   REM *** Create missile sprite ***
   CREATE ANIMATED SPRITE missile,
   ⮡"missile2.bmp",3,1,missile
   SPRITE missile,SPRITE X(1),900,missile
   PLAY SPRITE missile,1,2,10
   REM *** Calculate vertical distance ***
   verticaldistance = 900 - SPRITE Y(1)
   REM *** Record sprite width & height ***
   missilewidth# = SPRITE WIDTH(3)
   missileheight# = SPRITE HEIGHT(3)
ENDFUNCTION

FUNCTION HandleAlien()
   REM *** Move alien ***
   SPRITE alien,SPRITE X(2)+
   ⮡alienvelocity.xoffset,SPRITE Y(2) +
   ⮡alienvelocity.yoffset,alien
   REM ***Check for off screen situation ***
   WrapAlien()
ENDFUNCTION

FUNCTION WrapAlien()
   IF SPRITE X(2) > 1280
      SPRITE alien,0,SPRITE Y(2),alien
   ENDIF
   IF SPRITE X(2) < 0
      SPRITE alien,1280,SPRITE Y(2),alien
   ENDIF
   IF SPRITE Y(2) > 1024
      SPRITE alien,SPRITE X(2),0,alien
   ENDIF
   IF SPRITE Y(2) < 0
      SPRITE alien,SPRITE X(2),1024,alien
   ENDIF
ENDFUNCTION

FUNCTION HandleMissile()
   REM *** IF missile exists, move it ***
   IF SPRITE EXIST(missile)
      MOVE SPRITE missile,verticaldistance
      ⮡/15
      REM *** IF first 7, show engines ***
      IF missilemoves < 8
         PLAY SPRITE missile,1,2,10
      ENDIF
      REM *** IF 8th move, off engines ***
      IF missilemoves = 8
         SET SPRITE FRAME missile,3
      ENDIF
      REM *** Reduce size of missile ***
      missilewidth# = missilewidth# -
      ⮡missilewidth#/15
      missileheight# = missileheight# -
      ⮡missileheight#/15
      SIZE SPRITE missile,missilewidth#,
      ⮡missileheight#
      OFFSET SPRITE missile,
      ⮡SPRITE WIDTH(3)/2,0
      REM *** Increment number of moves ***
      INC missilemoves
      REM *** IF more than 15 moves THEN ***
```

```
         IF missilemoves > 15
            REM *** Check for hit on alien
            hit = SPRITE HIT(alien,missile)
            REM *** Delete missile & moves zero***
            missilemoves = 0
            DELETE SPRITE missile
            REM *** IF alien hit THEN ***
            IF hit = 1
               REM *** Move alien sprite to next frame ***
               displayframe = SPRITE FRAME(alien) + 1
               SET SPRITE FRAME alien,displayframe
               REM *** IF 5th frame, destroy alien ***
               IF displayframe = 5
                  PLAY SOUND explode
                  REM *** Show alien exploding ***
                  FOR c = 50 TO 250 STEP 10
                     SIZE SPRITE alien,c,c
                     OFFSET SPRITE alien,SPRITE WIDTH(2)/2,
                     ↳SPRITE HEIGHT(2)/2
                     SET SPRITE ALPHA alien,300-c
                     WAIT 1
                  NEXT c
                  DELETE SPRITE alien
               ENDIF
            ENDIF
         ENDIF
      ENDIF
   ENDIF
ENDFUNCTION
```

Appendix

The ASCII Character Set

	Second hex digit															
First hex digit	**0**	**1**	**2**	**3**	**4**	**5**	**6**	**7**	**8**	**9**	**A**	**B**	**C**	**D**	**E**	**F**
0	null							bell	back-space	H tab	line feed	V tab	form feed	return		
1											escape					
2	space	!	"	#	$	%	&	`	(	)	*	+	,	−	.	/
3	0	1	2	3	4	5	6	7	8	9	:	;	<	=	>	?
4	@	A	B	C	D	E	F	G	H	I	J	K	L	M	N	O
5	P	Q	R	S	T	U	V	W	X	Y	Z	[	\	]	^	_
6	`	a	b	c	d	e	f	g	h	i	j	k	l	m	n	o
7	p	q	r	s	t	u	v	w	x	y	z	{			}	~	delete

ASCII characters occupy the 7 least-significant bits of a byte and are coded as 00 to 7F (hexadecimal).
The characters coded 0 to 1F are non-printing control characters. Only those which may affect cursor position or produce audio output have been named in the table given above.

Index

X

Y

Z